"Tom Schreiner's new commentary on Hebrews, a Bible book that is considered difficult by many, will help both pastors and Christian believers in general appreciate the foundationally important theological emphases and spiritual challenges of this New Testament text. Readers will be enriched in their understanding of the manifold theological and exegetical traditions that feed into one of the New Testament's most consistently pastoral compositions. And they will be challenged to internalize strategies for revitalizing believers who are in danger of succumbing to the pressures that belonging to a minority entails. The volume is a worthy contribution to the expanding commentary literature on Hebrews."

Eckhard Schnabel
Mary F. Rockefeller Distinguished Professor
of New Testament Studies
Gordon-Conwell Theological Seminary

BIBLICAL THEOLOGY FOR CHRISTIAN PROCLAMATION

COMMENTARY ON
HEBREWS

Biblical Theology for Christian Proclamation

General Editors

T. DESMOND ALEXANDER
Senior Lecturer in Biblical Studies
Director of Postgraduate Studies
Union Theological College, Belfast, Northern Ireland

ANDREAS J. KÖSTENBERGER
Senior Research Professor of New Testament and Biblical Theology
Southeastern Baptist Theological Seminary, Wake Forest, North Carolina

THOMAS R. SCHREINER
James Buchanan Harrison Professor of New Testament Interpretation
Professor of Biblical Theology
Associate Dean of the School of Theology
The Southern Baptist Theological Seminary, Louisville, Kentucky

Assistant General Editors

JAMES M. HAMILTON
Professor of Biblical Theology
The Southern Baptist Theological Seminary, Louisville, Kentucky

KENNETH A. MATHEWS
Professor of Divinity/Old Testament
Beeson Divinity School, Birmingham, Alabama

TERRY L. WILDER
Professor of New Testament, Wesley Harrison Chair of New Testament
Southwestern Baptist Theological Seminary, Fort Worth, Texas

GENERAL EDITORS: T. DESMOND ALEXANDER,
ANDREAS J. KÖSTENBERGER, AND THOMAS R. SCHREINER

BIBLICAL THEOLOGY FOR CHRISTIAN PROCLAMATION

COMMENTARY ON
HEBREWS

THOMAS R. SCHREINER

HOLMAN
REFERENCE

NASHVILLE, TENNESSEE

Commentary on Hebrews
© Copyright 2015 by Thomas R. Schreiner

Published by B&H Publishing Group
Nashville, Tennessee
All rights reserved.

ISBN 978-0-8054-9613-0

Dewey Decimal Classification: 227.87
Subject Heading: BIBLE. N.T. Hebrews

Printed in the United States of America
20 19 18 17 16 15 • 8 7 6 5 4 3 2 1
SB

CONTENTS

General Editors' Preface ix
Acknowledgments xiii
Dedication xiv
List of Abbreviations xv
Introduction 1

    I. Author 2
    II. Date 5
    III. Destination and Addressees 6
    IV. Genre and Structure 10
    V. Purpose 13
    VI. Religious-Cultural Background 15
    VII. Hebrews Outline 17
    VIII. Hebrews and the Story Line of the Bible 20
    IX. Biblical and Theological Structures 29

Exposition
    Hebrews 1:1–4 51
    Hebrews 1:5–14 62
    Hebrews 2:1–4 78
    Hebrews 2:5–9 84
    Hebrews 2:10–18 93
    Hebrews 3:1–6 111
    Hebrews 3:7–11 120
    Hebrews 3:12–19 124
    Hebrews 4:1–5 132
    Hebrews 4:6–13 139
    Hebrews 4:14–16 149
    Hebrews 5:1–10 155
    Hebrews 5:11–14 167
    Hebrews 6:1–3 173
    Hebrews 6:4–8 178
    Hebrews 6:9–12 192
    Hebrews 6:13–20 196
    Hebrews 7:1–10 205
    Hebrews 7:11–12 214
    Hebrews 7:13–14 218
    Hebrews 7:15–17 220
    Hebrews 7:18–19 224
    Hebrews 7:20–22 228
    Hebrews 7:23–25 231
    Hebrews 7:26–28 235
    Hebrews 8:1–6 240
    Hebrews 8:7–13 247
    Hebrews 9:1–10 255

Hebrews 9:11–14 265
Hebrews 9:15–22 272
Hebrews 9:23–28 280
Hebrews 10:1–4 288
Hebrews 10:5–10 293
Hebrews 10:11–14 302
Hebrews 10:15–18 307
Hebrews 10:19–25 311
Hebrews 10:26–31 322
Hebrews 10:32–39 329
Hebrews 11:1–2 337
Hebrews 11:3–7 341
Hebrews 11:8–22 347
Hebrews 11:23–31 360
Hebrews 11:32–40 367
Hebrews 12:1–3 374
Hebrews 12:4–13 380
Hebrews 12:14–17 389
Hebrews 12:18–24 394
Hebrews 12:25–29 403
Hebrews 13:1–6 408
Hebrews 13:7–17 415
Hebrews 13:18–25 426

Biblical and Theological Themes 435
§1 God in Hebrews 435
§2 Jesus Christ. 441
§2.1 Divine Son 445
§2.2 The Humanity of the Son 452
§2.3 The Priesthood of Jesus 455
§2.4 Jesus' Better Sacrifice and Human Anthropology 460
§2.5 Perfection and Assurance 466
§2.6 Jesus' Resurrection and Exaltation 471
§3 The New Covenant 474
§4 The Spirit in Hebrews 477
§5 Warnings and Exhortations 480
§6 Sojourners and Exiles 491
§7 Faith, Obedience, and the Situation of the Readers 493
§8 Assurance 496
§9 The Future Reward 498

Bibliography 501
Name Index 519
Subject Index 523
Scripture Index 527

General Editors' Preface

In recent years biblical theology has seen a remarkable resurgence. Whereas, in 1970, Brevard Childs wrote *Biblical Theology in Crisis*, the quest for the Bible's own theology has witnessed increasing vitality since Childs prematurely decried the demise of the movement. Nowhere has this been truer than in evangelical circles. It could be argued that evangelicals, with their commitment to biblical inerrancy and inspiration, are perfectly positioned to explore the Bible's unified message. At the same time, as D. A. Carson has aptly noted, perhaps the greatest challenge faced by biblical theologians is how to handle the Bible's manifest diversity and how to navigate the tension between its unity and diversity in a way that does justice to both.[1]

What is biblical theology? And how is biblical theology different from related disciplines such as systematic theology? These two exceedingly important questions must be answered by anyone who would make a significant contribution to the discipline. Regarding the first question, the most basic answer might assert that biblical theology, in essence, is *the theology of the Bible*, that is, the theology expressed by the respective writers of the various biblical books *on their own terms* and *in their own historical contexts*. Biblical theology is the attempt to understand and embrace *the interpretive perspective of the biblical authors*. What is more, biblical theology is the theology of the *entire* Bible, an exercise in *whole-Bible theology*. For this reason biblical theology is not just a modern academic discipline; its roots are found already in the use of earlier Old

---

[1] D. A. Carson, "New Testament Theology," in *Dictionary of the Later New Testament and Its Developments,* ed. Ralph P. Martin and Peter H. Davids (Downers Grove, IL: InterVarsity, 1998), 810.

Testament portions in later Old Testament writings and in the use of the Old Testament in the New.

Biblical theology thus involves a close study of *the use of the Old Testament in the Old Testament* (that is, the use of, say, Deuteronomy by Jeremiah, or of the Pentateuch by Isaiah). Biblical theology also entails the investigation of *the use of the Old Testament in the New*, both in terms of individual passages and in terms of larger christological or soteriological themes. Biblical theology may proceed *book by book*, trace *central themes* in Scripture, or seek to place the contributions of individual biblical writers within the framework of the Bible's larger overarching *metanarrative*, that is, the Bible's developing story from Genesis through Revelation at whose core is *salvation* or *redemptive history*, the account of God's dealings with humanity and his people Israel and the church from creation to new creation.

In this quest for the Bible's own theology, we will be helped by the inquiries of those who have gone before us in the *history of the church*. While we can profitably study the efforts of interpreters over the entire sweep of the history of biblical interpretation since patristic times, we can also benefit from the labors of scholars since J. P. Gabler, whose programmatic inaugural address at the University of Altdorf, Germany, in 1787 marks the inception of the discipline in modern times. Gabler's address bore the title "On the Correct Distinction Between Dogmatic and Biblical Theology and the Right Definition of Their Goals."[2] While few (if any) within evangelicalism would fully identify with Gabler's program, the proper distinction between dogmatic and biblical theology (that is, between biblical and systematic theology) continues to be an important issue to be adjudicated by practitioners of both disciplines, and especially biblical theology. We have already defined biblical theology as whole-Bible theology, describing the theology of the various biblical books *on their own terms* and *in their own historical contexts*. Systematic theology, by contrast, is more topically oriented and focused on contemporary contextualization. While there are different ways in which the relationship between biblical and systematic theology can be construed, maintaining a proper distinction

---

[2] The original Latin title was *Oratio de iusto discrimine theologiae biblicae et dogmaticae regundisque recte utriusque finibus.*

between the two disciplines arguably continues to be vital if both are to achieve their objectives.

The present set of volumes constitutes an ambitious project, seeking to explore the theology of the Bible in considerable depth, spanning both Testaments. Authors come from a variety of backgrounds and perspectives, though all affirm the inerrancy and inspiration of Scripture. United in their high view of Scripture, and in their belief in the underlying unity of Scripture, which is ultimately grounded in the unity of God himself, each author explores the contribution of a given book or group of books to the theology of Scripture as a whole. While conceived as stand-alone volumes, each volume thus also makes a contribution to the larger whole. All volumes provide a discussion of introductory matters, including the historical setting and the literary structure of a given book of Scripture. Also included is an exegetical treatment of all the relevant passages in succinct commentary-style format. The biblical theology approach of the series will also inform and play a role in the commentary proper. The commentator permits a discussion between the commentary proper and the biblical theology it reflects by a series of cross-references.

The major contribution of each volume, however, is a thorough discussion of the most important themes of the biblical book in relation to the canon as a whole. This format allows each contributor to ground biblical theology, as is proper, in an appropriate appraisal of the relevant historical and literary features of a particular book in Scripture while at the same time focusing on its major theological contribution to the entire Christian canon in the context of the larger salvation-historical metanarrative of Scripture. Within this overall format, there will be room for each individual contributor to explore the major themes of his particular corpus in the way he sees most appropriate for the material under consideration. For some books of the Bible, it may be best to have these theological themes set out in advance of the exegetical commentary. For other books, it may be better to explain the theological themes after the commentary. Consequently, each contributor has the freedom to order these sections as best suits the biblical material under consideration, so that the discussion of biblical-theological themes may precede or follow the exegetical commentary. Moreover, contributors have some flexibility regarding format within these sections, as they consider their own biblical books and decide how best to help readers understand the text.

This format, in itself, would already be a valuable contribution to biblical theology. But other series try to accomplish a survey of the Bible's theology as well. What distinguishes the present series is its orientation toward Christian proclamation. This is the Biblical Theology *for Christian Proclamation* commentary series! As a result, the ultimate purpose of this set of volumes is not exclusively, or even primarily, academic. Rather, we seek to relate biblical theology to our own lives and to the life of the church. Our desire is to equip those in Christian ministry who are called by God to preach and teach the precious truths of Scripture to their congregations, both in North America and in a global context.

We hope and pray that the 40 volumes of this series, once completed, will bear witness to the unity in diversity of the canon of Scripture as they probe the individual contributions of each of its 66 books. The authors and editors are united in their desire that in so doing the series will magnify the name of Christ and bring glory to the triune God who revealed himself in Scripture so that everyone who calls on the name of the Lord will be saved—to the glory of God the Father and his Son, the Lord Jesus Christ, under the illumination of the Holy Spirit, and for the good of his church. To God alone be the glory: *soli Deo gloria.*

ACKNOWLEDGMENTS

I am grateful to Ray Clendenen, the editor for this series, for his assistance and help in writing this commentary and for his friendship that has spanned the years. Two of my PhD students have helped me immensely. Matt McMains checked out numerous books and scanned and sent me scores of articles, which saved me from spending many hours on such details. Aubrey Sequeira read an earlier draft of the commentary carefully, correcting errors and making numerous suggestions for improvement, and many of these suggestions have been incorporated into the commentary in one way or another. He also patiently organized my bibliography and painstakingly compiled the subject index. I can scarcely express my thanks for the love of these two students who have labored so graciously and willingly on my behalf. Also, my thanks to Desi Alexander for his keen comments on the commentary, which helped sharpen my thinking and helped me correct some mistakes. Finally, I am also so grateful to Chris Cowan, whose own work on Hebrews stimulated my thought in so many productive ways. Chris labored in a number of ways to make this commentary better than it would otherwise be and for that I am very thankful.

I am also thankful to The Southern Baptist Theological Seminary for supporting my writing and research so wonderfully. I finished the first draft of my commentary while I was on sabbatical, and I am thankful to Southern Seminary and to Southern Baptist church members who support scholarship in such a way. More specifically, I want to express my thanks to the president, R. Albert Mohler Jr., the vice president and provost, Randy Stinson, and the dean of the school of theology, Greg Wills, for their encouragement and support.

To my son, John,
and daughter-in-law, Brooke.

"I thank my God every time
I remember you." (NIV)

LIST OF ABBREVIATIONS

AB	Anchor Bible
ABD	*Anchor Bible Dictionary*. Edited by D. N. Freedman. 6 vols. New York, 1992
ALGHJ	Arbeiten zur Literatur Geschicte des hellenistischen Judentums
AnBib	Analecta biblica
AUSS	*Andrews University Seminary Studies*
BASOR	*Bulletin of the American Schools of Oriental Research*
BBR	*Bulletin of Biblical Research*
BDAG	Bauer, W., F. W. Danker, W. R. Arndt, and F. W Gingrich. *Greek-English Lexicon of the New Testament and Other Early Christian Literature*. 3rd ed. Chicago, 2000
Bib	*Biblica*
BJRL	*Bulletin of the John Rylands University Library of Manchester*
BSac	*Bibliotheca sacra*
BTB	*Biblical Theology Bulletin*
BZNW	Beihefte zur Zeitschrift für die neutestamentliche Wissenschaft
ca.	about
CBQ	*Catholic Biblical Quarterly*
CBQMS	Catholic Biblical Quarterly Monograph Series
CBR	*Currents in Biblical Research*
ch(s).	chapter(s)
CTJ	*Calvin Theological Journal*
CurBS	*Currents in Research: Biblical Studies*
EB	Echter Bibel

EDNT	*Exegetical Dictionary of the New Testament.* Edited by H. Balz, G. Schneider. ET. Grand Rapids, 1990–1993
ESV	English Standard Version
EvQ	*Evangelical Quarterly*
ExpT	*Expository Times*
GTJ	*Grace Theological Journal*
HCSB	Holman Christian Standard Bible
Herm	*Hermeneia*
Hist. eccl.	Eusebius, *Historia ecclesiastica*
HBM	Hebrew Bible Monographs
HTR	*Harvard Theological Review*
ICC	International Critical Commentary
JBL	*Journal of Biblical Literature*
JBMW	*Journal for Biblical Manhood and Womanhood*
JETS	*Journal of the Evangelical Theological Society*
JSJ	*Journal for the Study of Judaism in the Persian, Hellenistic, and Roman Periods*
JSNT	*Journal for the Study of the New Testament*
JSNTSup	Journal for the Study of the New Testament: Supplement Series
JTS	*Journal of Theological Studies*
KEK	Kritisch-exegetischer Kommentar über das Neue Testament (Meyer-Kommentar)
LHBOTS	Library of Hebrew Bible/Old Testament Studies
LN	Louw, Johannes P., and Eugene A. Nida. *Greek-English Lexicon of the New Testament Based on Semantic Domains.* 2nd ed. New York, 1989
LNTS	Library of New Testament Studies
LXX	Septuagint
MT	Masoretic Text (of the OT)
NABPRDS	National Association of Baptist Professors of Religion Dissertation Series
NA[28]	*Novum Testamentum Graece.* Edited by B. Aland, K. Aland, J. Karavidopoulos, C. M. Martini, and B. M. Metzger. 28th rev. ed. Stuttgart: Deutsche Bibelgesellschaft, 2012

NAC	New American Commentary
NACSBT	New American Commentary Studies in Bible and Theology
NET	New English Translation
NICNT	New International Commentary on the New Testament
NIGTC	New International Greek Testament Commentary
NIV	New International Version
NIVAC	NIV Application Commentary
NovT	*Novum Testamentum*
NovTSup	Novum Testamentum Supplement Series
NRSV	New Revised Standard Version
NT	New Testament
NTL	New Testament Library
NTS	*New Testament Studies*
OPTAT	*Occasional Papers of Translation and Textlinguistics*
OT	Old Testament
par.	parallels
PNTC	Pillar New Testament Commentary
PRSt	*Perspectives in Religious Studies*
ResQ	*Restoration Quarterly*
RTR	*Reformed Theological Review*
SBJT	*Southern Baptist Journal of Theology*
SBLDS	Society of Biblical Literature Dissertation Series
SBLMS	Society for Biblical Literature Monograph Series
SBT	Studies in Biblical Theology
SNTSMS	Society for New Testament Studies Monograph Series
SP	Sacra pagina
SPhilo	*Studia philonica*
STDJ	*Studies in the Texts of the Desert of Judah*
StudNeot	Studia neotestamentica
SubBi	Subsidia biblica
SuppNovT	Supplements to Novum Testamentum

TDNT	*Theological Dictionary of the New Testament.* Edited by G. Kittel and G. Friedrich. Translated by G. W. Bromiley. 10 vols. Grand Rapids, 1964–1976
Th	Theodotion
Thayer	*Thayer's Greek English Lexicon of the New Testament*
TNTC	Tyndale New Testament Commentary
TrinJ	*Trinity Journal*
TynBul	*Tyndale Bulletin*
v(v).	verse(s)
WBC	Word Biblical Commentary
WTJ	*Westminster Theological Journal*
WUNT	Wissenschaftliche Untersuchungen zum Neuen Testament
ZNW	*Zeitschrift für die neutestamentliche Wissenschaft und die Kunde der älteren Kirche*

INTRODUCTION

The words of Jesus on the cross, "It is finished!" (John 19:30), capture the theology of Hebrews. My aim in this commentary is to focus on the letter's biblical theology. The emphasis on biblical theology shows up especially in the introduction and conclusion of this commentary where I consider theological structures and themes. In the introduction I will examine four different structures that are woven into the entire letter: (1) promise/fulfillment; (2) eschatology; (3) typology; and (4) spatial orientation (which can also be described as the relationship between heaven and earth in the letter). The commentary will conclude, after presenting an exegesis of each chapter, with a discussion of some major theological themes in Hebrews.[1]

Most modern commentaries begin with significant introductions and then conduct an intensive exegesis of the text, chapter-by-chapter and verse-by-verse. By way of contrast, this introduction and the commentary are relatively brief and nontechnical. With the proliferation of commentaries today, a new commentary should have a distinctive approach. We now have many excellent commentaries on Hebrews that examine the letter in some detail. Many of these commentaries provide a useful function in that they draw on other parallels from both Jewish and Hellenistic literature to illuminate Hebrews. The advantage of such an approach is that the reader is plunged into the cultural world of the author. On the other hand,

---

[1] Given the constraints of this commentary, I cannot delve into the history of interpretation. For a start one should consult Jon C. Laansma and Daniel J. Trier, eds., *Christology, Hermeneutics, and Hebrews: Profiles from the History of Interpretation*, LNTS (London: T&T Clark, 2012); E. M. Heen and P. W. D. Krey, eds., *Hebrews*, Ancient Christian Commentary on Scripture (Downers Grove, IL: InterVarsity, 2005).

the careful sifting of various traditions may cause the reader to lose track of the letter's argument. At the same time, the author's theology may be muted, not because it isn't recognized but because it may be difficult to follow in the welter of information given to readers. I hope a commentary that probes the theology of Hebrews will prove to be helpful. I have been helped by many scholars in preparing this commentary, especially those who have written in-depth commentaries and those who have written monographs on the letter. No one writes from an objective standpoint, and hence I should state up front that I write as an evangelical Christian who believes that the Scriptures are the living and authoritative Word of God.

I. Author

The authorship of Hebrews is a fascinating issue that continues to interest Christians today. Clement of Alexandria (ca. AD 150–215) thought the letter was written by Paul in Hebrew and then translated into Greek by Luke.[2] Origen (ca. AD 185–253) said the thoughts are Pauline but suggested someone else made short notes and wrote up what the apostle taught and said.[3] Origen passed on the tradition that either Luke or Clement of Rome was the writer, but he remained noncommittal on the identity of the author. Most scholars believe Origen was agnostic about the author since he wrote, "But who wrote the epistle, truly only God knows."[4] David Alan Black, however, argues Origen believed Paul was the author but someone else was the penman.[5] Black's interpretation of Origen should be rejected. It has been shown that when Origen speaks of who wrote the epistle he was referring to the author, not merely the secretary.[6] Hence, the notion that Origen believed Paul was the author fails to persuade. As time passed, however, the notion that Paul was the

---

[2] Eusebius, *Hist. eccl.* 6.14.1.

[3] Eusebius, *Hist. eccl.* 6.25.13.

[4] This is my translation of Eusebius, *Hist. eccl.* 6.25.14.

[5] David Alan Black, "Who Wrote Hebrews? The Internal and External Evidence Re-examined," *Faith and Mission* 18 (2001): 3–26. See also David Alan Black, *The Authorship of Hebrews: The Case for Paul* (Gonzales, FL: Energion, 2013).

[6] See David L. Allen, *Hebrews*, NAC (Nashville: B&H, 2010), 32.

author gained credence, and by the third century Pauline authorship was accepted in the East.[7]

The situation in the West was different. Tertullian (ca. AD 155–220) suggested that Barnabas was the author, which indicates there was no inclination in the early centuries in the West to ascribe the letter to Paul.[8] Identifying the author as Barnabas is interesting since Barnabas was a Levite (Acts 4:36), which could explain the interest in and knowledge of priestly matters in Hebrews. Pauline authorship, however, finally triumphed in the West due to the influence of Jerome and Augustine.[9] Pauline authorship reigned as the view of the church until the time of the Reformation. Erasmus inclined against Pauline authorship but said he would submit to ecclesiastical authorities since the matter was inconsequential.[10] Luther rejected Pauline authorship, believing that Heb 2:3 proves the book could not have come from Paul. Luther had a novel but brilliant guess regarding authorship, proposing that the book was written by Apollos.[11] Hebrews is beautifully written and has an Alexandrian feel, fitting with Apollos's eloquence and Alexandrian roots (Acts 18:24). Calvin also agreed that Paul wasn't the writer based on Heb 2:3, suggesting that either Luke or Clement of Rome penned the letter.[12]

---

[7] See here Harold W. Attridge, *The Epistle to the Hebrews*, Hermeneia (Philadelphia: Fortress, 1989), 1–2, n7. See, e.g., Eusebius who accepts Hebrews as Pauline, though he thinks it was written originally in Hebrew and translated by Clement of Rome into Greek (*Hist. eccl.* 3.3.5 and 3.38.2–3).

[8] Attridge, *Hebrews*, 3.

[9] For the views of Jerome and Augustine, see Philip Edgecumbe Hughes, *A Commentary on the Epistle to the Hebrews* (Grand Rapids, MI: Eerdmans, 1977), 21–22.

[10] For Erasmus's comments on Hebrews, see ibid., 23.

[11] Guthrie nicely summarizes the evidence favoring Apollos, and he also provides a historical overview of those who have supported Apollos as the author (including Zahn, Lenski, Montefiore). Guthrie is not dogmatic on the matter but suggests Apollos as the author. George H. Guthrie, "The Case for Apollos as the Author of Hebrews," *Faith and Mission* 18 (2001): 41–56. For the development of Luther's views, see Hughes, *Hebrews*, 23; Attridge, *Hebrews*, 4. In support of Apollos, see Ceslas Spicq, *L'Épître aux Hébreux*, 2nd ed., 2 vols., EB (Paris: Gabalda, 1953), 1:197–219.

[12] See John Calvin, *Commentaries on the Epistle of Paul the Apostle to the Hebrews*, trans. J. Owen (repr.; Grand Rapids, MI: Baker, 2005), 54, 358. Despite the

In the contemporary period scholars continue to propose various authors, such as Priscilla, Silas, Epaphras, Jude, Aristion, etc.[13] In recent years a vigorous defense of Lukan authorship has been proposed by David Allen,[14] and there is also a significant defense of Pauline authorship by David Alan Black.[15]

Pauline authorship should be rejected despite the attempts, both ancient and modern, to mount a defense. First, in Paul's 13 letters he identifies himself by name, thus the absence of a name in Hebrews renders it doubtful that Paul wrote the letter. Second, stylistic arguments should not be relied on too heavily since the Pauline corpus is so limited. Still, the polished Greek style of Hebrews doesn't accord with what we find in the Pauline letters. Third, the writer separates himself from the original eyewitnesses in Heb 2:3. Paul, by way of contrast, emphasizes repeatedly his authority as an apostle of Jesus Christ and refuses to put himself in a subordinate position to the apostles and eyewitnesses. This last reason, in particular, rules out the notion that Paul was the author.

Once Paul is excluded, the door is pushed wide open for any number of candidates. David Allen argues intriguingly for Luke, but one can only say that he has shown that Lukan authorship is possible. He has certainly not proved his thesis. The linguistic evidence is not decisive, and the differences between Hebrews and Acts call into question Lukan authorship.[16] Barnabas is an attractive choice since he was a Levite, and the book has an interest in all things Levitical. Similarly, Luther's guess that the author was Apollos is appealing, for Apollos's eloquence accords with the letter's elegance, and his Alexandrian background fits with the character of

---

title of the commentary (which doubtless doesn't come from Calvin), Calvin clearly rejects Pauline authorship in his comments on 2:3 and 13:23.

[13] Adolf von Harnack defended Priscilla as the author (Adolf von Harnack, "Probabilia über die Addresse und den Verfasser des Hebräerbriefes," *ZNW* 1 [1900]: 16–41). For Silas, see Thomas Hewitt, *The Epistle to the Hebrews*, TNTC (Grand Rapids, MI: Eerdmans, 1960), 26–32. For Epaphras, see Robert Jewett, *Letter to Pilgrims: A Commentary on the Epistle to the Hebrews* (New York: Pilgrim, 1981), 7–9.

[14] Allen, *Hebrews*, 29–61. David L. Allen, *Lukan Authorship of Hebrews* (Nashville: B&H, 2010).

[15] See note 5 above.

[16] Rightly Gareth Lee Cockerill, *The Epistle to the Hebrews*, NICNT (Grand Rapids, MI: Eerdmans, 2012), 9.

the letter. Many scholars have seen an affinity between Hebrews and Platonic/Philonic thought, and Alexandria was a fertile center for such thought. But we come face-to-face here with the paucity of evidence in assigning an author. All the theories are guesses, though some are fascinating and alluring to be sure. We don't really know who wrote Hebrews. No theory of authorship has won the day and for good reason, for the answer to our quest lies outside the domain of historical knowledge. Origen's words about the author still ring true today: "God only knows." Hence, in this commentary I will refer to the writer as "the author." I will also use the title of the book as the subject so that the reader will find sentences like "Hebrews says."

II. Date

Dating NT documents is notoriously difficult, and Hebrews is no exception. No date was inscribed on the letter, and no historical referent in the letter gives us a definite date. Timothy was still alive (13:23) when the letter was written, and thus the letter was written in the first century. Since the author mentions the second generation of Christians (2:3), Timothy (13:23), and the death of some Christian leaders (13:7), the document was not written in the 30s or 40s. Furthermore, 5:12 indicates that the believers had been Christians for a while. The earliest date usually assigned is in the 60s.

Some date the book to the decades after AD 70, but there are reasons that suggest a date in the 60s, before AD 70.[17] The author refers often to the tabernacle and the ritual carried out there. In fact, he uses the present tense to describe the cultic system, indicating, perhaps, that the temple was still standing when he wrote. Against this, however, is the fact that 1 Clement also uses the present tense when referring to the temple, and he wrote in AD 96, well after the time when the temple was destroyed (AD 70).[18] Even though the argument from tense is not decisive, the reference to the tabernacle

---

[17] See e.g., Donald A. Hagner, *The New Testament: A Historical and Theological Introduction* (Grand Rapids, MI: Baker, 2012), 651–52.

[18] The dating of 1 Clement is not certain. Eisenbaum suggests a date late in the first century or early in the second. See Pamela M. Eisenbaum, "Locating Hebrews Within the Literary Landscape of Christian Origins," in *Hebrews: Contemporary Methods—New Insights*, ed. G. Gelardini (Leiden: Brill, 2005), 224–31.

is still significant in calculating the date. One of the fundamental arguments of the book is that Jesus' sacrifice is definitive and final so that the sacrifices of the old covenant belong to a former era.[19] The destruction of the temple in AD 70 would demonstrate conclusively (in accord with Jesus' prophecy; cf. Matthew 24) that temple sacrifices were no longer valid. Hence, it is improbable that the author would have failed to mention the destruction of the temple, suggesting that he wrote in the 60s before the temple was destroyed. A more definite date than this can't be assigned due to lack of evidence.

Another argument that may point to an early date also relates to 1 Clement. Most scholars date 1 Clement ca. AD 96, and Clement clearly cites Hebrews (e.g., 36:1–6). As noted above, this is not a knock-down argument since the date of 1 Clement is not certain either.[20] But if 1 Clement was written in AD 96, Hebrews had to have been around long enough to become part of the tradition, which suggests to me a pre-AD 70 date.[21]

III. Destination and Addressees

To whom was the letter written? It has been common to think it was written to a Jewish community since the readers, given the content of the letter, were tempted to revert to the sacrificial system from Judaism, perhaps to avoid persecution or to obtain assurance of forgiveness.[22] Attraction to Jewish rituals and practices, of

---

[19] The author probably refers to the rituals of the tabernacle rather than the temple worship of his day because he draws literarily from the account of the tabernacle in the Pentateuch.

[20] See William L. Lane, *Hebrews 1–8*, WBC (Dallas: Word, 1991), lxiii–lx; Attridge, *Hebrews*, 7–8.

[21] Cf. Luke Timothy Johnson, *Hebrews: A Commentary*, NTL (Louisville: Westminster/John Knox, 2006), 38–40; Barnabas Lindars, *The Theology of the Letter to the Hebrews*, New Testament Theology (Cambridge: Cambridge University Press, 1991), 20–21; Peter T. O'Brien, *The Letter to the Hebrews*, PNTC (Grand Rapids, MI: Eerdmans, 2010), 15–20; Paul Ellingworth, *The Epistle to the Hebrews: A Commentary on the Greek Text*, NIGTC (Grand Rapids, MI: Eerdmans, 1993), 33; Lane, *Hebrews 1–8*, lxvi.

[22] For a recent article that supports such a reading, see Susan Haber, "From Priestly Torah to Christ Cultus: The Re-Vision of Covenant and Cult in Hebrews," *JSNT* 28 (2005): 105–24. Cf. Lindars, *The Theology of Hebrews*, 11. Lindars argues that the readers struggled with their consciences and lacked confidence that their postbaptismal sins were forgiven (14, 59, 86). Selby shows that in Hebrews

course, does not necessarily point to Jewish readers. The presence
of God fearers in synagogues and Gentile proselytes who converted to Judaism indicates that Gentiles may have found Judaism alluring as well. Indeed, the readers were possibly a combination of
Jews and Gentiles.[23] Still, I side with the dominant view that the
letter was written to Jewish Christians.[24] The title of the book "to
the Hebrews" suggests that an address to Jewish readers is an old
interpretation. Koester says the title was affixed by the end of the
second century and hence isn't of much value in determining the
recipients.[25] Certainly the title doesn't resolve the question of addressees, but it is an ancient witness for the letter being addressed to
Jewish Christians, and it at least shows that the predominant view of
the addressees reaches back to the earliest interpreters of the letter.
At the end of the day, we can't rule out that the letter was intended
for Gentiles rather than Jews or included both Jews and Gentiles.[26]
Still the title of the letter and its contents (with the focus on the
Mosaic law and the Levitical priesthood) render it more likely that
the book was addressed to Jewish readers who wanted to revert to
Judaism.[27] Fortunately the interpretation of the letter doesn't depend

---

the conscience signifies one's "internal awareness of . . . sinfulness and guilt and
resulting in a guilty conscience which stands as the one effective barrier to enjoying
true fellowship with God." Jesus' sacrifice is superior since it has truly cleansed the
conscience. See Gary S. Selby, "The Meaning and Function of συνείδησις in Hebrews
9 and 10," *ResQ* 28 (1985–86): 153.

[23] So George Guthrie, *Hebrews*, NIVAC (Grand Rapids, MI: Zondervan, 1998),
20; David deSilva, *Perseverance in Gratitude: A Socio-Rhetorical Commentary on
the Epistle to the Hebrews* (Grand Rapids, MI: Eerdmans, 2000), 2–7.

[24] So O'Brien, *Hebrews*, 11–13; Hagner, *Introduction*, 646–48, and most commentators. See the helpful summary of the situation by Scott D. Mackie, *Eschatology
and Exhortation in the Epistle to the Hebrews*, WUNT 2/223 (Tübingen: Mohr
Siebeck, 2007), 9–17.

[25] Koester, *Hebrews*, 46, 171–73.

[26] In support of Gentile readers, see James A. Moffat, *A Critical and Exegetical
Commentary on the Epistle to the Hebrews*, ICC (New York: Scribner's,
1924), xv–xvii.

[27] Mason vigorously challenges this thesis (Eric F. Mason, "The Epistle [Not
Necessarily] to the 'Hebrews': A Call to Renunciation of Judaism or Encouragement
to Christian Commitment?" *PRSt* 37 [2010]: 7–20). He rightly says the author does
not specifically call on the readers to avoid reverting to Judaism. Mason shows the
main theme is a call to be committed to Christ and to avoid apostasy. So the interpretation of Hebrews offered here does not depend on the addressees being Jewish
Christians. Still, despite Mason's salutary cautions, it seems that the content of the

on the recipients. The meaning of the letter is fundamentally the same whether it addresses Jews or Gentiles, and thus the interpretation and biblical theology offered here do not rest on the identity of the addressees.

If we assume the letter was written to Jewish Christians, where were the Jews to whom the letter was addressed? Were they in Jerusalem, Palestine, Alexandria, or Rome? All of these locations make good sense. And scholars have also suggested Samaria, Antioch, Corinth, Cyprus, Ephesus, Bithynia, and Pontus.[28] It has even been argued that the letter was addressed to the Qumran community, but such a specific destination seems unlikely. No firm evidence in the letter ties it to Qumran, and the readers were almost certainly Christians, and there is no evidence of a Christian presence at Qumran.[29]

The most important clue for determining the location of the recipients comes from the letter itself, for the author closes the letter with the words, "Those who are from Italy greet you" (13:24). It is possible, of course, that he wrote *from* Italy, and those with the author in Italy sent their greetings. But it seems more probable that he wrote *to* those in Italy (cf. Acts 18:2), i.e., to Rome itself, so that

---

book is directed to those tempted to revert to the Jewish cult to obtain forgiveness. The apostasy warned against has a particular profile that has to do with Jewish ritual practices. Mason says the author engages in syncrisis to encourage and instruct the readers. This is certainly the case, but the *content* of the comparisons and the detailed attention to the OT cult suggest the author employs syncrisis to address readers who were tempted to find forgiveness through OT sacrifices. Incidentally, the author doesn't denigrate the OT or Judaism in making his argument. He argues salvation historically. The OT cultus was commanded and ordained by God, but its time, according to Hebrews, has expired. Now that Christ has come, the readers should not revert to the old covenant. The previous regulations were acceptable in their time and place, but they don't apply in the new period. Still, the old is not rejected, for the author believes the old covenant is fulfilled in the new.

[28] For these proposals, see Attridge, *Hebrews*, 10. Allen argues that the letter was addressed to converted priests who migrated to Syrian Antioch (*Hebrews*, 61–74; cf. Spicq, *L'Épître aux Hébreux*, 1:221–31).

[29] I am not saying that the worlds of Qumran and Hebrews are completely segregated. Some fascinating correspondences exist between Hebrews and the writings found at Qumran. See, e.g., Eric F. Mason, "Hebrews and the Dead Sea Scrolls: Some Points of Comparison," *PRSt* 37 (2010): 457–79. Mason notes parallels in cosmology, messianism, and the conception of Melchizedek.

those absent from Italy sent their greetings back to Rome.[30] If this is the case, then Hebrews was written to Jewish Christians in Rome. A Roman destination also fits with 1 Clement, for Clement wrote from Rome and knew the contents of Hebrews. His knowledge of Hebrews makes sense if the letter was directed to Rome. In addition, if we accept the nearly universal view that Paul didn't write Hebrews, it is suggestive that the West didn't accept Pauline authorship as early as the East did. If Hebrews was written to the Romans, they would have a more accurate historical memory regarding the author of the letter.

Carl Mosser, on the other hand, has made a sustained and powerful case for the letter's being written to Jewish Christians in Jerusalem.[31] He argues that what the author says about the tabernacle in the letter applies to the temple of his day.[32] The letter was written to persuade Jewish Christians to leave the city of Jerusalem, just as Rahab left the city of Jericho and identified with the people of God (11:31). Space is lacking, given the nature of this commentary, to investigate fully Mosser's thesis. He has certainly shown that a Jerusalem destination is possible, and such a destination has been rejected too quickly by scholars today. I still incline to a Roman destination, but the interpretation proposed here does not depend on such a hypothesis, and my reading of the letter in most respects could fit with a Jerusalem destination as well. We are reminded by Mosser's work that certainty often eludes us when it comes to historical reconstruction.

What we know from the letter is that the readers had experienced persecution in their early days as believers (10:32–34),[33] but they, apparently, had not suffered martyrdom (12:4). They were probably tempted to return to Judaism, perhaps to avoid persecution. Since Judaism was a legal religion under Roman law, it

---

[30] Cf. Lane, *Hebrews 1–8*, lviii–lx; Ellingworth, *Hebrews*, 29; O'Brien, *Hebrews*, 9.

[31] Carl Mosser, "No Lasting City: Rome, Jerusalem and the Place of Hebrews in the History of Earliest 'Christianity'" (Ph.D. diss., St. Andrews University, 2004).

[32] Ibid., 194–206.

[33] See here Bruce W. Winter, "Suffering with the Saviour: The Reality, the Reasons and the Reward," in *The Perfect Savior: Key Themes in Hebrews*, ed. J. Griffiths (Nottingham: InterVarsity, 2012), 147–67. Lane thinks it refers to Claudian expulsion in AD 49 (*Hebrews 1–8*, lxiv–lxvi), but such a suggestion, though fascinating, is probably too specific.

would afford protection from Roman imperial power.[34] If Hebrews was written to Rome, then it was composed before Nero lashed out against Christians, putting many to death. The author's bracing words about staying true to Christ prepared the readers for what was to come. Nevertheless, the situation posited here is a hypothesis that can't be established with certainty. We know *what* the author wrote, but we don't know all the *whys* and *wherefores*.

IV. Genre and Structure

The epistle to the Hebrews is elegantly written and structured. The quality of the writing might provoke us to think it is a literary essay, especially since the writing doesn't begin as a typical epistle by introducing the author and the recipients. Chapter 13, however, makes clear that the letter is an epistle, concluding with features (benediction, news, greetings, grace benediction) typical of letters. Some scholars have argued that chapter 13 was not originally part of the letter, but such a view is a historical curiosity, for it has been demonstrated that the themes in the chapter fit with the rest of Hebrews.[35] When we think of the warning passages that pervade the letter, calling Hebrews an essay doesn't fit. The admonitions have a practical and urgent tone that don't fit with an essay. In fact, the writer identifies his words as "a word of exhortation" (λόγου τῆς παρακλήσεως, 13:22). The same expression is used for Paul's sermon in Pisidian Antioch (Acts 13:15). Hebrews, then, is a sermon, an exhortation, in epistolary form.[36] The author urgently exhorts the readers to hold fast to their faith, to persevere to the end. The letter was read orally to the congregation; hence we should attend to the letter's oral character.[37] The oral character of the discourse is but-

---

[34] See here Winter, "Suffering with the Saviour," 147–67, though I think Winter probably overemphasizes the role that imperial authority played in the lives of the readers.

[35] See especially Floyd V. Filson, *"Yesterday": A Study of Hebrews in the Light of Chapter 13*, SBT 2/4 (Naperville, IL: Allenson, 1967). Despite the recent objections of A. J. M. Wedderburn, "The 'Letter' to the Hebrews and Its Thirteenth Chapter," *NTS* 50 (2004): 390–405.

[36] See the discussion in Lane, *Hebrews 1–8*, lxix–lxxv; Cockerill, *Hebrews*, 13–16. Cf. L. Johnson, *Hebrews*, 10. Against this see Mosser, "No Lasting City," 210–39.

[37] So Steve Stanley, "The Structure of Hebrews from Three Perspectives," *TynBul* 45 (1994): 248–50; Lane, *Hebrews 1–8*, lxxv; Cockerill, *Hebrews*, 11.

tressed particularly by two features:[38] (1) the emphasis on speaking and hearing that pervades the letter; (2) the alternation between exposition and exhortation, where the exhortations take precedence. As O'Brien says, "The author is skillfully conveying the impression that he is present with the assembly and actually delivering his sermon to them."[39]

NT letters have been examined as to whether they conform to Greek rhetoric, and Hebrews is no exception.[40] For instance, the commentaries by Attridge, Johnson, and Koester adopt a rhetorical stance, where the canons of Greek rhetoric are used to unlock the structure of the letter.[41] Certainly the writer is exceptionally well educated and was familiar with Greek rhetoric. Despite the rhetorical artistry in the letter and the rhetorical features of the writing, evidence that the writer followed the rhetoric found in Greek handbooks is lacking.[42]

Scholars have also investigated the structure of Hebrews carefully, and space is lacking to interact with the various structures

---

[38] Cf. O'Brien, *Hebrews*, 20–22. R. T. France rightly sees the oral and sermonic character of the letter but goes beyond the evidence in detecting seven discrete expositions in Hebrews ("The Writer of Hebrews as a Biblical Expositor," *TynBul* 47 [1996]: 245–76).

[39] O'Brien, *Hebrews*, 21.

[40] See the brief survey of scholarship in O'Brien, *Hebrews*, 24–27. See also Michael W. Martin and Jason A. Whitlark, "The Encomiastic Topics of Syncrisis as the Key to the Structure and Argument of Hebrews," *NTS* 35 (1989): 382–406, idem, "Choosing What Is Advantageous: The Relationship Between Epideicitic and Deliberative Syncrisis in Hebrews," *NTS* 58 (2012): 379–400; T. H. Olbricht, "Hebrews as Amplification," in *Rhetoric and the New Testament: Essays from the 1992 Heidelberg Conference*, ed. S. E. Porter and T. H. Olbricht, JSNTSup 90 (Sheffield: Sheffield Academic, 1993), 375–87; Duane F. Watson, "Rhetorical Criticism of Hebrews and the Catholic Epistles Since 1978," *CurBS* 5 (1997): 175–207, esp. 181–87; Barnabas Lindars, "The Rhetorical Structure of Hebrews," *NTS* 35 (1989): 382–406. Cf. Timothy W. Seid, "Synkrisis in Hebrews 7: The Rhetorical Structure and Strategy," in *The Rhetorical Interpretation of Scripture: Essays from the 1996 Malibu Conference*, ed. S. E. Porter and D. L. Stamps, JSNTSupS 180 (Sheffield: Sheffield Academic, 1999), 322–47. For a balanced approach, see deSilva, *Perseverance in Gratitude*, 39–58.

[41] Cf. Koester, *Hebrews*, 84–86; Johnson, *Hebrews*, 12–15.

[42] So Guthrie, *Structure of Hebrews*, 32–33; Lane, *Hebrews 1–8*, lxxv–lxxx; O'Brien, *Hebrews*, 26–27.

suggested.[43] Many outlines divide the letter up on the basis of content. Such approaches often ignore literary clues in the letter and underestimate the centrality of the exhortations. Hence, such outlines give the impression that Hebrews is a piece of systematic theology, which is misleading since it was addressed to a specific situation. The deficiencies evident in a content approach have been remedied by the careful studies of the structure of Hebrews in the work of Vanhoye,[44] Nauck,[45] Westfall,[46] Neeley[47] and Guthrie.[48] If anyone thought literary approaches would solve the problem, an analysis of the structures proposed by the scholars mentioned above demonstrates that such is not the case. It is evident from the diversity of opinion and the different outlines proposed that the outline of the letter is not an entirely objective issue. Indeed, the entire matter is remarkably complex and not easily solved, requiring a much longer discussion than is possible here.

The work of Vanhoye has been programmatic and suggestive, and yet virtually all scholars have concluded that it is not fully convincing.[49] Vanhoye set the course for future scholars through his careful analysis. He explored literary features that helped discern

---

[43] See the helpful survey and proposal of Barry C. Joslin, "Can Hebrews Be Structured? An Assessment of Eight Approaches," *CBR* 6 (2007): 99–129. Cf. Rodney J. Decker, "The Intentional Structure of Hebrews," *The Journal of Ministry and Theology* 4 (2000): 80–105; David J. MacLeod, "The Literary Structure of the Book of Hebrews," *BSac* 146 (1989): 185–97; Stanley, "The Structure of Hebrews," 245–71.

[44] See Albert Vanhoye, *La structure littéraire de l'épître aux Hébreux*, StudNeot 1, 2nd ed. (Paris: Desclée de Brouwer, 1976); idem, *Structure and Message of the Epistle to the Hebrews,* SubBi 12 (Rome: Pontifical Biblical Institute, 1989), 18–44. Cf. David Alan Black, "The Problem of the Literary Structure of Hebrews: An Evaluation and Proposal," *GTJ* 7 (1986): 163–77. Black focuses on Vanhoye's contribution.

[45] Wolfgang Nauck, "Zum Aufbau des Hebräerbriefes," in *Judentum-Urchristentum-Kirche: Festschrift für Joachim Jeremias*, ed. W. Eltester (Berlin: Alfred Töpelmann, 1960), 199–206.

[46] Cynthia Long Westfall, *A Discourse Analysis of the Letter to the Hebrews: The Relationship Between Form and Meaning*, LNTS 297 (London: T&T Clark, 2005).

[47] Linda Lloyd Neeley, "A Discourse Analysis of Hebrews," *OPTAT* 3–4 (1987): 1–146.

[48] George H. Guthrie, *The Structure of Hebrews: A Text-Linguistic Analysis*, NovTSup 73 (Leiden: Brill, 1994).

[49] For criticisms of Vanhoye, see O'Brien, *Hebrews*, 27–29; Guthrie, *Structure of Hebrews*, 34–35, 79.

the letter's structure, such as announcement of the subject (e.g., "angels" in 1:4 introduces the subsequent verses), framing devices (inclusio) which set the boundaries for a section, hook words (such as Melchizedek in 6:20 and 7:1), characteristic terms, shifts in literary genre (from exposition to exhortation), and chiasms (cf. the commentary on 5:1–10). Guthrie's work on the structure seems to have been the most convincing to scholars.[50] In any case, both literary features and content should be considered in determining the structure and outline of the letter. My approach here is rather eclectic and inevitably subjective. My outline takes into account rhetorical criticism, discourse analyses, and the content of the letter. Space is lacking to defend what is specifically proposed, but I hope it will prove to be illuminating in setting forth the message of Hebrews.

V. Purpose

Readers are immediately struck by the distinctive message and style of Hebrews, for it is different from anything else we read in the NT. By different I don't mean contradictory, for it fits well with Pauline theology. Still the theology is played in a different octave and a different key. In considering the theological message of the letter, it is important to locate the fundamental purpose of the writing. We may become dazzled and dazed by Melchizedek, angels, and the contrast between heaven and earth so that we fail to see why the letter was penned. The author isn't attempting to amaze us with his theological sophistication, his understanding of the relationship between the old covenant and the new, his reading of the Levitical and Melchizedekian priesthoods, and his construal of old and new covenant sacrifices. He writes for a practical reason, which becomes evident when we observe the warning passages that permeate the letter. The exact parameters of the warning passages are debated, but my concern here is not to delineate where the admonitions begin and end. What must be observed, regardless of where the warnings begin and end, is how pervasive the warnings are in Hebrews (2:1–4; 3:12–4:13; 5:11–6:12; 10:26–39; 12:25–29). Here we find the main

---

[50] E.g., Lane, *Hebrews 1–8*, lxxx–xcviii; O'Brien, *Hebrews*, 29–34; Joslin, "Can Hebrews Be Structured?"

purpose of the letter.[51] It is imperative to understand that the warnings, with all their diversity, essentially make the same point. In other words, the warnings should be read synoptically. They mutually cast light on one another. Hence the purpose of the letter becomes clear, for the warnings urge readers not to fall away. They must not turn away from Jesus and the new covenant and revert to the Mosaic law and the old covenant. The same message could be formulated positively. The readers are called on to persevere, to hold on, and to keep believing until the end. If they fall away, the author insists, they will face destruction and damnation.

The structure of the book also plays into the discussion. Some think Jesus' priesthood and sacrifice are the main point of the letter (cf. 8:1), while others see the main point as the exhortation. The strength of both positions can be acknowledged, for the priesthood and the sacrifice of Christ certainly pervade the letter. Still, to say that Christ's priesthood and sacrifice are central makes the letter too abstract and academic, and it misses the pastoral thrust of the work, for the theology of the book, the priesthood and sacrifice of Christ, serves the exhortation.[52] The author's point is that since the work of Christ is so great, it would be folly to turn away from him. The main point in the theology of the letter (8:1), then, provides a foundation for the central purpose of the letter: don't fall away.

Why were the readers tempted to fall away? We have several clues that aren't mutually exclusive. The readers were persecuted and discriminated against for their faith (10:32–34). Perhaps such persecution accounts for their moral lethargy and temptation

---

[51] Lane is particularly clear about this matter (*Hebrews 1–8*, xcviii–civ). See also Schenk, who notes that the exhortations are particularly linked to a loss of confidence in Christ's atonement relative to the Levitical cult. Kenneth L. Schenk, *Cosmology and Eschatology in Hebrews: The Settings of the Sacrifice*, SNTSMS 143 (Cambridge: Cambridge University Press, 2007), 24–47.

[52] Hooker argues that the letter was written after AD 70 and assures Jewish believers that they don't need the temple cult to obtain forgiveness of sins. Morna Hooker, "Christ, the 'End' of the Cult," in *The Epistle to the Hebrews and Christian Theology*, ed. R. Bauckham, D. R. Driver, T. A. Hart, and N. MacDonald (Grand Rapids, MI: Eerdmans, 2009), 189–212. If it was written before AD 70 (which I favor), readers were likely tempted to revert to the temple cult, but in either case the admonition is largely the same: readers must put their confidence in Christ's sacrifice and continue to follow Jesus Christ.

to renounce their commitment to Jesus Christ (cf. 5:11–6:12).[53] Judaism was a legal religion in the empire, and hence identification with the Jewish cult could spare them from further distress and from the shame and dishonor attached to a new religion. At the same time they may have pined for the concrete picture of forgiveness obtained through the Levitical cult. Perhaps they had lost the assurance of cleansing through Christ's blood, which would explain why the author emphasizes the boldness to enter God's presence through Christ's sacrifice.

VI. Religious-Cultural Background

Scholars have proposed a variety of backgrounds to the letter.[54] The matter is extraordinarily complex and hence can't be treated adequately here. Of course, the most important background is the OT itself since the author is clearly immersed in and familiar with OT Scriptures.[55] Along the same lines, Hebrews stands in close affinity to other NT documents; thus it is most fruitful to consider the message of Hebrews in light of the OT Scriptures and the witness to Christ in other NT documents.

A number of monographs have been devoted to tracing the religious-historical background of the letter. Some have postulated a Gnostic background,[56] but the Gnostic turn in NT scholarship is yesterday's news and has been abandoned by most scholars.[57] Others,

---

[53] See Attridge, *Hebrews*, 13.

[54] See the thorough discussion of this matter in Lincoln D. Hurst, *The Epistle to the Hebrews: Its Background of Thought*, SNTSMS 65 (Cambridge: Cambridge University Press, 1990). Hurst evaluates various alleged backgrounds, including Philonic, Qumranic, and Gnostic. He shows that the evidence is wanting for any of these to be postulated as the specific background for the letter. At the same time he demonstrates that the letter fits within the stream of other NT books. See also the compact but elegant survey in Lindars, *The Theology of Hebrews*, 21–25.

[55] See e.g., George B. Caird, "The Exegetical Method of the Epistle to the Hebrews," *Canadian Journal of Theology* 5 (1959): 44–51.

[56] Most notably, Ernst Käsemann, *The Wandering People of God: An Investigation of the Letter to the Hebrews*, trans. R. A. Harrisville and I. L. Sundberg (Minneapolis, MN: Augsburg, 1984).

[57] See e.g., Otfried Hofius, *Katapausis: Die Vorstellung vom endzeitlichen Ruheort im Hebräerbrief*, WUNT 11 (Tübingen: Mohr Siebeck, 1970); Jon Laansma, *"I Will Give You Rest": The Rest Motif in the New Testament with Special Reference to Mt 11 and Heb 3–4*, WUNT 2/98 (Tübingen: Mohr Siebeck, 1997); cf. Graham

detecting fascinating parallels with Plato's thought, have seen a Platonic worldview akin to the writings of Philo.[58] The Platonic and Philonic connection with Hebrews still lives on today, but the work of Williamson and Hurst, among others, has severely damaged the hypothesis.[59] Another possibility is to see a Qumranic background to Hebrews,[60] and it has even been suggested that the letter was written to the Essenes. Certainly Hebrews has many points of contact with Jewish literature in the Second Temple period, but assigning it specifically to Qumran goes beyond the evidence since there is no testimony of a Christian presence at Qumran.

Many scholars have also argued for the influence of eschatology or apocalyptic notions on Hebrews.[61] Schenk rightly suggests that Hebrews is fundamentally Christian, and yet such an admission does not rule out the influence of the OT or even Middle Platonism.[62]

Hughes, *Hebrews and Hermeneutics: The Epistle to the Hebrews as a New Testament Example of Biblical Interpretation*, SNTSMS 36 (Cambridge: Cambridge University Press, 1979), 137–42.

[58] For such a view, see Spicq, *L'Épître aux Hébreux*, 1:39–91; James W. Thompson, *The Beginnings of Christian Philosophy*, CBQMS 13 (Washington, D.C.: The Catholic Biblical Association of America, 1982). L. Johnson thinks scholars reject Philonic influence too dogmatically and sees many affinities between Neoplatonic thought and Hebrews in his commentary.

[59] Ronald Williamson, *Philo and the Epistle to the Hebrews*, ALGHJ (Leiden: Brill, 1970); Hurst, *Hebrews: Its Background of Thought*. Cf. Marie E. Isaacs, *Sacred Space: An Approach to the Theology of the Epistle to the Hebrews*, JSNTSup 73 (Sheffield: Sheffield Academic, 1992), 51–61; Kenneth L. Schenk, "Philo and the Epistle to the Hebrews: Ronald Williamson's Study After Thirty Years," *SPhilo* 14 (2002): 112–35.

[60] For discussion of this view with a careful attention to the evidence, see F. F. Bruce, "'To the Hebrews' or 'To the Essenes'?" *NTS* 9 (1962–63): 217–32.

[61] See C. K. Barrett, "The Eschatology of the Epistle to the Hebrews," in *The Background of the New Testament and Its Eschatology*, ed. W. D. Davies and D. Daube (Cambridge: Cambridge University Press, 1956), 363–93; Mackie, *Eschatology and Exhortation in Hebrews*. Barnard makes an interesting and learned case for apocalyptic mysticism. See Jody A. Barnard, *The Mysticism of Hebrews: Exploring the Role of Jewish Apocalyptic Mysticism in the Epistle to the Hebrews*, WUNT 2/331 (Tübingen: Mohr Siebeck, 2012). Still, weaknesses make the thesis less than convincing. See Nicholas J. Moore, review of *The Mysticism of Hebrews: Exploring the Role of Jewish Apocalyptic Mysticism in the Epistle of Hebrews*, by Jody A. Barnard, *Reviews of Biblical and Early Christian Studies*, November 13, 2012, http://rbecs.org/2012/11/13/barnard, accessed March 18, 2013.

[62] Cf. Schenk, "Philo and the Epistles to the Hebrews," 112–35; idem, *Cosmology and Eschatology in Hebrews*, 3–6. In making this comment I am not endorsing every

Hebrews belongs broadly to the cultural and religious world of early Christianity. Naturally, it has contacts with the Greco-Roman world and the Jewish world. It resonates in some respects with themes found in Plato or Philo without being Platonic or Philonic.[63] The author did not write in a vacuum; his work has some affinity with what we find in Philo, but such correspondences do not mean the writer was drawing from the same well as Philo. Similarly, it has contacts with other Jewish and Christian writings, even though it is not Qumranic or Pauline. The letter has a distinctive character and stamp (even though it corresponds with themes in other writings) that set it apart. At the same time, it belongs with the other NT writings that form the canon of the NT, for it proclaims the centrality of Jesus Christ and insists that forgiveness of sins and entrance into the heavenly city are only through him.

VII. Hebrews Outline

   I. Prologue: Definitive and Final Revelation in the Son (1:1–4)
  II. Don't Abandon the Son Since He Is Greater than Angels (1:5–2:18)
     A. The Son's Nature and Reign Show He Is Greater than Angels (1:5–14)
     B. Warning: Don't Drift Away (2:1–4)
     C. The Coming World Subjected to the Son (2:5–18)
       1. The Son of Man Exalted over Angels by Virtue of His Death (2:5–9)
       2. Jesus as the Merciful and Faithful High Priest Shares His Rule with His Brothers and Sisters (2:10–18)
 III. Don't Harden Your Hearts Since You Have a Son and High Priest Greater than Moses and Joshua (3:1–4:13)
     A. The Faithful Son Greater than the Servant Moses (3:1–6)

---

comment made by Schenk. Still, he rightly maintains that some have underemphasized the similarities and common background of Philo and the author of Hebrews.

  [63] Mackie rightly says that eschatology is central in Hebrews, but the author also draws upon the middle Platonism current in his day, though he did not embrace a Platonic worldview (*Eschatology and Exhortation in Hebrews*, 3–8, 105–20). See also Nash, who sees Philonic influence but carefully sets forth where the author of Hebrews differs from Plato. Ronald H. Nash, "The Notion of Mediator in Alexandrian Judaism and the Epistle to the Hebrews," *WTJ* 40 (1977): 100–109.

B. Warning: Continue Believing and Obeying to Enter Rest (3:7–4:13)
   1. The OT Text: Don't Harden Your Hearts as the Wilderness Generation Did (3:7–11)
   2. Application of OT: Beware of Unbelief and Disobedience (3:12–19)
   3. Fear Lest You Don't Enter His Rest (4:1–5)
   4. Be Diligent to Enter His Rest While It Remains (4:6–13)
IV. Don't Fall Away from Jesus' Melchizedekian Priesthood Since It Is Greater than the Levitical Priesthood (4:14–10:18)
   A. Exhortation in Light of Jesus' Priestly Status (4:14–5:10)
      1. Hold Fast Confession and Draw Near Since Jesus Is Son and High Priest (4:14–16)
      2. Jesus Appointed by God as Perfect High Priest (5:1–10)
   B. Warning and Assurance (5:11–6:20)
      1. Warning Against Falling Away from Jesus the High Priest (5:11–6:8)
         a. High Priesthood Hard to Explain Because of Readers' Sluggishness (5:11–14)
         b. Call to Maturity (6:1–3)
         c. Those Who Fall Away Can't Be Renewed to Repentance (6:4–8)
      2. Assurance and Comfort (6:9–20)
         a. Confident that Readers Will Be Diligent and Inherit the Promises (6:9–12)
         b. Assurance and Hope Through God's Oath (6:13–20)
   C. Jesus' Greater Priesthood as a Melchizedekian Priest (7:1–28)
      1. Melchizedek Greater than Levi (7:1–10)
      2. Arguments for a Changed Priesthood (7:11–28)
         a. Imperfection of Levitical Priesthood (7:11–12)
         b. Jesus from Tribe of Judah (7:13–14)
         c. Prophecy of Melchizedekian Priesthood (7:15–17)
         d. Setting Aside of Levitical Priesthood (7:18–19)

      e. Oath Accompanies Melchizedekian
         Priesthood (7:20–22)

      f. Jesus a Permanent Priest (7:23–25)

      g. A Sinless Priest and a Once-for-All
         Sacrifice (7:26–28)

  D. New Covenant Better than the Old (8:1–13)

    1. Jesus' Heavenly Priesthood Shows He Is Mediator of
       a Better Covenant (8:1–6)

    2. Prophecy of New Covenant Shows Weakness of
       Old (8:7–13)

  E. A Better Sacrifice Under the New Covenant (9:1–10:18)

    1. Free Access to God Not Granted Under Old
       Covenant (9:1–10)

    2. Jesus Entered Heaven Itself with His Blood (9:11–14)

    3. Jesus as Mediator of New Covenant Bestows an
       Eternal Inheritance (9:15–22)

    4. Jesus' Sacrifice: Better than OT Sacrifices
       (9:23–10:18)

      a. Jesus' Heavenly and Once-for-All
         Sacrifice (9:23–28)

      b. Repetition of OT Sacrifices Shows Their
         Inadequacy (10:1–4)

      c. Jesus' Once-for-All Sacrifice Canceled Old
         System (10:5–10)

      d. Jesus' Completed Sacrifice (10:11–14)

      e. Final Forgiveness Promised in New Covenant
         Realized (10:15–18)

V. Concluding Exhortations and Warnings (10:19–12:29)

  A. Exhortation to Draw Near, Hold Fast, and Help Others
     (10:19–25)

  B. Warning: No Hope of Forgiveness for Those Who Turn
     from Christ (10:26–31)

  C. Call to Persevere in Faith (10:32–12:3)

    1. Don't Abandon Confidence but Endure in Faith
       (10:32–39)

    2. Description and Examples of Persevering Faith
       (11:1–12:3)

      a. Nature of Faith (11:1–2)

      b. Creation Through Noah (11:3–7)

        c. The Faith of Abraham and His Heirs (11:8–22)

        d. The Faith of Moses and Those Entering the Land (11:23–31)

        e. A Closing Catalog of Faith (11:32–40)

        f. Run the Race Looking to Jesus as Supreme Exemplar of Faith (12:1–3)

    D. Exhortations to Readers to Endure (12:4–29)

        1. Endure Discipline for Holiness (12:4–13)

        2. Pursue Peace and Holiness for the Final Blessing (12:14–17)

        3. You Have Come to Mount Zion Instead of Mount Sinai (12:18–24)

        4. Final Warning: Don't Refuse the One Speaking (12:25–29)

VI. Epilogue: Final Exhortations (13:1–25)

    A. Practical Expressions of Love in the Church (13:1–6)

    B. Remember Your Leaders and Suffer with Jesus Outside the Camp (13:7–17)

    C. Final Words (13:18–25)

VIII. Hebrews and the Story Line of the Bible

The story line of the Scriptures can only be sketched here briefly, but it is important to put Hebrews in canonical context, for it is part of a library of books that constitute Holy Scripture. We won't truly understand Hebrews unless we see how it relates at least in some fashion to the rest of Scripture.

The Scriptures open in Genesis with God as the sovereign King creating the world and everything in it. Human beings are made in the image of God and appointed to rule the world for God (Gen 1:26–27). They are mandated to rule the world under God's lordship and for his glory. Instead of trusting and obeying God, Adam and Eve defied him and refused to submit to him (Genesis 3). Because of their transgression incited by the words of the serpent, they were spiritually separated from God and introduced death into the world. Nevertheless, death is not the final word, for God promises that the offspring of the woman will crush the serpent (Gen 3:15).

The initial optimism engendered by the promise collapses, for human beings are radically evil. Cain was the offspring of the serpent and murdered Abel.[64] The offspring of the serpent were triumphing over the offspring of the woman, though God granted Seth to Adam and Eve to continue the lineage through which the promise would be fulfilled (Gen 4:25). Because the corruption was so great, because the offspring of the serpent were spreading so rapidly, God had to destroy them with the flood, showing that he rules and reigns even when evil seems to have the upper hand. God established a covenant with Noah, pledging to preserve the world until he accomplished redemption (Genesis 6–9). Still, the story of the tower of Babel reveals that human beings had not changed (Gen 11:1–9); they were still inclined toward evil and lived to make a name for themselves instead of living for the glory and honor and praise of the one true God. Genesis 1–11 unveils the depth of human evil so that readers will grasp that victory over the serpent is a massive undertaking. The evil in human beings is no trivial matter. A demonic rejection of God and an embrace of evil afflict human beings.

Despite human evil, which defies the imagination, God is gracious. He chose one man through whom he would fulfill the promise made to the woman. He promises Abraham that he will have land (Canaan), offspring (Isaac), and universal blessing (Gen 12:1–3). Still the story rolls on slowly. Abraham, Isaac, and Jacob never possessed the land, and Abraham found it agonizingly difficult to have even one child! The Lord teaches him through the birth of Isaac that the promise will only be fulfilled through God himself, that human beings can't contribute to the promise's fulfillment. Isaac and Jacob learned the same lesson so that, when Genesis ends, Israel was in the wrong land (Egypt), there were only about 70 Israelites (when God promised they would be as many as the stars of the sky), and there was certainly not universal blessing. What is said here could be misunderstood, for there could scarcely be countless descendants in three generations, and Joseph as Pharaoh's right-hand man did bless the nations.

When Exodus opens, the promise of offspring for Israel is being fulfilled, for their population was exploding, which terrified the Egyptians. The Lord intended to show Israel again and again that salvation is his work, not theirs. Hence, he freed Israel from

---

[64] All the offspring of Adam and Eve come into the world as the offspring of the serpent, and hence those who belong to God are the recipients of his grace.

Egypt through Moses with great signs and wonders (Exodus 1–18). The Lord crushed the offspring of the serpent (Pharaoh), who attempted to annihilate the people from whom the offspring of the woman would come (Gen 3:15). Israel recognized that the Lord had redeemed them, fulfilling his promise to Abraham, Isaac, and Jacob. Israel was adopted as God's son (Exod 4:22), becoming his special possession and a kingdom of priests if they followed the Lord's instructions (Exod 19:5–6). The redemption from Egypt becomes a type and anticipation of the redemption that would be accomplished in Jesus Christ.

The Lord entered into a covenant with Israel, choosing them as his special people (cf. Exodus 19–24). If Israel obeyed the covenant stipulations, they would be blessed; but if they transgressed what the Lord commanded, they would experience the curses of the covenant (Leviticus 26, Deuteronomy 26–28). The Lord didn't demand perfection to remain in the covenant, for sacrifices were instituted to grant forgiveness for Israel's transgressions (Leviticus 1–7, 16). The Lord also impressed on Israel his holiness. He dwelt with his people in the tabernacle (Exodus 25–40), but those who treated the Lord with contempt would be destroyed (Leviticus 10), as the thunderstorm which gripped Mount Sinai clearly taught the people. Hebrews, of course, focuses on the final inadequacy of the sacrifices offered, and emphasizes the inauguration of the new covenant. Ultimately, the old covenant was a failure. The sacrifices didn't cleanse the conscience of sin and provide free access to God, nor did the old covenant inscribe the law on the heart. But we are getting ahead of the story here!

The next element of the promise of Abraham was ready to be fulfilled. Israel was about to take possession of Canaan. We read in Numbers how the people failed to follow the Lord's instructions. After seeing the Lord's signs and wonders that routed the Egyptians, Israel, amazingly enough, didn't believe the Lord could bring them into the land, and hence they disobeyed his instructions. Hebrews picks up on the sin of the wilderness generation (3:12–4:13), using it to warn his readers not to follow the example of Israel. The story wasn't over, however, for under Joshua Israel possessed the land of Canaan, though the story clarifies that they didn't possess the entirety of the land. Israel's triumphs are the Lord's work, for they win impossible victories over foes that are far stronger than they are. Joshua concludes by saying that the Lord has given rest to Israel (21:4; 22:4; 23:1). Hebrews picks up this theme, contending that the rest given to Israel under Joshua was not the final rest God promised. The rest under Joshua was a type and anticipation of a greater rest to come.

Upon opening Judges, we might think that paradise is around the corner. Two elements of the promise to Abraham are fulfilled: Israel had a large population and now inhabited the land of Canaan. Hundreds of years had passed since the promise was made to Abraham, but Israel now seemed to be on the cusp of blessing. It is rather stunning to see where the story goes next. Instead of moving forward, Israel slipped backward. They were in that sense like Adam in paradise. Instead of trusting and obeying the Lord, they turned toward idols so that the Lord unleashed their enemies upon them. Israel repeated a cycle of sin, defeat before enemies, repentance, and deliverance. Judges concludes with a story that echoes what happened to Lot in Sodom (Judges 20; Genesis 19). Israel was in the land, but they were not submitting to Yahweh's lordship. Instead of blessing the nations, they were being corrupted by the nations.

When 1 Samuel opens, Israel had a corrupt priesthood and was teetering toward collapse. Still the Lord was gracious, raising up Samuel to bring the nation back to him. The kingship was instituted under Samuel when Saul was installed as the first king. If we read perceptively, the theme of kingship is actually in the narrative from the beginning. The Lord promises that kings will come from Abraham and Jacob (17:6, 16; 35:11). Indeed, the scepter will belong to Judah, and the peoples of the world (universal blessing!) will obey him (Gen 49:10). Balaam prophesies that a star and scepter from Israel will crush (cf. Gen 3:15) the enemies of the Lord (Num 24:17–19). The offspring of the woman who will destroy the serpent will come from a king in Israel. The narrative poses an implicit question: is Saul that king? On first taking the reins of power, it looked as if he might be. But Saul turned out like Adam in the garden and like Israel after possessing Canaan. Instead of trusting and obeying the Lord, he followed his own desires, and hence the Lord pledges that there will not be a Saulide dynasty.

David was anointed as king instead of Saul, and Saul became David's mortal enemy, following the footsteps of Pharaoh (the offspring of the serpent!) who tried to destroy the chosen of the Lord. David was persecuted and on the run, but he trusted in the Lord to exalt him instead of wresting the kingdom from Saul. Finally, the Philistines killed Saul in battle, and David as king reigned over all Israel. David's kingship was marked by his trust and obedience to the Lord. Indeed, the Lord made a covenant with David that is central to the scriptural story line. The offspring of the woman who would triumph over the serpent would come from David's line. He would be a Davidic king, for the Lord promised David a perpetual dynasty (2 Samuel 7). According to Hebrews and the remainder of the NT, this promise finds its fulfillment in Jesus the Messiah.

Despite all of David's virtues, he was not the one who would crush the serpent, for he too was a sinner needing forgiveness since he violated the covenant with the Lord by committing adultery with Bathsheba and murdering Uriah (2 Samuel 11). Still, when David's son Solomon ascended to the throne, it seemed that paradise was around the corner. Israel was at peace. Solomon was a wise and judicious king, and a marvelous temple was erected to worship the Lord. Could universal blessing be far behind? But Solomon recapitulated the story we have seen over and over again. He followed the pattern of Adam in the garden, Israel in Canaan, and Saul as king. He ceased to trust in the Lord and turned to idols.

The kingdom, after Solomon's day and as a result of his sin, was divided between the north and the south, with Israel in the north and Judah in the south. Every single king in Israel followed the pattern of the first king, Jeroboam son of Nebat, and worshiped idols. The kings of Judah had a more mixed record, for some were faithful to the Lord, though even the best of them failed to do all the Lord commanded. At the end of the day, though, both Israel and Judah gave themselves over to sin, and thus both kingdoms experienced the curses of the covenant: Israel was exiled to Assyria in 722 BC and Judah to Babylon in 586 BC. We see from this brief recapitulation of the story that Hebrews rightly maintains that the new covenant is better than the old. Such a judgment is verified by the history of Israel. The kingdom was not realized through the old covenant since both Israel and Judah did not and could not keep the prescriptions of the covenant.

The prophets came to center stage after the kingdom was instituted in Israel, warning both Israel and Judah that exile would come unless they repented and turned to the Lord. The Day of the Lord will come, and it will not be a day of salvation but a day of judgment for disobedient Israel. The prophets, however, did not only proclaim a message of judgment. Israel would go into exile, but there would be a new exodus. Israel, by the grace of God, would return to the land. There would be a new start for the people of God, and the kingdom would come with the arrival of the new exodus. And that is not all. There will be a new covenant (Jer 31:31–34; Ezek 36:26–27) in which Israel's sins will be finally and fully forgiven. The Lord will write the law on Israel's heart by giving them the Holy Spirit, and so they will desire to do what the Lord says. The Lord will pour out his Spirit on his people, and a new age of salvation will arise (cf. Isa 32:15; 44:3; Joel 2:28). Creation will be renewed, and there will be a new exodus, a new covenant, and a new creation. The kingdom God promised has not been withdrawn. It will come, and a new David will reign on the throne (Hos 3:5; Mic 5:2–4; Isa 9:1–7; 11:1–10; 55:3; Jer 23:5–6; 30:9; 33:15–17; Ezek 34:23–24; 37:24–25; Zech 9:9). The new creation, the new exodus, and the new covenant will be fulfilled through a king! The serpent will be defeated, and the kingdom will come.

Israel returned from exile in 536 BC, and yet the promises of a new covenant, a new creation, and the coming kingdom were not realized. It seems that the prophecies found in the prophets only had an already-but-not-yet fulfillment. Remarkably Israel, by and large, did not surrender their faith. They continued to believe that the Lord would fulfill his promises to them. When the NT opens, there are a variety of opinions and sects in Israel, but there was a common belief that the Lord would keep his kingdom promises. Most believed that the great promises would be realized only if Israel was obedient to the Torah.

The events in the Gospels took place before Hebrews was written and hence are part of the theological backdrop of the letter. We can hardly do justice to the message of the Gospels here, but certain themes stand out. First, Jesus is the new David promised by the prophets. He is the one through whom the blessing promised to Abraham and David would be fulfilled. Second, Jesus teaches that the kingdom has arrived in his ministry. The kingdom has come because the king has come! Third, Jesus clearly teaches that he is the one who will give the Spirit to his people (cf. Matt 3:11–12 par.;

John 14–16); the promises of return from exile, a new covenant, and a new creation would come to pass through God's Spirit. Fourth, Jesus is the Son of Man who will receive the kingdom (cf. Dan 7:9–14). He is the Son of God who is Immanuel, God with us (Matt 1:23). He is the Word of God (John 1:1–18) who is fully divine (cf. John 5:23). He existed before Abraham was born (John 8:58). He is the Bread of the Life, the Light of the World, the Good Shepherd, the Resurrection and the Life, the Way and the Truth and the Life, and the True Vine. Fifth, at the Last Supper Jesus teaches that the new covenant is instituted with his death (Matt 26:26–29 par.). Jesus is the Servant of the Lord (cf. Isaiah 53) who took upon himself the sins of his people. The Gospels have been called passion narratives with an extended introduction, for the climax of the story comes with Jesus' death and resurrection, and all the Gospels teach that through Jesus' death and resurrection forgiveness is granted (e.g., Matt 1:21; 20:28; Mark 10:45; Luke 22:19–20; John 1:29; 6:51; 11:49–52).

Much more could be said. What is striking in the story of the Gospels is that the people of Israel, except for a few disciples, failed to see what was right before their eyes. The problem that plagued Israel throughout its history still persisted. They continued to resist God's revelation. Jesus wasn't embraced as Israel's deliverer. He was despised as a messianic pretender, especially since they thought his teaching didn't accord with the law. Hence, instead of crowning Jesus as the king, they crucified him on the cross. They didn't realize that Jesus was the Passover Lamb, the Son of Man, the Son of God, the Word of God, and the Servant of the Lord of Isaiah 53. They didn't understand that through Jesus' death on the cross the new covenant was instituted as he taught at the Last Supper. They didn't realize that the forgiveness that the new covenant promised (Jer 31:34) was accomplished through Jesus' death.

Death was not the end of the story. God vindicated Jesus by raising him from the dead. The resurrection (Isa 26:19; Ezekiel 37; Dan 12:2) signaled the arrival of the new creation and age to come. In Jesus the return from exile (which is the coming of the kingdom) had arrived, though it won't be consummated until the second coming. The new covenant was inaugurated with his death and the gift of the Spirit. The new creation had come with his resurrection, and he was most certainly the new David. The prophecies of the OT were all fulfilled in him. And yet there was a proviso. The new creation, the new covenant, and the new exodus were inaugurated but not consummated. The kingdom had come but not in its fullness. All nations would be blessed through him, so that there was an opportunity for salvation for all peoples before the final day.

We see in the Acts of the Apostles the gift of the Holy Spirit given to the church (Acts 2), signaling that the eschaton had arrived. The new covenant is the age of the Holy Spirit, which came at Pentecost. In Acts the good news about Jesus Christ is proclaimed to both Jews and Gentiles, so that the promise given to Abraham, Isaac, and Jacob of worldwide blessing began to be realized. As the gospel was proclaimed and believed, resistance arose from both Jews and Gentiles. The early Christians taught that salvation was only in Jesus (Acts 4:12) and that God raised him from the dead and would judge the world through him (Acts 17:31). Hence, people were required to believe in Christ and repent of their sins and receive baptism to be saved (e.g., Acts 2:38; 16:31). Interestingly, Jewish Christians continued to worship in the temple, apparently participating in the burnt offering (Acts 3:1–10), and Paul offered sacrifices in accord with the Nazirite vow (Acts 18:18; 21:23–26; cf. Num 6:9–21). Such practices did not mean that Christians were obligated to keep the law. The Apostolic Council determined that circumcision and observance of the law were not necessary for salvation (Acts 15:1–21). Furthermore, Peter was clearly instructed that the food and purity laws were no longer required (Acts 10:1–11:18). The early Christians apparently kept some of the laws for cultural reasons (not because they were required for salvation) and to facilitate fellowship with Jews they were trying to reach with the gospel.

The place of Hebrews in the canon and the NT is significant. It comes after the Gospels and the book of Acts. Having given a brief survey of the Bible's story line, we are not surprised that Hebrews picks up central themes from that story line. First, God's promises have been fulfilled in Jesus Christ. He is the Son of God, the Messiah, and the Melchizedekian high priest. The new covenant promised in the OT has been realized in him. Believers, therefore, are forgiven of their sins through the atoning work of Jesus Christ. Second, the fulfillment in Christ has an already-but-not-yet character. The new age has been inaugurated but not consummated. So the new covenant has indeed come, but believers are not yet perfectly free from sin. They are forgiven of their sins through Christ's sacrifice, but they still struggle with feelings of guilt. The age to come has arrived through Christ's resurrection, and yet believers still await the coming of the heavenly city. Third, the OT is typological so that the institutions, events, and persons in the OT forecast what is to come. The OT sacrificial system points forward to the final and definitive atonement accomplished in Jesus Christ's sacrifice. The Davidic king and Israel as God's son point ahead to Jesus as the Messiah, the unique Son of God who fulfilled what Adam was called to do in paradise. Fourth, the earthly reflects the heavenly. The tabernacle and its furnishings on earth point to a heavenly tabernacle above, to the presence of God. The OT should be read eschatologically, typologically, and spatially.

The story line rehearsed here reminds us of one of the most important themes in Hebrews. The OT should be read in light of the fulfillment in Jesus Christ. It does not apply in the same way to believers in Jesus Christ as it did to OT saints or even to those who lived when Jesus was on earth. Hence, one cannot depend on OT sacrifices to obtain forgiveness of sin, for such an activity denies the once-for-all sacrifice in Jesus Christ. To revert to OT sacrifices would be to march backward in salvation history. It would, in effect, deny that Jesus Christ has come. It would be a blatant rejection of his sacrifice. Practically speaking, then, a return to the OT cult would constitute a rejection of Jesus as Messiah, as the Son of God, and as the Melchizedekian priest. It would say that Moses and Joshua were greater than Jesus, that animal sacrifices were worth more than Jesus' sacrifice. It would mean returning to earth when Jesus has lifted believers to heaven, to the presence of God. The warnings are so strong in Hebrews because the readers were tempted to deny Jesus and all that he had accomplished. They were close to denying that the "last days" had come and that God has spoken definitively and finally in his Son (1:2). They were on the brink of hardening their hearts to what God had done in Jesus, just as the wilderness generation had done (3:12–4:13). They were perilously close to acting like Esau, who sold his birthright for a pot of porridge (12:16–17).

They were probably tempted to revert back to Judaism because they were suffering (cf. 10:32–34; 12:4–11). The writer reminds them of the pattern of OT saints and the pattern in the life of Jesus.

First comes suffering and then comes glory. Already-not-yet eschatology means the reward promised to believers, the heavenly city, still awaits them.

One question that arises when comparing Acts and Hebrews should be answered here. If Paul offered sacrifices for a Nazirite vow and other early Christians continued to participate in temple activities, why does Hebrews reject so dogmatically OT sacrifices? Doesn't that contradict what believers actually did in Acts? Answering this question is difficult since the circumstances and situation of the readers in Hebrews are not completely clear to us. I suggest the following. In the case of Paul and Peter, no one believed they were compromising their belief in Jesus Christ by participating in Jewish sacrifices. It was clear they believed Jesus was the Messiah and that his death was the only means by which one could be forgiven of sins (Acts 2:38; 4:12; 13:38–39). Apparently the readers of Hebrews were communicating something different. If they reverted to OT sacrifices, they were sending the message that Christ's sacrifice was not sufficient, that one needed to offer animal sacrifices to be saved. In other words, the readers were in effect saying that animal sacrifices were necessary for salvation and the sacrifice of Christ could be dispensed with. Participating in worship and sacrifice with other Jewish believers for cultural reasons to reach them with the gospel was one thing, but in Hebrews the readers were inclined toward something different. They were suggesting (if they continued on their path) that the sacrifice of animals and the OT cult was fundamental and crucial to obtain forgiveness of sins. They were in effect denying Christ's sacrifice and were placing their trust in the old covenant rather than the new.

IX. Biblical and Theological Structures

The intent in this section is to touch on some of the structural themes that undergird the biblical theology of Hebrews. The structures discussed here are not completely discrete entities, for they overlap to some extent. Still, it is helpful for the sake of clarity to look at the theology of Hebrews from a number of different angles. Here I will note the structures that inform Hebrews and at the conclusion of the commentary will focus on major themes. I hope these two different ways of exploring the theology of Hebrews will be enriching, indicating that the theology of the book can be explored from a variety of perspectives. I am not claiming that these are the only structures for examining Hebrews but that the structures here represent a helpful introduction to the letter. The structures explored here are: (1) promise-fulfillment; (2) already-but-not-yet eschatology; (3) typology; and (4) the spatial orientation of Hebrews.

Promise-Fulfillment

I understand promise-fulfillment in a particular way here. It refers to predictions or promises in the OT that, according to Hebrews, are now fulfilled. Even though promise-fulfillment is defined in such a way, there are instances where it is difficult to determine whether a particular passage is promise-fulfillment or typological. In some instances, since the categories overlap, I will argue that both categories apply.

The first verses of the book signal the theme of promise and fulfillment (1:1–2). God had spoken in a variety of modes in the OT, but he has spoken definitively and finally in his Son. The author communicates from the outset that OT revelation, which was diverse and incomplete, finds its fulfillment in Jesus Christ. It is clear in reading Hebrews that the entirety of the OT should be read in light of the fulfillment in Jesus, but for the sake of space the focus here will be on specific instances of fulfillment in Hebrews. We begin with what is perhaps the favorite OT Scripture for the author: Psalm 110. Verse 1 says, "This is the declaration of the LORD to my Lord: 'Sit at My right hand until I make Your enemies Your footstool.'" According to Hebrews this prophecy is clearly fulfilled in Jesus Christ, for he alludes to or quotes the verse five different times (1:2, 13; 8:1; 10:12–13; 12:2). The prophecy fits into the story line of the OT. God promises to reclaim his rule over the world through the offspring of the woman (Gen 3:15). As the story progresses, the promise is unpacked further, for the Lord reveals that the world will be blessed through Abraham's offspring (e.g., Gen 12:1–3). The identity of the one through whom the promise will be realized is explained further in the time of David, for God's rule over the world will be restored through a Davidic king according to the promise of the Davidic covenant (2 Samuel 7).

The citation of Psalm 110 fits into such a narrative, clarifying that according to Hebrews Jesus is the Davidic son and Lord (!)

through whom the kingdom will be established. The author quotes Ps 110:1, directly applying it to Jesus in 1:13. He also alludes at the outset of the book to Ps 110:1, declaring that Jesus "sat down at the right hand of the Majesty on high" (1:3). Hebrews returns to the fulfillment of this prophecy repeatedly, affirming that the "main point" in the letter is that Jesus as high priest "sat down at the right hand of the throne of the Majesty in the heavens" (8:1). Jesus' sitting at God's right hand is tied to his accomplishing final atonement for believers (10:12; 12:2) so that he now waits until his enemies are made the footstool for his feet (10:13). The author sees Jesus as the coruler of the universe with God, and as such he enjoys divine stature and worship (1:6).

Jesus also fulfills Ps 110:4, which reads, "The LORD has sworn an oath and will not take it back: 'Forever, You are a priest like Melchizedek.'" In Psalm 110 the one who is David's lord is also an eternal priest in the order of Melchizedek. The author of Hebrews sees this verse fulfilled in Jesus and exploits it to further his argument. Jesus' calling as a high priest is affirmed by citing Ps 110:4 (5:5–6). Jesus did not assert his selfish will, claiming that he should serve as high priest. He was called and identified by God as a Melchizedekian priest so that Jesus responded to God's claim on his life instead of deciding his own destiny.

Jesus also fulfilled the prophecy of serving as a priest like Melchizedek (5:10) because of his humanity and participation in suffering. He could not fulfill the priestly calling if he did not share the human condition. He knew anguish and misery, learning obedience and becoming perfect in the process (5:7–9). At the same time the author sees in Ps 110:4 a prophecy of the resurrection, for the verse says he will serve as a priest "forever" (7:17). Jesus fulfills this prophecy because he has "an indestructible life" (7:16), because he conquered death through the resurrection. Another element of the prophecy in Ps 110:4 is that it is accompanied by an oath. The author of Hebrews spies great significance in this, concluding that Jesus' priesthood is superior to the Levitical priesthood since the latter was not accompanied by an oath (7:20–22).

I noted above that God's kingdom, promised in the OT, would be realized through a Davidic king. Hebrews appropriates this theme and sees it as fulfilled in Jesus Christ. When the author says the Son is the "heir of all things" (1:2), he draws on a promise given to the anointed king of Israel (Ps 2:8). A few verses later Hebrews actually quotes Ps 2:7, which confirms that the writer identifies the Son and king of the psalm to be Jesus himself. The Messianic promise, granted to the Davidic king, finds its ultimate realization in Jesus.

In the same verse (1:5) Hebrews also quotes 2 Sam 7:14, which comes from the chapter where the Davidic covenant is inaugurated in which the Lord promises that David's dynasty will never end. The prophets pick up on this Davidic promise and reaffirm it regularly (Hos 3:5; Mic 5:2–4; Isa 9:1–7; 11:1–10; 55:3; Jer 23:5–6; 30:9; 33:15–17; Ezek 34:23–24; 37:24–25; Zech 9:9). Hebrews leaves us no doubt that Jesus is the true Son of David, that he is the Messiah, and thus the kingdom promised in the OT is realized in him.

The fulfillment of the new covenant stands out in Hebrews. The author quotes Jer 31:31–34 twice (8:8–12; 10:15–18), and it appears at the heart of his argument. The old covenant failed because Israel did not keep the covenant stipulations, and hence they were thrust into exile. The Lord promised, however, that he would make a new arrangement, a new covenant, with his people. He would implant the law within them so they could actually do what the Lord commanded. Furthermore, he would forgive the sins of his people. Interestingly Hebrews doesn't emphasize the ability to do what the law commands. Instead, it focuses on the fact that the covenant is called "new." If it is new, he concludes, then the fulfillment has come, and the old covenant is obsolete (8:13). Another dimension of the new covenant is exploited. God would not make a new covenant if the old one were adequate. So the new covenant is also a "better" covenant (7:22; 8:6). The new covenant has "a better hope" (7:19), "better promises" (8:6), and "better sacrifices" (9:23), since Jesus' blood "says better things than the blood of Abel" (12:24). The new covenant shows that believers should no longer live under the old, for the old is inferior and ineffectual. The inadequacy of the old comes to center stage when the author considers forgiveness. What makes the NT superior is that sins are forgiven definitively and fully and forever in the sacrifice of Jesus (9:11–10:18). It doesn't make sense to revert to OT sacrifices since the repetition of such sacrifices illustrates their inability to cleanse the conscience from sin.

We see the promise and fulfillment theme also in terms of the rest (3:12–4:13), the land promised to the people of God.[65] In God's covenant with the patriarchs, he promised them land (Gen 12:1–3; 13:14–17; 15:18–21; 26:3; 28:4, 13–15; 35:12). The promise of the land is fulfilled under Joshua when Israel possessed Canaan, though the land was surrendered again when the northern kingdom was sent into exile by Assyria in 722 BC and the southern kingdom by Babylon in 586 BC. In NT times Israel was still in exile in that the Romans ruled over her. Hebrews teaches that the land promise has not been fulfilled in its fullness, but it doesn't look forward to Israel's possessing the land of Canaan. Instead, a future rest is promised to the people of God (4:1–13), a heavenly rest that is greater than any earthly rest. The patriarchs did not obtain the entirety of what God promised, living as sojourners on the earth (11:13). The promise of land, the promise of eschatological rest, will be fulfilled in the heavenly city, in the new Jerusalem which is coming (11:10, 14–16; 12:22; 13:14).

Already-but-Not-Yet Eschatology

One of the common features of NT eschatology is its already-but-not-yet character.[66] What this means is that God's eschatological promises have been inaugurated through Jesus Christ but not consummated. Fulfillment has truly come in Jesus Christ, but the fulfillment isn't complete. Hence there is an eschatological tension that characterizes the NT witness. Hebrews shares such a perspective, and this reality will be outlined briefly.

We see eschatological tension in Jesus' reigning at the right hand of God. As noted above, the reign of Jesus at God's right hand fulfills Ps 110:1 (cf. 1:3, 13; 8:1; 10:12–13; 12:2). The last days have arrived (1:2), for the Messiah reigns as the OT prophesied.[67] It is striking for Christians today to realize that we have been in the last days for nearly 2,000 years. As Hebrews says elsewhere, the "end of the ages" has come through the sacrifice of Jesus Christ

---

[65] Oren Martin, *Bound for the Promised Land*, NSBT (Downers Grove: InterVarsity, 2015).

[66] For Hebrews, see especially Mackie, *Eschatology and Exhortation in Hebrews*, 29–152.

[67] See the discussion in Schenk, *Cosmology and Eschatology in Hebrews*, 78–111.

(9:26). But there is also eschatological reservation, for even though Jesus reigns in heaven, his enemies have not yet been completely vanquished (1:13; 10:13). "We do not yet see everything subjected to" Jesus (2:8), even though he is now "crowned with glory and honor" (2:8–9). We still await the coming new world that will be under Jesus' authority (2:5). Hebrews clarifies that the rule promised to human beings is fulfilled in and through Jesus. The present heavens will perish and be rolled up like a cloak (1:11–12). The created things, the present heavens and earth, will be shaken and removed, and only God's kingdom will remain (12:26–28).

The already-but-not-yet theme is also apparent with regard to salvation. On the one hand believers are waiting for Jesus to come again when he will bring salvation (9:28) and they will "inherit" the salvation promised (1:14; 9:15). The fullness of the promise has not yet become reality, but it will be realized when Jesus comes again (10:36–37). On the other hand salvation is also the present possession of believers (2:3; 5:9; 6:9–10). When we consider the temporal dimension of salvation, we find a both-and instead of an either-or. Believers *are* saved and *will be* saved. Both are true, and neither truth should be denied or neglected.

Similarly, believers are now "sanctified through the offering of the body of Jesus Christ once and for all" (10:10). They have been "sanctified" through "the blood of the covenant" (10:29; cf. 10:14), and thus sanctification is an already accomplished reality; it has been definitively accomplished through the sacrifice of Jesus Christ. But there is also eschatological reservation, a recognition that believers are not yet completely sanctified. They should "pursue . . . holiness," for apart from it they will not "see the Lord" (12:14). If sanctification were complete in every sense, there would be no need to pursue holiness. The urgent exhortation to holiness demonstrates that believers are not yet all they should be. Believers are already truly sanctified and set apart through Jesus Christ, and yet they await the fullness of their sanctification, the completion of holiness that God intends for his people to enjoy. The same kinds of things could be said about perfection. Believers are "perfected" (τετελείωκεν) now and forever by the once-for-all offering of Jesus Christ (10:14). One would think from such a statement that no further work was needed, yet the author also exhorts the readers to go on to perfection (τελειότητα, 6:1), indicating that perfection is not yet theirs in its entirety.

The provisional nature of the deliverance enjoyed by believers is evident in other ways in the letter. For instance, believers are "waiting" for the kingdom to come in all its fullness. The interval between the already and not yet is evident, for believers in Jesus Christ suffer (10:32–34) and experience discipline (12:4–11). Distress and affliction will not be the portion of believers when the kingdom is consummated. Another way to put it is that believers are freed from bondage to death and "the fear of death" now (2:14–15), and yet they are not spared physical death itself. They must die before enjoying new life in its fullness.

The eschatological tension in Hebrews is also communicated by the warning passages (2:1–4; 3:12–4:13; 5:11–6:8; 10:26–31; 12:25–29). The readers are admonished about the terrible consequences of falling away. If they turn away from Jesus Christ, there is no hope for them. Such admonitions are given to those who are "brothers" (3:12), to those who have been "enlightened" and have received the Holy Spirit (6:4–6). The Spirit, as the OT teaches, is an eschatological gift (Isa 32:15; 44:3; Ezek 36:26–27; 37:14; 39:29; Joel 2:28). Since the Hebrews had received the Spirit, they are members of the new age, participants in the new covenant (Jer 31:31–34). According to Jeremiah 31, beneficiaries of the new covenant have God's law implanted in them. But if that is the case, why the need for warnings? Certainly residents of the heavenly city won't need warnings. It seems here that we have another example of eschatological tension. The readers are members of the new covenant, the law is written on their hearts, and they are truly partakers of the Holy Spirit. And yet they need warnings to stimulate them to persevere until the end. The warnings are not inconsequential or insignificant. Even though the readers have already received eschatological promises, they must heed the warnings to obtain eschatological promises.

The call to faith is also a recognition of the "not yet" (10:39–11:40). Believers must continue to believe, as chapter 11 clarifies, to receive the promise, just as their ancestors believed in what God pledged to them. If the promise were visible (cf. 11:3) and the reward were given now (11:6), faith in God's future promises would be superfluous. Faith places its confidence in what God will do in the future. Faith recognizes, then, that God hasn't yet given everything he promised, and it reaches out to the future, believing that God will make good on everything he has said.

The rest promised in Hebrews is clearly eschatological (3:7–4:11). Believers must enter God's rest, and yet at the same time it seems that 4:3 teaches that those who believe have entered God's rest even now.[68] The word "today" (4:7) may also suggest that the rest can be entered now. Still the rest is fundamentally an end-time reality (4:11). Believers are still exiles and sojourners (11:13), and in that respect they are like the wilderness generation (cf. 3:12–19), which was "on the way" to receive God's promise.

Even if the rest is wholly future, which is the view of many scholars, believers enjoy many other present blessings, for they are members of God's people and enjoy his presence during their earthly sojournings (7:19). Associated with the notion of rest is the promise of the city to come (11:10). God has prepared a heavenly city for his own (11:16). Presently believers are members of the city of man, which will not endure (12:27). At the same time they are distinct from the people of this world, for they seek the city of God, which is "to come" (13:14). The notion of the heavenly city is eschatological, but there is also a suggestion that believers have now "come" to the heavenly Jerusalem, that they are members even now of a great heavenly assembly (12:22–23). Even though believers await the heavenly city in all its fullness and beauty, they are also currently members of it.

Typology

Typology exists when there is a historical correspondence between events, institutions, and persons found in the OT and the NT.[69]

---

[68] See the commentary on 4:3 for further discussion.

[69] In defense of the notion that Hebrews is characterized by allegory, see Stefan Nordgaard Svendsen, *Allegory Transformed: The Appropriation of Philonic Hermeneutics in the Letter to the Hebrews*, WUNT 2/269 (Tübingen: Mohr Siebeck, 2009). I suggest that the structure is better described as typological since there is a historical rootedness in the patterns discerned by the author. The author of Hebrews sees persons like Melchizedek and Aaron as historical, so too the tabernacle and sacrifices are anchored in the historical practices of Israel. Israel's failure to enter the land of promise was also a historical event that speaks typologically to later readers. Even if some modern historical-critical readers don't think such persons, events, or institutions are historical, it is certainly the case that the author of Hebrews believed they were.

I argue that typology does not merely represent correspondence but a correspondence *intended* by God.[70] In other words, there is a prophetic character to biblical typology. It is not merely retrospective but prospective. It is not merely the case that the author of Hebrews detects patterns and correspondences as he reflects on OT revelation. Since God is sovereign over all of history (e.g., Isa 46:9–11), he plans the end from the beginning. Hence, the events, institutions, and persons in which there is a typological relationship are not merely accidents of history, nor are they simply employed by God as helpful illustrations. On the contrary, the persons, events, and institutions were intended from the beginning as anticipations of what was to come.

Another element of biblical typology, clearly present in Hebrews, should be mentioned at the outset. Biblical typology is characterized by escalation. This means the fulfillment is always greater than the type. Indeed, this element of typology is absolutely crucial for Hebrews, for it is inconceivable that the readers would turn back to the type now that what God promised has become a reality, for the fulfillment is far superior to the type. We see, then, that escalation in typology fits with the main purpose of the letter: how can the readers turn away from Jesus Christ when his person and work are far superior to what was adumbrated in OT persons and institutions? Hebrews, then, reads the OT (rightly so), as forward looking. The OT itself points to a better priest, a better king, a better covenant, a better land, and better promises. Hence, the notion of escalation is not arbitrary or foisted upon the text but is intrinsic to the OT witness.

Typology in Hebrews centers on Jesus Christ. We see from the inception of the letter that ultimately all the types in the OT point to and climax in him. God spoke in various ways to the prophets, but the prophets direct us to and anticipate one greater than themselves (1:1–2). Finally and supremely God has spoken in his Son. He is the

---

[70] For a recent discussion of typology, see Benjamin J. Ribbens, "A Typology of Types: Typology in Dialogue," *Journal of Theological Interpretation* 5 (2011): 81–96.

Ribbens divides typology into three categories: christological, tropological, and homological. For the purpose of this discussion, I am limiting typology here to the category identified as christological in Ribbens. For further discussion on the matter, see also, Richard Ounsworth, *Joshua Typology in the New Testament*, WUNT 2/328 (Tübingen: Mohr Siebeck, 2012), 19–54.

greatest and final prophet. The author picks up this theme relative to Moses (3:1–6), for Moses is conceived of as the greatest prophet in the OT. Moses' greatness isn't attributed to his abilities but to his relationship with God, to his dependence on God for strength, and thus he is described as humbler than anyone else on earth (Num 12:3). Moses' humility manifests itself in his response to criticism, for he did not take umbrage when censured by Aaron and Miriam (Num 12:1–2).

The greatness of Moses as a prophet is emphasized in OT revelation. Moses is esteemed as "faithful" and as God's "servant" (Num 12:7–8). Therefore, God spoke to him "directly" and "openly" (Num 12:8). Indeed, the Lord "knew" him "face to face" (Deut 34:10). Despite the clarity of revelation given through Moses, Jesus is greater than he was, for Jesus like Moses was "faithful," but Jesus was faithful as "Son" (3:2, 6). Jesus was a greater prophet than Moses, for he was not merely a servant or merely a prophet. He was God's Son.

The title "Son" plays a major role in Hebrews relative to Jesus Christ (1:2, 5, 8; 3:6; 4:14; 5:5, 8; 6:6; 7:3, 28; 10:29), but the term is also used typologically. In the OT Israel was identified as God's son and firstborn (Exod 4:22; Jer 31:9), showing Israel's special relationship with God. As the OT story progressed, the Davidic king is appointed to be God's son and the firstborn (2 Sam 7:14; Ps 89:27). The promises given to Israel would become a reality through the covenant enacted with David. As God's son and firstborn, the Lord would rule the world through Israel and the Davidic king (cf. 1:5).

As the OT story progresses, we see that Israel as God's son was sent into exile since they failed to keep the stipulations of the covenant. The Davidic kings followed the same course, or perhaps it is better to say, given the message of 1–2 Kings, that the kings led the nation down the same path. They were appointed as kings to lead the nation in righteousness and justice and truth, but the kings forsook the Lord and failed to obey the instructions of the Lord. God's promise to bless the world through Abraham, therefore, did not become reality through the rule of the kings.

Hebrews, along with the rest of the NT, sets forth Jesus as the true Israel and the true Davidic king. He was the Son who invariably obeyed, never transgressing the will of the Lord (4:15; 7:26). The Lord promised Israel that his promises to them would be secured through obedience (Gen 18:18–19; cf. Gen 26:5), and Jesus as God's Son learned to obey in his suffering (5:8). His suffering did not propel him away from God but actually drew him closer to God. Israel was tested in the wilderness and sinned repeatedly, but when Jesus was tested, he didn't fall prey to sin (2:18; 4:15), and thus he was perfected via his sufferings (2:10). We see escalation in that Jesus was always the obedient Son in contrast to Israel and the Davidic kings. But there is also escalation in another sense, for Jesus is not only a human son but also the divine Son. He is not only the heir like the Davidic king but also the agent by whom the universe was created (1:2) and is "the radiance of God's glory and the exact expression of His nature" (1:3). Here is a Son who is worshiped (1:6) and is identified as God (1:8), showing that the Son shares in the divine identity.

The use of Psalm 45 in 1:8–9 is most interesting, for the psalm is originally a royal psalm about the Davidic king. It is a wedding song celebrating the king's majesty and greatness. When the king is identified as "God" in the psalm (Ps 45:6), we have an example of hyperbole. The king (cf. Exod 7:1) is identified as God in the psalm given his stature and rule. As God's vice-regent he is called "God," but no one in Israel interpreted the wording literally as if the Davidic king were actually divine. But what is said about the Davidic king was no accident, for it pointed forward in a deeper and truer sense to Jesus Christ. For this one truly is the Son of God, the one whom angels worship and who created the universe (1:2, 6, 10, 12). We see a prime example of escalation in typology here.

The Son typology is exploited in still another direction. In 2:5–8 the author cites Psalm 8, which is a creation psalm celebrating the dignity of human beings. Even though human beings seem to be small in the world, God made them to rule the world as his vice-regents (cf. Gen 1:26–27; 2:15). Psalm 8 celebrates the majesty of God and the dignity of human beings created in his image. Hebrews, however, reads the psalm eschatologically and typologically. The author recognizes that human beings didn't realize their potential. Human beings didn't rule the world for God. Instead they sinned against the Lord, plunging the world into chaos so that death reigned instead of life and joy (2:5–18). Death and sin prevented human beings from reaching their intended goal (2:14–15, 17).

The creation of human beings anticipates and points to the one human being (Jesus Christ) who was faithful to God, the one who succeeded where everyone else failed. Because of his obedience, the world will be subjected to him (2:5), even though that reality has not yet been realized (2:8). The original plan that human beings would rule the world for God is realized in Jesus Christ. Jesus functions as the representative human being, helping those who can't help themselves (2:18). His help consists supremely in his priestly work of offering himself as a sacrifice on the cross, by which he atoned for the sins committed against God (2:17). Jesus' victory over sin and death is shared with all who are his "brothers" (2:11–12), with "the children God gave" him (2:13), with "Abraham's offspring" (2:16). Human beings can't rule over the world if death triumphs over them, but Jesus conquered death for their sake.

The Melchizedekian priesthood of Jesus is also typological.[71] Melchizedek was not a preincarnate appearance of the Son of God, for Heb 7:3 says that Melchizedek was made like the Son of God. The wording here suggests that Jesus Christ as high priest was the goal and model of the priesthood from the beginning, and hence Melchizedek was always intended to point forward to him. This supports the claim made earlier that typology does not just happen to seize upon correspondences between persons, events, and institutions. Typology is prospective, reflecting God's sovereign plan for all of history.

Melchizedek's role as both a priest and a king (7:1) anticipates Jesus Christ who is both a priest after Melchizedek's order and the Davidic king.[72] The combination of the priestly and kingly offices is anticipated in Psalm 110, which identifies David's son as his lord but also as a Melchizedekian priest who will serve forever (Ps 110:1, 4). Hebrews, then, picks up on what the OT itself develops. The phrases "king of righteousness" and "king of peace" assigned to Melchizedek (7:2) also apply to Jesus, for ultimately he grants

---

[71] Against Cockerill, who limits typology to the Aaronic priesthood (*Hebrews*, 54). I would suggest that the author's typology is rather fluid so that he can argue that both the Aaronic and the Melchizedekian priesthood are typological.

[72] In defense of reading the reference to Melchizedek typologically, see Dale F. Leschert, *Hermeneutical Foundations of Hebrews: A Study in the Validity of the Epistle's Interpretation of Some Core Citations from the Psalms*, NABPRDS 10 (Lewiston, NY: Edwin Mellen, 1994), 228–41.

righteousness and peace to his people as their king and priest. When the text says that Melchizedek did not have a mother or father or genealogy, having no beginning or no end (7:3), we must beware of overinterpretation. The author isn't asserting that Melchizedek literally didn't have a father or mother, nor is he claiming that he wasn't born or that he didn't die. If Melchizedek didn't have a father or mother, he wouldn't even be a human being! Melchizedek is contrasted with Levitical priests here, for the genealogy of the latter is carefully traced; and if genealogical connections can't be proven, they can't serve as priests (Neh 7:64). It is remarkable, then, that Melchizedek served as a priest, though Genesis says nothing about his genealogy. The "silence" about Melchizedek's ancestry and birth and death is significant typologically, for it demonstrates that his priesthood is of a different character than the Aaronic priesthood. Certainly the language used here is not literally true of Jesus at every point, for he did have a mother.

The author contends that the Melchizedekian priesthood is superior to the Levitical, and thereby he establishes typologically that Jesus' priesthood is greater as well. Jesus cannot be a Levitical priest since he hails from the tribe of Judah (7:13–14). We see from Psalm 110 that the Melchizedekian priesthood is fulfilled in the Davidic king, so that the priesthood finds its ultimate fulfillment in the kingly office. Melchizedek's priesthood, according to Ps 110:4, remains "forever" (7:17). Certainly this wasn't literally true of Melchizedek, for he was dead and gone after his life ended. We see typological escalation here, for the word "forever" is literally true in Jesus' case, for he has "an indestructible life" (7:16). Jesus' priesthood never ends since he conquered death forever at his resurrection. The resurrection of Jesus is foundational to the superiority of his priesthood since the tenure of Levitical priests ends at death, whereas Jesus is a permanent and effective priest since he "remains forever" (7:24–25).

The author doesn't feel restricted or bound in considering the typological significance of Jesus. There is a sense in which the Levitical priests are types of Jesus as well (8:1–5). We see from 5:1–10 that the Levitical priesthood is the typological framework that anticipates Jesus' priesthood. Jesus, like the Levitical priests, was a human being appointed by God to his office. What is also emphasized, however, is the discontinuity between the two, for Jesus is a priest in the heavenly sanctuary, the true sanctuary, whereas the

Levitical priests are restricted to an earthly ministry. The earthly priests are "a copy and shadow of the heavenly things" (8:5). Moses himself signaled that the tabernacle pointed to a greater and more perfect tabernacle, for God instructed him to "make everything according to the pattern that was shown to you on the mountain" (8:5; Exod 25:40; cf. 25:9; 26:30; 27:8). The earthly priests point forward to a better priest, a heavenly one. Earthly priests stand because their work is never finished (10:11), but Christ sits because his sacrifice does not need to be repeated (10:12–14), for final forgiveness has been accomplished.

The author picks up on the typological significance of the tabernacle and its sacrifices in 9:1–10. The regulations for sacrifices are instructive, for the high priest was permitted to enter the most holy place only once a year on the Day of Atonement (9:7; Leviticus 16). The Spirit was revealing that the free access to God was lacking (9:8). Jesus' sacrifice was superior, for he did not enter an earthly tabernacle but a heavenly one, securing access to God's presence continually and forever (9:11–12). The animal sacrifices were a type of Jesus' greater sacrifice, and we clearly have an example of escalation since Jesus' sacrifice tore open the curtain in the temple/tabernacle separating human beings from God so that believers have constant access to God's presence (10:19–20).

The physical washings and sacrifices of the OT (9:10, 13) anticipate a greater washing and cleansing, one that is effectual. The external washings, after all, only cleanse the body (9:13), but Jesus' blood sprinkles the conscience clean of sin and washes the body with water so that the whole person is truly cleansed (9:14; 10:22). There is also a typological relationship in terms of covenantal practice. The old covenant was ratified by the blood of animals, signifying that forgiveness only comes with the spilling of blood, with the death of sacrificial victims (9:15–22). The typological connection is clear. The blood of animal sacrifices points forward to a greater and more effective sacrifice, to the blood of Jesus, which is a "better" sacrifice (9:23–24) since it brings access to God. Jesus' once-for-all sacrifice secured forgiveness of sins forever (9:25–28).

The law and the sacrifices therein are "shadows" pointing to a greater reality (10:1), to a greater sacrifice. Animal sacrifices direct us to the sacrifice of Christ (10:2–10), for it is obvious that the blood of animals can't atone for sin. True atonement can only be secured by a human being, not by brute animals who are offered unwillingly and without any consciousness of what is going on. Christ, on the other hand, gave himself personally and gladly for the sake of his people. Animal sacrifices simply remind people of their sins year after year. The sacrifice of Christ, on the other hand, sanctifies once for all (10:10). What is offered at Jesus' altar (the cross) is better than the food of OT sacrifices (13:9–10), for the former brings grace while the latter is an external practice that points forward to a better sacrifice and a better altar.

The author suggests a correspondence with the life of Christ in a few other texts. For instance, the sacrifice of Christ is compared to the slaying of Abel (12:24). Both died as innocent victims, but Christ's blood speaks better than Abel's, for Christ washes clean those who trust in him. Abel's blood cries out for justice, but Christ's blood does something far more wonderful and startling. Through his death human beings can boldly enter God's presence. Similarly, the sacrifice of Isaac anticipated Christ's resurrection typologically (παραβολῇ, 11:17–19), for Abraham was convinced that God would raise Isaac from the dead if he sacrificed him (Gen 22:4), but Jesus, in contrast to Isaac, was truly raised from the dead, fulfilling what was adumbrated in the "sacrifice" of Isaac.

Typology also plays an important role in the letter's warning passages. We see again here the prospective nature of typology and escalation. For instance, under the old covenant those who transgressed covenant stipulations received a "just punishment" on earth (2:2). The punishment could be death for sins like adultery or homosexuality (Lev 20:10, 13) or covenant curses for departing from the Lord (Deut 28:15–68). They were banished and sent into exile for their failure to abide by the covenant. Such earthly punishments, however, anticipated the final judgment that would be experienced by those who drifted away from the salvation given by the Lord (2:3). In this case the punishment is escalated, for the readers are threatened with the eschatological wrath of God.

The same pattern of argumentation surfaces in 10:26–31. Those who violate the Mosaic law die without mercy. Such an earthly punishment forecasts a future and greater punishment if one tramples God's Son under his feet, considers the blood of the covenant unclean, and insults the Holy Spirit. The judgment in this case is more terrifying than physical death, for those who reject the Son will "fall into the hands of the living God" (10:31). The warning in 12:25–29 runs along similar lines. Israel didn't escape judgment when God warned them on earth, and so it is even more the case that those who ignore a heavenly word will not be spared God's judgment.

We see the same paradigm in 3:7–4:13. The wilderness generation didn't obtain rest in Canaan because they refused to obey the Lord's will (3:11, 18; 4:3). The unbelief and disobedience of the wilderness generation function as an example to avoid for believers in Jesus Christ (3:12, 15, 18–19; 4:2–3). Parenthetically, but along the same lines, Esau also functions as a type in the same way as the wilderness generation. Esau surrendered an earthly birthright, but believers are admonished not to throw away their eternal birthright for temporal joys (12:16–17). When we consider the wilderness generation, the rest promised in Canaan was an earthly rest, but there is a better rest, a heavenly rest available for believers in Jesus Christ (4:1). The rest theme is complex and variegated, for it doesn't only relate to the promise that Israel would inherit Canaan. The author also hearkens back to creation, where "God rested from all His works" on the seventh day (4:4; Gen 2:3). God's rest on the seventh day, when he completed his creation work, has an anticipatory element to it. God rested because his work was completed, and hence his Sabbath rest points to and anticipates the new creation to come. When God's kingdom is realized in its fullness, those who belong to God will enjoy Sabbath rest in its fullness, for then human beings will cease from their labor and work (4:10). The rest God enjoyed upon completing his work at creation anticipates the rest which will come when the new creation dawns.

The author pulls on another thread regarding the rest. The wilderness generation didn't find rest, but under Joshua the people obtained the rest promised in Canaan (Josh 22:4). God's promises regarding rest were fulfilled under Joshua (21:44–45; cf. 23:1). The author notes, however, that the rest Joshua gave to the people could hardly be ultimate (4:8). At the end of the day, the rest in Joshua is provisional, temporal, and earthly. Otherwise, the rest referred to in Psalm 95 would be extraneous (Ps 95:11). It would be pointless to offer rest at a later period under David if earthy rest was already secured under Joshua. It follows, then, that the rest under Joshua is a type of a better rest to come, which is identified as "a Sabbath rest" (4:9).[73] Indeed, the name "Joshua" (Ἰησοῦς) here is actually the name "Jesus." Jesus is a new and better Joshua, and the writing of Psalm 95 after the days of Joshua signifies that a new and better rest is coming, a rest that is given by Jesus the Christ, a rest that can never be disturbed by anyone. The author argues typologically, therefore, from God's Sabbath rest and Israel's rest (or lack thereof) in Canaan, seeing a future rest for those who believe and obey, and a future judgment for those who fall away. We have escalation in both instances: the future judgment and future rest are eternal.

The typology of a future homeland is picked up elsewhere in the letter. Abraham, Isaac, and Jacob were promised the land of Canaan (11:8). Canaan becomes a type of a heavenly homeland, a heavenly city that will be granted to believers (11:10, 13–16). Believers are exiles and resident aliens here, but the city to come is far better than any earthly city, for it is an enduring city (12:22; 13:14).

This brief foray into typology demonstrates that typology plays a significant role in Hebrews. The author often sees a typological connection between the OT and the NT, and he regularly sees an escalation between the type and its fulfillment.

The Spatial Orientation of Hebrews

Some scholars place the spatial orientation of Hebrews under the subject of typology or eschatology.[74] Creating a distinct section is useful, however, since typology is characteristic of many of the books in the NT, whereas the author's spatial emphasis is distinctive. Hebrews quite frequently contrasts the earthly and the heavenly, so we have a vertical or spatial contrast. Hence, the author, in accord with the OT, "works with a two-story model of the created cosmos— heaven/s and earth" (cf. Gen 1:1; 2:1; Jer 10:11).[75] It also seems that

---

[73] Some argue that the author doesn't argue typologically since he doesn't have any interest in the land, but such a judgment is overstated. For the typological nature of the author's conception of land, see David M. Allen, *Deuteronomy and Exhortation in Hebrews: A Study in Narrative Representation*, WUNT 2/238 (Tübingen: Mohr Siebeck, 2008), 143–55.

[74] Steyn says we have both a spatial and a linear eschatology in Hebrews. See Gert J. Steyn, "The Eschatology of Hebrews: As Understood Within a Cultic Setting," in *Eschatology of the New Testament and Some Related Documents*, ed. J. G. van der Watt, WUNT 2/315 (Tübingen: Mohr Siebeck, 2012), 429–31.

[75] Edward Adams, "Cosmology in Hebrews," in *The Epistle to the Hebrews and Christian Theology*, ed. R. Bauckham, D. R. Driver, T. A. Hart, and N. MacDonald

the author distinguishes between the sky, the visible heavens, and heaven as God's dwelling place.[76] Such a distinction is borne out since Jesus "passed through the heavens" (4:14), is "exalted above the heavens" (7:26), and has entered "heaven itself" (9:24). The last phrase refers to the presence of God. The nature of the heavens here can't be described adequately, for God's dwelling place is mysterious and beyond human access. We need to acknowledge here the symbolic character of the language found in Hebrews. Discerning where the language is symbolic is, of course, difficult. For instance, Christ truly has a resurrection body; the author doesn't engage in symbolism here. The language about a heavenly tent (8:2; 9:11, 24) and a city, however, should not be pressed to say there is a literal tent or a literal heavenly city.[77] Spatial imagery may be appropriated to express the inexpressible, to convey a reality that transcends our understanding in symbolic language. Hence, the reference to God's throne in the heavens points the readers to God's transcendence (1:3; 8:1–2; 10:12; 12:2).[78]

Some in the history of interpretation have interpreted the writer's contrast between the earthly and heavenly sanctuary in Platonic terms, for what is heavenly is superior to what is earthly.[79] The notion sounds Platonic at first glance, as if the earthly is a pale replica of the perfect archetype which is in heaven. Furthermore, what the author says could be understood as critical of the physical creation, as if the author longs for a transcendent world undefiled by

---

(Grand Rapids, MI: Eerdmans, 2009), 130. Paul Ellingworth maintains that angels belong to an intermediate sphere, but it seems more accurate to say that angels belong to the highest sphere where God dwells in heaven ("Jesus and the Universe in Hebrews," *EvQ* 58 [1986]: 349). But such a perspective doesn't mean angels aren't also active on earth (so Adams, "Cosmology in Hebrews," 131–32).

[76] I am following Adams closely here ("Cosmology of Hebrews," 131), though I am not claiming he would agree with all the steps I make.

[77] I will argue further for this view in the commentary proper.

[78] Steyn, "The Eschatology of Hebrews," 437.

[79] On the cosmology of Hebrews, see Jon Laansma, "The Cosmology of Hebrews," in *Cosmology and New Testament Theology*, ed. J. T. Pennington and S. M. McDonough, LNTS 355 (London: T&T Clark, 2008), 125–43; idem, "Hidden Stories in Hebrews: Cosmology and Theology," in *Cloud of Witnesses: The Theology of Hebrews in Its Ancient Contexts*, ed. R. Bauckham, D. Driver, T. Hart, and N. MacDonald, LNTS 387 (London: T&T Clark, 2008), 9–18; Adams, "Cosmology in Hebrews," 122–39.

material reality.[80] Certainly the language is reminiscent of what we find in Plato or Philo.[81] Still the worldview is dramatically different, and most scholars now agree that the writer was not appropriating Platonic notions in any technical sense, and hence he is ultimately world affirming instead of world denying. Most significantly, the language of heaven and earth is plotted on an eschatological time line. The eschatological and spatial are complementary, and we have no such conception in Plato.

According to the author, the heavenly realm is superior to the earthly.[82] Jesus' priesthood, in contrast to the Levitical priesthood, is heavenly (8:4), and therefore Jesus' priesthood is infinitely more valuable than the ministry conducted by the Levitical priests. Similarly, the message conveyed from heaven, from Mount Zion, represents God's final and definitive word (1:2; 12:25). The author doesn't reject the word given through Moses and the prophets, but the heavenly message is the consummation and completion and fulfillment of what God has revealed. Hence, those who reject such a heavenly message will face severe judgment if they renounce the word proclaimed to them.

Believers have a "heavenly calling" (3:1), and Jesus has "passed through the heavens" (4:14), entering God's presence as high priest. The earthly tabernacle established by Moses is contrasted with "the true tabernacle," which is in heaven (8:2). The author is clearly saying that the heavenly is superior to the earthly. Similarly, the earthly priests who offer sacrifices according to the law are contrasted with Jesus, who is a heavenly priest (8:3–4). Earthly priests, then, are "a copy and shadow of heavenly things" (8:5). Since the earthly reflects the heavenly, when Moses constructed the tabernacle, he did so according to the pattern specified by God (8:5; Exod 25:40). The earthly is again inferior, but the argument isn't that it is inferior

---

[80] Adams argues that Plato himself actually valued the physical cosmos, and hence the polarity is not apt; but he goes on to show how Hebrews claims in a number of places that God created the world, showing that the world of creation is good and not inferior ("Cosmology in Hebrews," 123–30).

[81] See the careful and restrained conclusions of Adams ("Cosmology of Hebrews," 132–33). Adams points out that the term "copy" (ὑπόδειγμα, 8:5) is not used by Plato, nor is it evident that the term "model" or "copy" (NRSV) (ἀντίτυπος) was Platonic. Plato does use the term "shadow" (σκιά, 10:1), but, given the author's eschatology, it is unclear that Hebrews uses it in a Platonic sense.

[82] See again, Adams, "Cosmology of Hebrews," 133–34.

because it comes from the material world. Its inferiority is linked to eschatology, for the superiority of Christ's priesthood is tied to the inauguration of the new covenant in his ministry (8:7–13). The earthly tabernacle points above to "a greater and more perfect tabernacle" in heaven (9:11), a tabernacle that is "not of this creation." The author isn't claiming that there is a literal tabernacle or place in heaven.[83] He simply uses the language of tabernacle to communicate the truth that the earthly tabernacle symbolizes God's presence in heaven. Jesus' sacrifice is better than animal sacrifices, for he entered the presence of God and cleansed the conscience of sin (9:12–14).

The "copies" (ὑποδείγματα, 9:23) of what is in heaven were purified with the sacrifices of animals. But "the heavenly things" (ἐπουράνια) needed "better sacrifices" (9:23). The blood of animals could not avail in heaven, in the presence of God. Since the earthly sanctuary is a "model of the true one" (ἀντίτυπα τῶν ἀληθινῶν), Jesus could not content himself with entering such a sanctuary (9:24). He entered a better sanctuary, a heavenly one, to "appear in the presence of God for us" (9:24). The law on earth is "a shadow" (Σκιάν) of the heavenly world, which is the "actual form" (εἰκόνα) of things (10:1). Similarly, Mount Sinai was terrifying when God came down on it, rocking with thunder and blazing with lightning so that those present were awe stricken (12:18–21). But believers have come to a better mountain: Mount Zion (12:22), a heavenly mountain where the "living God" resides. Indeed, it is nothing other than "the heavenly Jerusalem." It follows, then, that no one will escape if they turn away from a message given from heaven (12:25), for even those who rejected the message from Sinai received an earthly punishment.

God will shake the created world so that created things are removed (12:26–27) and only the kingdom remains (12:28). Hence, the author departs from Plato, for in contrast to the latter he does not believe this world is eternal.[84] The author underscores the transience and impermanence of the present world by citing Ps 102:25–27 (1:10–12). But Edward Adams rightly remarks that the temporary

---

[83] Against William L. Lane, *Hebrews 9–13*, WBC (Dallas: Word, 1991), 237–38; Barnard, *The Mysticism of Hebrews*, 104–9.

[84] Adams, "Cosmology of Hebrews," 136.

character of the world does not mean the author of Hebrews believes the physical world is intrinsically evil.[85]

Scholars debate whether the writer of Hebrews believes in a new creation or thinks the heavenly realm is nonmaterial. Adams rightly argues it is more convincing to say the author looks forward to a new creation.[86] As Jon Laansma says, "Creation has not been removed but rather cleansed (1:3) and reconstituted as God's temple, city, fatherland, world, and kingdom."[87] The Son will be heir of all things (1:2), "which implies that in the eschaton there will be a cosmos . . . for him to inherit."[88] Furthermore, in Heb 2:6–8 the author cites Ps 8:4–6 when he predicts that Jesus will fulfill the destiny for human beings recorded in the psalm. But this destiny, according to Psalm 8, involves rule over the world, indicating that Jesus will rule over a physical cosmos. Indeed, Jesus will reign over the "coming world" (2:5; cf. 1:6).[89] The term "world" (οἰκουμένη) here designates "inhabited earth,"[90] signifying that the coming city (13:14; cf. 12:22) designates a renewed cosmos (cf. 6:5). Such a view fits with Revelation 21–22, where the heavenly city also describes a new creation.

Believers should follow the example of Abraham, Isaac, and Jacob and look forward to a heavenly city instead of longing to fit into the present social order (11:13–16).[91] They should recognize that they are exiles and resident aliens in the present world. This present earth is not their home. They long for the city that is coming (13:14). This world is not rejected as inherently evil, for this is the place where Christ came to save his people (10:5–10). He is the incarnate Son (2:10–18) who suffered for the sake of his people, and he will return to earth to complete his saving work (9:28).

---

[85] Ibid., 135–36.

[86] Ibid., 137–38; cf. also Laansma "Hidden Stories in Hebrews," 12–18.

[87] Ibid., 14.

[88] Adams, "Cosmology of Hebrews," 137.

[89] I am not suggesting that 2:6–9 restricts the rule to Jesus, for his brothers and sisters will rule with him and because of him.

[90] So Adams, "Cosmology of Hebrews," 137.

[91] Cf. ibid., 134. Adams contests the idea that the author uses Platonic conceptions here.

Exposition

Hebrews 1:1–4

Outline

I. **Prologue: Definitive and Final Revelation in the Son (1:1–4)**

II. Don't Abandon the Son Since He Is Greater than Angels (1:5–2:18)

Scripture

¹Long ago God spoke to the fathers by the prophets at different times and in different ways. ²In these last days, He has spoken to us by His Son. God has appointed Him heir of all things and made the universe through Him. ³The Son is the radiance of God's glory and the exact expression of His nature, sustaining all things by His powerful word. After making purification for sins, He sat down at the right hand of the Majesty on high. ⁴So He became higher in rank than the angels, just as the name He inherited is superior to theirs.

Context

The opening of Hebrews is elegant and eloquent, demonstrating the literary artistry of the author. The introduction gives no evidence that the writing is an epistle, for the author doesn't introduce himself, the recipients aren't identified, and there isn't a greeting. The opening suggests a literary work, something like a literary essay on the significance of Jesus Christ. We know from the conclusion of the work, however, that Hebrews has epistolary features, and thus the book should not be classified as a literary essay. Still, the artistry and beauty that characterize the entire letter are evident from the opening. The author invites the reader via the elevated style of the letter to reflect on and apply his theology.

The main point of the first four verses is that God has spoken finally and definitively in his Son. The author beautifully contrasts the past era in which God spoke to the ancestors and prophets with the last days in which God spoke to us in his Son. A table should illustrate the contrast in the first two verses.

Long ago	In these last days
God spoke to the fathers	He has spoken to us
by the prophets	by His Son
at different times and in different ways	

Verses 2–4 focus on the identity of the Son and what he has done. Here we have a chiasm.

A He has spoken to us by His Son	D¹ He is the exact expression of His nature
B God has appointed Him heir of all things	C¹ sustaining all things by His powerful word
C He made the universe through Him	B¹ After making purification for sins, He sat down at the right hand of the Majesty on high
D The Son is the radiance of God's glory	A¹ He became higher in rank than the angels, just as the name He inherited is superior to theirs

The main point of the chiasm is found under A and A¹: the Son is superior to angels since he is the Son. Indeed, he is the heir and ruler of the universe since he is the Creator of the universe and shares God's nature.

Exegesis

1:1

God is a speaking God, and he has spoken to the prophets in a variety of ways and modes in the OT. The first verse is marked by alliteration in the Greek, with five different words beginning with "p":

"at different times" (πολυμερῶς); "in different ways" (πολυτρόπως); "long ago" (πάλαι) "fathers" (πατράσιν); and "prophets" (προφήταις). From the outset the literary skill and the deft style of the author are apparent so that the reader sees a master craftsman at work. The diversity of revelation in the former era is featured. God spoke "at different times" and "in different ways." OT revelation was transmitted through narrative, hymns, proverbs, poetry, parables, and love songs, through wisdom and apocalyptic literature. God communicated with his people for hundreds of years, speaking to Abraham, Isaac, and Jacob, to Moses and Joshua, Samuel and Saul, David and the kings of Judah and Israel, and to the prophets, and to the people who returned from exile.

One of the major themes in Hebrews emerges: "God spoke to the fathers." The one true God is a speaking God, one who communicates with his people and reveals his will and his ways to them. The "fathers" can't be limited to Abraham, Isaac, and Jacob but include and encompass all those addressed in OT revelation.[1] Similarly, the word "prophets" should not be restricted to books that are labeled as "prophetic" in our English Bibles.[2] The writer identifies the entire OT as prophetic. Finally, the revelation given in the past is described as occurring "long ago" (πάλαι). The author is not emphasizing primarily that the revelation occurred in the distant past. His main point, given the remainder of the book, is that OT revelation belonged to a previous era. A new day has arisen, a new covenant has arrived, and the old is no longer in force. The "first" covenant is "old" (παλαιούμενον) and hence obsolete (8:13). The words of the previous era are authoritative as the word of God, but they must be interpreted in light of the fulfillment realized in Jesus Christ.

1:2

The God who spoke in the past still speaks, but "in these last days" he has spoken finally and definitively in his Son. This Son is the Davidic heir promised in the Scriptures, and he is also the agent of all creation. He is the Davidic heir and more since as Creator he shares God's nature.

---

[1] So Harold W. Attridge, *The Epistle to the Hebrews*, Hermeneia (Philadelphia: Fortress, 1989), 38.

[2] Ibid., 38–39. The word ἐν in the phrase "in the prophets" (literally) is instrumental and is rightly translated by the HCSB as "by the prophets" (cf. Attridge, *Hebrews*, 38n41).

The last days (Gen 49:1; Num 24:14; Isa 2:2; Jer 23:20; 25:19; Dan 10:14; Hos 3:5; Mic 4:1) represent the days in which God's saving promises are fulfilled, and they have now commenced with the coming of the Son. Believers no longer live in the days when they await the fulfillment of what God has promised. They live in the eschaton; "the ends of the ages have come" (1 Cor 10:11). It is inconceivable that the readers would embrace the old era with its sacrifices and rituals now that the new has come in Jesus Christ.

God has spoken in his Son. If we look at the table introducing this section, we see that the one phrase with no corresponding phrase is "at different times and in different ways." Still the author expects the readers to fill in the gap. The revelation in the former era was diverse and partial, but the revelation in the Son is unitary and definitive.[3] The final revelation has come in the last days for God has spoken his last and best word. No further word is to be expected, for the last word focuses on the life, death, and resurrection of the Son. As 9:26 says of Jesus, "But now He has appeared one time, at the end of the ages, for the removal of sin by the sacrifice of Himself." Believers await the return of the Son (9:28), but they don't expect a further word from God. No more clarification is needed. The significance of what the Son accomplished has been revealed once for all, and hence the readers must pay attention (2:1) to this revelation.

The author also emphasizes that God has spoken "by his Son." In the OT Israel is the Lord's son, his firstborn (Exod 4:22). And the Davidic king is also identified as God's son (2 Sam 7:14; Ps 2:7). The author implies that Jesus is the true Israel and the true king. But the subsequent verses indicate that sonship transcends these categories, for Jesus is also the unique and eternal Son of God, one who shares the nature of God. Indeed, the following verses indicate why the readers must pay heed to the word spoken in the Son, for the Son is far greater than angels. He is the exalted and reigning Son, the one who rules the universe.

The reference to the Son begins the chiasm represented in the second table above, and it matches 1:4, which emphasizes that Jesus as the Son is greater than the angels because he has inherited a more excellent name. The author desires the readers to see the majesty of

---

[3] Cf. also Luke Timothy Johnson, *Hebrews: A Commentary*, NTL (Louisville: Westminster/John Knox, 2006), 66.

Jesus as the Son so they understand that he is supreme over angels and any other entity in the universe.

Jesus as the Son was appointed (ἔθηκεν) by God as "heir of all things."[4] In the OT, inheritance language is typically used with reference to the land of Canaan, which was promised to Israel as an inheritance (cf. Deut 4:38; 12:9; Josh 11:23). But the Son is the heir of "all things," which echoes the promise given to the Davidic king in Ps 2:8: "Ask of Me, and I will make the nations Your inheritance and the ends of the earth Your possession." The Son is the heir because he is the Davidic king, the fulfillment of the covenant promise made to David that he would never lack a man to sit on the throne. The Son as heir matches in the chiasm his sitting down "at the right hand of the Majesty on high" (1:3). The Son's heirship is tied to his kingship, to his rule over all, and hence it commences with his exaltation to God's right hand.[5]

Jesus' rule as the Son demonstrates that he is the Messiah, the Davidic king, the one through whom God's promises to Israel are fulfilled. As the son of David, he is a human being, but he is more than a human being, for "God made the universe through him" (see §2.1). The phrase "the universe" (τοὺς αἰῶνας) is most often temporal, but here it designates the world God has made (cf. Wis 13:9), and the author features the Son as the agent of creation (cf. John 1:3; 1 Cor 8:6; Col 1:16).[6] The author likely draws here upon wisdom traditions, for we see in the OT that the Lord created the world in wisdom (Prov 3:19; 8:22–31; Ps 104:24; Jer 10:12; cf. Wis 7:22; 9:2). The Son is greater than wisdom, however, for wisdom is a personification, but the Son existed as a person before the world was formed.[7] We can easily fail to see how astonishing this statement is.

---

[4] The word τίθημι means "appoint" in other contexts as well (1 Thess 5:9; 1 Tim 2:7; 2 Tim 1:11; 1 Pet 2:8).

[5] So Peter T. O'Brien, *The Letter to the Hebrews*, PNTC (Grand Rapids, MI: Eerdmans, 2010), 52.

[6] Amy L. B. Peeler says that God chose to include the Son in creating, but this notion sounds a bit adoptionistic, as if the Son isn't equally God. Peeler actually strongly emphasizes the Son's deity elsewhere in her work (*You Are My Son: The Family of God in the Epistle to the Hebrews*, LNTS 486 [New York: Bloomsbury T&T Clark, 2014], 16).

[7] Against Kenneth L. Schenk, *Understanding the Book of Hebrews: The Story Behind the Sermon* (Louisville: Westminster/John Knox, 2003), 17. Rightly Cockerill, *Hebrews*, 99.

The one who was put to death in Jerusalem on a cross a few decades earlier is now praised as the one who created the world![8]

1:3

Verse 3 unpacks further the nature and supremacy of the Son. First, the author speaks ontologically about the Son, maintaining that he fully shares the divine nature and identity. Second, the Son's role in sustaining the cosmos is affirmed. Third, and most crucial for his argument, the Son's reign at God's right hand is featured. The Son reigns and rules as the one who has accomplished full cleansing for sin.

The first two clauses in verse 3 focus on the nature of the Son,[9] showing that the Christology here is not merely functional but also ontological.[10] The Son is the King and the Creator because of who he is because he shares the nature of God. Similarly, the author grounds Christ's atoning work as high priest in who he is. Sometimes scholars focus on functional Christology and minimize ontology, but Hebrews makes ontology the basis for function so that Christ saves because of who he is.

The author begins by claiming that Christ "is the radiance of God's glory" (see §2.1). The word "radiance" (ἀπαύγασμα) could mean "reflection," so that the Son mirrors God's glory.[11] Or it could be defined as "radiance" or "outshining" to emphasize the manifestation of God's glory.[12] The use of the term in Wis 7:26 doesn't settle the issue,[13] for the same interpretive issues arise there. It is difficult to determine which meaning is correct, though the active radiance

---

[8] So L. Johnson, *Hebrews*, 68.

[9] Some scholars detect dependence on a hymn here (see Attridge, *Hebrews*, 41–42).

[10] John P. Meier says the participle "stands out like a metaphysical diamond against the black crepe of narrative" ("Structure and Theology in Heb 1,1–4," *Bib* 66 [1985]: 180). He rightly notes that the author here probes "speculative, philosophical implications" of the person of Christ (180). Against Caird and Hurst who limit what Hebrews 1 says to Christ's humanity. See G. B. Caird, "Son by Appointment," in *The New Testament Age: Essays in Honor of Bo Reicke*, ed. W. Weinrich, 2 vols. (Macon, GA: Mercer University Press, 1984), 1:73–81; Lincoln D. Hurst, "The Christology of Hebrews 1 and 2," in *The Glory of Christ in the New Testament: Studies in Christology*, ed. L. D. Hurst and N. T. Wright (Oxford: Clarendon, 1987), 151–64.

[11] So O. Hofius, "ἀπαύγασμα," *EDNT*, 1:117–18.

[12] See LN 14.48; G. Kittel, "ἀπαύγασμα," *TDNT* 1:508.

[13] Rightly Attridge, *Hebrews*, 42.

seems slightly more likely.[14] In either case God's glory is revealed in the Son, and it really doesn't matter much which we choose, for as Johnson says, "Reflection becomes radiance, and radiance is what is reflected."[15]

The Son is also "the exact impression of his nature." The word translated "exact impression" (χαρακτήρ) is used of the impression or mark made by coins.[16] Here it denotes the idea that the Son represents the nature (ὑπόστασις) and character of the one true God.[17] He reveals who God is, and thus he must share the divine identity. The Son cannot represent God to human beings unless he shares in the being, nature, and essence of God. The Son of God reveals the reality of the one true God.

Hebrews is not alone in the sentiments expressed in the previous two phrases. John's Gospel emphasizes that God speaks to human beings in Jesus Christ. He is the "Word" of God (John 1:1) through whom the world was created (John 1:3). John directly tells us in John 1:1 that the "Word was God" (1:1). God is invisible and in that sense inaccessible, but Jesus Christ explains to human beings who God is (John 1:18). In the same way Jesus instructs Philip that the one who has seen him has also seen the Father (John 14:9). Paul in Colossians celebrates and affirms the truth that Christ is "the image of the invisible God" (Col 1:15), and in Philippians he says Christ "was in the form of God" (2:6 ESV).

After affirming the Son's ontological divinity, Hebrews returns to the Son's role in the created world. He is not only the one through whom the world was made but also sustains the universe "by His powerful word." The thought is similar to Col. 1:17, "And by him

---

[14] Ellingworth slightly prefers "radiance" (Paul Ellingworth, *The Epistle to the Hebrews: A Commentary on the Greek Text*, NIGTC [Grand Rapids, MI: Eerdmans, 1993], 98–99). See also O'Brien, *Hebrews*, 69–70; Gareth Lee Cockerill, *The Epistle to the Hebrews*, NICNT (Grand Rapids, MI: Eerdmans, 2012), 94. The Son's radiance is eternal and should not be limited to the time following his exaltation (rightly Cockerill, *Hebrews*, 95).

[15] L. Johnson, *Hebrews*, 69. Barnard says the main point here is "the unique unity of the Son with the Divine glory" (Jody A. Barnard, *The Mysticism of Hebrews: Exploring the Role of Jewish Apocalyptic Mysticism in the Epistle to the Hebrews*, WUNT 2/331 [Tübingen: Mohr Siebeck, 2012], 151).

[16] G. Kelber, "χαρακτήρ," *TDNT* 9:418; K. Berger, "χαρακτήρ," *EDNT* 3:456.

[17] See H. Koester, "ὑπόστασις," *TDNT* 8:572–89.

all things hold together."[18] Not only did the created world come into being through the Son; it also continues, "And is upheld because of the Son. The created world does not run by "laws of nature," so that the Son's continued superintendence is dispensed with. The author of Hebrews does not embrace a deistic notion of creation. The universe is sustained by the personal and powerful word of the Son, so that the created world is dependent on his will for its functioning and preservation. Implied in the expression is that the universe will reach its intended goal and purpose.[19]

The author reprises the idea that the Son reigns over all, presaging one of the major themes of the book in doing so. The Son's rule commences "after making purification of sins." The word for "purification" (καθαρισμός) is cultic (cf. Exod 29:36; 30:10; Lev 14:32; 15:13; 1 Chr 23:28), anticipating the discussion on the efficacy of Levitical sacrifices in chs. 7–10 (see also Heb 9:14, 22–23; 10:2). The Son's once-for-all sacrifice cleanses the sins of those who believe in him. Hence, those who are "purified" (κεκαθαρισμένους) "no longer have any consciousness of sins" (10:2). They are free from the stain of guilt that defiled them. Since atonement has been accomplished, the Son has now "sat down at the right hand of the Majesty on high." The allusion as noted above is to Psalm 110 in the letter, a psalm that pervades the entire letter and plays a fundamental role in the author's argument.

The allusion, as noted above, is to Ps 110:1, where David's Lord sits down at God's right hand (see also 1:13; 8:1; 10:12; 12:2).[20] The right hand signifies power (Exod 15:6, 12), protection (Pss 16:8; 73:23; Isa 41:10), and triumph (Pss 20:6; 21:8). Indeed, it signifies that Jesus shares the same identity as God, as Bauckham argues. The "potent imagery of sitting on the cosmic throne has only one attested significance: it indicates his participation in the unique sovereignty

---

[18] Against Peeler, the reference here is not to the Father's powerful word (*You Are My Son*, 18).

[19] O'Brien, *Hebrews*, 56.

[20] See here David M. Hay, *Glory at the Right Hand: Psalm 110 in Early Christianity*, SBLMS 18 (Nashville: Abingdon, 1973); Martin Hengel, *Studies in Early Christology* (Edinburgh: T&T Clark, 1995), 119–225; W. R. G. Loader, "Christ at the Right Hand—Ps. cx.l in the New Testament," *NTS* 24 (1977–78): 199–217.

of God over the world."[21] Here the author emphasizes the forgiveness of sins, for the Son is seated at God's right hand since his work is finished. And he reigns at God's right hand as the Lord of the universe and as the Davidic Messiah. The exaltation of Christ is a common theme in the NT (see Phil 2:9–11; Col 1:15–18; Eph 1:21; 1 Pet 3:22), and thus we see Hebrews shares the worldview of the NT generally in presenting Christ as the exalted and reigning king over the universe.

1:4

Verse 4 is tied closely to 1:3. The Son who is seated at God's right hand and rules the world as the Davidic Messiah and Lord has become greater than angels. Israel was called as God's son to rule the world for God (Exod 4:22–23). David and his heirs had a special calling as God's son and the king to mediate God's rule to the world (2 Sam 7:14; Pss 2:7–12; 72:1–20). The kingly role of both Israel and David is fulfilled in Jesus as the one who rules over all. Clearly the author is not suggesting that he has become greater than angels as the eternal Son of God. His argument, anticipating chapter 2 as well, is that the Son has become greater than the angels as the God-Man. The author introduces here one of his favorite words: "better" (κρείττων).[22] Believers in Christ have a "better hope" (7:19), a "better covenant" (7:22; 8:6), "better sacrifices" (9:23), a "better possession" (10:34), a "better resurrection" (11:35), and "better" blood than Abel's (12:24). The one who shares God's nature and manifests his glory has purified believers of sins and now reigns at God's right hand. In other words his reign commenced at a certain point in history. He began to rule at his resurrection and exaltation.

The author introduces angels here, which play a major role in the ensuing argument (1:5–2:16). Why does the author emphasize Jesus' superiority to angels? Were the Hebrews assigning a particular significance to angels?[23] If we examine the letter as a whole, and what the author says in the next chapter, we discover the most

---

[21] Richard Bauckham, "The Divinity of Jesus Christ in the Epistle to the Hebrews," in *The Epistle to the Hebrews and Christian Theology*, ed. R. Bauckham, D. R. Driver, T. A. Hart, and N. MacDonald (Grand Rapids, MI: Eerdmans, 2009), 33 (see his whole discussion, 32–33).

[22] My translation.

[23] Cf. F. F. Bruce, *The Epistle to the Hebrews*, rev. ed., NICNT (Grand Rapids: Eerdmans, 1990), 9. It is unlikely that the readers were tempted to identify Jesus as an

probable answer. The angels were the mediators of the Mosaic law (2:2; cf. Acts 7:53; Gal 3:19). In stressing the Son's superiority to the angels, the author features Jesus' supremacy over the Mosaic law and the Sinai covenant.[24] Hence, the reference to the angels ties into one of the central themes of the letter. The readers should not transfer their allegiance to the law mediated by angels. Such a gambit should be rejected, for they would be opting for what is inferior since the Son rules over angels as one who has "inherited" a name better than theirs. God promised to make Abraham's name great (Gen 12:2), and the same promise is given to David (2 Sam 7:9). And this covenant promise, first given to Abraham and then channeled through David, finds its final fulfillment in Jesus Christ. The word "inherited" (κεκληρονόμηκεν) reaches back to "heir of all things" (1:2). Such an inheritance has been *gained* through his suffering and death, signifying again the rule of the Son at his resurrection.[25]

The more excellent name is typically understood to be Son.[26] But others argue that the name here is probably Yahweh, the name of God revealed to Israel. Joslin, in particular, makes a powerful argument supporting a reference to Yahweh.[27] First, the term "name" elsewhere in Hebrews almost certainly refers to Yahweh (2:12; 6:10; 13:5). Hence, the presumption is that the same name is in view here as well. Second, Joslin says that the term "Son" is not a name but

---

angel in order to soften a reference to his deity (against Donald A. Hagner, *Hebrews* [New York: Harper & Row, 1983], 10).

[24] Hence, the author is not countering those who unduly venerated angels, as if Hebrews addresses a problem similar to what Paul opposed in Colossae (against Robert Jewett, *Letter to Pilgrims: A Commentary on the Epistle to the Hebrews* [New York: Pilgrim, 1981], 5–13; Thomas W. Manson, "The Problem of the Epistle to the Hebrews," *BJRL* 32 [1949]: 1–17). Nor is there any evidence that he combats an angelic Christology (against Ronald H. Nash, "Mediator in Alexandrian Judaism and the Hebrews," *WTJ* 40 (1977): 89–115, esp. 109–12).

[25] Schenk rightly says the author features the rule and enthronement of Christ over angels here, though he mistakenly suggests the Christology does not involve preexistence. See Kenneth L. Schenk, "A Celebration of the Enthroned Son: The Catena of Hebrews 1," *JBL* 120 (2001): 469–86.

[26] E.g., Attridge, *Hebrews*, 47; Cockerill, *Hebrews*, 98; Meier, "Structure and Theology," 187.

[27] Barry Joslin, "Whose Name? A Comparison of Hebrews 1 and Philippians 2 and Christ's Inheritance of the Name," unpublished paper. Cf. also L. Johnson, *Hebrews*, 71; Bauckham, "The Divinity of Jesus Christ in the Epistle to the Hebrews," 21–22; Barnard, *The Mysticism of Hebrews*, 157–70.

a title or a description of Jesus (1:2, 5, 8; 2:6; 3:6; 4:14; 5:5, 8; 6:6; 7:3, 28; 10:29). The word "name" echoes the name of God that plays a central role in biblical tradition (cf. Exod 3:13–15), for God's name signifies his character and in revealing his name God reveals himself. The superiority of Jesus' name in a context where his exaltation and divine identity are communicated points to his deity.

It is difficult to decide between Son and Yahweh here, though I prefer the former for the following reasons. First, the word "Son" occurs four times in the chapter (1:2, 5 [twice], 8), so that the reader naturally thinks of the word "Son." Second, in the chiasm of verses 2–4 presented in the table above the term "Son" (v. 2) matches the inheriting a more excellent name (v. 4). Third, the word "name" refers to the Lord elsewhere in the letter, but all these references are to the Father rather than to the Son, so the parallel isn't as close as claimed. Fourth, verse 5 supports and grounds verse 4 with the word "for" ($\gamma\acute{\alpha}\rho$), and the verse twice calls attention to Jesus' sonship, suggesting that Son is the name that makes Jesus greater than angels. Fifth, the author speaks of Jesus inheriting the name. It is difficult to see how Jesus could inherit the name of Yahweh. Such a state of affairs would suggest that there was a period when Jesus wasn't divine and that he inherited such deity at some point. But doesn't the same objection apply to the word *Son*? No, for in using the word *Son,* the author would be referring to Jesus' exaltation and rule as God *and* man, and such a rule only commenced at his resurrection.[28]

Bridge

Jesus is the culmination of God's revelation. The OT Scriptures point to him and are fulfilled in him. We see in the introduction of Hebrews that Jesus is the prophet, priest, and king. He is the

---

[28] Perhaps there is also an echo of 2 Samuel 7 where "name" (7:9, 13, 23, 26) and God's greatness (7:21, 26; cf. Heb 1:3) point to the "honor conferred by God on the Messiah as the Davidic heir at the establishment of his throne and in association with God himself" (so George H. Guthrie, "Hebrews," in *Commentary on the New Testament Use of the Old Testament*, ed. G. K. Beale and D. A. Carson [Grand Rapids, MI: Baker, 2007], 925). See also his discussion on p. 924. Guthrie maintains that the title here is "name," which could fit with the view stated above (George Guthrie, *Hebrews*, NIVAC [Grand Rapids, MI: Zondervan, 1998], 50), though it seems to me that "Son" is the more natural reading.

prophet, for God's final word is spoken by him and in him.[29] He is the priest by whom final cleansing of sins is accomplished. He is the king who reigns at God's right hand. The last days have arrived in Jesus and the final word has been spoken, and hence there will be no further revelation until Jesus' return. The great revelatory events have taken place in Jesus' ministry, death, resurrection, and exaltation. Believers do not need any other word from God for their lives. They are to put their faith in what God has revealed in and through Jesus the Christ.

Hebrews 1:5–14

Outline

I. Prologue: Definitive and Final Revelation in the Son (1:1–4)
II. **Don't Abandon the Son Since He Is Greater than Angels (1:5–2:18)**
   A. **The Son's Nature and Reign Show He Is Greater than Angels (1:5–14)**
   B. Warning: Don't Drift Away (2:1–4)
   C. The Coming World Subjected to the Son (2:5–18)

Scripture

⁵ For to which of the angels did He ever say, You are My Son; today I have become Your Father, or again, I will be His Father, and He will be My Son? ⁶ When He again brings His firstborn into the world, He says, And all God's angels must worship Him.

⁷ And about the angels He says: He makes His angels winds, and His servants a fiery flame, ⁸ but to the Son: Your throne, God, is forever and ever, and the scepter of Your kingdom is a scepter of justice. ⁹ You have loved righteousness and hated lawlessness; this is why God, Your God, has anointed You with the oil of joy rather than Your companions. ¹⁰ And: In the beginning, Lord, You established the earth, and the heavens are the works of Your hands; ¹¹ they will perish, but You remain. They will all wear out like clothing; ¹² You will roll them up like a cloak, and they will

---

[29] In saying God's final word is spoken in and by Jesus, I am including the entirety of the NT canonical witness to Jesus as the Son.

be changed like a robe. But You are the same, and Your years will never end. [13] Now to which of the angels has He ever said: Sit at My right hand until I make Your enemies Your footstool? [14] Are they not all ministering spirits sent out to serve those who are going to inherit salvation?

Context

The author picks up on angels from verse 4, demonstrating in verses 5–14 that the Son is greater than angels, using many of the same arguments advanced in 1:1–4. I would structure the argument in 1:5–14 as follows.

The Son's Rule over All (1:5–9)
The Son as Creator (1:10)
The Eternal Nature of the Son (1:11–12)
The Exaltation of the Son over Angels (1:13–14)

Lane relates 1:1–4 to 1:5–14 as follows.[30]

A Appointment as royal heir (v. 2b)	A¹ Appointment as God's Son and heir (vv. 5–9)
B Mediator of creation (v. 2c)	B¹ Mediator of creation (v. 10)
C Eternal nature and preexistent glory (v. 3ab)	C¹ Unchanging, eternal nature (vv. 11–12)
D Exaltation to God's right hand (v. 3c)	D¹ Exaltation to God's right hand (v. 13)

The table makes clear that the author puts forward the same kind of arguments we saw in 1:1–3. But here the author advances his case by citing the OT so that every argument is made by appealing to the OT for support. Hence, we can say that what is asserted in 1:1–4 is elaborated upon and scripturally supported in 1:5–14. The central theme is the Son's superiority to the angels. The content of 1:5–14

---

[30] William L. Lane, *Hebrews 1–8*, WBC (Dallas: Word, 1991), 22. See also Meier, "Structure and Theology," 168–89; idem, "Symmetry and Theology in the Old Testament Citations of Heb 1,5–14," *Bib* 66 (1985): 504–33. Cf. also Victor (Sung Yul) Rhee, "The Role of Chiasm for Understanding Christology in Hebrews 1:1–14," *JBL* 131 (2012): 341–62. Attridge doubts the parallels are so precise (*Hebrews*, 50n14).

also forecasts the remainder of the letter, and it may function, as Jipp contends, as an inclusio with 12:18–29.[31]

Exegesis

1:5

Jesus is greater than the angels because the OT Scriptures designate him as God's Son, which is a title not given to angels. Angels are designated as "sons" but are never identified as God's Son. Quite remarkably the author claims that God was speaking to *Jesus* in the OT Scriptures quoted here, though they were originally directed to the Davidic king. The attribution "Son" in Ps 2:7 and 2 Sam 7:14 is ultimately addressed to Jesus.

The word "for" (γάρ) introducing 1:5 indicates that the author supports what he asserts in 1:4, which suggests, as I argued regarding verse 4, that the more excellent name that makes Jesus better than the angels is "Son." The author's goal is to support this claim from the OT Scriptures. He begins by noting that none of the angels was ever addressed as God's Son. Angels were identified as "sons" but never as the Son (cf. Gen 6:2, 4; Job 1:6; 2:1; 38:7). Furthermore, two texts that in their historical context address the Davidic king are applied to Jesus as the Son of God, showing that he is superior to the angels as the reigning and ruling Son of God.[32]

The first quotation hails from Ps 2:7, which is a messianic psalm.[33] The Davidic king will inherit the nations and rule the entire world (Ps 2:8–9), fulfilling the promise made to Abraham, Isaac, and Jacob that the entire world would be blessed through one of their offspring (Gen 12:3; 18:18; 22:18; 26:4; 28:14; cf. Ps 72:17). Verse 7 of the psalm refers to the installation of the Davidic king. The language of begetting is not literal in the context of the psalm but refers to the appointment of the king, to his accession to the

---

[31] Joshua W. Jipp, "The Son's Entrance into the Heavenly World: The Soteriological Necessity of the Scriptural Catena in Hebrews 1:5–14," *NTS* 56 (2010): 557–75.

[32] Jesus' royal authority over human beings as the exalted Son of God is especially emphasized by David M. Moffitt (*Atonement and the Logic of the Resurrection in the Epistle to the Hebrews*, SuppNovT 141 [Leiden: Brill, 2011], 47–53). He underestimates, however, the argument from deity present here. It seems to me that the author makes *both* arguments in this context.

[33] The citation here matches the LXX, though it functions well as a translation of the MT as well.

throne. The nations should fear, for God has decreed that the kings of the world serve his Son. The author of Hebrews picks up the sonship theme, identifying Jesus as the Son installed by the Father as the messianic king (cf. Acts 13:33).[34] The reference is not to the eternal begetting of the Son by the Father, though this reading is rather common in the history of interpretation.[35] Nor is the reference to the virgin birth.[36] The author of Hebrews actually interprets the verse in light of the entire message of Psalm 2. In context the verse refers to the reign of the messianic king, which Hebrews sees as commencing at Jesus' resurrection and ascension.[37] Jesus is greater than the angels because he now reigns as the messianic king.

The second citation is from 2 Sam 7:14. Once again the quotation matches the LXX but also fits as a literal translation of the MT.[38] The quotation is embedded in the chapter (2 Samuel 7) in which the covenant with David is inaugurated, where Yahweh promises David an irrevocable dynasty.[39] Hence, the author has not randomly found the word *Son* and applied it to Jesus. He applies a text to Jesus that relates to kingship, so Jesus fulfills the covenant promise that a man will always reign on David's throne. Sonship is again tied closely to ruling and reigning. As Lane says, "Although Jesus was the

---

[34] The text is also alluded to at Jesus' baptism (Matt 3:16–17 par.), but in Hebrews Jesus' exaltation rather than his baptism is in view.

[35] Against, apparently, Bauckham, "The Divinity of Jesus Christ in the Epistle to the Hebrews," 34.

[36] Athanasius saw a reference here to the Son's eternal generation and Gregory of Nyssa to the incarnation (see D. Stephen Long, *Hebrews*, Belief: A Theological Commentary on the Bible [Louisville: Westminster John Knox, 2011], 47).

[37] Cf. Craig R. Koester, *Hebrews: A New Translation with Introduction and Commentary*, AB (New Haven, CT: Yale University Press, 2001), 191; Philip Edgecumbe Hughes, *A Commentary on the Epistle to the Hebrews* (Grand Rapids, MI: Eerdmans, 1977), 55.

[38] Most scholars agree that the author worked primarily from the Septuagint. The use of the OT in Hebrews is complex and can't be treated adequately here. See George H. Guthrie, "Hebrews' Use of the Old Testament: Recent Trends in Research," *CBR* 1 (2003): 271–94. For a careful study of 1:5–13, see Herbert W. Bateman IV, *Early Jewish Hermeneutics and Hebrews 1:5–13: The Impact of Early Jewish Exegesis on the Interpretation of a Significant New Testament Passage* (New York: Peter Lang, 1997). See most recently, Georg Q. Walser, *Old Testament Quotations in Hebrews*, WUNT 2/356 (Tubingen: Mohr Siebeck, 2013).

[39] For the messianic character of 2 Sam 7:14, see Lane, *Hebrews 1–8*, 25 (cf. John 7:42).

preexistent Son of God . . . , he entered into a new experience of sonship by virtue of his incarnation, his sacrificial death, and his subsequent exaltation."[40] Jesus is greater than angels because he is the enthroned Davidic king, because he is God's unique Son, and as the Son he rules over all.

We should also note the promise in 2 Sam 7:13 that the future Davidic king will build a house for the Lord's name.[41] Later we are told that Jesus is the one who builds the house (Heb 3:3), which stands for the people of God (3:6). Jesus, as the builder of the new temple, as the elder brother (2:10–16), rules over the people of God.

1:6

We come to one of the most disputed verses in Hebrews, so before plunging in, we should set the context. The central theme in this section is that the Son is greater than angels, and hence the readers should not revert to an earlier period of salvation history, for they are no longer under the Sinai covenant. That covenant has been fulfilled in the new covenant that has arrived in the ministry, death, resurrection, and exaltation of Jesus Christ. The author probably cites Deut 32:43, observing that the angels worshiped Jesus upon his resurrection and exaltation, showing Jesus' superiority to angels (see §2.1). In its OT context, Deut 32:43 refers to Yahweh, but NT writers often apply to Jesus texts that refer to Yahweh (see 1:10–12 below). Apparently, they felt free to do so since Jesus shares the same identity as Yahweh.

Scholars dispute whether the author draws here upon Ps 97:7 or Deut 32:43. It is also possible that we have a conflation of both texts in which they are merged together, but it is a bit more likely that we have a citation from Deut 32:43.[42] The MT of Deut 32:43 lacks any reference to angels, but a Qumran manuscript of Deuteronomy found in Cave 4 supports the reading in Hebrews, for it says the "sons of God" worship the Lord.[43] "Sons of God" in the plural almost always refers to angels (cf. Gen 6:2, 4; Job 1:6; 2:1; 38:7; cf.

---

[40] Lane, *Hebrews 1–8*, 26.

[41] So L. Johnson, *Hebrews*, 79.

[42] See David M. Allen, *Deuteronomy and Exhortation in Hebrews: A Study in Narrative Representation*, WUNT 2/238 (Tübingen: Mohr Siebeck, 2008), 44–51. For the use of the OT here, see also Bateman, *Hebrews 1:5–13*, 142–44.

[43] See Patrick W. Skehan, "A Fragment of the 'Song of Moses' (Deut. 32) from Qumran," *BASOR* 136 (1954): 12–15.

Ps 29:1; 89:6; 138:1). Hence, in the Hebrew textual tradition we find evidence for a reference to angels even if it is lacking in the MT. The LXX also concurs with the Hebrew tradition from Qumran ("sons of God," υἱοὶ θεοῦ), whereas Hebrews has "God's angels" (ἄγγελοι θεου). The difference between the LXX and Hebrews is not significant in terms of meaning, for as we have seen "sons of God" is another way of speaking of angels.[44]

Whether Hebrews draws on Ps 97:7 or Deut 32:43, the context is similar, for both texts speak of the Lord's sovereignty and rule over all, especially in his judgment over his adversaries. The author of Hebrews, as I will argue below, sees a reference to Jesus Christ and his exaltation at God's right hand. The angels worshiped the Son as the one exalted over all, as the one who would be the final judge on the last day.

Hebrews describes Jesus here as the "firstborn." Such language hearkens back to Exod 4:22 where Israel is identified as God's "firstborn." The notion of Jesus' sonship surfaces here, for just as Israel was God's firstborn son, now Jesus is God's firstborn par excellence. Indeed, we see an allusion to God bringing his people up from Egypt at the exodus (cf. Exod 3:8; 6:8; Deut 4:30; 6:10).[45] God liberated his people from Egypt and brought them into Canaan where they were to reign as God's vice-regents. Israel as God's firstborn failed to rule the world as God intended, but now he has brought his firstborn Son into his heavenly habitation where he rules at God's right hand, fulfilling the promise of victory over the serpent found in Gen 3:15. Because of the Son's obedience, God vindicated him by raising him from the dead and by seating him at his right hand, and thus he brought the Son into the heavenly world to reign over all. When the angels saw the Son exalted in fulfillment of God's promises that began in Gen 3:15, they were stunned, responding in worship and praise and adoration.

I have presented some evidence to support a reference to Jesus' exaltation, but other commentators believe the author refers to Jesus' incarnation or his *parousia*, and hence we should consider those interpretations. First, some see a reference to the incarnation instead

---

[44] We don't have to resolve here which textual tradition Hebrews depends on. It is enough to note that the reading found here is represented in both Hebrew and Greek texts of the OT.

[45] Cf. O'Brien, *Hebrews*, 69.

of his exaltation at the resurrection.[46] The word "again" (πάλιν) on this reading simply introduces another OT quotation, for other citations from the OT in the letter are also introduced with "again" (1:5; 2:13; 4:5; 10:30). According to this interpretation, the author reflects on Jesus' coming into the world at his incarnation, alluding to the worship of angels in accord with Luke 2:13–14. Second, others see a reference to Jesus' future coming.[47] Apparently, the HCSB (cf. NET) understands the verse in this way, "When He again brings His firstborn into the world, He says." This reading fits with the notion that the world here refers to the place where human beings reside, and it connects the word "again" with the verb "brings."

Finally, the emphasis on the Son's exaltation in the context of chapter 1 supports the notion that the angels worshiped the Son when he was exalted.[48] On this reading "again" belongs with the verb "says," as we see in the ESV (cf. NIV, NRSV), "And again, when he brings the firstborn into the world, he says."[49] The last option is preferable for several reasons.

First, the use of "again" (πάλιν) is ambiguous and hence not decisive in construing the meaning.[50] It could well be linked to the verb "says," as was pointed out above. Second, there is no clear evidence that the angels worshiped Jesus at the incarnation. In Luke the angels worship God, not Jesus. Indeed, Jesus' time on earth indicates that he was lower than angels during his time on earth (2:6–9), and so a reference to the incarnation as the time when he

---

[46] E.g., Ceslas Spicq, *L'Épître aux Hébreux*, 2nd ed., 2 vols., EB (Paris: Gabalda, 1953), 2:17. A reference to Jesus' baptism is unlikely (against Bateman, *Hebrews 1:5–13*, 222).

[47] E.g., B. F. Westcott, *The Epistle to the Hebrews: The Greek Text with Notes and Essays* (repr.; Grand Rapids, MI: Eerdmans, 1977), 22–23.

[48] So Ardel B. Caneday, "The Eschatological World Already Subjected to the Son: The Οἰκουμένη of Hebrews 1:6 and the Son's Enthronement," in *Cloud of Witnesses: The Theology of Hebrews in Its Ancient Contexts*, ed. R. Bauckham, D. Driver, T. Hart, and N. MacDonald, LNTS 387 (London: T&T Clark, 2008), 28–39; Moffitt, *Atonement and the Logic of the Resurrection in the Epistle to the Hebrews*, 56–69; Meier, "Symmetry and Theology," 507–11; Bruce, *Hebrews*, 17; L. Johnson, *Hebrews*, 79; Koester, *Hebrews*, 192; Lane, *Hebrews 1–8*, 26–27. It seems unlikely that the word *firstborn* denotes here that Jesus was also a priest, but see Peeler (*You Are My Son*, 52) for support of that notion.

[49] See Caneday, "The Eschatological World," 32–33.

[50] The phrase here is ὅταν δὲ πάλιν, which is not found anywhere else in Hebrews.

was worshiped doesn't fit as well with the theology of Hebrews.[51] Third, the "world" (οἰκουμένη) in 2:5 refers to the heavenly world, and hence it is likely that it has the same referent here.[52] As Caneday points out, we have numerous indications of a coming world before 2:5:[53] (1) salvation as a future inheritance (1:14–2:4); (2) "the consummation of the Son's reign" (1:13); (3) the eternity of the Son over against creation (1:10–12); (4) "the Son's enduring dominion" (1:8–9); and (5) the worship of the Son by angels when he enters the heavenly world (1:5–6).

Fourth, the use of the word "firstborn" (πρωτότοκον), as noted earlier, strengthens the case for the Son's being brought into the world at his exaltation. The word "firstborn" doesn't emphasize Jesus' incarnation (as in Luke 2:7) but his sovereignty and rule. The previous verse in Hebrews (1:5) describes Jesus' rule as the messianic king, and therefore we have grounds for expecting a similar theme here. The word "firstborn" is used of the Davidic king in Ps 89:27: "I will also make him My firstborn, greatest of the kings of the earth." In Psalm 89 "firstborn" designates sovereignty and rule. Such a notion fits well with angels worshiping the Son, for they worship him as their sovereign; and his sovereign rule began, as chapter 2 will also emphasize, at his resurrection/exaltation.

1:7

We saw in verse 6 that angels worshiped the Son when he was exalted as the messianic king. Angels, on the other hand, are messengers and servants and hence are clearly subordinate to the Son. The use of the OT here is fascinating. The author cites Ps 104:4 where the Lord's creative power is celebrated for "making the winds His messengers, flames of fire His servants." Hebrews departs from the LXX only at the last word, though what we find in Hebrews and

---

[51] Moffitt, *Atonement and the Logic of the Resurrection in the Epistle to the Hebrews*, 55–56.

[52] See especially ibid, 58–63. He gives seven reasons for linking the two uses. The most compelling are these: (1) the author continues the discussion of angels from chapter 1; (2) the salvation to be inherited (1:14) and the great salvation (2:3) are other ways of referring to the "world" in 1:6; (3) when the author says he speaks of the world to come (2:5), he most naturally refers back to the same word used in 1:6. For a fuller study of "world" (οἰκουμένη), see Moffitt's discussion (ibid., 63–118).

[53] Caneday, "The Eschatological World," 34.

the LXX functions as literal translation of the MT as well.[54] In the OT the author refers to physical forces in the world. Yahweh rules over all so that the winds do not blow by chance or even by the laws of nature but at God's personal direction.[55] Similarly, the flames that consume are God's servants. The Scriptures regularly ascribe what happens in nature to God. He is personally involved in the created order (cf. Heb 1:3).

The author of Hebrews reads the verse a bit differently from the way it is translated in Ps 104:4. It should be noted at the outset that the meaning presented by Hebrews fits with the wording of the verse in the MT as well. His construal of the verse is not exegetical fantasy but represents a legitimate reading of the text. The author of Hebrews likely believed both readings of the text were legitimate ways of construing its wording. According to Hebrews, the creaturely nature of angels is featured. God has made "his angels winds" and "his ministers a flame of fire." The statement should not be interpreted literally, as if the winds are actually angels and the flame that burns should be identified as God's messengers. The author *could* be making such an assertion, but it seems unlikely that he is teaching that winds *are* angels and that flames *are* his ministers. So I understand Hebrews to be saying that angels are God's ministers who serve God in the natural order. In other words God uses angels as his agents in sending wind and fire and presumably other natural phenomena like rain and sunshine as well. Regardless of what we think of such an interpretation, the verse's main purpose is clear: angels are God's messengers and servants. They are not worshiped as the Son is, for they did not create the world, but are part of the created order. They are not the Son but couriers who carry out the will of God.

1:8

Jesus as the Son is contrasted with the angels, for in distinction to them, he does not serve but rules as the divine king. The divinity

---

[54] See here L. Timothy Swinson, "'Wind' and 'Fire' in Hebrews 1:7: A Reflection upon the Use of Psalm 104 (103)," *TrinJ* 28 (2007): 215–28. Swinson observes that the translator of the LXX may have been influenced to render the text the way he does because of the clear references to angels in the preceding psalm (Ps 103:20–21).

[55] Cockerill (*Hebrews*, 108–9) thinks the emphasis is on the angels' temporality, and this is certainly possible, but I would suggest that the focus is on their role as servants.

of the Son and his reign over all are heralded here. Jesus' reign will not be limited but will endure forever, for as the obedient Son he has been rewarded with an eternal reign.

The author cites Ps 45:6–7 in Heb 1:8–9. Psalm 45 is a royal psalm penned in honor of the king of Israel. Truth and righteousness and justice are ascribed to the king. The psalmist envisions the triumph of the king over his enemies so that the cause of truth is advanced. Because of the king's righteousness, he has been exalted. The daughters of foreign kings should find their delight in the king, and their children, their sons, will reign in the land as princes. In the story line of the OT, the psalm is about the Davidic king, and David comes closest to living out the high ideals of the psalmist. In identifying the king as "God" (Ps 45:6), the psalmist is not literally identifying the king as divine.[56] The author anticipates royal succession (Ps 45:16), which hardly makes sense if the king is literally God. What we have here is similar to what we see in Exod 7:1 where Moses is as "God" to Pharaoh in that he speaks God's authoritative word to him. So too, judges in Israel are identified as "gods" in the sense that they pronounce (or are supposed to pronounce) God's judgment for the people (Ps 82:1, 6).[57]

The author of Hebrews appropriates the psalm, seeing it as fulfilled in the Son. Even though the psalm says nothing about the Son, in the words introducing the citation, he says, "But to the Son," indicating that the king is none other than the Son, Jesus Christ. The writer picks up the words where the king is identified as God, "Your throne, God, is forever and ever." Clearly divinity is ascribed to the Son (see §2.1). It makes little sense to translate the phrase, "Your throne is God." Furthermore, the deity of the Son fits with the Son's role as Creator (1:2, 10), his divine nature (1:3, 11–12), his preservation of the world (1:3), and his being worshiped by angels (1:6). The use of the OT is instructive here. The author argues typologically.

---

[56] For a careful study of Psalm 45 in its historical context and for arguments that fit closely with what is argued here, see Dale F. Leschert, *Hermeneutical Foundations of Hebrews: A Study in the Validity of the Epistle's Interpretation of Some Core Citations from the Psalms*, NABPRDS 10 (Lewiston, NY: Edwin Mellen, 1994), 23–78.

[57] Attridge understands Ps 45:7 to say, "Your throne is (a throne of God), eternal" (*Hebrews*, 58), but this reading of the verse is unpersuasive. See Murray J. Harris, *Jesus as God: The New Testament Use of* Theos *in Reference to Jesus* (Grand Rapids, MI: Eerdmans, 1992), 190–202.

Jesus as the greatest king in the Davidic line literally fulfills the words of the psalm. The wording of the psalm can be construed poetically (so in the original context of Psalm 45) or literally. Psalm 45 is read in light of the revelation of God in Jesus Christ, in light of the entire story line of Scripture. The Davidic king, as he is revealed in Jesus Christ, is himself God (Isa 9:6–7). All the threads of OT revelation are woven together to proclaim that the king that has come is both divine and human.

The NT doesn't often identify Jesus Christ as "God" explicitly, but such a statement is clearly made in John 1:1 and 20:28. Furthermore, such an ascription is the most probable reading of Rom 9:5; Titus 2:13; 2 Pet 1:1.[58]

As readers we can so concentrate on the ascription of deity to the Son that we miss the emphasis on kingship. The throne, the rule, of this divine king lasts forever. He is greater than the angels because he enjoys eternal sovereignty. Furthermore, his rule is righteous, for the "scepter" of his kingdom is characterized by rectitude (εὐθύτητος). Often kings rule with cruelty and selfishness, mistreating and taking advantage of their subjects. The Son's rule, however, is dramatically different, for he rules justly and righteously.

1:9

The humanity and deity of the Son are closely intertwined in Hebrews. The rectitude of the Son's kingdom is elaborated upon in verse 9. Because he has loved what is righteous and hated what is wicked, he has been anointed by God with a position above his companions.[59] Here the author refers to the exaltation, presumably at the resurrection, of the Son as King. In the OT priests (Exod 28:41; 29:7; 30:30), prophets (1 Kgs 19:16), and kings were anointed (1 Sam 9:16; 15:1; 16:3, 12) to signify that they were appointed to office. In the Gospels Jesus' anointing for ministry occurs at his baptism (Matt 3:16–17), and Jesus proclaims in Luke at the outset of his ministry that God has anointed him (Luke 4:18).

According to Hebrews, Jesus is anointed to serve as king and is superior to the angels and all others because he has received a

---

[58] See the careful and convincing work on this matter by Harris, *Jesus as God*.

[59] Alternatively, the anointing refers to gladness in God's justice (O'Brien, *Hebrews*, 74).

position that exalts him above all other human beings.[60] The reason for this exaltation is his pursuit of and love for what is righteous. Conversely, he detested and rejected evil in all its forms. The one exalted above other human beings was exalted because of his goodness and his devotion to righteousness. Here we have a foreshadowing of Jesus' obedience, faithfulness, and sinlessness in testing, topics that run like a thread throughout the letter (2:18; 3:2, 6; 4:15; 5:8–9; 7:26, 28; 9:14; 10:7–10; 12:3). We have a preview of what we find elsewhere in Hebrews. Jesus learned obedience from what he suffered (5:8). He was tested and tried but never succumbed to sin (4:15). As 7:26 says, Jesus was "holy, innocent, undefiled, separated from sinners, and exalted above the heavens." Though 1:8 speaks of the divinity of the Son, here the humanity of the Son is featured (see §2.2). The two references to "God" (θεός) in verse 9 both refer to the Father.[61] The Father rewarded him with rule over all because he was the obedient Son, because he never strayed from doing God's will.

1:10

The author cites Ps 102:25–27, showing that the Son is greater than angels because he is the Creator of all and because he is eternal in contrast to the created world which is temporary (see §2.1). In Psalm 102 the psalmist laments the distress he faces, the brevity of his life, the opposition of his enemies, and the indignation of the Lord. Yet he has hope that the Lord will restore Zion, for the Lord reigns and will fulfill his covenant promises. The psalmist pleads with the Lord to show mercy, knowing that the Lord has the power to do so as the Creator of all and as the eternal God. Hence, he has confidence that the Lord will establish and protect Israel in coming generations.

It is fascinating to see that a psalm about Yahweh is appropriated by the author of Hebrews and applied to Jesus Christ as the

---

[60] In the psalm the king is exalted over his other earthly companions. In Hebrews the "companions" could be identified as angels (Meier, "Symmetry and Theology," 516; Barnard, *The Mysticism of Hebrews*, 262; Bateman, *Hebrews 1:5–13*, 229). Alternatively and more likely, he refers to the sons and companions of 2:10 and 3:14 (so Bruce, *Hebrews*, 21; O'Brien, *Hebrews*, 74–75; Cockerill, *Hebrews*, 111; Moffitt, *Atonement and the Logic of the Resurrection in the Epistle to the Hebrews*, 51). Hughes thinks Jesus' exaltation over other kings is intended, but he goes on to say the referent is general (*Hebrews*, 66).

[61] For the view that the vocative refers to the Son, see Attridge, *Hebrews*, 59–60.

Son. Apparently the author, since he has identified Jesus as divine, feels free to cite a psalm about Yahweh and apply it to Jesus Christ as well. Such a move is typical of NT Christology, where texts that refer to Yahweh as Lord in the LXX are applied to Jesus Christ (e.g., Rom 10:13; 14:11; 1 Cor 1:31; 2:16; 10:22, 26; 2 Cor 10:17; Phil 2:10–11; 1 Thess 3:13; 4:6; 2 Thess 1:7–8; 2 Tim 2:19). Ellingworth suggests several reasons the author may have selected Psalm 102. He sees thematic similarities between Psalm 45 and Psalm 102, including the reference to divine rule (Pss 45:6; 102:12) and divine victory (Pss 45:4–5; 102:15). In addition, we see connections between Hebrews and the psalm with references to Christ's exaltation (Ps 102:12), "the renewal of Zion" (vv. 13, 16), freedom from the fear of death (v. 20), and the claim that what was written will be fulfilled in a later generation (v. 18).[62]

We have in seed form here what has been called in Trinitarian theology "coinherence." Whatever is true of one member of the Trinity in terms of the shared divine nature is true of the others. The Father is divine by virtue of being Creator, and hence it follows that the Son, since he is divine, is the Creator as well. Elsewhere in the NT (e.g., John 1:3; Col 1:16) and Hebrews (1:3), of course, we have explicit statements that the Son is the Creator.

The psalm is introduced in verse 10 merely by the word "and." The Son is greater than the angels because he created the earth and the heavens. Metaphorical language is used to depict the creation of the world. The Son laid the foundations for the earth as a builder erects a foundation for a building. The heavens, which here represent the sky and the sun, moon, and stars, are fashioned by the hands of the Son, as an artist fashions a vase or a sculpture. The creative work of the Son was accomplished at the beginning, when history began, when the heavens and the earth were created. The language echoes Gen 1:1 where God is said to create the heavens and the earth at the beginning (cf. also Prov 8:22–31). All of created reality was made by the Son.

1:11

The created world is temporary and will not last forever. Here it stands in contrast to the Son who is eternal and remains forever. The author foreshadows his argument in chapter 7, which features Jesus

---

[62] Ellingworth, *Hebrews*, 125–26.

as an eternal Melchizedekian priest.[63] Creation is compared to a garment that grows old as time elapses, as it is subject to the elements and wear and tear of everyday life. The temporary character of the present creation is also taught in 2 Peter: "The heavens will pass away with a loud noise" (2 Pet 3:10), and "The elements will melt with the heat" (2 Pet 3:12). The changelessness and eternality of the Son demonstrate his divinity, indicating that he shares the same identity as God (1:3). God never changes in his character (Mal 3:6; Jas 1:17) and will always fulfill his promises. The author anticipates 13:8 where he proclaims that Jesus is the same yesterday, today, and forever.[64]

1:12

Verse 12 reiterates and drives home what was said in 1:11. The created world will come to an end and will not persist forever, but Jesus as the Son will never change and is eternal. The author portrays the end of this world as a cloak that is rolled up. The same Greek verb "roll up" (ἑλίσσω) is used elsewhere to denote the cessation of the present creation. "The skies will roll up like a scroll" (Isa 34:14) on the day of the Lord when the Lord judges the world for its evil. Revelation picks up the same image, describing the "sky" as a scroll that is "rolled up" on the final day of the Lord (Rev 6:14).

In Hebrews the present creation comes to an end, just as one rolls up a cloak when it is no longer useful (cf. 12:27). The created world is compared to a garment that wears out and changes over time. By way of contrast, the Son remains the same. He does not grow old or grow weary or wear out, but as 13:8 powerfully affirms, he remains the same forever. The passing years do not detract from his person, for he does not grow "older" with the years.

Statements about the temporary nature of this present creation should be placed against the promise of the coming new creation (Rev 21:1–22:5). A new heaven and earth are promised to believers (2 Pet 3:13). Believers realize they are sojourners on this earth (11:10, 13–16), and hence they desire a better homeland, the city to come (13:14). The author describes it as "the city of the living God (the heavenly Jerusalem)" (12:22). Scholars have long debated whether the present universe is destroyed and God makes a new one,

---

[63] Attridge, *Hebrews*, 61.

[64] So L. Johnson, *Hebrews*, 81.

or the present world is transformed and purified. It is probably the latter, though space is lacking to pursue that matter here.[65] In any case the world as it is now is temporary and evanescent in contrast to the Son who is unchanging and never ending.

1:13

The author cites Ps 110:1 to demonstrate that the Son is greater than the angels, for the Son sits at the right hand of God, reigning with him; no privilege like this was ever given to angels. The contrast with angels is paramount, for the OT text is introduced with the words, "Now to which of the angels has He ever said . . ." The rule given to the Son was never intended for angels.

The superiority of the Son is established by quoting Ps 110:1. The psalm is clearly a favorite for the author, for the psalm speaks of a priest-king, and this king functions as a priest according to the order of Melchizedek (Ps 110:4). The author alludes to Psalm 110 in 1:3 where he declares that the Son "sat down at the right hand of the Majesty on high." The letter elaborates upon the Melchizedekian priesthood of Jesus (5:6; 6:20; 7:1–28), drawing on Ps 110:4. When the author summarizes his "main point," he alludes to Ps 110:1 again, claiming that Jesus as the "high priest" "sat down at the right hand of the throne of the Majesty in the heavens" (8:1). The psalm verifies one of the fundamental themes of the letter. Jesus' priestly work is finished, and hence he now reigns as king at the right hand of God. The author finds incredible that the readers would turn away from the forgiveness achieved once for all by Jesus as the priest-king and latch onto the law and its sacrifices to experience forgiveness of sins.

Psalm 110:1 was also cited by Jesus during his ministry (Matt 22:41–46 par.). He befuddled the Pharisees by asking how the Messiah could be both David's Lord and son since according to verse 1 David's heir was also his Lord. Hebrews, among other books in the NT, supplies the answer. Jesus is both human and divine. He is both David's son as a human being and his Lord as the Son of God. New Testament writers regularly quote or allude to Ps 110:1 to indicate that God exalted Jesus (Acts 2:34; 5:31; Rom 8:34; 1 Cor

---

[65] In defense of the notion that this world is renovated rather than annihilated and recreated, see Douglas J. Moo, "Nature in the New Creation: New Testament Eschatology and the Environment," *JETS* 49 (2006): 459–69.

15:25; Eph 1:20; Col 3:1; 1 Pet 3:22). The reference to Jesus' exaltation, therefore, draws on a common Christian theme, a staple of NT theology. Jesus reigns at God's right hand.

The message of Psalm 110 as a whole should be summarized briefly here. Yahweh will extend the rule of David's Lord from Zion so that he will triumph over his enemies. The people will gladly join this ruler who will introduce a new day of victory for Israel, a new dawn. He will reign as a priest-king. Since he sits at the Lord's right hand, he will crush his enemies. It is difficult in vv. 5–7 to distinguish where the text refers to Yahweh and where it refers to the priest-king who triumphs in Yahweh's name. This close identification suggests that the priest-king has the same stature as Yahweh. In other words, the ambiguity is itself intentional, for the king's victories are Yahweh's victories. The king will "lift up His head" in triumph and exultation (110:7), restoring Yahweh's rule over the world.

In verse 13 the author cites verse 1 of the psalm. The quotation follows the LXX, which in turn is a literal translation of the MT. The Son is invited to sit at God's right hand while Yahweh makes his enemies submit at the footstool of the Son. One of the prominent themes of chapter 1 is the Son's sovereignty and rule. Through the Son the victory promised to Israel and the Davidic king becomes a reality.[66]

1:14

By way of contrast, angels do not rule but serve. They are sent by God to carry out his wishes. Indeed, they are not greater than human beings but subservient to them, for they carry out God's bidding for the salvation of human beings. Angels are identified as "ministering spirits" (λειτουργικὰ πνεύματα), underscoring that their role is to serve. The ministering function of angels is underscored throughout the verse, for they are commissioned to fulfill the will of the one who sent them. Their service is for the sake of human beings, for angels do their work for "those who are going to inherit salvation." The salvation of human beings is conceived of here as eschatological, as something human beings will receive on the final day.

---

[66] The author probably envisions the rule of the Son until the day of victory (so Ellingworth, *Hebrews*, 131; O'Brien, *Hebrews*, 78n211), but others think the reign of the Son will last forever (e.g., Hughes, *Hebrews*, 70–71).

Bridge

The supremacy of Jesus as the Son is the theme of this section. Jesus' sonship is tied to his being the Davidic king and the ruler over the world. The divinity and the humanity of the Son are both central to the argument. He rules as the Davidic king and as one who is fully divine. The angels worshiped him when he was raised from the dead and exalted, and as God he rules over all. Indeed, the Son is the eternal and unchanging Creator. By way of contrast angels are servants, carrying out God's will. Since the Son is superior to angels, since he is divine and rules over all, why would the readers consider returning to a revelation (the Mosaic law) mediated by angels?

Hebrews 2:1–4

Outline

I. Prologue: Definitive and Final Revelation in the Son (1:1–4)
II. **Don't Abandon the Son Since He Is Greater than Angels (1:5–2:18)**
    A. The Son's Nature and Reign Show He Is Greater than Angels (1:5–14)
    B. **Warning: Don't Drift Away (2:1–4)**
    C. The Coming World Subjected to the Son (2:5–18)

Scripture

[1] We must therefore pay even more attention to what we have heard, so that we will not drift away. [2] For if the message spoken through angels was legally binding, and every transgression and disobedience received a just punishment, [3] how will we escape if we neglect such a great salvation? It was first spoken by the Lord and was confirmed to us by those who heard Him. [4] At the same time, God also testified by signs and wonders, various miracles, and distributions of gifts from the Holy Spirit according to His will.

Context

The reason for the elegant theological argument in 1:1–14 now surfaces. The author warns the readers that they should not drift away from the message they received. The main point of the paragraph is the warning given to the readers (see §5). Connections between this paragraph and chapter 1 surface; both emphasize that God has spoken through the Son, and thus the readers must heed what was proclaimed to them.[67] Verses 2–4 explain why the warning is so crucial. In verses 2–3 we have an argument from the lesser to the greater. If those who violated the word given by angels were punished with earthly punishments, those who reject such a great salvation will experience even more dire consequences. When we put the pieces together, the main point of the paragraph can be summarized as follows: pay attention and don't drift away from the message proclaimed by the Son, for there is no escape for those who neglect such a great salvation. The paragraph concludes with an affirmation of the truth received. It was "spoken by the Lord" and confirmed by eyewitnesses. Signs and wonders and other miracles attested to the truthfulness of the revelation. The readers should have no doubts about the veracity of the revelation and therefore must not turn away from the truth.

Exegesis

2:1

The readers are exhorted, in this first warning passage, to continue to pay attention to the gospel proclaimed to them so they don't drift away. The word translated "drift away" ($\pi\alpha\rho\alpha\rho\upsilon\tilde{\omega}\mu\epsilon\nu$) is used to describe "a ring slipping off a finger."[68] Perhaps there is a nautical metaphor here so that we picture a ship not anchored slowly drifting out to sea.[69] The word "therefore" ($\Delta\iota\grave{\alpha}\ \tauο\tilde{\upsilon}\tau o$) links 2:1–4 with the preceding argument.[70] The logic is as follows: since Jesus as the divine Son and Davidic king is greater than the angels and since he has cleansed the readers of their sins, they must stand by what they have heard.

What they heard, of course, was the message about Jesus Christ, particularly the efficacy of his sacrifice for sins. They heard the final and definitive word that God had spoken by his Son (1:2). They faced the danger of ceasing to pay heed to this authoritative word and slipping away from the truth. The remainder of the letter,

---

[67] Cf. O'Brien, *Hebrews*, 82–83.

[68] Attridge, *Hebrews*, 64n19.

[69] Koester, *Hebrews*, 205; Lane, *Hebrews 1–8*, 35.

[70] It encompasses the whole of ch. 1 (so Ellingworth, *Hebrews*, 135).

especially the remaining warning passages, clarifies that the drifting away described here is not a temporary defection from the truth. Drifting away is another way of describing apostasy, the denial and rejection of the gospel.

2:2

The author gives the reason ("for," γάρ) in an "if-then" construction why the readers should not defect from the word they heard. The message transmitted by angels was binding, and those who violated its stipulations were punished. The argument moves from the lesser to the greater, with the lesser reason given in verse 2 and the greater reason in verse 3. Verse 2 features the revelation transmitted by angels. The message given by angels was binding on its hearers so that those who violated its provisions were justly punished.

Angels reappear here in the text after playing a prominent role in chapter 1, which emphasized the Son's superiority to angels. The connection to the first chapter should not be missed. The message mediated by the angels was clearly the Mosaic law, a notion stated elsewhere in the NT (cf. Acts 7:53; Gal 3:19). Apparently such a tradition was commonplace, though it is not clearly articulated in the OT (but cf. Deut 33:2).[71]

We see from the link between angels and the Mosaic law why angels surface in chapter 1. The readers were not interested in angels because they were entranced by angels in some kind of mystical way or because of a polemic against angel Christology.[72] Instead, the reference to angels fits with the letter as a whole. It accords with the readers' desire to live under the old covenant, to find forgiveness in Levitical sacrifices.[73] Hence the superiority of the Son to angels demonstrates that he is superior to the old covenant mediated by angels.

There is no thought, however, that the word conveyed by angels was flawed. No, it was "reliable" (βέβαιος, ESV) and sure and hence "legally binding" on the hearers. In light of the contrast between

---

[71] For the allusion to Deut 33:2, see Allen, *Deuteronomy and Exhortation in Hebrews*, 105–6. The notion of angelic mediation was present in Jewish tradition as well. See Attridge, *Hebrews*, 65n28.

[72] Rightly Koester, *Hebrews*, 200; Hughes, *Hebrews*, 52.

[73] See here Barnabas Lindars, *The Theology of the Letter to the Hebrews*, New Testament Theology (Cambridge: Cambridge University Press, 1991), 38.

1:1 and 1:2, we can say that the angelic word was partial and provisionary. It was not the last and definitive word spoken through the Son. Nevertheless, it was still a reliable and sure word. Indeed, those who violated the covenant stipulations "received a just punishment." The punishment accorded with the nature of the crime, and this is a fundamental principle of the Torah. Leviticus 26 and Deuteronomy 27–28 rehearse in some detail the curses of the covenant and specify the punishments imposed for transgressions. Furthermore, the case law (Exod 21:1–22:20) articulates the penalties assessed for breaking the law. The author emphasizes that the punishments were "just" and deserved.

2:3

The author now completes the if-then argument, the argument from the lesser to the greater. If the word spoken by angels was sure and those who violated it were punished, then those who neglect the greater revelation given through the Son will not escape. Indeed, the readers would be foolish to reject the word spoken by the Lord, for there is no doubt about its truthfulness since it is a word from heaven. The first generation of Christians heard the message directly from Jesus, and those eyewitnesses confirmed the message for the readers.

The author presses home his argument. The readers will not "escape" (ἐκφευξόμεθα) if they turn away from such a great salvation. The salvation is great because it represents God's final word (1:2). Jesus' sacrifice has accomplished cleansing of sin once for all (1:3; 7:1–10:18), and hence he now sits at God's right hand (1:13; 8:1), triumphant and reigning over all. Those who repudiate such a salvation will face certain judgment. In the OT (2:2) the punishments were earthly: Israel suffered exile for its sin. But the revelation through the Son is heavenly (e.g., 12:25–27), so that those who reject him will receive a more intense punishment, a final and eternal punishment from which there is no exit.[74] The use of the word "escape" places a frame around this warning passage and the last warning in 12:25–29, for in both cases the readers are warned that they will not "escape" (ἐκφεύγω, 2:3; 12:25). Elsewhere in the

---

[74] Rightly O'Brien, *Hebrews*, 86n29. Against Cockerill (*Hebrews*, 120–21), who thinks Israel suffered from the same punishment (an eternal one) with which the author threatens the readers here, but the author specifically contrasts the earthly judgments of Israel with the eternal punishments threatened for the church.

NT the word "escape" is used in relation to the end-time judgment (Luke 21:36; Rom 2:3; 1 Thess 5:3). The framing device also supports the notion that the warning passages should be read together, that they all make the same point. The readers are admonished not to "neglect" such a great salvation. The word "neglect" (ἀμελέω) in Matt 22:5 is used to describe those who failed to attend the wedding banquet because they found their farm or business more interesting. The "neglect" here is malignant, for they will face judgment for disregarding such a great salvation.[75]

The remainder of verses 3–4 unpacks why it is utter folly to neglect the salvation accomplished in Jesus Christ. First of all, it is an authoritative word, for "it was first spoken by the Lord." The "Lord" here refers to Jesus himself; he is the Son by whom God has spoken his final word (1:2). The Creator and Sustainer of the world, the heir of all things, has himself entered history and spoken to human beings through word and deed. Jesus Christ has revealed finally and definitively who God is to human beings.

Second, not only was the word spoken personally by the Lord himself in history, this word was also "confirmed" to the readers by eyewitnesses who heard and saw Jesus. Legal language is prominent in the next two verses, underscoring the truth of the message proclaimed. If believers are going to stake their lives on the gospel, they need to be assured of its truthfulness and reliability. The word spoken through angels was "legally binding" (βέβαιος), and the word spoken by Jesus was "confirmed" (ἐβεβαιώθη). The author and readers, though they were not ear- and eyewitnesses, can be sure of the message spoken through the Lord because it was corroborated by those who heard Jesus. We see from this verse that the early church was concerned about the reliable transmission of what Jesus said and did. They did not look kindly upon those who freely invented the words and works of Jesus Christ.

In addition, this verse functions as strong evidence against Pauline authorship. Even though he wasn't an eyewitness, he nowhere describes himself as dependent on others for the gospel he proclaimed. He emphasizes instead that Jesus called him to be an apostle on the Damascus Road and that his knowledge of the gospel was not dependent on the other apostles (Gal 1:11–17).

---

[75] Rightly Ellingworth, *Hebrews*, 140.

2:4

The author now gives the third reason for putting their trust in their great salvation. First, the Lord Jesus spoke it in history. Second, those who heard Jesus during his ministry confirmed the message of Jesus to the readers and to the author. Third, God also bore witness to the truth of the revelation by miracles and gifts of the Holy Spirit.

The author emphasizes that God has added his own witness (συνεπιμαρτυροῦντος) to the truth of the gospel. The truth was verified "by signs and wonders, various miracles." The miracles given accredited the revelation, demonstrating that it was genuinely given by God. Jesus' miracles authenticated his ministry according to the Gospels, and they were also signs of the presence of the kingdom. The three words used to denote miracles are roughly synonymous, though the term "signs" (σημείοις) suggests that human beings should discern the significance of the miracles. The word "wonders" (τέρασιν) communicates the unprecedented and astonishing nature of God's work, while "miracles" (δυνάμεσιν) features the power of God. During the Exodus the Lord performed many "signs and wonders" so both Egypt and Israel realized that he was the Lord of history, that he was the only true God, and that he was fulfilling his covenant in liberating Israel from Egypt (cf. Exod 7:3; Deut 6:22; 26:8; 29:3; 34:11; Ps 135:9; Jer 32:20, 21). God also granted signs and wonders to the apostles, demonstrating that they were truly his messengers (Acts 2:43; 4:30; 5:12; 14:3; 15:12). Paul emphasizes the validity of his apostleship by appealing to the "signs and wonders" in his ministry (Rom 15:19; 2 Cor 12:12). So too, the readers in Hebrews can be assured that the salvation they initially trusted is true. The miracles and signs and wonders demonstrate that God has put his imprimatur, his seal of approval, upon the message the Hebrews received initially.[76] Also verifying the truth of the gospel is "the distribution of gifts from the Holy Spirit" (see §4). The word "apportionments" (μερισμοῖς) probably refers to the gifts of the Spirit as the HCSB translates it (cf. also NIV, ESV, NRSV). Here the particular argument is that the gifts of the Spirit accredit the

---

[76] Perhaps the miracles described here were also ongoing in the life of the readers. So Lane, *Hebrews 1–8*, 39–40; Steve Motyer, "The Spirit in Hebrews: No Longer Forgotten?" in *The Spirit and Christ in the New Testament and Christian Theology: Essays Presented in Honor of Max Turner*, ed. I. H. Marshall, V. Rabens, and C. Bennema (Grand Rapids, MI: Eerdmans, 2012), 214–15, 219–20.

revelation given by God. Elsewhere, both Paul (Gal 3:1–5) and Peter (Acts 15:7–11) claim that the gift of the Holy Spirit demonstrates that Gentile believers truly belong to the people of God. In other contexts the gifts of the Spirit are granted to edify believers (cf. Rom 12:3–8; 1 Cor 12:1–31; 14:1–40; Eph 4:11–16; 1 Pet 4:10–11), but here the author appeals to the gifts of the Spirit to support the veracity of the gospel.

Bridge

The NT nowhere teaches that an initial acceptance of the saving message is sufficient without perseverance in faith. We must not drift from the faith or neglect our great salvation. If the people of God in the OT received earthly punishments for transgressing the Mosaic law mediated by angels, then those who repudiate the heavenly revelation given by the Son will not escape final judgment. Nor can we say that the revelation spoken by the Son is uncertain, for the Lord himself came to earth to speak the word. And it was then confirmed by those who heard the Lord in history. Finally, God attested to the truth of the revelation through miracles, signs, and wonders and gifts of the Holy Spirit. Apostasy, then, would constitute a rejection of a clear word from God. No one can make the excuse that the revelation was not sufficiently certified so that doubts were permissible. Koester rightly remarks, "Warnings are not designed to rob people of hope, but to steer them away from danger in order to preserve them so that they might persevere and inherit what has been promised."[77]

Hebrews 2:5–9

Outline

   I. Prologue: Definitive and Final Revelation in the Son (1:1–4)
  II. **Don't Abandon the Son Since He Is Greater than Angels (1:5–2:18)**
      A. The Son's Nature and Reign Show He Is Greater than Angels (1:5–14)
      B. Warning: Don't Drift Away (2:1–4)

---

[77] Koester, *Hebrews*, 209.

C. **The Coming World Subjected to the Son (2:5–18)**
   1. **The Son of Man Exalted over Angels by Virtue of His Death (2:5–9)**
   2. Jesus as the Merciful and Faithful High Priest Shares His Rule with His Brothers and Sisters (2:10–18)

Scripture

⁵ For He has not subjected to angels the world to come that we are talking about.

⁶ But one has somewhere testified: What is man that You remember him, or the son of man that You care for him? ⁷ You made him lower than the angels for a short time; You crowned him with glory and honor ⁸ and subjected everything under his feet. For in subjecting everything to him, He left nothing that is not subject to him. As it is, we do not yet see everything subjected to him. ⁹ But we do see Jesus—made lower than the angels for a short time so that by God's grace He might taste death for everyone—crowned with glory and honor because of His suffering in death.

Context

The "for" (γάρ) connects 2:5–18 (and 2:5–9 particularly) with the previous paragraph. The line of argument is as follows. Believers won't escape judgment if they neglect such a great salvation and devote themselves to the law mediated by angels.[78] Verses 5–9 explain why. Rule over the world hasn't been given to angels, and thus human beings will only reach their destiny if they belong to Jesus as the son of man. Psalm 8 clearly attests that rule has been given to human beings instead of angels. The psalmist reflects on the creation narrative. Human beings are lower than the angels, but they are destined for glory and honor. Everything in creation is to be subject to human beings. The author reads the creation narrative and Psalm 8 through the lens of redemptive history. All things in creation are not subjected to human beings. The world is flawed and fallen. Still one human being has fulfilled the purpose for which he was created: Jesus. He was lower than angels in his incarnation but now is

---

[78] Rightly L. Johnson, *Hebrews*, 89. What binds ch. 2 to ch. 1 is the reference to angels (cf. 1:5 and 2:16). Hebrews 2:17–18 transitions to the next section (rightly O'Brien, *Hebrews*, 63).

crowned with glory and honor. The path to the crown, however, was the cross. Because of his suffering, his death, he is now the exalted one. Hence, his death was not for himself alone but for every human being who belongs to him. Human beings will only rule the world as God intended when they triumph over death. But Jesus is the only human being who reigns over death by virtue of his suffering. The rest of humanity will only share in that victory if they belong to Jesus. It is inconceivable, then, that readers would turn to an angelic revelation that does not promise rule over the world and forsake the revelation that secures victory over death!

Exegesis

2:5

The world to come, which has been the subject of the letter thus far, will not be subjected to angels. Human beings will rule the world for God.[79] Hence, what the author describes is another way of referring to "a kingdom that cannot be shaken" (12:28).[80] The author makes his case from Psalm 8, which appeals to the creation tradition. Paul makes a similar argument to what we find here in Hebrews, claiming that believers will judge angels (1 Cor 6:3). Some texts in the biblical tradition demonstrate that angels exercised authority and rule over human beings (cf. Deut 32:8 LXX; Dan 10:13, 20; Herm. *Vis.* 12:1), and if this is in the author's mind, it fits with the emphasis on angels in chapters 1–2.

In any case angels haven't left the author's mind, showing that chapters 1–2 belong together. It follows, then, that the warning in 2:1–4 is related to both 1:1–14 and 2:5–18. We saw in chapter 1 that the rule of Jesus as divine and as the Davidic king, i.e., his sonship, reveals that he is greater than angels. The author reminds us now that the world to come will not be subjected to angels. The words "that we are talking about" are important, for they reveal that

---

[79] The author thinks here of human beings in general and not Jesus in particular (so Moffitt, *Atonement and the Logic of the Resurrection in the Epistle to the Hebrews*, 122). Moffitt says angels ruled the world before Jesus was exalted as a human being (119–22). Such a rule by angels may be the case (see the commentary on this verse), but the text is not completely clear on this point. Moffitt rightly contends that Jesus is exalted and rules as a human being. I would simply add that he is exalted and rules as the God-man, as one who is fully human and fully divine.

[80] So Lane, *Hebrews 1–8*, 46.

1:1–2:4 were a discussion about the world to come (τὴν οἰκουμένην τὴν μέλλουσαν; cf. also 1:6). Elsewhere in the letter he refers to the future "homeland" (πατρίδα, 11:14) and to the city to come (11:16; 13:14), which is also described as "the heavenly Jerusalem" (12:22).

2:6

The writer in the subsequent verses quotes Ps 8:4–6, showing that rule over the world wasn't given to angels but to human beings. He then argues that this rule has become a reality in Jesus, the human being par excellence.[81] In verse 6 the author quotes Ps 8:5 which poses a question about the significance of human beings. Why does God remember them or care for them? The text here follows the LXX but represents a literal translation of the MT as well. We shall see in verse 7 below, however, that the writer follows the LXX instead of the MT.[82]

The introductory formula is interesting. At first glance the wording seems cavalier, "But one has somewhere testified." The author is not betraying ignorance, as if he doesn't know the text he cites. The letter as a whole demonstrates that he is sophisticated and knowledgeable in his use of the OT. These are not the words of an uneducated novice. Hebrews doesn't focus on the person who uttered the words or the exact place where they are found. The author wants us to pay heed to the OT Scripture as testimony (διεμαρτύρατο),

---

[81] Cockerill argues that these verses refer exclusively to Jesus (*Hebrews*, 129). See also the robust defense of this view by Barry Joslin, "'Son of Man' or 'Human Beings'? Hebrews 2:5–9 and a Response to Craig Blomberg," *JBMW* 14 (2009): 42–45. I would suggest that we have a both-and in vv. 6–8. The text refers both to human beings in general and to Jesus in particular, and this is scarcely surprising since Jesus himself was human. See Kenneth L. Schenk, *Cosmology and Eschatology in Hebrews: The Settings of the Sacrifice*, SNTSMS 143 (Cambridge: Cambridge University Press, 2007), 54–59; George H. Guthrie and Russell D. Quinn, "A Discourse Analysis of the Use of Psalm 8:4–6 in Hebrews 2:5–9," *JETS* 49 (2006): 235–46. For the notion that it doesn't refer to Jesus until v. 9, see Craig L. Blomberg, "'But We See Jesus': The Relationship Between the Son of Man in Hebrews 2.6 and 2.9 and the Implications for English Translations," in *Cloud of Witnesses: The Theology of Hebrews in Its Ancient Contexts*, ed. R. Bauckham, D. Driver, T. Hart, and N. MacDonald, LNTS 387 (London: T&T Clark, 2008), 88–99.

[82] Leschert rightly argues that the use of Psalm 8 in Hebrews, even though it extends the meaning of the psalm, accords well with its meaning in its historical context (*Hermeneutical Foundations of Hebrews*, 79–121).

as the word spoken by God, and hence the human author remains unnamed.[83]

The psalm from which these words are taken celebrates the majesty of God and the dignity of human beings. The psalmist considers the universe God created, the moon and stars, and reflects on the dignity of mankind. Human beings seem so trivial and insignificant in light of the grandeur of the world God has made. The two lines, reflecting Hebrew parallelism, are roughly synonymous. So "man" and "son of man" both refer to human beings in the original meaning of the psalm. The words "son of man" do not reflect a messianic title in the psalm, nor do they have that meaning in Hebrews.[84] Still the translation (so HCSB, ESV, NIV) should retain "son of man" (against "mortals," NRSV), for there may be echoes here of "One like a son of man" in Dan 7:13. A translation should preserve such echoes if possible, particularly since "Son of Man" is such a common title for Jesus in the Gospels. The verb "remember" (μιμνήσκῃ) is better rendered as "are mindful of" (ESV, NIV, NRSV), for the author is inquiring whether God is concerned about and cares for (ἐπισκέπτῃ) human beings.

2:7

The question asked in verse 6 is now answered in verses 7–8. Who and what are human beings? For a limited period of time they are lower than the angels, but they are ultimately destined for glory and honor. The reference to the angels reflects the LXX of Ps 8:5. The MT reads, "you made him little less than God" (cf. NRSV), though the ESV and NIV adopt the LXX reading, seeing a reference to angels. A reference to angels fits with what the author of Hebrews does in chapters 1–2, but the MT probably preserves the original text. The MT emphasizes the qualitative difference between God and human beings, but Hebrews, in dependence on the LXX, argues that the subordination of humans to angels is temporary.[85] Ultimately, human beings are "crowned . . . with glory and honor" since they are the crown of creation. Psalm 8 is a meditation on the

---

[83] Rightly Lane, *Hebrews 1–8*, 46; Ellingworth, *Hebrews*, 148; Hughes, *Hebrews*, 83–84.

[84] Rightly O'Brien, *Hebrews*, 95–96; Cockerill, *Hebrews*, 128. Against Guthrie and Quinn, "A Discourse Analysis," 243–44; Moffitt, *Atonement and the Logic of the Resurrection in the Epistle to the Hebrews*, 122–29.

[85] Cf. O'Brien, *Hebrews*, 98; Ellingworth, *Hebrews*, 154.

creation account where human beings are made in the divine image and are summoned to rule the world for God. They are intended to rule the world, and that rule will include rule over angels.

2:8

Verse 8 begins with the last line cited from Psalm 8: "and subjected everything under his feet," and then the author offers commentary on the psalm. "Everything" really means "everything." Everything is subject to human beings. But this immediately leads the author to another comment: It is obvious at the present time that the world isn't under the rule of humans. The rule promised to human beings has not yet been realized in history.

If we pick up from verse 7, human beings are crowned with glory in honor in a specific sense, i.e., everything in the world has been subjected to human beings. Human beings may seem trivial and insignificant, but God has appointed them to rule the world. Everything is to be subject to them. Such was the role of Adam and Eve in the garden. They were called upon to rule the earth and to domesticate it for the glory of God and for the good of creation (Gen 1:28).

The author of Hebrews reads Psalm 8, which is itself a meditation on creation, in light of the fall into sin. He doesn't read the Scriptures abstractly but in light of the whole story line found in the OT, for Psalm 8 was written after the fall into sin by Adam and Eve, a fall which brought pain, frustration, futility, and death into the world. Yes, human beings were destined to rule the entire world for God. Everything was supposed to be under the rule and dominion of human beings, but sin intervened to frustrate this rule. The subsequent argument will clarify that death (which is due to sin) thwarts human dominion over the world. The glory designed for human beings has not become a reality in human history. Instead, human history is littered with the wreckage of destruction and death—a world gone mad.

2:9

The destiny for human beings, however, is revealed in the person of the true human being—Jesus.[86] He was lower than angels

---

[86] As the last word in the clause, the reference to Jesus is final and climactic (so Kevin B. McCruden, *Solidarity Perfected: Beneficent Christology in the Epistle to the Hebrews*, BZNW 159 [Berlin: Walter de Gruyter, 2008], 47).

during his incarnation, but now he rules at God's right hand and is therefore crowned with glory and honor. The rule he enjoys is because of the death that he died, and the death that he died was not for himself alone: he experienced death for everyone.[87]

Jesus is the "representative" man who has "fulfilled the vocation intended for humankind" (see §2.2).[88] Hebrews uses the name Jesus when referring to "the Son's humanity and suffering."[89] The author begins with Jesus' earthly ministry as he continues to apply the message of Psalm 8 to his readers. Jesus was "made lower than angels for a short time."[90] Here the author reflects on Jesus' life on earth, his incarnation. As a human being he was not superior to angels during his life on earth but placed beneath them, for he, like all other human beings, was subject to death. Jesus' death, however, was for the sake of others, for he did not deserve to die since he was the sinless one (4:15; 7:26–27). His death, therefore, represented the grace of God.[91] In other words, the rest of the human race deserved to die because of its sin, but God poured out his grace by rescuing human beings from sin and death through the death of Jesus.

The word "taste" (γεύσηται) here means "experienced," signifying that Jesus faced death in its fullness with all its horrors.[92] There are no grounds for the notion that "taste" suggests death was partial or limited (cf. Matt 16:28 par.; Luke 14:24; John 8:52). Death signifies the frustration, futility, and despair of human existence, and

---

[87] As O'Brien says, "That death is the ground or reason for God's exalting him (see also Phil. 2:9), rather than the purpose of his incarnation" (*Hebrews*, 99).

[88] Lane, *Hebrews 1–8*, 47.

[89] Cockerill, *Hebrews*, 132.

[90] Most commentators agree that the expression "for a short time" (βραχύ τι) in Hebrews is temporal. The MT says that human beings are a little lower than God, but Hebrews interprets the text temporally, teaching that human beings are for a short time lower than angels (against Westcott, *Hebrews*, 44; Bruce, *Hebrews*, 34n23 [perhaps]).

[91] The text is disputed here. Some favor the reading χωρίς (so Ellingworth, *Hebrews*, 155–57; Alan C. Mitchell, *Hebrews*, SP [Collegeville, MN: Michael Glazier, 2007], 67), but χάριτι is to be preferred (Hughes, *Hebrews*, 94–97). The disagreement goes back to the earliest history of the church; see E. M. Heen and P. W. D. Krey, eds., *Hebrews*, Ancient Christian Commentary on Scripture (Downers Grove, IL: InterVarsity, 2005, 38–40). Mitchell, then, is mistaken in saying that "apart from God" was "the patristic understanding" (*Hebrews,* 67). Actually, the fathers were divided on which reading was to be preferred.

[92] Rightly Ellingworth, *Hebrews*, 157; Hughes, *Hebrews*, 91.

hence Jesus died to free us from the consequences of sin. The author emphasizes that Jesus died for the sake of "everyone" (ὑπὲρ παντός). The subsequent context will clarify what the writer means by "everyone." It seems that he has in mind everyone without distinction instead of everyone without exception. Jesus' death frees from futility and the fear of death the sons brought to glory (2:10), his brothers (2:11–12), the children given to him by God (2:13), i.e., all those who belong to Abraham's family (2:16).

Jesus' death, however, was not the end of the story. He has now been exalted to God's right hand, as Ps 110:1 prophesied (cf. 1:3, 13; 8:1; 10:12–13; 12:2)! The role ascribed to human beings in creation, which Psalm 8 reaffirms, has now been realized in Jesus Christ. He currently reigns at God's right hand, crowned with glory and honor. Certainly his reign has not come in its fullness.[93] All his enemies are not yet subjected to him. Nevertheless, in the reign of Jesus, we see the destiny of the human race, the destiny of all those who belong to Jesus. Death will not conquer. Remarkably, Jesus' rule over all and his exaltation take place because he suffered death. Death can only be conquered through death. The death deserved by human beings can only be undone by one who dies as a human being. The dominion of death is severed only through the suffering and death of the high priest. The author of Hebrews does not provide a full argument here, but it is evident that death is due to sin. Sins can only be cleansed through death (1:3; 2:17; 5:1–3; 7:27; 8:12; 9:26, 28; 10:2–4, 11–12, 17–18). Jesus died in the place of human beings, thus securing their triumph over sin so they can rule with him.

What Hebrews teaches here about Jesus' death fits with what we find elsewhere in the NT (e.g., Mark 10:45; Luke 22:20; Mark 14:24; John 6:51; Rom 3:24–26; 5:6–10; 1 John 2:2; 4:10). The rule of sin over humanity has been dethroned through the death of Jesus as he took upon himself the penalty we deserve for our transgressions. Hebrews fits with the mainstream message of the NT, for salvation is obtained through the redeeming and reconciling work of Jesus Christ.

---

[93] "The final clause, *so that by the grace of God he might taste death for everyone*, expresses purpose, not the purpose of the crowning by itself, but rather the purpose of the whole sequence of preceding events, the humiliation, passion, and glory combined" (O'Brien, *Hebrews*, 100).

The reference to the son of man in these verses has provoked discussion as to whether there is a Son of Man Christology here along the lines of Daniel 7. In recent years most commentators have argued in the negative, though there is not universal agreement. Strictly speaking, there is no clear evidence here that the author connects Psalm 8 to Daniel 7, for there isn't a clear allusion to Daniel 7 in the letter. Most recent commentators are correct, then, in maintaining that the author himself doesn't draw on the Son of Man Christology of Daniel, a theology that is so prominent in the Gospels.[94] On the other hand, there is a canonical link between Psalm 8 and Daniel 7, for the son of man in the latter is the true human being who stands in contrast to the brutal kings and regimes who have held sway over the world. This son of man, who represents the saints, will reign with peace and justice and bring in a world where the saints will flourish. One can easily see that the flow of thought in Daniel 7 is remarkably similar in some respects to Psalm 8. Both Psalm 8 and Daniel 7 speak of the rule of human beings. According to the NT, Jesus fulfills what is said about the Son of Man in both texts. The rule intended for human beings becomes a reality through his suffering and death. Since Jesus represents human beings (Psalm 8) and the saints (Daniel 7), the rule and dominion intended for human beings is realized through him.

Jesus is the true human being in the sense that he lived his life under God's rule, always doing his will. The role prescribed for human beings in Psalm 8 was fulfilled in him. Those who belong to him participate in the victory he won, and thus they too enjoy the reign intended for them from creation.

Bridge

We learn from this text that human beings are magnificent. As Francis Schaeffer said, "Human beings are wonderful because they are made in God's image."[95] In a world where human life is cheap and is often discarded casually or destroyed brutally, the author of Hebrews reminds us that human beings are the crown of creation. They were made to rule the world for God. Still the world has gone

---

[94] See e.g., Lindars, *The Theology of Hebrews*, 39.

[95] See Francis Schaffer, *Escape from Reason* (Downers Grove: InterVarsity, 1968), 29–31.

awry. More precisely, human beings have strayed from their calling. They were meant to rule the world and even to rule over angels, but sin and death have intervened. The world is not marked by peace, order, and harmony but by chaos and massive evil. The solution to the evil that has broken into the world comes from one man since Jesus Christ has tasted death for everyone. Through his death he now reigns at God's right hand, showing that death has been dethroned.

Hebrews 2:10–18

Outline

I. Prologue: Definitive and Final Revelation in the Son (1:1–4)
II. **Don't Abandon the Son Since He Is Greater than Angels (1:5–2:18)**
    A. The Son's Nature and Reign Show He Is Greater than Angels (1:5–14)
    B. Warning: Don't Drift Away (2:1–4)
    C. **The Coming World Subjected to the Son (2:5–18)**
        1. The Son of Man Exalted over Angels by Virtue of His Death (2:5–9)
        2. **Jesus as the Merciful and Faithful High Priest Shares His Rule with His Brothers and Sisters (2:10–18)**

Scripture

[10] For in bringing many sons to glory, it was entirely appropriate that God—all things exist for Him and through Him—should make the source of their salvation perfect through sufferings. [11] For the One who sanctifies and those who are sanctified all have one Father. That is why Jesus is not ashamed to call them brothers, [12] saying: I will proclaim Your name to My brothers; I will sing hymns to You in the congregation.

[13] Again, I will trust in Him. And again, Here I am with the children God gave Me.

[14] Now since the children have flesh and blood in common, Jesus also shared in these, so that through His death He might destroy the one holding the power of death—that is, the Devil—[15]and free those who were held in slavery all their lives by the fear

of death. [16] For it is clear that He does not reach out to help angels, but to help Abraham's offspring. [17] Therefore, He had to be like His brothers in every way, so that He could become a merciful and faithful high priest in service to God, to make propitiation for the sins of the people. [18] For since He Himself was tested and has suffered, He is able to help those who are tested.

Context

The subjection of the world to human beings is only realized through the Son who tasted death for human beings.[96] Verse 10 picks up the argument by explaining that it was fitting for God to perfect the originator of salvation through suffering, and through such suffering, he brings many sons to glory. The appropriateness of suffering is explained in the following verses. Both Jesus as the sanctifier and human beings as those being sanctified share the same human nature (v. 11). Since Jesus shares the same human nature, he is not ashamed to call human beings his brothers and sisters (v. 11). The author supports the common humanity, the brotherly and sisterly connection, by appealing to Ps 22:22 where Jesus as the Davidic king proclaims God's name to his brothers (v. 12). And in Isa 8:17–18 human beings are the children given to Jesus by God (v. 13). Now the author explains more precisely why it is fitting for Jesus to be perfected through suffering (vv. 14–15). He shares in flesh and blood and endured suffering to nullify the one having the power of death, i.e., the devil. By suffering death, he broke the power of death and reconciled to God those who feared death constantly. The significance of human nature is highlighted, for Jesus came to help Abraham's offspring, not angels (v. 16). The rule over the world, after all, was given to human beings and not to angels. Jesus could only help human beings if he became like them—if he lived a human life like us (v. 17) and suffered the death we deserved. Only in this way could he be a merciful and faithful high priest and appease God for the sins of the people. Verse 17 clarifies that the reign of death finds its roots in sin, and therefore the power of death is only broken when sin is forgiven. Because Jesus himself faced suffering and temptation, he can come to the aid of those who are tempted (v. 18).

---

[96] For a useful discussion of the history of religions background, see Attridge, *Hebrews*, 79–82.

Exegesis

2:10

The author explains why it is fitting and appropriate for God to perfect Jesus through sufferings (see §2.5). Through Jesus' sufferings believers are glorified. In the Greco-Roman world to associate the divine with suffering and perfection with suffering would be utterly shocking.[97] But this is precisely what Hebrews does in speaking of the sovereign God of the universe, of the one for whom and through whom all things exist.

The death Jesus tasted for everyone (v. 9) accords with the way things should be, harmonizing with God's nature and character. This God who is working out his plan in history is the center of the universe: "All things exist for Him and through Him." God is both the end and the means to the end, both the goal of history and the agent of history (see §1). Paul speaks similarly, saying all things are to him, through him, and for him (Rom 11:36). History is not anthropocentric but theocentric, not man centered but God centered. And one of God's primary goals in history is to bring "many sons to glory." The glory destined for human beings includes the rule over all described in the previous verses, and it also "refers to God's own being and presence."[98] We should not miss that God is the one who brings many sons to glory.[99] The same Lord who led Israel in the exodus, freeing them from Egypt, is leading his people to glory through Jesus Christ.[100] The author does not say that "all" are glorified but "many."[101] The tasting of death for everyone does not lead to universalism, to the salvation of everyone without exception, but to the salvation of those who are God's sons and daughters.

Jesus is described as the "source" (ἀρχηγός) of salvation for the many sons who are brought to glory. This word is also translated as

---

[97] So L. Johnson, *Hebrews*, 95. He says Greco-Roman writers "would have found it incomprehensible to associate suffering with the Divine" (95).

[98] Ibid.

[99] Some think Christ brings many sons to glory (e.g., Hughes, *Hebrews*, 101–2), but most commentators agree that the reference here is to God (e.g., Ellingworth, *Hebrews*, 159). Grammatically, both views are possible. If one takes Hughes's view, the participle is related to "source" (ἀρχηγόν), but if the participle refers to God, it hearkens back to "for him" (δι' ὃν).

[100] Cf. Lane, *Hebrews 1–8*, 56; O'Brien, *Hebrews*, 104.

[101] Though it is possible to conclude that "many" means "all" here.

"pioneer" (NIV, NRSV) or "founder" (ESV), indicating that Jesus is the pathfinder of salvation for the sons whom God brings to glory. He is the trailblazer who secures salvation for his brothers; but the word also carries the idea of leader, and hence "pioneer" is perhaps the best rendering for the term.[102] The reference to Jesus as a pioneer forecasts the comparison with Moses in 3:6, for Moses was the "pioneer" (cf. Num 14:4) who led Israel out of Egypt.[103] It also anticipates Joshua, who led Israel into the promised land (Num 13:2–3).[104]

Jesus as the source and pioneer is perfected through his sufferings. Perfection here does not denote, given the insistence on Jesus' sinlessness elsewhere in Hebrews (4:15; 7:26–27), that Jesus was perfected morally in the sense that he was deficient previously.[105] The word "perfect" in the OT is used of the consecration of priests to indicate that they are qualified for office (cf. Exod 29:22, 26; Lev 7:37; 8:22). Jesus is perfected in that he reaches God's intended goal by his obedience, suffering, death, and exaltation.[106]

---

[102] For the meaning of the word, see R. J. McKelvey, *Pioneer and Priest: Jesus Christ in the Epistle to the Hebrews* (Eugene, OR: Pickwick, 2013), 171–86; L. Johnson, *Hebrews*, 96. Pioneer is a better designation than Lane's "champion" (*Hebrews 1–8*, 57), for the latter doesn't convey as clearly that Jesus blazes the way for others (see here O'Brien, *Hebrews*, 107n27). The claim that it should be rendered "prince," designating a messianic title, doesn't fit well with Heb 12:2 (against George Johnston, "Christ as Archegos," *NTS* 27 [1980–81]: 381–85).

[103] See Cockerill, *Hebrews*, 138.

[104] Cf. Moffitt, *Atonement and the Logic of the Resurrection in the Epistle to the Hebrews*, 129–30.

[105] For a history of religions survey, see Attridge, *Hebrews*, 83–87. The definitive work is by David G. Peterson (*Hebrews and Perfection: An Examination of the Concept of Perfection in the "Epistle to the Hebrews,"* SNTSMS 47 [Cambridge University Press, 1982]), whose conclusions are followed here. Moisés Silva emphasizes the eschatological character of perfection ("Perfection and Eschatology in Hebrews," *WTJ* 39 [1976–77]: 60–71). But Silva wrongly excludes any notion of "moral progression in Jesus' character" so that his view does not "do justice to the full scope of our writer's presentation" (Peterson, *Hebrews and Perfection*, 226n130).

[106] McCruden surveys the different ways perfection has been understood in Hebrews: (1) glorification; (2) cultic; (3) moral/ethical development; and (4) vocational/experiential (*Solidarity Perfected*, 5–24). McCruden turns to the papyri to understand perfection (25–44) and sees there the notion of divine attestation that he applies to Hebrews. He goes on to link Jesus' perfection to his solidarity with human beings in which he shows his beneficence and love for humans (45–121). McCruden underestimates the extent to which Jesus' glorification qualifies him to be a priest and hence misses the eschatological significance of the term. Koester

Perfection, then, is best characterized as *vocational* so that, like the priests in the OT, he is qualified for his office as priest-king. Even though perfection is not Jesus' moral improvement, it has an experiential and existential dimension and in that sense includes the obedience and sufferings that qualified Jesus to serve as high priest. Ellingworth says that Jesus' perfection is "telic, cultic, and ethical," so that "God accomplished his purpose whereby the Son would become a high priest, able to cleanse God's people from their sins, thus enabling them to approach God in true worship."[107] Or as Peterson says, "Perfecting involved a whole sequence of events: his proving in suffering, his redemptive death to fulfill the divine requirements for the perfect expiation of sins and his exaltation to glory and honour."[108] Peterson summarizes it this way: Jesus' perfection consists in "his proving in temptation, his death as a sacrifice for sins and his heavenly exaltation."[109] By his obedience in the anguish of his sufferings Jesus proved that he always trusted God.

2:11

Jesus' perfection through sufferings is fitting, for both he and human beings share the same origin. Both the one sanctifying (Jesus) and those being sanctified (the sons being brought to glory) have the same Father and belong to the same family. Since they belong to the same family, Jesus is not ashamed to call them brothers and sisters.

The "for" (γὰρ) introducing the verse explains further why it is appropriate for Jesus to be perfected through sufferings. Both Jesus and those being sanctified, i.e., those being brought to glory,

---

rightly notes that McCruden doesn't do justice to the "full range of usage" for perfection in Hebrews, even though he rightly emphasizes Jesus' identification with human beings. Koester also aptly remarks, "What is less clear is that language used for the attestation or execution of a document can be transferred to Jesus. Although McCruden makes every effort to address that problem, the case would be stronger if closer precedents could be found for perfection as the attestation of a person's character. It would also be helpful to see more clearly why *philanthropia* was selected as key to Hebrews' Christology, since the term itself is not used in Hebrews and the concept was used in various ways in Greco-Roman sources." See Craig R. Koester, review of *Solidarity Perfected: Beneficent Christology in the Epistle to the Hebrews*, by Kevin B. McCruden, *Review of Biblical Literature*, February 2012, http://www.bookreviews.org/pdf/7407_9193.pdf, accessed March 27, 2013.

[107] Ellingworth, *Hebrews*, 163.

[108] Peterson, *Hebrews and Perfection*, 73. See also his fuller discussion, 67–73.

[109] Ibid., 118. In Peterson these words are italicized.

share the same nature. The author literally says, "They are all of one." English versions provide an interpretation, rendering it "all have one Father" (HCSB, NRSV), or "all have one source" (ESV), or they "are of the same family" (NIV), or "all have the same origin."[110] The translations render the phrase in various ways, but they actually make the same point, though a reference to God as Father is the most probable since Adam isn't mentioned in the text and Abraham doesn't crop up until verse 16. In any case those who have the same Father belong to the same family and have the same source and origin.

The common origin between Jesus and his brothers and sisters doesn't mean all distinctions between Jesus and others are erased, for Jesus does the sanctifying, and the rest of the human race is sanctified. Jesus as the ever-obedient one didn't need to be placed into the realm of the holy. He was always and ever the holy one and was dedicated to God throughout his life. All other human beings, as those subject to death and sin (2:17), need to be sanctified, for they are unholy and have given themselves over to evil. Indeed, the author states here that Jesus is the one who sanctifies them. To say that Jesus sanctifies them is a remarkable statement, for in Leviticus we read, in a virtual refrain, that the Lord sanctifies his people (Lev 20:8; 21:8, 15, 23; 22:9, 16, 32).[111] We have another indication of the remarkably high Christology of the letter. Jesus and human beings

---

[110] The Greek here is ambiguous, for it literally says "from one" (ἐξ ἑνὸς). A number of suggestions have been made as to the identity of the one. The most likely are Adam (Moffitt, *Atonement and the Logic of the Resurrection in the Epistle to the Hebrews*, 130–38); Abraham (Christopher A. Richardson, *Pioneer and Perfecter of Faith: Jesus' Faith as the Climax of Israel's History in the Epistle to the Hebrews*, WUNT 2/338 [Tübingen: Mohr Siebeck, 2012], 18–19; James Swetnam, *Jesus and Isaac: A Study of the Epistle to the Hebrews in Light of the Aqedah*, AnBib 94 [Rome: Pontifical Biblical Institute, 1981], 132–34; L. Johnson, *Hebrews*, 97–98); or God (Bruce, *Hebrews*, 44n64; Peterson, *Hebrews and Perfection*, 59–60; Koester, *Hebrews*, 229). Hughes takes it as neuter and sees a reference to human nature (*Hebrews*, 104–6). Most commentators think God is the referent. A reference to Adam seems unlikely, for we actually expect a reference to Adam in v. 16, and we find Abraham instead. A reference to Abraham is more promising given v. 16, but since Abraham isn't named until v. 16, the most likely referent is God. Fortunately, the meaning doesn't change remarkably whether we choose Abraham or God here.

[111] Cf. Lane, *Hebrews 1–8*, 581.

share the same nature, but Jesus stands apart in the sense that he does the sanctifying, and they are the sanctified.[112]

Because Jesus and those being sanctified by him have the same Father, he is not ashamed to call them brothers and sisters. We should not fail to note that the word "brothers" includes "sisters" since the term "brothers" is generic referring to both "brothers and sisters" (cf. NRSV and NIV), to all those who belong to the family of God.

Shame, which played a significant role in the ancient world, could prevent someone from acknowledging a father, a son, a wife, or a daughter. But Jesus is not ashamed of his brothers and sisters. He gladly acknowledges that they belong to the same family. Clearly "brothers" here does not refer to all human beings, for not all human beings have God as their Father in the sense that they are saved. Not all human beings are brought to glory. Not all human beings are sanctified. The family is restricted here to those who are consecrated and dedicated to God through the sanctifying work of Jesus, through his atoning death that freed them from the fear of death.

2:12

The notion that Jesus and believers belong to the same family is supported by Ps 22:22. Hebrews understands the speaker in the verse to be Jesus himself. Jesus will proclaim God's name to his brothers and sisters and will praise God in the assembly along with fellow believers. What particularly interests the author is that Jesus identifies fellow believers as "my brothers." The solidarity between Jesus and his brothers is emphasized, which supports the author's claim that the rule given to Jesus is not restricted to him but also is granted to his brothers and sisters.

The citation comes from Psalm 22, a well-known messianic psalm. The citation accords with the LXX except for the first word ("I will recount," διηγήσομαι, Ps 22:22; "I will proclaim," ἀπαγγελῶ, in Heb 2:12). The citation may represent a literal translation of the MT of Ps 22:22.[113] Jesus uttered the words of the first verse of the psalm ("My God, My God, why have you forsaken Me?") when he was dying upon the cross (Matt 27:46; Mark 15:34). Other verses from the psalm are alluded to during Jesus' passion (Ps 22:7 and

---

[112] As Cockerill says, "Thus, the Son's role in sanctification, as well as in creation and consummation (1:2, 8–12) confirms his deity" (*Hebrews*, 141).

[113] Against this, see Attridge, *Hebrews*, 90.

Mark 15:29; Ps 22:28 and Matt 27:43; Ps 22:15 and John 19:28; Ps 22:18 and Mark 15:24; Luke 23:34; John 19:23–24). Hebrews doesn't cite the verses that recount Jesus' sufferings. It is likely, however, that the sufferings rehearsed in the psalm are part of the furniture of his thought, for we have significant evidence that Psalm 22 was widely accepted as messianic. In addition, the context of Hebrews 2 calls attention to Jesus' suffering, emphasizing that through Jesus' death the power of the devil was broken. The story line of Psalm 22 is probably in the author's mind, for it fits with what Hebrews is doing. The suffering one has become the exalted one. Jesus, who suffered death for the sake of his brothers and sisters, is now crowned with glory and honor at God's right hand. The rule over the world promised to human beings has been realized through the death and resurrection of Jesus Christ.

Hebrews quotes the key transitional verse in Psalm 22, the verse where the story changes. Throughout Psalm 22 the speaker, whom Hebrews identifies as Jesus, pleads with God to save him from his overwhelming distress, from the suffering that is tearing him apart. His pleas for help are punctuated by confessions of trust in God, which reaffirm God's faithfulness to deliver his own. When we come to verse 22, the corner is turned. The call for help has been answered. The psalmist (and Jesus!) for the remainder of the psalm praises the Lord for answering his prayer and for rescuing him from his enemies. The victory, however, is not reserved for Jesus alone; he shares it with those who are his family members, so we have a family celebration, a family feast (Ps 22:26, 29).

In the historical context of the psalm, deliverance is granted to David as king; and his victory means triumph for Israel and indeed for the whole world (Ps 22:27), fulfilling the promise to Abraham. Still the psalm finds its final fulfillment in Jesus as the inheritor of the promise made to David. Thus, Jesus' victory at his resurrection and exaltation means victory for all those who belong to Jesus, for his brothers and sisters. Hence, just as David praised Yahweh in the congregation of the saints, so too Jesus praises the Lord with his brothers and sisters. Indeed the victory for the king anticipates the final vanquishing of all foes. The entire earth will bow before the Lord (Ps 22:27). The promise of blessing for all peoples made to Abraham (Gen 12:3; 18:18; 22:18; 26:4; 28:14; cf. Ps 72:8) will be realized. The Lord will rule over all as the mighty king (Ps 22:28).

Again, it is not far-fetched to see an echo of such a promise in the reference to Psalm 22 here, for Hebrews 2 is about the restoration of right rule to human beings through Jesus. Jesus does not praise God alone. He does it in the assembly, in "the eschatological congregation of God, which from one perspective is already assembled around the exalted Christ (12:22–24) but is still very much part of this world (2:14–18)."[114] He praises God with his brothers and sisters whom he has ransomed from Satan's power.

2:13

The solidarity between Jesus and his brothers and sisters is confirmed as well by Isaiah. Hebrews again understands the "I" from the citations to refer to Jesus himself. Jesus puts his confidence and trust in the Lord, and this trust is inseparable from the promise of a larger family.[115] God has given him children who will share together the victory and deliverance that God will bring.

The quotations hail from Isa 8:17–18.[116] The wording from Isa 8:17 is again remarkably close to the LXX.

Isa 8:17	Heb 2:13
"I will put my trust in him" (NIV)	"I will put my trust in him"
πεποιθὼς ἔσομαι ἐπ᾽ αὐτῷ	ἐγὼ ἔσομαι πεποιθὼς ἐπ᾽ αὐτῷ

The only difference is that Hebrews added "I" (ἐγώ) and reversed the order of two of the words. What we find in the LXX and Hebrews represents a literal translation of the MT as well. The quotation from Isa 8:18 matches the LXX exactly but also is a literal translation of the MT.

The quotations come from a section in Isaiah (chapters 7–12) where Judah is threatened by Israel and Syria, who are attempting

---

[114] O'Brien, *Hebrews*, 111.

[115] In support of the notion that Jesus trusted in God, see Richardson, *Pioneer and Perfecter of Faith*. Cf. also Todd D. Still, "*Christos as Pistos:* The Faith(fullness) of Jesus in the Epistle to the Hebrews," in *Cloud of Witnesses: The Theology of Hebrews in Its Ancient Contexts*, ed. R. Bauckham, D. Driver, T. Hart, and N. MacDonald, LNTS 387 (London: T&T Clark, 2008), 40–50. Richardson overstates the importance of this theme but rightly sees its presence.

[116] It is also possible that the author cites 2 Sam 22:3 or Isa 12:2, but most agree that, since the next verse cites Isa 8:18, Isa 8:17 is likely in view (against Cockerill, *Hebrews*, 143–44).

to put a rival on the throne of Ahaz.[117] The Lord promises Ahaz that the plot will not succeed. God's covenant is with the Davidic dynasty, not with these upstart kings who are trying to overthrow the Davidic ruler. The futility of their attempt to displace Ahaz will soon become evident, for Assyria will sweep in and conquer both Syria and Israel. Indeed, the real threat here is Assyria (not Israel and Syria), for Assyria will almost succeed in capturing Judah as well, but Jerusalem and Judah will be spared. On the basis of God's promises, Isaiah summons the people not to fear political and military contrivances. God's kingdom will triumph through a Davidic ruler (Isa 9:2–7; 11:1–10), while the Lord's enemies will face judgment (cf. Isa 10:5–34). The righteous kingdom promised through David will ultimately triumph; a new world of peace and justice will dawn under the rule of a son of David.

It is instructive to see that Hebrews cites words spoken by the prophet Isaiah in chapter 8. In the midst of political turmoil in which Ahaz and Judah are terrified of Syria and Israel, Isaiah summons the people to fear the Lord instead of worrying about the conspiracy hatched against their kingdom (Isa 8:11–13). The Lord is a "sanctuary" for those who trust in him (Isa 8:14), and hence there is no need to turn to the dead to decipher the future (Isa 8:19). Isaiah says he will wait for and hope in the Lord (Isa 8:17), for he has promised that the enemies poised against Judah will not succeed. An interesting parallel exists between Isaiah and Jesus, for just as Isaiah was rejected by his contemporaries, so too Jesus was rejected by his. Still, Isaiah became "a rallying point for faith," and Jesus functions supremely as such.[118] Indeed, the children God has given to Isaiah function as "signs and wonders in Israel" (Isa 8:18), for they represent the remnant that belongs to the Lord. Isaiah's children testify to ultimate victory, to the promise that the Lord's rule and blessing for his people will become a reality.

Now we turn to what Hebrews does with this citation. We saw that in Isa 8:17–18 the "I" is Isaiah himself, but Hebrews identifies the "I" as Jesus. Jesus is the one who trusts in God, as Isaiah trusted him of old. Isaiah trusted that the Lord would triumph even though Judah was imperiled by foes on every side. Jesus trusted that God

---

[117] The OT context is not ignored here (against Attridge, *Hebrews*, 91n137).
[118] Lane, *Hebrews 1–8*, 60.

would rescue and deliver him in his suffering, even though he faced the greatest peril of all: death.[119] Death frustrates human beings from ruling the world as God originally ordained, but Jesus trusts that God will rescue him from death.

The second citation from Isa 8:18 also plays a key role in Hebrews. The victory for which Jesus trusts God is not his alone. It also belongs to his brothers and sisters, to the children whom God has given to him. They will share with Jesus the rule over death and exercise the dominion promised in Psalm 8 to human beings. It is remarkable that the children are described as those whom God gave to Jesus. Their salvation and liberation is God's work and cannot be attributed to their own moral capacities. The author emphasizes here that the reconciliation of human beings is the work of God and of Jesus the high priest. Belonging to God is a work of grace and mercy; it can't be attributed to the virtue and moral goodness of human beings.

2:14

Jesus' solidarity with human beings is not superficial but profound and genuine. Like us he shares flesh and blood, and he identifies with us and takes on the same nature to destroy the devil's power by yielding up his life in death.

Since the children God gave to Jesus share in flesh and blood, Jesus does the same. He is fully and truly human, beset by the physical weaknesses and mortality that characterize human existence. We saw in Hebrews 1 some of the strongest statements in the NT on the deity of Christ. Chapter 2, on the other hand, contains some of the most profound verses on Christ's humanity (see §2.2). He identifies fully and completely with the children God gave to him since he shares the same human nature with them. There is no basis for the complaint that God does not truly understand the human predicament since Jesus experienced fully the travails of mortal existence. We naturally think here of what John says in his Gospel: "The Word became flesh" (John 1:14). Hebrews shares this sentiment, even though he expresses it in a different manner.

The reason Jesus shared human nature is so that he could destroy through death the one who has the power of death, i.e., the

---

[119] The author particularly emphasizes that Jesus trusted God in his suffering (see Richardson, *Pioneer and Perfecter of Faith*, 23–25).

devil. One of the fascinating statements here is the claim that the devil exercises authority (τὸ κράτος) over death. We might expect the author to say that God has the power of death as the Creator and Sovereign over all. As Lane rightly says, "The devil did not possess control over death inherently but gained his power when he seduced humankind to rebel against God."[120]

The authority of the devil is matched by other statements in the NT. John says that "the whole world is under the sway of the evil one" (1 John 5:19). In the Gospel he says twice that Satan is "the ruler of this world" (John 12:31; 14:30). Paul identifies Satan as "the god of this age" (2 Cor 4:4) and as "prince of the power of the air, the spirit that is now at work in the sons of disobedience" (Eph 2:2 ESV). We see in the book of Job that Satan unleashes terrible attacks on Job, but everything Satan inflicts on Job passes through the hands of God, i.e., God grants Satan permission. As Hughes says, "Death is held by the devil in a secondary and not in an ultimate sense."[121] Still, such a state of affairs does not nullify the demonic rule and destruction perpetrated by the devil. We see in the Synoptic Gospels that the kingdom of God in and through Jesus Christ waged war on the kingdom of darkness, which included freeing those under demonic powers. Ultimately, God as the sovereign Creator is Lord of all, but recognizing this does not exclude the notion that death is also under the domain of Satan. Perhaps the writer reflects on Genesis 2–3 here. God threatened death if Adam and Eve transgressed, but their sin and death came at the impetus of the serpent (cf. John 8:44; Wis 2:24). Death prevents human beings from obtaining the rule over the world promised in Psalm 8. Human beings can hardly serve as God's vice-regents over the world if they die under Satan's domain.

What Hebrews teaches here is that death is only undone through death. Death dies only through the death of Jesus. Or, more precisely, the one who has the power of death is dethroned through the death of Jesus. As Owen says: "All of Satan's power over death was founded on sin. The obligation of the sinner to death gave Satan his power. If this obligation was removed, Satan's power would also be

---

[120] Lane, *Hebrews 1–8*, 61.
[121] Hughes, *Hebrews*, 112.

taken away."[122] Such a claim resonates, as noted previously, with the teaching on the kingdom in the Synoptics. Jesus has come to bind the strong man and to plunder his house (Matt 12:29). The devil's reign over death has been removed through the death of Christ. The word "destroy" (καταργήσῃ) "does not mean that the devil has been annihilated or obliterated."[123] His power has been removed; "The overthrow of death and the devil has begun but is not yet complete."[124] Jesus' sharing in humanity does not exempt him from death and all its terrors. Indeed, by subjecting himself to death, he conquers the one who enjoys dominion over death.

In early church history some appealed to this text to argue that a ransom was paid to Satan. Such a notion goes beyond what the verses say, for there is no evidence in the NT that Satan received payment for the liberation of human beings. On the other hand there is clearly a Christus Victor theme here. The devil exercised power over human beings, and those who belong to Jesus Christ are freed through Jesus' death. It seems here that Christus Victor and substitutionary themes come together, for only through Jesus' death is the devil's reign over death cancelled. If the devil's rule over death ends only through Jesus' death, it seems that Jesus' death functions as the means by which death's reign is destroyed. The penalty for sin is death, and Jesus paid that penalty. This is not to say that a penalty is paid to Satan, but there is the implicit notion that Jesus took the penalty upon himself that sinners deserved. His death took the place of their death.

2:15

The second purpose for Jesus' becoming a human being is explained here. He became a man to dethrone the devil who had the power of death. But the Son also took on humanity so that through his death he would free those who were captive to the fear of death all their lives.[125] Psalm 8 proclaims that human beings were made

---

[122] John Owen, *Hebrews*, Crossway Classic Commentaries (Wheaton, IL: Crossway, 1998), 46.

[123] O'Brien, *Hebrews*, 115.

[124] Ibid.

[125] The word ἀπαλλάξῃ here means "free" (cf. L. Johnson, *Hebrews*, 100). Perhaps the readers feared death because they were experiencing persecution (cf. Lane, *Hebrews 1–8*, 54), but more likely the universal experience of humanity is in view: the angst and horror of death that afflicts all of us.

to rule the world for God, but instead of exercising dominion over the world, they are subject to slavery (δουλείας). For death casts a shadow over the entirety of life, hovering like a specter over every dimension of existence. Death means that human beings do not reign but are ruled over by a foreign power, for they fear their eventual demise that comes inexorably upon them. In every moment of happiness, death is our dark shadow, reminding us that our joy is short-lived.

Jesus, however, has freed those who are his brothers and sisters from the fear of death. The author doesn't fully unpack his argument here, but he apparently believes that death can only be defeated through a human being. Hence, Jesus had to become a human being to destroy death. It wasn't enough for Jesus to become human. He had to endure death himself. Death would only die through the death of a human being. Through Jesus' death those who are part of Jesus' family are freed from the fear of death. If Jesus' death frees his brothers and sisters from the dominion and fear of death, it seems that he dies in their place. The death they deserve he took upon himself so that they are now free from the fear of death that haunts human existence.

2:16

Suddenly angels come back into the argument. Jesus does not help angels but only those who are part of Abraham's family. How does this verse fit into the flow of the argument? The author explains why (γάρ) Jesus became a human being, why he nullified the devil's power over death, and why he freed human beings instead of angels from the fear of death.

The reference to angels is not entirely unexpected, for they have played a major role in chapters 1–2. Rule over the world has not been promised to angels but to human beings, and Christ came to free human beings from the devil and from the fear of death. Actually, the author doesn't speak of human beings in general. Release from the tyranny of death is limited to those who belong to the offspring of Abraham (σπέρματος Ἀβραάμ). The offspring of Abraham here isn't limited to Jewish Christians;[126] all who believe in Jesus are chil-

---

[126] Against Charles P. Anderson, "Who Are the Heirs of the New Age in the Epistle to the Hebrews?" in *Apocalyptic in the New Testament: Essays in Honor of J. Louis Martyn*, ed. J. Marcus and M. L. Soards, JSNTSup 24 (Sheffield: Sheffield Academic, 1989), 257–68.

dren of Abraham. Here Hebrews accords with Pauline teaching, for Paul emphasizes that those who put their trust in Jesus Christ are Abraham's children (Rom 4:9–12; Gal 3:6–9).

Rule over the world will not be given to all those who are the children of Adam. Jesus came to take hold of the children of the promise, to those who are the offspring of Abraham. The blessing is limited to the sons brought to glory (2:10), to those being sanctified (2:11), to those who are Jesus' brothers and sisters (2:11–12, 17), and to "the children God gave Me" (2:13). The promises made to Abraham are fulfilled for those who are Jesus' brothers and sisters. Jesus took hold of them so that the dominion over the world originally promised to Adam would be realized in the children of Abraham. The word translated "help" (ἐπιλαμβάνεται) doesn't typically have such a meaning; it usually means to "take hold" or "grasp."[127] Still, the word "help" makes good sense in context, for Jesus took hold of Abraham's offspring to help them.

The author probably draws on Isa 41:8–10,[128]

> "But you, Israel, my servant, Jacob, whom I have chosen, the offspring of Abraham, my friend; you whom I took (ἀντελαβόμην) from the ends of the earth, and called from its farthest corners, saying to you, 'You are my servant, I have chosen you and not cast you off'; fear not, for I am with you; be not dismayed, for I am your God; I will strengthen you, I will help (ἐβοήθησά) you, I will uphold you with my righteous right hand." (ESV)

It seems that he takes hold of the children of Abraham to help them (cf. Sir 4:11).[129] We see that the verbs "take hold of" and "help" are both used here, suggesting that they are closely related conceptually. Interestingly, Hebrews uses the verb "take hold of" (ἐπιλαμβάνεται) in verse 16 and "help" (βοηθῆσαι) in verse 18, and thus it matches the Isaiah citation well, even if the terms aren't exactly the same. Perhaps the author also draws on the new covenant

---

[127] See Attridge, *Hebrews*, 94; L. Johnson, *Hebrews*, 102; Cockerill, *Hebrews*, 148–49n116. Some early interpreters saw a reference to Jesus' assuming a human nature. For a modern advocate of this historic view, see Hughes, *Hebrews*, 115–18, but the text refers to the children of Abraham, not to Jesus.

[128] Ellingworth, *Hebrews*, 176.

[129] So Koester, *Hebrews*, 232; Lane, *Hebrews 1–8*, 52, 63–64. Cf. Ellingworth, *Hebrews*, 176–78.

text in Jeremiah where the Lord refers to his taking Israel by the hand (Jer 31:32; 38:32 LXX).[130] Once again he took hold of Israel to assist them. Finally one other observation should be made about verse 16. In anticipation of 3:1–6 Jesus is compared to Moses, for like Moses he led his people to freedom.[131] But the freedom and help he gave to the offspring of Abraham was far greater than Moses could give, for he delivered them from death by his sacrifice.

2:17

The author now draws an inference ("Therefore," ὅθεν) from the preceding argument. Jesus had to be like his brothers and sisters in every way to function as a faithful and merciful high priest. For only one who is fully human can make propitiation for the sins of the people.

The author started this section (2:5) by emphasizing from Psalm 8 that dominion over the world was granted to human beings. Jesus now rules over the world at God's right hand, being crowned with glory and honor. He is qualified to rule, for he is fully human. He is flesh and blood like all other human beings (2:14). Or, as the author says here, "He had to be like His brothers in every way." Jesus wasn't partially human or mainly human but fully human. And it had to be this way, for the rule promised to human beings can only be restored through a human being.

The full humanity of Jesus qualifies him to serve as the high priest (see §2.2). This is the first of 17 times that "high priest" (ἀρχιερεύς) occurs in Hebrews.[132] The author anticipates his future discussion of Jesus' high priesthood (cf. 3:1; 4:14–15), which is explained in some detail in 5:1–10 and 7:1–10:18. To be a high priest one must be fully human (cf. 5:1), and Jesus meets that prerequisite. Of course, as Hebrews makes clear, Jesus is a different type of high priest in that he is like Melchizedek. But he also distinguishes himself in that he is both the priest and the offering. He doesn't offer "other" sacrifices as OT priests did; rather, he offers himself. No priest in the OT ever imagined that he would be the priest and the offering.

---

[130] O'Brien, *Hebrews*, 117; Lane, *Hebrews 1–8*, 64.

[131] Cf. O'Brien, *Hebrews*, 117–18.

[132] For traditions that may inform the notion of priesthood in Hebrews, see Attridge, *Hebrews*, 97–103.

Jesus is merciful to human beings, offering them forgiveness for their sins. But he is also faithful to God in that he invariably did the will of God instead of pursuing his own desires (cf. 4:15; 5:7–9; 7:26–28). Perhaps we have an allusion to Ps 145:8 in the words "merciful" and "faithful" where the Lord is described as merciful and compassionate.[133] He was faithful to God and to his people, showing mercy through his sacrifice.

He made "propitiation for the sins of the people." Scholars dispute the meaning of the word "propitiated" (ἱλάσκεσθαι). Some argue that it means "expiated" so that the focus is on forgiveness of sins.[134] The object of the verb, after all, is "sins" (τὰς ἁμαρτίας), fitting with the idea that sins are erased or wiped away.[135] It is likely, however, that there is also the notion of the appeasement of God's wrath.[136] Hebrews draws on sacrificial language from the cultus, and in the OT the failure to abide by what God commands provokes his wrath (cf. Lev 10:1–2). Another way of putting it is that we don't have an either-or here. The word designates both forgiveness of sins and appeasement and satisfaction of God's wrath. In the OT, if sins aren't expiated (wiped away), God pours out his holy and just wrath on those who have transgressed.

The reference to sin and propitiation helps us pull some threads together in this text. The author has argued that death frustrates human beings from fulfilling their destiny. But he hasn't said thus far why human beings die. The answer to that question appears here. They die because of sin. The author doesn't make this point explicitly, but the connection seems obvious, especially since the inception of death in the world is traced to sin (Gen 2:17; 3:3). Death

---

[133] O'Brien, *Hebrews*, 120.

[134] E.g., Attridge, *Hebrews*, 96; Ellingworth, *Hebrews*, 188–89.

[135] The accusative "sins" (τὰς ἁμαρτίας) may be an accusative of respect. See Simon J. Kistemaker, "Atonement in Hebrews," in *The Glory of the Atonement: Biblical, Historical and Practical Perspectives: Essays in Honor of Roger Nicole*, ed. C. E. Hill and F. A. James III (Downers Grove, IL: InterVarsity, 2004), 166–67. In either case the notions of propitiation and expiation are both present.

[136] See the helpful discussion in Benjamin J. Ribbens, "Levitical Sacrifice and Heavenly Cult in Hebrews" (Ph.D. diss., Wheaton College, 2013), 280–88. Koester sees a reference to both expiation and propitiation with the focus on the former (*Hebrews*, 241; cf. also Cockerill, *Hebrews*, 151). Perhaps the author also draws on martyr traditions from 4 Maccabees (6:28–29; 17:21–22) for the notion that the death of a victim could provide atonement (so Koester, *Hebrews*, 241n106).

can be conquered, therefore, only if sin is atoned for and forgiven. The devil's authority over death ended with the death of Jesus, but the nature of Jesus' death should be explained. His death was the means by which sins were expiated and propitiated. The nature of Jesus' death helps us with another important theological issue noted in verse 14. Jesus did not appease the devil in atoning for sins. God was appeased; God forgave sin through Jesus' sacrifice on the cross.

Jesus atoned for the sins of "the people" (τοῦ λαοῦ). In the OT sacrifices were offered for the people of Israel. According to Hebrews the people of God consists of those members of the new covenant who have been cleansed of their sins through the sacrifice of Jesus Christ (cf. 4:9; 7:27; 8:10; 13:12). Those who enjoy forgiveness of sins are described here as "sons" brought to glory (v. 10), as those "who are sanctified" (v. 11), as Jesus' brothers (vv. 11–12), as "the children God gave" Jesus (v. 13), and as "Abraham's offspring" (v. 16). We see, then, that the "everyone" of verse 9 should be interpreted to refer to everyone without distinction instead of everyone without exception. Jesus' propitiatory sacrifice is limited to his people, to the children given to him by God, to the offspring of Abraham.

2:18

Jesus' priestly qualifications are presented here, for he is a merciful high priest who knows what it is like to be tempted and to suffer. His solidarity with human beings is not an abstraction, for he knows first-hand the anguish of human existence, and thus he can grant help to those who are suffering. As Hughes says, Jesus' resistance of all temptation demonstrates that he knows the "full force of temptation in a manner that we who have not withstood it to the end cannot know it."[137] The "help" (βοηθῆσαι) envisioned in this context refers to Jesus' high priestly work, his atoning sacrifice for the sins of the people. We have seen throughout that Jesus' death is the means by which the rule of human beings over the world is restored. He helps his people by nullifying the power of death and freeing them from the slavery entailed in death.

The help provided for Jesus' brothers can only be given because he too is fully human. He also suffered and was tempted to depart from God. As Vos points out, the author doesn't focus on Jesus'

---

[137] Hughes, *Hebrews*, 124.

temptation in general but Jesus' temptation to sin in suffering.[138] Jesus knows the angst and sorrow of human experience. The temptation we face he has encountered as well. The suffering of Jesus here probably focuses on the cross since verse 17 speaks of his propitiatory work and the verses are joined by "for" (γάρ). He extends mercy (v. 17) to the offspring of Abraham through his suffering on the cross. Those who are tempted are also encouraged to endure suffering as Jesus did so that they too will be rewarded by God. By persevering to the end, they will be members of the heavenly city (see §8).

Bridge

The full humanity of Jesus leaps out to readers in this text. Believers are his brothers and sisters, for Jesus lived a flesh-and-blood life. He knew the agony of temptation and the pain of suffering. Most important, he died for our sake so that we would be freed from the power of death. Jesus is our elder brother, and his victory over death and sin means we have conquered death and sin through him. As C. S. Lewis said, "The Son of God became a man to enable men to become sons of God."[139] Indeed, believers no longer fear death because of the atoning work of their great high priest.

Hebrews 3:1–6

Outline

I. Prologue: Definitive and Final Revelation in the Son (1:1–4)
II. Don't Abandon the Son Since He Is Greater than Angels (1:5–2:18)
III. **Don't Harden Your Hearts Since You Have a Son and High Priest Greater than Moses and Joshua (3:1–4:13)**
   A. **The Faithful Son Greater than the Servant Moses (3:1–6)**

---

[138] Geerhardus Vos, "The Priesthood of Christ in Hebrews," in *Redemptive History and Biblical Interpretation: The Shorter Writings of Geerhardus Vos*, ed. R. B. Gaffin Jr. (Phillipsburg, NJ: Presbyterian & Reformed, 1980), 149.

[139] C. S. Lewis, *Mere Christianity* (rev. ed.; San Francisco: HarperCollins 2001), 178.

B. Warning: Continue Believing and Obeying to Enter Rest
(3:7–4:13)

Scripture

¹ Therefore, holy brothers and companions in a heavenly calling, consider Jesus, the apostle and high priest of our confession;
² He was faithful to the One who appointed Him, just as Moses
was in all God's household. ³ For Jesus is considered worthy of
more glory than Moses, just as the builder has more honor than
the house. ⁴ Now every house is built by someone, but the One
who built everything is God. ⁵ Moses was faithful as a servant
in all God's household, as a testimony to what would be said in
the future.

⁶ But Christ was faithful as a Son over His household. And we
are that household if we hold on to the courage and the confidence
of our hope.

Context

In the first section of the letter, the author argues that the Son is
superior to the angels who mediated the Mosaic law. From 3:1–4:13
he continues with a similar theme, contending that the Son is greater
than Moses and Joshua.[140] We find many contacts with what has preceded:[141] (1) Jesus' high priesthood is picked up from 2:17; (2) his
faithfulness, noted in 2:17, is a major theme in 3:1–6; (3) those who
belong to Jesus are part of his family (2:11–12; 3:1, 6); (4) believers
are holy (3:1) because they have been sanctified by Jesus (2:11).
The section, as O'Brien rightly notes, combines both exposition and
exhortation,[142] though exhortation is more dominant.

The first verse of chapter 3 picks up the argument from chapter
2. Believers in Jesus, those who are Jesus' brothers and sisters, share
the heavenly calling with him. Nevertheless, the main point of this
paragraph isn't the shared calling of believers and Jesus. The central
theme in verses 1–6 is Jesus' role as the apostle and high priest. The
readers are on the verge of forgetting Jesus' role as the one sent by
God to cleanse them of their sins. Jesus was faithful in his mission,

---

[140] For the view that the second section of the letter includes 3:1–4:13, see O'Brien,
Hebrews, 125.

[141] For these parallels, see ibid., 126.

[142] Ibid., 127.

just as Moses was faithful in his (v. 2). Still, Jesus deserves greater honor than Moses, for Moses is a member of the house (the people of God), but Jesus is the builder of the house (v. 3). Jesus' building of the house points to his deity since God shapes and directs all things (v. 4). Moses should be honored as a faithful servant, but it is a serious mistake to see him as the terminus of revelation, for he pointed forward to a greater word (v. 5). Moses was a faithful servant, but Jesus is the faithful Son (v. 6), and believers are part of his house if they endure in faith to the end.

Exegesis

3:1

The "therefore" (Ὅθεν) links this section with the previous one. Since Jesus has conquered death and sin, fulfilling the destiny for human beings by ruling the world as God's vice-regent, those who belong to him are his "holy brothers." Here the author picks up on the previous paragraph, which emphasized that those who are sanctified and who are the offspring of Abraham are Jesus' brothers and sisters. Indeed, they are his "holy" brothers and sisters since they have been cleansed of their sin through Jesus' propitiatory sacrifice. Furthermore, as brothers and sisters they share a heavenly calling. Their destiny is not confined to present earthly realities, for believers are promised a future reward (10:35). They have "tasted the heavenly gift" (6:4), and "the heavens" in Hebrews refers to the presence of God (9:23). The heavenly calling for believers is also described as a heavenly city (11:16), which is also called "the heavenly Jerusalem" (12:22). The heavenly calling of believers focuses on the future, for believers "seek the city that is to come" (13:14 ESV).

The main point of the paragraph emerges with the summons to consider Jesus as the apostle and high priest of our confession (see §2.3). Jesus is the emissary sent by God to fulfill God's covenant promises. He is the one sent by God to accomplish salvation, "to enable humanity to have access to God."[143] Such a notion fits with the Gospel of John, in which Jesus regularly says he was sent by the Father into the world (John 3:34; 4:34; 5:23, 24, 30, 36–38; 6:29, 38–39, 44; 7:18, 28–29, 33; 8:16, 18, 26, 29, 42, etc.; cf. 1 John 4:9–10, 14), a concept found in other NT writings as well

---

[143] Ellingworth, *Hebrews*, 199.

(Matt 10:40; 15:24; Mark 9:37; Luke 4:18, 43; 9:48; 10:16; Acts 3:26; Gal 4:4).[144] The sending of Jesus echoes the thought that he served as the pioneer (2:12).[145] The Lord sent Moses to deliver his people from Egypt (Exod 3:10); Jesus, as God's final and definitive messenger (cf. 1:1–2), is the great deliverer of the Lord's people.[146]

Cockerill says Jesus' apostleship captures the themes of 1:1–2:4.[147] He is God's final word to human beings, superior to Moses, the prophets, or angels. He also undertakes a commission as high priest, as the one who took on human nature and offered himself as a sacrifice for the cleansing of sins. When the author says that Jesus is the apostle and high priest of the believer's "confession" (ὁμολογίας), the word "confession" denotes the truth embraced by the readers (4:14; 10:23).[148] The teaching accepted by the readers focuses on Jesus as God's high priest, as the one sent by God. The confession is not an abstract list of doctrines. It focuses on Jesus himself and his work on the cross for the readers' salvation. If the readers limited themselves to the revelation mediated through Moses, they would be guilty of forgetting Jesus and would repudiate his sacrificial work on their behalf, and as a result they would be turning against the one whom God sent as high priest.

3:2

In the subsequent verses the author explains why the readers should consider Jesus as their apostle and high priest. The reason provided here is that Jesus was faithful to the one who appointed him as an apostle and high priest, just as Moses was faithful.[149] Perhaps

---

[144] So Hughes, *Hebrews*, 127.

[145] So O'Brien, *Hebrews*, 129.

[146] Lane, *Hebrews 1–8*, 76; cf. Richardson, *Pioneer and Perfecter of Faith*, 58–64.

[147] Cockerill, *Hebrews*, 159. He goes on to say, "'Apostle' contrasts the Son with Moses as the source of revelation; 'High Priest' anticipates comparison with Aaron as the source of salvation" (160).

[148] The word includes both the act of confessing and the content of the confession (rightly Attridge, *Hebrews*, 108n42).

[149] L. Johnson argues that the verb "appointed" (ποιήσαντι) should be translated "made," so that it refers to the creation of Jesus (*Hebrews*, 107). This reading is certainly possible since Jesus as a human being was created by God, but the emphasis on Jesus' apostleship and high priesthood in this context (3:1) suggests that the idea of appointment is preferable.

we have allusions here to both 1 Sam 2:35 and 1 Chr 17:14.[150] In 1 Sam 2:35 the Lord promises to raise up a faithful priest, and in the LXX of 1 Chr 17:14 he promises to raise up a faithful king. This text, of course, emphasizes Jesus' role as a faithful priest. Jesus carried out the commission entrusted to him by God as an apostle and high priest. The readers were attracted to Moses and to the revelation entrusted to him and were in danger of exalting Moses over Jesus. Hebrews does not denigrate Moses, nor does it deny that God revealed himself to him (cf. 1:1!). Indeed, Moses was faithful in God's house as well. "House" in this context refers to the people of God. As a member of God's people Moses was faithful. In that sense he anticipated the greater ministry of Jesus.

3:3

Moses and Jesus are not on the same level. They were both faithful to their callings, but Jesus is worthy of more glory than Moses. Why is this so? The author uses an illustration from everyday life. When a house is built, honor goes to the one who built the house. No one thinks the house deserves more honor than the one who built it. The application of the illustration is evident given verse 2. Jesus as "the builder" (ὁ κατασκευάσας) of the house warrants more honor than Moses as a member of the house.

The author likely alludes to Zech 6:12 where the one called the Branch will build the Lord's temple.[151] Identifying the Branch in Zech 6:12 is difficult. The reference could be to Joshua as high priest (Zech 6:11) or to Zerubbabel as king. Probably the reference is to Zerubbabel, for he "will sit on His throne and rule" (Zech 6:13). Zechariah 3:8 seems to confirm this, for Joshua the high priest is promised by the Lord, "I am about to bring my servant, the Branch" (Zech 3:8). The Branch seems to be distinct from Joshua here, and the most likely candidate is Zerubbabel. Such a high position for Zerubbabel fits with Hag 2:20–23, where he is promised that the Lord will shake the heavens and earth, overthrow enemy rulers, and establish him as God's "signet ring."[152] Still the matter is complicated

---

[150] Cf. Lane, *Hebrews 1–8*, 72. See here Karl Deenick, "Priest and King or Priest-King in 1 Samuel 2:35," *WTJ* 73 (2011): 325–39.

[151] For the OT background to both texts mentioned here, see Hughes, *Hebrews*, 132, 135.

[152] The author of Hebrews was certainly familiar with this prophecy of Haggai, for he cites it in 12:26–27.

since Zerubbabel shares his rule with Joshua, for "there will also be a priest on His throne" (Zech 6:13). Zerubbabel and Joshua are probably the two olive trees and two anointed ones through whom the Lord will build his temple (Zech 4:10, 13). Sorting out which texts refer to Zerubbabel or Joshua is difficult, but in the final analysis Hebrews clearly sees Jesus as King and High Priest, so what is said about both of them is finally fulfilled in Jesus. As God's king and high priest, he builds God's house, which refers to the people of God (cf. 3:6).

There is probably also an allusion to 1 Chr 17:11–12, which is a prophecy regarding David's dynasty, the text where the Davidic covenant is established. David's heirs are promised perpetual rule as long as they obey the Lord. In particular David's son would build a house for Yahweh. Solomon, of course, fulfilled this prophecy, but it was ultimately fulfilled in Jesus as the obedient Son.[153]

Both Jesus and Moses were faithful, but Jesus was faithful as the one who built the house, as the one who established the people of God.[154] Moses, on the other hand, was faithful as a member of the people of God. The argument is complex here and operates at a number of levels.[155] On the one hand Jesus as a human being and as the high priest is faithful to God. On the other hand, as the divine Son he is the builder of the house—the Creator of all! The weaving together of these two themes is stitched into the letter, as noted previously, from its outset (1:2). We are not surprised, then, to find both the humanity and deity of Jesus proclaimed here. At the same time the house here seems to refer both to the people of God (3:2, 5–6) and to the creation of the universe (3:3–4). A verse that looked rather simple on first glance holds a number of hidden treasures.

3:4

The author pauses to make a comment about building. Every building that exists has been prepared and built by someone. For every effect there is a cause. Ultimately, however, everything that exists has been built by God himself. He is sovereign over all that is and is the ultimate cause for everything in the universe (see §1). Hence, God receives the glory for all that exists and for all that has

---

[153] Cf. here Guthrie, "Hebrews," 952.

[154] Attridge thinks the analogy is general, and the author is not saying that Jesus built the people of God (*Hebrews*, 110).

[155] Rightly L. Johnson, *Hebrews*, 109.

been created. The author doesn't say specifically here that Christ is the Builder of the house;[156] rather, he constructs an analogy between Christ and God. God as the Creator of the universe deserves glory and honor, so too Christ as the Builder of the house is honored above Moses. Hence, he implies, when we put this verse together with the previous one, Jesus is the divine Builder of the house.

3:5

Verses 5–6 contrast Moses and Christ. Moses was a faithful servant in the house, functioning as a prelude and anticipation of Christ as the faithful Son. Hebrews again underscores that Moses was not the builder of the house; i.e., Moses did not establish the people of God. Instead, he was a member of the people of God. He stands out as a faithful servant in the house, but he wasn't inherently superior to those whom he led, for he too was under God's rule as a human being and as a member of Israel.

The OT background here is illuminating. Hebrews alludes to Num 12:7 where the Lord commends Moses as his faithful servant: "Not so with My servant Moses; he is faithful in all My household." The words "servant" (θεράπων), "faithful" (πιστός), and "house" (οἶκός) from Num 12:7 are repeated in Heb 3:5. A comparison of the LXX of Num 12:7 (ὁ θεράπων μου Μωυσῆς ἐν ὅλῳ τῷ οἴκῳ μου πιστός ἐστιν) and the text of Heb 3:5 (Μωϋσῆς μὲν πιστὸς ἐν ὅλῳ τῷ οἴκῳ αὐτοῦ ὡς θεράπων) demonstrates that the author draws on Num 12:7, even if there is not an introductory formula. The context of Numbers 12 is also important. Miriam and Aaron criticized Moses because he married a Cushite woman. They were apparently jealous of Moses, claiming that God did not speak through Moses alone. The Lord appeared to them, indicating that he spoke to prophets in visions and dreams, but Moses was distinctive as the faithful servant of God. God spoke to him "directly" (literally, "mouth-to-mouth," ESV), "not in riddles" (Num 12:8). Indeed, Moses saw "the form of the Lord" (Num 12:8). It is imperative to see that when the author speaks of Moses as God's "servant," he is using an exalted title. The context of Numbers 12 shows Moses' superiority and greatness in comparison to others. Moses stands out as the greatest prophet and perhaps the greatest leader in the OT.

---

[156] Against Spicq, *L'Épître aux Hébreux*, 2:68.

Hebrews does not argue for the superiority of the new covenant by denigrating Moses as the mediator of the old covenant. On the contrary he is praised as God's servant.[157] Despite Moses' greatness we look forward to something better. Moses was God's servant as a witness "to the things that were to be spoken later" (ESV). God spoke, as Heb 1:1 attests, in a variety of ways and modes under the old covenant, but his final and definitive revelation has arrived in his Son (Heb 1:2). This text likely alludes to Deut 18:15, 18–19 as well, for Moses himself predicted that God would raise up a future prophet to whom the people must listen, and thus Moses himself anticipated a future and better word from God. Moses is not the terminus and goal of revelation but a pointer along the way to something better.

3:6

Moses was God's faithful servant, but he looked forward to when God would speak a better and final word through his Son. Jesus is not just a faithful servant in the house. He is the faithful Son "over (ἐπί) God's house" (ESV). He is the sovereign ruler over the people of God, the Davidic Messiah who reigns at God's hand, the Creator and Preserver of the universe (Heb 1:2–3). As a human being he always did the will of his Father, faithfully obeying and submitting to him. The readers should not turn back to Moses the faithful servant, for Moses himself spoke of a coming day. Moses himself looked forward to the arrival of the faithful Son, and the readers should remain loyal to the Son. In this sense Moses functions as the type of the one to come, Jesus.

The last part of the verse communicates the importance of faithful endurance. The readers are members of God's house; they are truly members of the people of God if they endure to the end. The author urges them to hold fast and to hold on with a word that he uses two other places to designate the need to "hold on" (κατέχω, 3:14; 10:23). They are to hold onto their "boldness" (παρρησία), which in light of other texts in Hebrews (4:16; 10:19, 35) focuses on their free access to God through Jesus' high priestly work.[158] The words "confidence of our hope" (τὸ καύχημα τῆς ἐλπίδος) should

---

[157] Against Attridge, who claims that Hebrews "takes the passage out of context and accords a very different sense to its key term" (*Hebrews*, 111). I would suggest the argument is more profound. The honor in Moses' identification as a servant is retained, but Christ is greater since he is the Son.

[158] There are both an objective and a subjective element to the term (Attridge,

be understood as the NET Bible renders it: "the hope we take pride in." Hope refers here to the "content [of hope] rather than the act of hoping."[159] Believers must not abandon their confidence and their hope, for they belong to the Son who reigns over all.

How should we interpret the words "we are" (ἐσμεν ἡμεῖς) in the conditional sentence? Some understand the present tense and the conditional to say that believers already belong to the people of God if they persevere to the end.[160] If that is the case, then perseverance functions as evidence of an already existing right relationship to God. It seems significant that the author doesn't use a future tense here. He doesn't teach that believers *will belong* to the people of God if they persevere.

Despite the appeal of the interpretation explained above, it probably puts too much emphasis on the tense of the verb. It seems unlikely that the author is making such a nuanced point here. The sentence should be interpreted as a simple condition. So I suggest reading the sentence as follows: if the readers endure to the end, they are God's house. The author is not attempting to affirm that if they endure *they already belong* to God's house, but he is not denying such an affirmation either. Nor is he saying that if they endure to the end *they will be* his house. The purpose here is not to speak to or resolve such temporal questions. The author isn't contemplating whether the readers were already Christians; his point is pastoral: the readers must persevere to belong to God's house. The conditional here should be interpreted in the same way as the other conditionals in Hebrews: if the readers persevere to the end, they belong to God's household.

Bridge

Believers in Jesus Christ must hold onto their faith until the end. It would be lamentable to revert to the revelation given through

---

Hebrews, 111–12; Ellingworth, *Hebrews*, 211). Since believers have objective reasons to be bold, they can draw near to God with confidence.

[159] O'Brien, *Hebrews*, 137.

[160] Fanning understands the condition to be one from evidence to inference, so that those who persevere show they are already members of the people of God. Buist M. Fanning, "A Classical Reformed View," in *Four Views on the Warning Passages in Hebrews*, ed. Herbert W. Bateman IV (Grand Rapids, MI: Kregel, 2007), 206–18. Against this view see Cockerill, *Hebrews*, 170–72.

Moses, for Moses was a faithful servant of the Lord, but Jesus is God's faithful Son. He is the apostle and high priest of our confession. Moses himself looked forward to a further word from God, to the fulfillment of what was proclaimed, and Jesus constitutes that fulfillment. The boldness to enter God's presence through Jesus' high priestly work would be surrendered if believers abandoned Jesus.

Hebrews 3:7–11

Outline

   I. Prologue: Definitive and Final Revelation in the Son (1:1–4)
  II. Don't Abandon the Son Since He Is Greater than Angels (1:5–2:18)
 III. **Don't Harden Your Hearts Since You Have a Son and High Priest Greater than Moses and Joshua (3:1–4:13)**
     A. The Faithful Son Greater than the Servant Moses (3:1–6)
     B. **Warning: Continue Believing and Obeying to Enter Rest (3:7–4:13)**
       1. **The OT Text: Don't Harden Your Hearts as the Wilderness Generation Did (3:7–11)**
       2. Application of OT: Beware of Unbelief and Disobedience (3:12–19)
       3. Fear Lest You Don't Enter His Rest (4:1–5)
       4. Be Diligent to Enter His Rest While It Remains (4:6–13)

Scripture

[7] Therefore, as the Holy Spirit says: Today, if you hear His voice, [8] do not harden your hearts as in the rebellion, on the day of testing in the wilderness, [9] where your fathers tested Me, tried Me, and saw My works [10] for 40 years. Therefore I was provoked with that generation and said, "They always go astray in their hearts, and they have not known My ways." [11] So I swore in My anger, "They will not enter My rest."

Context

The superiority of Jesus the Son to Moses the servant is not a theological abstraction. The previous text concluded with a call to stand firm until the end. Now the author continues in this vein, proceeding to warn his readers in a long section extending from 3:7–4:13, beginning with a fairly long citation from Ps 95:7–11. The warning takes center stage: they must not harden their hearts as the wilderness generation did. The Israelites tested the Lord and resisted him, even though they saw his gracious and saving work for 40 years. As a result, God poured his anger out on them and swore that they would not enter his rest, which is the land of promise.

Exegesis

3:7

The author commences his exhortation with the word "therefore" (Διό). Since Jesus the Son is superior to Moses, they should not harden their hearts to the message given through him. In this verse the author begins to quote from Ps 95:7–11. The citation is introduced with the words "as the Holy Spirit says." Hebrews regularly emphasizes that in Scripture God speaks to his people, and here that speaking is attributed to the Holy Spirit (see §4). This is a remarkable indication of the Spirit's deity, for the Scriptures represent the voice and word of God, and here that word is attributed to the Holy Spirit.

The citation begins with Ps 95:7: "Today, if you hear His voice." The word "today" (σήμερον) plays a significant role in the text before us. The Spirit addresses the people of God, admonishing them not to harden their hearts today.

It is fitting here to summarize the message of Psalm 95. The text is close to the LXX with a few minor changes, though it should also be said that the LXX reflects a close translation of the MT. The psalm begins with a call to cry out joyfully to God for his saving work in Israel. The Lord should be thanked, for he is a great God and King over all. God's lordship over all is evident, for he is the Creator and Owner of the sea and dry land. All the earth belongs to him; therefore, Israel should worship the one who is their Creator and Lord. Indeed, he is the Shepherd of Israel and tends them as his people, promising to supply their every need as Israel's Deliverer.

Therefore, Israel should not harden their hearts like the wilderness generation did, or they will face his wrath and fail to enter his rest.

3:8

The psalmist addresses his generation, admonishing them not to harden their hearts today, as the rebellious generation in the wilderness hardened theirs. The wilderness generation provoked the Lord through unbelief and disobedience repeatedly and refused to enter the land of Canaan when they were commanded to do so (so Numbers 13–14). Such actions signaled that their hearts had grown cold against the Lord. When they were tested in the wilderness, they resisted his admonitions and failed to believe his promises.

3:9

The wilderness generation tested God instead of trusting him. Instead of believing God cared for them, they became convinced that he despised them. Their unbelief is astonishing since they experienced God's gracious work for 40 years.[161] The Lord liberated them from Egypt and preserved them from the perils of the desert for 40 years. Seeing the Lord's gracious work and turning against him can only be explained by a rebellious and resistant heart. They did not want the Lord to be their God.

3:10

The wilderness generation hardened their hearts, testing and doubting the Lord for 40 years. As a consequence ("therefore," διό) God became angry with them, for they did not trust him or love him after all he had done for them.[162] Israel's problem was irreme-

---

[161] It is also possible to read the text to say that God was angry for 40 years instead of saying that Israel saw God's works for 40 years (cf. Koester, *Hebrews*, 256), but it seems most likely that the focus is on God's gracious work in Israel for 40 years. In 3:17, however, it seems that the focus is on God's wrath being poured out on Israel for 40 years. The content of v. 17 supports Koester's reading here. The matter is difficult, and I slightly lean toward both themes coexisting: God both showed his gracious work to Israel for 40 years (as here in 3:9), and they also experienced his wrath (so 3:17).

[162] Some detect significance in the shift from "that" (ἐκείνῃ) to "this" (ταύτῃ), arguing that the author subtly indicts his readers (Bruce, *Hebrews*, 60n28; Ellingworth, *Hebrews*, 218). This reading seems unlikely (rightly Attridge, *Hebrews*, 115; Koester, *Hebrews*, 255). The text describes the wilderness generation—not the readers—in the past tense. Furthermore, the readers were not yet the objects of God's anger, for they were being *warned* about being like the wilderness generation. The author doesn't say they were in the same place as the wilderness generation. Indeed, he writes so that they won't fall into the same error.

diable: "They always go astray in their hearts." The word "always" (ἀεί) indicates that Israel's wandering from the Lord was not temporary or occasional but was the constant refrain of their lives. As Num 14:22 says, they "tested" the Lord "10 times" and refused to listen to his voice.[163] Defection from the Lord characterized them. Fundamentally, Israel did not know God's "ways" (ὁδούς). Often we find in the OT the need to "walk" in God's "ways" (cf. Deut 8:6; 10:12; Jos 22:5; 1 Kgs 2:3). The psalmist prays that God's ways—his faithful and true ways (Ps 25:10)—would be disclosed to him (Ps 25:4; cf. Isa 2:3). God made his ways known to Moses (Ps 103:7), which probably refers to his saving acts for Israel (cf. NET, which translates it as "his faithful acts"). God repeatedly revealed his saving ways to Israel, showing them his mercy and love and grace. The wilderness generation, despite seeing God's ways, did not truly learn who he is. Since they didn't know God's ways, they didn't know God.

3:11

Since Israel strayed from God, hardening themselves against him, he swore with an oath that they would not enter his rest. The particle at the beginning of the verse ("So," ὡς) designates result.[164] The Lord's wrath against his people was provoked by their continual wandering from him, by their failure to trust and rely on him. His anger reached a point where he took an oath, pledging that they would not enter his rest. The "rest" here refers to the land of Canaan that was promised to Israel in fulfillment of the covenant enacted with Abraham, Isaac, and Jacob. The text alludes again to Numbers 14. The Lord said they would never "see the land I swore to their fathers" (Num 14:23), and "I swear that none of you will enter the land I promised to settle you in" (Num 14:30).[165] The promise would be fulfilled for a later generation, but the wilderness generation would not enjoy the land since they rebelled against the Lord.

---

[163] For the parallel, see Lane, *Hebrews 1–8*, 85–86. The HCSB translation of Num 14:22 is apposite, but readers miss the parallel to Hebrews, for literally it says, "They did not obey my [God's] voice" (οὐκ εἰσήκουσάν μου τῆς φωνῆς). For the many parallels to Numbers 14 in 3:1–4:13, see Richard Ounsworth, *Joshua Typology in the New Testament*, WUNT 2/328 (Tübingen: Mohr Siebeck, 2012), 56–59.

[164] See LN 89.52; BDAG.

[165] Again see Lane, *Hebrews 1–8*, 86.

Bridge

The author quotes from Psalm 95 and identifies its words as those which were spoken by the Holy Spirit. The OT is conceived of as the written word of God. Indeed, what was spoken by David so long ago speaks afresh to the author's generation. The old covenant is obsolete, but the OT Scriptures continue to be the living voice of God. Both the readers addressed in Hebrews and we must hear God's voice with faith. We should beware of hardening our hearts against God. A rebellious person puts the Lord to the test, showing that he doesn't know God since he doesn't know God's saving ways.

Hebrews 3:12–19

Outline

I. Prologue: Definitive and Final Revelation in the Son (1:1–4)

II. Don't Abandon the Son Since He Is Greater than Angels (1:5–2:18)

III. **Don't Harden Your Hearts Since You Have a Son and High Priest Greater than Moses and Joshua (3:1–4:13)**

    A. The Faithful Son Greater than the Servant Moses (3:1–6)

    B. **Warning: Continue Believing and Obeying to Enter Rest (3:7–4:13)**

        1. The OT Text: Don't Harden Your Hearts as the Wilderness Generation Did (3:7–11)

        2. **Application of OT: Beware of Unbelief and Disobedience (3:12–19)**

        3. Fear Lest You Don't Enter His Rest (4:1–5)

        4. Be Diligent to Enter His Rest While It Remains (4:6–13)

Scripture

[12] Watch out, brothers, so that there won't be in any of you an evil, unbelieving heart that departs from the living God. [13] But encourage each other daily, while it is still called today, so that none of you is hardened by sin's deception. [14] For we have become companions of the Messiah if we hold firmly until the end the reality that we had at the start. [15] As it is said: Today, if you hear His voice, do not harden your hearts as in the rebellion. [16] For who

heard and rebelled? Wasn't it really all who came out of Egypt under Moses? [17] And who was He provoked with for 40 years? Was it not with those who sinned, whose bodies fell in the wilderness? [18] And who did He swear to that they would not enter His rest, if not those who disobeyed? [19] So we see that they were unable to enter because of unbelief.

Context

The author applies the message of Psalm 95 to his readers in verses 12–19. They must be watchful lest a heart of unbelief surfaces in them, leading them to apostasize and to fall away from God (see §5). The antidote to apostasy is given in verse 13. Believers should exhort one another daily so that they are not deceived by sin that would lead them to abandon the Lord. Verse 14 explains verses 12–13. If they persevere to the end, they will belong to Christ. The need for perseverance explains why the author quotes Psalm 95. Like David's readers many generations ago, the readers of the letter must not harden their hearts and rebel against God (v. 15). Verses 16–19, as the author's interpretive commentary on Psalm 95, function similarly to the pesher interpretations well known from Qumran. Verses 16–18 pose questions with the words of Psalm 95, and then the author answers these queries with his own words in each of the verses. So, who rebelled when hearing God's word (v. 16)? Answer: those who were delivered from Egypt with Moses. With whom was God angry (v. 17)? Answer: with those who sinned and died in the wilderness. And who won't enter God's rest (v. 18)? Answer: those who disobeyed. The author draws a conclusion in verse 19, explaining the reason for Israel's apostasy and judgment. They didn't enter God's rest because of their unbelief because they failed to trust God. The reference to unbelief forms an inclusio with verse 12, where the author began his admonition by warning the readers about falling prey to an evil heart of unbelief.

Exegesis

3:12

The words addressed to the wilderness generation and David's own generation are applied to the readers of the letter. The author is concerned that the readers will fall prey to unbelief so that they would fall away from God. The HCSB captures nicely the imperative which begins the verse: "Watch out" (Βλέπετε). The warning is addressed to believers, to the brothers and sisters in the church (or churches) receiving the letter. In fact, every single person should take the admonition seriously, for he directs it to "any of you." No member of the church is exempted from the warning. The readers must guard their hearts and be vigilant so that their hearts do not turn toward evil. Unbelief—the failure to trust in God and to believe his promises—is the essence of an evil heart that refuses to "trust" (πιστεύουσίν) in him (Num 14:11). Lack of trust leads to failure to obey. As Cockerill says, "The pastor envisions no faith that does not lead to obedience, nor does he conceive of any obedience that does not stem from faith."[166]

An evil heart of unbelief results in apostasy, in abandoning the living God. Numbers 14 recounts how Israel refused to trust in God and failed to enter the land. In Num 14:9, as Israel stood at the crossroads determining whether to obey the Lord or not, Joshua and Caleb exhorted them not to "rebel (ἀποστάται) against the LORD" (14:9). The author of Hebrews, recalling that event, makes a similar plea to his readers, summoning them not to repeat the error of the wilderness generation. The infinitive construction ("that departs," ἐν τῷ ἀποστῆναι) could designate "content," so that departing from the living God defines and explains a heart of unbelief.[167] Wallace, however, is probably correct in understanding this as a result clause.[168] Apostasy is the consequence or result of an unbelieving heart. Apostasy captures well the meaning of the word used here (ἀποστῆναι).[169] The author warns them against departing from God (HCSB), about the danger of falling away (ESV), about forsaking him (NET), about turning away from him (NIV). Such turning away is not a temporary deviation but a rejection of God's lordship. Indeed, it is the height of foolishness, for he is "the living God" (cf. Heb 9:14; 10:31; 12:22). In the OT the Lord is described as the "living God" when Israel is in a conflict with

---

[166] Cockerill, *Hebrews*, 183.

[167] A. T. Robertson, *A Grammar of the Greek New Testament in the Light of Historical Research,* 2nd ed. (Nashville: Broadman, 1934), 1073; Ellingworth, *Hebrews*, 222; Cockerill, *Hebrews*, 184n40.

[168] Daniel B. Wallace, *Greek Grammar Beyond the Basics: An Exegetical Syntax of the New Testament* (Grand Rapids, MI: Zondervan, 1996), 593n12. Wallace says it is the only example in the NT where ἐν τῷ designates result.

[169] Rightly Hughes, *Hebrews*, 145.

other nations (e.g., Josh 3:10; 1 Sam 17:26; 2 Kgs 19:4, 16), or to designate his reality in contrast to idols (Jer 10:10; cf. Acts 14:15), or to emphasize that their fellowship is truly with the Lord (Ps 42:2; 84:2). Falling away from the true and living God is an unmitigated disaster, comparable to trying to make it to the top of Mount Everest without proper equipment.

3:13

Falling away from God can be prevented if believers encourage one another daily. Encouragement can stave off a spiritual hardness incited by sin's deception. Encouragement and exhortation, the author believes, are a community project and a mutual endeavor. Believers should gather together, as the author says later (10:25), to strengthen and encourage one another. They should be reminded of the goodness of God and the dangers of unrepentant sin. Occasional encouragement does not suffice. Instead it is needed daily. The author pauses to highlight the word "today" from Ps 95:7. The day of final rest has not yet arrived. It is still "today," a day when mutual exhortation and encouragement are needed. Every day matters to the author. There is no such thing as a routine day without significance.

The author explains why constant encouragement is necessary. He does not want the readers to be hardened by sin's deceitfulness. "The pastor does not write so that his hearers will ask, 'Have I been hardened and thus irrevocably lost to God's rest?' He writes, 'Lest any of you be hardened.'"[170] Again the importance of each individual to pay heed is underscored in the words "none of you" (τις ἐξ ὑμῶν). No one is exempt from the warning given here; everyone needs encouragement. The word "hardened" (σκληρυνθῇ) is taken from Ps 95:8, reflecting the sin of the wilderness generation. A calloused heart no longer hears the admonition of God. Such a heart steels itself against the stabs of conscience that bring one back to God. The means of deception is the deceitfulness of sin. Sin may blind the readers to the danger before them. They may mistakenly think they are safe when they are actually on the precipice. Advice, correction, and encouragement from others are the means by which the deception of sin can be unmasked.

---

[170] Cockerill, *Hebrews*, 187. He goes on to say, "Those seriously concerned for their spiritual welfare have not 'fallen away from the living God'" (187n58).

3:14

The author explains that the readers must not fall away or be hardened by sin's deception, for they share in Christ truly only if they hold firm their confidence until the end. The "for" (γάρ) connects verse 14 to verses 12–13, indicating that the final rest will be granted only to those who persevere to the end. The word rendered "companions" (μέτοχοι) by the HCSB is better translated as "partners" (NET) or as those who "share in Christ" (ESV, NIV). The word is used elsewhere in Hebrews of Christ's partners (1:9; 3:1) and of those who share in the Holy Spirit (6:4) and in discipline (12:8). The verb is translated "we have become" (γεγόναμεν), but the perfect tense here designates an existing state[171] and thus can also be translated "we are."[172] Some interpreters read too much into the perfect tense, interpreting the condition here as evidence to inference.[173] It is preferable to read the condition here in accord with the other conditional statements in Hebrews. It is certainly possible that the author makes the point that those who have truly become Christians in the past are those who will persevere in the future. Theologically, I have no objection to that reading. It is questionable, however, whether such nuanced reading fits the context of Hebrews. Elsewhere in the letter the author doesn't make the point that only true Christians persevere.[174] Instead, he admonishes believers to persevere until the end so they will receive the final reward. In other words we should beware of imposing a theological reading on the text that goes beyond the boundaries of what the author wants to do here. He is simply saying that the readers are sharers of Christ if they persevere to the end. He is not arguing here that true believers will definitely persevere, for it is a conditional statement. Nor is he saying that those who are truly believers *will* persevere. It is better to read the text as a simple condition.[175]

---

[171] Cf. also Wallace, *Greek Grammar*, 576.

[172] See here O'Brien, *Hebrews*, 150n146.

[173] So Fanning, "Classical Reformed," 206–18.

[174] Other texts, of course, teach that true believers persevere. See, for instance, Andrew J. Wilson, "Hebrews 3:6b and 3:14 Revisited," *TynBul* 62 (2011): 247–67. I am not convinced, however, that the author is teaching in this particular text that genuine believers endure until the end.

[175] For a fuller discussion, see the discussion on the warning passages in the theological section below (§5).

Verse 14, then, should be interpreted similarly to 3:6. Indeed, the same verb for "holding on" (κατάσχωμεν) is used in 3:6 and 3:14. Believers share in Christ if they hold firm the confidence they exercised in the beginning until the end. The HCSB in using the word "reality" rejects the idea that the author speaks of "confidence" (τῆς ὑποστάσεως) here. Many scholars support this view, contending that the term never means "confidence" and thus should be translated as realization or foundation.[176] However, there is evidence that the term means something like "confidence" or "hope" in some instances in the OT (Ps 39:7; Ezek 19:5), and the same meaning is possible in Paul as well (2 Cor 9:4; 11:17). Perhaps Attridge is correct in merging the two renderings together, in that believers put their trust in that which is real and stable.[177] When we come to 11:1, I will argue that the subjective experience of faith cannot be ruled out and fits well in context. The parallel with 3:6, where believers are exhorted to retain their "courage and the confidence of our hope," functions as a close parallel, lending support to the notion that confidence is in view here.[178] The author calls upon the readers to hang onto their confidence until the end, for such perseverance is necessary to share in Christ.

3:15

Verse 15 restates the main point in verses 12–14 by citing again Ps 95:7–8. The words "as it is said" (ἐν τῷ λέγεσθαι) introduce the OT citation and tie the quotation back to verses 12–14.[179] The call to remain faithful to the end still echoes "today," according to the author. If the readers have heard God's voice, then they should not harden their hearts against the Lord and should continue to listen to him. The readers are enjoined to be pliable, attentive, and eager to do what the Lord commands. They should not imitate the wilderness generation, which hardened themselves against the Lord and resisted his instructions so that they failed to enter Canaan.

---

[176] Cf. BDAG; O'Brien, *Hebrews*, 151; Cockerill, *Hebrews*, 189. See the important study by H. Koester, "ὑπόστασις," *TDNT* 8:572–89.

[177] Attridge, *Hebrews*, 118–19. Cf. Hughes, *Hebrews*, 152.

[178] Ellingworth, *Hebrews*, 227–28.

[179] In support of the notion that v. 15 relates to vv. 12–14 as a whole, see Attridge, *Hebrews*, 119–20; Lane, *Hebrews 1–8*, 88. Some scholars argue that v. 15 belongs with what follows (Ellingworth, *Hebrews*, 228; Otfried Hofius, *Katapausis: Die Vorstellung vom endzeitlichen Ruheort im Hebräerbrief*, WUNT 11 (Tübingen: Mohr Siebeck, 1970), 134–35; Otto Michel, *Der Brief an die Hebräer*, 13th ed., KEK (Göttingen: Vandenhoeck & Ruprecht, 1975), 190.

3:16

The author engages here and in the next several verses in an interpretation of the OT. In each verse he cites from Psalm 95, which he quoted extensively in 3:7–11, providing a commentary on its meaning. He begins by citing Ps 95:8, asking who heard God's voice and rebelled against what he commanded. The author provides the answer. It was the entire generation led by Moses who left Egypt. Remarkably, the same people who saw God's signs and wonders in Egypt, who witnessed Pharaoh being brought to his knees, and who experienced freedom at the Red Sea rebelled against God. They heard God speaking to them and knew his will but refused to do what he commanded (see Num 14:1–38).[180] Perhaps there is a hint here of Christ's superiority to Moses in that those who were freed through Moses never entered the land. Jesus Christ gives his people rest and a better rest than Moses as well. Still the main point is that if Israel didn't escape punishment when they disobeyed the message given by Moses, then those who turn against the message of Jesus will not be spared either.

3:17

Verse 17 continues the pattern of quoting from Psalm 95 with commentary. Here the author cites Ps 95:10. He asks with whom was God angry for 40 years. The emphasis here is on the extensive period of time during which the wilderness generation faced God's wrath. Their rebellion had consequences in history. The author of Hebrews answers his own question. The Lord was angry with those who sinned. The word "sinned" calls attention to their evil, to their refusal to carry out what the Lord commanded. Israel was called to enter the land and refused to do so since they feared death if they submitted to God's command. The consequences were disastrous. As a result of their sin, the wilderness generation died in the wilderness (cf. Num 14:29, 32). They sinned against God because they feared death, and they experienced death because they didn't do what he mandated. They didn't die in the land of promise but in the wilderness. They didn't experience God's favor in the land but his wrath in the wilderness.

---

[180] The influence of Numbers 14 here is pervasive. See Jon Laansma, *"I Will Give You Rest": The Rest Motif in the New Testament with Special Reference to Mt 11 and Heb 3–4*, WUNT 2/98 (Tübingen: Mohr Siebeck, 1997), 262–64.

3:18

The full import of their sin is explicated in this verse. Here the author merges together the question (with words from Ps 95:11) and the answer in one sentence. He poses a question so that the readers will grasp the significance of Israel's sin and see its implications for their own lives. The wilderness generation didn't enter the rest promised in Canaan. They didn't experience the promise of the land pledged to Abraham, Isaac, and Jacob. Despite being delivered from Egypt with signs and wonders, they never made it to Canaan.[181] Indeed, God swore on an oath that they would not enter the land. Later in Hebrews (6:13–18) the author stresses that God made an oath to Abraham, which provides assurance of his faithfulness. But here the oath functions in a different way. God's swearing relates here to judgment, not salvation. The oath indicates God's anger over Israel's disobedience. The oath indicates there will be no second chance for Israel. God's patience was exhausted since they disobeyed him in the wilderness repeatedly. Their disobedience constituted blatant rebellion, and hence they were banned from the land.

3:19

The author concludes by explaining the reason Israel didn't enter God's rest: unbelief. The defect of the wilderness generation is described as hardness of heart (3:8, 13, 15), testing God (3:9), going astray (3:10), rebellion (3:15–16), sin (3:17), and disobedience (3:18). Here the author identifies it as unbelief, forming an envelope or inclusio with 3:12 where the readers are warned about having an evil and unbelieving heart. The author, as will be evident throughout the letter and especially in chapter 11, believes faith and obedience are inseparable.[182] Faith and obedience can be distinguished from each other because they aren't the same entity. Still all true faith inevitably results in obedience. The wilderness generation failed to put

---

[181] Against Cockerill, the failure to enter Canaan is not equivalent to the eternal punishment with which the readers are threatened (*Hebrews*, 194). Instead, the earthly failure of the Israelites is analogous to and typological of the eternal judgment the readers face if they fall away. It may well be the case that many or most of the wilderness generation also experienced eternal punishment. It is possible, however, that some repented and believed. The author makes a typological point here and does not consider the final fate of the wilderness generation.

[182] L. Johnson collapses faith into faithfulness or obedience, and hence he doesn't see the fundamental role faith plays here (*Hebrews*, 117, 119).

their trust in God's promises. Consequently, they rebelled, sinned, and disobeyed. Apostasy at its heart is unbelief, and perseverance becomes a reality when one trusts God and what he has promised.

Bridge

The warning addressed to early Christians still applies today. Believers should be vigilant so that unbelief does not begin to invade our hearts. One of the marks of the church should be daily, mutual encouragement so we aren't hardened by sin. Such encouragement means believers know one another and share struggles. Perseverance until the end is necessary for salvation. When we read about the wilderness generation, we see what happens to those who disbelieve and disobey. They failed to enter God's earthly rest. How much more terrible it is to fail to enter the heavenly rest.

Hebrews 4:1–5

Outline

I. Prologue: Definitive and Final Revelation in the Son (1:1–4)
II. Don't Abandon the Son Since He Is Greater than Angels (1:5–2:18)
III. **Don't Harden Your Hearts Since You Have a Son and High Priest Greater than Moses and Joshua (3:1–4:13)**
    A. The Faithful Son Greater than the Servant Moses (3:1–6)
    B. **Warning: Continue Believing and Obeying to Enter Rest (3:7–4:13)**
        1. The OT Text: Don't Harden Your Hearts as the Wilderness Generation Did (3:7–11)
        2. Application of OT: Beware of Unbelief and Disobedience (3:12–19)
        3. **Fear Lest You Don't Enter His Rest (4:1–5)**
        4. Be Diligent to Enter His Rest While It Remains (4:6–13)

Scripture

[1] Therefore, while the promise to enter His rest remains, let us fear that none of you should miss it. [2] For we also have received the good news just as they did; but the message they heard did

not benefit them, since they were not united with those who heard it in faith [3] (for we who have believed enter the rest), in keeping with what He has said: So I swore in My anger, they will not enter My rest. And yet His works have been finished since the foundation of the world, [4] for somewhere He has spoken about the seventh day in this way: And on the seventh day God rested from all His works.

[5] Again, in that passage He says, They will never enter My rest.

Context

The author continues to apply Psalm 95 to his readers. The main point of 3:12–19 is that the readers should be on guard against an unbelieving heart, for that would lead them to fall away from God so that they don't enter God's rest. The same concern animates 4:1–5. Here the main point emerges in verse 1. The readers should fear, and their fear should motivate them to enter God's rest. The author reminds them in verse 2 that merely hearing the good news proclaimed will not rescue them, for the wilderness generation failed to believe what they heard. The rest, as verse 3 explains, is only accessed by those who have faith, and God swore that the wilderness generation would not enter his rest since they failed to believe and obey. The need to believe to enter God's rest dominates this paragraph, but at the same time the author argues that the rest has been available since creation when God finished his creative work. He cites Gen 2:2 to establish that God's rest was instituted from the seventh day of creation. The paragraph ends with the sobering reminder of the words spoken to the wilderness generation (Ps 95:11). Even though God's rest was accessible, they didn't enter it because of their rebellion and persistent unbelief.

Exegesis

4:1

The author applies afresh, as he did in 3:12, the story of the wilderness generation to his readers, warning them to take seriously his words so that they don't fall short while the promise of entering God's rest remains. The "therefore" (οὖν) in verse 1 indicates that a conclusion or exhortation is drawn from the experience of the wilderness generation. The readers are summoned to fear lest they fail to enter God's rest.[183] The rest certainly includes the notion of place.[184] I would suggest that this view is strengthened if one accepts that the rest is also described as "the city that has foundations" (11:10), as a "homeland" (11:14), a "heavenly" one (11:16). It is "the city of the living God (the heavenly Jerusalem)" (12:22), the "kingdom that cannot be shaken" (12:28), and the city "to come" (13:14). That the rest also includes the idea of a state is evident if there is an already-but-not-yet character to the rest (4:3).[185] It seems that the rest can't be limited to a place since God rests from his works, and such rest doesn't designate a place. The notion of Sabbath rest (4:9) also suggests that rest transcends the notion of a place, though the idea of place is not abandoned.

The verb "let us fear" (φοβηθῶμεν) is a first person plural, showing that the author includes himself in the admonition. The warning is not restricted to so-called weak Christians but is addressed to all Christians everywhere. We saw in 3:12 that Christians should be on guard, and here they are called upon to fear. The reference is not to paralyzing fear that disables and enervates. The fear commanded here is a stimulus to action, like the fear that motivates mountain climbers to ensure all their equipment is working properly, provoking readers to enter God's rest and stimulating them to believe and obey. God's rest began after the seventh day and thus probably

---

[183] For a brief survey of various religious historical parallels, see Attridge, *Hebrews*, 126–28. A Philonic or Gnostic background is unlikely. See Laansma, *I Will Give You Rest*, 327–35, 338–42. This does not preclude, as Laansma observes, a Platonic coloring of the author's language. The issue is whether the conception of rest is fundamentally Middle Platonic or Gnostic. Even though Laansma is more sympathetic with Hofius's view that the author's conception of rest is derived from Jewish apocalyptic, he shows the weaknesses in Hofius's attempt to delineate the background as well (342–47). Laansma argues in his work that the background of the term is broadly Christian, rooted in a Christian understanding of the OT.

[184] See Laansma, *I Will Give You Rest*, 277–83. But there is a sense in which the rest is both a place and a state (see Ounsworth, *Joshua Typology*, 78–88). Laansma rightly shows that Hofius's view (*Katapausis*, 49–50) that "rest" (κατάπαυσις) is a technical term for the temple fails to convince (see Laansma, *I Will Give You Rest*, 94–101, 314–16). Laansma agrees that the term is often associated with the temple, but this is different from saying that it is a technical term. Since writing this, Laansma inclines a bit more to Hofius's view, though he does not embrace it entirely ("Hidden Stories in Hebrews," 12n16).

[185] See here Leschert for an insightful discussion on the nature of rest (*Hermeneutical Foundations of Hebrews*, 133–37).

includes the idea of fellowship with God as well. Adam and Eve enjoyed such fellowship in the garden, and believers also enjoy such rest in fellowship with Jesus (Matt. 11:28-30), and will experience rest and fellowship in a consummated way in the future.

The readers should consider their place in history. The opportunity to enter God's rest still lies before them. They have not yet been rejected as the wilderness generation was. Nor has the rest yet been consummated. It has been promised but is not yet realized. The heavenly city, which is such a prominent theme in Hebrews, has not yet arrived. The readers, therefore, should seize the day. They must not fall short of the promised rest. In contrast to the wilderness generation, they must believe and obey.

4:2

Both the readers and the wilderness generation were the recipients of good news, but the proclamation of God's saving goodness did not benefit the wilderness generation because they failed to believe. The author reminds the readers that the proclamation of the good news has no inherent benefit. Simply hearing the gospel will not guarantee that they enter God's rest on the last day.[186] After all, the wilderness generation heard the good news about entrance into Canaan, but they never entered the land. They heard what God promised, but they were not united with those (like Joshua and Caleb) who heard the message in faith.[187] The wilderness generation is repeatedly held up to the readers as a warning on account of their disbelief. Merely hearing the good news does not guarantee future security. The message heard is only useful if it is believed. Otherwise, it remains an abstraction instead of a living reality.

4:3

The author explains previous statements. Clearly believers enter God's rest, for Psalm 95, which the author expounds here, clarifies

---

[186] The HCSB rendering "the message they heard" (ὁ λόγος τῆς ἀκοῆς) rightly understands the genitive to be descriptive so that the author refers to the message that was heard (so Attridge, *Hebrews*, 125; Hofius, *Katapausis*, 179n338).

[187] So Westcott, *Hebrews*, 93–94; Lane, *Hebrews 1–8*, 98. The accusative "united" (συγκεκερασμένους), modifying the accusative "those" (ἐκείνους), is clearly the best textual reading. For a discussion of the textual evidence, see Attridge, *Hebrews*, 122n2. Attridge maintains that the wilderness generation did not share the faith of the recipients of the letter (125–26). This interpretation is certainly possible, but it seems unlikely the author refers to the faith of the readers in the midst of a warning, so I suspect he refers to the faith of Joshua and Caleb.

that God swore that the wilderness generation, which failed to trust God, would never enter his rest. He goes on to add that the rest is still available for a new generation since God has been resting since the creation of the world.

The first part of the verse reiterates a central theme of this section. Believers enter God's rest. The promise will not become a reality for those who dishonor God by refusing to trust what he says. It is difficult to decipher the significance of the present tense verb "enter" (εἰσερχόμεθα). Is Hebrews suggesting that the rest is entered both now and eschatologically? Is there an already-but-not-yet dimension to the rest? Certainly the author emphasizes that the rest is eschatological since it lies ahead of believers, and they must persevere to the end to enjoy it. Since the focus is on end-time rest, the question is whether there is a present dimension to the rest as well. A decision should not be made on the basis of the present-tense verb "enter" (εἰσερχόμεθα). Recent work on verbal aspect has demonstrated conclusively that the present tense does not necessarily designate "present time." A decision here is difficult. Even though the emphasis is on the future rest,[188] it seems that an already-but-not-yet dimension of the rest is also present.[189] Such a reading fits with what the author writes about the heavenly city. The city is eschatological, and believers await its coming (11:10, 13–16; 13:14; cf. *T. Dan* 5.12; 4 Ezra 8:52), but at the same time the author says (12:22) that the readers have now "come (προσεληλύθατε) . . . to the city of the living God (the heavenly Jerusalem)." In one sense believers have

---

[188] For the view that the rest is only future, see Laansma, *I Will Give You Rest*, 305–10; Hofius, *Katapausis*, 57; Koester, *Hebrews*, 270; Ellingworth, *Hebrews*, 246; Cockerill, *Hebrews*, 205; Richard B. Gaffin Jr., "A Sabbath Rest Still Awaits the People of God," in *Pressing Toward the Mark: Essays Commemorating Fifty Years of the Orthodox Presbyterian Church*, ed. C. G. Dennison and R. C. Gamble (Philadelphia: The Committee for the Historian of the Orthodox Presbyterian Church, 1986), 41–46.

[189] Cf. C. K. Barrett, "The Eschatology of the Epistle to the Hebrews," in *The Background of the New Testament and Its Eschatology*, ed. W. D. Davies and D. Daube (Cambridge: Cambridge University Press, 1956), 372; A. T. Lincoln, "Sabbath, Rest, and Eschatology in the New Testament," in *From Sabbath to Lord's Day: A Biblical, Historical, and Theological Investigation*, ed. D. A. Carson (Grand Rapids, MI: Zondervan, 1982), 210–13; Attridge, *Hebrews*, 126; Westcott, *Hebrews*, 95; Lane, *Hebrews 1–8*, 99; Hughes, *Hebrews*, 158; Ounsworth, *Joshua Typology*, 62; Schenk, *Cosmology and Eschatology in Hebrews*, 60–63.

even now arrived and come to the heavenly city, but in another sense it is future. They still experience the suffering that constitutes life in "the city of man." It seems that the same is true of the rest. The rest is fundamentally eschatological, and yet the eschaton has penetrated the present. Believers enter God's rest, which has been accessible since the day of creation; but they have not entered the fullness of his rest, for they must continue to believe and obey until the end to obtain it. Such a reading fits with what we find elsewhere in the NT. For instance, the kingdom of God is both a present and a future reality. Hence the already-not-yet dimension of the rest fits with the eschatology we see elsewhere in the NT.[190]

The connection between the clauses in 4:3 is not easy to discern. The HCSB identifies the first clause as parenthetical, but it is difficult to see how the second clause in verse 3 relates to verse 2 conceptually. So it seems slightly preferable to relate the comparative clause here to the first clause in verse 3. The logic of the verse would be as follows: those who believe enter God's rest, and the necessity of belief is evident, for God swore in his wrath that the wilderness generation would not enter the rest. In other words they didn't enter the rest because of their unbelief. God swore that they

---

[190] O'Brien thinks the rest is exclusively future for a variety of reasons (*Hebrews*, 165–66): (1) the promise to enter the rest remains; (2) the promise is not yet obtained (Heb 10:32–39); (3) the present tense doesn't necessarily designate present time; (4) the context of chs. 3–4 clarifies that one must persevere to obtain the final reward; (5) a corporate entering of the rest is only fulfilled eschatologically; (6) entering the rest is dependent on striving to do so; and (7) believers don't rest from their works now. These excellent arguments may indeed demonstrate that the rest is only future. Certainly the emphasis is on the future nature of the rest. Still most of the arguments made by O'Brien stand if the rest has an already-not-yet character. This is seen most clearly when we compare the rest to the heavenly city. Believers are already members of the city (12:22), and yet they seek the city to come and must strive to enter it. If they fall away, they will not be members of the city. Believers are even now part of the corporate eschatological gathering (12:22–23), and yet there is an eschatological fulfillment still to come for such a gathering. It seems as if the same tension could be true of the rest, particularly since the rest describes the final reward for believers from a different angle. O'Brien's best argument is that believers don't rest from their labors until the eschaton. I would concur. Still it seems that here the author focuses on the eschatological character of that rest. When we speak of the already-not-yet character of rest, it isn't necessary to argue that every aspect of the rest has a present fulfillment. In the same way, believers are now members of the heavenly Zion, but they don't fully enjoy the benefits of their citizenship.

would not enjoy the rest since they persistently refused to trust in him.

The HCSB links the concessive clause ("and yet His works have been finished since the foundation of the world") to verse 4. Grammatically, however, the concessive clause is more likely attached to verse 3. What is the verse's logic? It seems that the writer asserts that Israel could have entered God's rest. They didn't enter it, but the possibility was open to them, for God's rest began from the foundation of the world, from the seventh day of creation as we learn in the next verse. Israel's failure to enter, then, was not because God's rest was unavailable to them. They failed to enter because they refused to enter, because they did not believe God's promises.

4:4

By quoting Scripture, the author supports the notion that God's rest has been available from the foundation of the world, for Scripture says God rested on the seventh day from his works. As is typical in Hebrews, God "speaks" in Scripture, declaring his word to human beings. The word "somewhere" does not betray ignorance of the context or the location of the text cited. The citation from Gen 2:2 matches the LXX but represents a clear translation of the MT as well. The author is not concerned to specify from where the verse comes; what he emphasizes is that God speaks through this word. Almost certainly the source of the quotation wasn't hard to find since it is in the first book of the Bible and is drawn from the seventh day of creation. When God completed the creative work of the six days, he rested from his work. He didn't rest because he was exhausted or weary but because his work was completed.[191] Furthermore, God's rest doesn't mean he refrained from all activity but from his work in creation. Hence, there is the suggestion that the rest, though it refers to a place, also includes the notion of fellowship with God.[192] The author makes the point that God's rest has been available since creation. While human history lasts, there is opportunity to enter God's rest. The author circles back, therefore, to verse 1: the promise of entering God's rest still remains.

---

[191] Cf. Lane, *Hebrews 1–8*, 99.

[192] Hughes, *Hebrews*, 161.

4:5

Given how the previous verse ends, it is rather surprising to return to the words of Ps 95:11: "They will not enter My rest." For the third time the author quotes Ps 95:11 (see also 3:11, 18), indicating the importance of the verse in his argument. What is the import of the verse? Why does the author cite it here? He has just emphasized that God's rest has been available since the beginning of the world. But he then turns and emphasizes that the wilderness generation will never enter God's rest. He addresses his readers by juxtaposing these two. On the one hand they live in the day of opportunity. The rest is still open to them. The door has not been closed for entering the rest of God. On the other hand the wilderness generation demonstrates that some have repudiated the rest God offers. The readers should not follow the example of those Israelites who refused to believe in and obey God. The decision before them is of immense importance, and hence he exhorts them to fear (v. 1), warning them about the consequences of falling away.

Bridge

The Christian life is complex. Believers are called upon to love, but we see from these verses that we are also called upon to fear. God has promised heavenly rest to believers, but believers should fear missing out on what he has promised. The fear to which the readers are summoned is not disabling but rather is intended to stimulate them to action. Merely hearing the good news does not guarantee life, for the wilderness generation heard good news but failed to believe it. They did not enter the rest of the land of Canaan, and believers will only enter the heavenly rest if they trust in God and obey him.

Hebrews 4:6–13

Outline

   I. Prologue: Definitive and Final Revelation in the Son (1:1–4)
  II. Don't Abandon the Son Since He Is Greater than Angels (1:5–2:18)
 III. **Don't Harden Your Hearts Since You Have a Son and High Priest Greater than Moses and Joshua (3:1–4:13)**

A. The Faithful Son Greater than the Servant Moses (3:1–6)
B. **Warning: Continue Believing and Obeying to Enter Rest (3:7–4:13)**
    1. The OT Text: Don't Harden Your Hearts as the Wilderness Generation Did (3:7–11)
    2. Application of OT: Beware of Unbelief and Disobedience (3:12–19)
    3. Fear Lest You Don't Enter His Rest (4:1–5)
    4. **Be Diligent to Enter His Rest While It Remains (4:6–13)**

Scripture

⁶ Since it remains for some to enter it, and those who formerly received the good news did not enter because of disobedience, ⁷ again, He specifies a certain day—today—speaking through David after such a long time, as previously stated: Today, if you hear His voice, do not harden your hearts. ⁸ For if Joshua had given them rest, God would not have spoken later about another day. ⁹ Therefore, a Sabbath rest remains for God's people. ¹⁰ For the person who has entered His rest has rested from his own works, just as God did from His. ¹¹ Let us then make every effort to enter that rest, so that no one will fall into the same pattern of disobedience. ¹² For the word of God is living and effective and sharper than any double-edged sword, penetrating as far as the separation of soul and spirit, joints and marrow. It is able to judge the ideas and thoughts of the heart. ¹³ No creature is hidden from Him, but all things are naked and exposed to the eyes of Him to whom we must give an account.

Context

This section continues the warning that commenced in 3:7. In 3:7–11 the readers are warned about hardening their hearts. In 3:12–19 he admonishes them about the danger of having an evil and unbelieving heart. The same truth is communicated in a different way in 4:1–5: the recipients of the letter should fear so that they do not fail to enter God's rest. The main point in 4:6–13 runs along the same lines. The readers should be diligent to enter God's rest so that they do not miss out on it by disobedience. We see in the various sections of 3:7–4:13 that the author reiterates the main theme repeatedly, stating it from different angles so that the readers grasp what he is saying and are impressed with the gravity of the situation.

Verse 6 begins by summarizing the import of verses 1–5: a rest still remains for the people of God, and the wilderness generation did not enter it because of disobedience. The availability of rest is confirmed by the use of the word "today" in Psalm 95 (v. 7), for it confirms that God's rest is still accessible "today." The author supports what he said in verse 7 by appealing to the import of Psalm 95 in verse 8. He explains that if Joshua had given full and final rest to the people, then Psalm 95 would not have spoken of a rest that is still available. Hence he concludes in verse 9 that there is still a Sabbath rest for the people of God. Interestingly, he ties the rest that remains to God's seventh-day rest, seeing in the seventh-day rest a preview of what is to come for the people of God. Verse 10 explains the nature of the Sabbath rest: just as God rests from his activity on the seventh day, so too human beings will rest from their works when they enter God's rest. Having spoken of the rest, the author drives home his main point in verse 11. They should be assiduous about entering God's rest while the opportunity remains. They must not turn against God as the wilderness generation did. Verses 12–13 explain why they should be diligent to enter God's rest. God's word is living and active, judging and destroying those who turn against him. No creature can hide from God, for he is the all-knowing One as our Creator, and our lives are laid bare before him.

Exegesis

4:6

The author sums up and restates the previous discussion, linking the present verse with what has gone before with the words "since therefore" (ESV, ἐπεὶ οὖν). The rest God promised still remains. It is still accessible and available for the people of God, for those who trust in him and obey him. At the same time, not all those who received the good news entered the rest. The good news proclaimed by Moses centered on God's rescue of Israel from Egypt and the promise that he would bring them into the land of Canaan, confirming the promises made to Abraham, Isaac, and Jacob. Israel, however, failed to enter Canaan because of their disobedience. The author continues to forge a close link between faith and obedience, for those who fail to trust in God also refuse to do what he commands (cf. 3:12, 18–19; 4:2–3, 11).

4:7

The continuing availability of God's rest is evident since rest is offered to Israel again by David (Ps 95:7–11) hundreds of years after the rest offered in the days of Moses and Joshua. The historical nature of OT revelation and the sequence of events become a major feature of the argument here. The author assumes the historical facticity of Moses, Joshua, and the events surrounding the land of Canaan during those days. Along the same lines he accepts that David wrote Psalm 95 at a certain juncture in history. The historical and temporal interval is crucial to his argument. After so many years rest is still offered to Israel.

The author seizes upon the word "today" from Ps 95:7 and gives it great significance. Since the Lord exhorted Israel not to harden their hearts anew and afresh in David's day, it follows that the rest promised by Moses and Joshua has not been terminated. It was still available for Israel in David's day, and by the same token it is open for the recipients of the letter. Hence the readers must not let their hearts grow hard today. They should hear God's voice and believe and obey so that they will receive the final reward.

4:8

The author continues to explain why the rest is still available for the readers of his day. The rest given by Joshua can't be the final rest since David hundreds of years later speaks of another rest, of a rest that is still available for the people of God.[193] If the rest given by Joshua was final and definitive, no further rest would be offered. The author often makes the argument that the new is better, contrasting it with the old.[194] In Joshua rest is linked to entering and possessing the land of Canaan (Josh 1:13, 15; 11:23; 14:15; cf. also Deut 3:20; 12:10; 25:19). After Joshua had defeated his enemies and Israel in-

---

[193] Whitfield intriguingly argues that the author emphasizes the priestly theme in Hebrews. He also maintains that the author does not only draw on Joshua who led Israel into Canaan but also Joshua the priest from Zechariah 3. Bryan J. Whitfield, *Joshua Traditions and the Argument of Hebrews 3 and 4*, BZNW 194 (Berlin: de Gruyter, 2013). His proposal warrants more consideration than can be given here. Still the links with Joshua the priest aren't clearly evident.

[194] See James W. Thompson, "The New Is Better: A Neglected Aspect of the Hermeneutics of Hebrews," *CBQ* 73 (2011): 547–61.

herited the land, we read that "the LORD gave them rest on every side according to all He had sworn to their fathers" (Josh 21:44; cf. 22:4; 23:1).

The typological nature of the rest given by Joshua is evident here.[195] Joshua anticipates Jesus Christ. Indeed, the name "Joshua" (Ἰησοῦς) here in Greek is spelled exactly as "Jesus" is spelled in the NT. Jesus is the new and final and better "Joshua." The salvation and rest given through Joshua were never intended to be the final rest for the people of God. The earthly rest in the land under Joshua points forward to the heavenly rest given in Jesus Christ, to the heavenly country and city (11:10, 13–16; 12:22; 13:14) awaiting believers in Jesus Christ.

4:9

The threads of the preceding verses are picked up here and the author draws a conclusion about the nature of the rest God promised. The word "therefore" (ἄρα) signals that a conclusion is drawn from the preceding verses. Another link with the preceding verses is the repetition of the verb "remains" (ἀπολείπεται; cf. 4:6). The rest continues to be open for God's people. The word spoken to Israel so long ago has a continuing relevance for believers in Jesus Christ. Israel's entrance into the land (and refusal to enter it as well) is not just a historical fact. That event and word address believers throughout history, for the rest described there has a predictive and typological character.

Indeed the author pulls together the rest promised to Israel in the land with God's rest on the seventh day of creation. The word translated as "Sabbath rest" (σαββατισμός) does not actually use the word "rest," though rest was closely linked with the Sabbath in Jewish tradition (Exod 16:23, 30; 20:11; 23:12). The reference to the Sabbath here points to the celebration and joy of the Sabbath.[196] A link between the Sabbath and God's rest on the seventh day is suggested in 4:4, and here the joy and praise that mark the end-time rest are featured. The connection between joy and rest is featured in

---

[195] Against Ellingworth, *Hebrews*, 253, 256. Ounsworth, in his work, ably defends the notion that the rest given by Joshua functions typologically (Ounsworth, *Joshua Typology*).

[196] So Lane, *Hebrews 1–8*, 101–2; O'Brien, *Hebrews*, 170–71; Laansma, *I Will Give You Rest*, 276–77. For a helpful discussion on the Sabbath rest, see Harold Weiss, "*Sabbatismos* in the Epistle to the Hebrews," *CBQ* 58 (1996): 674–89, esp. 685–89.

Deut 12:9–12.[197] Israel is about to experience rest in the land ("the resting place and inheritance," Deut 12:9). God promises to give them "rest" (Deut 12:10), and when he does so, they are to "rejoice before the LORD your God" (Deut 12:12). The joy of rest in the land, described in Deut 12:9–12, finds its eschatological fulfillment for those who find rest in Jesus Christ.

The author's reading of the Bible's story line is fascinating. God's rest in creation and the rest of Israel in the land have an eschatological character. God's creation rest anticipates the rest that will become a reality in the new creation. The rest realized under Joshua can't be the full and final rest since God still speaks of rest after the days of Joshua. The ultimate rest will match God's seventh-day rest as we shall see further in the next verse. Perhaps we have a hint here that the rest has an already-but-not-yet character. Israel, in the land, experienced God's rest to some degree. In the same way believers in Jesus Christ enjoy God's rest in part, but the fullness of that rest will only be theirs in the heavenly city.[198]

Another typological connection should be made explicit. The writer refers here to "God's people" (τῷ λαῷ τοῦ θεου). The rest given to Israel was a rest for a particular people in a specific location. But just as the rest points forward to a rest that embraces the whole creation, the new creation, the heavenly city, so Israel functions as a type for the new people of God, the church of Jesus Christ. The new people of God is not restricted to Israel but consists of Jewish and Gentile believers scattered throughout the world. The author doesn't erect a distinction between Israel and Gentile believers, indicating that he envisions one people of God.[199]

4:10

The nature of the Sabbath rest is unfolded by the author. Just as God rests from his works on the seventh day of creation, so when

---

[197] See Ounsworth, *Joshua Typology*, 87.

[198] The author doesn't address observance of the Sabbath specifically. It seems that his theology leads to the conclusion that literal observation of the Sabbath isn't necessary, for the Sabbath points to the eschatological rest believers enjoy in Jesus Christ. For a fuller discussion see Thomas R. Schreiner, "Goodbye and Hello: The Sabbath Command for New Covenant Believers," in *Progressive Covenantalism*, ed. S. Wellum and B. Parker (Nashville: B&H Academic, forthcoming).

[199] So L. Johnson, *Hebrews*, 129.

human beings enter God's rest, they rest from their works.[200] The "for" (γάρ) introducing the verse indicates that the nature of the Sabbath rest is unpacked for the readers. The rest envisioned is patterned after God's rest on the seventh day when God rested from his works. I already noted that God rested from his works because he was finished with his work, not because he was tired or exhausted.

The comparison furnished here is crucial and fundamental for understanding the rest promised to believers. It transcends the rest given to Joshua and Israel in the land. Their rest was an earthly rest, a rest in the land of Canaan, but the rest envisioned for those who belong to Jesus Christ is a greater rest than what was given under Joshua. The author declares that those who enter the rest promised by God rest from their works. The reference to works here has nothing to do with works righteousness. The author is not making a Pauline point about the danger of works righteousness. He is not saying believers rest from relying on their own works and start relying on God and his grace when they enter God's rest. Such notions are quintessentially Pauline but are beside the point here. After all, the author says believers rest from their works in the same way God rested from his works on the seventh day of creation. Certainly God did not rest from works righteousness! The first six days of creation were not an exercise in works righteousness, which is a concept that really makes no sense at all when speaking of God.

The comparison shows that any idea of refraining from works righteousness is foreign to what the author of Hebrews says. Resting from works means, then, that human beings stop working because their works are completed, just as God ceased working on the seventh day because his work of creation was completed. Clearly human beings only cease from works or activity at death. Hence we enter the rest finally and definitively after our death. Entering the rest is complementary with entrance into the heavenly city (11:10, 13–16; 12:22; 13:14). The parallel to Rev 14:13 is apt.[201] "Then I heard a voice from heaven saying, 'Write: The dead who die in the

---

[200] For the view that the one who entered into rest here is Jesus, see Nicholas J. Moore, "Jesus as 'The One who Entered his Rest': The Christological Reading of Hebrews 4.10," *JSNT* 36 (2014): 1–18. Moore makes an interesting and fascinating case for his reading, but the participle is more likely timeless here, and more contextual evidence is needed to substantiate a reference to Jesus.

[201] Rightly O'Brien, *Hebrews*, 172.

Lord from now on are blessed.' 'Yes,' says the Spirit, 'let them rest from their labors, for their works follow them!'" The author designates the final reward that Christians will enjoy (cf. 10:35; 11:26), so that the Christian's final rest means his works on earth are completed. The time of labor and suffering has ended, and believers enjoy their eternal inheritance (6:12; 9:15).

4:11

The day of final rest has not yet arrived; hence the author relays the main point of the paragraph, drawing an inference ("then," οὖν) from the promise of the future rest. Believers (and the author includes himself here with the first-person plural) should be diligent to enter into rest. They must not take God's promises for granted as if they could inherit the rest even while straying from the message of Jesus Christ.

The author returns to where he began (3:7–11), reminding his readers of the example set by the wilderness generation. They disobeyed God's commands and failed to enter Canaan. The rest was available to them, just as it is accessible to the recipients of the letter, and yet they did not take advantage of their privileges.

4:12

Verses 12–13 explain why the readers should strive to enter God's rest and why they should avoid unbelief and disobedience. Disobedience is fatal, for the word of God is powerful and effective, so that those who disobey it will not escape punishment.

The word of God, i.e., the word God speaks, is like God himself. God is, so to speak, what God says.[202] Hence the word of God, like God himself, is living (cf. Heb 3:12; 9:14; 10:31; 12:22) and active. It has an inherent power and dynamism that cannot be thwarted. In context the focus is on the effectiveness of God's judgment, but what is said here also applies more broadly to God's word in general. Whether the focus is on judgment or salvation, God's word accomplishes what God intends. The effectiveness of God's word is a regular theme of the OT, for the world was created by the word of God (cf. Gen 1:1–31; cf. Ps 33:6). Isaiah emphasizes that God's

---

[202] Still there is no reference to Christ's being the Logos here. Rightly Attridge, *Hebrews*, 134; L. Johnson, *Hebrews*, 136; Lane, *Hebrews 1–8*, 103; Ellingworth, *Hebrews*, 261. Against James Swetnam, "Jesus as λόγος in Hebrews 4,12–13," *Bib* 62 (1981): 214–24; Ronald Williamson, "The Incarnation of the Logos in Hebrews," *ExpT* 95 (1983): 4–8.

word accomplishes what God intends it to accomplish (Isa 55:10–11; cf. Ps 107:20).

God's word is compared to a double-edged sword. It seems here that the word's role in judgment is brought to the forefront. Perhaps the author thinks of the swords of Amalekites and Canaanites, which cut down Israel when they attempted to enter the land after the Lord told them they could not enter because of their disobedience (Num 14:39–45).[203] So too, the Lord's word hews down any and all those who disobey him.[204]

When the author speaks of the word "penetrating as far as the separation of soul and spirit, joints and marrow," the word here continues to be compared to a sword. As Louw and Nida remark, "Strictly speaking there is no one point at which joints and marrow may be separated."[205] It is difficult to know as well what the author could possibly mean by "the separation of soul and spirit." It is not apparent elsewhere from the OT or the NT that clear distinctions should be erected between the soul and spirit. In some popular and devotional literature, this verse is used to justify distinguishing between the soul and the spirit, and sometimes a whole spirituality springs up that separates the spirit, the soul, and the body. These tripartite understandings of human beings are speculative, testifying to the creativity of their authors more than they reflect the teaching of the NT. In context the author highlights the efficacy of God's word. Nothing can withstand its power. As Hughes says, "Our author is not concerned to provide here a psychological or anatomical analysis of the human condition, but rather to describe in graphic terms the penetration of God's word to the innermost depth of man's personality."[206]

A focus on the inherent potency of God's word is confirmed by the last phrase in the verse. God's word "judges the thoughts and

---

[203] So Lane, *Hebrews 1–8*, 102; O'Brien, *Hebrews*, 175.

[204] Alternatively, Scott D. Mackie argues that the word here doesn't connote judgment but is intended to remind the readers of the circumcision Israel experienced before entering the land (Josh 5:2–9) ("Heavenly Sanctuary Mysticism in the Epistle to the Hebrews," *JTS* 62 [2011]: 108–9). This suggestion, however, seems unlikely since it is more distant contextually.

[205] LN 8.62. Cf. O'Brien, *Hebrews*, 177. The whole matter is complex. For further discussion, see Attridge, *Hebrews*, 134–35.

[206] Hughes, *Hebrews*, 165.

attitudes of the heart" (NIV). God's word penetrates to the core of the human heart, for God's word represents God himself. Just as God knows our thoughts and attitudes, so God's word judges our thoughts and intentions. God knows reality so that he knows whether we are believing or disbelieving, obeying or disobeying.

4:13

This verse features God's infallible knowledge of human beings (see §1). The shift from the word of God to God himself confirms the close connection between God and his word so that the latter is an expression of the former. God knows the thoughts and attitudes of the heart, for nothing in the created order is hidden from him. God's judgments are always according to the truth, for he knows exhaustively everything that occurs in the world. Such a notion is derived from the OT. As Job says, "Sheol is naked before God, and Abaddon has no covering" (Job 26:6), and "For He looks to the ends of the earth and sees everything under the heavens" (Job 28:24). Or, the psalmist says, "The LORD looks down from heaven; He observes everyone" (Ps 33:13). God's judgments never suffer from superficiality since he sees and knows all, and everything is "laid bare" (NIV) before him. All human beings will give account to this God who knows all and judges their hearts infallibly.[207] God is never duped by the stratagems and devices of human beings. Thus, no one should think he can disobey God and fall away and escape judgment.

Bridge

This text underscores the importance of history. The promise of rest "today" in Psalm 95 indicates that the rest given under Joshua cannot be the final and definitive rest, for David promises that a rest still remains for God's people. Indeed the rest under Joshua figuratively anticipates the rest that will be secured under the new Joshua (Jesus). Since Jesus grants a better rest, he is superior to Joshua. Indeed, the rest Jesus gives is a Sabbath rest, which is defined as an everlasting rest, a rest that means the cessation from the toil and labor of life in this world. We have seen that the rest will be enjoyed in the city to come, the heavenly city. At the same time the rest can be

---

[207] The expression πρὸς ὃν ἡμῖν ὁ λόγος most likely means that humans must give an account to God for their lives (see Koester, *Hebrews*, 275).

described as the reward that will be granted to those who persevere to the end.

Perseverance is the author's main concern. The readers should not disobey as the wilderness generation did. They should strive to enter the rest while the opportunity still remains. The same applies to us today. The Lord is gracious and compassionate, but we should continue to trust in him and to obey him until the end. God's word is powerful in judging (and saving) those who turn against him. It penetrates to the deepest secrets of our lives. God knows who and what we are and will judge us if we depart from him.

Hebrews 4:14–16

Outline

I. Prologue: Definitive and Final Revelation in the Son (1:1–4)
II. Don't Abandon the Son Since He Is Greater than Angels (1:5–2:18)
III. Don't Harden Your Hearts Since You Have a Son and High Priest Greater than Moses and Joshua (3:1–4:13)
IV. **Don't Fall Away from Jesus' Melchizedekian Priesthood Since It Is Greater than the Levitical Priesthood (4:14–10:18)**
  A. **Exhortation in Light of Jesus' Priestly Status (4:14–5:10)**
    1. **Hold Fast Confession and Draw Near Since Jesus Is Son and High Priest (4:14–16)**
    2. Jesus Appointed by God as Perfect High Priest (5:1–10)
  B. Warning and Assurance (5:11–6:20)

Scripture

[14] Therefore, since we have a great high priest who has passed through the heavens—Jesus the Son of God—let us hold fast to the confession. [15] For we do not have a high priest who is unable to sympathize with our weaknesses, but One who has been tested in every way as we are, yet without sin. [16] Therefore let us approach the throne of grace with boldness, so that we may receive mercy and find grace to help us at the proper time.

Context

In the first two sections of the book, the author argues that Jesus is superior to the angels (1:1–2:18) and that he is superior to Moses and Joshua (3:1–4:13). In the third major section of the book (4:14–10:18), he maintains that Jesus' priesthood is better than the Levitical priesthood. Hebrews 4:14–16 introduces this section even though many acknowledge that the verses are transitional. It has often been pointed out that the content of 4:14–16 is parallel in many respects to 10:19–25.[208]

4:14–16	10:19–25
"great high priest" (v. 14)	"great high priest" (v. 21)
"who has passed through the heavens" (v. 14)	"enter the sanctuary through the blood of Jesus" (v. 19) . . . "through the curtain" (v. 20)
"let us hold fast our confession" (v. 14)	"let us hold fast on to the confession of our hope without wavering" (v. 23)
"let us approach the throne of grace with boldness" (v. 16)	"since we have boldness to enter the sanctuary" (v. 19) . . . "let us draw near with a true heart in full assurance of faith" (v. 22)

In the third section of the letter, the author comes to the heart and soul of his argument, contending that the Melchizedekian priesthood of Jesus is superior to the Levitical priesthood of Aaron (4:1–10:18), though he foreshadowed and anticipated his theme in 2:17–18 and 3:1.

We should note the common thesis that informs the first three sections of the letter, for in every instance there is a contrast between the old covenant focusing on the law and the new covenant inaugurated by Jesus. The angels were the mediators of the law given to Moses and the people (1:5–2:18). Moses instituted the Sinai covenant with Israel that contained the covenant stipulations for Israel (3:1–4:13). And the Levitical priesthood is inextricably tied to the Sinai covenant (4:14–10:18; cf. 7:11–12). We see from this that the author is making the same argument throughout the book, but that

---

[208] See the programmatic study of Wolfgang Nauck, "Zum Aufbau des Hebräerbriefes," in *Judentum-Urchristentum-Kirche: Festschrift für Joachim Jeremias*, ed. W. Eltester (Berlin: Alfred Töpelmann, 1960), 199–206.

argument is advanced from different angles or by considering various persons or institutions in the old covenant. If readers keep this in mind, they will be able to trace the main theme and not get lost in a welter of details as the author progresses. We should also remember that the superiority of Jesus over angels, over Moses and Joshua, and the superiority of his priesthood is not a theological abstraction. In other words the theology of the book serves the warning passages. Since Jesus is superior to the old covenant in all its dimensions, since the new covenant is better than the old, forsaking Jesus is fatal.

Since the three themes of Jesus' superiority (to angels, to Moses and Joshua, and to the Levitical priesthood) are closely intertwined, we are not surprised to see that the transition to the superiority of Jesus' priesthood does not represent a radical change in the author's argument. Indeed, the author has already referred to Jesus' priesthood in the preceding argument (2:17; 3:1; cf. 1:3). We are not surprised, then, that the new section begins with the word "therefore" (οὖν, 4:14). The "therefore" is probably resumptive, picking up the theme of Jesus' priesthood introduced in 2:17–3:1,[209] though it also seems to encompass all that has been said up to this point. Since Jesus is greater than the angels and Moses and since he grants a better rest than Joshua, then the readers should "hold fast to the confession" (4:14). The readers should not dispense with the one who has given them such a great salvation.

At the same time, the author begins in verse 14 to support the warning and admonition to persevere by appealing to Jesus' priesthood. Abandoning their confession would be folly, for Jesus is the Son of God. The reference to Jesus as the Son resonates with the themes of 1:1–4:13 where Jesus as the Son is superior to angels and Moses. Furthermore, Jesus is the great high priest who has entered God's presence. If the readers renounce him, they are cut off from God himself. Verse 15 explains the high priesthood of Jesus in terms of his sympathy with the human condition. He knows our weaknesses and experienced temptation in the same way we do, though he never sinned. The author draws a conclusion from Jesus' priesthood in verse 16: readers should come to God's throne boldly to receive grace and mercy in a needy time.

---

[209] Cockerill, *Hebrews*, 221; Ellingworth, *Hebrews*, 266.

Exegesis

4:14

The high priesthood of Jesus now takes center stage. Believers must hold on to their confession of the faith since Jesus as the great high priest and God's Son has passed through the heavens. The priestly ministry of Jesus (2:17; 3:1) was noted briefly earlier in the letter, but now the author begins to develop the theme in more detail,[210] although he breaks off to warn the readers in 5:11–6:20 before resuming the theme in more detail. We have already seen the priestly theme in 1:3 where Jesus accomplished cleansing for sins and sat down at God's right hand. The same idea is implicit here. Jesus "passed through the heavens." We have spatial and vertical language here, representing the notion that God is transcendent and separate from human beings, removed from us, so to speak, by the sky. But Jesus as the supreme and great high priest has traveled through the heavens.[211] He has entered the presence of God by virtue of his sacrifice. The author here anticipates a common theme, although the terminology varies. Jesus has entered the sanctuary or presence of God (6:19–20; 8:1–2; 9:11, 24; 10:20).[212] As the Son of God, who is superior to angels (1:1–2:18) and Moses (3:1–6), he has brought believers near to God so we can enjoy fellowship with him (see §8).

Given what Jesus has accomplished as the great high priest and Son of God (these two titles tie together the two sections of the letter: 4:14–10:18 and 1:1–4:13 respectively), they should not renounce their confession. The word "confession" (ὁμολογίας, cf. 3:1; 10:23) denotes the faith the readers have embraced and promised to uphold. They should hold fast to it and not let it slip away, for retaining their confession is not merely a matter of adhering to a set of doctrines about Jesus as the Son and high priest. Jesus has secured for his people access to God's presence, and the presence of God is not available by any other means. If they turn away from Jesus' priestly sacrifice and seek to find forgiveness in the sacrifices of the Levitical cult, they are sundered from God.

---

[210] The "therefore" here is resumptive (Attridge, *Hebrews*, 139).

[211] "The pastor uses the name 'Jesus' when he wants to direct our attention to the earthly life and humanity of our Lord" (Cockerill, *Hebrews*, 224n13).

[212] Cf. Attridge, *Hebrews*, 139.

4:15

The author draws attention to the nature of Jesus' high priest-hood. Even though he has entered God's presence by passing through the heavens, he can identify with human beings. Here the author picks up the emphasis on Jesus' humanity, which was rehearsed in 2:5–18, and especially in 2:17–18. Jesus is not only a majestic high priest who has entered the heavens and sits at God's right hand. He is also a tender high priest. He sympathizes "with our weaknesses." The word sympathy is not limited to compassion and empathy but also denotes Jesus' ability to help those who are afflicted (cf. Heb 10:34; 4 Macc 5:25).[213]

As a human being he knows the frailties and groaning that beset the human race. He is not a distant and aloof high priest but is himself intimately acquainted with the human condition. Indeed he experienced the full range of temptation. The delight and joys offered by sin were no stranger to Jesus. He was cognizant of and experienced the attractiveness of sin, realizing that it brought pleasure (cf. Heb 11:25). He understands every temptation we face since he experienced something similar. Nevertheless he never surrendered to sin's power. He shared in our weaknesses and frailty, but he did not—not even once—give himself over to sin. He always obeyed the will of his Father.[214] "The writer nowhere suggests that Jesus had to become identical to fallen humanity in order to redeem it. In fact, in 7:27 he denies that Jesus had to offer sacrifice 'first for his own sins, and then for the sins of the people.'"[215] As Hughes says, "What we, and they, needed was not a fellow loser but a winner; not one who shares our defeat but one who is able to lead us to victory; not a sinner but a savior."[216] The notion that Jesus was sinless is a common theme in the NT. Even where it is not stated, it is presupposed. Nonetheless, a number of texts explicitly affirm his sinlessness (Luke 23:41; John 7:18; 8:46; 14:30; 2 Cor 5:21; 1 Pet 1:19; 2:22; 3:18; 1 John 3:5). It is evident from this text that sin is

---

[213] Lane, *Hebrews 1–8*, 114; O'Brien, *Hebrews*, 182–83.

[214] The notion that Hebrews teaches that Jesus was not sinless is a historical curiosity but is hardly convincing. Against Ronald Williamson, "Hebrews 4:15 and the Sinlessness of Jesus," *ExpT* 86 (1974): 4–8. See Peterson, *Hebrews and Perfection*, 188–90.

[215] Lane, *Hebrews 1–8*, 115.

[216] Hughes, *Hebrews*, 177.

not intrinsic and inherent to human nature. Jesus was fully human in every respect, and yet he never sinned.

4:16

The "therefore" (οὖν) hearkens back to verses 14–15. Since Jesus is both a transcendent (having gone into God's presence in the heavens) and tender (sharing our frail and weak nature) high priest, believers are exhorted to draw near to God boldly to receive grace and mercy at a needy time.

The verb "approach" (προσερχώμεθα) is used often in Hebrews (7:25; 10:1, 22; 11:6; 12:18, 22). In 12:22 the recipients are told they have already "come" (προσεληλύθατε) to Mount Zion, which is the heavenly realm where Christ reigns. Here, however, believers are exhorted to approach the throne of grace.[217] The closest parallel to 4:16 is 10:22, where the readers are exhorted to "draw near with a true heart in full assurance of faith." The readers are encouraged to approach the throne of grace boldly (παρρησίας). As L. Johnson says, the word "expresses the joyful confidence with which they can approach God because of Christ."[218] Both texts emphasize the confidence and joy with which believers approach God. The word *boldness* is used in a similar text in 10:19: "Therefore, brothers, since we have boldness (παρρησίαν) to enter the sanctuary through the blood of Jesus." "Entering the sanctuary" (εἴσοδον τῶν ἁγίων) in 10:19 is equivalent to "the throne of grace" in 4:16. Jesus' priestly work in shedding his blood accounts for believers' confidence in drawing near to God's throne.

The throne is designated as one "of grace." Believers draw near to the throne boldly, for they know it is a throne of grace by virtue of Jesus' work, not a throne of wrath. Hence they confidently and gladly ask God to grant them "mercy," presumably for sins they have committed. At the same time they petition God for "grace" for the strength and power to face every situation in life.[219] God's grace is poured out as believers request help when they are overwhelmed.

---

[217] Mackie rightly emphasizes the importance of drawing near in Hebrews, highlighting the importance of experiencing God's presence. Scholars dispute whether this experience should be called mystical, but what can't be doubted is the centrality of drawing near to God in the letter. See Mackie, "Heavenly Sanctuary Mysticism," 77–117.

[218] L. Johnson, *Hebrews*, 140.

[219] Or perhaps "mercy" and "grace" here are simply synonymous.

The term for "help" here (βοήθειαν) echoes 2:18 where Jesus as high priest "is able to help" (βοηθῆσαι) those in temptation. The author emphasizes in 4:16 that help is granted when the need is greatest.

Bridge

These verses are among the most comforting in the Bible. Believers suffer from all the temptations and agonies that characterize the human condition. Does God care? Can he do anything to help if he does? We are given the answer here. We have a high priest who is fully human. He experienced the full range of temptations. No temptation was foreign to his experience. He can relate to all of our temptations. He sympathizes with our weaknesses because he experienced those weaknesses as well. We can't say that our God doesn't know what it is like to be human. He is not a transcendent deity who is far removed from us, but he also dwells among his people. His full humanity, however, did not involve failure. We would hardly be helped by one who knew what it was to be human but failed as we have. No, here is one who suffered all the pains and anguish of human life without ever yielding to sin. He knows what it is like to be tempted by sin with all its allure and charm, but he never turned to selfishness. He always did the will of the Father.

Our great high priest, Jesus, the Son of God, knows and cares what our lives are like. But he is also powerful. He has passed through the heavens. He has come into the presence of God. He is tender and transcendent. He not only cares, but he also reigns at the right hand of God. He passed through the heavens and atoned for our sins with his blood, thus solving our problem with guilt and shame. He has expunged our guilt with his blood. Therefore, we do not shrink back from God's presence. We approach him gladly and confidently, knowing that he offers mercy and grace, longing for us to know his forgiveness and his power in every circumstance of life.

Hebrews 5:1–10

Outline

I. Prologue: Definitive and Final Revelation in the Son (1:1–4)
II. Don't Abandon the Son Since He Is Greater than Angels (1:5–2:18)

III. Don't Harden Your Hearts Since You Have a Son and High
Priest Greater than Moses and Joshua (3:1–4:13)
IV. **Don't Fall Away from Jesus' Melchizedekian Priesthood
Since It Is Greater than the Levitical Priesthood
(4:14–10:18)**
  A. **Exhortation in Light of Jesus' Priestly Status
(4:14–5:10)**
    1. Hold Fast Confession and Draw Near Since Jesus Is
Son and High Priest (4:14–16)
    2. **Jesus Appointed by God as Perfect High
Priest (5:1–10)**
  B. Warning and Assurance (5:11–6:20)

Scripture

[1] For every high priest taken from men is appointed in service
to God for the people, to offer both gifts and sacrifices for sins.
[2] He is able to deal gently with those who are ignorant and are
going astray, since he is also subject to weakness. [3] Because of
this, he must make a sin offering for himself as well as for the
people. [4] No one takes this honor on himself; instead, a person is
called by God, just as Aaron was. [5] In the same way, the Messiah
did not exalt Himself to become a high priest, but the One who
said to Him, You are My Son; today I have become Your Father,
[6] also said in another passage, You are a priest forever in the order of Melchizedek. [7] During His earthly life, He offered prayers
and appeals with loud cries and tears to the One who was able to
save Him from death, and He was heard because of His reverence.
[8] Though He was God's Son, He learned obedience through what
He suffered. [9] After He was perfected, He became the source of
eternal salvation for all who obey Him, [10] and He was declared by
God a high priest in the order of Melchizedek.

Context

What is the logical relationship between 4:14–16 and 5:1–10?
The main point in 4:14–16 is that believers should hold fast their
confession and draw near to God to receive grace and mercy. In
5:1–10 we discover why believers should hold fast the confession.
They have a better high priest, one who is appointed by God and is

a Melchizedekian priest. Turning away from such a priesthood, as 5:11–6:8 explains, is disastrous.

Lane detects a chiasm in 5:1–10, which helpfully captures its structure and message. My chiasm derives from Lane, though I rephrase his description in C.[220]

A The old office of high priest (5:1)	C¹ The appointment of Christ as high priest (5:5–6)
B The solidarity of the high priest with the people (5:2–3)	B¹ The solidarity of Christ with his people (5:7–8)
C The appointment of the high priest under the old covenant (5:4)	A¹ The new office of high priest (5:9–10)

I will use the chiasm above to explain briefly the flow of the text. In the OT high priests were chosen among human beings to offer gifts and sacrifices for sins (v. 1/A). Jesus, on the other hand, is a Melchizedekian priest (vv. 9–10/A¹). Indeed, his priesthood, in contrast to OT priests, was perfect, and hence he secured "eternal salvation" for his people. Verses 2–3 convey the solidarity of the high priest with the people (B). Since the high priest is also weak and sinful, he identifies with the people and needs to offer sacrifices for his own sins as well. Jesus is also able to identify with his people as a high priest (vv. 7–8/B¹), not because he was a sinner but because of the intensity of his sufferings. He learned to obey in his suffering, and hence believers can be assured that he knows the travails of human experience. Finally, in the OT one did not choose to be a high priest (v. 4/C). Aaron was called by God to serve as a priest. Similarly, Jesus did not honor himself and decide to serve as a high priest (vv. 5–6/C¹). The author appeals to two OT texts (Pss 2:7; 110:4) to support the notion that God appointed him to be a priest like Melchizedek.

Exegesis

5:1

The author begins by explaining the conception of high priest found in the OT. High priests were selected from men and were

---

[220] See Lane, *Hebrews 1–8*, 111. Many scholars recognize a chiasm here, though the exact pattern differs (e.g., Attridge, *Hebrews*, 138). O'Brien says we shouldn't press the chiasm, even though it is present (*Hebrews*, 188).

appointed to represent human beings before God with gifts and sacrifices that atone for sins. An angel would not qualify for the office since it is restricted to human beings. High priests must be human beings since they are chosen to represent human beings before God. In other words they have the special privilege and responsibility to serve as mediators between human beings and God. The origin of the priesthood is traced to Exodus 28–29, which records the instructions for Aaron and his sons to serve as priests for Israel.

High priests carry out their office with gifts of thanksgiving and devotion that are offered up to God. We see examples of such gifts in burnt offerings (Lev 1:1–17), grain offerings (2:1–16), fellowship offerings (3:1–17), and thank offerings (Lev 7:12–13, 15; 2 Chr 29:31; Ps 50:14). High priests also offered sacrifices to atone for sins. The burnt offering also atoned for sin (Lev 1:4), as did sin offerings (Lev 4:1–35) and restitution offerings (Lev 5:1–19). Transgressions were particularly atoned for on the Day of Atonement when sins committed during the entire year were forgiven (Lev 16:1–34). The author fixes his attention on OT sacrifices and the Day of Atonement in chapters 9–10.

5:2

The solidarity of the high priest with human beings is featured here.[221] The high priest does not belong to a different class of humanity. He is able to relate and minister to those who are ignorant and led astray since he was also stained with sin. The verb "deal gently" (μετριοπαθεῖν) indicates that the priests avoided anger (at least ideally), since they themselves were sinners. The term is not precisely synonymous with "sympathize" (συμπαθῆσαι) in 4:15, for the latter has the notion of helping whereas here the focus is on the high priest's identification with the people.[222]

"Those who are ignorant" (τοῖς ἀγνοοῦσιν) probably refers to those who committed sins out of ignorance (Lev 4:2, 13; 5:18; Num 5:22–29) and those "going astray" to those wandering from the things of God. Defiant sins are not included here, for such sins are equivalent to the apostasy against which the author warns, and

---

[221] It seems unlikely that his point here is that high priests were unable to deal effectively with sin, though there is a hint that such is a problem since high priests were also sinners (against Cockerill, *Hebrews*, 234). Rather their solidarity with human beings is featured here.

[222] Rightly Attridge, *Hebrews*, 143–44.

he makes clear that there is no forgiveness for such rebellion (see Num 15:30–31; Deut 17:12–13). The high priest is able to identify with those who sin, for he himself is beset by "weakness." The word "weakness" (ἀσθένειαν) here includes the notion of sinfulness.[223] The high priest has to offer sacrifices for his own sins as well, as the next verse and 7:27 specifically indicate. The high priest, then, is able to deal gently and compassionately with sinners since he shares the same human condition as they.

5:3

It is clear from this verse that the weakness of the high priest includes his own sin. Therefore, he is required to make an offering both for his own sin and for the sin of the people. In the ordination of Aaron, atonement is secured for both Aaron as high priest and for the people: "Then Moses said to Aaron, 'Approach the altar and sacrifice your sin offering and your burnt offering; make atonement for yourself and the people'" (Lev 9:7). In Leviticus 16, on the Day of Atonement, which comes to center stage in Hebrews 9, the high priest is required to "present the bull for his sin offering and make atonement for himself and his household" (16:6; cf. also 16:11).[224] On the same day he also "slaughters the male goat for the people's sin offering" (16:15). Hebrews reflects on this annual ritual. The word used for "offering" (προσφέρω) appears 29 times in Leviticus 1–7 alone. The phrase "must make a sin offering" (προσφέρειν περὶ ἁμαρτιῶν), which is literally translated "to offer concerning sins," is rightly translated by the HCSB as designating a sin offering. The close parallels between Heb 5:3 and Lev 16:6 support this interpretation. Aaron offered a bull for a sin offering for himself (προσάξει Ααρων τὸν μόσχον τὸν περὶ τῆς ἁμαρτίας). Further, the phrases in Greek (περὶ τῆς ἁμαρτίας and περὶ ἁμαρτίας) regularly refer to the sin offering in Leviticus (Lev 4:3, 14, 28, 35; 5:6–9, 11, etc.). Hebrews, of course, uses the plural (περὶ ἁμαρτιῶν), so the parallel isn't exact, but the sacrificial context and the close parallels to Leviticus 16 suggest that the sin offering is in view. In any case the main point of the verse is clear. The high priest identifies with the people, for he transgresses just as they do and must offer sacrifices for his sin.

---

[223] Cf. Cockerill, *Hebrews*, 235.

[224] For a reference to the Day of Atonement here, see O'Brien, *Hebrews*, 192.

5:4

No one chooses to be the high priest. It isn't a democratic office in which one puts forward his name, nor is it an elected office in which people choose the high priest. The high priest is called and chosen by God, just as Aaron was chosen by him. The calling of Aaron as high priest is evident from Exod 28:1, "Have your brother Aaron, with his sons, come to you from the Israelites to serve Me as priest" (cf. 1 Chr 23:13; Ps 105:26). In NT times Herod and the Roman authorities chose the high priest, but such a political move offended Jews devoted to the OT, for they were convinced that the high priest should be in the line of Zadok, so that no human being could appoint the high priest.

5:5

Just as Aaron didn't appoint himself as high priest, neither did Jesus the Christ. He didn't seek his own glory and exalt himself to be high priest. As the Son of God, he was appointed by God as the words of Ps 2:7 attest. Hebrews doesn't pinpoint the moment when Jesus became high priest. Certainly he functioned as a high priest on earth since his once-for-all sacrifice atoned for sin. At the same time, "he did not enter into the full exercise of that office until 'he sat down at the right hand of the Majesty in heaven' (8:1; cf. 1:3)."[225]

The humility of Jesus the Christ comes to the forefront here. He didn't seek his own glory but the glory of God (cf. John 5:44; 7:18; 8:50, 54), and God exalted him and appointed him as high priest because he sought the glory of God instead of pursuing his own honor. For proof that God appointed Jesus as a high priest, the author appeals to Ps 2:7, a verse which he cited in 1:5 to support Jesus' superiority to the angels as the Son.[226] It is a bit surprising that the author turns to Ps 2:7, for the text says nothing about Jesus as a priest; it emphasizes his kingship instead. Further, as we saw in the discussion of 1:5, the verse refers to Jesus' resurrection, to his being installed at God's right hand as Lord and king over all. It seems that the author quotes Ps 2:7 because Jesus is a priest-king like Melchizedek. In other words Jesus is a particular kind of priest,

---

[225] Cockerill, *Hebrews*, 239. The discussion as to when Jesus became a priest is complicated and difficult. See Michael Kibbe, "Is It Finished? When Did It Start? Hebrews, Priesthood, and Atonement in Biblical, Systematic, and Historical Perspective," *JTS* 65 (2014): 25–61.

[226] See the commentary on 1:5 for further discussion on Ps 2:7.

a priest who also serves as a king just as Melchizedek did. The word "order" (τάξιν) could refer to an order where there is succession or simply mean that Jesus is a priest like Melchizedek.[227] The latter is probably in view here. Hence, Jesus' priestly status is proved not only by his sacrifice but also by his resurrection and his reign at the Father's right hand.

Scholars have long discussed when Jesus became the high priest.[228] The reference to Ps 2:7 could suggest that he became such at his exaltation, but the emphasis on Christ's death on earth indicates that he served as a priest during his earthly ministry. The author of Hebrews does not answer precisely when Jesus' priestly ministry began. Hebrews focuses on Jesus' death and exaltation as high priest. Perhaps we could say that Jesus' obedience and ministry were crucial for his priestly sacrifice, but we must admit that the author doesn't specify when Jesus' priesthood was inaugurated, though the emphasis on his death indicates that we can't restrict his priesthood to the time of his exaltation. It is certainly the case that Jesus, on his exaltation, was installed as the heavenly high priest.

5:6

Jesus' appointment as high priest is confirmed by Ps 110:4, where David prophesies that the one who is his Lord (Ps 110:1) is also a priest forever according to the order of Melchizedek. Here we have the first mention of Melchizedek in the letter. Melchizedek first appears in the biblical story in Gen 14:18–20 where Abraham gives him a tenth of the spoils won in battle and Melchizedek blesses him.[229] Melchizedek then vanishes from the scene until his name suddenly appears in Ps 110:4. In fact, this is the only other text in the OT that mentions this mysterious and puzzling character.

When we consider the context of Psalm 110, it is clear that David prophesies about the coming of a future king, for he will sit at God's right hand ruling and reigning (Ps 110:1). He will "rule" with his "scepter" over his enemies (Ps 110:2). He will crush and destroy his enemies (Ps 110:5–7). The king is certainly a Davidic king, fulfilling the promise of a future Davidic ruler (cf. e.g., Psalms 89, 132). Psalm 110:4, however, adds another dimension. The future ruler is

---

[227] See L. Johnson, *Hebrews*, 144–45; Koester, *Hebrews*, 287.

[228] See the helpful discussion in Peterson, *Hebrews and Perfection*, 191–95.

[229] Technically, of course, his name was still "Abram," but for ease of reference, I will identify him as Abraham throughout the commentary.

not only a king, but he is also a priest, and yet he is not a priest in the line of Aaron. His priesthood stems from an entirely different order, for he is a Melchizedekian priest. The word "order" doesn't signify a line of succession as if there were many Melchizedekian priests; it refers to the nature of Jesus' priesthood.[230]

Hebrews, of course, sees in Jesus the fulfillment of these prophecies. He is the Messiah, the son of David, who sits at God's right hand by virtue of his resurrection. Indeed we saw that in the previous verse Ps 2:7 is cited to support the notion that Jesus is the risen and exalted King. The citation of Ps 110:4 indicates that he is more than a king. He is a king-priest. Jesus is a Melchizedekian priest. Indeed, there is also an indication here of the resurrection of Jesus Christ, for he serves as a priest "forever." In any case the main point of the verse is that God appointed him as a Melchizedekian priest. Jesus did not take that honor upon himself.

5:7

Just as the high priest could identify with human beings, so too could Jesus. Even though he was without sin, he knew the anguish of human experience. He pleaded with God to deliver him from death, and God answered his prayers because of his piety.

The phrase "during his earthly life" reads literally "in the days of his flesh" (ESV). The word "flesh" ($\sigma\alpha\rho\kappa\acute{o}\varsigma$) denotes the frailty and weakness characterizing life on earth. As one who was fully human, Jesus shared with other human beings "flesh and blood" (2:14) and was plagued with the sorrows and heartache of human existence. He "offered up prayers and petitions" (NIV) during his life on earth, for he, like any other human being, was completely dependent on God. He looked to God to meet his needs and to answer his pleas, praying "with loud cries and tears." The intensity of grief and sorrow described here recalls Jesus' experience in the garden of Gethsemane (Matt 26:36–45 par.). Indeed, some interpreters maintain that Hebrews refers specifically to Gethsemane since it matches so well the reference to "loud cries and tears."[231] Such a reading is certainly possible, and no doubt Gethsemane is included within the

---

[230] Cf. Ellingworth, *Hebrews*, 283.

[231] Cf. Bruce, *Hebrews*, 98–100 (though Bruce thinks what is said applies more widely as well); Hughes, *Hebrews*, 182; O'Brien, *Hebrews*, 198.

author's purview.[232] Still the text speaks of "the days of his flesh" (ESV). The plural "days" shouldn't be limited to just one experience and one day. Certainly the author isn't saying that Jesus' life was restricted to crying and tears. But he is suggesting that sorrow and tears were a regular experience for him. As Cockerill says, "It is better to see this entire verse as a depiction of the utter dependence upon God that characterized the Son's earthly life and came to its climax in Gethsamene and on the cross."[233] The readers were experiencing suffering and persecution, but Jesus knew suffering as well. They weren't encountering anything that was foreign to his own time on earth.

We can see also why some see a reference to Gethsemane since he prayed "to the One who was able to save Him from death."[234] Certainly such an experience could fit Jesus' prayer in the garden, though there his prayer to be rescued from death was not heard.[235] It seems more likely that the author describes a regular feature of Jesus' prayer during his earthly ministry, so we can't isolate what is said to any particular event in his life. According to the Gospel accounts, he often predicted his death (e.g., Mark 8:31; 9:31; 10:32–34), and hence it makes sense that he would also ask God to deliver him from the death that was coming.

Jesus' prayers for deliverance from death were answered: "He was heard because of His reverence." The word for "reverence" is only found in Hebrews in the NT (cf. also 12:28) and occurs only twice in the OT (Josh 22:24; Prov 28:14; cf. Wis 17:8). Some think the word means that Jesus was rescued from his "anxiety," but the use of the same word in 12:28 suggests the meaning "reverence" or "awe,"[236] which is also translated as "devotion" (NET) or "reverent

---

[232] Richardson argues that the reference is to Jesus' sufferings on the cross, but the general nature of the description suggests that it can't be limited to Calvary (*Pioneer and Perfecter of Faith*, 74–89).

[233] Cockerill, *Hebrews*, 244.

[234] The word "offered" (προσενέγκας) in relation to prayers should not be understood technically, even though it is used elsewhere for offering sacrifices (cf. 5:1, 3). The word can also be used metaphorically to denote something presented to God (rightly Attridge, *Hebrews*, 149; Peterson, *Hebrews and Perfection*, 84; against Lane, *Hebrews 1–8*, 119).

[235] Against Swetnam, Jesus does not ask to die here ("The Crux at Hebrews 5:7–8," *Bib* 81 [2000]: 347–61).

[236] See BDAG; LN 53.7; Ellingworth, *Hebrews*, 290.

submission" (NIV, NRSV). The meaning "anxiety" should be rejected since it is not well attested. God answered Jesus' prayers because of his fear of God, because he had given his life completely into God's hands. But how did God answer his prayer to be delivered from death?[237] Certainly not by sparing him from death, for he endured the cruelty of death by crucifixion. His prayer was answered at the resurrection by deliverance from the realm of the dead, for when God raised him from the dead, he was rescued from death once for all (see §2.6).[238] The reference to the resurrection fits well with 5:5–6, which alludes to Jesus' resurrection and ascension. The resurrection shows that Jesus is a priest "forever," and at the resurrection he was begotten by God, i.e., he was appointed to rule at God's right hand.

5:8

Even as God's Son, Jesus learned obedience through his sufferings. The sonship of Jesus is a major theme in Hebrews. In chapter 1 Jesus is superior to angels because he is the Son of God. Jesus' sonship denotes his unique relationship with God and his kingly authority. But even though he is specially related to God, he learned obedience in his sufferings. The word "learned" ($\xi\mu\alpha\theta\varepsilon\nu$) suggests a process. There is no suggestion that Jesus ever disobeyed (cf. 4:15; 7:26), as if he had to learn to obey because he disobeyed previously. As Koester says, "To say that Jesus 'learned obedience' does not mean that he was formerly disobedient any more than saying that he 'became a merciful and faithful high priest' means that he was formerly callous or faithless."[239] The verse, however, emphasizes Jesus' humanity (see §2.2). He learned how to obey in the anvil of human experience, as he experienced life day by day. In particular he learned obedience in his sufferings. When suffering strikes, human beings are inclined to do whatever it takes to avoid it, to find another path where there is joy and refreshment. Jesus, however, learned

---

[237] The content of the prayer, as the context shows, is deliverance from death. Hence, Attridge rightly rejects the idea that Jesus prayed for other people, for his own perseverance under trial, or for triumph over the devil (*Hebrews*, 150).

[238] So Koester, *Hebrews*, 288–89; Lane, *Hebrews 1–8*, 120; Hughes, *Hebrews*, 184.

[239] Koester, *Hebrews*, 295. He says elsewhere, "Although Jesus was never disobedient to God, he could not demonstrate obedience until he was placed in situations where the will of God was challenged and obedience was required" (299).

how to trust God and do his will in the midst of his suffering. His first aim was not his own pleasure and comfort but the will of God.

5:9

Jesus was perfected by his sufferings and thereby became the source of salvation for those who submit to him (see §2.5).[240] The phrase "after He was perfected" (τελειωθείς) is closely related to Jesus' obedience in verse 8, for he was perfected through his suffering and obedience. The word "perfected" is also used in 2:10 where we read that Jesus was made "perfect (τελειῶσαι) through sufferings." After speaking of Jesus' offering himself in death, 7:28 declares that Jesus as the Son "has been perfected (τετελειωμένον) forever." Conversely, "the law perfected (ἐτελείωσεν) nothing" (7:19). The "gifts and sacrifices" of the old covenant "cannot perfect (τελειῶσαι) the worshiper's conscience" (9:9; cf. also 10:1). The perfection of Jesus in Hebrews is tied to his sufferings and death, his obedience, and his exaltation.

Jesus was perfected in his experience by learning obedience in his sufferings. His perfection was an abstraction until he obeyed God in the concrete realities and travails of everyday human experience. His sufferings and death equipped and qualified him to serve as a priest.[241] He learned what it was to please God as a child, a teenager, and an adult. Hebrews does not teach the recapitulation theology found in Irenaeus, and yet Irenaeus's conception is fundamentally right. Jesus' perfecting and obedience had to be worked out in everyday life and at every stage of his life. He wasn't qualified to serve as priest as a young boy or teenager. It is certainly fitting to see an eschatological dimension to Jesus' perfection as well. He fulfilled what God intended for human beings in his suffering and is now crowned as God's king-priest. In his testing and obedience, Jesus exemplified what God intended when he created human beings. Jesus' suffering was not merely moral. It is also vocational, fitting him for his role as high priest.[242]

Jesus' suffering has a representative and saving character. Those who "obey him" (ὑπακούουσιν αὐτῷ) will experience salvation.

---

[240] "'Having been perfected' describes the result of the Son's obedience in vv. 7–8 as the cause of his becoming 'the Source of eternal salvation' in v. 9" (Cockerill, *Hebrews*, 248).

[241] Lane, *Hebrews 1–8*, 122; O'Brien, *Hebrews*, 202.

[242] Cf. Attridge, *Hebrews*, 153.

According to Hebrews there is no salvation apart from obedience. The wilderness generation perished (3:18) because of their disobedience (ἀπειθήσασιν). They did not enter Canaan "because of [their] disobedience" (ἀπείθειαν, 4:6; cf. 4:11). We saw in 3:12–4:11 that faith and obedience are inseparable, even though they are distinguishable, for the author often emphasizes that Israel failed to enter the rest because of their unbelief (3:12, 19; 4:2–3). The relationship between faith and obedience is captured well by 11:8, "By faith Abraham, when he was called, obeyed and went out to a place he was going to receive as an inheritance." Because Abraham trusted in God, he obeyed him.

Only those who obey Jesus will experience eternal salvation. They will experience eschatological salvation because Jesus is "the source" (αἴτιος) of such salvation. As the one who suffered and was perfected, he grants salvation to those who follow him (see §9). The term "source" here is akin to a different word for "source" (ἀρχηγός, 2:10; 12:2) used elsewhere in Hebrews.[243] Jesus as the Davidic king and as the high priest grants salvation to his brothers and sisters who belong to him (2:5–18). Since he is their brother and king and priest, his obedience becomes their obedience, his perfection is granted to them. Hence, those who belong to Jesus are not merely saved from earthly harm. They are rescued from the punishment that will be meted out on the wicked eschatologically.

5:10

Jesus was the source of eternal salvation (v. 9) because he was made perfect by his obedience (vv. 8–9) and because he was designated as a priest after the order of Melchizedek (v. 10). Here the author takes up what he introduced in verse 6, identifying Jesus as a Melchizedekian priest. Fitting with the theme of the paragraph, God declared and named Jesus as a Melchizedekian priest. Jesus did not assume the office himself; it was bestowed upon him by God. It was a responsibility and calling granted to him. The salvation of the readers is founded on Jesus' priesthood. The author explains in detail how Jesus' Melchizedekian priesthood accomplishes salvation for the readers in 7:1–10:18. Actually, it was his desire to explain the nature of Jesus' priesthood in 5:11, but he pauses to warn the readers since he is concerned about their spiritual state, which

---

[243] Attridge, *Hebrews*, 154.

makes it difficult for him to expound upon the significance of Jesus' priesthood for their lives.

Bridge

The author contrasts the old and new priesthood in these verses. We and the readers live under the new priesthood, the Melchizedekian priesthood of Jesus Christ. And the new is far better than the old, for Jesus bestows eternal salvation since he reigns at God's right hand and serves as a priest forever. God appointed Jesus as a Melchizedekian priest, and the appointment was fitting, for Jesus in his suffering and anguish obeyed God. He wasn't spared from the misery that besets humanity. His suffering extended to his death. We have a high priest who identifies with us, but more importantly, we have a high priest who is able to save and deliver us.

Hebrews 5:11–14

Outline

  I. Prologue: Definitive and Final Revelation in the Son (1:1–4)
  II. Don't Abandon the Son Since He Is Greater than Angels (1:5–2:18)
  III. Don't Harden Your Hearts Since You Have a Son and High Priest Greater than Moses and Joshua (3:1–4:13)
  IV. **Don't Fall Away from Jesus' Melchizedekian Priesthood Since It Is Greater than the Levitical Priesthood (4:14–10:18)**
    A. Exhortation in Light of Jesus' Priestly Status (4:14–5:10)
    B. **Warning and Assurance (5:11–6:20)**
      1. **Warning Against Falling Away from Jesus the High Priest (5:11–6:8)**
        a. **High Priesthood Hard to Explain Because of Readers' Sluggishness (5:11–14)**
        b. Call to Maturity (6:1–3)
        c. Those Who Fall Away Can't Be Renewed to Repentance (6:4–8)
      2. Assurance and Comfort (6:9–20)

Scripture

> [11] We have a great deal to say about this, and it's difficult to explain, since you have become too lazy to understand. [12] Although by this time you ought to be teachers, you need someone to teach you the basic principles of God's revelation again. You need milk, not solid food. [13] Now everyone who lives on milk is inexperienced with the message about righteousness, because he is an infant. [14] But solid food is for the mature—for those whose senses have been trained to distinguish between good and evil.

Context

The author has embarked on explaining the greatness of Jesus' priesthood. It is a superior priesthood, for Jesus has been appointed by God as a Melchizedekian priest, not as a priest after the order of Aaron. Jesus as high priest has accomplished eternal salvation for his people. But the author interrupts the flow of argument here to warn and assure his readers (5:11–6:20). "He uses the exhortation of 5:11–6:12 to arouse and encourage them to enthusiastically embrace his teaching on this subject before he expounds Ps 110:4 (6:20) and explains the nature of the Son's high-priestly ministry."[244] Indeed, he doesn't take up again the theme of the Melchizedekian priesthood until chapter 7. The readers are warned in the most sobering terms about the danger of falling away (5:11–6:8). Cockerill rightly splits up the argument into the following sections: the author shames the readers (5:11–6:3), warns them (6:4–8), encourages them (6:9–12), and then assures them (6:13–20).[245] Hebrews 6:9–12 is transitional, for the readers are consoled but are at the same time exhorted to persevere until the end. The section closes (6:13–20) with the assurance of God's promises for those who take refuge in Jesus.

In 5:11–14 the author indicates that his desire is to speak more about Jesus' priesthood, but he is unable to do so because of the readers' spiritual sluggishness. Incidentally, the word "sluggish" (νωθροί, NET) frames this section, appearing in both 5:11 and 6:12. The readers *are*, so to speak "sluggish" (5:11), and he writes so they won't *be* "sluggish" (6:12). The recipients of the letter should be teachers, and yet they need to be instructed all over again with

---

[244] Cockerill, *Hebrews*, 220.
[245] Ibid., 252.

elementary teachings. They are like infants who can only handle milk and can't digest solid food. Those who are mature can digest solid food, and maturity belongs to those who are able to distinguish between good and evil.

Exegesis

5:11

The author's desire is to explain in more detail the significance of Jesus' Melchizedekian priesthood, "but it is hard to make it clear to you because you no longer try to understand" (NIV).[246] The author will, in fact, expand upon the Melchizedekian priesthood of Jesus in chapter 7, but he pauses to note the difficulty he is encountering. The problem isn't the readers' lack of intelligence, nor is it even the case that the subject is intellectually stretching. The entire problem lies in the spiritual inclination, or better disinclination, of the readers. They are "sluggish" (νωθροί, NET) or "dull" (ESV) or "lazy" (HCSB) and lethargic in their hearing. As mentioned above, the word "sluggish" (νωθροί) frames this section, concluding it in 6:12. The author writes hyperbolically and rhetorically. The readers are verging toward lethargy, and hence he warns them against it so they won't be lethargic (6:12).[247] The readers won't understand the truth if they don't want to understand it, and so the fundamental issue facing the readers isn't intellectual but moral.

5:12

The readers have had adequate time to become teachers, but now they need to be taught the fundamental and elementary truths of God's revelation all over again. They are unable to eat solid food and can only digest milk.

The readers should have grown sufficiently to be able to instruct others in the truths of God's oracles. God's oracles "probably means the Scriptures interpreted in the light of the death and exaltation of

---

[246] The antecedent of the pronoun "this" (οὗ) is Christ's Melchizedekian priesthood noted in the previous verses and not a particular word, such as Melchizedek, Christ, or high priest (so Attridge, *Hebrews*, 156). L. Johnson sees a reference to Christ here (*Hebrews*, 154).

[247] Attridge, *Hebrews*, 157–58. Cf. Lane, who says the language is ironic (*Hebrews 1–8*, 135–39). It seems better to describe it as hyperbolic. For another view, see Ellingworth, *Hebrews*, 298.

Jesus."[248] When he says that they should be "teachers" (διδάσκαλοι), he does not use the word "teachers" in its technical sense, as if they should all be teachers able to instruct the congregation publicly. He doesn't expect every member of the congregation to be a pastor or elder. What he means is that every member should be able to explain the elementary and basic elements of God's word to others.[249] The context here clarifies that it is the fundamental truths of God's revelation that they should know and be able to communicate. In that sense they should be able to teach others.

But instead of being able to teach the fundamentals of the Christian faith to others, they need to relearn what they were taught at the beginning. They need to learn the "elementary truths of God's word" (NIV; τὰ στοιχεῖα τῆς ἀρχῆς τῶν λογίων τοῦ θεου). The word "principles" (στοιχεῖα) refers to the elements that make up something. For instance, in Greek philosophy the word often is used to discuss the "elements" from which the world is made: earth, air, fire, and water.[250] The word may also denote the elementary or fundamental principles or rules of life (Plato, *Leg.* 7.790C; Xenophon, *Mem.* 2.1.1; Plutarch, *Lib. Ed.* 16.2).[251] It clearly has the latter meaning here, and in context the elementary principles are those found in God's "oracles" (τῶν λογίων, ESV). The principles they need to learn are "basic" (τῆς ἀρχῆς) or "elementary" (NIV). As Christians we need to review the basics of our faith, but in this case the readers are indicted for needing to be taught when they should be teachers. They need to relearn all over again the basic teachings of the Christian faith, which are derived from the Scriptures.

The author uses milk and solid food to illustrate his point. Infants can only digest milk and are unable to handle solid food. The readers are like spiritual infants in that they are only able to digest spiritual milk, not solid food. What does the author have in

---

[248] O'Brien, *Hebrews*, 207.

[249] Rightly Attridge, *Hebrews*, 158; L. Johnson, *Hebrews*, 155; Hughes, *Hebrews*, 190.

[250] Plato, *Timaeus* 48B; Diogenes Laertius 7.134–135; 4 Macc 12:13; Philo, *Dec.* 31; *Op. Mund.* 146; 2 Pet 3:10, 12. See Dietrich Rusam, "Neue Belege zu dem τὰ στοιχεῖα τοῦ κόσμου (Gal 4,3.9; Kol 2,8.20)," *ZNW* 83 (1992): 119–25; Josef Blinzer, "Lexikalisches zu dem Terminus τὰ στοιχεῖα τοῦ κόσμου bei Paulus," in *Studiorum Paulinorum Congressus Internationalis Catholicus*, 2 vols., AnBib 17–18 (Rome: Pontifical Biblical Institute, 1961), 2:429–43.

[251] Blinzer, "τὰ στοιχεῖα τοῦ κόσμου," 430–31.

mind by spiritual milk? Are we able to identify the basic teachings he has in mind? The most satisfactory answer is that the list found in 6:1–2 represents the elementary teachings with which they should already be familiar.

5:13

In verses 13–14 a contrast is drawn between those who live on milk and solid food. Those whose diet is milk remain unacquainted with the message of righteousness.[252] They are still spiritual infants. Those who live on milk are spiritually immature and are "not acquainted with the teaching about righteousness" (NIV).[253] The author doesn't mean that they have never been taught what it means to live righteously, as if they were ignorant of God's standards. The point is that they haven't put into practice what they were taught. They haven't lived righteously to the extent they should as believers in Jesus Christ. They are living as if they are still spiritual infants, when they should have progressed beyond that stage.

The text could easily be misread. The author does not believe there is a permanent state of spiritual infancy that believers can occupy. The entire purpose of the book is to warn believers about the danger of falling away. Indeed, this text segues into one of the strongest warning passages in the whole of the NT. What worries the writer about the spiritual infancy of the readers is the danger of slipping into apostasy. He doesn't contemplate the possibility of drinking spiritual milk for years and years and still obtaining eternal life. It is urgent, rather, to leave spiritual infancy behind, for one is either drawing nearer to God or falling away from him. Their spiritual slackness is a matter of greatest concern to the author.

5:14

If milk is for infants, then solid food is for those who are mature. Milk designates the items mentioned in 6:1–2, and solid food

---

[252] For the view that the referent is the Christian message generally, see Peterson, *Hebrews and Perfection*, 181–82. Ellingworth thinks he refers to Christian ethics informed by a Christian worldview (*Hebrews*, 307).

[253] Against Westcott (*Hebrews*, 138) and Hughes (*Hebrews*, 191), there is no reference to Christ being our righteousness here (rightly O'Brien, *Hebrews*, 208–9; Cockerill, *Hebrews*, 259n23). Cockerill says, "It is the revelation of Christ's high priesthood as the means by which the pastor's hearers will be able to follow the 'righteous' (10:38; 11:4, 7) of ch. 11 and thus persevere in faithfulness" (258).

has to do with the teaching about Christ's Melchizedekian priest-hood.[254] Those who are mature have their faculties trained to discern good from evil. In the illustration those who eat solid food are those who are spiritually mature. They have no need to relearn basic and elementary teachings, and hence they are able to instruct others in spiritual truths. "There is no contradiction between the pastor's statement that his hearers have come to 'need milk' and his insistence on feeding them 'solid food.' One weans infants by feeding them adult fare."[255]

The translation "because of their maturity" (διὰ τὴν ἕξιν) captures the meaning of the phrase used here. The word "maturity" (ἕξις) is often translated as "habit" or "custom."[256] We see this interpretation in the ESV "by constant practice," NET "by practice," and the NIV "by constant use." But the word often refers to that which is grown up and mature (e.g., Judg 14:9; 1 Sam 16:7; Sir 30:14; Dan 1:15), referring to the state of a person because of their training.[257] The HCSB supports this interpretation, for it omits any idea of regular use or habit in its translation.

The writer's purpose is to emphasize the capacity of those who are mature to discern between good and evil. Those who are mature and able to discern what is good and evil perceive that returning to the Levitical cult isn't the pathway of righteousness. They understand that such a move is actually deleterious, even if on first glance it seemed to be helpful. The idea here is similar to what we find in Proverbs. Those who seek wisdom will understand the fear of the Lord (Prov 2:1–5). They "will understand righteousness, justice, and integrity" (Prov 2:9). They will be able to determine what is righteous because "wisdom will enter your mind, and knowledge will delight your heart" (Prov 2:10). In other words wisdom will become a constituent part of their personality. It will inhabit and dwell in them so that they are able to distinguish good from evil. So too here, those who are spiritually mature, those who have eaten solid food, will choose what is good rather than evil. Their "tastes" and desires will incline them to what is good, just as wisdom brings delight to those who pursue it.

---

[254] Ellingworth, *Hebrews*, 304; Cockerill, *Hebrews*, 259.

[255] Cockerill, *Hebrews*, 260.

[256] See Thayer; LN 42.10.

[257] Ellingworth, *Hebrews*, 309; O'Brien, *Hebrews*, 210.

Bridge

Spiritual maturity, the author teaches, doesn't depend fundamentally on intellectual ability. It isn't correlated with theological depth or the ability to grasp theological truths. The readers were spiritual infants because they weren't putting into practice what they had learned. They needed to be instructed in the fundamentals of the faith because they hadn't progressed on to spiritual maturity. There is no idea here that we can be confident of the salvation of those who remain "spiritual infants" for years and years. The readers, because of their infancy, are slipping toward apostasy. Those who are spiritual infants can't remain where they are. They will either go forward or fall away and be destroyed forever. Hence the warning that follows is urgent since death and life are at stake.

Hebrews 6:1–3

Outline

I. Prologue: Definitive and Final Revelation in the Son (1:1–4)
II. Don't Abandon the Son Since He Is Greater than Angels (1:5–2:18)
III. Don't Harden Your Hearts Since You Have a Son and High Priest Greater than Moses and Joshua (3:1–4:13)
IV. **Don't Fall Away from Jesus' Melchizedekian Priesthood Since It Is Greater than the Levitical Priesthood (4:14–10:18)**
   A. Exhortation in Light of Jesus' Priestly Status (4:14–5:10)
   B. **Warning and Assurance (5:11–6:20)**
      1. **Warning Against Falling Away from Jesus the High Priest (5:11–6:8)**
         a. Priesthood Hard to Explain Because of Readers' Sluggishness (5:11–14)
         b. **Call to Maturity (6:1–3)**
         c. Those Who Fall Away Can't Be Renewed to Repentance (6:4–8)
      2. Assurance and Comfort (6:9–20)

Scripture

> [1] Therefore, leaving the elementary message about the Messiah, let us go on to maturity, not laying again the foundation of repentance from dead works, faith in God, [2] teaching about ritual washings, laying on of hands, the resurrection of the dead, and eternal judgment. [3] And we will do this if God permits.

Context

The author continues to shame the readers, so these verses belong with the previous section conceptually. The readers must not remain in spiritual infancy. They must progress to maturity and understand the significance of Jesus' Melchizedekian priesthood and apply it to their lives. Progressing onto maturity should not be understood as the goal of elite Christians who are particularly godly. All believers must pursue maturity to avoid apostasy. In verses 1–2 the author indicates the foundational teachings that are assumed but beyond which they should progress. The first pair relates to the inception of the Christian life: teaching about dead works and faith in God. The last pair refers to the final day: the last judgment and the resurrection. The middle two items are particularly difficult. Perhaps they relate to the inception of the Christian life as well with teaching about baptisms and the laying on of hands (by which the Spirit was often given). In any case the author realizes that the readers will only progress if God permits. Human beings are responsible for spiritual growth, but such growth ultimately comes from God himself.

Exegesis

6:1

The readers should go on to maturity and not focus on the foundational elements of their faith, such as the need to repent and trust in God at conversion. The word "therefore" ($\delta\iota\acute{o}$) links the text with the previous paragraph. In 5:11–14 the writer lamented the spiritual immaturity and infantile state of his readers. He draws a conclusion from the previous discussion here, exhorting them to go on to maturity. The call to progress on to maturity ($\tau\epsilon\lambda\epsilon\iota\acute{o}\tau\eta\tau\alpha$) is another way of saying they should hold fast their confession (4:16). The readers cannot and must not remain in their infantile state. They will either go forward to maturity or fall into apostasy (6:4–8). What it means to mature is to leave behind "the elementary teachings about Christ"

(NIV; τὸν τῆς ἀρχῆς τοῦ Χριστοῦ λόγον). The phrase hearkens back to 5:12: "the basic principles of the oracles of God" (ESV; τὰ στοιχεῖα τῆς ἀρχῆς τῶν λογίων τοῦ θεου), which confirms the notion that the basic principles have to do with a Christian understanding of the OT.

The word "leaving" does not mean abandoning the fundamental teachings about Christ.[258] The context helps us understand what is intended. They should get beyond the place where the foundational teachings are rehearsed over and over (cf. 5:11–14). They should never leave the foundational teachings behind, precisely because they are fundamental. On the other hand, such teachings should be the basis and platform for further growth.

The author divides the foundational teachings into three pairs. A number of interpretations of the pairs have been proposed.[259] Some have suggested that the teachings are not even Christian but are fundamentally Jewish since nothing about Christ is included and all the matters mentioned are found in the OT.[260] Such a reading is certainly possible, but it seems doubtful, for the readers should see Christ as the fulfillment of the OT and must not revert to the OT cult. Indeed, the writer specifically says the elementary teachings are about Jesus Christ. It seems, then, that the list here pertains to the revelation mediated through Jesus Christ.

The first pair is "not laying again a foundation of repentance from dead works and of faith toward God." As noted above, the author is not minimizing the importance of repentance and faith. He objects to reiterating the same things repeatedly, to going over again the same basic teachings without any indication that the readers are grasping it. The first pair pertains to the inception of the Christian life, consisting of repentance and faith. The meaning of the phrase "repentance from dead works" (μετανοίας ἀπὸ νεκρῶν ἔργων) is captured nicely by the NIV: "repentance from acts that lead to death."[261] The works are dead in the sense that they result in death, which is

---

[258] The teachings about Christ don't refer to Christ's teaching in the Gospels or oral tradition about Christ handed down. The author refers to basic Christian teachings (so Cockerill, *Hebrews*, 261).

[259] For the structure adopted here, see ibid., 263–64. For a concise survey, see Ellingworth, *Hebrews*, 310.

[260] Hagner suggests that the readers may have emphasized what they held in common with Judaism to avoid estrangement from their Jewish roots (*Hebrews*, 67).

[261] So also Ellingworth, *Hebrews*, 314.

both physical and spiritual (i.e., separation from God; see §2.4).[262] When one becomes a believer, one turns away from such evil works and gives himself to God. Repentance and faith are two sides of the same coin. They are distinguishable but inseparable. Salvation is given to those who put their faith in God, trusting in him to deliver them on the day of wrath. We have here a staple of the NT message. The evangelistic preaching in Acts calls unbelievers to repent and believe (e.g., Acts 2:38; 3:19; 5:31; 8:12; 10:43; 11:18, 21; 13:39; 15:7; 16:31; 17:30; 19:4; 20:21; 26:20; cf. Mark 1:14–15). The centrality of repentance (cf. Rom 2:4; 1 Thess 1:10; 2 Tim 2:25) and faith (cf. Rom 3:22, 28; 4:24; 9:33; 10:9; 1 Cor 15:2; Gal 2:16; Phil 3:9) is also prominent in the Pauline letters. Hebrews reflects here a fundamental and shared teaching among early Christians.

6:2

The last two pairs of elementary teachings about Christ are stated here: teachings about washings and laying on of hands, and instruction about the resurrection and the final judgment. The first pair is particularly difficult to decipher. The word translated "ritual washings" (βαπτισμῶν) could refer to the cleansing rites required in the OT. We also know that such washings were practiced regularly in Judaism and in the Qumran community. Mark 7:4 notes that the Pharisees washed "cups, pitchers, and kettles." A related text in John 3:25 records a dispute John's disciple had with a Jewish person over purification. Later in the letter, when speaking of the OT cult, the author mentions the requirement of "various washings" (9:10). The importance of washing for cleansing is hard to overestimate in Jewish circles. It is also possible that the washing in view relates particularly to baptism. Both John and the early Christians baptized their disciples, as is well known. We don't know the exact date, but proselyte baptism came also to be practiced in Judaism. The plural for washings here probably indicates that the readers were instructed on how Christian baptism was distinct from the cleansing common in Jewish circles (cf. 9:10).[263]

Hands were laid on people in the OT for blessing (Gen 48:14), on sacrificial animals who atoned for sin (Exod 29:10, 15, 19; Lev

---

[262] There is no polemic against Jewish legalism here (against Hughes, *Hebrews*, 197).

[263] So Koester, *Hebrews*, 305; Hughes, *Hebrews*, 199–202; Lane, *Hebrews 1–8*, 140.

4:15; 8:14, 18, 22; 16:21; Num 8:12), to commission someone for service (Num 27:23; Deut 34:9; Num 8:10), or on one about to suffer the death penalty (Lev 24:14). In the NT the laying on of hands was for blessing (Matt 19:13, 15; Mark 10:16), healing (Mark 5:23; 6:5; 8:23, 25; Luke 4:40; 13:13; Acts 9:12; Acts 28:8), to commission people for service (Acts 6:6; 13:3; 1 Tim 5:22), for receiving the Holy Spirit (Acts 8:17–19; 9:17; 19:6), and for receiving spiritual gifts (1 Tim 4:14; 2 Tim 1:6), although this last one may fit with commissioning someone for ministry. The sheer diversity of matters associated with laying on of hands makes it difficult to determine what the author had in mind. If the washings refer to baptism, which seems likely, then the laying on of hands would perhaps refer to the idea of receiving the Spirit, for then the pair would both refer to what occurs at the inception of the Christian life.[264] If that is the case, then this pair would also be closely related to repentance and faith.

The last pair clearly belongs together, looking forward to the final day of salvation and judgment. The "resurrection of the dead" refers to the physical resurrection that will occur on the last day. The future physical resurrection is an essential element in Christian preaching (e.g., Acts 4:2; 17:18; 23:6; 24:22; Rom 8:11; 1 Cor 6:14; 15:12–19; 2 Cor 4:14; Phil 3:11; Heb 11:35). "Eternal judgment" refers to the final judgment on the last day. The word "eternal" signifies that the judgment is definitive. There will be no second chance (Heb 9:27). Again, a final judgment is a widely shared Christian teaching (e.g., Acts 24:25; Rom 2:2–3; 1 Pet 4:17; 2 Pet 2:3; Jude 4; Rev 20:11–15). Both of these teachings are fundamental to Christian proclamation, so we have further evidence that the writer is not relegating these issues to secondary matters. Instead, the readers should now be at the point where such teachings do not have to be elaborated and defended to them. Such teachings should be part of the stable foundation of their faith.

6:3

The author will proceed to build on the foundation that has been laid "if God permits." As Hughes says, we don't just have a "pious cliché" here.[265] On the one hand, the readers are held responsible

---

[264] Cf. Koester, *Hebrews*, 305.
[265] Hughes, *Hebrews*, 206.

for their spiritual infancy and immaturity. They should be able to grasp what is being taught. They are only drinking milk and need to hear the elementary truths of the faith repeatedly because of their own dullness and spiritual sluggishness. At the same time the writer acknowledges that a spiritual breakthrough will only come "if God permits." Spiritual maturity is given by God and is a result of his gracious work in the lives of his people. It is imperative to see that these two themes are complementary. The Scriptures regularly teach that human beings are responsible for their actions and that God is sovereign over all that occurs (e.g., Gen 45:5, 7–8; 50:20; Isa 10:5–34; Acts 2:23; 4:27–28). Here the writer acknowledges that progress will only be made if God allows it. True spiritual understanding is always a miracle.

Bridge

Christians never leave or abandon the elementary teachings of the faith. They are, as Hebrews says, foundational and fundamental. On the other hand, something is radically wrong if the same teachings need to be defended and explicated repeatedly. The fundamental teachings should become the platform for further growth and understanding. We are responsible for our spiritual growth and understanding. We should progress in the faith and in maturity. At the same time the author acknowledges that growth only comes "if God permits." Finally and ultimately, we are not in control of our destiny. Spiritual maturity is a gift of God. This truth does not cancel out human responsibility and the authenticity of our choices, but it does remind us that God rules over all things and that any growth in holiness results from his grace.

Hebrews 6:4–8

Outline

I. Prologue: Definitive and Final Revelation in the Son (1:1–4)
II. Don't Abandon the Son Since He Is Greater than Angels (1:5–2:18)
III. Don't Harden Your Hearts Since You Have a Son and High Priest Greater than Moses and Joshua (3:1–4:13)

IV. **Don't Fall Away from Jesus' Melchizedekian Priesthood
Since It Is Greater than the Levitical Priesthood
(4:14–10:18)**
   A. Exhortation in Light of Jesus' Priestly Status (4:14–5:10)
   B. **Warning and Assurance (5:11–6:20)**
      1. **Warning Against Falling Away from Jesus the
         High Priest (5:11–6:8)**
         a. High Priesthood Hard to Explain Because of
            Readers' Sluggishness (5:11–14)
         b. Call to Maturity (6:1–3)
         c. **Those Who Fall Away Can't Be Renewed to
            Repentance (6:4–8)**
      2. Assurance and Comfort (6:9–20)

Scripture

⁴ For it is impossible to renew to repentance those who were
once enlightened, who tasted the heavenly gift, became companions with the Holy Spirit, ⁵ tasted God's good word and the powers of the coming age, ⁶ and who have fallen away, because, to
their own harm, they are recrucifying the Son of God and holding
Him up to contempt.

⁷ For ground that has drunk the rain that has often fallen on it
and that produces vegetation useful to those it is cultivated for
receives a blessing from God. ⁸ But if it produces thorns and thistles, it is worthless and about to be cursed, and will be burned
at the end.

Context

The author strongly warns the readers in this paragraph (see
§5). The spiritual sluggishness and infancy of the readers is not a
neutral state, nor can they continue to live as spiritual infants. They
must get to the place where they can digest solid food. In other
words they must progress on to maturity so that the fundamental
teachings of the faith do not need to be repeated constantly. In verses
4–8 the author explains why the readers should go on to maturity,
for if those who have experienced such astonishing blessings fall
away and crucify again the Son of God, then there is no room for
repentance for them. He compares the readers to land refreshed by
the rain falling upon it. If the land produces fruit, it is blessed by

God. But if the land yields weeds, then the land will be rejected and is near the time when it will be cursed. Ultimately, it will be burned. So too, if the readers do not progress on to maturity, but fall away, then they, like the land, will be rejected and cursed by God. There will be no hope for them on the final day.

Exegesis

6:4

The "for" (γάρ) explains why it is imperative that the readers progress on to maturity and do not remain spiritual infants. They are in a perilous position, for they are in danger of apostasy.[266] The author warns them that if they fall away they cannot be renewed to repentance. "The pastor would not be issuing this warning had his hearers come to this terrible end. His exhortation is not counsel of despair but a timely wake-up call."[267] The author addresses the readers pastorally and doesn't assume a divine perspective of their ultimate fate.[268] If the readers apostatize and turn away from Jesus Christ, there will be no opportunity of salvation for them. Is the writer saying that they can't come back to Christ even if they wish to do so? If we think of the context of the letter, the readers were being persecuted and were growing weary and exhausted with the trials of the Christian life. The author sees that they are at a crossroads. He perceives that if they turn away from Christ, there will be no future repentance for them.[269] It isn't the case that God would not and could not forgive them. Rather, the readers, if they repudiate Christ, will have no desire to return to him.[270] They will have left that "phase"

---

[266] For parallels, see Attridge, *Hebrews*, 168–69.

[267] Cockerill, *Hebrews*, 268. Against Matheson who thinks those addressed have already fallen away "and have come under the covenantal curse" (Dave Matheson, "Reading Hebrews 6:4–6 in Light of the Old Testament," *WTJ* 61 [1999]: 223).

[268] Rightly Martin Emmrich, "Hebrews 6:4–6—Again! (A Pneumatological Inquiry)," *WTJ* 65 (2003): 89. But Emmrich is right and wrong in saying that the possession of the Spirit is contingent on obedience (94). At one level what he says is certainly the case, but he doesn't clarify that the new covenant guarantees future obedience. See the theological exposition of the warnings in the last section of this work for an explanation of how these two truths cohere.

[269] The author doesn't say that repentance is merely difficult but impossible (so Attridge, *Hebrews*, 167; Hughes, *Hebrews*, 213).

[270] So Cockerill, *Hebrews*, 276. Koester argues, on the other hand, that the writer is speaking objectively, not subjectively (*Hebrews*, 312–13). Parallels include the

of their life behind. Hence, the urgency of the current situation provokes the author to admonish them severely.[271]

The language of renewing to repentance makes clear that the sin is apostasy.[272] The danger isn't simply that the readers would live unfruitful lives and thus not gain a greater reward. Repentance and faith are regularly used in the NT to describe the human response necessary to enter the people of God. So by saying that they couldn't repent again, the author indicates that they would be outside the people of God if they fall away, that there would be no room for coming back in through repentance and faith. Such language precludes the notion that rewards are intended.

To whom is the warning addressed?[273] The author describes the recipients of the warning in five ways in verses 4–5. As Lane says, "The recital of what occurred with the reception of the gospel does not describe a succession of salvific events but the one event of salvation that is viewed from different aspects and manifestations."[274] The central dispute is whether those addressed are described as Christians or as those who are almost Christians. I will argue here that the language used points to Christians.

---

following: the author says it is impossible for God to lie (6:18), for the blood of bulls and goats to remove sins (10:4), and to please God without faith (11:6).

[271] L. Johnson sketches in well and briefly how this text was received in the early church (*Hebrews*, 163). The Shepherd of Hermas suggests that a second chance was available (*Mand.* 4.3.1–7; *Vis.* 2.2.4–5; *Sim.* 9.26.5–6). Tertullian rejected Hermas's second chance option (*On Modesty*, 20). Later Novatian refused readmission to the church of those who fell away (Epiphanius, *Panarion*, 59.1.1–3.6.). Cyprian and Ambrose, however, counseled that mercy should be offered (Cyprian of Carthage, *Letter* 51; Ambrose of Milan, *On Penance*, 2.2). See also Patrick Gray, "The Early Reception of Hebrews 6:4–6," in *Scripture and Traditions: Essays on Early Judaism and Christianity in Honor of Carl R. Holladay*, ed. Patrick Gray and Gail R. O'Day, NovTSup 129 (Leiden: Brill, 2008), 321–39.

[272] In other words the sin is equivalent to blasphemy against the Holy Spirit. According to Koester, Tyndale interpreted the warning passages similarly (*Hebrews*, 37).

[273] The warning could be understood as corporate rather than individual. See Verlyn D. Verbrugge, "Towards a New Interpretation of Hebrews 6:4–6" *CTJ* 15 (1980): 61–73. The warnings, however, are also individual in nature and hence can't be limited to a corporate group (see 3:12; 4:1; 10:25). Rightly Attridge, *Hebrews*, 172n69.

[274] Lane, *Hebrews 1–8*, 141. So also Hughes, *Hebrews*, 212.

Some maintain that a mixed audience composed of both believers and unbelievers is addressed.[275] Such an observation is almost certainly true on one level. It is difficult to believe that every single person in the congregation was truly a believer. Such an observation, however, skirts the fundamental question the text raises, and that question should still be answered. The question that must be resolved is whether the author *describes* the recipients as believers or unbelievers. When we look at the specific terms the author uses, does he address his readers as believers or as those who were almost but not quite believers? No doubt the audience was mixed, but the question being asked here is how the author describes the readers, and I will argue that he describes them as Christians. He doesn't address them as a mixed audience.

Grudem, following a long line of Reformed interpreters, gives the best defense for the readers being almost Christians.[276] According to Grudem, the author doesn't use language that clearly demonstrates that those described are Christians. For instance, he doesn't say they are forgiven of their sins or sanctified. Indeed, Grudem lists 18 different ways the author could have communicated clearly that the readers are Christians, all of which are lacking in the text. A couple of brief responses must suffice here. First, Grudem's list demands more than is reasonable.[277] We can't expect that a writer uses terms to describe believers that fit our criteria. What must be determined is whether what is written accords with those being described as believers or unbelievers. Outside criteria can't be imposed on the text as an abstraction to determine who is addressed. Second, we shall see that the readers are described as those who have received the Holy Spirit and as those who are sanctified (10:29). There is no clearer mark in the NT that one is a believer than receiving the Holy

---

[275] See C. Adrian Thomas, *A Case for Mixed-Audience with Reference to the Warning Passages in the Book of Hebrews* (New York: Peter Lang, 2008).

[276] See also Wayne Grudem, "Perseverance of the Saints: A Case Study from the Warning Passages in Hebrews," in *Still Sovereign*, ed. T. R. Schreiner and B. A. Ware (Grand Rapids, MI: Baker, 2000), 133–82; Guthrie, *Hebrews*, 223–32.

[277] See Allen for a critique of Grudem (David L. Allen, *Hebrews*, NAC [Nashville: B&H, 2010], 348–54). Allen rightly says we would expect the author to call for the hearers' conversion instead of exhorting them to press on to maturity if they were truly unconverted (358).

Spirit (6:4), so there are excellent reasons for thinking believers are addressed here.

Each of the five descriptions should now be considered. First, they "were once enlightened." Some see an echo of the light that illumined the exodus generation (Exod 13:21; Neh 9:12; Ps 105:39),[278] but the parallel seems too attenuated to be convincing.[279] In any case, there is no contextual indication that the enlightenment was partial or inadequate or insufficient in any way. The word "once" (ἅπαξ) suggests a decisive event, which is naturally interpreted to be at conversion, for at their conversion they were illuminated in that they received the knowledge of God. Later the term was used for baptism.[280] A reference to baptism here is unclear, but what is evident is that the author refers to conversion. The word "enlightened" (φωτισθέντας) is also used in Heb 10:32. The author thinks back to previous experiences of the readers: "Remember the earlier days when, after you had been enlightened, you endured a hard struggle with sufferings." In 10:32, then, the word "enlightened" naturally refers to the conversion of the readers, for the most natural interpretation is that the readers suffered after turning to God in faith and repentance. Neither in 10:32 nor in 6:4 does the author hint in any way that they were "almost enlightened." Elsewhere in the NT conversion is portrayed in terms of light shining on one so that they truly see the truth (2 Cor 4:4–6).

Second, the readers "tasted the heavenly gift." It is difficult to be sure what the writer means by "gift" (δωρεᾶς). Some see a connection with the gift of manna in the OT,[281] but the parallel doesn't seem terribly clear or illuminating. As Cockerill says, "One cannot draw significant theological conclusions from such very tenuous OT allusions."[282] Elsewhere in the NT, the word is used for the gift of the

---

[278] So O'Brien, *Hebrews*, 221; Matheson, "Reading Hebrews 6:4–6 in Light of the Old Testament," 215; Emmrich, "Hebrews 6:4–6—Again," 84.

[279] Rightly Cockerill, *Hebrews*, 272n21.

[280] Cf. Attridge, *Hebrews*, 169n44. In support of such a reference, see, e.g., Ernest Käsemann, *The Wandering People of God: An Investigation of the Letter to the Hebrews*, trans. R. A. Harrisville and I. L. Sundberg (Minneapolis, MN: Augsburg, 1984), 187–88; Spicq, *L'Épître aux Hébreux*, 2:150.

[281] O'Brien, *Hebrews*, 222; Matheson, "Reading Heb 6:4–6," 216–17; Emmrich, "Hebrews 6:4–6—Again," 84–85.

[282] Cockerill, *Hebrews*, 272n21.

Holy Spirit (John 4:10[283]; Acts 2:38; 8:20; 10:45; 11:17), or the gift of righteousness (Rom 5:17). A reference to the Holy Spirit is possible but seems unlikely since he mentions the Holy Spirit in the next verse. The gift is "heavenly," i.e., it is transcendent, coming down from above.[284] It seems most satisfying to say the author thinks generally of the new life or salvation of the readers.[285] The words used give no indication that the gift was partial. Instead, the gift was "heavenly," i.e., it was from the God who reigns over all. Some have maintained that the readers are not described here as truly saved because they "tasted (γευσαμένους) the heavenly gift." The metaphor of "tasting" could signify partiality, for we may "sip" something or take just a taste of something without swallowing it down. The word "taste" does have that meaning in some texts (e.g., Matt 27:34). But normally the word *taste* means "to experience fully" or is another way of describing eating (cf. Matt 16:28; Luke 14:24; John 8:52; Acts 20:11; 23:14; Col 2:21). Most important, elsewhere in Hebrews the word clearly means to experience fully. The author refers to Jesus' "tasting" (γεύσηται) death (2:9). Certainly Jesus did not just sip death or dabble with it a bit. He died! He experienced fully all the horrors of death. So, when the author says the readers "tasted the heavenly gift," the expression most naturally means they experienced the salvation that comes from above.

Third, the author describes those who "have shared in" (ESV, NIV) or "become partakers" (NET) of the Holy Spirit.[286] The HCSB rendering is off target here: "companions with the Holy Spirit." This seems to suggest that believers are friends of the Holy Spirit, but the

---

[283] Cf. Ellingworth, *Hebrews*, 320.

[284] Attridge is probably right in saying "heavenly" denotes both the "source and goal" of the gift (*Hebrews*, 170).

[285] So Attridge, *Hebrews*, 170; Cockerill, *Hebrews*, 270. A reference to the Eucharist is unlikely, despite its popularity in the history of interpretation (cf. the discussion in Hughes, *Hebrews*, 209).

[286] Some see an allusion to the gift of the Spirit given to the elders (Num 11:16–30). See Emmrich, "Hebrews 6:4–6—Again," 85; Matheson, "Reading Heb 6:4–6," 218–19. But the parallel isn't evident (rightly Cockerill, *Hebrews*, 272n21), for the gift of the Spirit in Numbers was for the sake of uttering God's word. Participation in the Holy Spirit signifies something stronger and more permanent. On the whole matter of the difference between the OT and the NT with regard to the Holy Spirit, see James M. Hamilton Jr., *God's Indwelling Presence: The Holy Spirit in the Old and New Testaments*, NACSBT (Nashville: B&H, 2006).

point is that they have partaken or shared in the Spirit, not that they are his companions or partners or friends.[287] Does the word "shared" suggest experiences with the Spirit that fell short of a saving experience with the Spirit? Certainly there are experiences with the Holy Spirit that do not constitute salvation. The story of Simon the sorcerer in Acts 8:9–24 fits such a pattern. This interpretation should be rejected, however, for the word "shared in" (μετόχους) denotes full participation. The use of the word group in Hebrews makes this clear. In 3:1 believing human beings share a heavenly calling, while in 3:14 they are truly sharers of Christ if they persevere to the end. The author tells us that those who are truly sons share in discipline (12:8). The verb "share" or "partake" (μετέχω) is used to say that Jesus shared flesh and blood with human beings (2:14). There is no doubt that Jesus fully shared flesh and blood, i.e., humanity, with us. The closest reference is 5:13, where the readers partake of milk. Again they were ingesting milk instead of solid food. There is no evidence whatsoever that the word refers to a partial sharing or partaking.

Here Grudem's reading fails to convince. *The* sign that one was a Christian in the NT was the reception of the Holy Spirit (see §4). As Motyer says, the Spirit is "center-stage" here.[288] When the Galatians were tempted to succumb to circumcision to ensure that they belonged to the people of God, Paul instructs them that they are truly believers apart from the works of the law because they received the Holy Spirit when they believed (Gal 3:1–5). Similarly, in Acts 15 the church called a council to determine whether circumcision was required for salvation. Peter declares that circumcision is unnecessary and defends his claim by appealing to the salvation of Cornelius (Acts 15:7–11). Peter tells those gathered that the salvation of Cornelius and his friends apart from the law was certain, for God gave them the Holy Spirit just as he did to Jewish believers in the beginning (Acts 15:8). Paul says in Rom 8:9 that those who don't have the Holy Spirit don't belong to God, whereas those who have the Spirit are members of the people of God. The point being made here is simple: the gift of the Holy Spirit is the clearest

---

[287] The HCSB probably makes this decision in light of the use of the same word in Heb 1:9, but the context is completely different, and the rendering makes little sense here.

[288] Motyer, "The Spirit in Hebrews: No Longer Forgotten?," 221.

indication in the NT that one is a Christian, so for the author to say that the readers were sharers of the Holy Spirit demonstrates that he is saying they were Christians. In fact, it is hard to imagine a clearer way of saying that the readers were believers. Now this is not to deny that the congregation had some false believers in it. Doubtless, the congregation was mixed in this sense. Surely some were not authentically Christian. But it is crucial to make an important distinction here. The writer specifically addresses believers in the warning. The terms he uses don't suggest inadequate or partial belief. Instead, he uses expressions that designate Christian believers in the fullest sense of the word.

6:5

Fourth, those described "tasted God's good word." The word "taste" (γευσαμένους) is the same word investigated in the previous verse. Perhaps there is a reference to the good promises of God that were fulfilled during Joshua's days (Josh 21:43; 23:15; cf. Neh 9:13),[289] but the parallel isn't terribly illuminating or even closely matched in wording. Here the author says they fully ingested God's word by receiving the gospel of Jesus Christ. It is this "word" that the leaders taught them as new believers (Heb 13:7).[290] Again there is nothing to suggest that their initial reception was false or superficial. Instead, the author reminds them elsewhere of their love and service to the saints at the beginning (6:10). He recalls their early sufferings, their solidarity with others who suffered, and their joy when stripped of their possessions (10:32–34). He doesn't cast doubts upon their reception of the word but warns those who initially embraced it.

Fifth, they also "tasted the powers of the coming age." The word "taste" does double-duty here for both this phrase and the previous one. Again, some see resonance with the signs and wonders by which Israel was liberated from Egypt.[291] But the actual terms "signs and wonders" aren't replicated, and so the parallel is general if present at all. In any case, it is clear that the readers truly experienced the power of the age to come. The distinction between this age and

---

[289] So O'Brien, *Hebrews*, 223; Matheson, "Reading Hebrews 6:4–6," 218–19; Emmrich, "Hebrews 6:4–6—Again," 85–86.

[290] In 6:5 we find the term ῥῆμα and in 13:7 the term λόγον, but they are synonyms.

[291] O'Brien, *Hebrews*, 223; Matheson, "Reading Heb 6:4–6," 220; Emmrich, "Hebrews 6:4–6—Again," 86.

the age to come is a typical feature of NT eschatology.[292] In Jesus Christ's death and resurrection the new age has penetrated history. The eschaton has invaded history before the end of history arrived. The readers were catapulted into the future age of God's reign in the midst of the present evil age. They had experienced God's end-time blessings in a powerful way. The word "powers" (δυνάμεις) suggests a real and dynamic experience, not something that was ineffectual.

6:6

In this verse the danger of falling away is emblazoned on the minds of the readers. Those who fall away can't be renewed to repentance since their apostasy recrucifies God's Son and dishonors him.

The final of the six descriptors is found in the words, "who have fallen away" (παραπεσόντας). The word only occurs here in the NT. The verb in Ezekiel (παραπίπτω) clearly designates apostasy (Ezek 14:13; 15:8; 18:24; 20:27; 22:4).[293] Judah suffers exile for forsaking the Lord. The text in Ezek 18:24 is particularly clear. Those who devote themselves to iniquity will die because of their transgressions since they have repudiated the Lord and his ways. Context is determinative for assigning a particular meaning in any case, and the word used here is parallel to the different words for falling away elsewhere in the warning passages.[294] In other words the author refers here to apostasy, to abandoning the gospel of Jesus Christ. As L. Johnson remarks, "This is not a matter of faults and errors, in

---

[292] E.g., Matt 12:32; 13:39–40, 49; 24:3; 28:20; Mark 10:30; Luke 18:30; 20:35; Rom 12:2; 1 Cor 1:20; 2:6; 3:18; 7:31; 2 Cor 4:4; Gal 1:4; Eph 1:21; 1 Tim 6:17; 2 Tim 4:10; cf. also 4 Esdr. 2:36, 39; 4:27; 6:9; 7:113; 9:18–19.

[293] Allen argues (*Hebrews*, 359–62) that the word doesn't mean apostasy in Jewish literature, and he is correct in saying that it doesn't mean apostasy in every instance (cf. Esth 6:10; Wis 6:9; 12:2). For a similar view see Rodney D. Decker, "The Warning of Hebrews 6," *The Journal of Ministry and Theology* 5 (2001): 26–48. But the references in Ezekiel clearly designate apostasy on account of which Judah is sent into exile. Thus, contrary to Allen, apostasy is part of the semantic domain of the word, and the context of Hebrews shows that such is in view, as almost all interpreters agree. Since Allen goes astray here, the text can't be speaking of loss of rewards as he maintains (*Hebrews*, 377).

[294] As Ellingworth says, "The context virtually requires a reference to apostasy here" (*Hebrews*, 322).

other words, but of apostasy, of making a deliberate choice not to participate in the gift once given."[295]

A crucial question is how the participle "falling away" should be interpreted. Some understand it to be parallel to the rest of the list so that he describes those who have actually fallen away. Such an understanding of the participle is improbable, for elsewhere in the letter the writer admonishes the readers not to fall away in the warning passages. He doesn't assume they *have already fallen away.* The participle is not conditional *grammatically*, but functionally and *interpretively* the word found here is to be construed as a condition. Attridge remarks: "Our author does not accuse his addressees of being in this condition. . . . It is a warning that should remind them of the seriousness of their situation and the importance of renewing their commitment. Apostasy is where their 'sluggishness' could lead."[296]

If the readers fall away, they can't be renewed to repentance. They will not retrace their steps and put their faith in Christ anew. It is possible that the author has in mind the wilderness generation and Esau who departed from God.[297] Still the wilderness generation and Esau do not stand in the same place as new covenant members, for as we shall see, all members of the new covenant are regenerate. Hence, we must be careful not to see an exact parallel between the OT examples given and the application to the hearers of the letter. I argue in the theological analysis of the warning passages at the close of the commentary that the warnings are a means by which believers are preserved by God. They stimulate and provoke believers to heed the admonition so they don't apostatize.

If any fall away, they can't be renewed to repentance, for "they are recrucifying the Son of God."[298] The word "recrucify" (ἀνασταυροῦντας) often simply means crucify.[299] In this case the nuance may be the lifting up to public shame.[300] In context, however,

---

[295] L. Johnson, *Hebrews*, 161. See also Lane, *Hebrews 1–8*, 142; Hughes, *Hebrews*, 216.

[296] Attridge, *Hebrews*, 171. So also O'Brien, *Hebrews*, 219.

[297] So Cockerill, *Hebrews*, 273.

[298] The HCSB rightly interprets the phrase as a dative of disadvantage: "to their own harm" (ἑαυτοῖς).

[299] See BDAG; Attridge, *Hebrews*, 171.

[300] So L. Johnson, *Hebrews*, 161; Koester, *Hebrews*, 315.

the idea of crucifying again seems to be present. Those who abandon the Son of God can't be reconverted all over again, for that would be like crucifying Jesus all over again.[301] Hebrews emphasizes the superiority of Jesus as God's Son, and hence the notion of crucifying him again is particularly outrageous. A similar idea is expressed in 10:29 where believers are warned not to "profane the blood of the covenant by which [they were] sanctified." The severity of the language here also rules out "the rewards" view. Jesus would need to be crucified twice if those who fall away were to be saved, but Hebrews is clear that he dies only once (7:27; 9:12, 27–28; 10:10), and they can't be renewed to repentance. Christ can't be crucified twice for them.

The participles here could be construed as temporal so that the author teaches they can't be renewed to repentance as long as they are recrucifying Christ and holding him up to shame.[302] More likely the participles provide the reason apostates can't be renewed to repentance, and the other warnings in the letter don't fit with the notion that apostates can be brought back to repentance (cf. esp. 12:17).[303]

They also can't be renewed to repentance since they would be "holding Him up to contempt" ($\pi\alpha\rho\alpha\delta\epsilon\iota\gamma\mu\alpha\tau\acute{\iota}\zeta o\nu\tau\alpha\varsigma$). The notion is parallel to recrucifying God's Son, for crucifixion in the ancient world was the ultimate expression of shame. To abandon God's Son is to say that his death didn't save, that it was for nothing. Or to put it another way, apostasy concedes that Jesus should have been crucified, that the penalty was warranted. Instead of finding salvation in Jesus' death, they reject it and thereby confess that the shame and dishonor Jesus received was deserved.

6:7

Verses 7–8 give an illustration of the consequences of apostasy. The writer asks the readers to envision land that has often received refreshing rain. If it yields crops useful for those who tended it, then it receives a blessing from God. The last phrase indicates that the

---

[301] Rightly Lane, *Hebrews 1–8*, 133; Ellingworth, *Hebrews*, 324. Against Allen, who argues the untenable position that Christians recrucify Jesus by their daily sins (*Hebrews*, 365), for he implausibly contends that the sin here isn't apostasy.

[302] So J. K. Elliott, "Is Post-Baptismal Sin Forgivable?" *Bible Translator* 78 (1977): 330–32.

[303] Attridge, *Hebrews*, 172n68.

author is illustrating his point, for we could see the author saying that God blesses the land and then it yields useful crops. Instead, he says that *if* the land produces crops that are helpful, then it is blessed by God, showing that he continues to warn the readers. The point of the illustration is clear. The land represents the readers and the refreshing rain the blessings God poured out upon them.[304] In response to God's goodness, they should produce good fruit in their lives and persevere in faith.

6:8

In verse 7 the author portrays a picture where good fruit appears because of refreshing rain. Now in verse 8 he looks at another situation where refreshing rain does not produce good crops. Instead, "thorns and thistles" appear. If thorns and thistles appear, even when there is refreshing rain, the land is "worthless" and "about to be cursed" and will finally be "burned." The language here resonates with themes from Deuteronomy, including the watering of the land (11:11; 28:12), its curse (29:27), and its burning (29:23).[305]

The purpose of the illustration is clear. The participle "produces" (ἐκφέρουσα) is conditional: "if it produces" (cf. ESV, NET). The writer addresses the readers, and hence the illustration continues the warning of verses 4–6. If the readers yield weeds in their lives after receiving God's blessings, then they are "worthless." The word "worthless" (ἀδόκιμος) is regularly used in the NT for those who are disqualified on the last day, for those who will not be saved, but judged, by God (cf. Rom 1:28; 1 Cor 9:27; 2 Cor 13:5–7; 2 Tim 3:8; Titus 1:16).[306] The HCSB's "about to be cursed" (κατάρας ἐγγύς)

---

[304] There is no clear allusion here to the promised land of Deut 11:11 (against Matheson, "Reading Hebrews 6:4–6," 221–22; Guthrie, "Hebrews," 962; rightly Cockerill, *Hebrews*, 279n53), but a broad reference to the blessings and cursings in the OT is plausible (see Allen, *Deuteronomy and Exhortation in Hebrews*, 126–34).

[305] See O'Brien, *Hebrews*, 229–30; Allen, *Deuteronomy and Exhortation in Hebrews*, 127–34.

[306] So also O'Brien, *Hebrews*, 229. The OT background from Deuteronomy sketched in above supports such a reading. Against Allen (*Hebrews*, 378–86) and Gleason (Randall C. Gleason, "A Moderate Reformed View," in *Four Views on the Warning Passages in Hebrews*, ed. Herbert W. Bateman IV [Grand Rapids, MI: Kregel, 2007], 336–77) who see only a loss of rewards here. Both Allen and Gleason consistently make the mistake of thinking the judgment threatened is temporal since the judgment levied on the wilderness generation and Esau were temporal. What they fail to see is the typological escalation present here. The promise of land in the

captures well the meaning of the text. Another way of translating the phrase is "near to being cursed" (ESV). The author is not thinking spatially, as if they are near to being cursed but will actually avoid it. Instead the expression has a temporal dimension. If one's life is dominated by weeds, if one falls away, then the day when one will be cursed by God, the day of judgment, is coming.[307]

The reference to the judgment is confirmed by the words, "and will be burned at the end." The author says the land will be burned, which applies to people who will be consumed on the final day. Those who think the text speaks of losing rewards instead of final damnation appeal to the illustration to support their view. But such a reading fails, for it is not the fruit that is burned but the land itself! It would make sense to see a reference to rewards if it were the crops that were destroyed at the end. The author, however, describes the destruction of the *land*, not its fruit. The land refers to the persons in the illustration, and hence there is no doubt that the threat is eternal punishment, not loss of rewards.

Bridge

Warnings and admonitions are integral to the proclamation of the gospel of Christ. The gospel not only provides comfort and consolation. Those who have received the stunning blessings of salvation, who have seen and known the power of the gospel, who have received the Holy Spirit, are warned that if they fall away there will be no turning back. If they renounce Jesus Christ, after embracing him and after tasting the power of God's word, they in effect crucify him again. To receive such blessings and then to repudiate God's goodness leaves no other option but irrevocable judgment. Those who reject what is supremely good will find that they have welcomed evil, and it will be their destiny.

OT designates the final rest for the author of Hebrews, and thus more than temporal rewards and fruitfulness are intended by the author of Hebrews.

[307] "The adjective is not meant to suggest that the land is not subject to a curse, as if there were still hope for it" (Attridge, *Hebrews*, 173).

Hebrews 6:9–12

Outline

I. Prologue: Definitive and Final Revelation in the Son (1:1–4)

II. Don't Abandon the Son Since He Is Greater than Angels (1:5–2:18)

III. Don't Harden Your Hearts Since You Have a Son and High Priest Greater than Moses and Joshua (3:1–4:13)

IV. **Don't Fall Away from Jesus' Melchizedekian Priesthood Since It Is Greater than the Levitical Priesthood (4:14–10:18)**

    A. Exhortation in Light of Jesus' Priestly Status (4:14–5:10)

    B. **Warning and Assurance (5:11–6:20)**

        1. Warning Against Falling Away from Jesus the High Priest (5:11–6:8)

        2. **Assurance and Comfort (6:9–20)**

            a. **Confident that Readers Will Be Diligent and Inherit the Promises (6:9–12)**

            b. Assurance and Hope Through God's Oath (6:13–20)

        3. Jesus' Greater Priesthood as a Melchizedekian Priest (7:1–28)

Scripture

⁹ Even though we are speaking this way, dear friends, in your case we are confident of the better things connected with salvation. ¹⁰ For God is not unjust; He will not forget your work and the love you showed for His name when you served the saints— and you continue to serve them. ¹¹ Now we want each of you to demonstrate the same diligence for the final realization of your hope, ¹² so that you won't become lazy but will be imitators of those who inherit the promises through faith and perseverance.

Context

The warning that began in 5:11 concludes with this paragraph. After admonishing the readers so severely in 6:4–8, the author now steps back and comforts them. He assures them that he is convinced they will not fall away but be saved (v. 9). The reason for his assurance is provided in verse 10. The past and current care and concern for fellow believers attests to the love of the readers for God's name. So, why does he warn them if he has such confidence? He wants the readers to be diligent and persevere to the end so their hope would be fully realized (v. 11). In this way they would not fall prey to the sluggishness that elicited such concern (v. 12) and would inherit the promises through faithful patience.

Exegesis

6:9

The severe admonition is followed up by a word of assurance and comfort. As Koester says, "The warning disturbs while the promise gives assurance—but they serve the same end, which is that listeners might persevere in faith."[308] The author addresses the readers as "beloved" only here in the entire book, reminding them that they are loved by God. Indeed, despite the strong admonition in verses 4–8, he is confident and persuaded "of the better things connected with salvation." In other words the author is confident that his admonition will have the desired effect and they will not fall away.[309] The readers will take heed of what he has said so they will not apostatize.[310] L. Johnson remarks that "the author's warning in the previous verses was truly a caution concerning the possibility of their falling away, rather than a response to those who had already apostatized."[311]

The interpretation proposed here is more plausible than Grudem's interpretation, where "the better things connected with salvation" are contrasted with being enlightened, tasting the heavenly gift, being sharers of the Holy Spirit, etc.[312] For Grudem the blessings listed in verses 4–5 are not quite saving so that those described in those verses are "almost Christians." According to Grudem's reading, the author affirms that he is persuaded that the readers are not merely "almost Christians"; he is persuaded that they are truly saved. Such an interpretation should be rejected, for then the warning in verses 4–6 is not truly for the readers since he is

---

[308] Koester, *Hebrews*, 321.

[309] So Hughes, *Hebrews*, 225.

[310] So ibid., 174.

[311] L. Johnson, *Hebrews*, 164.

[312] Grudem, "Perseverance of the Saints," 133–82.

persuaded they are truly believers. Strictly speaking, according to Grudem, the words in 6:4–6 are not a warning at all; they describe a certain group of people who are not Christians. But why include such words for readers who are Christians? In addition, the words "even though we are speaking this way" more naturally fit with the warning about the consequences of falling away instead of referring to the blessings described in verses 4–5. That is, the experiences related in verses 4–5 are actually taken by Grudem to be negative, but it is scarcely apparent that they are benefits that fall short of salvation. The negative words come in the warning and the consequences for believers if they fail to heed it. Finally, such a view fails, for the words in 6:4–8 become distinct from all the other warning passages in Hebrews, which seems unlikely. As I argue in the theology section at the conclusion of the commentary, the warnings should be interpreted synoptically.

6:10

The author explains why ("for") he is convinced that the readers will heed his warnings and be saved on the last day. He appeals to God's justice. God will not forget the work and love of the readers manifested in their past and current ministry to fellow believers.

God is "not unjust." He righteously rewards those who do what pleases him, and final judgment will not be poured out on those who live righteously. How we live our lives matters, and God does not forget the righteous and loving actions undertaken for others. The past obedience of the readers signals that they have new life in Christ. The love evident in the readers' lives was not merely horizontal. It revealed their concern for God's "name." What animated the readers was the glory and honor of God. But they did not obey merely out of a sense of duty. They were inspired by love for God and love for his reputation. One of the key indications that one belongs to God is a genuine love for his name and his glory.

Their vertical love for God expressed itself in practical ways. They served (διακονήσαντες) fellow believers in the past and are continuing to serve (διακονοῦντες) them. The author's confidence in the readers' salvation is anchored to their service to the saints, a service that endured, beginning in the past and continuing until the day the author writes.

6:11

After the expression of confidence, the author explains why he gave the warning. He wants the "diligence" (σπουδὴν) that characterized their lives at the beginning to continue so that they will be full of hope until the final day. Assurance of faith is obtained through the activity of believers; they are not called to passivity or to laxity. They should be intentional and diligent in their faith. Such words remind us of 2 Pet 1:5–11, where Peter says believers must diligently pursue virtue if they wish to enter the eternal kingdom on the last day.

It is difficult to determine whether the author speaks of "final realization" (so HCSB, πληροφορίαν), understanding the term more objectively,[313] or if the word has a more subjective meaning, such as "full assurance" (ESV) or confidence.[314] The latter reading fits with the boldness with which the readers are to approach God (4:16; 10:19; cf. 3:6, 14) and with the use of the same word in 10:22 where believers enjoy full assurance since their "hearts" are "sprinkled clean from an evil conscience." Perhaps we don't have an either-or here, so that the word designates both the subjective and objective dimension of assurance. Their diligence in virtue assures them that they belong to God, but it is also the means by which they will realize their eschatological hope.

The author picks up the verb from verse 10, "show" (ἐνδείκνυμι), and uses it again in verse 11. They "showed" love for God's name by ministering to the saints (v. 10). Now he wants them to "show" the same kind of diligence they had in the beginning until the end.[315] Perseverance is necessary so that the hope they have now will be realized on the final day. The warning, therefore, is intended by the author to be the means by which they persevere.

6:12

The readers' spiritual "sluggishness" (νωθροί, 5:11) precipitated the strong admonition and warning. The readers must be diligent so they will not fall prey to "sluggishness." For, as we have seen, those who are spiritually idle are in danger of falling away. They are on the precipice of destruction, despite the zeal and love that

---

[313] Lane, *Hebrews 1–8*, 130; Attridge, *Hebrews*, 135–36.

[314] So O'Brien, *Hebrews*, 232; Cockerill, *Hebrews*, 282n11.

[315] The words "we passionately want" (NET) are a bit overwrought. We "want" (HCSB, NIV) and we "desire" (ESV) capture the meaning.

first characterized their Christian lives. They should recover the eagerness of their former days as believers and imitate those who inherited the promises through "faith and patience." Here the author anticipates chapter 11, where he gives many examples of those who trusted God in the midst of their difficulties. The promises inherited here are eschatological so they will be obtained on the final day. But the promises are reserved for those who endure in faith. Initial "faith" does not guarantee the reception of the promises if they do not believe until the end.

Bridge

The author mixes together encouragement and rebuke in the letter. Believers need warnings and admonitions to remain faithful, but at the same time they also need encouragement. The readers are reminded that their obedience is not trivial or forgettable. God notices what they do in their everyday lives. He knows whether they truly love his name, and that love is expressed in service for the saints. All believers should continue such love and service to the end. The Christian life is a journey that requires patience and continued faith. The reward of eternal life will not be given to those who drop out of the race. Retribution will be meted out for those who cease loving God and fellow believers. Hence we need to be provoked to be diligent until the final day. We must not give into spiritual torpor. The flames of spiritual life should be fanned by trusting the promises of God.

Hebrews 6:13–20

Outline

I. Prologue: Definitive and Final Revelation in the Son (1:1–4)
II. Don't Abandon the Son Since He Is Greater than Angels (1:5–2:18)
III. Don't Harden Your Hearts Since You Have a Son and High Priest Greater than Moses and Joshua (3:1–4:13)
IV. **Don't Fall Away from Jesus' Melchizedekian Priesthood Since It Is Greater than the Levitical Priesthood (4:14–10:18)**
   A. Exhortation in Light of Jesus' Priestly Status (4:14–5:10)

B. **Warning and Assurance (5:11–6:20)**
1. Warning Against Falling Away from Jesus the High Priest (5:11–6:8)
2. **Assurance and Comfort (6:9–20)**
   a. Confident that Readers Will Be Diligent and Inherit the Promises (6:9–12)
   b. **Assurance and Hope Through God's Oath (6:13–20)**
C. Jesus' Greater Priesthood as a Melchizedekian Priest (7:1–28)

Scripture

[13] For when God made a promise to Abraham, since He had no one greater to swear by, He swore by Himself: [14] I will indeed bless you, and I will greatly multiply you. [15] And so, after waiting patiently, Abraham obtained the promise. [16] For men swear by something greater than themselves, and for them a confirming oath ends every dispute.

[17] Because God wanted to show His unchangeable purpose even more clearly to the heirs of the promise, He guaranteed it with an oath, [18] so that through two unchangeable things, in which it is impossible for God to lie, we who have fled for refuge might have strong encouragement to seize the hope set before us. [19] We have this hope as an anchor for our lives, safe and secure. It enters the inner sanctuary behind the curtain. [20] Jesus has entered there on our behalf as a forerunner, because He has become a high priest forever in the order of Melchizedek.

Context

Verses 11–12 conclude with an exhortation to be diligent so that the hope given to believers will be realized, so that they will inherit the promises through faith and patience. Verses 13–20 consider the nature of God's promise, the need for patience to obtain the promise, and the hope that belongs to believers by virtue of the promise. The main point of the section is found in verse 18. He wants the readers to be encouraged so they will seize the hope set before them, so they will not miss out on the promise pledged to them.

Verses 13–14 contemplate the nature of the promise. God's pledge to bless Abraham is inviolable, for he swore by himself, and there is no one greater to swear by. Abraham received the promise by patience (v. 15). Abraham didn't obtain the promise immediately. In fact, years passed before the promise became a reality, but Abraham patiently waited on and trusted in the promise. In verses 16–18 the author reflects further on why God sealed the promise with an oath. Among human beings oaths testify that someone greater and more trustworthy is invoked. Hence it confirms the truth of what is said and is intended to bring disputes about truthfulness to a conclusion. God, of course, doesn't need to undertake an oath to display his truthfulness. The oath was for the sake of believers, to certify unmistakably his unchangeable purpose. God, after all, cannot lie, but he underscored his truth to those inheriting the promise by making a promise and then swearing he would fulfill it. God's purpose in doing this (v. 18) was to grant encouragement to those who have taken hold of the hope before them. The nature of this hope is unpacked in verses 19–20. The hope is unmovable and secure. It is an anchor for believers that reaches into the innermost part of the veil, i.e., it has access to the presence of God. The reason believers have access is explained in verse 20. Jesus entered through the veil into God's presence as our forerunner, and he was able to do so because he is a Melchizedekian priest. So the author returns to where he started (4:14–5:10) before he stepped aside to warn believers. He needs to explain to them Jesus' Melchizedekian priesthood, for that priesthood brings them into God's presence. That priesthood brings them a hope that nothing can conquer. That priesthood will fill them with encouragement and consolation. And that priesthood is like an anchor nothing can dislodge.

Exegesis

6:13

The notion of promise links this verse to the previous section (cf. v. 12). Believers are encouraged in verse 12 to inherit the promises through faith and patience. Now the author wants them to contemplate the nature of the promise and the grandeur and faithfulness of the one who made it by reflecting on the promise made to Abraham. The promise made to Abraham is a central theme in Genesis. God promises Abraham land, offspring, and universal blessing (Gen 12:1–3; 18:17–18; 22:17–18). Such promises drive the story line in the Pentateuch and indeed all of Scripture, for the promises made to Abraham are the vehicle by which the offspring of the woman will triumph over the serpent (Gen 3:15). Blessing is promised for the whole world through the offspring of Abraham; and the NT, of course, proclaims that Jesus Christ is the one through whom the stunning blessings granted to Abraham become a reality.

Here the focus is on Gen 22:17, where God swears to Abraham that he will bless him. The blessing comes after the most dramatic and terrifying test in Abraham's life, for the Lord summoned him to sacrifice the son of the promise, Isaac. Abraham's faith in God shines, for he takes the Lord at his word and is prepared to sacrifice his son, the son of the promise, if God so commands. The Lord, of course, spares Isaac and pronounces the words of promise that Hebrews reflects on.

The purpose here is to underline the certainty of the promise. God took an oath to certify the promise to Abraham. But by what did God swear? On what basis did he affirm his truthfulness? God can't swear by anyone greater than himself, for there is no being in heaven or on earth greater than God. God possesses all perfections and is infinitely perfect in all of them. Hence, since no being is greater than God, God swore by himself. God is the definition of greatness, and since no one surpasses him or can surpass him, he couldn't swear by any higher entity.

6:14

The oath God swore to Abraham is cited from Gen 22:17, assuring him that he would bless him and multiply his offspring. The citation is close to the LXX but matches the MT as well. In the LXX and the NT we have a strong assertion, which the author understands as an oath. God promises Abraham that he will certainly bless and multiply him. The author cuts off the citation here, but the promise is that Abraham's offspring will multiply like the stars of heaven, that his offspring will inherit the cities of his enemies, and that the blessing will extend to all peoples (Gen 22:17–18).

The link between the "promise" in verse 13 and "blessing" in verse 14 shows that these two terms mutually interpret each other. What the writer particularly emphasizes is that God's promise was accompanied with an oath. This is no ordinary promise, for God underscores it with an oath, and thus the promise and the blessing will certainly come to pass. There is no question about whether the blessing will come to pass since God swore that he would do so.

The oath differs from the promise, according to Griffiths, in that the oath is accompanied by an action that secures what is promised.[316] Hence, God's oath in Genesis 22 is joined with his deliverance of Isaac, which certifies that God will bless Abraham and multiply his offspring through Isaac.

6:15

Verse 15 seems to interrupt the flow of the argument. Verses 13–14 emphasize the inviolability of God's word, for he swore to Abraham that he would bless him. We expect the author to say, therefore, that the promise is guaranteed by virtue of the promise of God. Instead the text turns to the response of Abraham, affirming that he obtained the promise because he was patient. What is the author up to here? Even though the wording is brief, he catches us up into Abraham's story. Abraham received the promise of land, offspring, and blessing in Gen 12:1–3, but years and years passed before even one aspect of the promise was fulfilled. The story in Genesis concentrates on how many years passed before Abraham and Sarah even had one child. The birth of Isaac is the promise he has in mind here.[317] What strikes the writer is Abraham's patience. He endured in faith as the years passed. Though there were ups and downs in his life, he persevered in believing. How often it seemed as if the promise would not be realized, for Isaac was a long time coming, and then after he arrived, God asked Abraham to sacrifice him!

The writer wants the readers to imitate (cf. v. 12!) Abraham. The circumstances and sufferings of life suggest that God's promises are a charade, that they are disconnected from reality. But Abraham faced the same temptation as the readers, for he too was tempted to think that God's promise would not come true. Like Abraham they should continue to believe even when their situation suggests that God's promises are false. It is precisely here that we should see a connection between verses 13–14 and verse 15. The readers should be patient, but their patience is founded on the promise of God, a promise that will not be broken. The summons to patience and perseverance is not a call ultimately to human virtue. Abraham

---

[316] Jonathan Griffiths, "The Word of God: Perfectly Spoken in the Son," in *The Perfect Savior: Key Themes in Hebrews*, ed. J. Griffiths (Nottingham: InterVarsity, 2012), 39.

[317] So most commentators. Against Lane, it is not the promise of many offspring, for Abraham did not obtain that promise (*Hebrews 1–8*, 151).

was patient precisely because of the unbreakable promise of God. His faith was grounded and established in the word of God, and thus what God pledged to him fueled his patience.

But what does God's promise to Abraham have to do with the readers? Apparently, the promises made to Abraham belong to the readers. After all, God helps the offspring of Abraham instead of angels (2:16). The promise to Abraham included the notion that the whole world would be blessed, as was noted in 6:13. That is to say, the rule over the entire world, which was destined for human beings (see 2:5–9), will be realized through Abraham's offspring. As 2:5–18 explains, all those who are the brothers and sisters of Jesus share in that promise. They, like Abraham, will be blessed. If we consider the remainder of Hebrews, they will enjoy the heavenly rest (4:1–11) and the city to come (11:10, 13–16; 12:22; 13:14). It follows, then, that what God swore to Abraham pertains to the readers. The promises made to Abraham belong to them as well.

6:16

The significance of God taking an oath is taken up again in verses 16–18. First, the significance of oaths among human beings is considered. Why do human beings take oaths? What is their significance? When an oath is taken, one who is greater or superior is invoked. Swearing by someone greater underscores the truthfulness of what is said and seals the solemnity of the occasion. An oath confirms and ratifies what is uttered and thus resolves what is disputed. Those who take an oath swear that their words truly accord with what happened, bringing to a conclusion a debated matter. Of course, human beings may lie, even under oath. But the author doesn't focus on that fact here. Ordinarily, a word under oath is trusted and becomes the basis on which controversies are decided.

6:17

If human beings end disputes with oaths, it certainly doesn't follow that God needs to take one. It is all the more remarkable, then, that God swears an oath.[318] The oaths of human beings, though they may resolve disputes, are not infallible, for one may be lying. But God's oaths are of a different character and nature. God doesn't

---

[318] The words in Greek rendered "because" (ἐν ᾧ) do not have a particular antecedent but refer to the thought of the previous verse as a whole (so Attridge, *Hebrews*, 180). The phrase is likely causal (Ellingworth, *Hebrews*, 340–41).

need to take an oath since his word is truth and his promises never fail. Still he swore an oath to Abraham to underline his unchangeable purpose. His promise to bless and multiply Abraham would certainly come to pass. No doubt about its future fulfillment could be entertained. God's intention in making an oath was to grant assurance and bold confidence to those who are "heirs of the promise."

Since God's unalterable promise was the foundation of Abraham's patient endurance, the same should be true for the readers of the letter. Any doubt about being inheritors of the promise should be removed, for what God has pledged will certainly be fulfilled (see §8). The verb "guaranteed" (ἐμεσίτευσεν) signifies that God as mediator pledges to fulfill his promise.[319] God's oath is accompanied by an action that secures what he has promised. The author suggests in using the language of mediator Jesus' role as "mediator" (μεσίτης, 8:6; 9:15; 12:24) of what God has promised so the oath is ultimately grounded and fulfilled in Jesus' atonement.[320] Hence he is the "guarantee" (ἔγγυος) of the new covenant (7:22). The readers need not fear that the promise would fail, for it is grounded in God's oath and Jesus' atoning work that secures what God has sworn.

6:18

The oath is given to confirm the certainty of the promise, which is designed to encourage the readers to persevere in faith and hope. The "two unchangeable things" are God's word and his oath. God's word itself is irrevocable, but his oath will never be rescinded either. The consolation of the readers is the author's purpose, and so he goes further, affirming that "it is impossible for God to lie." God's word alone is sufficient for faith since he never deviates from the truth. Nevertheless, he adds to his word his oath. The oath isn't given to substantiate God's truthfulness since he can't lie. The oath was given, then, for the sake of human beings, to underscore God's faithfulness.

When we speak of God's omnipotence, the meaning of his almightiness should be defined by the entirety of Scripture. There are some things God cannot do, for to do such things would be a denial of his divinity. We read in Num 23:19, "God is not a man who lies, or a son of man who changes His mind. Does He speak and not act,

---

[319] Attridge, *Hebrews*, 181.
[320] So Griffiths, "The Word of God," 40–41.

or promise and not fulfill?" What separates God from human beings, according to this text, is his unchangeableness. He does not change course, nor does he lie. Human beings prevaricate and deviate from the truth. God is inherently good and defines what is good. God can't be God and deviate from his nature. He wouldn't be God if he could lie. It is not as if there is a law above God that dictates his nature. Instead, the inability to do evil constitutes God's nature; goodness is intrinsic to and inherent in his being.

The inviolable promise of God is not an abstract truth unrelated to life. It is intended to give "strong encouragement" (ἰσχυρὰν παράκλησιν) for believers. They are assured that God will fulfill what he has promised. They turned to Jesus to find refuge by taking hold of the hope set before them. The encouragement furnished to the readers is that the hope they have staked their lives on will become a reality. They should persevere to the end with confidence and joy, knowing that God will fulfill his eschatological promises.

6:19

The author continues to elaborate on the certainty of the hope belonging to believers. This hope is an anchor for their lives, and it is "firm and secure" (NIV).[321] Nothing can dislodge their hope, for hope is an objective reality. As the author has indicated, the hope is stable and solid because it is founded on God's promise and oath. Since there is no doubt that God will keep his promises, the hope is a sure and stable anchor. Indeed, their hope "enters the inner sanctuary behind the curtain."[322] The inner sanctuary in the temple, the holy of holies, represents the presence of God. Indeed, the only other place where the words "inside behind the curtain" (ἐσώτερον τοῦ καταπετάσματος) occur is in Lev 16:2. Leviticus 16 speaks of the Day of Atonement, which is the only day in the year that the high priest entered the holy of holies.[323] For the writer, the holy of holies

---

[321] The HCSB rendering "safe" doesn't seem to fit as well the image of an anchor grasping onto something so that it holds firm.

[322] Hope, then, rather than the anchor, enters inside the veil (O'Brien, *Hebrews*, 241n187; Ellingworth, *Hebrews*, 345).

[323] Against Davidson, who sees a reference to the inauguration of the sanctuary rather than the Day of Atonement. Richard M. Davidson, "Christ's Entry 'Within the Veil' in Hebrews 6:19–20: The Old Testament Background," *AUSS* 39 (2001): 175–90. For a convincing critique of Davidson, see Norman H. Young, "The Day of Dedication or the Day of Atonement? The Old Testament Background to Hebrews

represents the presence of God.[324] The hope of believers is like an anchor that reaches within the veil, i.e., it brings believers into contact with God himself. "Hope penetrates behind the curtain, that is, believers *in hope* may now enter where Jesus has already gone in reality, into the heavenly sanctuary."[325] Here is a far better hope than what we find in the old covenant where access to God was limited to one day a year by the high priest (cf. 9:6–8). Now believers have "boldness to enter the sanctuary through the blood of Jesus" (10:19).

6:20

Believers have no warrant to obtain access to God's presence. Such access is given to them because Jesus is their Melchizedekian high priest. And as high priest he entered God's presence, offering his own blood to secure access to God for believers. The hope of believers is anchored in the work of Jesus as high priest. Their hope is secure, for Jesus as the Melchizedekian priest has atoned for their sins so that they can enter God's presence joyfully and boldly. He is their "forerunner" (πρόδρομος) or "precursor."[326] We think of the claim made elsewhere that Jesus is the pioneer (ἀρχηγός) of salvation (2:10; 12:2). The hope of believers, then, depends on the atoning work on the cross. The author doesn't call upon the readers to look to themselves and to their resources but to the cross of Jesus Christ.

Bridge

God promises eschatological blessings for those who belong to him, but we need patience like Abraham to obtain the promise. We need encouragement to continue along the pathway God has marked out for us. Such encouragement comes from God's promises. Just as God promised and swore an oath to Abraham, so too believers in Jesus Christ are the offspring of Abraham. The promises made to Abraham belong to them as well. Believers should be full of boldness and confidence, for not only did God promise blessing and multiplication to Abraham; he swore that he would fulfill the promise.

6:19–20 Revisited," *AUSS* 40 (2002): 61–68. Young rightly sees a reference to the Day of Atonement.

[324] The writer doesn't believe there is a literal curtain in heaven but speaks metaphorically. Rightly Hagner, *Hebrews*, 79.

[325] O'Brien, *Hebrews*, 242; cf. Cockerill, *Hebrews*, 290n21.

[326] L. Johnson, *Hebrews*, 173.

An oath is superfluous for the one true God who always keeps his word. The oath was for the benefit of human beings, underscoring the fidelity of his promises, so that we would put our hope and confidence in God. The hope believers possess is an anchor for their lives, for it is based on Jesus' priestly work inasmuch as he brings believers into God's presence based on his sacrificial work.

Hebrews 7:1–10

Outline

I. Prologue: Definitive and Final Revelation in the Son (1:1–4)
II. Don't Abandon the Son Since He Is Greater than Angels (1:5–2:18)
III. Don't Harden Your Hearts Since You Have a Son and High Priest Greater than Moses and Joshua (3:1–4:13)
IV. **Don't Fall Away from Jesus' Melchizedekian Priesthood Since It Is Greater than the Levitical Priesthood (4:14–10:18)**
    A. Exhortation in Light of Jesus' Priestly Status (4:14–5:10)
    B. Warning and Assurance (5:11–6:20)
    C. **Jesus' Greater Priesthood as a Melchizedekian Priest (7:1–28)**
        1. **Melchizedek Greater than Levi (7:1–10)**
        2. Arguments for a Changed Priesthood (7:11–28)

Scripture

¹ For this Melchizedek—King of Salem, priest of the Most High God, who met Abraham and blessed him as he returned from defeating the kings, ² and Abraham gave him a tenth of everything; first, his name means king of righteousness, then also, king of Salem, meaning king of peace; ³ without father, mother, or genealogy, having neither beginning of days nor end of life, but resembling the Son of God—remains a priest forever. ⁴ Now consider how great this man was—even Abraham the patriarch gave a tenth of the plunder to him! ⁵ The sons of Levi who receive the priestly office have a command according to the law to collect a tenth from the people—that is, from their brothers—though they have also descended from Abraham. ⁶ But one without this

lineage collected tenths from Abraham and blessed the one who had the promises.

⁷ Without a doubt, the inferior is blessed by the superior. ⁸ In the one case, men who will die receive tenths, but in the other case, Scripture testifies that he lives. ⁹ And in a sense Levi himself, who receives tenths, has paid tenths through Abraham, ¹⁰ for he was still within his ancestor when Melchizedek met him.

Context

The writer's desire has been to explicate the significance of Jesus' Melchizedekian priesthood, for the hope and confidence of the readers is based on Jesus' entering the presence of God for them. Before unfolding the significance of such a priesthood, he warns the readers about the danger of spiritual sluggishness (5:11–6:12). If they fall away, they will not receive the blessings God has promised. Now that he has given the warning, he is ready to unpack Jesus' Melchizedekian priesthood for them.

Melchizedek plays a unique role in the Scriptures and the biblical story line, for he is a priest-king (7:1–3). As a priest-king he blessed Abraham, and Abraham gave him a tenth of the spoils. Melchizedek's priesthood was unique, for it wasn't based on a genealogy, and thus he was a perpetual priest. In this sense he was like Jesus, the Son of God.

The greatness of Melchizedek is evident, for he received a tenth from Abraham and blessed Abraham (vv. 4–10), and the greater person blesses and receives gifts from the lesser. The Levitical priests who descended from Abraham also collected a tenth from fellow Israelites, but Melchizedek was superior to Levi as well, for Levi, so to speak, paid a tenth to Melchizedek. The logic is as follows: Abraham gave a tenth to Melchizedek, and Levi was a child of Abraham, and thus there is a sense in which Levi paid tithes to Melchizedek. The excellence of Melchizedek is also evident, for his priesthood never ends, for he is a living priest, whereas Levitical priests are constantly replaced since they die. The discussion on Melchizedek seems foreign to contemporary readers, but it is designed for a pastoral purpose. Since the Melchizedekian priesthood is clearly superior to the Levitical one, the readers must not abandon or forsake Jesus.

Exegesis

7:1

The author is now prepared to explain the significance of the Melchizedekian priesthood in more detail. He identifies Melchizedek as the king of Salem and the priest of the Most High God. After Abraham defeated the kings who captured Lot and rescued him, Abraham returned to the King's Valley (Gen 14:17). Without any explanation Melchizedek suddenly appears in the story as "a priest to God Most High" (Gen 14:18), bringing out bread and wine in celebration of Abraham's victory. He proceeds to bless Abraham, proclaiming that he was blessed "by God Most High, Creator of heaven and earth" (Gen 14:19). In response Abraham gave a tenth to Melchizedek (Gen 14:20), and the name Melchizedek vanishes from the scene in the OT until he appears in Ps 110:4.

The only place Melchizedek is mentioned in the NT is in Hebrews. Melchizedek does appear, however, in the Dead Sea Scrolls in 11QMelch.[327] According to this document, Melchizedek will proclaim at the final judgment the liberty of Jubilee to Israel and declare that they are forgiven of their sins. He is identified as "God" and will also assess people at the final judgment. Probably the identification of Melchizedek as "God" (cf. Exod 7:1) should not be read

---

[327] For a wider discussion on Melchizedek, including references to him in other sources, see M. Delcor, "Melchizedek from Genesis to the Qumran Texts and the Epistle to the Hebrews," *JSJ* 2 (1971): 115–35; Hughes, *Hebrews*, 237–45. Mason argues that Melchizedek is an angelic figure and that the portrait of Melchizedek at Qumran is the most significant religious-historical parallel. See Eric F. Mason, *"You Are a Priest Forever": Second Temple Jewish Messianism and the Priestly Christology of the Epistle to the Hebrews*, STDJ 74 (Leiden: Brill, 2008). Horton, on the other hand, maintains that Melchizedek was conceived of as a human being in Hebrews, and hence the Qumran conception of Melchizedek as an angelic figure was not shared by the author of Hebrews. Horton's work helpfully summarizes and examines the portrait of Melchizedek in the OT, Josephus, Philo, Qumran, rabbinic literature, and in Gnosticism. Fred L. Horton Jr., *The Melchizedek Tradition: A Critical Examination of the Sources to the Fifth Century A.D. and in the Epistle to the Hebrews*, SNTSMS 30 (Cambridge: Cambridge University Press, 1976). The dispute over whether Melchizedek in Hebrews was a human being or an angelic or supernatural figure of some kind hearkens back to the earliest church. For instance, Epiphanius of Salamis was insistent that he was a human being and should not be identified as Shem (some early fathers also argued that Melchizedek was the same person as Shem in the OT), but there was not universal agreement on these matters. See Heen and Krey, *Hebrews*, 98–107.

literally. It simply designates the significant role he plays in the final judgment. The exalted position of Melchizedek at the final judgment indicates that discussion and speculation over his role were in the air when Hebrews was written. The reference to Melchizedek, then, would not have shocked the readers because we see from other sources that Jews discussed his significance and his role.

In verse 1 the author of Hebrews introduces Melchizedek in accord with what was written about him and Abraham in Gen 14:17–18. As a king-priest he met Abraham and blessed him when he returned victorious from his battle with the kings.

7:2

The writer continues to remind the readers about what Genesis says about Melchizedek and Abraham. Abraham gave a tenth of the spoils of his victory to Melchizedek. The significance of Melchizedek's name is then unfolded. In explicating the meaning of Melchizedek's name, the author continues to draw literally on the Genesis account. The author introduces (Gen 14:18) Melchizedek (מַלְכִּי־צֶדֶק) and translates the meaning of his name for his readers. He is "king of righteousness" (βασιλεὺς δικαιοσύνης). The genitive should be understood as attributive, meaning that he was a righteous king. Of course, Melchizedek points to one greater than he, and the author has already told us that Jesus is a righteous king, informing us that Jesus was exalted and crowned as king because he "loved righteousness and hated lawlessness" (1:9).[328] Rooke also points out a connection to Ps 72:7, which is a messianic psalm, where peace and righteousness characterize the reign of the king.[329] Most kings don't rule righteously, but Melchizedek did, and his reign anticipated the righteous reign of a better king (Jesus), who will secure "a kingdom that cannot be shaken" (12:28).

Melchizedek is also "king of Salem" (Gen 14:18, מֶלֶךְ שָׁלֵם, βασιλεὺς Σαλήμ, Heb 7:2). Salem may refer to what eventually became Jerusalem. The author of Hebrews does not tie the name specifically to Jerusalem but translates it as "king of peace." Perhaps in Genesis Melchizedek's irenicism is tied to his not waging war, for

---

[328] Cf. here Deborah W. Rooke, "Jesus as Royal Priest: Reflections on the Interpretation of the Melchizedek Tradition in Heb 7," *Bib* 81 (2000): 81–94. See also Dae-I Kang, "The Royal Components of Melchizedek in Hebrews 7," *Perichoresis* 10 (2012): 95–124.

[329] Rooke, "Jesus as Royal Priest," 85–86.

he did not engage in war like the other kings in Genesis 14.[330] After all, Abraham fought the battle instead of Melchizedek. Surely for the author of Hebrews the significance of "Salem" points to Jesus: the king of peace who brings peace between human beings and God through his priestly work. We think of Isaiah where the Davidic ruler is the "Prince of Peace" (Isa 9:6). Isaiah also promises eschatological peace and righteousness, which will come with the Davidic ruler, for "a king will reign righteously" (Isa 32:1), and he goes on to say in the same chapter, "The result of righteousness will be peace" (Isa 32:17). Indeed, Isaiah takes it further, for peace for the people of God comes through the Servant of the Lord (Isa 53:5), and it is clear from the NT that this Servant is also the Son of David, the King of Israel and of the entire world.

7:3

What is left unsaid about Melchizedek in Genesis is mined for meaning. He served as a priest, but nothing is said about his father, mother, or genealogy (see §2.1). The omission of his genealogy doesn't mean he wasn't a human being. The author detects significance in the silence of Genesis, for Genesis identifies Melchizedek as a priest but says nothing about his genealogical qualifications to serve as a priest. In other words, Melchizedek stands out as a priest in that there is no genealogy relative to his priesthood.[331] One could not serve as Levitical priest, on the other hand, unless one could demonstrate that one was genealogically qualified. We think of those who were prohibited from serving as priests in Nehemiah because they could not prove their lineage (Neh 7:64–65). Melchizedek, on the other hand, appears on the scene not as one who was born or as one who dies. In the text as scripted, he continues as a priest forever, like Jesus the Son of God.

Some interpreters adopt a different perspective, arguing that Melchizedek was actually a preincarnate appearance of Jesus as the Son of God. That is, Melchizedek truly didn't have a father, mother, and was not born, nor did he die, for he was actually the Son

---

[330] So Kang, "Royal Components of Melchizedek," 101.

[331] See Horton, who also notes that Jewish writers spied special significance in Melchizedek because he was the first priest recorded in Scripture (*The Melchizedek Tradition*, 157–62).

of God, taking a human form and appearing on earth before the incarnation.[332]

Despite the popularity of this reading, it should be rejected for a number of reasons. First, the author of Hebrews regularly argues typologically, seeing Jesus as the greater David, the greater Moses, the greater Joshua, and the greater priest. The tabernacle points to and corresponds with God's dwelling in heaven. So too, Melchizedek's priesthood foreshadows and anticipates Jesus' Melchizedekian priesthood. Second, the author describes Melchizedek as "resembling the Son of God" (ἀφωμοιωμένος δὲ τῷ υἱῷ τοῦ θεου). The author doesn't say that Melchizedek *is* the Son of God but that he was *like* him.[333] The two are compared, not identified.[334]

The writer spies significance in what the text doesn't say about Melchizedek as a priest.[335] One couldn't serve as a Levitical

---

[332] Some think the wording here points to Melchizedek in the OT as deity (Bauckham, "The Divinity of Jesus Christ in the Epistle to the Hebrews," 27–39; Kiwoong Son, *Zion Symbolism in Hebrews: Hebrews 12:18–24 as a Hermeneutical Key to the Epistle*, Paternoster Biblical Monographs [Waynesboro, GA: Paternoster, 2005], 153–60). The problem with this, as O'Brien notes, is that if one sees Melchizedek as a divine being, then his "priesthood would encroach upon the eternal priesthood of Christ" (O'Brien, *Hebrews*, 248).

Cockerill understands (*Hebrews*, 305–6) Melchizedek to be a human being, comparing him to God's appearance to Abraham (Gen 18:1–15), the appearances of the Angel of the Lord, and the appearance of the captain of the Lord's army to Joshua (Josh 5:13–15). He argues that Melchizedek was a human being, concluding that there is no evidence that the author indulged in Melchizedek speculation, and his argument derives from Genesis 14. See also Gareth Lee Cockerill, "Melchizedek without Speculation: Hebrews 7.1–25 and Genesis 14.17–24," in *Cloud of Witnesses: The Theology of Hebrews in Its Ancient Contexts*, ed. R. Bauckham, D. Driver, T. Hart, and N. MacDonald, LNTS 387 (London: T&T Clark, 2008), 128–44. At the same time Cockerill also says that Melchizedek is an eternal being. How can he be an eternal being but also human? He suggests that Melchizedek was a preincarnate appearance of the Son. See Gareth Lee Cockerill, "The Melchizedek Christology in Hebrews 7:1–28" (Ph.D. diss., Union Theological Seminary, Richmond, Virginia, 1976), 484–93.

[333] Gaffin argues that Melchizedek here is made like the eternal Son of God, not the incarnate Christ. See Richard B. Gaffin Jr. "The Priesthood of Christ: A Servant in the Sanctuary," in *The Perfect Savior: Key Themes in Hebrews*, ed. J. Griffiths (Nottingham: InterVarsity, 2012), 64–66. Gaffin says that Christ's "divine, eternal Sonship makes his priesthood what it is in distinction from every other kind of priesthood" (65).

[334] Rightly Koester, *Hebrews*, 349.

[335] Rightly Hughes, *Hebrews*, 248.

priest without establishing one's genealogy. One had to know one's father to be qualified for the priesthood; yet nothing is said about Melchizedek's father, mother, or genealogy. The author is not suggesting that he didn't have such. His point is that, according to the text of Genesis, such things were irrelevant, for he is constituted as a priest without any mention of his paternity. Indeed, his birth and death are not recorded, signifying that "he remains a priest forever."

Jesus also serves as a Melchizedekian priest. It is not the case that his genealogy is unknown. In fact, the author is keenly aware that Jesus was from the tribe of Judah (7:13–14). The point is that Jesus' priesthood, like Melchizedek's, is not established on the basis of his genealogy. Instead, the focus is on his eternal priesthood (anticipating Ps 110:4) as the Son of God. By virtue of his resurrection from the dead, he continues as a priest forever, in contrast to the Levitical priests whose priesthood ends upon death.

7:4

The author wants the readers to rivet their eyes on Melchizedek. With an imperative verb he summons them to "consider (Θεωρεῖτε) how great this man was."[336] It would be easy to read the narrative in Genesis and forget about Melchizedek. Most readers would concentrate on Abraham since the narrative focuses on him, and he was the progenitor and patriarch of Israel. Still, Abraham was clearly not as great as Melchizedek since he gave him one-tenth of his plunder. The author of Hebrews invites us to read the OT with discernment and care, helping us grasp the significance of the narrative.

7:5

The previous verse featured the greatness of Melchizedek. He is exalted above Abraham, the founder of the Jewish people. On the other hand the priesthood was bequeathed to the sons of Levi. The Lord specially set them apart to serve and minister to him, and in particular the Aaronic priesthood derived from the Levites.

The Lord instructed the Levites to collect a tithe from Israel. "Look, I have given the Levites every tenth in Israel as an inheritance in return for the work they do, the work of the tent of meeting" (Num 18:21; cf. also Num 18:26; 2 Chr 31:4–5; Neh 10:37–38). The tenth collected by the Levites was from fellow Israelites, their

---

[336] The verb could be construed as an indicative, but in context an imperative is preferable.

brothers and sisters. Like the Levites the rest of Israel, which gave a tenth to the Levites, descended from Abraham. In turn the Levites were to give a tenth of what they collected to the Aaronic priests (cf. Num 3:5–9; 18:1–32; Neh 10:37–39). Since the author's focus is on the Aaronic priesthood, he speaks rather generally in saying that they collect a tenth from the people since strictly speaking they received it from the Levites; but we have seen elsewhere that the author generalizes and is often imprecise when referring to the OT.[337]

7:6

Melchizedek, however, stands outside such boundaries, for he wasn't an Israelite. He wasn't a son of Abraham. His receiving a tithe from Abraham wasn't comparable to the Levites receiving tithes from fellow Israelites. In the case of Melchizedek, there is a completely different category as one who stands outside Israel. And yet he collected a tenth from Abraham. Not only that; he blessed Abraham. The author underscores the significance of Melchizedek's blessing Abraham, for he "blessed the one who had the promises." As was noted previously (see 6:14), there is a close relationship between "blessing" and "the promises." The promises pledged to Abraham were dependent, at least in part, on Melchizedek's blessing. Such statements confirm Melchizedek's greatness (7:4).

7:7

In case we missed the point, the author makes it explicit. The one who blesses is greater than the one receiving the blessing. Since Melchizedek blessed Abraham, he is greater than Abraham. The wording of Gen 14:19 is significant: "He [Melchizedek] blessed him and said: Abram is blessed by God Most High, Creator of heaven and earth." Melchizedek as a priest mediated the blessing of "God Most High." His blessing had the imprimatur and the authority of heaven, of the maker of all things. Since the author exploits what the text says about Melchizedek, it is fascinating that he makes no comments about Melchizedek giving Abraham bread and wine. In church history bread and wine have often been identified as anticipations of the Eucharist. Cockerill rightly remarks that the author leaves out any reference to the bread and wine because they "did not facilitate demonstration of Melchizedek's 'superiority.'"[338]

---

[337] Cf. the discussion in Hughes, *Hebrews*, 252.

[338] Cockerill, *Hebrews*, 297.

7:8

The author shifts from Abraham to the Levites, from the fount of Israel to his descendants. He returns to their role, adumbrated in verse 5, of receiving tithes from fellow Israelites. But he latches on to another matter in which they are distinguished from Melchizedek. Previously, it was noted that Levites collected a tenth from fellow Israelites, while Melchizedek was not a descendant of Abraham. Now he picks up on a matter that will receive sustained attention as the argument progresses. The Levites who collected a tenth from their brothers eventually died. Their priesthood concluded with their death, for they were mortal men. But the text says nothing about Melchizedek's death. Nothing is said about priests succeeding him. The text testifies, then, to a living priesthood; for the writer Melchizedek points to Jesus Christ as the resurrected one. Do the readers want to attach themselves to priests who die or to a great high priest who has conquered death and lives forever?

7:9

The superiority of the Melchizedekian priesthood is the author's aim so he continues to pursue his argument, recognizing that what he is about to say isn't literally true. Still, Abraham's paying a tenth to Melchizedek has implications for the Levitical priesthood, for the Levites "through Abraham" paid a tenth to Melchizedek. And if they paid Melchizedek a tenth, then Melchizedek's priesthood is superior to the Levitical one. It follows, then, that they should not revert to the Levitical priesthood when they enjoy a better priesthood.

7:10

But in what sense can be it be said that Levi paid a tenth to Melchizedek? The author explains that when Abraham gave a tenth to Melchizedek, Levi was, so to speak, in his body. As a descendant of Abraham, Levi through Abraham gave a tenth to Melchizedek. If this is true, then all the arguments relative to Abraham also apply to Levi. The lesser (Levi) paid a tenth to the greater (Melchizedek).

Bridge

What concerns the author is that the readers might fall away, and the reference to the law mediated by angels (2:2), to Moses (3:1–6), to the contrast between the Levitical and Melchizedekian priesthood (7:1–28), to the old and new covenant (8:1–13), to the earthly and true tabernacle (9:1–14), and to two kinds of sacrifices

(9:15–10:18) demonstrate that the readers were inclined to revert to the Mosaic cult. The author argues here that such a move would be senseless. After all, the Melchizedekian priesthood is clearly superior to the Levitical one. Melchizedek was greater than Abraham, for he blessed Abraham and collected a tenth from him. Furthermore, his priesthood has a different character. It doesn't depend on a particular genealogy. It is a living and permanent priesthood. Levitical priests die, but Melchizedek's priesthood is endless. Indeed, even Levi paid a tenth to Melchizedek through Abraham. Melchizedek anticipates and corresponds to Jesus Christ. He is the ever-living one, the priest whose priesthood never ends. If the readers desire life and true forgiveness of sins, they must continue to hold fast to the confession that proclaims Jesus as the Melchizedekian priest.

Hebrews 7:11–12

Outline

   I. Prologue: Definitive and Final Revelation in the Son (1:1–4)

  II. Don't Abandon the Son Since He Is Greater than Angels (1:5–2:18)

 III. Don't Harden Your Hearts Since You Have a Son and High Priest Greater than Moses and Joshua (3:1–4:13)

 IV. **Don't Fall Away from Jesus' Melchizedekian Priesthood Since It Is Greater than the Levitical Priesthood (4:14–10:18)**

    A. Exhortation in Light of Jesus' Priestly Status (4:14–5:10)

    B. Warning and Assurance (5:11–6:20)

    C. **Jesus' Greater Priesthood as a Melchizedekian Priest (7:1–28)**

       1. Melchizedek Greater than Levi (7:1–10)

       2. **Arguments for a Changed Priesthood (7:11–28)**

          a. **Imperfection of Levitical Priesthood (7:11–12)**

          b. Jesus from Tribe of Judah (7:13–14)

          c. Prophecy of Melchizedekian Priesthood (7:15–17)

          d. Setting Aside of Levitical Priesthood (7:18–19)

          e. Oath Accompanies Melchizedekian Priesthood (7:20–22)

f. Jesus a Permanent Priest (7:23–25)

g. A Sinless Priest and a Once-for-All
Sacrifice (7:26–28)

D. New Covenant Better than the Old (8:1–13)

Scripture

¹¹ If then, perfection came through the Levitical priesthood (for under it the people received the law), what further need was there for another priest to appear, said to be in the order of Melchizedek and not in the order of Aaron? ¹² For when there is a change of the priesthood, there must be a change of law as well.

Context

In 7:1–10 the author argues that Melchizedek's priesthood is superior to the Levitical priesthood, and he continues along the same lines in 7:11–19. Verses 11–19 set forth the inadequacy of the Levitical priesthood. If perfection were realized through the Levitical priesthood, a new priesthood, a Melchizedekian priesthood, would not have been promised. The promise of a new priesthood demonstrates the inferiority of the old. In verse 11 the law is intertwined with the Levitical priesthood. Verse 12 unfolds the inextricable relationship between the Mosaic law and the priesthood. It follows, then, that a change in the priesthood also means a change in the law.

Exegesis

7:11

Verses 11–19 are closely tied to the preceding argument. The author begins by drawing an inference, "then" (μὲν οὖν), from the preceding verses. Since Melchizedek was greater than Abraham and Levi, which was evident from his blessing of Abraham and receiving tithes from him and from his perpetual priesthood, and since a priest like Melchizedek is prophesied (Ps 110:4), perfection will clearly not be achieved through the Levitical priesthood. The word "perfection" (τελείωσις) refers here to eschatological perfection.[339]

---

[339] Lane, *Hebrews 1–8*, 181. L. Johnson says, "Perfection is a matter of human transformation rather than cultic transaction. It combines elements of maturity and moral growth. . . . Negatively, perfection means abandoning or overcoming sin (9:27; 10:4) and cleansing the conscience (9:9). Positively, it means a process

In Hebrews the concept of perfection is broad, including the forgiveness of sins, ethical righteousness, and the rule human beings were to exercise over the universe as priest-kings.[340] If eschatological perfection could be realized under the Levitical priesthood, there would be no need to designate the arrival of another priesthood, a Melchizedekian one. Another priesthood would be superfluous if the Levitical priesthood could bring about the new creation and bring human beings to the heavenly city. So it is clear that the Levitical priesthood is inadequate: it doesn't truly and finally forgive sins and provide access to God. It doesn't transform human beings so they become righteous. It doesn't restore the rule human beings lost when Adam sinned. Instead the Levitical priesthood had an interim character and nature so that it adumbrated and prepared the way for a better priesthood, a Melchizedekian one.

Two other comments should be added here. First, the author says the law and the Levitical priesthood are entwined together.[341] The law here is clearly the law of Moses, the law given to Israel at Sinai. The writer probably has in mind the fundamental character of the priesthood relative to the Mosaic law. In other words, apart from the sacrifices offered, there would be no forgiveness of sins under the old covenant. Hence the priesthood was essential for the law and Israel's covenant with Yahweh. Second, the priesthood in view here is the one made with Aaron. When the author refers to the Levitical priesthood, he thinks particularly of the unique role given to Aaron and his sons as priests to offer sacrifices to atone for Israel's sins.

---

of sanctification (9:13; 10:10, 14)—entering into a state of holiness—through an opening to God's power and presence through faithful obedience (5:7–10; 12:1–2)" (*Hebrews*, 185–86).

[340] Cf. Peterson, *Hebrews and Perfection*, 126–30.

[341] It is disputed whether the author actually argues that the law is *based* on the priesthood. The words "upon it" (ἐπ' αὐτῆς) may indicate that the law was "about" the Levitical priesthood (Koester, 353; Lane, *Hebrews 1–8*, 174). Still the author is most likely saying that the law is based on the priesthood (cf. Ellingworth, *Hebrews*, 372; O'Brien, *Hebrews*, 258). Such a statement seems strange since the law instituted the priesthood, but as Cockerill says, "Although the law given at Sinai established the priesthood, living under that law was based on and dependent upon its perpetual functioning" (*Hebrews*, 316). He continues, "Before the advent of Christ God's people could not live under the law without the priesthood as a means of approaching God through atonement" (317).

Levites had other priestly duties as well in the OT, but the focus is on the sacrifices offered by Aaronic priests to procure atonement.

7:12

The indissoluble relationship between the priesthood and the law is explained. Since the law and the priesthood are bound together, a change in one means a change in the other. Now it is clear from verse 11 that eschatological perfection is not achieved through the Aaronic priesthood. Indeed, God planned all along that a new priesthood would arrive, a Melchizedekian one. Hence the Aaronic priesthood is passé. But if the priesthood has changed, then the Mosaic law is no longer in force either. Hence there is no basis for saying that Hebrews limits what he says about the law to priesthood and sacrificial instructions.[342] The law and the priesthood are entwined together, and thus the passing of the priesthood also means that the law as a whole is no longer in force.[343]

Bridge

The prediction and arrival of the Melchizedekian priesthood means the Aaronic priesthood and the Mosaic law are no longer in force. Christians no longer live under the old covenant. The OT is still authoritative Scripture, but the OT should be read in light of the new covenant and the new priesthood, which have arrived in Jesus Christ. Eschatological perfection (forgiveness of sins and the arrival of the new creation) come only through Jesus Christ. Hence the readers should not turn back to the Levitical priesthood when it cannot bring such perfection.

---

[342] Against Anderson, "Who Are the Heirs of the New Age in the Epistle to the Hebrews?" 268–72. Barry C. Joslin rightly criticizes those who posit absolute discontinuity between the law and the age of the new covenant ("Hebrews 7–10 and the Transformation of the Law," in *Cloud of Witnesses: The Theology of Hebrews in Its Ancient Contexts*, ed. R. Bauckham, D. Driver, T. Hart, and N. MacDonald, LNTS 387 [London: T&T Clark, 2008], 100–117). But against Joslin (100–106), the author of Hebrews argues that the law as a whole has passed away in 7:11–19. To say that the law has passed away does not preclude the notion that there is also a sense in which the law is fulfilled in that it is written on the heart. See the commentary on Heb 8:8–12 and 10:15–18.

[343] See here Koester, *Hebrews*, 114–15; Lane, *Hebrews 1–8*, 182. Against Ellingworth, *Hebrews*, 374.

Hebrews 7:13–14

Outline

I. Prologue: Definitive and Final Revelation in the Son (1:1–4)
II. Don't Abandon the Son Since He Is Greater than Angels (1:5–2:18)
III. Don't Harden Your Hearts Since You Have a Son and High Priest Greater than Moses and Joshua (3:1–4:13)
IV. **Don't Fall Away from Jesus' Melchizedekian Priesthood Since It Is Greater than the Levitical Priesthood (4:14–10:18)**
  A. Exhortation in Light of Jesus' Priestly Status (4:14–5:10)
  B. Warning and Assurance (5:11–6:20)
  C. **Jesus' Greater Priesthood as a Melchizedekian Priest (7:1–28)**
     1. Melchizedek Greater than Levi (7:1–10)
     2. **Arguments for a Changed Priesthood (7:11–28)**
        a. Imperfection of Levitical Priesthood (7:11–12)
        b. **Jesus from Tribe of Judah (7:13–14)**
        c. Prophecy of Melchizedekian Priesthood (7:15–17)
        d. Setting Aside of Levitical Priesthood (7:18–19)
        e. Oath Accompanies Melchizedekian Priesthood (7:20–22)
        f. Jesus a Permanent Priest (7:23–25)
        g. A Sinless Priest and a Once-for-All Sacrifice (7:26–28)
  D. New Covenant Better than the Old (8:1–13)

Scripture

[13] For the One these things are spoken about belonged to a different tribe. No one from it has served at the altar. [14] Now it is evident that our Lord came from Judah, and Moses said nothing about that tribe concerning priests.

Context

The main point in verses 11–12 is that the priesthood has been changed. Clearly a new priesthood has arisen because God ordained a priesthood according to the order of Melchizedek. Verses 13–14 confirm that the priesthood of Jesus is indeed new, for he is not from the tribe of Levi. He is from the tribe of Judah, and Moses says nothing about anyone from the tribe of Judah serving as a priest. Hence, Jesus' priesthood is of a new and different character.

Exegesis

7:13

The author confirms that a new priesthood has been established. Jesus is the great high priest, but he does not belong to the tribe of Levi. In the OT the priesthood is given specifically and exclusively to the tribe of Levi, and more specifically the high priesthood is restricted to Aaron and his sons (cf. Exod 28:1, 3–4, 41; 29:9, 30, 44; 30:30; 31:10; 40:13–15). There is no precedent or permission from God for other tribes to bring offerings. As O'Brien points out, the author doesn't appeal to OT texts where David and Solomon engaged in priestly functions, and thus he doesn't defend Jesus' priesthood by suggesting that he functions as priest in ways similar to David or Solomon.[344] Jesus is a priest, but he is a priest from another order and sphere.

7:14

The author restates and amplifies verse 13. In verse 13 Jesus is said to be from another tribe, and in verse 14 the tribe is specified: it is clear that Jesus descended from the tribe of Judah. Verse 13 noted that the tribe from which Jesus came never officiated at the altar. Verse 14 restates the same idea by indicating that a priestly ministry was not ascribed to Judah in the law. Verses 13–14 confirm that a new priesthood has arisen since Jesus is a priest from another tribe. Jesus' priesthood is not in accord with the law and its prescriptions, since he hails from the tribe of Judah. The reference to Judah brings to mind the kingly nature of Jesus' priesthood. He is a Davidic priest-king, a Messianic priest-king. There is likely an echo here of Balaam's prophecy, for he predicted that "a star will come from Jacob, and scepter will arise in Israel. He will smash the forehead of Moab" (Num 24:17). The verb for the star "coming" (ἀνατελεῖ) is

---

[344] O'Brien, *Hebrews*, 260.

used here for Jesus coming from (ἀνατέταλκεν) Judah.[345] The scepter rising (ἀναστήσεται, Num 24:17) also suggests Jesus' resurrection, which fits with the emphasis in Hebrews on Jesus' reigning as the risen priest-king (cf. also Isa 11:1; Jer 23:5; 33:15; Zech 3:8; 6:12; Mal 4:1–2).[346]

Bridge

A new order has come since Jesus is a Melchizedekian priest, the priest-king prophesied in the OT. It is evident that a new day has come, for Jesus is from the tribe of Judah instead of the tribe of Levi. As believers we live in the day of fulfillment, and thus we should rejoice in and cling to our priest-king, the Lord Jesus Christ.

Hebrews 7:15–17

Outline

   I. Prologue: Definitive and Final Revelation in the Son (1:1–4)
  II. Don't Abandon the Son Since He Is Greater than Angels (1:5–2:18)
 III. Don't Harden Your Hearts Since You Have a Son and High Priest Greater than Moses and Joshua (3:1–4:13)
 IV. **Don't Fall Away from Jesus' Melchizedekian Priesthood Since It Is Greater than the Levitical Priesthood (4:14–10:18)**
    A. Exhortation in Light of Jesus' Priestly Status (4:14–5:10)
    B. Warning and Assurance (5:11–6:20)
    C. **Jesus' Greater Priesthood as a Melchizedekian Priest (7:1–28)**
      1. Melchizedek Greater than Levi (7:1–10)
      2. **Arguments for a Changed Priesthood (7:11–28)**
        a. Imperfection of Levitical Priesthood (7:11–12)
        b. Jesus from Tribe of Judah (7:13–14)
        c. **Prophecy of Melchizedekian Priesthood (7:15–17)**

---

[345] Cockerill argues that the verb used here does not mean "descend" but "arise" and that he chose this term to echo Balaam's words (*Hebrews*, 319–20).

[346] Cf. Attridge, *Hebrews*, 201; L. Johnson, *Hebrews*, 187; Hughes, *Hebrews*, 259. Cockerill, however, says the text is limited to Jesus' coming here (*Hebrews*, 320n37).

    d. Setting Aside of Levitical Priesthood (7:18–19)

    e. Oath Accompanies Melchizedekian
       Priesthood (7:20–22)

    f. Jesus a Permanent Priest (7:23–25)

    g. A Sinless Priest and a Once-for-All
       Sacrifice (7:26–28)

  D. New Covenant Better than the Old (8:1–13)

Scripture

¹⁵ And this becomes clearer if another priest like Melchizedek appears, ¹⁶ who did not become a priest based on a legal command concerning physical descent but based on the power of an indestructible life. ¹⁷ For it has been testified: You are a priest forever in the order of Melchizedek.

Context

Verses 15–17 are part of an argument that stretches through verses 11–28. Verses 11–12 indicate that there has been an alteration of the priesthood. Verses 13–14 confirm that a change has occurred since Jesus is not from the tribe of Levi but the tribe of Judah. A new priesthood is even more evident according to verses 15–17, for the Scripture clearly indicates that a priest according to the order of Melchizedek is coming. Jesus' priesthood is far superior to the Levitical priesthood, for he is appointed as a priest by virtue of his resurrection. Levitical priests, on the contrary, were appointed genealogically, even though they were unable to conquer death. The perpetuity and resurrection of Jesus is apparent in the prophecy of Ps 110:4, for he is a priest *forever*.

Exegesis

7:15

The words "and this becomes clearer" introduce verse 15. What has become clearer? God has unmistakably communicated that a new priesthood has arrived, and thus the old Levitical priesthood is no longer applicable.[347] The readers of the letter were not facing an ambiguous and complex situation where the will of God was difficult to discern, where they could legitimately claim that perhaps the

---

[347] So also Attridge, *Hebrews*, 202.

Levitical system was the best option for them. The superiority of the Melchizedekian priesthood and the obsolescence of the Levitical priesthood are plain to see, for God has now fulfilled—as the resurrection of Jesus makes especially evident—his promise to bring in a priest according to the order of Melchizedek.[348]

The word "arises" (ESV, ἀνίσταται), which is obscured by the HCSB/NIV "appears," is likely polyvalent so that it refers not only to Jesus' appearing on the scene as priest but also to his resurrection.[349] Jesus' resurrection vindicated his priesthood, and upon his resurrection his priesthood was established in all its fullness.

7:16

The author continues to explain why Jesus' priesthood is superior and permanent, whereas the Levitical arrangement is inferior and temporary. Levitical priests served on the basis of a "fleshly commandment" (ἐντολῆς σαρκίνης). The HCSB captures what the author means. Levitical priests were appointed "based on a legal command concerning physical descent." Even better here is the NRSV: they were priests because of "a legal requirement concerning physical descent." No intrinsic virtue qualified one to be a Levitical priest. All one needed was the right family tree, the appropriate genealogical roots.

Jesus' priesthood, however, was of a radically different nature. He didn't qualify as priest by virtue of his genealogy. Indeed he failed the genealogical test, for he was clearly not from the tribe of Levi (vv. 13–14). Jesus didn't merely meet an external legal requirement. The criteria were much higher for him, for he became a priest because of "the power of an indestructible life." The word "indestructible" (ἀκαταλύτου) refers to a life "that cannot be brought to an end."[350] In 4 Macc 10:11 the word is used to describe "unceasing" torments (NRSV). Jesus, of course, died, and hence the reference is

---

[348] The word "order" here does not refer to a succession of priests, as if there would be many Melchizedekian priests. The idea is that Jesus' priesthood is of the same nature and quality as Melchizedek's (so Lane, *Hebrews 1–8*, 183).

[349] L. Johnson, *Hebrews*, 186–87; Moffitt, *Atonement and the Logic of the Resurrection in the Epistle to the Hebrews*, 203.

[350] LN 13.47.

likely to his resurrection, to his victory over death (see §2.6).[351] So his resurrection and exaltation are in view.[352]

Cockerill, on the other hand, says we have a reference here to Jesus' deity, to the indestructible life he possesses as a divine being.[353] According to Cockerill, Jesus' exaltation refers to his perfection, not to his "deification." The divine eternity of the Son contrasts him with Levitical priests, according to Cockerill. On both interpretations, Jesus is now the living and reigning high priest. It is difficult to choose between the two options, for certainly Hebrews highlights Jesus' deity. Nevertheless, I would suggest that the emphasis here is on his resurrection instead of his deity per se. The author doesn't reflect on Jesus' intrinsic ability to conquer death as a divine being but on his resurrection as a human being.

All Levitical priests die, but Jesus is a priest who has triumphed over death forever. His life will never be brought to an end. Surely such a priesthood is superior to one where death leads to an endless succession of priests.

7:17

The author supports the claim that Jesus had an indestructible life, confirming it from Scripture itself. He cites Ps 110:4, the only other place in the Scripture that names Melchizedek. The inclusion of this verse in Psalm 110 indicates that the Melchizedek priesthood was no anomaly. It was intended by God to last forever, as the prophetic word demonstrates. Furthermore, what the psalmist wrote applies to Jesus Christ. The author has already applied Ps 110:1 to Jesus, and he regularly alludes to or quotes it in the letter (1:3, 13; 8:1; 10:12; 12:2). If we put Ps 110:1 and Ps 110:4 together, it is evident that Jesus is a king-priest. Here the author quotes Ps 110:4 to support the claim that Jesus possesses an indestructible life. The key word from the OT citation is "forever." Jesus is a priest in the Melchizedekian order, and what distinguishes him from the Levitical priests is that he serves as a priest forever. Death did not and could not conquer him.

---

[351] So also Koester, *Hebrews*, 355; Lane, *Hebrews 1–8*, 184.

[352] Peterson, *Hebrews and Perfection*, 110–11.

[353] Cockerill, *Hebrews*, 323–24.

Bridge

Psalm 110:4 demonstrates that another priesthood would arise, a Melchizedekian priesthood. Jesus served as a priest according to the order of Melchizedek. He is superior to Levitical priests because of his indestructible life. The readers must hold fast to their confession, for they belong to a priest who has conquered death. They would not be pursuing life if they attached themselves to a priesthood (the Levitical one) where priests die.

Hebrews 7:18–19

Outline

I. Prologue: Definitive and Final Revelation in the Son (1:1–4)
II. Don't Abandon the Son Since He Is Greater than Angels (1:5–2:18)
III. Don't Harden Your Hearts Since You Have a Son and High Priest Greater than Moses and Joshua (3:1–4:13)
IV. **Don't Fall Away from Jesus' Melchizedekian Priesthood Since It Is Greater than the Levitical Priesthood (4:14–10:18)**
   A. Exhortation in Light of Jesus' Priestly Status (4:14–5:10)
   B. Warning and Assurance (5:11–6:20)
   C. **Jesus' Greater Priesthood as a Melchizedekian Priest (7:1–28)**
      1. Melchizedek Greater than Levi (7:1–10)
      2. **Arguments for a Changed Priesthood (7:11–28)**
         a. Imperfection of Levitical Priesthood (7:11–12)
         b. Jesus from Tribe of Judah (7:13–14)
         c. Prophecy of Melchizedekian Priesthood (7:15–17)
         d. **Setting Aside of Levitical Priesthood (7:18–19)**
         e. Oath Accompanies Melchizedekian Priesthood (7:20–22)
         f. Jesus a Permanent Priest (7:23–25)
         g. A Sinless Priest and a Once-for-All Sacrifice (7:26–28)
   D. New Covenant Better than the Old (8:1–13)

Scripture

¹⁸ So the previous command is annulled because it was weak and unprofitable ¹⁹ (for the law perfected nothing), but a better hope is introduced, through which we draw near to God.

Context

Verses 18–19 conclude verses 11–17 and sum up the main point of the paragraph. The author began in verses 11–12 by saying a new priesthood was needed to achieve perfection, that the Levitical priesthood had been replaced by a Melchizedekian one. Verses 13–14 confirm that the priesthood is indeed new. Jesus is not a priest from the tribe of Levi but a priest-king from the tribe of Judah. Indeed, the arrival of a new and better priesthood is clear (vv. 15–17) because Ps 110:4 prophesies that the Melchizedekian priesthood will endure forever, and that prophecy is now fulfilled, which is particularly evident by virtue of Jesus' resurrection. Jesus is a better priest because, in contrast to the Levitical priests, he triumphed over death. The author assesses the situation in verses 18–19. The regulation and command concerning Levitical priests has been set aside. A new day has arrived. The previous order has been annulled because of its intrinsic defects, i.e., it was unable to bring perfection. The word "perfected" (ἐτελείωσεν) here is a framing device. The paragraph began with the claim that the Levitical priesthood could not bring "perfection" (τελείωσις 7:11). The author returns to that theme here, emphasizing the inferiority of the Levitical order. By way of a contrast, a new order has arrived with a new priesthood. What sets it apart is that there is a better hope. The reference to the hope draws in 6:18–19 where hope is construed as an anchor for the lives of believers. Indeed, 7:19 resonates with 6:18–20, for what makes the hope better is that believers actually draw near to God through Jesus' priesthood. The Levitical priesthood did not have the same efficacy. Instead, it reminded believers of their sins and failings.

Exegesis

7:18

The contrast between the Levitical and Melchizedekian priesthood continues in verses 18–19. There is an "on the one hand" and "but on the other hand" (μέν-δέ) construction here. The "previous command" here refers not to any particular command in the Mosaic law, but the previous administration, the Levitical order that was in force during the old covenant.[354] So what has been "set aside" (NIV) or "annulled" (HCSB, ἀθέτησις) is the Levitical priesthood. The term is legal, designating the "abrogation" (NRSV) of a previous requirement.[355] The reason given for the setting aside of the Levitical priesthood centers on its deficiencies. It is faulted for being "weak and unprofitable," i.e., "weak and ineffectual" (NRSV). The weakness, given the flow of the argument, relates to its inability to give human beings hope. The Levitical priesthood doesn't bring people near to God with confidence and boldness.

7:19

The weakness of the Levitical priesthood is elaborated upon: "for the law perfected nothing." As noted above, the use of the word "perfected" (ἐτελείωσεν) functions as an inclusio with the word "perfection" (τελείωσις) in 7:11. In 7:11 the inability of the Levitical priesthood to bring perfection is asserted, but here he says that the "law" (ὁ νόμος) cannot bring perfection. The priesthood and law are tied together in any case since the author indicated in 7:11 that the law is based on the priesthood. We have a package deal here; what is true of the law is also true of the priesthood and vice versa. In asserting that the law perfected nothing, he means (cf. 7:11 above) that eschatological perfection could not be achieved via the law.[356] The law did not accomplish final and full forgiveness of sins and cleanse their consciences. "The institutions of priesthood, sacrifice, and atonement were not able to achieve a definitive arrangement of the relationship to God."[357] Nor were human beings transformed via the law. Nor was human rule over the world restored via the law.

Given its liabilities, the Levitical priesthood was annulled, and a better and new hope has been introduced. The word "better" (κρείττονος) captures the author's intention: Jesus is "better" than angels (1:4); the readers have experienced "better things" (6:9); Melchizedek is "better" than Abraham (7:7); Jesus guarantees a

---

[354] Cf. 7:16 and the use of the term "fleshly commandment" (ἐντολῆς σαρκίνης) to designate the Levitical order.

[355] BDAG; Attridge, *Hebrews*, 203; L. Johnson, *Hebrews*, 189; Ellingworth, *Hebrews*, 380–81.

[356] So Lane, *Hebrews 1–8*, 185.

[357] Ibid., 185.

"better covenant" (7:22; 8:6), which has "better promises" (8:6); he offered "better sacrifices" (9:23); the readers have a "better possession" (10:34); a "better country" (11:16); await a "better resurrection" (11:35); OT saints will experience what is "better" and "perfect" only in fellowship with NT saints (11:40); Jesus' blood speaks "better" than Abel's (12:24). It is inconceivable, according to the author, that the readers would forsake what is better and cling to the law and the Levitical priesthood.

The "better hope" picks up on the theme of hope in 6:18–20. "What is introduced is a *better* hope, which refers not to the quality of hope (in the sense that God has made us more hopeful), but the thing hoped for, its content or ground. It is better because of its effectiveness."[358] In 6:18–20 the author encourages the readers with the promise of God, with the oath that he swore to them as the offspring of Abraham. They have a hope that is an anchor, for through Jesus they have access to God (see §8). The veil in the old covenant, which separated human beings from God, has been breached through Jesus. The author makes a similar point here. The hope is better because through it believers "draw near to God" (see §1). Jesus' sacrifice, as will be explained in more detail as the letter progresses, cleanses believers from sin so they can boldly enter God's presence. The Levitical priesthood did not bring people near to God. Instead, it reminded people that they were distant from him, that their sins were not atoned for fully and finally.

Bridge

The Levitical priesthood has been set aside because of its inferiority and weakness. It ultimately doesn't and can't bring people into God's presence. It doesn't and can't cleanse people of their sins. A new priesthood has been inaugurated, a Melchizedekian one. It is far superior to the Levitical priesthood, for it actually brings hope and draws people into God's presence. The author of Hebrews is not attempting to write an abstract theological tract on the superiority of the new covenant to the old. He worries that the readers will fall away. He wants his readers to enjoy the boldness and confidence of a personal relationship with God. Only Jesus and his priesthood, only Jesus and his sacrifice, can do that.

---

[358] O'Brien, *Hebrews*, 266.

Hebrews 7:20–22

Outline

I. Prologue: Definitive and Final Revelation in the Son (1:1–4)
II. Don't Abandon the Son Since He Is Greater than Angels (1:5–2:18)
III. Don't Harden Your Hearts Since You Have a Son and High Priest Greater than Moses and Joshua (3:1–4:13)
IV. **Don't Fall Away from Jesus' Melchizedekian Priesthood Since It Is Greater than the Levitical Priesthood (4:14–10:18)**
    A. Exhortation in Light of Jesus' Priestly Status (4:14–5:10)
    B. Warning and Assurance (5:11–6:20)
    C. **Jesus' Greater Priesthood as a Melchizedekian Priest (7:1–28)**
        1. Melchizedek Greater than Levi (7:1–10)
        2. **Arguments for a Changed Priesthood (7:11–28)**
            a. Imperfection of Levitical Priesthood (7:11–12)
            b. Jesus from Tribe of Judah (7:13–14)
            c. Prophecy of Melchizedekian Priesthood (7:15–17)
            d. Setting Aside of Levitical Priesthood (7:18–19)
            e. **Oath Accompanies Melchizedekian Priesthood (7:20–22)**
            f. Jesus a Permanent Priest (7:23–25)
            g. A Sinless Priest and a Once-for-All Sacrifice (7:26–28)
    D. New Covenant Better than the Old (8:1–13)

Scripture

[20] None of this happened without an oath. For others became priests without an oath, [21] but He became a priest with an oath made by the One who said to Him: The Lord has sworn, and He will not change His mind, You are a priest forever. [22] So Jesus has also become the guarantee of a better covenant.

Context

The superiority of the Melchizedekian priesthood to the Levitical continues to be argued. First, the change of priesthood demonstrates that the Levitical priesthood is inferior (vv. 11–12). Second, the priesthood has truly changed since Jesus comes from the tribe of Judah instead of the tribe of Levi (vv. 13–14). Third, Jesus' priesthood is better because he possesses an indestructible life (vv. 15–17). Fourth, the Melchizedekian priesthood is better because it brings human beings into God's presence (vv. 18–19). Here we find the fifth argument. Jesus is the guarantor of a better covenant because the covenant was accompanied by an oath (vv. 20–22). Levitical priests never received an oath, showing that the priesthood was not of the same caliber. Psalm 110:4 confirms that the Melchizedekian priesthood was established on the basis of an oath: the Lord swore that the king would serve as a Melchizedekian priest forever.

Exegesis

7:20

Jesus' priesthood, his Melchizedekian priesthood, was distinctive, for his priesthood was based on an oath. The author previously explained the significance of God's taking an oath in 6:13–18. An oath isn't necessary for God's sake but for the sake of human beings, confirming and underscoring the unalterable character of God's purpose. God's oath demonstrates that the Melchizedekian priesthood is permanent. By way of contrast, no oath accompanied the Levitical priesthood, showing that the Levitical order was restricted to a certain period in salvation history. The author is not suggesting that the Levitical priesthood was contrary to God's will or intention; he is simply emphasizing that it had a built-in obsolescence.

7:21

By way of contrast, Jesus became a priest with an oath. Once again the wording of Psalm 110 is consulted, where the author finds an oath (Ps 110:4). We cannot help but notice how virtually every word in this verse is ransacked for its significance. The attention paid to the specific wording of the text is quite remarkable. The Lord did not only say, "You are a priest forever." He swore (ὤμοσεν) that Jesus would serve as a priest forever. The emphatic nature of the utterance leaps out to the reader. Not only did God swear that the

Melchizedekian priesthood would endure forever; the verse also stresses that God will not change his mind. God swears there is no going back on the Melchizedekian priesthood so he will never revoke what he has sworn. The content of the oath is important as well. Jesus is a Melchizedekian priest "forever" (εἰς τὸν αἰῶνα). The Levitical priesthood was established for a limited period of time, but the Melchizedekian priesthood will never come to an end.

7:22

The author concludes the comparison begun in verse 20. If we put the two parts of the comparison together, the argument runs as follows: "To the degree that this was not without an oath, to the same degree Jesus became the guarantor of a better covenant." The superiority of the Melchizedekian priesthood and the new covenant is based on the oath which accompanied Jesus' priesthood. As noted previously, the word "better" (κρείττονος) plays a major role in the author's argument, and the covenant established through Jesus is far better than the old covenant.[359]

Jesus is "the guarantee" (ἔγγυος) of a better covenant inasmuch as it was established with an oath (see §3). The verb is used of those who guarantee the debts of another so they pay what is owed (Prov 17:18; 22:26). The word "guarantee" along with "oath" drives home the certainty of what was promised. But in what sense does Jesus stand as a guarantee? The author doesn't say here that Jesus fulfills the debts human beings owe to God. Rather he emphasizes that Jesus guarantees God's fidelity and faithfulness, indicating that God will certainly fulfill his promise of forgiving the sins of his people.[360] The word is closely related to another word translated "guaranteed" in 6:17 (ἐμεσίτευσεν). Ellingworth understands the two words to be synonyms, saying the term in 6:17 refers to "Christ's past action in the setting up of the new covenant," while the word here designates Christ as the "guarantee . . . for the future."[361] Another way of saying this is that the term (ἔγγυος) means that Christ "is a pledge of a

---

[359] Ellingworth defines *covenant* in Hebrews as "a free manifestation of divine love, institutionalized in an 'economy' whose stability and consummation are guaranteed by a cultic ratification, the death of Christ, and whose aim is to make men live in communion with God, to impart to them the treasure of grace and the heavenly inheritance" (*Hebrews*, 388).

[360] For the interpretation offered here, see Koester, *Hebrews*, 370.

[361] Ellingworth, *Hebrews*, 388.

new covenant, guaranteeing its eternal effectiveness. A 'mediator' [ἐμεσίτευσεν] of a covenant is involved in the means of establishing the covenant."[362]

Bridge

Returning to the Levitical priesthood violates God's intention, for it is inferior to the Melchizedekian priesthood, for the latter is accompanied by an oath. The oath certifies that the Melchizedekian priesthood will never cease. In contrast to the Levitical order, it will endure forever. Hence, Jesus is the guarantor of a better covenant, one in which sins are truly and finally forgiven. How can the readers and how can we turn away from such a full and final cleansing?

Hebrews 7:23–25

Outline

I. Prologue: Definitive and Final Revelation in the Son (1:1–4)
II. Don't Abandon the Son Since He Is Greater than Angels (1:5–2:18)
III. Don't Harden Your Hearts Since You Have a Son and High Priest Greater than Moses and Joshua (3:1–4:13)
IV. **Don't Fall Away from Jesus' Melchizedekian Priesthood Since It Is Greater than the Levitical Priesthood (4:14–10:18)**
   A. Exhortation in Light of Jesus' Priestly Status (4:14–5:10)
   B. Warning and Assurance (5:11–6:20)
   C. **Jesus' Greater Priesthood as a Melchizedekian Priest (7:1–28)**
      1. Melchizedek Greater than Levi (7:1–10)
      2. **Arguments for a Changed Priesthood (7:11–28)**
         a. Imperfection of Levitical Priesthood (7:11–12)
         b. Jesus from Tribe of Judah (7:13–14)
         c. Prophecy of Melchizedekian Priesthood (7:15–17)
         d. Setting Aside of Levitical Priesthood (7:18–19)

---

[362] O'Brien, *Hebrews*, 271–72. Cf. also Cockerill, *Hebrews*, 330.

e. Oath Accompanies Melchizedekian
   Priesthood (7:20–22)
f. **Jesus a Permanent Priest (7:23–25)**
g. A Sinless Priest and a Once-for-All
   Sacrifice (7:26–28)
D. New Covenant Better than the Old (8:1–13)

Scripture

²³ Now many have become Levitical priests, since they are prevented by death from remaining in office. ²⁴ But because He remains forever, He holds His priesthood permanently. ²⁵ Therefore,
He is always able to save those who come to God through Him,
since He always lives to intercede for them.

Context

The author continues to pile up arguments for the superiority of
the Melchizedekian priesthood: a change was prophesied (vv. 11–
12); Jesus belongs to a different tribe (vv. 13–14); he has an indestructible life (vv. 15–17); he brings people into God's presence (vv.
18–19); he received his priesthood with an oath (vv. 20–22). The
main point in verses 23–25 is that Jesus is able to save completely
those who come into God's presence through him. Levitical priests
can't match this, for they all die. Dead priests can't accomplish salvation! Jesus' priesthood, on the other hand, never ends, and thus the
saving efficacy of his priesthood is perpetual. Believers can be full
of confidence that they are truly entering into God's presence, for
Jesus as the ever-living priest intercedes for them.

Exegesis

7:23

The inferiority of the Levitical priesthood is evident because
death was the master of every Levitical priest. There were scores of
priests, priest after priest, through the roll call of history. But each
and every one died. No Levitical priest lasted more than a genera-
tion, and each one in succession died. The "many" ($\pi\lambda\epsilon\acute{\iota}ον\acute{\epsilon}ς$) are
contrasted with the one. What is needed is one effective priest, one
priest that conquers death, but such a priest did not hail from the
tribe of Levi.

7:24

In marked contrast to Levitical priests, Jesus' priesthood continues forever. "He holds his priesthood permanently." The word "permanently" (ἀπαράβατον) means his priesthood never ends. Remaining forever refers implicitly to the resurrection. His priesthood endures because he conquered death, and as the one who triumphed over death, his priesthood persists. Cockerill, however, takes it as a reference to "the eternal character of the Son's person affirmed in the opening chapter of Hebrews."[363] On this reading the author doesn't focus on Jesus' triumph over death but his inherent superiority as a divine being. Still it seems more likely that the author thinks of Jesus' humanity as a priest, and hence the focus is on his humanity instead of his inherent divine properties. Certainly Jesus as high priest is both divine and human, and the two ultimately can't be separated from each other. Nevertheless, it seems that the author here focuses on Jesus' humanity, and hence his permanence is most likely ascribed to his resurrection.

7:25

Since Jesus has a permanent priesthood, it follows (ὅθεν) that he is able to save "for all time" (NRSV, εἰς τὸ παντελές) those who come to God through him (see §9).[364] Alternatively, the sense is that he is able to save "completely" (NIV, εἰς τὸ παντελές) those approaching God through him (cf. Luke 13:11). Probably both ideas are intended here, for they are not mutually exclusive, and both fit the context.[365] Christians are saved forever and fully through the priesthood of Jesus Christ.

The phrase "able to save" (σῴζειν . . . δύναται) does not simply convey the idea of potentiality, as if he is able to save but he might not do so. On the contrary the efficacy of Jesus' saving work is featured here. Those who draw near to God through Jesus are assured that they will be saved. The word "approach" (NRSV, προσερχομένους) is often used in the letter for drawing near to God (4:16; 10:1, 22; 11:6; 12:18, 22). One of the central issues in Hebrews is fellowship with God. The author reminds them that true fellowship with God, genuine access to God, is only possible through Jesus Christ.

---

[363] Cockerill, *Hebrews*, 333.

[364] So Ellingworth, *Hebrews*, 391.

[365] So Attridge, *Hebrews*, 210.

In the last phrase of the verse, the readers receive further assurance. Their salvation is complete and final because Jesus "always lives to intercede for them."[366] The contrast with the Levitical priests continues, for their ministry on behalf of the readers can't continue after they die. The benefits of Jesus' priestly work endure, for he intercedes as the ever-living one, as the one who has triumphed over death forever, as the risen one. It is probable that Jesus' intercession is based on his sacrifice, for Jesus' priestly ministry is the theme here, and the subsequent verses (vv. 26–28) focus on his offering as a priest.[367] His intercession, then, is linked with and based on what he accomplished in his death. Indeed, the drawing near to God (cf. 10:22) is only made possible through Jesus' blood and sacrifice.[368] As Koester says, "The strongest reasons for assuming that intercession in Hebrews involves petitions for forgiveness are that Heb 7:26–27 mentions human sin, that Christ's priestly work involves making atonement (2:17), and that the new covenant brings forgiveness (Heb 8:12; 10:17)."[369] The parallel text in Rom 8:33–34 also plays a confirmatory role, for Jesus' intercession, as is the case in Hebrews, is joined with his death and resurrection. At the same time, there is no reason intercession could not also involve the notion of help and assistance so that Jesus intercedes to help those being tempted (2:17–18; 4:14–16). Jesus' intercession includes his help for those in need and a plea for forgiveness.[370] The language of intercession is analogous language, and thus there is no idea of the Son literally interceding before the Father forever and ever.[371]

---

[366] Virtually all translations rightly take the participle "lives" (ζῶν) as causal here.

[367] "The idea of Christ's intercession can best be understood to be an application of Christ's once-for-all sacrifice" (Koester, *Hebrews*, 372n249). See also Hughes, *Hebrews*, 270.

[368] Hay says that intercession "embraces everything needed to give believers access to God" (*Glory at the Right Hand*, 132).

[369] Koester, *Hebrews*, 366.

[370] Rightly Koester, *Hebrews*, 366. Lane focuses almost solely on the need for assistance (*Hebrews 1–8*, 190). But Hengel rightly says there is no need to choose between intercession for assistance and intercession for forgiveness. Both are included (Hengel, *Studies in Early Christology*, 146n65).

[371] Cf. here Cockerill, *Hebrews*, 336–37.

Bridge

What is striking in verses 23–25 is that Jesus is a living priest in contrast to the Levitical priests. The readers should not cling to the Levitical priesthood, for dead priests can't save. Jesus, as the resurrected one, triumphed over death forever, and thus he is a permanent priest. And as a permanent priest he secures a complete and unending salvation to those who come to God through him, interceding for them and for all who believe in him. We can be assured of our forgiveness of sins through Jesus' atoning death and his intercession for us.

Hebrews 7:26–28

Outline

I. Prologue: Definitive and Final Revelation in the Son (1:1–4)

II. Don't Abandon the Son Since He Is Greater than Angels (1:5–2:18)

III. Don't Harden Your Hearts Since You Have a Son and High Priest Greater than Moses and Joshua (3:1–4:13)

IV. **Don't Fall Away from Jesus' Melchizedekian Priesthood Since It Is Greater than the Levitical Priesthood (4:14–10:18)**

  A. Exhortation in Light of Jesus' Priestly Status (4:14–5:10)

  B. Warning and Assurance (5:11–6:20)

  C. **Jesus' Greater Priesthood as a Melchizedekian Priest (7:1–28)**

    1. Melchizedek Greater than Levi (7:1–10)

    2. **Arguments for a Changed Priesthood (7:11–28)**

      a. Imperfection of Levitical Priesthood 97:11–12)

      b. Jesus from Tribe of Judah (7:13–14)

      c. Prophecy of Melchizedekian Priesthood (7:15–17)

      d. Setting Aside of Levitical Priesthood (7:18–19)

      e. Oath Accompanies Melchizedekian Priesthood (7:20–22)

      f. Jesus a Permanent Priest (7:23–25)

      g. **A Sinless Priest and a Once-for-All Sacrifice (7:26–28)**

  D. New Covenant Better than the Old (8:1–13)

Scripture

²⁶ For this is the kind of high priest we need: holy, innocent, undefiled, separated from sinners, and exalted above the heavens. ²⁷ He doesn't need to offer sacrifices every day, as high priests do—first for their own sins, then for those of the people. He did this once for all when He offered Himself. ²⁸ For the law appoints as high priests men who are weak, but the promise of the oath, which came after the law, appoints a Son, who has been perfected forever.

Context

The final argument for the superiority of Jesus' Melchizedekian priesthood is given here. First, since perfection isn't achieved through the Levitical priesthood, it is clear that the priesthood would change (vv. 11–12). Second, the new priesthood has arrived in Jesus since he is from a different tribe—the tribe of Judah (vv. 13–14). Third, since Jesus' priesthood represents a new order (Melchizedekian) and since he has an indestructible life, his priesthood is superior (vv. 15–17). Fourth, whereas the Levitical priesthood has been set aside because of its weakness, Jesus' priesthood brings people hope so they enjoy fellowship with the living God (vv. 18–19). Fifth, the Melchizedekian priesthood was accompanied with an oath in contrast to the Levitical priesthood (vv. 20–22). Sixth, Jesus' priesthood is living and hence accomplishes a complete and definitive salvation (vv. 23–25).

These verses celebrate the greatness of Jesus' Melchizedekian priesthood. In contrast to Levitical priests, Jesus is a sinless and perfect priest (v. 26). Therefore, he did not have to offer sacrifices to obtain forgiveness for his own sins, as the Levitical priests were required to do (v. 27a). Instead, he offered himself once for the sake of others, securing by his one sacrifice forgiveness forever (v. 27b). The law appointed men as priests who were weak and sinful, who themselves needed atonement (v. 28a). But a new era after the law has arrived. Jesus' priesthood is in accord with the oath about the Melchizedekian priesthood (Ps 110:4), and he is a perfect priest. The use of the word "perfected" (τετελειωμένον) closes out this section nicely, for we saw in 7:11 the Levitical priesthood did not bring perfection (τελείωσις), and the law "perfected" (ἐτελείωσεν) nothing

(7:19). The age of perfection, of eschatological realization, has arrived with the death, resurrection, and exaltation of Jesus Christ.

Exegesis

7:26

The superiority of Jesus' priesthood is evident from his qualifications. He is a "fitting" (ESV) high priest, one that matches what humans "need" since he is a sinless high priest. The author uses a number of terms to describe Jesus' virtues. He is "holy" (ὅσιος), always living righteously in a way that pleases God. He is "innocent" (ἄκακος) and devoted to what is good. The word "undefiled" (ἀμίαντος) means he is unstained by sin. The same word is used for the sexual purity demanded in marriage (Heb 13:4).

Jesus was also "separated (κεχωρισμένος) from sinners." Probably the author has in mind here Jesus' separation in that he was exalted by God as priest-king.[372] The last line ("exalted above the heavens") is similar, but Cockerill captures nicely the significance of the last two clauses. "The first describes the exaltation as Christ's final triumph over sin. The second underscores the dazzling heights he has attained."[373] What does Jesus' purity of life have to do with his exaltation? The most likely answer is that his exaltation was the fitting reward for his righteousness. Jesus' exaltation picks up what we find in Ps 110:1: Jesus' reigning at God's right hand. As the sinless one, he is now the triumphant and reigning one.

7:27

Because Jesus was without sin, he had no need to offer a sacrifice first for his own sin and then for the sin of the people. Jesus atoned for sin once for all by the sacrifice of himself.

Jesus' sinlessness (v. 26) stands in sharp contrast to all other human beings. Their sin requires sacrifices "every day." We have an implicit recognition here that the sacrifices offered do not truly atone for sin (cf. 10:1–4). Indeed, the fallibility of the high priests is also evident. The author has already emphasized their impermanence:

---

[372] Attridge, *Hebrews*, 213; Michel, *Der Brief an die Hebräer*, 90. Though perhaps both notions are in view, i.e., both qualitative separation (he was without sin) and spatial separation (he is exalted in heaven) (so Koester, *Hebrews*, 367; Peterson, *Hebrews and Perfection*, 116). Hughes argues that there is only separation from sin here (*Hebrews*, 273–75).

[373] Cockerill, *Hebrews*, 342.

they all die (7:23). But here he reminds us of their sins. Despite the reputation and holiness of high priests, they were required to offer sacrifices for their own sins (cf. Lev 9:7; 16:6). Then they were to proceed to offering a sacrifice to atone for the sins of the people (Lev 16:15). The Day of Atonement was limited to once a year, but the author speaks generally, merging together the sacrifices offered daily with the Day of Atonement.[374]

Jesus as a high priest is different, showing that he belongs to a different category. As the sinless one, he didn't need to offer a sacrifice for his own sins. Furthermore, a new sacrifice wasn't required every day. Instead, forecasting one of the major themes of chapters 9–10, Jesus offered himself as a sacrifice "once for all" (ἐφάπαξ). His one sacrifice definitively and finally dealt with sin, and thus no further sacrifices were needed, showing that sin had been truly cleansed through the sacrifice of Christ. Forgiveness was obtained not through the offering of animals but the sacrifice of Jesus Christ.[375] The priests did not offer themselves but animals. Jesus secured forgiveness by offering himself, and so unlike the priests he was both the priest and the victim offered in sacrifice.

7:28

The final verse in the chapter and in the argument that commenced in 7:11 rounds out the discussion. We see here again that the law and the priesthood are intertwined, for the law, as was noted previously, appointed men to serve as high priests (cf. Exodus 28–29).

---

[374] Cf. the discussion in Attridge, *Hebrews*, 213–14; O'Brien, *Hebrews*, 282. Cockerill says the author is simply indicating the need for repeated sacrifices since the Day of Atonement ritual doesn't actually remove sin (*Hebrews*, 342–43). The author may have in mind burnt offerings that were offered twice a day for atonement and thanksgiving (Exod 29:38–42; Lev 1:4). Strictly speaking the high priest didn't offer the daily sacrifices for his own sin. Ellingworth remarks that "the author was interested in the theology of rather than the details of the temple liturgy," and so "he assimilated the meaning and ritual of the daily rites to those of the annual festival, assuming that the high priest, like other priests would officiate in them all" (*Hebrews*, 395). Ellingworth goes on to note that in Numbers 28–29 the daily offerings conclude with the Day of Atonement (*Hebrews*, 395). Hughes says we have a general reference to daily offerings, though the offering on the Day of Atonement is particularly in view (*Hebrews*, 277).

[375] Against Moffitt (*Atonement and the Logic of the Resurrection in the Epistle to the Hebrews*, 278–79), the sacrifice offered here is on earth, not in heaven. On the historical actuality of Jesus' death, see Mackie, *Eschatology and Exhortation in Hebrews*, 175–77.

What is noteworthy is that the men who served as priests were characterized by "weakness" (ESV, ἀσθένειαν). Their weakness, as is apparent from the preceding verses, includes their sinfulness (v. 27) and their being subject to death (v. 23). The word "weakness" picks up a thread in the previous discussion. The previous regulation regarding the priesthood is annulled because of its "weakness" (ESV, ἀσθενές). A new order has arrived which does not suffer from the liabilities inherent in the old order.

The superiority of the new order is also evident, for the author characterizes what has come in Jesus Christ as "the promise of the oath." The word "oath" echoes the previous argument, where the superiority of the Melchizedekian priesthood is confirmed by its being accompanied by an oath (7:20–22), a feature that was lacking relative to the Levitical priesthood. The oath was subsequent to the law, and yet the newness of the oath does not suggest inferiority but superiority. That the oath came after the law was instituted (Ps 110:4) reveals that the law is temporary in contrast to the priesthood affirmed with an oath.

The oath is directed to the Son. We might expect him to say a priest or a king, for he is also, as Psalm 110 itself affirms, a king and priest; but here he picks up the term *Son*, which is so important from the outset of the book, for the Son is greater than the angels. The oath was not spoken merely to a priest or to a king but to God's unique Son.[376] The Son "has been perfected forever" (εἰς τὸν αἰῶνα τετελειωμένον). Earlier the author taught that Jesus "was perfected" (τελειωθείς) through his obedient sufferings (5:8–9). Obviously, this does not mean Jesus was sinful before he was perfected, for the author just affirmed his sinlessness (7:27; cf. 4:15). The perfection here is eschatological and experiential. Jesus, in the anvil and agony of human experience, trusted and obeyed his Father. He demonstrated that he was qualified to be the perfect sacrifice for sins. The word "perfected" also resonates with the themes of 7:11–28. The Levitical priesthood could not bring "perfection" (7:11, τελείωσις), and "the law perfected (ἐτελείωσεν) nothing." Believers in Jesus Christ, however, have a perfect priest who ushers them into the presence of God.

---

[376] For this emphasis on the Son's deity, see Cockerill, *Hebrews*, 344. We should also note, however, that Jesus' sonship also includes his kingship as the exegesis of chapter 1 demonstrates.

The perfecting of Jesus refers "to the whole process by which Jesus was personally prepared and vocationally qualified for his continuing ministry in the presence of God."[377] His once-for-all sacrifice testifies that the old order has been terminated and a new day has begun.

Bridge

It seems that one of the main purposes of the letter is to assure believers that their sins are forgiven. We have no need to go anywhere else to secure a clean conscience. The author reminds the readers and us that we have a perfect and sinless priest and one who reigns at God's right hand. His once-for-all sacrifice atoned for our sins forever. Why would the readers think of trusting in priests who were sinful and mortal when they are beneficiaries of the work of God's Son, who has been perfected and offers complete and final cleansing from sin?

Hebrews 8:1–6

Outline

I. Prologue: Definitive and Final Revelation in the Son (1:1–4)
II. Don't Abandon the Son Since He Is Greater than Angels (1:5–2:18)
III. Don't Harden Your Hearts Since You Have a Son and High Priest Greater than Moses and Joshua (3:1–4:13)
IV. **Don't Fall Away from Jesus' Melchizedekian Priesthood Since It Is Greater than the Levitical Priesthood (4:14–10:18)**
  A. Exhortation in Light of Jesus' Priestly Status (4:14–5:10)
  B. Warning and Assurance (5:11–6:20)
  C. Jesus' Greater Priesthood as a Melchizedekian Priest (7:1–28)
  D. **New Covenant Better than the Old (8:1–13)**
    1. **Jesus' Heavenly Priesthood Shows He Is Mediator of a Better Covenant (8:1–6)**

---

[377] Lane, *Hebrews 1–8*, 196.

2. Prophecy of New Covenant Shows Weakness of
   Old (8:7–13)
V. A Better Sacrifice Under the New Covenant (9:1–10:18)

Scripture

¹ Now the main point of what is being said is this: We have this kind of high priest, who sat down at the right hand of the throne of the Majesty in the heavens, ² a minister of the sanctuary and the true tabernacle that was set up by the Lord and not man. ³ For every high priest is appointed to offer gifts and sacrifices; therefore it was necessary for this priest also to have something to offer. ⁴ Now if He were on earth, He wouldn't be a priest, since there are those offering the gifts prescribed by the law. ⁵ These serve as a copy and shadow of the heavenly things, as Moses was warned when he was about to complete the tabernacle. For God said, Be careful that you make everything according to the pattern that was shown to you on the mountain. ⁶ But Jesus has now obtained a superior ministry, and to that degree He is the mediator of a better covenant, which has been legally enacted on better promises.

Context

The readers should not and must not fall away, for the Melchizedekian priesthood of Jesus is far superior to the Levitical priesthood (7:1–28). In 8:1–6 the relationship of Jesus' priesthood to the tabernacle and the new covenant is explored. Jesus introduces believers to the true sanctuary, to God's dwelling in heaven, and he is also the mediator of a new and better covenant. The author pauses in 8:1 to underscore the main point, and as readers we must pay particular attention when we are told by the author himself what the main point is! He affirms that believers in Christ now enjoy the benefits of the Melchizedekian priest (8:1) described in the previous chapter.[378] Indeed, Jesus is now seated at the right hand of the one who reigns in the heavens, demonstrating that he is king-priest (Ps 110:1). His rule in the heavens indicates that he is a minister of the true sanctuary and tabernacle in the heavens (8:2). The priests, by way of contrast, ministered at the earthly tabernacle with gifts and

---

[378] The author makes his argument for the existential and psychological benefit of his readers (Attridge, *Hebrews*, 216).

sacrifices (v. 3). Since Jesus was a priest, he also had to offer a sacrifice. He is not merely an earthly priest, for on earth sacrifices had to be offered in accord with the Mosaic law (v. 4). The sanctuary at which the priests serve, however, functions as a pattern of the heavenly tabernacle (v. 5) in accord with Exod 25:40. Jesus' heavenly ministry is better than the priest's earthly ministry (v. 6), for he mediates a better covenant, and it is a better covenant because it is enacted on the basis of better promises.

Exegesis

8:1

The "main point" (Κεφάλαιον) of the preceding is now set forth for the readers.[379] The main point is: "We have this kind of high priest" (see §2.3). What the author means by this is that Jesus matches the description of the Melchizedekian priest in chapter 7. He is the ever-living one, the one who always did the will of God, and the one whose sacrifice accomplished forgiveness of sins. The oath and promise of Ps 110:4 find their fulfillment in him. In addition, what is written in Ps 110:1 points to Jesus. He is David's Lord and sits at God's right hand until his enemies are made his footstool. The author alludes to Ps 110:1, affirming that Jesus sat down at God's right hand in the heavens. Jesus is the reigning and ruling priest-king and exercises authority as the messianic king. The words "Majesty in the heavens" point to God's awesomeness and his transcendence. Since Jesus sits at the right hand of one who is so great, he also exercises transcendent power.

8:2

Jesus serves as the minister in the holy place (τῶν ἁγίων), i.e., God's sanctuary. God's sanctuary where Jesus serves is also

---

[379] In defense of the notion that the term means "main point," see Attridge, *Hebrews*, 217. L. Johnson says it is the main point from 5:1 onward (*Hebrews*, 197; cf. also Koester, *Hebrews*, 375; Ellingworth, *Hebrews*, 400). Against Bruce, who thinks it means "summary" (*Hebrews*, 161). Cockerill rightly argues that it is the main point of the book (*Hebrews*, 350–51). Or perhaps it is better to put it this way. Jesus' sitting at the right hand of the Father signifies that the consciences of believers are cleansed, and therefore they should not fall away. Hence, the main point of the book is don't fall away, but here we have the main theological point undergirding that command.

described as "the true tabernacle" (τῆς σκηνῆς τῆς ἀληθινῆς).[380] Jesus sits at the right hand of the one who rules in the heavens (v. 1), and the true tabernacle is not earthly but heavenly. Here we see an example of the writer's spatial and eschatological theology. On the one hand the earthly is not ultimate; it points up spatially to what is heavenly. At the same time there is an eschatological dimension to the writer's thought, for the tabernacle erected in Israel pointed forward to the tabernacle Jesus would enter upon his death and resurrection. Hence the earthly tent is not "false" but rather temporary and points to something greater.[381] When the writer says the Lord "pitched" the tabernacle, he is scarcely suggesting that there is a literal tabernacle in the heavens. The language is analogical instead of univocal. The true tabernacle, then, designates the presence of God, the place where God reigns and rules. Jesus is the greatest priest since he dwells in God's presence and ministers in the heavenly realm where God dwells.

8:3

Jesus is the minister of God's true tabernacle, but a minister must carry out a specific ministry, and 8:1 and 7:1–28 emphasized Jesus' priestly ministry. The author reflects generally here on the responsibility of high priests. They were ordained in Israel to offer gifts and sacrifices, both to express thanksgiving to God and to atone for sins committed in Israel. Since Jesus is a priest, he must also offer a sacrifice, for it is the nature of a priesthood to offer a sacrifice to God. The author's side comment here is illuminating, for it clarifies that the fundamental role of the priest in his estimation is to procure access to God through sacrifices, just as the high priest in Israel offered sacrifices to obtain atonement and the forgiveness of sins (Leviticus 16).

8:4

Jesus was a priest, but his priesthood was distinct from the priests who served under the Mosaic law. The author characterizes

---

[380] I am taking "sanctuary" and "true tabernacle" as referring to the same entity (Hughes, *Hebrews*, 281–82n55; Peterson, *Hebrews and Perfection*, 130–31; Koester, *Hebrews*, 376, Lane, *Hebrews 1–8*, 205; Ellingworth, *Hebrews*, 402). Others posit a distinction in the heavenly sanctuary (Michel, *Der Brief an die Hebräer*, 95–96; Attridge, *Hebrews*, 218; Barnard, *The Mysticism of Hebrews*, 110–18). For a fuller discussion, see Hughes, *Hebrews*, 283–90.

[381] Cf. Koester, *Hebrews*, 376; Lane, *Hebrews 1–8*, 205–6.

Jesus' priesthood in a fascinating way, saying that "if He were on earth, He wouldn't be a priest." Jesus' humanity, as noted previously (cf. 2:5–18), is a major theme in Hebrews, and in that sense his priesthood had an earthly dimension. Indeed, as Hebrews regularly affirms, he suffered and died on earth. Still, the author asserts that Jesus was not an earthly priest. What he means must be discerned by the broader argument.[382] It is apparent, by way of contrast, that an earthly ministry was exercised by the Levitical priests who offered sacrifices in accord with the Mosaic law.[383] Jesus, on the other hand, ministers in the true tabernacle, the heavenly tabernacle where God rules. Levitical priests offered their sacrifices at the earthly tabernacle, which is ultimately not the true tabernacle. However, Jesus was not an earthly priest, i.e., he was not a priest in accord with the Mosaic law. His priesthood has a different location (heaven) and is thus more effective. But this does not mean Jesus' sacrifice was actually in heaven. Instead "his singular death on earth is the basis for his heavenly ministry."[384]

8:5

Earthly priests serve at the earthly sanctuary, at the tabernacle God commanded Israel to build (cf. Exodus 25–31; 35–40). The NIV captures most clearly the verse's meaning: "They serve at a sanctuary that is a copy and shadow of what is in heaven." Even though the word "sanctuary" is absent in Greek, it is clearly implied by the reference to Exod 25:40 and by the flow of the argument. The earthly sanctuary, however, was never meant to be ultimate. It served

---

[382] Against Moffitt, who claims that Jesus wasn't an earthly priest at all (*Atonement and the Logic of the Resurrection in the Epistle to the Hebrews*, 198–99). Moffitt rightly sees the importance of heaven in Jesus' priestly ministry but wrongly downplays the role of his earthly offering. In defense of Jesus' sacrifice on earth, see Richardson, *Pioneer and Perfecter of Faith*, 36–45. Vos says the point here is that Jesus' priestly ministry "as a whole" wasn't exercised on earth ("The Priesthood of Christ in Hebrews," 159).

[383] The word "priests" (τῶν ἱερέων) is added by some witnesses in the textual tradition to clarify the text, but its absence represents the harder reading, and hence the words were not present in the original text. Interpretively, however, the words are present by implication. Hence the scribal insertion represents a correct interpretation.

[384] Koester, *Hebrews*, 382. Even though Jesus' priesthood is heavenly, his sacrifice is offered on earth (rightly Attridge, *Hebrews*, 216–17). The Socinians maintained that Christ offered himself in heaven rather than on earth (see Koester, *Hebrews*, 35, 382n264).

as "a copy and shadow" of the heavenly sanctuary. We see again the spatial or vertical thought of the author. It has affinities with Plato's thought, but the notion that Hebrews mediates Platonic thought via Philo or any other thinker has been discredited.[385] Still, the author views the earthly as an inferior reflection of what is heavenly. Once again, however, what is vertical is also eschatological. The law and the earthly tabernacle were intended to be in force under the old covenant; they were set in place for a limited period of salvation history.

We see here the role of the divine author in the history of revelation. When Moses was instructed to complete the tabernacle, he was commanded to make everything "according to the pattern (τύπον) shown to you on the mountain."[386] The typological role of the tabernacle is communicated through three different terms: "copy" (ὑποδείγματι), "shadow" (σκιᾷ), and "pattern" (τύπον). The original plan for the tabernacle (Exod 25:40) reveals from the beginning that it signified a greater reality, that the earthly place of God's residence figurally represented his residence in the heavens.

8:6

If one word were to summarize this verse, it is the word "better." There is a "better covenant" (κρείττονός . . . διαθήκης), "better promises" (κρείττοσιν ἐπαγγελίαις), and "a superior ministry" (διαφορωτέρας . . . λειτουργίας). The last phrase, of course, uses a different term, but it carries the same idea. In fact, the same word is used earlier to say that Jesus has a name superior to angels (1:4, διαφορώτερον . . . ὄνομα). Jesus has a ministry that is more excellent than the ministry of Levitical priests, for the preceding verses have clarified that his ministry is carried out in God's presence, in the true sanctuary. The word "now" (νυν) introducing the verse is eschatological: what is better has arrived in the last days (cf. 1:2).

Jesus' better ministry is tied to a better covenant of which he is the covenant mediator (see §3). The better covenant is the new covenant, as the author will make plain in the subsequent verses (8:7–13). Jesus' role as the covenant mediator is effected through

---

[385] See Ronald Williamson, *Philo and the Epistle to Hebrews*, ALGHJ (Leiden: Brill, 1970).

[386] It doesn't follow from the wording here that there is a literal tabernacle in the heavens (rightly Schenk, *Cosmology and Eschatology in Hebrews*, 171–73).

the sacrifice of himself.[387] We can compare 1 Tim 2:5 where Christ is the only mediator between God and humanity. On two other occasions the author refers to Jesus as the mediator of the new covenant, and in both places his role as a mediator is tied to his death. Such a connection reflects the Gospel traditions where Jesus inaugurates the new covenant by shedding his blood (Matt 26:28; Mark 14:24; Luke 22:20). Moses mediated the old covenant, but we have already seen that Jesus is superior to Moses (3:1–6), and this is no surprise since he as the Son of God establishes the covenant by sacrificing himself.

The reason the new covenant is better is because it is established on the basis of better promises (see §3). The relative pronoun "which" (ἥτις) actually gives the reason the new covenant is better than the old.[388] Both the ESV and the NIV reflect this interpretation by translating the relative pronoun with the word "since." The better promises are revealed in the terms of the new covenant, for God will write the law on the hearts of his people (8:10), all covenant members will know the Lord (8:11), and sins are forgiven fully and definitively (8:12).

Bridge

Believers enjoy a high priest who sits at God's right hand and has access to God's true sanctuary, his presence, in the heavens. Jesus is not in the same category as the Levitical priests. His ministry is not earthly but heavenly. He has introduced a better ministry and a better covenant that is established on the basis of better promises. Why would the readers consider trading away what Jesus has done for them, as if a ministry and tabernacle on earth could be better than a ministry and tabernacle in heaven?

---

[387] Attridge notes that Socinians argued that Hebrews emphasizes Christ's offering in the heavens and reject the notion that his death had atoning significance (*Hebrews*, 221n60). Attridge rightly remarks, "Such interpretations fail to do justice to the way our author manipulates the categories in which he speaks of Christ's sacrifice" (220–21).

[388] For a causal understanding of ἥτις, see Lane, *Hebrews 1–8*, 201.

Hebrews 8:7–13

Outline

I. Prologue: Definitive and Final Revelation in the Son (1:1–4)

II. Don't Abandon the Son Since He Is Greater than Angels (1:5–2:18)

III. Don't Harden Your Hearts Since You Have a Son and High Priest Greater than Moses and Joshua (3:1–4:13)

IV. **Don't Fall Away from Jesus' Melchizedekian Priesthood Since It Is Greater than the Levitical Priesthood (4:14–10:18)**

    A. Exhortation in Light of Jesus' Priestly Status (4:14–5:10)

    B. Warning and Assurance (5:11–6:20)

    C. Jesus' Greater Priesthood as a Melchizedekian Priest (7:1–28)

    D. **New Covenant Better than the Old (8:1–13)**

        1. Jesus' Heavenly Priesthood Shows He Is Mediator of a Better Covenant (8:1–6)

        2. **Prophecy of New Covenant Shows Weakness of Old (8:7–13)**

    E. A Better Sacrifice Under the New Covenant (9:1–10:18)

Scripture

[7] For if that first covenant had been faultless, there would have been no occasion for a second one. [8] But finding fault with His people, He says: Look, the days are coming, says the Lord, when I will make a new covenant with the house of Israel and with the house of Judah—[9] not like the covenant that I made with their ancestors on the day I took them by their hands to lead them out of the land of Egypt. I disregarded them, says the Lord, because they did not continue in My covenant. [10] But this is the covenant that I will make with the house of Israel after those days, says the Lord: I will put My laws into their minds and write them on their hearts. I will be their God, and they will be My people. [11] And each person will not teach his fellow citizen, and each his brother, saying, "Know the Lord," because they will all know Me, from the least to the greatest of them. [12] For I will be merciful to their wrongdoing, and I will never again remember their sins. [13] By saying, a

new covenant, He has declared that the first is old. And what is old and aging is about to disappear.

Context

In 8:6 we are told that Jesus is a mediator of a better covenant, and in 8:7–13 the author explains why the new covenant is better than the old, citing Jer 31:31–34. The new covenant is better than the old one, for a new one would not have been instituted if the old was adequate (v. 7). The defectiveness of the old covenant is demonstrated by the weakness and sin of the covenant people under the old administration, for the promise of a new covenant witnesses to the deficiency of the old (v. 8). In the old covenant the Lord delivered Israel from Egypt, but Israel did not remain faithful to the covenant stipulations (v. 9). The new covenant is entirely different, for now the obedience of covenant members is a divine work. The Lord will write his law upon the hearts of his people and will be their God (v. 10). Since God will write his law on the heart, it follows that every member of the covenant in the new administration will know the Lord (v. 11). There will be no unconverted members in the new covenant, and their new life will be based on the forgiveness of sins (v. 12). The right conclusion to draw, then, is that the coming of the "new" means the dismissal of the old. The new and the old are incompatible, though the old is fulfilled in the new; the old has passed away since the new has arrived.

Exegesis

8:7

Jesus is the mediator, says 8:6, of a better covenant, and now in 8:7–13 he explains the reason the covenant he mediates is better. The "better covenant" is identified here as the "second" one. By way of contrast, the "first covenant" was faulty. We encountered this line of argument previously in Hebrews. If the first covenant was adequate, a second one would not have been instituted. The same line of reasoning was used relative to the priesthood. If the Levitical priesthood truly brought perfection, there would be no need for a Melchizedekian priesthood (7:11). Or, if sacrifices offered according to the law truly brought forgiveness, there would be no need for Christ's sacrifice (10:1–18). Each one of these matters is closely related, of course, for the old covenant, the Levitical priesthood, the law, and animal sacrifices are intertwined.

8:8

The new covenant was instituted because God found fault with Israel, and hence he prophesies that a new covenant will be instituted with Israel and Judah.

The textual evidence is disputed here, and if we accept the variant in NA[28], the fault is with the Mosaic covenant rather than the people.[389] The NET translation reflects the variant so that in the phrase "showing its fault," the "its" is the old covenant. Such an interpretation fits well in the context since the inferiority of the old covenant is being emphasized. The textual evidence, however, supports the more difficult reading so that the fault is found "with them," i.e., the people. In context, however, a wedge should not be driven between the sin of the people and the defectiveness of the covenant.[390] By stressing the disobedience of Israel, the author calls attention to their moral responsibility, to their refusal to do the will of God. Still the context also draws attention to the weakness of the old covenant, for the covenant didn't provide the resources to renew the people. At the end of the day, the author finds fault with both the people and the old covenant, though in this phrase he concentrates upon the sin of the people.

The spiritual state of Israel, i.e., their endemic refusal to do God's will, showed that a new covenant was necessary. The author cites Jer 31:31–34 to support the notion that a new covenant is mandatory. The new covenant text comes from Jeremiah 30–33, where Jeremiah promises hope and restoration for the people after exile. Exile is not the last word, for the Lord will bring Israel back to the land and will fulfill the promises made to Abraham and David.

Israel's hope is not rooted in their piety, but in the Lord's transforming grace, in his changing the hearts of his people by his

---

[389] In defense of the idea that the problem is with the covenant, see Hughes, *Hebrews*, 298–99; Guthrie, *Hebrews*, 281. Significant early evidence supports the dative "to them" (αὐτοῖς) instead of the accusative "them" (αὐτούς). Koester argues, however, that in either case the pronoun refers to the people (*Hebrews*, 385). Fortunately, the meaning isn't affected in either case as I explain above.

[390] Against Attridge, *Hebrews*, 227. See Lane, *Hebrews 1–8*, 209.

power.[391] The promise in Ezekiel that the Lord will put his Spirit in Israel and cause them to obey his law (Ezek 36:26–27) runs thematically along the same lines. The significance of the prophecy in Jeremiah should be noted, for the OT Scriptures themselves recognize that the old covenant was inadequate. The author doesn't invent the notion of the new covenant, for the OT promises that new days are coming for Israel and Judah. A new agreement, a new administration, would be enacted with Israel and Judah. Other NT writers as well taught that the new covenant was inaugurated with the death of Jesus Christ (Matt 26:28; Mark 14:24; Luke 22:20; 1 Cor 11:25; cf. 2 Cor 3:6), and thus Hebrews fits well with the witness of the remainder of the NT.

8:9

The old covenant and the new covenant are different. The covenant made with Israel on Mount Sinai had gracious elements. It would be a mistake to identify it as a legalistic covenant. God by his grace liberated Israel from Egyptian bondage. The Lord carried them "on eagles' wings" (Exod 19:4). He tenderly "took them by their hands to lead them out of the land of Egypt" (Heb 8:9). The summons to keep the law was given *after* the Lord had saved them from slavery to Egypt (Exod 20:1). The call to keep the Lord's commands was to be in *response* to the Lord's gracious intervention on their behalf.

Even though the Sinai covenant wasn't legalistic, it was still defective and is inferior to the new covenant. Israel had to keep the stipulations of the covenant to be blessed. If Israel obeyed, they would receive the blessings of the covenant; but if they disobeyed, they would experience the cursings of the covenant (Leviticus 26; Deuteronomy 26–28). By the time Jeremiah wrote, it was apparent that Israel "did not continue in My covenant." The northern kingdom of Israel had already been exiled by Assyria in 722 BC, and the southern kingdom of Judah experienced the final hammer of exile to Babylon in 586 BC. The claim that Israel and Judah did not

---

[391] Perhaps the shift to "I will accomplish" (συντελέσω) a new covenant signifies the idea of perfection attested often in Hebrews and thus represents a conscious intensification over "I will make" (διαθήσομαι) a new covenant. So Attridge, *Hebrews*, 227. What calls into question Attridge's reading is that the shift from "made" (διεθέμην) to "make" (ἐποίησα) in 8:10 seems insignificant. The lexical meaning of the latter does not signify a more effective "making" of the covenant.

keep the covenant was not an abstract theological proposition. Both kingdoms faced exile because of their disobedience; the curses of the covenant had become a reality. The consequence of Israel's disobedience is that the Lord "turned away from them" (NIV). God's "not caring" (ἠμέλησα) for them is another way of saying they experienced the curses of the covenant.

Israel and Judah were responsible for their disobedience, and at the same time their disobedience reflected the inadequacy and limitations of the old covenant. Israel, of course, returned from exile. Still the fundamental problem with Israel remained, for the people didn't obey the Lord and the covenant promises weren't realized. When the NT opens, Israel is under the dominion of Rome and is not experiencing the freedom and joy promised by the Lord, and their dismal state is due to their sin.

8:10

The nature of the new covenant over against the old begins to be elaborated in verse 10. In Jeremiah's context, establishing a new covenant would solve the problem of Israel's continual violation of covenant stipulations. The promises made to Abraham can hardly become a reality if Israel continues to transgress what God commands. The Lord declares, however, that he will remedy the problem, promising to make a new agreement, a new covenant, with Israel. The author of Hebrews believes the new covenant has been fulfilled in his day, in the cross and resurrection of Jesus Christ.

The new covenant is distinct from the old in that God inscribes his law on their hearts and minds.[392] Under the old covenant Israel knew the law as a written statute external to them, but knowing the commands did not give them any inclination to keep what God commanded. Jeremiah complained that they had an uncircumcised heart (Jer 4:4; 9:25–26). The new covenant is an entirely different state of affairs, for now God circumcises the hearts of his people in accord with the promise of Deut 30:6 ("The LORD your God will circumcise your heart and the hearts of your descendants, and you will love Him with all your heart and all your soul so that you will live"). God's commands are not an onerous burden but reflect the desires

---

[392] Attridge denies that there is any notion of the Torah being inscribed here (*Hebrews*, 227). For a more convincing reading, see Joslin, "Transformation of the Law," 112.

of their heart since God has imprinted the law upon their hearts. The fundamental flaw in God's people has been remedied, for now they delight to do the will of God.[393]

The covenant formula would, under the terms of the new covenant, become a reality. God would be their God, and Israel would be his people (cf. Gen 17:8; Exod 6:7; Jer 30:22; 32:38; Ezek 11:20; 36:28; 37:23, 27). God would meet every need of his people, protecting and guarding them from all that would harm them. At the same time Israel would be the people of God. In the NT, this promise is fulfilled in the church of Jesus Christ, which is understood to be the new Israel.

8:11

The new covenant differs from the old and is superior to the old in that the law is written on the heart instead of merely being an external word (see §3). Another dimension of the new covenant over against the old comes to the forefront here. The old covenant people of God were a mixed community. In other words Israel under the old covenant was composed of both believers and unbelievers in the covenant community. Hence members of the covenant community had to be exhorted to know the Lord, for many were unregenerate. Under the new covenant an entirely new situation is envisioned. There will be no need to summon a "fellow citizen" ($\pi o\lambda i\tau\eta\nu$) or "brother" to know the Lord, for every member of the covenant community will know the Lord. In other words, every member of the covenant community "from the least to the greatest" will be regenerate.[394]

---

[393] Joslin rightly argues that the author doesn't restrict himself to forgiveness of sins here and in his subsequent discussion of the implication of the new covenant (cf. chs. 9–10 in particular). Hebrews also teaches that the hearts of God's people have been transformed. Barry C. Joslin, *Hebrews, Christ, and the Law: The Theology of the Mosaic Law in Hebrews 7:1–10:18*, Paternoster Biblical Monograph Series (Carlisle, England: Paternoster, 2008), 132–262. Still, Hebrews doesn't emphasize this theme but instead focuses on the forgiveness of sins in the new covenant.

[394] Koester says this dimension of the covenant is "unrealized" since believers need to be taught (*Hebrews*, 387), but this misunderstands the purpose of what is being said. For the argument isn't that teaching is unnecessary in the new covenant but that new covenant members don't need to be taught about regeneration since they already enjoy new life via the work of the Holy Spirit. In other words, all new covenant members know the Lord. Understanding what the author says here has important implications for the warning passages: the admonitions against apostasy don't lead to the conclusion that some in the new covenant aren't truly saved or that some could abandon the salvation they now enjoy. The warnings are a means by which those who

The difference between the covenants could easily be misunderstood. Israel's covenant with Yahweh was theocratic, so that all those who were circumcised were members of the covenant community (cf. Genesis 17). Not all of those who were circumcised, however, were regenerate. Israel under the old covenant was both the people of God and a political entity. Under the new covenant the political dimension of the people of God falls away, which is to say that the church isn't a theocratic entity; it isn't a church and state combined together. The church consists of believers from every tribe, tongue, people, and nation. To say that every new covenant member knows the Lord doesn't deny that some claim to be believers and do not truly belong to Christ. In fact, such claimants are not truly and genuinely members of the new covenant, for the new covenant by definition means the law is inscribed on one's heart, that one has been given new life by the Holy Spirit. The parallel passage to the new covenant in Ezek 36:26–27 bears this out: "I will give you a new heart and put a new spirit within you; I will remove your heart of stone and give you a heart of flesh. I will place My Spirit within you and cause you to follow My statutes and carefully observe My ordinances." The genius of the new covenant, then, is that the Spirit causes new covenant members to obey the will of God. They won't apostatize since the law is implanted within them, since the Spirit has regenerated them.

Hence, no one who is truly a new covenant member will ever fall away, and all new covenant members are regenerate. So, if someone does not know the Lord, then, by definition, they are not members of the new covenant. The text is clear here: all the members of the new covenant, from the greatest to the least, know the Lord.[395]

Nor does it work to say that some new covenant members can apostatize because of the already-but-not-yet character of NT eschatology. This is a mistaken application of the already-not-yet. Some do fall away from the new covenant community, but they show thereby that they were not truly regenerated, as 1 John 2:19 demonstrates: "They went out from us, but they did not belong to us; for if they had belonged to us, they would have remained with

---

are regenerated are preserved in the faith (for this view, see the discussion on the warning passages in the last section of the book).

[395] As O'Brien says, what is new in the new covenant is its universal and personal knowledge of God (*Hebrews*, 298–300).

us. However, they went out so that it might be made clear that none of them belongs to us." The already-but-not-yet applies in that those who are members of the new covenant are not yet perfected, for they are still liable to sin. But the eschatological schema doesn't mean genuine covenant members can apostatize, for if this were the case, then the new covenant actually doesn't differ from the old covenant. The situation would be precisely the same as under the old covenant, and hence it is difficult to see how the new covenant constitutes an improvement.

8:12

The NIV captures well the meaning of the verse: "For I will forgive their wickedness and will remember their sins no more." The "for" (ὅτι) explains the basis upon which God's people truly know the Lord, giving the reason they are regenerate. Their new life finds its roots in the forgiveness of their sins, and when sins are truly forgiven, they are remembered no more. The author will expand upon this matter in some detail in the following chapters: old covenant sacrifices do not fully and finally forgive sins. By way of contrast, Christ's sacrifice brings genuine and lasting forgiveness. The new heart implanted in believers is based on the sacrificial work of Christ, on the forgiveness secured through his atoning death. Such forgiveness was never accomplished by OT sacrifices. Indeed, the OT cult could not accomplish forgiveness (10:4).[396]

8:13

The prophecy of a new covenant entails the obsolescence of the old. The author doesn't envision a situation where the old and new coexist.[397] The two covenants are not complementary to each other in that sense. Instead they are successive. The Sinai covenant is designated in this verse as "first" (πρώτην). Three times it is described as "old." Clearly the old isn't better but inferior. The old has been superseded and "is about to disappear." The author isn't suggesting that the old covenant is still in force. Its imminent disappearance is forecast by the prophecy in Jeremiah.[398] Now that the new covenant has arrived, the old one is obsolete and no longer plays a role.

---

[396] Cf. Attridge, *Hebrews*, 226.

[397] Against L. Johnson, *Hebrews*, 209–10; Koester, *Hebrews*, 388. It seems Hughes agrees with the point being made here, though he says the reference might be to continuing temple service before AD 70 (*Hebrews*, 302).

[398] So Attridge, *Hebrews*, 229.

Jeremiah's prophecy that the old was about to disappear has now become a reality, and thus Hebrews is not suggesting that the old covenant still exists and is close to disappearing. Its days as a legally binding contract are over. As Cockerill says, "Since the New has come in Christ, the Old is no longer 'near to' but *has* definitively passed away as a way of relating to God."[399]

Bridge

The prophecy and promise of the new covenant entails the passing away of the old. The old was clearly inferior to the new, for it did not empower Israel to observe the law. With the coming of the new covenant, the law is inscribed on the heart so believers desire to do the will of God. In addition, the new covenant differs from the old in that every covenant member knows the Lord. All those who are truly covenant members are regenerate. The new heart of believers is based on the forgiveness of sins accomplished in the new covenant. Jesus' sacrifice atones for sins once for all. As believers we can rejoice that our sins are forgotten and that we are new creatures.

Hebrews 9:1–10

Outline

I. Prologue: Definitive and Final Revelation in the Son (1:1–4)
II. Don't Abandon the Son Since He Is Greater than Angels (1:5–2:18)
III. Don't Harden Your Hearts Since You Have a Son and High Priest Greater than Moses and Joshua (3:1–4:13)
IV. **Don't Fall Away from Jesus' Melchizedekian Priesthood Since It Is Greater than the Levitical Priesthood (4:14–10:18)**
   A. Exhortation in Light of Jesus' Priestly Status (4:14–5:10)
   B. Warning and Assurance (5:11–6:20)
   C. Jesus' Greater Priesthood as a Melchizedekian Priest (7:1–28)
   D. New Covenant Better than the Old (8:1–13)

---

[399] Cockerill, *Hebrews*, 370.

  E. **A Better Sacrifice Under the New Covenant (9:1–10:18)**
  1. **Free Access to God Not Granted Under Old Covenant (9:1–10)**
  2. Jesus Entered Heaven Itself with His Blood (9:11–14)
  3. Jesus as Mediator of New Covenant Bestows an Eternal Inheritance (9:15–22)
  4. Jesus' Sacrifice: Better than OT Sacrifices (9:23–10:18)
V. Concluding Exhortations and Warnings (10:19–12:29)

Scripture

¹ Now the first covenant also had regulations for ministry and an earthly sanctuary. ² For a tabernacle was set up, and in the first room, which is called the holy place, were the lampstand, the table, and the presentation loaves. ³ Behind the second curtain, the tabernacle was called the most holy place. ⁴ It contained the gold altar of incense and the ark of the covenant, covered with gold on all sides, in which there was a gold jar containing the manna, Aaron's staff that budded, and the tablets of the covenant. ⁵ The cherubim of glory were above it overshadowing the mercy seat. It is not possible to speak about these things in detail right now. ⁶ With these things set up this way, the priests enter the first room repeatedly, performing their ministry. ⁷ But the high priest alone enters the second room, and he does that only once a year, and never without blood, which he offers for himself and for the sins of the people committed in ignorance. ⁸ The Holy Spirit was making it clear that the way into the most holy place had not yet been disclosed while the first tabernacle was still standing. ⁹ This is a symbol for the present time, during which gifts and sacrifices are offered that cannot perfect the worshiper's conscience. ¹⁰ They are physical regulations and only deal with food, drink, and various washings imposed until the time of restoration.

Context

The main point of this long section is found in the warning (5:11–6:12). The readers must not fall away by adopting the old covenant rather than the new. The author assures them of the certainty of God's promises (6:13–20). He teaches them that they have a better priesthood (Melchizedekian, 7:1–28), a better covenant (new rather than old, 8:1–13), and now a better sacrifice (9:1–10:18). The section begins with the furniture and placement of items in the tabernacle (9:1–5). The ministry of the priests in the tabernacle is then considered (9:6). What is most significant, however, is that the holy of holies is entered only once a year and by only one person (the high priest, 9:7). Such a limitation signifies that access to God was not yet available as long as the tabernacle remained (9:8). The gifts and sacrifices and other regulations of the old administration are figural (9:9–10). They show that the conscience of worshipers is not yet cleansed and point toward a new day when everything will be changed.

Exegesis

9:1

The focus shifts to the sacrifices offered under the old covenant. The word "now" (μὲν οὖν) may designate "a resumption of the theme of the old covenant" from 8:7.[400] The word "first" (ἡ πρώτη) refers back to the same word in 8:13, where it clearly refers to the old covenant.[401] The old covenant was to be administered in a particular way. Indeed, many commands or "regulations for worship" (ESV) were specified under the old covenant. Israel could not worship God according to its own wisdom and preferences. Worship was regulated and defined so that they followed God's instructions in worshiping him. The worship required took place at "an earthly sanctuary." The sanctuary here is clearly the tabernacle. It is "earthly" (κοσμικόν), pertaining to this world rather than the heavenly world where God dwells,[402] pointing forward and upward to something better.[403]

9:2

The author zeros in on the holy place and the most holy place, beginning with the holy place. Other features relating to the tabernacle, such as the courtyard or the altar for sacrifices and offerings are not considered here. The "tabernacle" (σκηνή) or "tent" (ESV) was set up according to the directions given by God (Exodus 25–31;

---

[400] So Ellingworth, *Hebrews*, 420.

[401] Rightly Attridge, *Hebrews*, 23.

[402] The word "earthly" has a negative connotation (Attridge, *Hebrews*, 232; Peterson, *Hebrews and Perfection*, 132).

[403] Cf. O'Brien, *Hebrews*, 306–7.

35–40). Probably the author refers to the tabernacle rather than the temple because the former was associated with the enactment of the Sinai covenant,[404] and the instructions about priestly offerings are associated with the tabernacle in the OT. First, the furniture in the holy place is considered: the lampstand (Exod 25:31–39; 37:17–24), the table (Exod 25:23–29; 37:10–16), and the bread presented on the table (Exod 25:30). The lampstand and the table are clearly put in the holy place: "Place the table outside the veil and the lampstand on the south side of the tabernacle, opposite the table; put the table on the north side" (Exod 26:35; cf. 40:22–24).

9:3

From the holy place the author moves inward, inside the veil to "the most holy place" (Ἅγια Ἁγίων).[405] The holy of holies was behind the curtain separating the holy place from the most holy place. "Hang the veil under the clasps and bring the ark of the testimony there behind the veil, so the veil will make a separation for you between the holy place and the most holy place" (Exod 26:33; cf. Exod 40:21).

9:4

The items in the most holy place are now recorded, including the altar of incense, the ark of the covenant, the golden jar with the manna, the rod of Aaron which sprouted, and the tablets of the covenant. The furniture will be considered in reverse order since the altar of incense is the most difficult to explain here.

The tablets of the covenant were placed in the ark at the beginning (Exod 25:16; Deut 10:5) and continued to be in the most holy place in the temple and were in fact the only items left in the ark when the temple was built (1 Kgs 8:9; 2 Chr 5:10), which confirms that the author thinks historically about what was in the most holy place in the tabernacle and does not reflect on what was in the most holy place of the temple in his day. The tablets, which had the Ten Commandments inscribed on them, represented the main covenant stipulations required for Israel (Exod 31:18; 34:28; Deut 4:13; 5:22; 10:4).

---

[404] Ibid., 307.

[405] The textual tradition is varied here. It is possible that ἁγία is the best reading, but even so the referent is still the most holy place.

The sprouting and blossoming of Aaron's staff indicated that the Lord had chosen him for the priesthood (Num 17:1–13). Aaron's staff was placed in the most holy place to deter those rebelling against the Lord. The Lord provided manna to sustain Israel for its 40 years in the wilderness (Exod 16:31–35; cf. Deut 8:3, 16; Ps 78:24), and a sample was placed before the tablets as a witness of God's care for Israel (Exod 16:34). Strictly speaking, Aaron's staff and the manna were not placed in the ark but were in the most holy place, though it is possible that as time progressed such items were put in the ark along with the tablets of the covenant.[406]

The ark of the covenant was constructed according to the Lord's instructions (Exod 25:10–16; 37:1–5). The ark was in the most holy place: "Hang the veil under the clasps and bring the ark of the testimony there behind the veil, so the veil will make a separation for you between the holy place and the most holy place" (Exod 26:33; cf. 40:3, 21). The ark is linked with the covenant the Lord made with Israel, with his promise to bless them and to be their God.[407]

The instructions for the altar of incense are also detailed (Exod 30:1–5; cf. 37:25–28).[408] Twice a day Aaron was to burn incense on the altar in the morning and at twilight (Exod 30:7–9). Almost certainly the author, who was so familiar with the Day of Atonement, would realize from this text alone that the incense altar was not in the most holy place.[409] The altar was to be purified once a year (Exod 30:10), and when there was a sin offering, blood had to be applied to the altar of incense (Lev 4:7). Exodus is clear that the altar is in the holy place, not the most holy place: "You are to place the altar in front of the veil by the ark of the testimony—in front of the mercy seat that is over the testimony—where I will meet with

---

[406] Ellingworth points out, however, that in rabbinic tradition the items were not said to be put into the ark (*Hebrews*, 428). Perhaps the author was unconcerned about precision here.

[407] Cf. Num 10:33; 14:44; Deut 10:8; 31:9; Josh 3:3, 6, 8, 11; 4:7, 9; 8:33; Judg 20:27; 1 Sam 4:3–4, 5; 2 Sam 15:24; 1 Kgs 3:15; 8:1; 1 Chr 15:25–26, 28; Jer 3:16.

[408] Some have argued that the reference is to the incense burner since the term used (θυμιατήριον) typically denotes a censer (2 Chr 26:19; Ezek 8:11; 4 Macc 7:11), but there are decisive reasons for seeing a reference to the incense altar here (Ellingworth, *Hebrews*, 425–26; Hughes, *Hebrews*, 311).

[409] Against Lindars, *The Theology of Hebrews*, 86. Rightly Hughes, *Hebrews*, 312. Incense was burned twice a day, but the offerings for the Day of Atonement were once a year.

you" (Exod 30:6; cf. Lev 16:8–19), though some verses, taken out of context, could suggest that the altar was in the most holy place: "Place the gold altar for incense in front of the ark of the testimony" (Exod 40:5).

Hebrews, of course, places the altar of incense in the most holy place. It is difficult to believe the author, who was familiar with the OT and likely knew Jewish tradition, didn't know where the altar of incense was located.[410] After all, the priest had to tend to it twice a day, and the blood of sin offerings was constantly applied to the horns of the altar. The location of the altar was common knowledge in Judaism (cf. Jdt 9:1; 1 Macc 4:49–50; 2 Macc 10:3).[411] Both Philo and Josephus put the incense altar in the outer sanctum instead of the most holy place.[412] Zechariah's ministry in the temple confirms this (Luke 1:5–23), for his ministry at the altar of incense could not have been in the most holy place since it was accessible only once a year. It seems likely, then, that the author links the incense altar closely with the most holy place (cf. also 1 Kgs 6:20, 22) since the incense altar is associated with God's presence.[413] "On the Day of Atonement incense from the altar was taken in (Lev. 16:12–13), and the blood of the sin offering was sprinkled on the horns of the incense altar as well as on the mercy seat (Exod. 30:10; Lev. 16:15)."[414] As Hagner says, "Yet so vital was the burning of incense on the Day of Atonement . . . that the author automatically associates the altar of incense with the Holy of Holies."[415]

By the time of the NT, the ark was no longer present (cf. Jer 3:16; 2 Macc 2:4–5), and when Pompey went into the temple, he was shocked to discover that there was nothing there at all.

---

[410] For helpful discussions, see Hughes, *Hebrews*, 309–14; Cockerill, *Hebrews*, 375–77. Traditions that place the altar of incense in the most holy place are neither clear nor dominant (against Attridge, *Hebrews*, 235), though one could read the LXX to draw such a conclusion (L. Johnson, *Hebrews*, 220).

[411] Cf. here Attridge, *Hebrews*, 234.

[412] Philo, *On the Life of Moses* 2.93–95, 101–4; *Who Is the Heir?*, 226; Josephus, *J.W.* 5:216–19; *Ant.* 3.139–47, 198–99.

[413] Alternatively, Ellingworth suggests the author is simply imprecise since he isn't concerned with such details (*Hebrews*, 426–27).

[414] O'Brien, *Hebrews*, 309.

[415] Hagner, *Hebrews*, 108.

9:5

The glorious cherubim were above the mercy seat (ἱλαστήριον), guarding the presence of God (Exod 25:18–20; cf. 37:7–9; 1 Kgs 6:23–28; 2 Chr 3:10–13), a task which belonged to the cherubim in the garden of Eden (Gen 3:24). The ark is where the Lord has fellowship with his people: "I will meet with you there above the mercy seat, between the two cherubim that are over the ark of the testimony; I will speak with you from there about all that I command you regarding the Israelites" (Exod 25:22; cf. 1 Sam 4:4; 2 Sam 6:2). All these articles of furniture could be explored in some detail, but it is not the author's purpose to do so.

9:6

It is evident that the author selectively appropriates the tradition, focusing on what is relevant for his readers. After explaining the arrangement of the furniture in the holy and most holy place, the ministry of the priests in the tabernacle is related. The priests regularly ministered in "the outer room" (τὴν πρώτην σκηνήν), i.e., "the outer tent" (NET). They were to perform their various duties in the holy place, including placing the bread of the presence on the table (Exod 25:30), which according to 1 Chr 9:32 was changed every Sabbath (Lev 24:8; 1 Chr 9:32; cf. 2 Chr 4:19; 13:11). Instructions were given for baking, how the bread was to be arranged, and for putting frankincense on the table as well (Lev 24:5–7). In the same way they had to tend to the lampstand to shed light in the holy place (Lev 24:4; Num 8:2–3; 2 Chr 13:11). Incense was to be offered daily (Exod 30:8), and the lamps were to be attended to daily as well (Exod 27:20; Lev 24:2). Twice a day sacrifices were to be offered (Exod 29:38–42; Num 28:3–8). What is particularly emphasized is that they engaged in this service "repeatedly" (διὰ παντός). Their work was never done and had to be reduplicated each day.

9:7

Every day the priests minister in the holy place, but the most holy place is an entirely different matter. Only the high priest can enter the inner sanctuary, and he is not allowed to enter whenever he wishes. As Lev 16:2 says, "Tell your brother Aaron that he may not come whenever he wants into the holy place behind the veil in front of the mercy seat on the ark or else he will die." The most holy place is restricted to one day a year, the Day of Atonement (Exod 30:10; Lev 16:34; 23:27; Num 29:7), which Leviticus 16 describes in detail. Nor does the high priest enter the room boldly. The sprinkling of blood is necessary for forgiveness to be secured (Exod 30:10; Lev 16:14–15, 18–19, 27). He offers a bull for a sin offering for himself (Lev 16:3) and two male goats for a sin offering for the people (Lev 16:5). Thereby atonement was secured both for Aaron (Lev 16:6, 11) and for the people (Lev 16:9, 15, 21–22). The word used for "offer" (προσφέρει) here, as O'Brien observes, is never used for what the priests offered, and thus the term anticipates and typifies Christ's offering of himself on the cross (Heb 9:14, 25, 28; 10:12).[416] Ellingworth thinks the author wrongly restricts forgiveness to sins committed in ignorance.[417] But the author of Hebrews does not misread the OT here, for defiant sins were not amenable to forgiveness (Num 15:30; cf. Deut 1:43; 17:12–13; Ps 19:13), and for the author they are comparable to the apostasy he warns against.

9:8

The writer clues the readers into the significance of the Day of Atonement ritual. The Holy Spirit is revealing the difference between the old covenant and the new. Perhaps there is the notion here that the Spirit unveils what was hidden previously.[418] When reading about the Levitical priesthood and the administration of its sacrifices, the rituals should be read with spiritual perception. One must attend, therefore, to what the Spirit says through the OT ritual and covenant. In this instance the limitation of access to the most holy place only once a year on the Day of Atonement indicates that access to God's presence was not yet freely available. As long as the first tabernacle continued, the people could only meet with God once a year and only through the mediation of the high priest.[419] The continuation of the tabernacle does not refer to its remaining in existence but to its continued validity.[420] Now that Christ has come and sacrificed himself, its viability has ended.

---

[416] O'Brien, *Hebrews*, 312.

[417] Ellingworth, *Hebrews*, 435 (despite Ellingworth's qualifications on 436).

[418] L. Johnson, *Hebrews*, 223.

[419] The reference is to the whole of the tabernacle here (Bruce, *Hebrews*, 194–95; Hughes, *Hebrews*, 322–23), in contrast to those who see reference to the outer sanctuary alone (Attridge, *Hebrews*, 240; Westcott, *Hebrews*, 252; Schenk, *Cosmology and Eschatology in Hebrews*, 149–50; Norman H. Young, "The Gospel According to Hebrews 9," *NTS* 27 [1981]: 200).

[420] So Attridge, *Hebrews*, 240.

9:9

Again the readers are summoned to be discerning, to grasp what the Holy Spirit is saying.[421] Limited access to God via the sacrificial cultus functions as a "symbol" (παραβολή) or "illustration" (NIV). As long as the earthly sanctuary remained valid, there was no regular access to God in either the earthly or the heavenly sanctuary.[422] The recipients of the letter face the danger of superficiality. In considering the sacrifices under the old covenant, they may not truly understand what is being communicated for the present day. Such sacrifices were ordained by God for a particular period of salvation history, but a new era has arrived ("the present time") where such sacrifices give way to a greater and perfect sacrifice. The HCSB interprets "the present time" (see above) as a reference to the old covenant period.[423] But the NIV is to be preferred here: "This is an illustration for the present time, indicating that the gifts and sacrifices being offered were not able to clear the conscience of the worshiper." Hence, the present time designates the era of the new covenant. Such an interpretation fits with what the author says elsewhere, for the Sinai covenant is "old" in contrast to the newness of the new covenant (8:8, 10, 13; 9:15; 12:24). It is the "first" covenant, not the present one (8:7; 9:1, 15, 18).

The gifts and sacrifices offered under the Sinai covenant (Leviticus 1–7; 16) could not "perfect the worshiper's conscience." The perfection (τελειῶσαι) of the conscience involves the full forgiveness of sins. In 7:19 the law's inability to perfect (ἐτελείωσεν) means it can't bring people near to God. In 10:1 the author uses the same verb that we find in this verse: the same sacrifices can't "make perfect (τελειῶσαι) those who draw near" (ESV). Hence, those who rely on the law have a continual "consciousness" (συνείδησιν) of sins (10:2) and are reminded of sins daily (10:3). The parallel with 9:9 is remarkable, for here the author speaks of perfecting the conscience

---

[421] The pronoun "this" (ἥτις) that begins the verse could have as its antecedent "way," "tabernacle," or "standing" from 9:8 (so Ellingworth, *Hebrews*, 439), but it probably refers to the entire thought from verse 8 (so L. Johnson, *Hebrews*, 225). Young thinks it refers to the holy place, reflecting his interpretation of verse 8 ("The Gospel According to Hebrews 9," 201).

[422] For this point, see Steve Stanley, "Hebrews 9:6–10: The 'Parable' of the Tabernacle," *NovT* 37 (1995): 385–99.

[423] So also William L. Lane, *Hebrews 9–13*, WBC (Dallas: Word, 1991), 234.

(συνείδησιν). We find a similar idea in 9:14 where Christ's blood "cleanse[s] our consciences." The flaw with the OT cultus, then, is that it did not truly cleanse the conscience of sin.

9:10

Old Testament regulations were fundamentally external. They dealt with foods (cf. Lev 11:1–44; Deut 14:3–21), drinks (cf. Num 6:3), and regulations for cleansing and different kinds of washing and cleansing (e.g., Exod 29:4; 30:19–21; 40:12; Lev 11:25; 13:6; 14:8–9; 15:5–8; 16:26; 17:16; Num 19:7–8; Deut 23:11). Such "regulations" are "physical" (σαρκός) or "external" (NIV). In other words they point to a greater washing and cleansing, to truly being washed and cleansed from sin. In the OT itself "washing" and "cleansing" become a metaphor for true forgiveness of sins (e.g., Pss 19:12; 51:2, 7; Ezek 36:25, 33; 37:23; Zech 13:1). Such external regulations had their place for a certain period in salvation history. The author doesn't denigrate the regulations, as if they were not from God. He argues temporally and eschatologically. They were appropriate during the old covenant, but they were intended to cease when the day of fulfillment arrived. Since the "time of restoration" (καιροῦ διορθώσεως), or better "the time of the new order" (NIV), has arrived, the old regulations are dismissed, for that to which they pointed has come.[424]

Bridge

The author considers the tabernacle: its furniture and compartments. What is striking is that the tabernacle does not provide full and free access to God. Only once a year does the high priest actually enter God's presence. Further, the regulations of the old covenant have to do with external matters like food, drink, and washings. The Holy Spirit speaks to us through these matters. The new covenant rather than the old brings us into God's presence. Our consciences aren't cleansed and perfected through the old covenant rituals, for those rituals point to a sacrifice that is better and truly brings us into God's presence.

---

[424] "The present time" (v. 9) and the time of restoration (v. 10) both refer to the days of fulfillment that have arrived in Jesus Christ (cf. here Ellingworth, *Hebrews*, 440–41; Cockerill, *Hebrews*, 384n60).

Hebrews 9:11–14

Outline

I. Prologue: Definitive and Final Revelation in the Son (1:1–4)
II. Don't Abandon the Son Since He Is Greater than Angels (1:5–2:18)
III. Don't Harden Your Hearts Since You Have a Son and High Priest Greater than Moses and Joshua (3:1–4:13)
IV. **Don't Fall Away from Jesus' Melchizedekian Priesthood Since It Is Greater than the Levitical Priesthood (4:14–10:18)**
   A. Exhortation in Light of Jesus' Priestly Status (4:14–5:10)
   B. Warning and Assurance (5:11–6:20)
   C. Jesus' Greater Priesthood as a Melchizedekian Priest (7:1–28)
   D. New Covenant Better than the Old (8:1–13)
   E. **A Better Sacrifice Under the New Covenant (9:1–10:18)**
      1. Free Access to God Not Granted Under Old Covenant (9:1–10)
      2. **Jesus Entered Heaven Itself with His Blood (9:11–14)**
      3. Jesus as Mediator of New Covenant Bestows an Eternal Inheritance (9:15–22)
      4. Jesus' Sacrifice: Better than OT Sacrifices (9:23–10:18)
V. Concluding Exhortations and Warnings (10:19–12:29)

Scripture

[11] But the Messiah has appeared, high priest of the good things that have come. In the greater and more perfect tabernacle not made with hands (that is, not of this creation), [12] He entered the most holy place once for all, not by the blood of goats and calves, but by His own blood, having obtained eternal redemption. [13] For if the blood of goats and bulls and the ashes of a young cow, sprinkling those who are defiled, sanctify for the purification of the flesh, [14] how much more will the blood of the Messiah, who through the eternal Spirit offered Himself without blemish

to God, cleanse our consciences from dead works to serve the living God?

Context

The main point in 9:1–10:18 is that Christ's sacrifice is better than the sacrifices of the old covenant. In 9:1–10 the inadequacy of old covenant sacrifices comes to the forefront. They don't usher people into God's presence, nor do they truly cleanse the conscience from guilt. The sacrifice of Christ is contrasted with the sacrifices of the old covenant in 9:11–14. Christ entered into the presence of God with his own blood, thereby securing eternal redemption (9:11–12). The blood of animals cleanses the flesh, but Christ's blood is far superior. He cleanses the conscience of those who belong to him, purging them of their guilt so they are free to serve the living God (9:13–14).

Exegesis

9:11

A new era has arrived in the high priesthood of Jesus Christ (see §2.3). He has entered God's presence, i.e., the true and perfect tabernacle. This tabernacle is not earthly but heavenly (see §2.4). Jesus' priesthood signaled the realization, at least in part, "of the good things to come" (NET; τῶν γενομένων ἀγαθῶν). In Christ the eschatological good things have dawned, but they are not yet completed until the arrival of the heavenly city. We have another indication that the old era has been superseded, and in Christ that which is better has commenced.

The earthly tabernacle was a picture of the heavenly tabernacle.[425] The conception is both spatial and eschatological. The earthly tabernacle points to a "greater and more perfect tabernacle." That which is heavenly, then, is far better than what is earthly. For the tabernacle Jesus entered does not belong to this creation, for it is

---

[425] The tabernacle here doesn't refer to Christ's physical body (Vanhoye, *Structure and Message of Hebrews*, 66–67) nor the eucharist (James Swetnam, "'The Greater and More Perfect Tent': A Contribution to the Discussion of Hebrews 9,11," *Bib* 47 [1966]: 91–106). Rightly Attridge, *Hebrews*, 246; Peterson, *Hebrews and Perfection*, 141–43.

not made with hands.[426] Strictly speaking, there isn't a tabernacle at all in the heavenly realm.[427] The heavenly tabernacle becomes a vehicle for describing the indescribable, for depicting the presence of God.[428]

> In the New there is no need for a heavenly 'Holy Place' since Christ brings his people into the very presence of God. Thus, any suggestion that 'the greater and more perfect Tent' represents a heavenly 'Holy Place' is nothing more than a vestigial remnant from the parallel the pastor has drawn between Old Tent and the New.[429]

There is an eschatological reality as well here, for the more perfect and heavenly tabernacle has been accessed in the last days through the cross, resurrection, and exaltation of Jesus Christ.[430]

---

[426] The word "through" (διά) is local here, emphasizing movement. Cf. Attridge, *Hebrews*, 246; Lane, *Hebrews 9–13*, 236–38; Ellingworth, *Hebrews*, 450–551. But see Koester for a defense of an instrumental rather than a spatial reading (*Hebrews*, 408–9). Even though we have a local use of the preposition, we shouldn't conclude from this that Jesus literally passed through a tabernacle in heaven. The language here is analogical instead of being univocal.

[427] Against Otfried Hofius, *Der Vorhang vor dem Thron Gottes: Eine exegetisch-religionsgeschichtliche Untersuchung zu Hebräer 6,19f. und 10,19f.*, WUNT 14 (Tübingen: Mohr Siebeck, 1972), 50–73; Moffitt, *Atonement and the Logic of the Resurrection in the Epistle to the Hebrews*, 223–25. Also, "the greater and more perfect tabernacle" refers to the whole sanctuary (Koester, *Hebrews*, 409; Ellingworth, *Hebrews*, 446–47; Schenk, *Cosmology and Eschatology in Hebrews*, 159), not to the forecourt of the sanctuary (against Lane, *Hebrews 9–13*, 237–38; O'Brien, *Hebrews*, 320; W. Michaelis, "σκηνή," *TDNT* 7:376–77). We should note that the author is often imprecise in describing features of the OT cult, and hence we should not make the mistake of pressing his language here (cf. Schenk, *Cosmology and Eschatology in Hebrews*, 164).

[428] Cf. here the comments of Ounsworth (*Joshua Typology*, 94) who warns us about taking the author's language too literally.

[429] Cockerill, *Hebrews*, 391.

[430] We should note here the fine study of Ribbens, who argues that the heavenly sanctuary is real. He defends his case by noting the presence of a heavenly sanctuary in Jewish apocalyptic literature, by the references to sacrifices in a heavenly sanctuary in a couple of texts in Second Temple Jewish literature, and by providing an exegesis of key texts in Hebrews. See Ribbens, "Levitical Sacrifice and Heavenly Cult in Hebrews," esp. 1–182. Ribbens should also be distinguished from Moffit, for he sees both a heavenly and an earthly role in Jesus' sacrifice. Space is lacking to respond in detail to Ribbens here, so a couple of comments will have to suffice.

9:12

The earthly tabernacle was entered with "the blood of goats and calves" (cf. Exod 29:10; Lev 1:5; 3:12; 4:3, 23; 8:2; 16:3). The blood of the animals "represented the lives of those who offered them poured out in death."[431] Jesus, however, entered the heavenly tabernacle because of a sacrifice far more valuable than the blood of animals. He offered his own blood; he surrendered his own life in death for the sake of his people. Furthermore, he entered "the most holy place" (εἰς τὰ ἅγια) "once for all" (ἐφάπαξ). Jesus did not literally bring his blood into heaven. The blood stands for the giving up of his life which was offered as a sacrifice.[432] Again the most holy

---

First, the evidence from Jewish literature isn't decisive, for the evidence for sacrifices in heaven is limited to a couple of examples. Given the diversity of Judaism in NT times, it is unclear that these examples exercised influence upon the author of Hebrews. The parallels aren't pervasive and compelling enough to prove the case. Certainly Ribbens's reading is possible, but it is not established by the evidence presented. Even if the author of Hebrews was aware of such traditions, he may not have interpreted them literally. Second, and more important, as with so much else in Hebrews' scholarship, one's understanding is influenced by the alleged background. I agree with Ribbens that Hebrews isn't directly dependent on Philo or Middle Platonism. But I am not as convinced that Jewish apocalyptic is the primary background against which one should interpret the letter. As I suggested earlier in this commentary, there is a Philonic and Platonic character to the letter that suggests some influence from Middle Platonism. I am not suggesting the book represents Philonic or Middle Platonic thought in any technical sense, but I am suggesting the background of the book represents a creative fusion of the OT apocalyptic traditions and Middle Platonic thinking. Hence it is equally possible that the temple and sacrificial language in heaven shouldn't be interpreted literally. We can't say that the author is either Philonic or apocalyptic. He is a unique blend, and the Platonic features of the letter can't be washed out altogether. So, third, it seems less likely to me that the language about a heavenly sanctuary should be interpreted literally. Instead, the author is probably using analogical language that shouldn't be pressed to say that Jesus literally brought his blood into a heavenly temple.

[431] Cockerill, *Hebrews*, 393.

[432] So also Attridge, *Hebrews*, 248. "The pastor, however, is careful to avoid giving the impression that Christ carried his blood into heaven" (Cockerill, *Hebrews*, 394). Moffitt maintains that blood doesn't signify Jesus' obedient death but the presentation of his life to God (*Atonement and the Logic of the Resurrection in the Epistle to the Hebrews*, 218–19, 256–78). Such an interpretation is flawed and confusing. First of all, the shedding of blood points to death (rightly Guthrie, *Hebrews*, 318). When one's blood is shed, a person dies. Second, there is a notion of life here, but the notion that is present is this: when Jesus shed his blood, he gave up his life so others would live. For a more convincing explanation of the role of Jesus' blood,

place in the tabernacle points to the holiest place of all: the presence of God in the transcendent realm. Jesus did not repeatedly offer his blood to procure forgiveness of sins. After all, as a human being he could only die once. As a result of Jesus' once-for-all sacrifice, he secured "eternal redemption" (αἰωνίαν λύτρωσιν).[433] The one sacrifice was an effective and definitive sacrifice, securing forgiveness of sins.[434] In the OT redemption is related to Passover (Exodus 12–14), the Jubilee (Lev 25:29, 48), and to liberation from Egypt (Ps 111:9). Freedom at Jubilee or liberation from Egypt is not eternal, and hence the redemption Jesus accomplished is far superior to what happened in the year of Jubilee or at the exodus. Both of these events point typologically to the redemption accomplished in Jesus Christ.

9:13

The author argues from the lesser to the greater here (9:13–14), from the earthly to the heavenly. Blood from goats and bulls sprinkles "those who are ceremonially unclean" (NIV; τοὺς κεκοινωμένους). In the same way the ashes of a heifer remove defilement. The ceremony regarding the heifer is explained in Numbers 19. The ashes remove impurity as a sin offering (Num 19:9, 17) and also remove corpse impurity (Num 19:12). All these sacrifices, however, did not truly cleanse the inner person or the conscience. They cleansed the flesh or body of those who were defiled. They removed ceremonial uncleanness. The flesh does not represent here, then, a sin principle against God as we find in Paul but that which is external and outward.[435]

---

see Leon Morris, *The Apostolic Preaching of the Cross,* 3rd ed. (London: Tyndale, 1965), 112–29. For the notion that blood stands for life (not death), see Christian A. Eberhart, "Characteristics of Sacrificial Metaphors," in *Hebrews: Contemporary Methods—New Insights,* ed. G. Gelardini (Leiden: Brill, 2005), 37–64; Ekkehard W. Stegemann and Wolfgang Stegemann, "Does the Cultic Language in Hebrews Represent Sacrificial Metaphors? Reflections on Some Basic Problems," in *Hebrews: Contemporary Methods—New Insights,* ed. G. Gelardini (Leiden: Brill, 2005), 18–23.

[433] The participle here could designate subsequent action (so Lane, *Hebrews 9–13,* 230; Hughes, *Hebrews,* 328n84), but it is better to see it as "coincident" (so Ellingworth, *Hebrews,* 453).

[434] Redemption here may involve both deliverance from bondage and forgiveness of sins (Koester, *Hebrews,* 408; Cockerill, *Hebrews,* 395). O'Brien says the emphasis is on forgiveness of sins (*Hebrews,* 322).

[435] Rightly Hughes, *Hebrews,* 356.

9:14

The blood of Christ is far better than the sacrifice of bulls, goats, and heifers. After all, it is the blood of a human being, and not just any human being; it is the blood of the Messiah—the King of Israel and the entire world (Ps 110:1). The blood here designates Jesus' death, referring to the "principle of life, offered to God in death."[436] Animals offered in sacrifice had to be "without blemish" (ἄμωμον).[437] Animals were physically unblemished, but Christ was morally unblemished (cf. 1 Pet 1:19). Here the author picks up again the notion that Christ was sinless (Heb 4:15; 7:26–28).

Jesus "offered (προσήνεγκεν) himself," and the word for offering is often used to designate offerings in the OT (e.g., Exod 32:6; Lev 1:2, 5, 13–15; 3:6, etc.), and so it is clear that we have the language of sacrifice here. The offering was "through the eternal Spirit" (διὰ πνεύματος αἰωνίου). The reference could possibly be to his human spirit, so that Jesus offered himself without reserve to God.[438] But the word "eternal" doesn't fit well with a reference to Jesus' humanity and seems to fit better with a reference to the Holy Spirit (see §4).[439] Furthermore, the author by adding the word "his" would have made clear that Jesus' human spirit is intended, and its omission suggests a reference to the Holy Spirit.[440] Most of the references to the Spirit in Hebrews clearly refer to the Holy Spirit (2:4; 3:7; 6:4; 9:8; 10:15, 29; but cf. 4:12). We see elsewhere in Hebrews that the Spirit is closely connected with the inauguration of the last days, either by verifying the gospel (2:4), or as the gift of the new age

---

[436] Ellingworth, *Hebrews*, 456. Cf. also Morris, *Apostolic Preaching of the Cross*, 112–29; J. Behm, "αἷμα," *TDNT* 1:174–75; Hughes, *Hebrews*, 335–36. As Behm says, "The interest of the NT is not the material blood of Christ, but in His shed blood as the life violently taken from Him" (174). There is no notion here of the blood literally being brought into the sanctuary and being preserved forever (rightly Hughes, *Hebrews*, 329–34; O'Brien, *Hebrews*, 321).

[437] Exodus 29:1; Lev 1:3, 10; 3:1, 6; 4:3, 23, 28, 32; 5:15; 9:2; 14:10; 22:19; Num 6:14; 19:2; 28:3, 9, 11, 19, 27, 31; Ezek 43:22, 23, 25.

[438] This view was rather popular in the history of interpretation. See Westcott, *Hebrews*, 261–62. Cf. the discussion in Hughes, who seems to favor the same position presented here (*Hebrews*, 358–60).

[439] So Koester, *Hebrews*, 410–11; Lane, *Hebrews 9–13*, 240. Against Attridge, *Hebrews*, 250–51. L. Johnson doesn't see a reference to the Holy Spirit and thinks the reference is to "the mode of Christ's offering" (*Hebrews*, 236).

[440] Hagner, *Hebrews*, 120.

(6:4), or as speaking through the Scriptures to the new community (3:7; 9:8; 10:15). Insulting the Spirit (10:29) is an egregious sin, for it rejects the salvation accomplished by Jesus Christ and applied by the Holy Spirit. Why does he refer to the "eternal" Spirit? Before answering that question, it seems that the Spirit empowered and strengthened Jesus to give himself to God as a sacrifice.[441] Such a notion fits with the Lukan conception of the Spirit's work in the life of Jesus, where his ministry was empowered by the Holy Spirit (Luke 1:35; 3:22; 4:1, 14, 18; 10:21). It also seems that the word "eternal" emphasizes the deity of the Spirit. Perhaps there is also an emphasis on the fulfillment of prophecy so that Jesus' self-offering was in accord with the eternal plan of God. Furthermore, there is the suggestion that someone who is merely a human being cannot atone for sin. Atonement must be secured by someone who is both human and divine for the sacrifice rendered to be efficacious.[442] The offering through "the eternal Spirit" secures "eternal redemption" (9:12), "eternal salvation" (5:9), and an "eternal inheritance" (9:15).

In the last part of the verse, the benefits of Jesus' offering are considered. He cleanses consciences stained with guilt by his blood.[443]

---

[441] So Ellingworth, *Hebrews*, 457; cf. Martin Emmrich, *Pneumatological Concepts in the Epistle to the Hebrews: Amtscharisma, Prophet, and Guide of the Eschatological Exodus* (Lanham, MD: University Press of America, 2003), 1–13.

[442] Hughes, *Hebrews*, 359.

[443] Moffitt questions whether "blood" refers to Jesus' death since blood doesn't procure forgiveness without the ritual application of the blood (*Atonement and the Logic of the Resurrection in the Epistle to the Hebrews*, 271–73). The objection doesn't stand, for Jesus' death (the shedding of his blood) has a transcendent effect, i.e., both his death and the presentation/application of the blood are necessary for atonement. It doesn't logically follow from the necessity of ritual application and manipulation that blood has to do with life instead of death. Nor is it correct to say that atonement is procured with the manipulation of the blood as if the death is only preparatory and hence not part of the sacrifice (against Walter Edward Brooks, "The Perpetuity of Christ's Sacrifice in the Epistle to the Hebrews," *JBL* 89 [1970]: 208–9). Separating death from the sacrifice is artificial and unpersuasive. The blood (the death of Christ) must be applied for forgiveness to be granted, but the blood is integrally related to his death. Such picturesque language doesn't mean the blood was literally presented in heaven. Rightly Barry C. Joslin, "Christ Bore the Sins of Many: Substitution and Atonement in Hebrews," *SBJT* 11 (2007): 82. Such an interpretation is guilty of reading the typological language too rigidly. Joslin rightly points out that no OT institution, whether the Day of Atonement (Leviticus 16), covenant inauguration (Exodus 24), or the red heifer purification (Numbers 19) matches perfectly with Christ's sacrifice. The fulfillment is greater than the type, showing that

The conscience refers to "removing sin from the 'heart,' that is, from the inner reality of the faithful."[444] Cleansing is often referred to in the OT, such as the purification of altars (Exod 29:36–37; 30:10; Lev 8:15; 16:18) and cleansing human beings from uncleanness (Lev 12:7–8; 13:6–7, 13, 17; 14:2, 4; 15:13, 28) and from sin (Lev 16:30). Typically uncleanness in the OT is from physical defilement. Such defilement is related to sin, but the cleansing Jesus accomplished is deeper, for he cleansed the conscience from the works that lead to death (cf. Heb 6:1). The new covenant looked forward to a definitive cleansing of sin (see §2.4). "I will purify (καθαριῶ) them from all the wrongs they have committed against Me, and I will forgive all the wrongs they have committed against Me, rebelling against Me" (Jer 33:8). Those who are thus cleansed are liberated to serve the living God. They are not saddled with guilt but purified from it, and thus they can live in confidence and joy before God and serve him gladly.

Bridge

Jesus entered the heavenly tabernacle, God's presence, with his own blood. As believers, therefore, we enjoy eternal redemption. Our consciences are cleansed by his blood from all that defiles us, and thus we are liberated from our past and are free to serve the living God. The readers must not turn back to OT sacrifices and ritual, for they are merely external and point forward to Jesus' sacrifice, to the blood that truly cleanses us from sin.

Hebrews 9:15–22

Outline

I. Prologue: Definitive and Final Revelation in the Son (1:1–4)
II. Don't Abandon the Son Since He Is Greater than Angels (1:5–2:18)

Christ's atoning sacrifice is greater than what was effected in any OT ritual or practice. Hebrews merges together various OT texts and practices so the readers see that the OT is fulfilled in the cross of Jesus Christ. Hebrews appropriates a number of OT rituals and practices to emphasize that the conscience must be cleansed by the blood of Christ for sinners to be forgiven. Another way of putting this is that Christ fulfills all the ritual and sacrificial practices in the OT.

[444] Cockerill, *Hebrews*, 401.

III. Don't Harden Your Hearts Since You Have a Son and High Priest Greater than Moses and Joshua (3:1–4:13)

IV. **Don't Fall Away from Jesus' Melchizedekian Priesthood Since It Is Greater than the Levitical Priesthood (4:14–10:18)**
   A. Exhortation in Light of Jesus' Priestly Status (4:14–5:10)
   B. Warning and Assurance (5:11–6:20)
   C. Jesus' Greater Priesthood as a Melchizedekian Priest (7:1–28)
   D. New Covenant Better than the Old (8:1–13)
   E. **A Better Sacrifice Under the New Covenant (9:1–10:18)**
      1. Free Access to God Not Granted Under Old Covenant (9:1–10)
      2. Jesus Entered Heaven Itself with His Blood (9:11–14)
      3. **Jesus as Mediator of New Covenant Bestows an Eternal Inheritance (9:15–22)**
      4. Jesus' Sacrifice: Better than OT Sacrifices (9:23–10:18)

V. Concluding Exhortations and Warnings (10:19–12:29)

Scripture

[15] Therefore, He is the mediator of a new covenant, so that those who are called might receive the promise of the eternal inheritance, because a death has taken place for redemption from the transgressions committed under the first covenant. [16] Where a will exists, the death of the one who made it must be established. [17] For a will is valid only when people die, since it is never in force while the one who made it is living. [18] That is why even the first covenant was inaugurated with blood. [19] For when every command had been proclaimed by Moses to all the people according to the law, he took the blood of calves and goats, along with water, scarlet wool, and hyssop, and sprinkled the scroll itself and all the people, [20] saying, This is the blood of the covenant that God has commanded for you. [21] In the same way, he sprinkled the tabernacle and all the articles of worship with blood. [22] According to the law almost everything is purified with blood, and without the shedding of blood there is no forgiveness.

Context

Christ's sacrifice is far better than OT sacrifices, for worshipers were not cleansed from their sins, and free access to God was not granted when the tabernacle and temple system were still valid (9:1–10). Christ, on the other hand, entered the true tabernacle, God's presence in heaven, cleansing with his blood the conscience of those belonging to him (9:11–14). Because of Jesus' atoning sacrifice, he is the mediator of the new covenant, so that those who are called may enjoy the promise of an eternal inheritance (9:15). The author then explains why death was necessary under the old covenant (9:15). After all, one's last will and testament (by analogy to a covenant) are only established on the basis of death (9:16–17). It follows, therefore, that the first covenant was inaugurated with the blood (the death) of sacrificial victims (9:18). The author supports this by appealing to Exod 24:8 where Moses established the covenant with Israel, sprinkling blood on the book of the covenant and on the people (9:19–20). Moses proclaims, "This is the blood of the covenant" (9:20), demonstrating that the covenant depends on the sprinkling of blood. Indeed, virtually every cultic object, along with the tabernacle, was sprinkled with blood (9:21), showing that without the shedding of blood there is no forgiveness of sins (9:22).

Exegesis

9:15

Since Jesus entered God's presence and cleansed the conscience through his blood, he is the mediator of a new covenant (cf. also 12:24).[445] In 8:6 Jesus is said to be "the mediator of a better covenant." The newness of the covenant is evident since Jesus enters the presence of God, which is something that was not accomplished under the old covenant. The new covenant, then, was inaugurated by Jesus' death, signifying that the former covenant established in Exodus 24 is no longer operative.

The purpose of Jesus' covenantal work is the main point of the verse. As the mediator of the new covenant, he ensured that those who are called would receive the promise of eternal inheritance (see §9). "Those who are called" (οἱ κεκλημένοι) likely has the same meaning

---

[445] The word "therefore" (διὰ τοῦτο) looks back to what precedes (so Ellingworth, *Hebrews*, 460).

that calling does in the Pauline literature (e.g., Rom 4:17; 8:30; 9:7, 12, 24–26; 1 Cor 1:9; Gal 1:6, 15; Eph 4:1; 1 Thess 5:24; 2 Thess 2:14; 2 Tim 1:9), where it designates God's powerful, life-changing, and effectual call in the life of believers (see §2.5). Because of Jesus' mediatorial new covenant work, those who are called by God are guaranteed that they will obtain "the eternal inheritance" (αἰωνίου κληρονομίας).[446] The one who offered himself through the *eternal* Spirit has secured an *eternal* inheritance. Originally the inheritance was promised to Abraham at the beginning (cf. 6:17; 11:8), but that inheritance belongs to all who are Abraham's offspring. The inheritance is another way of describing the heavenly city pledged to believers (11:10, 13–16; 12:22; 13:14).[447] Since Jesus has entered the heavenly tabernacle with his blood, believers have grounds to enter the heavenly city. All the promises made to Abraham, Isaac, and Jacob will be fulfilled for those who belong to Jesus Christ. Such promises did not become a reality through the old covenant, but they have been secured through the new.

The author, as has been the custom through the letter, detects both continuity and discontinuity between the two covenants. The old covenant was not effective in bringing people into God's presence, but there is a typological and figural relationship between the two covenants. The old anticipated and foreshadowed the new. Under the first covenant death was necessary to be redeemed (by which he probably means forgiven) from the transgressions committed under that covenant. That death was required is evident from the sacrifices that were offered for sin, purification, reparation, and the Day of Atonement (Leviticus 1–7; 16).

9:16

Death was necessary for redemption (i.e., forgiveness) under the old covenant. The connection between death and the covenant is pressed further. A will is only established on the basis of the death of

---

[446] The "eternal inheritance" defines what the promise is. In other words the eternal inheritance is appositional to the promise (O'Brien, *Hebrews*, 328). The inheritance is fundamentally future, but believers may enjoy some of the benefits now (Ellingworth, *Hebrews*, 461) since they are part of the heavenly city now (12:22).

[447] So also Koester, *Hebrews*, 417. For the inheritance theme in Hebrews, see Dana M. Harris, "The Eternal Inheritance in Hebrews: The Appropriation of the Old Testament Inheritance Motif by the Author of Hebrews" (Ph.D. diss., Trinity Evangelical Divinity School, 2009).

the one making it. Analogously, such is true under the old covenant as well, for sacrificial animals represent the death of the one making the covenant. Under the new covenant, of course, the covenant is established on the basis of Jesus' death.

Some commentators argue, contrary to most interpreters (see HCSB, NIV, ESV) that the reference in verses 16–17 is to the covenant rather than a will.[448] They support this reading for a number of reasons. First, wills in the Greco-Roman world were valid when written down, and hence they didn't require a death to be instituted. Second, the argument makes the best sense if there is no transition from covenant to will, for nowhere else in Hebrews does the word "covenant" (διαθήκη) refer to a will. Third, the word "dead" (ἐπὶ νεκροῖς) in verse 17 is plural, and thus the verse may teach that a covenant is "confirmed on the basis of dead animals," demonstrating that a covenant rather than a will is in view. Fourth, the verb translated "established" (φέρεσθαι) never means a death is confirmed or validated.

Deciding this matter is difficult, but I slightly favor a reference to a will or testament in verses 16–17.[449] First, we have often seen that the writer isn't technical or precise, and hence he probably refers to what is normally the case. A will doesn't usually take effect until someone dies. By way of contrast, covenants are often enacted without the death of the one making the covenant.[450] So it is difficult to see how the author could be speaking of covenants in general here. Second, it is unlikely that the plural for "dead" (ἐπὶ νεκροῖς)

---

[448] See Lane, *Hebrews 9–13*, 231–32, 242–44; J. J. Hughes, "Hebrews IX 15ff. and Galatians III 15ff.: A Study in Covenant Practice and Procedure," *NovT* 21 (1976–77): 27–96; O'Brien, *Hebrews*, 329–32; Cockerill, *Hebrews*, 405–7. Hahn proposes more specifically that there is a reference to the Sinai covenant. See Scott W. Hahn, "Covenant, Cult, and the Curse-of-Death: Διαθήκη in Hebrews 9:15–22," in *Hebrews: Contemporary Methods—New Insights*, ed. G. Gelardini (Leiden: Brill, 2005), 65–88. For a qualified critique of Hahn, see O'Brien, *Hebrews*, 331–32. O'Brien maintains that ἐπὶ νεκροις refers to the bodies of the slain animals instead of referring to the Israelites who transgressed the covenant. He also argues that verses 18–22 refer to the Sinai covenant but verses 16–17 to a broken covenant in general.

[449] Attridge, *Hebrews*, 255–56; Bruce, *Hebrews*, 209–14.

[450] Rightly Ellingworth, *Hebrews*, 462; Schenk, *Cosmology and Eschatology in Hebrews*, 101. Those seeing a reference to covenant, however, maintain that the presentation of sacrifices symbolizes the death of the one making the covenant (J. Hughes, *Hebrews*, 40–46; Lane, *Hebrews 9–13*, 243).

can be pressed since the plural for "dead" is often abstract.[451] The reference to dead animals, in other words, isn't clear. Third, analogies are analogies. They don't apply to or explain every situation. The author establishes a point of contact between wills and covenants without implying that in every instance wills demand the death of the one who enacts the will.[452] As Ellingworth says, the language is fluid here, and the author is illustrating by using an analogy.[453] Fortunately, the meaning of the paragraph as a whole isn't greatly affected whether one sees a reference to a covenant or a will here. In either case the importance of death for the receiving of an inheritance is the main point.

9:17

In the context of discussing a will, the author, not surprisingly, resorts to legal language. A will typically takes effect at death, and when one is alive, the provisions of the will are not yet in effect. The author constructs an analogy between a will and a covenant here. Covenant benefits (like the benefits of a will) are generally granted to those who are covenant members only upon the death of the one making the covenant.

9:18

The analogy is now applied to the old covenant or to what the author calls "the first" (ἡ πρώτη) covenant. The word "first" is important, indicating that a successor follows and that the first covenant is temporary. Even the first covenant, i.e., the Sinai covenant, was inaugurated or "put into effect"[454] with blood. The covenant was established by virtue of the death of sacrificial animals.

9:19

The author demonstrates from the OT that the first covenant was established with blood. The covenantal stipulations were enshrined in the law, which Moses spoke to all the people (Exod 24:3, 7). Israel corporately affirmed that they would keep the covenant and do what the Lord instructed (Exod 24:3, 7). Moses then wrote

---

[451] Against J. Hughes, "A Study in Covenant Practice and Procedure," 43–46; Lane, *Hebrews 9–13*, 243.

[452] The word "established" (φέρεσθαι) here means something like "registered" (Attridge, *Hebrews*, 256) or "proved" (Ellingworth, *Hebrews*, 464). The meaning of the term must be established in context.

[453] Ellingworth, *Hebrews*, 462–63.

[454] So O'Brien, *Hebrews*, 332.

down the Lord's words and built an altar (Exod 24:4). Half the blood was sprinkled on the altar (Exod 24:6). Hebrews says that "water, scarlet wool, and hyssop" were present. None of these things are mentioned in Exodus 24, though all three are included in the ceremony of the heifer (Num 19:6, 18), and perhaps the author assumed the same were used for the ceremony in Exodus 24.[455] Exodus says that Moses sprinkled the altar and the people (Exod 24:6, 8), while Hebrews says he sprinkled the people and the book of the covenant. In either case the blood purified both the people and other elements of the covenant. Since Hebrews links blood with the forgiveness of sins (Heb 9:22), the sprinkling of blood is conceived of as removing the defilement of Israel. On this basis Israel could enter into a covenant relationship with the Lord.

9:20

The text of Exod 24:8 is quoted. The quotation doesn't reflect precisely the LXX or the MT. Instead of making or cutting the covenant (διέθετο, בָּרַת), the author uses the word "commanded" (ἐνετείλατο). The use of the verb "commanded" puts the emphasis on the covenant requirements Israel had to fulfill. But what the author really stresses is "blood" (αἷμα). The covenant had validity only because blood was sprinkled on the people and other covenant objects.

9:21

The necessity of blood for purification continues to be pursued. Both the tabernacle and other items of worship were sprinkled with blood at the inauguration of the covenant. The practice of sprinkling blood for purification was a common procedure, for blood was sprinkled on the altar (Lev 8:19, 24, 30; 9:12), on the garments of the high priests (Exod 29:21; Lev 8:30), before the tent of meeting (Num 19:4), before the veil of the sanctuary (Lev 4:6, 17), on the mercy seat once a year (Lev 16:14–15), and the doorposts of the temple (Ezek 45:19). It doesn't seem that all the items of worship had to be sprinkled with blood, but perhaps the author is generalizing or reflects the practice of his day. In any case the author underscores that purification isn't granted without the sprinkling of blood.

---

[455] The author may draw on Lev 14:1–9 as well (so Ellingworth, *Hebrews*, 468).

9:22

The importance of blood is driven home in the concluding statement of the paragraph. We have already seen that the first covenant was inaugurated and ratified with blood. In other words death was necessary for the covenant to take effect. Blood was fundamental for the covenant. Virtually everything is cleansed by blood according to the law. The pervasiveness of blood is evident in sacrificial practices. Indeed the sacrificial cultus of the OT teaches that there is no forgiveness apart from the shedding of the blood.[456] This is evident from the various sacrifices in Leviticus 1–7 and the Day of Atonement (Leviticus 16). This is not to say that all sacrifices were bloody, for it is evident that grain offerings were not (Lev 2:1–16). Some sacrifices were offered to express thanksgiving or commitment to God. Nevertheless, to be forgiven of sin, as the Day of Atonement indicates, blood had to be spilt. A death had to occur.[457]

A few scholars have argued that the blood provided forgiveness because life is in the blood (Lev 17:11). In other words the focus on blood is actually not death but the release of life.[458] Such a reading is almost certainly wrong, for the shedding and pouring out of blood meant the death of the victim. People in the ancient world saw such things firsthand more than modern people, for they witnessed often the death of animals when their blood was shed. Hence, the life being

---

[456] The word "shedding of blood" (αἱματεκχυσίας) may have been coined by the author, though it is difficult to be sure (Attridge, *Hebrews*, 259). The etymology of the word suggests that pouring of blood is in view here, for we have "blood" (αἷμα) and the verbal noun from the verb "pour" (ἐκχέω). We also see in 1 Kgs 18:28 and Sir 27:15 the phrase "pouring out of blood" (ἐκχύσεως αἵματος and ἔκχυσις αἵματος respectively). The word coined in Heb 9:22 functions as a combination of these two words, which shows that the shedding of blood is in view. Such a view does not necessarily rule out the ritual application of the blood or the priestly manipulation of the blood (Koester, *Hebrews*, 420). Ellingworth says the pouring out of blood and the ritual application of the blood "are closely associated, and in the death of Christ they coincide" (*Hebrews*, 474; see also Ribbens, "Levitical Sacrifice and Heavenly Cult in Hebrews," 209). Others say that the shed blood was poured out at the base of the altar, and this practice must be distinguished from death of the sacrificial animal (so, e.g., T. C. G. Thornton, "The Meaning of αἱματεκχυσίας in Heb. ix.22," *ExpT* 15 [1964]: 63–65).

[457] Graham Hughes argues that the need for sacrifice is removed in the new covenant, but this is surely mistaken (*Hebrews and Hermeneutics*, 88–89). See the decisive refutation by Ellingworth, *Hebrews*, 472.

[458] Against this view, see Morris, *Apostolic Preaching of the Cross*, 112–29.

in the blood in Lev 17:11 indicates that forgiveness comes from the death of victims. It is hard to avoid the idea that the death of the animal functions as a substitute for the death of the human being. The animal suffered the fate that the human being deserved, showing the seriousness of sin and the great cost of forgiveness.[459]

Bridge

Jesus is the mediator of a new and better covenant because the covenant is established by the shedding of his blood. Therefore, those who belong to Jesus will receive an eternal inheritance. Those under the old covenant were limited to an earthly inheritance, which is temporary and foreshadows a better inheritance, i.e., a heavenly one. The author explains in some detail that the old covenant was ratified and inaugurated with blood, just as wills become effective at death. The close link between blood and death in the paragraph demonstrates that the shedding of blood signifies death. Forgiveness comes at the expense of the death of the victim. The author's point is that the readers have an eternal inheritance because they have a better sacrifice. The blood of the Messiah avails far better than the blood of any animal. Still the sacrificial ritual of the old covenant forecasts and anticipates the death of Christ, demonstrating that death is necessary for sins to be forgiven.

Hebrews 9:23–28

Outline

I. Prologue: Definitive and Final Revelation in the Son (1:1–4)
II. Don't Abandon the Son Since He Is Greater than Angels (1:5–2:18)
III. Don't Harden Your Hearts Since You Have a Son and High Priest Greater than Moses and Joshua (3:1–4:13)
IV. **Don't Fall Away from Jesus' Melchizedekian Priesthood Since It Is Greater than the Levitical Priesthood (4:14–10:18)**

---

[459] Some scholars have argued that ἄφεσις doesn't denote "forgiveness" here but release or purification. See Ribbens for decisive arguments that support forgiveness ("Levitical Sacrifice and Heavenly Cult in Hebrews," 210–12).

A. Exhortation in Light of Jesus' Priestly Status (4:14–5:10)
B. Warning and Assurance (5:11–6:20)
C. Jesus' Greater Priesthood as a Melchizedekian Priest (7:1–28)
D. New Covenant Better than the Old (8:1–13)
E. **A Better Sacrifice Under the New Covenant (9:1–10:18)**
  1. Free Access to God Not Granted Under Old Covenant (9:1–10)
  2. Jesus Entered Heaven Itself with His Blood (9:11–14)
  3. Jesus as Mediator of New Covenant Bestows an Eternal Inheritance (9:15–22)
  4. **Jesus' Sacrifice: Better than OT Sacrifices (9:23–10:18)**
    a. **Jesus' Heavenly and Once-for-All Sacrifice (9:23–28)**
    b. Repetition of OT Sacrifices Shows Their Inadequacy (10:1–4)
    c. Jesus' Once-for-All Sacrifice Canceled Old System (10:5–10)
    d. Jesus' Completed Sacrifice (10:11–14)
    e. Final Forgiveness Promised in New Covenant Realized (10:15–18)
V. Concluding Exhortations and Warnings (10:19–12:29)

Scripture

[23] Therefore it was necessary for the copies of the things in the heavens to be purified with these sacrifices, but the heavenly things themselves to be purified with better sacrifices than these. [24] For the Messiah did not enter a sanctuary made with hands (only a model of the true one) but into heaven itself, so that He might now appear in the presence of God for us. [25] He did not do this to offer Himself many times, as the high priest enters the sanctuary yearly with the blood of another. [26] Otherwise, He would have had to suffer many times since the foundation of the world. But now He has appeared one time, at the end of the ages, for the removal of sin by the sacrifice of Himself. [27] And just as it is appointed for people to die once—and after this, judgment—[28]so also the Messiah, having been offered once to bear the sins of many, will

appear a second time, not to bear sin, but to bring salvation to those who are waiting for Him.

Context

In the previous paragraph we saw that Jesus is the mediator of a better covenant, ensuring that those who are called will receive an eternal inheritance. The author, then, explains that even under the first covenant the shedding of blood (death) was necessary for atonement. The old covenant functions here typologically, pointing to a better and more effective sacrifice. Similarly, the earthly tabernacle functions as a copy of what is heavenly, and Jesus with his blood did not cleanse the earthly, but the heavenly (9:23–24). In other words he brought us into the presence of God. Jesus' offering differs from the Day of Atonement offering of the high priest in another respect. In both instances we have an offering, but the Day of Atonement offering had to be repeated every year. By way of contrast, Jesus has set aside sin forever through his one offering (9:25–26). Finally, just as there is one death and one judgment, so Christ's death removed sins forever, and thus when he comes again it will not be to die for sins but to grant final salvation to those waiting for him (9:27–28).

Exegesis

9:23

What is the function of "therefore" (οὖν) here? It reaches back to 9:15–22. Since blood was necessary for the old covenant to be enacted and is required for believers to receive an eternal inheritance under the new covenant as well, it demonstrates that death was indispensable for the forgiveness of sins. The word "necessary" (Ἀνάγκη) reveals God's perspective and demand. Even the "copies" (ὑποδείγματα) of the things in the heavens had to be purified with blood. Earlier the word "copy" was used of tabernacle under the old covenant (8:5), which functioned as a copy and shadow of what was in heaven. Once again the author thinks of the tabernacle on earth and all the things related thereto which had to be purified with blood (9:19–22).[460] Such cleansing was necessary even though they were merely copies of a transcendent and heavenly reality. In other words

---

[460] For a helpful summary and evaluation of interpretations of this verse, see David J. MacLeod, "The Cleansing of the True Tabernacle," *BSac* 152 (1995): 60–71.

they were not the substance and reality itself; they pointed both vertically and temporally to a greater reality.

Heavenly realities, on the other hand, warrant better sacrifices. The sacrifices under the old covenant suffice to cleanse what is earthly, but they can hardly suffice for what is heavenly. It isn't convincing to say that the author thinks here of the inauguration of the heavenly sanctuary, for he speaks of purification dealing with forgiveness rather than the establishment of the heavenly sanctuary.[461] The heavenly things don't refer to the people of God or to the conscience.[462] Nor is there any notion here that the heavenly places are defiled and literally need cleansing.[463] The reference is to heaven itself, the presence of God.[464] The key word "better" (κρείττοσιν), which we have seen repeatedly (see 7:19 in particular), appears again. Still the imagery should not be pressed, as if somehow heaven itself is defiled by human sin. The writer uses spatial and typological language to communicate the effectiveness of Christ's sacrifice, but it is unwarranted to conclude that he actually believes there are heavenly places that literally need cleansing. As Hughes says, the presence of God doesn't need "any kind of purification."[465] We have seen that the author often writes typologically when citing the OT, and thus the reference to the cleansing of heavenly places should not be understood literally or univocally but analogically.

9:24

Verse 24 further explains verse 23. Christ did not enter into a holy place made with hands. Earlier the word rendered "holy place"

---

[461] Against Ellingworth, *Hebrews*, 477.

[462] So Bruce, *Hebrews*, 218–19; Attridge, *Hebrews*, 262; O'Brien, *Hebrews*, 337.

[463] Against Lane, *Hebrews 9–13*, 247. Schenk rightly suggests, "The author was not actually picturing the cleansing of a literal structure in heaven" (*Cosmology and Eschatology in Hebrews*, 8; cf. also Hagner, *Hebrews*, 129). He recognizes here the presence of metaphorical language (168–81). Cf. also Aelred Cody, *Heavenly Sanctuary and Liturgy in the Epistle to the Hebrews: The Achievement of Salvation in the Epistle's Perspectives* (St Meinrad, IN: Grail, 1960). In support of the notion that the heavenly tabernacle is literal, see Mackie, *Eschatology and Exhortation in Hebrews*, 157–68; George W. MacRae, "Heavenly Temple and Eschatology in the Letter to the Hebrews," *Semeia* 12 (1978): 179–99. For a brief discussion on the heavenly temple in Jewish sources, see McKelvey, *Pioneer and Priest*, 202–5.

[464] As Cockerill says, "This statement is definitive evidence that the pastor is not dealing with a two-part heavenly Sanctuary" (*Hebrews*, 418n19).

[465] Hughes, *Hebrews*, 379.

(ἄγια) referred to the outer compartment of the tabernacle (9:2) in contrast to the most holy place (Ἅγια Ἁγίων), which is the innermost compartment (9:3). But it seems that the term ἄγια may also refer to the most holy place without the genitive being added (9:12), for the writer says Jesus entered into the most holy place (which of course is heaven itself) with his own blood. The next verse confirms such a reading, for once again the term used here refers to "the most holy place" (NIV; ἄγια). Apparently, the author does not use his terms technically, trusting that the readers would be able to discern his meaning from the context.

The holy place on earth is "made with hands" (χειροποίητα). Remarkably, this term is regularly used of idolatry in the OT (Lev 26:1, 30; Isa 2:18; 10:11; 16:2; 19:1; 21:9; 31:7; 46:6; Dan 5:4, 23; 6:8; cf. Jdt 8:18; Wis 14:8; Bel 1:5). Paul uses the term to indict Athenian idolatry in Acts 17:24, referring to their temples made with hands. It doesn't seem likely that the author of Hebrews is making precisely the same point here. After all, the tabernacle was commanded by God and typologically points to God's presence in heaven. Nevertheless there is a criticism implied in the use of the word. If the recipients of the letter turn to the Levitical cult and sacrifices now that the "better" has come, then such a move would be comparable to idolatry. Stephen uses the word "made with hands" with the same import in his critique of those who gave undue prominence to the temple (Acts 7:48), as does Paul regarding circumcision (Eph 2:11). The critique of the tabernacle, then, is both spatial (it is earthly and not heavenly) and eschatological (it belongs to the old age, not the new). Still, Hebrews does not criticize the tabernacle per se. It had a legitimate function for a certain period of salvation history. The tabernacle has a typological function; it is a "model" (ἀντίτυπα) of the "true" holy place, which is heaven itself (the dwelling place of God). Hence, Jesus appears in God's presence for us. He does not just appear in an earthly tabernacle that represents God's residence in heaven. Believers trust in one who has by his blood provided access to God himself.

It should also be noted that the language employed here is symbolic. It is not as if there is literally a heavenly tabernacle or heavenly furniture that needs to be cleansed. "Nor does our author continue with the imagery of the Yom Kippur ritual and suggest that Christ in the heavenly realm sprinkles his blood, even in some metaphorical sense, as an act independent of his death on the cross."[466] Such language is used analogically (not univocally) to denote the residence of God in the transcendent sphere and to emphasize that one must be clean to approach him.

9:25

Another contrast between the heavenly and earthly tabernacle is exploited. When Jesus entered into heaven (the presence of God), he didn't need to offer himself repeatedly (πολλάκις). What the author says could be misconstrued here. "The pastor has no intention of identifying Christ's self-offering with his entrance into heaven."[467] Cockerill goes on to say, "However, his self-offering on the cross is the basis of his entrance into heaven, and that entrance brings his offering to fulfillment, thus demonstrating its effectiveness."[468] Young rightly observes that the offering had to occur on earth, for it is parallel to dying (v. 27) and suffering (v. 26).[469] Indeed, 13:12 clarifies that Jesus' suffering and hence his death and offering took place on earth, for he clearly says that Jesus died (sacrificed himself) outside the gates of Jerusalem. The author contrasts the offering of the high priest with the offering of Jesus. The high priest entered the "the most holy place" (τὰ ἅγια) every year and needed a new offering every time (Lev 16:3, 5–11, 14–20, 24–25). But Jesus' offering doesn't need to be renewed. By one definitive offering he procured cleansing once for all so that further offerings were superfluous.

9:26

If more than one offering were required so that Jesus had to offer himself repeatedly, then he would be required to suffer often from the foundation of the world. His sacrificial and cleansing work would never be finished if his one offering wasn't sufficient.

---

[466] Attridge, *Hebrews*, 263; O'Brien, *Hebrews*, 339. See also here Hughes in response to the Socinian view that the sacrifice was in heaven rather than on earth (*Hebrews*, 337, 341–44). See also Stott, who says the author understands the offering to be one offered on earth instead of heaven (Wilfrid Stott, "The Conception of 'Offering' in the Epistle to the Hebrews," *NTS* 9 [1962–63]: 62–69). For the contrary view, see Moffitt, though Moffitt isn't defending Socinianism (*Atonement and the Logic of the Resurrection in the Epistle to the Hebrews*, 280–81). For a helpful discussion of the entire matter, see Kibbe, "Is It Finished? When Did It Start?," 25–61.

[467] Cockerill, *Hebrews*, 421n8.

[468] Ibid.

[469] Young, "The Gospel According to Hebrews 9," 209.

Such a state of affairs doesn't pertain to reality. The efficacy of what Jesus accomplished in his incarnation stands out. He "appeared" (πεφανέρωται) at a particular juncture in history. Here we have an indication of the incarnation, which is expressed more clearly in John 1:14. Indeed, Jesus' appearance was "at the end of the ages" (ἐπὶ συντελείᾳ τῶν αἰώνων), which echoes the opening of the letter: "In these last days, He has spoken to us by His Son" (1:2). The last days, the end of the ages, and the fulfillment of God's promises have arrived in Jesus Christ. The readers were tempted to go back to the Levitical cult, but the author wants them to live in the "now" (νυνί), i.e., in the age to come which has dawned in Jesus Christ. Peter argues similarly that the end time has arrived with the coming of Jesus Christ (1 Pet 1:20). Paul also says that the end of the ages has arrived (1 Cor 10:11). Certainly the notion that the last days have come in Jesus Christ is taught pervasively in the NT. Hebrews reminds us what Christ accomplished and what he did when he came to earth. He removed (ἀθέτησιν) sin by the sacrifice of himself. Sin has been set aside not through animals offered by the high priest but through the self-sacrifice of the Messiah.

9:27

A comparison is introduced between the life of human beings and the work of Jesus Christ. The first part of the comparison is found in verse 27, and it is completed in verse 28. Reflecting on human life, the author posits that human beings are appointed to die once and then comes the judgment. Human life is not repeated over and over again. There is a finality and distinctiveness about human existence. Certainly what is said here rules out any notion of reincarnation. The worldview is theistic. Life is lived once before the one true God who is the Creator of all, and then comes the judgment. Death is not followed by nothingness, nor is there a promise of happiness without reservation. Rather, when human beings die, they encounter the Creator God as the Judge of all. He will assess the lives of all and determine their future existence.

9:28

The other half of the comparison is completed here, and the central point in verse 27–28 is set forth. Since death is a once-for-all event, so too Christ's death cannot be repeated. His singular death definitively removed sins forever. Hence he will not come again to die (since death is a one-time event). Instead he will come to establish final and complete salvation.

In describing Christ's death, the author doesn't use the word "die" (ἀποθανεῖν), as he did in verse 27. He uses the verb "offered" (προσενεχθείς), focusing on the sacrificial character of his death. Every human being dies, but Jesus' death was distinctive in that he died as a sacrificial offering, giving his life for the sake of others. The word "once" (ἅπαξ) is, therefore, emphatic, conveying the finality of Jesus' sacrifice. The sacrificial character of Jesus' death is affirmed by the phrase "to bear the sins of many" (εἰς τὸ πολλῶν ἀνενεγκεῖν ἁμαρτίας). The clause designates purpose, explaining why Jesus offered himself, confirming that his death was sacrificial. The phrase almost certainly alludes to Isa 53:12, where the Servant of the Lord "bore the sins of many" (ἁμαρτίας πολλῶν ἀνήνεγκεν). The substitutionary character of the Servant's sacrifice is patently clear in Isaiah 53 (vv. 4–6, 8, 10–12).[470] The author implicitly suggests here that the OT itself envisions in the suffering of the Servant the setting aside of Levitical sacrifices. For the Servant by his sacrifice bears the sins of all, and thus the need for Levitical sacrifices is cancelled.

The notion of a second coming of Christ is also explicitly communicated here. Jesus is coming again, but he is not coming to offer his life as a sacrifice again. His sacrificial work has been completed forever. Hence he will not be coming the second time "to bear sin" since the penalty for sin has been fully atoned for. Literally the words are "without sin" (χωρὶς ἁμαρτίας): Jesus will appear a second time "without sin." Obviously this phrase does not mean Jesus was sinful at his first coming. Hebrews is most emphatic about Jesus' freedom from all sin during his earthly life (4:15; 7:26–28; 9:14). The HCSB (and virtually all English translations) rightly interpret this to mean that Jesus will not come the second time to deal with or atone for sin. When Jesus appears the second time, he will bring salvation to those who await him. By salvation the author means here eschatological deliverance. Believers, who are cleansed and forgiven through Jesus' sacrifice, will enjoy the new creation at Jesus' second coming (11:10, 13–16; 12:22; 13:14). The word "waiting"

---

[470] For substitutionary atonement in Hebrews, see Joslin, "Christ Bore the Sins of Many," 74–103. Joslin rightly argues that in Hebrews human beings face death (2:14–15) and God's wrath and final judgment if their sins are unforgiven (cf. 2:1–4; 3:7–4:13; 6:4–8; 10:26–31; 12:25–29; see pp. 91–95).

(ἀπεκδεχομένοις) in every case but one has an eschatological significance in the NT (Rom 8:19, 23, 25; 1 Cor 1:7; Gal 5:5; Phil 3:20).

Bridge

Christ's sacrifice is far better than the sacrifices offered under the old covenant. First, his sacrifice brings us into the presence of God. The Christian life is ultimately about fellowship with God, about enjoying him, and such a relationship becomes a reality through Christ's offering. Second, sin has been decisively and finally dealt with through the sacrifice of Jesus the Christ. There is no need to wonder or doubt whether sins have been forgiven. Jesus' sacrifice doesn't need to be repeated since he fully atoned for sin. Third, believers have nothing to fear from death. They don't face the coming judgment with dread and anxiety but with hope and confidence, knowing that Jesus is bringing final salvation to those who belong to him.

Hebrews 10:1–4

Outline

I. Prologue: Definitive and Final Revelation in the Son (1:1–4)
II. Don't Abandon the Son Since He Is Greater than Angels (1:5–2:18)
III. Don't Harden Your Hearts Since You Have a Son and High Priest Greater than Moses and Joshua (3:1–4:13)
IV. **Don't Fall Away from Jesus' Melchizedekian Priesthood Since It Is Greater than the Levitical Priesthood (4:14–10:18)**
    A. Exhortation in Light of Jesus' Priestly Status (4:14–5:10)
    B. Warning and Assurance (5:11–6:20)
    C. Jesus' Greater Priesthood as a Melchizedekian Priest (7:1–28)
    D. New Covenant Better than the Old (8:1–13)
    E. **A Better Sacrifice Under the New Covenant (9:1–10:18)**
        1. Free Access to God Not Granted Under Old Covenant (9:1–10)
        2. Jesus Entered Heaven Itself with His Blood (9:11–14)

3. Jesus as Mediator of New Covenant Bestows an
   Eternal Inheritance (9:15–22)
4. **Jesus' Sacrifice: Better than OT Sacrifices
   (9:23–10:18)**
   a. Jesus' Heavenly and Once-for-All
      Sacrifice (9:23–28)
   b. **Repetition of OT Sacrifices Shows Their
      Inadequacy (10:1–4)**
   c. Jesus' Once-for-All Sacrifice Canceled Old
      System (10:5–10)
   d. Jesus' Completed Sacrifice (10:11–14)
   e. Final Forgiveness Promised in New Covenant
      Realized (10:15–18)
V. Concluding Exhortations and Warnings (10:19–12:29)

Scripture

[1] Since the law has only a shadow of the good things to come, and not the actual form of those realities, it can never perfect the worshipers by the same sacrifices they continually offer year after year. [2] Otherwise, wouldn't they have stopped being offered, since the worshipers, once purified, would no longer have any consciousness of sins?

[3] But in the sacrifices there is a reminder of sins every year. [4] For it is impossible for the blood of bulls and goats to take away sins.

Context

Hebrews 10:1–4 is in the midst of a section where the author argues that Jesus' sacrifice is better than Levitical sacrifices. The OT cult was inferior because it did not truly bring one into the presence of God (9:1–10). Christ, on the other hand, entered God's presence and cleansed the conscience with his blood (9:11–14). Believers, as beneficiaries of the new covenant, enjoy the promise of an eternal inheritance through Christ's sacrifice, for God's covenant promises in both the old covenant and the new are based on the shedding of blood (9:15–22). Since blood was necessary, Christ shed his own blood to grant believers access to heaven itself (9:23–24). Furthermore his sacrifice atoned for sins once for all and hence does not need to be repeated (9:25–26). Believers await now the experience of final salvation (9:27–28). In 10:1–4 the dramatic difference between Christ's sacrifice and Levitical sacrifices is sketched in. The law could never perfect those drawing near to God with its repeated sacrifices, for it is only a shadow and not the substance (10:1). If old covenant sacrifices truly cleansed the conscience of sins, there would be no need to keep sacrificing (10:2). The repetition of sacrifices illustrated the problem: the people were reminded of their sins, annually (10:3). The reason such sacrifices can't atone for sins is then explained: animal sacrifices could never remove sins (10:4).

Exegesis

10:1

The inadequacy of the law and its accompanying sacrifices is explained (see §2.4). The law points forward to something better, to genuine forgiveness of sins; but the law itself doesn't truly forgive sins, and this is evident since the sacrifices are repeated continually.

The law is only a "shadow" (Σκιάν) of the good things that are coming. The law isn't evil; it isn't contrary to the will of God. It actually foreshadows the good things that are coming and in that sense partakes of goodness.[471] Still the law is not ultimate or final. It is a shadow portending the arrival of something else; the law, eschatologically, belongs to yesterday, for the good things the law anticipated have come.[472] The last days and the end of the ages have arrived in Jesus Christ (1:2; 9:26). Earlier the author said that Aaronic priests served "as a copy and shadow" of what was heavenly (8:5). In Col 2:17 Paul uses an expression similar to what we find here, declaring that the Sabbath was "a shadow of what was to come." Hebrews insists that the readers must not turn back from "the good things" to the shadow. The law is not "the actual form" (εἰκόνα) or "the true form" (NRSV) of the realties that have now dawned in Jesus Christ. The word here is often translated "image." An image to our minds does not participate in the reality of what is imaged, but that is clearly not what the author means here. In fact he means precisely the opposite. The law is a shadow, but what has come in Christ is, as the NIV says, "the realities themselves."[473] The word "image" bears the

---

[471] "The good things" referred to here are future from the standpoint of the law, but the future has arrived (at least in inaugurated form) for believers in Jesus (Attridge, *Hebrews*, 259).

[472] For the Platonic character of the expression here, see L. Johnson, *Hebrews*, 249.

[473] So also Attridge, *Hebrews*, 270.

same meaning as it does in Col 1:15 where Christ is said to be "the image of the invisible God." In Colossians, Christ being the image means he partakes in the essence or nature of what it means to be God. So too here, the law is inferior because it doesn't participate in the reality of what it foreshadows or forecasts.

The fundamental problem with the law and its sacrifices is disclosed here.[474] It can't "perfect" (τελειῶσαι) those drawing near to God. Earlier we saw that "perfection" (τελείωσις) could not be obtained through the Levitical priesthood (7:11). "The law perfected (ἐτελείωσεν) nothing" (7:19). The sacrifices ordained in the law can't "perfect (τελειῶσαι) the worshiper's conscience" (9:9) in contrast to the sacrifice of Christ (10:14). The word "perfect" here, then, communicates the idea of a true cleansing of the conscience that brings one into God's presence.[475] The law and its sacrifices did not and cannot accomplish such, and hence they function as a shadow of the good that has come in Jesus Christ, where such perfection becomes a reality.

What is striking is how emphatic the language is to underscore the law's inferiority. Temporal words are piled up to express the idea. The law can "never" (οὐδέποτε) perfect worshipers. Sacrifices under the old covenant are offered "continually" (εἰς τὸ διηνεκές), but true forgiveness is not attained. Indeed, the "same" sacrifices are brought "year after year" (κατ᾽ ἐνιαυτόν). The law is not identified as evil, and yet there is a futility and frustration in the law and its sacrifices, for it is like a merry-go-round that never stops.

10:2

The law and its sacrifices can never perfect those drawing near to God according to verse 1. Now in verse 2 support is adduced for the notion that the law doesn't bring perfection. If perfection were truly achieved, the sacrifices would have ceased. There would no longer be a need for them. The nub of the issue is addressed here. If the sacrifices were effective, the worshipers, having been

---

[474] Joslin rightly emphasizes the complexity of the author's understanding of the law, warning against those who see no continuity ("Transformation of the Law," 100–117). But against Joslin (114–15) the author sees the entire law as a shadow of what is to come, not just the cultic law. Still, see Joslin's excellent dissertation for his complete exposition (Joslin, *Hebrews, Christ, and the Law*).

[475] "To 'perfect' something is to bring it to its intended goal" (Cockerill, *Hebrews*, 430).

cleansed (κεκαθαρισμένους), would no longer be conscious of their sins. They would be assured that full and final forgiveness had been accomplished and would be free from the defiling guilt of sin. The content of Heb 9:14 is remarkably similar, though there the author speaks positively about the efficacy of Christ's sacrifice. Two words from 10:2, "purified" (κεκαθαρισμένους) and "consciousness" or "conscience" (συνείδησιν), are also used in 9:14: Christ's blood "cleanse[s] our consciences" (καθαριεῖ τὴν συνείδησιν ἡμῶν) so that believers can serve God. Or as 10:22 says, the hearts of believers are "sprinkled clean from an evil conscience" (10:22) by the blood of Christ. Old Testament sacrifices, on the other hand, "cannot perfect the worshiper's conscience" (9:9). They don't truly cleanse one from sin.

10:3

Instead of cleansing and purifying from sin, OT sacrifices remind people of their sins. And the reminder comes "every year" (κατ᾽ ἐνιαυτόν). This phrase is picked up from verse 1 and clearly refers to the Day of Atonement. Undergoing the entire ritual specified in Leviticus 16 year after year testifies to the continuing presence of sin. Perhaps the readers were attracted to Levitical sacrifices because they concretely and clearly "offered" forgiveness of sins. But it is just the opposite according to the author. They summon sins to mind, showing that genuine purification has not occurred under the Levitical system.

10:4

But why is it the case that Levitical sacrifices don't cleanse the conscience? Why must they be repeated year after year? The answer given is that it is impossible for the blood of sacrificial animals to remove sin. The author doesn't expand on his answer, but the reason for his assertion seems clear, especially when it is contrasted with the sacrifice of Christ (10:5–10). Animals could scarcely provide atonement. They didn't realize why they were slain and had no consciousness of the significance of their death. They certainly didn't give their life voluntarily for the sake of sinners but were coerced to die against their will.[476] One thinks here of the prophetic criticisms of the cult (Isa 1:10–15; 66:3; Jer 7:21–23; Hos 6:6; Amos 5:22;

---

[476] Cf. Hughes, *Hebrews*, 392.

Mic 6:6–8), though strictly speaking the authors didn't repudiate the sacrifices themselves.

Hebrews doesn't claim that the death of animals was a mistake from the beginning or contrary to the will of God. The sacrificial system was, after all, instituted by God himself. Hence the blood of animals functioned typologically and symbolically, pointing forward to the blood of Christ, which truly cleanses from sins. OT sacrifices had their place before the coming of Christ, but now that the good things have come (v. 1), they are no longer needed. Something better, someone better, is needed to cleanse the heart from sin.

Bridge

The author focuses on the inadequacy of the law and its sacrifices. The conscience is not cleansed of sin but reminded of its presence every year. Ultimately animal sacrifices cannot remove sins. The law and its sacrifices typologically anticipate the sacrifice of Christ. Most believers today, of course, aren't tempted to obtain forgiveness through animal sacrifices. Nevertheless, Hebrews still speaks to us today. Hebrews declares that any pathway to forgiveness outside the sacrifice of Jesus Christ doesn't avail. Only Jesus' death truly cleanses the heart of its sin and provides assurance of a right relationship with God.

Hebrews 10:5–10

Outline

I. Prologue: Definitive and Final Revelation in the Son (1:1–4)
II. Don't Abandon the Son Since He Is Greater than Angels (1:5–2:18)
III. Don't Harden Your Hearts Since You Have a Son and High Priest Greater than Moses and Joshua (3:1–4:13)
IV. **Don't Fall Away from Jesus' Melchizedekian Priesthood Since It Is Greater than the Levitical Priesthood (4:14–10:18)**
   A. Exhortation in Light of Jesus' Priestly Status (4:14–5:10)
   B. Warning and Assurance (5:11–6:20)
   C. Jesus' Greater Priesthood as a Melchizedekian Priest (7:1–28)

D. New Covenant Better than the Old (8:1–13)

E. **A Better Sacrifice Under the New Covenant (9:1–10:18)**

   1. Free Access to God Not Granted Under Old Covenant (9:1–10)

   2. Jesus Entered Heaven Itself with His Blood (9:11–14)

   3. Jesus as Mediator of New Covenant Bestows an Eternal Inheritance (9:15–22)

   4. **Jesus' Sacrifice: Better than OT Sacrifices (9:23–10:18)**

      a. Jesus' Heavenly and Once-for-All Sacrifice (9:23–28)

      b. Repetition of OT Sacrifices Shows Their Inadequacy (10:1–4)

      c. **Jesus' Once-for-All Sacrifice Canceled Old System (10:5–10)**

      d. Jesus' Completed Sacrifice (10:11–14)

      e. Final Forgiveness Promised in New Covenant Realized (10:15–18)

V. Concluding Exhortations and Warnings (10:19–12:29)

Scripture

⁵ Therefore, as He was coming into the world, He said: You did not want sacrifice and offering, but You prepared a body for Me. ⁶ You did not delight in whole burnt offerings and sin offerings. ⁷ Then I said, "See—it is written about Me in the volume of the scroll—I have come to do Your will, God!" ⁸ After He says above, You did not want or delight in sacrifices and offerings, whole burnt offerings and sin offerings (which are offered according to the law), ⁹ He then says, See, I have come to do Your will. He takes away the first to establish the second. ¹⁰ By this will of God, we have been sanctified through the offering of the body of Jesus Christ once and for all.

Context

The author continues to contrast the inadequacy of the OT sacrifices over against the sacrifice of Christ. The substance of his case in chapter 9 is that Christ truly brings believers into God's presence by his blood over against OT sacrifices. In 10:1–4 the inability of the law and its sacrifices to purge sins is featured. Hence, 10:5–10 explains why the death of Christ was absolutely necessary, using Psalm 40 to support the case. Upon coming into the world, Christ realized that God was not calling upon him to offer sacrifices but to give his own life (vv. 5–6). Hence he came to do the will of God (v. 7). The significance of Psalm 40 is unpacked further. The sacrifices and offerings referred to in the psalm are offered in accord with the law of Moses (v. 8). The psalm says, however, that Jesus came to do God's will, after already stating that God did not delight in sacrifices and offerings (v. 9). It follows, according to the author, that the former (sacrifices offered according to the Mosaic law) are displaced by the latter (Jesus' fulfilling God's will by offering himself as a sacrifice). The climax of the argument comes in verse 10: believers are sanctified through the offering of Jesus Christ once for all. Believers stand in the realm of the holy by virtue of the sacrifice of Jesus Christ. They are clean before God instead of being defiled.

Exegesis

10:5

Christ, upon entering the world, realized that God did not desire sacrifice or offerings. Instead, God summoned Jesus to sacrifice his own body for the sake of his people. The word "therefore" (Διό) reaches back to the previous paragraph. Since the law and its sacrifices can't perfect worshipers and cleanse the conscience of sins and since animal sacrifices can't atone for sins, "therefore" Jesus did not come into the world to offer animal sacrifices but to give of himself.

The coming of Christ into the world refers to the incarnation.[477] To speak of an incarnation does not impose an alien theology on the letter, for the first two chapters of the letter clearly set forth both the deity and the humanity of Jesus Christ. Preexistence is probably implied here, for the one coming into the world speaks, declaring his intention upon entering into the world. The author introduces Psalm 40, beginning with verse 6 to support his argument. According to the Hebrews, the words of the psalmist are the words of Jesus at his incarnation. Christ realized upon coming into the world that God did not desire sacrifices or offerings. He was not being asked to make the offerings mandated in the OT. Instead, God had prepared

---

[477] See Attridge, *Hebrews*, 273.

a "body" for Jesus. In other words Jesus was being asked to give himself as a sacrifice to God.

The use of Psalm 40 here is most interesting.[478] Psalm 40 is a lament psalm where David asks the Lord to rescue him from his enemies (vv. 11–17). In the first part of the psalm, David remembers past instances of God's deliverance when he was in desperate straits (vv. 1–5). In the middle of the psalm, we have the verses appropriated by Hebrews (vv. 6–8) and the reminder that David has proclaimed the Lord's righteousness, faithfulness, and salvation among the people of God (vv. 9–10). What role do verses 6–8 play in the psalm? It seems that David gives another reason God should deliver him. David is not merely offering sacrifices and offerings. He has given himself and the entirety of his life to God. He has pledged himself to do God's will, and God in his righteousness will deliver and rescue the one who belongs to him.

How can the author of Hebrews relate this psalm to Jesus when in its historical context it isn't an evident prophecy?[479] It doesn't refer to Jesus as the Messiah in any direct way. Indeed, David admits his many sins in the psalm (40:12). Nor is it evident in reading the psalm that it teaches the setting aside of the sacrificial system of the OT. Certainly neither David himself nor other Jews understood the psalm in this way.

Several things can be said in reply. First, NT writers read the psalms in light of the fulfillment realized in Jesus Christ. They didn't believe the psalms should only be read historically. They also thought they should be read christologically and eschatologically. It is increasingly recognized today that a historical grammatical hermeneutic isn't the "only right way" to read Scripture. The Scriptures are also to be read in terms of a divine author, i.e., the meaning of the OT is clarified now that the Messiah has come. Second, I am not suggesting, however, that the psalm is interpreted arbitrarily or fancifully. What the psalms say about David points to the greater David, Jesus the Christ. Psalms about David do not merely concern

---

[478] The author draws particularly upon the LXX (see Attridge, *Hebrews*, 274).

[479] For another approach to the use of the OT here, which is compatible in some respects with what is said here, see Walter C. Kaiser Jr., "The Abolition of the Old Order and Establishment of the New: Psalm 40:6–8 and Hebrews 10:5–10," in *Tradition and Testament: Essays in Honor of Charles Lee Feinberg*, ed. J. S. and P. D. Feinberg (Chicago: Moody, 1981), 19–37.

David as a historical person, for David was the king, and David had received the promise that his dynasty would never end (2 Samuel 7; 1 Chronicles 17; Psalms 89, 132, etc.). Hence, psalms about David were read typologically and eschatologically and messianically. What was said about David anticipated the coming of the Christ. Typology also usually includes escalation, so Jesus is the greater David. Hence, the reference to David's sins doesn't preclude the notion that the psalm points to Jesus. It was easily recognized that Jesus was greater than David, that David's faults were not replicated in the life of Jesus.

Third, how do we explain the author seeing here support for the setting aside of the sacrificial system? Again it seems that the answer is eschatological and christological. Historically, as noted above, there is no warrant for understanding the psalm to teach that the sacrifices of the OT are no longer necessary. David continued to offer sacrifices! The author of Hebrews, however, reads the psalm in the light of the Christ event. Jesus is the greater, indeed the greatest, Davidic king. Hence the words of the psalm are uttered by Jesus himself as he addresses the Lord. The Lord did not desire from Jesus sacrifices and offerings. Instead he asked for Jesus to give of himself, to give of his own body in sacrifice. Hebrews understands the words of the psalm literally insofar as they relate to Jesus Christ. Certainly he didn't need to offer sacrifices and offerings since he was without sin. God is doing something new, though it is in continuity with the old, with the coming of Jesus. David's recognition that sacrifices and offerings are insufficient is grasped more clearly and sharply in the new era.

Interestingly, Hebrews, which follows closely the LXX and MT here, diverges from both of them. The meaning of the MT is rendered well by the HCSB: "You open my ears to listen" (Ps 40:6). In other words the Lord worked in David so that he was obedient and compliant to God's will. In Hebrews, however, the word "body" ($\sigma\tilde{\omega}\mu\alpha$) is substituted for the notion of opening the ear.[480] What we

---

[480] It is unlikely that the word "body" was first inserted by the author of Hebrews and was later put into the LXX. So Karen H. Jobes, "Rhetorical Achievement in the 'Misquote' of Psalm 40," *Bib* 72 (1991): 387–96. Cf. Karen H. Jobes, "The Function of Paronomasia in Hebrews 10:5–7," *TrinJ* 13 (1992): 181–91. Rightly Jared Compton, "The Origin of $\sigma\tilde{\omega}\mu\alpha$ in Heb 10:5: Another Look at a Recent

have here is the part (ears) standing for the whole (the body).[481] Actually the meaning of the verse remains largely the same. God didn't ask Jesus to give sacrifices and offerings but instead desired obedience. More specifically, however, he called upon Jesus to give his body in sacrifice, and hence the word "body" fits nicely with the focus on Jesus' sacrificial death in the letter.

10:6

Verse 6 expands upon the content of verse 5. God didn't delight in or take pleasure in burnt offerings or sin offerings.[482] In the psalm we don't have an absolute rejection of sacrifices. The psalmist is scarcely suggesting that sacrifices were contrary to God's will from the beginning. Burnt offerings, after all, were a regular part of Israelite worship (cf. Lev 1:1–17). A burnt offering was to be offered every morning and evening (Exod 29:40–42). So too, sin offerings were regularly given to the Lord (Lev 4:1–35) and were included on the Day of Atonement (Lev 16:3, 5, 9, 11, 15, 25, 27). David is saying that such offerings without obedience and consecration to the Lord are meaningless. Religious ritual without a change of heart doesn't avail before God.

These same words, however, are applied in a different sense with reference to Jesus Christ. God didn't want animal sacrifices from him. Obedience to God for Jesus meant that he wasn't called upon to offer animal sacrifices but his own life. We naturally think of Isaiah 53 here. For the Servant of the Lord "was pierced because of our transgressions, crushed because of our iniquities; punishment for our peace was on Him" (Isa 53:5). The Servant was clearly put to death as "an offering for sin" (Isa 53:10 NIV). The Servant's sacrifice was final and effective, for he bore the iniquities of the people (Isa 53:11–12), but if he bore the sins of his people, then the need for animal sacrifices vanishes. It seems that Hebrews reads Psalm 40 in light of the coming of Jesus Christ and Isaiah's words about the Servant whose sacrificial offering obtains redemption for his people.

Proposal," *TrinJ* 32 (2011): 19–29; Koester, *Hebrews*, 432–33; Richardson, *Pioneer and Perfecter of Faith*, 92n310.

[481] Cf. Koester, *Hebrews*, 433; Cockerill, *Hebrews*, 436.

[482] The only significant difference between Hebrews and the OT is in the verb. In both the MT and the LXX the verb is "ask," but Hebrews introduces the word "delight."

10:7

The author continues to quote Psalm 40 (here vv. 7–8), and the differences between the MT and LXX and Hebrews are relatively minor. The temporal adverb "then" (τότε) is important to the author, as we shall see shortly. Jesus' mission isn't to bring animal sacrifices to the altar but to do something profoundly different. He announces the mission and purpose of his life: he has come to do the will of God. The words "I have come" (ἥκω) point to Jesus' incarnation and his mission, matching the phrase "coming into the world" (εἰσερχόμενος εἰς τὸν κόσμον) in verse 5.

The most intriguing phrase in the verse is the reference to "the volume of the scroll." What writing does the author of Hebrews have in mind? It is difficult to be certain. The inclusion of the phrase indicates that Jesus' coming to do God's will was his destiny. His submission to the divine will accords with what has been written. Perhaps the author of Hebrews has the entire OT in view. In the context of Psalm 40, David may be referring to the covenant the Lord made with him. The promise of an eternal dynasty points to Jesus as well, and perhaps Hebrews also has in mind specifically the promises made to David. The Davidic king as the representative of the people had a special calling to give himself entirely to God and to do his will. But David, as the psalm itself testifies (Ps 40:12), failed. The Davidic covenant would ultimately be fulfilled through an obedient king, through an obedient Son (2 Sam 7:14; Pss 89:30–32; 132:12). What is written about the Davidic dynasty and the Davidic king finds its fulfillment in one who gave himself unreservedly to God instead of pursuing his own selfish will.

10:8

The author now provides an explanation of the verses cited from Psalm 40, summoning the readers to what was written above (vv. 5–6). God did not desire or take pleasure in the sacrifices of the Levitical cult, which included whole burnt offerings and sin offerings. The author then offers his comment on such sacrifices: they were "offered according to the law." The sacrifices in which God did not delight stemmed from the old covenant. God's not delighting in them doesn't mean the sacrifices during the old covenant era were contrary to God's will. The point is that such sacrifices are provisional instead of permanent. They did not truly and finally atone for sin, demonstrating the inadequacy of the old covenant. A greater sacrifice must be coming since God did not delight in what was offered according to the law.

10:9

Hebrews pays close attention to the wording of the text, particularly to the sequence implied in the text. He sees a setting aside of animal sacrifices that are replaced by (or perhaps better "fulfilled by") the sacrifice of Jesus Christ. The "then" in the text is important, showing that the doing of God's will by Jesus is subsequent to the era of the law where OT sacrifices were required. God's will for Jesus consisted in the offering of his body, the giving up of his life. As I noted concerning verse 6 above, the self-offering of Jesus naturally leads us to think of Isaiah 53. Nor is such a reference an imposition, for the author clearly alludes to Isa 53:12 in 9:28, showing that he was cognizant of the sacrificial import of Isaiah 53.

We return here to the sequence Hebrews discerns in the text: the "first" is taken away, i.e., the sacrifices and offerings mandated in the law. The "first covenant" (8:7, 13; 9:1, 15, 18) and the "first tabernacle" (9:8) and the "first" sacrifices have given way to the "second" covenant (8:7), the heavenly tabernacle, and the final and definitive sacrifice. That which is second and later is "better" and superior.[483] The "first" anticipates and points to the second, but once the second has come, believers should not revert to the first. Now that the Servant of the Lord has given himself as an offering for the people, there is no going back. OT sacrifices will never be reinstituted now that the great and final forgiveness has come in Jesus Christ.

10:10

The superiority of the second and final sacrifice is explained further. Jesus did the will of God by giving his whole person, his body and soul, so to speak, over to death as an offering to God.[484] God's will was that Jesus himself would be the final and effective sacrifice.[485] His sacrifice is the second, the better, the new sacrifice

---

[483] The author is not specifically and directly referring here to the first and second covenant (against Käsemann, *Wandering People*, 57) but to the passing away of OT sacrifices, which are no longer required now that the sacrifice of Christ has been offered (O'Brien, *Hebrews*, 352).

[484] The reference here is to Jesus' death, not his entire life (Hughes, *Hebrews*, 399; Peterson, *Hebrews and Perfection*, 148).

[485] Against Moffitt, the author does not speak exclusively here of Jesus' presentation of himself before God in heaven (*Atonement and the Logic of the Resurrection*

which inaugurates the new covenant. His sacrifice was effective and definitive, for he was sinless, without spot and blemish. And, as noted earlier in these verses, he was a willing victim, in contrast to animals who were forced to give up their lives and who had no idea why they were being slain. Jesus, on the other hand, gave himself willingly and voluntarily so that others could be cleansed and forgiven. Hence his sacrifice is "once and for all." It was the definitive and final sacrifice so that no further sacrifices are needed. It would be folly to revert to animal sacrifices now that the Davidic king, the Son of God, and the high priest has given his life as an atonement for sinners. The author emphasizes here that believers "have been sanctified" (ἡγιασμένοι ἐσμέν) through Jesus' self-offering. Sanctification here is positional, something true of believers upon conversion. The author does not have in mind progressive sanctification by which believers become more like Jesus Christ.[486] Believers, on account of Jesus' sacrifice, are now in the realm of the holy. They are not unclean or defiled before God but holy before him because of the work of Jesus Christ. Since believers stand before God as holy and clean by virtue of Christ's sacrificial offering, they don't need to offer any other sacrifices to obtain forgiveness of sins.

Bridge

When Jesus Christ came, God did not instruct him to show his devotion by offering animals in sacrifice. Instead, he summoned him to give his own body, his own life, as an offering. Jesus' self-offering signaled that the day of animal sacrifices had terminated. A new era, a new covenant, a new arrangement had begun. The former covenant and its sacrifices passed away. Jesus' offering was effective. As believers we are sanctified and in the realm of the holy because of his

---

in the Epistle to the Hebrews, 230–56). Moffitt rightly sees that Jesus' exaltation in heaven is an embodied exaltation. But the word "offering" refers to what Jesus accomplished on earth. Moffitt's analysis of Psalm 40 and other OT texts in this section is most illuminating and full of many pertinent insights. The language of Heb 10:5–10 is most important for discerning the author's meaning, and the close relationship between OT sacrifices and Jesus' offering demonstrates that Jesus' offering on earth is intended.

[486] Rightly Peterson, Hebrews and Perfection, 148. According to Cockerill, the author reserves the phrase "Jesus Christ" for the climax of his argument (Hebrews, 444).

once-for-all sacrifice. God does not look on us as guilty or defiled but as pure and clean because of Jesus Christ.

Hebrews 10:11–14

Outline

I. Prologue: Definitive and Final Revelation in the Son (1:1–4)
II. Don't Abandon the Son Since He Is Greater than Angels (1:5–2:18)
III. Don't Harden Your Hearts Since You Have a Son and High Priest Greater than Moses and Joshua (3:1–4:13)
IV. **Don't Fall Away from Jesus' Melchizedekian Priesthood Since It Is Greater than the Levitical Priesthood (4:14–10:18)**
   A. Exhortation in Light of Jesus' Priestly Status (4:14–5:10)
   B. Warning and Assurance (5:11–6:20)
   C. Jesus' Greater Priesthood as a Melchizedekian Priest (7:1–28)
   D. New Covenant Better than the Old (8:1–13)
   E. **A Better Sacrifice Under the New Covenant (9:1–10:18)**
      1. Free Access to God Not Granted Under Old Covenant (9:1–10)
      2. Jesus Entered Heaven Itself with His Blood (9:11–14)
      3. Jesus as Mediator of New Covenant Bestows an Eternal Inheritance (9:15–22)
      4. **Jesus' Sacrifice: Better than OT Sacrifices (9:23–10:18)**
         a. Jesus' Heavenly and Once-for-All Sacrifice (9:23–28)
         b. Repetition of OT Sacrifices Shows Their Inadequacy (10:1–4)
         c. Jesus' Once-for-All Sacrifice Canceled Old System (10:5–10)
         d. **Jesus' Completed Sacrifice (10:11–14)**
         e. Final Forgiveness Promised in New Covenant Realized (10:15–18)
V. Concluding Exhortations and Warnings (10:19–12:29)

Scripture

¹¹ Every priest stands day after day ministering and offering the same sacrifices time after time, which can never take away sins. ¹² But this man, after offering one sacrifice for sins forever, sat down at the right hand of God. ¹³ He is now waiting until His enemies are made His footstool. ¹⁴ For by one offering He has perfected forever those who are sanctified.

Context

The sacrifices of the old covenant did not bring believers into the presence of God, whereas the blood of Christ effectively cleanses believers once for all (9:1–28). Animal sacrifices were inferior, for they could never truly remove sins (10:1–4). Jesus did not come, therefore, to offer animals but to give his own body as an offering (10:5–10). Thereby believers are sanctified. By way of contrast, the priests and their sacrifices never end. They continue offering them in perpetuity (10:11). Jesus, on the other hand, since his sacrificial work is finished, has sat down at God's right hand (10:12). Now he awaits the denouement, the day when all his enemies will be placed under his feet (10:13). It is abundantly clear that Jesus' sacrificial work is completed, for it was effective: his one offering perfected for all time those who are sanctified (10:14).

Exegesis

10:11

The contrast with the old covenant and its accompanying sacrifices continues to be explained. Every priest under the old covenant stands (cf. Deut 10:8; 18:7). They stand because their work is never completed, because they must continue to offer sacrifices. The burnt offering, which is offered in part to obtain forgiveness (Lev 1:4), must be offered every day (Exod 29:38; Num 28:3). The author can't be much more emphatic about the inadequacy of such sacrifices, for the priests stand "day after day." Nor does their work progress so that they move on to new tasks. They offer "the same sacrifices" (τὰς αὐτὰς . . . θυσίας), and they do so "repeatedly" (πολλάκις), which illustrates the futility of their ministry. If the same sacrifices are offered, they are obviously not securing final and definitive forgiveness. The author restates the idea of 10:4, where he asserts that the blood of animals can't remove sins. Here he observes that the sacrifices of the old covenant cannot remove sins.

10:12

The effectiveness of Christ's sacrifice and priesthood stands in stark contrast to the sacrifices offered by the priests under the old covenant. They offer "many sacrifices," but he offered "one sacrifice." His one sacrifice was "for sins" (ὑπὲρ ἁμαρτιῶν), i.e., it cleansed human beings of their sins. The benefits of the sacrifice never end, for it secures forgiveness "forever" (εἰς τὸ διηνεκές),[487] whereas the priestly sacrifices of the old covenant "never" (οὐδέποτε) remove sins (10:11). The author's favorite psalm now surfaces. Since Jesus' sacrifice achieved its goal, his work is finished. And since his work is finished, he has no need like the priests of the old covenant to keep standing (10:11). Rather he sat down at God's right hand (Ps 110:1) since as a priest-king he triumphed over sin and death. Jesus' sitting at God's right hand, sharing the rule of God, indicates his deity and confirms that his work is completed.[488]

10:13

Since Jesus' sacrificial work is finished, he sits triumphantly at God's right hand. As the risen Lord, he now waits for the last act in the drama of redemption. The verse echoes 9:28 where we are told that Jesus' one sacrifice atones for the sins of many, thus believers now await (ἀπεκδεχομένοις) the completion of their salvation when Jesus appears on earth again. The parallel to 9:28 is evident in 10:13, for Jesus is waiting (ἐκδεχόμενος) for his enemies to be subjugated before returning again to complete his saving work. The author clearly alludes to his favorite psalm (110:1) in speaking of the domestication and removal of Jesus' enemies (cf. Matt 22:44; 1 Cor 15:25). Oscar Cullmann rightly compared NT eschatology to D Day and V Day.[489] Jesus' death and resurrection are D Day, in that they represent the decisive victory of the Christ of God. Still, the final

---

[487] The word "forever" could also modify "sat down" (so Attridge, *Hebrews*, 280; Ellingworth, *Hebrews*, 509–10; Cockerill, *Hebrews*, 449n9). For the view adopted here, see Peterson, *Hebrews and Perfection*, 148–49; O'Brien, *Hebrews*, 355.

[488] On the broader christological significance of Jesus sitting at the right hand, see Hengel, *Studies in Early Christology*, 119–225.

[489] Oscar Cullmann, *Christ and Time: The Primitive Christian Conception of Time and History*, trans. F. V. Filson (Philadelphia: Westminster, 1950), 84.

mopping up operation hasn't occurred. V Day isn't here yet, but it is most certainly coming.

10:14

The reason Jesus' work is finished is set forth in one of the most famous sentences of the letter. The "one offering" of Jesus, the offering of his body (10:5, 10), the shedding of his blood (9:14), has perfected believers forever (see §2.5). The word "perfected" (τετελείωκεν) is a favorite of the author. The law and its sacrifices didn't bring perfection (7:19; 10:1; cf. 7:11) since they can't perfect the conscience (9:9). Perfection in Hebrews has the idea that sins are cleansed and removed, so that the conscience is no longer defiled by guilt. Believers, by virtue of Christ's sacrifice, can now enter God's presence freely and boldly. The work of perfection is objective and has been accomplished "forever" (εἰς τὸ διηνεκές). Here the author emphasizes the present consequences the perfecting work accomplished, but this doesn't preclude the future, for perfection will only be achieved finally and fully when believers enter the heavenly city.[490] We have an implication here, therefore, that the perfecting work of Christ secures the final reward for believers.

The perfecting work has been accomplished for "those who are sanctified" (τοὺς ἁγιαζομένους). Hebrews doesn't use the language of justification (but cf. 10:38; 11:7), but the terms *perfection* and *sanctification* are akin to the way Paul speaks of justification. Paul emphasizes that justification is a completed work in the lives of believers (e.g., Rom 5:1; 8:30), even though justification is an eschatological reality. A similar thing may be said about perfection in Hebrews. Believers are perfected because of the work of Jesus Christ, which includes his death, resurrection, and exaltation. Perfection, then, isn't fundamentally a subjective reality but an objective one, denoting God's saving work in the lives of those who belong to Jesus.

The objective and definitive nature of perfection isn't contradicted by the sin that continues to stain the everyday life of believers.

---

[490] Perhaps the perfect here should be described as stative. For the category, see Constantine R. Campbell, *Basics of Verbal Aspect in Biblical Greek* (Grand Rapids, MI: Zondervan, 2008), 106–7. See Peterson, *Hebrews and Perfection*, 149–53. He notes: "The terminology of perfection itself quite naturally suggests some eschatological or ultimate adjustment to the nature and situation of man. However, 10:14 clearly locates this perfecting *in the past with respect to its accomplishment and in the present with respect to its enjoyment*" (167, emphasis original).

The warnings in the letter show that this absolute perfection isn't yet theirs. They are perfect before God because of what Christ has done, even though they still struggle with sin. What we have here is characteristic of the NT tension between the already and the not yet, between what is true of believers in Christ Jesus and what is true in their everyday experience.

The sanctifying work of Jesus is a frequent theme in Hebrews (10:10, 29; 13:12), especially when we realize that the word is in the same semantic domain with the word "cleansing" (9:14, 22, 23; 10:2, καθαρίζω; 10:22, καθαρός), "washing" (10:22, λούω), and "sprinkling" (9:13, 19, 21; 10:22, ῥαντίζω; 12:24, ῥαντισμός). Jesus' blood has purified believers. They are now in the realm of the holy. The present participle is translated by the ESV as "those who are being sanctified" (τοὺς ἁγιαζομένους) and by the NIV as "those who are being made holy" (cf. NLT).[491] On the other hand a number of versions don't emphasize the tense of the participle: "those who are sanctified" (HCSB; NRSV); "those who are made holy" (NET). It seems unlikely that the tense of the participle should be pressed here, for the author typically uses the words *sanctification, cleansing*, and *washing* to depict the pure and holy state believers already enjoy.[492] The participle denotes here, then, a "finished state" and not an ongoing process.[493] As stated above, Hebrews uses cultic terms much as Paul speaks of justification, in order to emphasize that believers are pure and clean before God. That is probably what the author is saying here as well. Believers are sanctified through the one offering of Jesus Christ. They are not unclean or besmirched but pure and spotless in God's presence.

Bridge

One of the greatest comforts for believers is that they are perfected forever by the one offering of Jesus Christ. Believers aren't

---

[491] For such a reading, see Ellingworth, *Hebrews*, 511; cf. also Cockerill, *Hebrews*, 452.

[492] The participle should be construed, then, as timeless (see O'Brien, *Hebrews*, 357; Peterson, *Hebrews and Perfection*, 150). It should be noted that most scholars now agree that Greek verbs don't designate time inherently, but aspect. This is commonplace in studies of NT Greek. For an excellent introduction, see Campbell, *Basics of Verbal Aspect*.

[493] Rightly Ribbens, "Levitical Sacrifice and Heavenly Cult in Hebrews," 292–93.

perfected because of what they have accomplished. The old covenant doesn't provide final assurance, for the priests' work is never done. They have to keep standing, keep sacrificing, and keep offering every day. Jesus, however, doesn't stand but sits at God's right hand, and he sits because his work is finished. Now he waits until the day all his enemies are put under his feet. Believers put their trust in Jesus as their reigning priest-king. They don't rest in what they have done to secure forgiveness. They realize their purity, cleanness, and sanctification derive from the once-for-all sacrifice of Jesus the Christ.

Hebrews 10:15–18

Outline

I. Prologue: Definitive and Final Revelation in the Son (1:1–4)
II. Don't Abandon the Son Since He Is Greater than Angels (1:5–2:18)
III. Don't Harden Your Hearts Since You Have a Son and High Priest Greater than Moses and Joshua (3:1–4:13)
IV. **Don't Fall Away from Jesus' Melchizedekian Priesthood Since It Is Greater than the Levitical Priesthood (4:14–10:18)**
   A. Exhortation in Light of Jesus' Priestly Status (4:14–5:10)
   B. Warning and Assurance (5:11–6:20)
   C. Jesus' Greater Priesthood as a Melchizedekian Priest (7:1–28)
   D. New Covenant Better than the Old (8:1–13)
   E. **A Better Sacrifice Under the New Covenant (9:1–10:18)**
      1. Free Access to God Not Granted Under Old Covenant 9:1–10)
      2. Jesus Entered Heaven Itself with His Blood (9:11–14)
      3. Jesus as Mediator of New Covenant Bestows an Eternal Inheritance (9:15–22)
      4. **Jesus' Sacrifice: Better than OT Sacrifices (9:23–10:18)**
         a. Jesus' Heavenly and Once-for-All Sacrifice (9:23–28)

  b. Repetition of OT Sacrifices Shows Their
     Inadequacy (10:1–4)
  c. Jesus' Once-for-All Sacrifice Canceled Old
     System (10:5–10)
  d. Jesus' Completed Sacrifice (10:11–14)
  e. **Final Forgiveness Promised in New Covenant
     Realized (10:15–18)**
V. Concluding Exhortations and Warnings (10:19–12:29)

Scripture

[15] The Holy Spirit also testifies to us about this. For after He says: [16] This is the covenant I will make with them after those days, says the Lord: I will put My laws on their hearts and write them on their minds, [17] He adds: I will never again remember their sins and their lawless acts. [18] Now where there is forgiveness of these, there is no longer an offering for sin.

Context

The final section on the superiority of Christ's sacrifice concludes here. We have seen in chapter 9 that the old covenant sacrifices didn't bring access to God while the blood of Christ secured such access. The flow of the argument in 10:1–18 is captured well by Lane, whom I am quoting in the chiasm below:[494]

A   The inadequacy of the provisions of the law for repeated sacrifices (10:1–4)

   B   The repeated sacrifices have been superseded by the one sacrifice of Christ in conformity to the will of God (10:5–10)

   B[1]   The Levitical priests have been superseded by the one priest enthroned at God's right hand (10:11–14)

A[1]   The adequacy of the provisions of the new covenant, which render a sacrifice for sins no longer necessary (10:15–18)

The Holy Spirit, according to verse 15, testifies to the superiority of the new covenant in the words of Jer 31:33–34. God pledges to inscribe his law on the hearts and minds of his people (vv. 15–16). Indeed, he promises to forget the sins and failures of his

---

[494] Lane, *Hebrews 9–13*, 258.

people (v. 17). The author seizes upon the last line. Since forgiveness has been obtained under the new covenant, an offering for sin is no longer needed (v. 18). The definitive and final sacrifice has come in Jesus Christ.

Exegesis

10:15

That the definitive and final sacrifice has been offered is confirmed by the testimony of the Holy Spirit. The Holy Spirit speaks through the words of OT prophecy, particularly here in Jer 31:33–34. For the notion that the Holy Spirit speaks through the Scriptures, see also Heb 3:7 where the Spirit speaks through the words of Psalm 95 (see §4). Similarly, the Spirit reveals through the OT cultus that there was not free access to God's presence (9:8). In 2 Pet 1:21 a similar idea is communicated: true prophecy occurs when people speak from God as they are moved and carried along by the Holy Spirit. The OT itself often traces prophecy to the work of the Holy Spirit (Num 11:25–26, 29; 24:2; 1 Sam 10:6, 10; 19:20, 23; 23:2; 1 Chr 12:18; 2 Chr 15:1; 2 Chr 20:14; 24:20; Isa 61:1; Ezek 11:5; Joel 2:28; Mic 2:7; 3:8; Zech 7:12). Nothing is said about the Spirit speaking through Jeremiah, but the author of Hebrews rightly draws this conclusion from the frequent references to the Spirit's speaking through the prophetic word. Indeed the Holy Spirit continues to speak to the church of Jesus Christ in the Scriptures by the power of the Holy Spirit.

10:16

Earlier the author cited Jer 31:31–34 (8:8–12). The text is cited again, though in this case the author is more selective. The citation is close to the LXX and MT with some minor changes. Instead of the covenant being made "with the house of Israel" (Jer 31:33), it was made "with them" (Heb 10:16), which presumably refers to the recipients of the letter, suggesting that the readers are conceived of as the new Israel. The covenant in Jeremiah 31 is a "new covenant" (Jer 31:31), and God takes the initiative in establishing the covenant. The newness of the covenant is confirmed by the words "after those days," signifying that the new covenant succeeds the old, for it is a new arrangement and dispensation and economy for the people of God.

The sovereign grace of God is featured in the covenant. He inscribes his law on the hearts and minds of his people.[495] The desire to obey doesn't come from human beings but is ascribed to the power of God. "This points to an obedience from the heart that was expected under the old covenant, but which now will be accomplished by God."[496] The author probably has in mind especially the great commandments to love God and neighbor (Deut 6:4–5; Lev 19:18).[497]

10:17

The author then skips several lines from Jer 31:33–34, which he cited earlier (Heb 8:10–11), concluding with the words that speak of the forgiveness of sins. The Lord will write his law on their hearts, and he will no longer remember their sins and lawless deeds. The word "remember" ($\mu\nu\eta\sigma\theta\dot{\eta}\sigma\omega\mu\alpha\iota$) is often used in the OT to indicate that God cares for his people, acting on their behalf (Gen 8:1; 30:22; 1 Sam 1:19; Neh 5:19; 13:14; Jer 15:15). In a number of texts, it is joined together with the notion that God acts on their behalf because of his covenant with them (cf. Gen 9:15–16, 29; Exod 2:24; 6:5; 32:13; 26:14, 45; Deut 9:27; Pss 74:2; 105:8, 42; 106:45; 111:5; Jer 14:21; Lam 5:1; Ezek 16:60). More particularly, it can be used to denote forgiveness of sins: "Do not remember the sins of my youth or my acts of rebellion" (Ps 25:7). "Do not remember against us our former iniquities" (Ps 79:8 ESV). "It is I who sweep away your transgressions for My own sake and remember your sins no more" (Isa 43:25). "Lord, do not be terribly angry or remember our iniquity forever" (Isa 64:9). "None of the transgressions that he has committed shall be remembered against him" (Ezek 18:22 ESV). Or conversely, the Lord says, "I remember all their evil" (Hos 7:2), i.e., they won't be forgiven (cf. Hos 8:13; 9:9). What is distinctive about the new covenant, then, is the forgiveness of sins.

10:18

The author draws a ringing conclusion from the new covenant promise of Jeremiah, focusing especially on the promise that God will no longer remember the sins of his people. He has already shown previously that the promise of forgiveness belongs to the new covenant rather than the old (8:7–13). Hence, what is said here can't

---

[495] Attridge says the law inscribed is Christ's voluntary obedience, not the old covenant law (*Hebrews*, 281), but the text doesn't actually make this point.

[496] O'Brien, *Hebrews*, 359.

[497] So Cockerill, *Hebrews*, 457.

be applied to old covenant sacrifices. It only applies to the new covenant sacrifice of Jesus the Christ.

Since the new covenant pronounces forgiveness,[498] there is no longer a need for any other offering. Final and full forgiveness has been achieved in the offering of Jesus Christ. Nothing else should be done or needs to be done for sins to be wiped away. Since God doesn't remember our sins any longer, believers should enjoy the forgiveness that has been given freely to them.

Bridge

The author wants to give his readers assurance so that they don't fall away from Christ, so that they don't turn to the Levitical cult to find forgiveness of sins and peace in their hearts. He reminds them, therefore, of the words of the Holy Spirit, who testifies to what God is doing in the words of the new covenant (Jer 31:33–34). What makes the new covenant new, among other things, is that sins are definitively cleansed once for all through the offering of Jesus Christ. If they renounce Jesus, they lose their claim to the only offering that can truly cleanse. If they remain with Jesus, they can be confident that their sins have been removed and cleansed forever.

Hebrews 10:19–25

Outline

I. Prologue: Definitive and Final Revelation in the Son (1:1–4)
II. Don't Abandon the Son Since He Is Greater than Angels (1:5–2:18)
III. Don't Harden Your Hearts Since You Have a Son and High Priest Greater than Moses and Joshua (3:1–4:13)
IV. Don't Fall Away from Jesus' Melchizedekian Priesthood Since It Is Greater than the Levitical Priesthood (4:14–10:18)
V. **Concluding Exhortations and Warnings (10:19–12:29)**
   A. **Exhortation to Draw Near, Hold Fast, and Help Others (10:19–25)**

---

[498] The word "forgiveness" (ἄφεσις) here or "release" focuses on the absolving of transgressions so it doesn't also include the power to live a new life (against Cockerill, *Hebrews*, 459), though it is certainly true theologically that those who are forgiven are also enabled by God and called by him to live in a way that pleases him.

   B. Warning: No Hope of Forgiveness for Those Who Turn
       from Christ (10:26–31)
   C. Call to Persevere in Faith (10:32–12:3)
   D. Exhortations to Readers to Endure (12:4–29)

Scripture

[19] Therefore, brothers, since we have boldness to enter the sanctuary through the blood of Jesus, [20] by a new and living way He has opened for us through the curtain (that is, His flesh), [21] and since we have a great high priest over the house of God, [22] let us draw near with a true heart in full assurance of faith, our hearts sprinkled clean from an evil conscience and our bodies washed in pure water. [23] Let us hold on to the confession of our hope without wavering, for He who promised is faithful. [24] And let us be concerned about one another in order to promote love and good works, [25] not staying away from our worship meetings, as some habitually do, but encouraging each other, and all the more as you see the day drawing near.

Context

From 5:1–10:18 the author has been expounding on Jesus' Melchizedekian priesthood. He was anxious to explain this subject to the readers, though he feared they were too spiritually dull to grasp what he had to say (5:11–14; 6:12). He argued that Jesus is a better priest, for he is a Melchizedekian priest, one who brings people near to God and is able save them completely (7:1–28). Jesus is not only a high priest who has completed his saving work and sat down at God's right hand, but he is also the mediator of a better covenant, the new covenant (8:1–13). In the new covenant the law is written on the heart and sins are forgiven, and thus it is clear that the old covenant is no longer in force. Finally, Jesus offered a better sacrifice. His blood actually brings believers into the heavenly tabernacle: God's presence. Believers are truly cleansed in their conscience through Jesus' sacrificial blood. The work of priests under the old covenant is never finished: they stand and offer the same sacrifices daily. But Jesus sits at God's right hand because his one sacrifice brought forgiveness of sins once for all.

After this long exposition the author is ready to exhort the readers. As noted earlier, 10:19–25 has many points of contact with

4:14–16. Cockerill rightly maintains that these verses, though functioning as an inference and conclusion of the preceding argument (5:1–10:18), also introduce the sustained exhortation section in the letter.[499] Hebrews 4:14–16 prepared readers for the high priest argument to follow. As Cockerill says, "4:14–16 is tailored to bring the hearers into Christ's high priesthood, but 10:19–25 is shaped in order to direct them from that high priesthood to faithful endurance."[500] Indeed, the rest of the letter constitutes an exhortation, and that is hardly surprising since the main purpose of the letter is to warn the readers not to fall away from Jesus. Given the greatness of Jesus' Melchizedekian priesthood, the readers are urged to draw near, hold fast, and encourage others to persevere (10:19–25).

Perseverance is absolutely crucial, for if they turn away, there will be no forgiveness for them but only judgment (10:26–31). He encourages the readers to remember their fervor and spiritual vitality at their conversion so they do not throw away their boldness (10:32–39). They must endure and believe to receive final salvation. Those who persevere trust in God, and those who fall away fail to trust him. The ancestors of faith, then, are recorded for hortatory purposes (11:1–40). The readers are to imitate their faith and continue believing even when things look as if they will not be fulfilled. Jesus, naturally, is the supreme exemplar of such persevering faith (12:1–3). The readers should endure as those who are being disciplined for the sake of their maturity and holiness (12:4–11). They should strengthen weak hands and make straight paths for their feet and pursue sanctification so that they are not like Esau who didn't receive the reward (12:12–17). The author explains in 12:18–24 why they should persevere. They have come to something better than Sinai! They have come to Zion, the city of God, the heavenly Jerusalem. Indeed they have come to Jesus, whose blood speaks a better word than the blood of angels. Since the readers have had such privileges, they must beware of refusing to heed the voice that came from heaven (12:25–29). A kingdom is coming that can't be

---

[499] Cockerill, *Hebrews*, 461n2. Over against Guthrie, *Structure of Hebrews*, 117, 136, 144; Cynthia Long Westfall, *A Discourse Analysis of the Letter to the Hebrews: The Relationship Between Form and Meaning*, LNTS 297 (London: T&T Clark, 238–44.

[500] Cockerill, *Hebrews*, 461n2.

shaken, and the readers don't want to face the wrath of God who is a consuming fire.

Having summarized the landscape of the exhortation section as a whole, we need to look a bit closer at the logic of 10:19–25. Verses 19–21 reach back into the previous argument (7:1–10:18) and pick up some of the main points, explaining why the readers should persevere to the end. First, believers can boldly enter the holy place, the presence of God, through Jesus' blood (v. 19). The curtain separating people from God has been torn down through the flesh of Jesus (v. 20). The author has labored to explain in the preceding chapters that access to God's presence that was not available under the old covenant is now theirs through Jesus. Second, Jesus is the great priest over God's house (v. 21). He is the Melchizedekian priest who brought perfection. Here is a priest who secures access to God and is able to save completely those who draw near to God through him (7:25). Since believers have access to God and a great priest, they are given three exhortations: draw near (v. 22), hold fast (v. 23), and stimulate others to love and good works (vv. 24–25).

We will look at each exhortation briefly. First, they are to draw near with assurance and confidence because they have been purified and washed by Christ's blood (v. 22). No shame and guilt should prevent them from drawing near. Second, believers must hold fast the confession of faith and not waver (v. 23). The God who called them is faithful and will sustain them. Third, they are to stimulate one another to love and good works (vv. 24–25). They should not forsake their meetings, for that is the road to apostasy. Instead, as they consider the final day (the day of judgment and salvation), they should encourage one another in the faith.

Exegesis

10:19

The "therefore" (οὖν) here commences a new section, as explained above. The exhortations that begin in this paragraph are grounded in Jesus' priesthood and sacrifice. In fact, those realities are so important that the author pauses to rehearse them again before exhorting the readers. The readers are addressed here as "brothers" (cf. 3:1, 12; 13:22). They are not merely "readers" or recipients or even friends. They are family and are the brothers and sisters of the author.

The readers are full of boldness (παρρησίαν) and confidence, and it is a particular kind of boldness,[501] a boldness to enter "the most holy place" (τῶν ἁγίων, NIV) by the blood of Jesus. The word could also be translated "authorization," which emphasizes the right of access for believers.[502] Earlier in the letter the readers are encouraged to approach the throne of grace boldly since Jesus is their high priest (4:15–16). The word rendered "sanctuary" here refers to "the Most Holy Place" (NIV). The author alludes to the most holy place in the tabernacle, but he is using the term typologically, for the tent where God meets his people points to a heavenly sanctuary where there is access to God's presence. The language here shouldn't be read literally as if there is a literal most holy place or sanctuary in heaven. The earthly tabernacle points to a heavenly tabernacle, to the presence of God. Entering God's presence isn't joyful but terrifying because of human sin. God, as the author reminds us, is a consuming fire (12:29)! Therefore, believers enter his presence only through the blood of Jesus, as the author has argued in some detail in 7:1–10:18. Jesus is a Melchizedekian priest and far better than the Levitical priests, for his blood actually secures forgiveness of sins once for all and brings people into God's presence. Confidence and boldness to enter God's presence doesn't stem from human virtue but from God's grace.

10:20

Jesus has opened a new way to God through the veil that separates human beings from God,[503] and they gain access to God through the flesh, i.e., through the death of Jesus. The entrance believers enjoy is "a new and living way." Even though the author uses a different word for "new" (πρόσφατον), he almost certainly has the new covenant in mind. Jesus is a mediator of a new covenant, which

---

[501] Lane wrongly understands boldness only objectively and fails to see its subjective dimension (*Hebrews 9–13*, 274). There is no need for an either-or here. Rightly Ellingworth, *Hebrews*, 517.

[502] Cockerill, *Hebrews*, 466.

[503] The verb "opened" (ἐνεκαίνισεν) could mean that Christ inaugurated a new way to God with his sacrifice (Attridge, *Hebrews*, 285; Ellingworth, *Hebrews*, 518). Or it could mean that he "opened" access to God (O'Brien, *Hebrews*, 363–64; Lane, *Hebrews 9–13*, 284). The latter is slightly preferable on the basis of the parallel to 6:19–20.

is better than the old one because it secures forgiveness of sins.[504] The word "living" (ζῶσαν) probably refers to Jesus' resurrection. Jesus is a Melchizedekian priest and a better priest because he is a priest "forever" (Ps 110:4). Jesus always lives (7:25) and has an indestructible life (7:16). Believers enjoy fellowship with God because Jesus has conquered death (cf. 2:14–15), because he is the ever-living one.

The last part of the verse is harder to interpret. Jesus brings believers "through the curtain." The "curtain" (καταπετάσματος) here is the veil that separates the holy place from the most holy place (Heb 6:19; 9:3; cf. Exod 26:33; 30:6; 35:12; 40:3, 21–22, 26; Lev 16:2, 12, 15; 24:3; Num 3:10). The author again uses the furniture of the tabernacle typologically. The curtain separating the holy place from the most holy place represents restricted access to God under the old covenant, and the writer makes clear in 9:6–10 that access to God was limited to one day a year (the Day of Atonement) by only one person (the high priest). All believers now have access to God but not by going through a literal veil.

The veil is described in an appositional statement as Jesus' "flesh" (σαρκὸς αὐτου). But what does the author mean by this statement? It seems awkward and a bit strange to say that Jesus' flesh was like the curtain of the tabernacle that separated the holy place from the most holy place. It is tempting to say that "His flesh" modifies "way" (ὁδόν). On this reading the new and living way through the veil is Jesus' flesh, his death on the cross. The problem with such a reading is that the word "way" is farther away from the word "flesh" than the word "curtain." Furthermore, the word "way" is in the accusative case, while the words "curtain" and "flesh" are genitive, which makes us think that "flesh" describes the "curtain." Even though "flesh" modifies the word "curtain," the expression shouldn't be taken literally. The author isn't saying that Jesus' flesh separates us from God. He is probably saying that access to God is not ultimately granted by passing through a curtain. It is granted through

---

[504] Hence the new covenant is not just "new" but "qualitatively different" (O'Brien, *Hebrews*, 364).

the torn and bloody and dead flesh of Jesus (cf. John 6:50–58).[505] "Jesus secured access to God's presence 'by means of' his flesh."[506]

10:21

Believers have access to God through the blood and death of Jesus, and they also have a great priest over God's house (cf. 3:6). The author has argued throughout the letter that Jesus is a Melchizedekian priest (Ps 110:1 Heb 5:6, 10; 6:20; 7:17, 21; see §2.3). He expiated the sins of the people as "a merciful and faithful high priest" (2:17). As a sinless priest and as the Son of God (1:4–14; 3:1; 7:26), he offered himself to God as a sacrifice (9:11, 26), atoning for the transgressions of others. As the risen one he has ascended into heaven and sits at the right hand of God, reigning as high priest (4:14; 7:16; 8:1; 10:12). No Levitical priest could match such priestly qualifications, for the high priest only had access to God once a year on the Day of Atonement (Lev 16:1–34; Heb 9:6–8), and previous high priests all died and could not continue their priestly ministry. But Jesus' priesthood lasts forever since he has conquered death, and thus the efficacy of his sacrifice will never be extinguished.

10:22

Since believers have access to God through Jesus' death and since he is their great high priest who reigns at God's right hand and intercedes for them (7:25), they are to draw near to God assured that their sins are forgiven (see §8). The word translated "draw near" (προσερχώμεθα) is one of the author's favorites. He encourages the readers to "approach (προσερχώμεθα) the throne of grace with boldness" (4:16). Believers have not "drawn near" to Mount Sinai but Mount Zion (12:18, 22), for the law can't perfect those drawing near (10:1). Only the resurrected Lord can do that (7:25). The readers are encouraged to draw near with "a true heart in full assurance of faith." This is another way of saying that they are to approach

---

[505] See L. Johnson, *Hebrews*, 257. The meaning of this expression is contested (see Attridge, *Hebrews*, 286–87), but the Greek construction should be taken appositionally. So Norman H. Young, "Tout Estin Sarkos Autou' (Heb. X.20): Apposition, Dependent, or Explicative?" *NTS* 20 (1973): 100–104. The context in which this statement is found indicates that we don't have a reference to the incarnation here. Against Mark A. Jennings, "The Veil and the High Priestly Robes of the Incarnation: Understanding the Context of Heb 10:20," *PRSt* 37 (2010): 85–97.

[506] Koester, *Hebrews*, 443. Cf. Lane, *Hebrews 9–13*, 284.

God boldly (4:16), confidently, and joyfully.[507] They should not let doubts bedevil them, for their "hearts are sprinkled clean from an evil conscience."

Their assurance and confidence do not reside in themselves. If readers considered their own worthiness to enter God's presence, they would rightly be filled with fear. But fear has no place, for they have been sprinkled clean by the blood of Christ (12:24). Just as the blood sprinkled Israel under the old covenant (Exod 24:8), so the blood of Christ sprinkles clean believers under the new covenant. The evil that defiled the conscience is washed away.[508] But Jesus' blood avails forever in contrast to the blood spilt under the new covenant, for the sacrifices offered under that covenant did not perfect the conscience of the worshiper (9:9). Jesus' blood, on the other hand, cleanses the conscience (9:14) so that there is no longer consciousness of sins (10:2). Saying that the body is "washed in pure water" is another way of describing the cleansing that comes through Jesus' offering of himself. The language of "washing" goes back to the OT where washings were required for cleanliness (Exod 29:4; 40:12; Lev 8:6; 11:40; 14:8–9; 15:5–6; 16:4, 24, 26; 17:15; 22:6; Num 19:7–8; Deut 23:12). Physical washing in the OT does not truly cleanse people before God as Heb 9:10 attests. Such washings were "fleshly ordinances" (NKJV) appointed to last until the time of reformation. They pointed to a more significant washing, the cleansing of sin accomplished through Jesus Christ. Jesus "cleansed" his people of their sins by his death (1:3) and cleansed their consciences (9:14) once for all (10:4).

Most commentators think there is a reference here to baptism that symbolizes cleansing from sin.[509] Others maintain that baptism

---

[507] Koester says, "'Full assurance' includes a personal disposition and its external expression" (*Hebrews*, 444). In defense of full assurance and not just fullness, see Ellingworth, *Hebrews*, 523.

[508] The two expressions here (sprinkling and washing) are to be taken together (so Ellingworth, *Hebrews*, 523). They are two different pictures of the same reality.

[509] Attridge, *Hebrews*, 289; Koester, *Hebrews*, 449; Lane, *Hebrews 9–13*, 287. Peter J. Leithart rightly sees a reference to baptism here but mistakenly draws the conclusion that those who are baptized are initiated as priests ("Womb of the World: Baptism and the Priesthood of the New Covenant in Hebrews 10.9–22," *JSNT* 78 [2000]: 49–65). The author of Hebrews, however, reserves the priesthood to Jesus Christ and does not argue from the priesthood of Christ for the priesthood of all believers. This also stands against the view of Scholer that believers in Hebrews are

shouldn't be read into the text here, claiming that the writer draws on Ezek 36:25–26 which speaks of the cleansing believers enjoy through the death of Jesus.[510] But appeal to the latter doesn't exclude the former, for baptism as an initiation rite reminds believers of the cleansing received through the cross. It seems natural that believers would think of baptism when the washing of the body is mentioned. The term "body" doesn't mean that baptism cleanses people physically. The physical washing of the body that took place in baptism symbolizes the cleansing of the heart, as in the first part of the verse, which takes place when the sins of believers are forgiven. The "body," then, stands for the whole person who stands before God clean because of the cleansing work accomplished in the cross. The author is hopeful that his readers will be confident and bold in God's presence, knowing that their sins have been forgiven through Jesus Christ.

10:23

We see, secondly, that the readers are exhorted to hold on to the faith they confessed "without wavering." For the third time in the letter, the readers are exhorted to "hold on" (κατέχωμεν; cf. 3:6, 14). And there is a similar expression in 4:14, "Let us hold fast (κρατῶμεν) to the confession." The "confession" refers (cf. also 3:1) to the faith, to the doctrine the believers have acknowledged as the truth. Here it is designated as a confession of hope. Hope is the sure promise of eschatological joy for those who persevere to the end, and elsewhere the author encourages them to hang on to their hope

---

conceived of as proleptic priests. See John M. Scholer, *Proleptic Priests: Priesthood in the Epistle to the Hebrews*, JSNTSup 49 (Sheffield: Sheffield Academic, 1991); cf. also John Dunnill, *Covenant and Sacrifice in the Letter to the Hebrews*, SNTSMS 75 (Cambridge: Cambridge University Press, 1992), 259; Emmrich, *Pneumatological Concepts in Hebrews*, 13–16. In one sense believers do engage in priestly activities since they approach God as priests. Theologically, in terms of the entirety of the NT (cf. 1 Pet 2:9), there is no objection to describing believers as priests. The author of Hebrews, however, deliberately avoids identifying believers as priests. In the OT there were many priests, but in the NT there is one priest: Jesus Christ. The author jealously reserves the priesthood for Jesus Christ alone so that the glory of our relationship with God rests on his priestly work alone.

[510] Cf. O'Brien, *Hebrews*, 367–68. Against Barnard, the author doesn't refer to repeated ritual washings as was common in Judaism (*The Mysticism of Hebrews*, 196–208). The once-for-all character of the cleansing accomplished by Christ, which is so prominent in chapters 9–10, rules out such a conception.

(3:6; 6:11, 18; cf. also 6:19; 7:19). Hope here is conceived of as an objective reality.[511] They are to remain true to that upon which they initially set their hope. The heavenly city beckons for those who keep trusting until the end (11:10, 13–16; 12:22; 13:14). The words "without wavering" should not be confused with sinlessness. It is simply another way of describing perseverance in faith. Those who will enjoy the end-time rest (4:1–11) will continue to believe and obey until the end. The author encourages endurance with the truth that the one who promised life is faithful (cf. 11:11). God will surely grant the reward he pledged to his people, thereby motivating perseverance.

10:24

The third admonition is now given. Believers should reflect and consider how to provoke one another to love and good works. Encouraging others, therefore, is not invariably spontaneous. The author calls upon the readers to contemplate ways in which they could stimulate others to love and good works. The word "promote" (παροξυσμόν) is perhaps a bit too tame for the meaning of the Greek word used here. The NIV's "spur" or the ESV's "stir up" catch the meaning more accurately. The word is used for the strong disagreement that led to a parting of ways between Paul and Barnabas (Acts 15:39). Here the term is used in the positive sense of impelling one another to love and good works.[512] The Hebrew Christians demonstrated their love for one another by serving the saints (6:10) and by showing concern for those in prison (10:32). Love is the mark of Christian discipleship (John 13:34–35), and the supreme virtue for believers (Matt 22:34–40; 1 Cor 13:1–13; Col 3:15). Those who persevere in faith also persevere in love. Love is not merely a feeling or emotion. It manifests itself in "good works." "Dead works" lead to spiritual death (6:10; 9:14), while good works testify to God's grace among believers. Such good works are necessary for final salvation, expressing a living and vital faith. Such good works, of course, should not be confused with perfection. The foundation for their assurance is the blood of Christ, but good works constitute evidence that believers authentically trust in Christ.

---

[511] The focus here is on "the objective content of hope" (O'Brien, *Hebrews*, 368).

[512] As L. Johnson notes the word is also used in a positive sense in Greek literature (*Hebrews*, 259; see Xenophon, *Memorabilia* 3.3.13).

10:25

Community encouragement and love and good works can scarcely occur if believers cease to meet with one another. The fear of discrimination and persecution explains, at least in part, why some believers were inclined to abandon their meetings. Refusing to meet with other believers in this context signifies apostasy, the renunciation of the Christian faith. If believers renounce meeting with other Christians, especially because they fear discrimination and mistreatment, they are in effect turning against Christ. Apparently, some were following this course of action, for they had made it a habit of not attending. For the author of Hebrews, this isn't a light matter. Forsaking such meetings signaled great danger, for if they did not return to the assembly of fellow believers, they would face final judgment and destruction. Meeting together with other believers on earth looks forward to the eschatological gathering. O'Brien comments on the significance of the church meeting together: "Their gathering together" anticipates "the final ingathering of God's people. The assembly is the earthly counterpart to the heavenly 'congregation' (*ekklēsia*) of God's people."[513]

Instead of abandoning meeting together, believers should encourage (παρακαλοῦντες) one another. Encouragement is vital for perseverance, as 3:13 attests: "But encourage each other daily, while it is still called today, so that none of you is hardened by sin's deception." The urgency of encouragement is indicated by the nearness of the eschatological day. The day here is the day of the Lord. In the OT the day of the Lord is the day of judgment and salvation (Isa 13:6–13; 34:8; Ezek 13:5; 30:2–3; Joel 1:15; 2:1–2, 11, 28–31; 3:14; Amos 5:18, 20; Obad 15; Zeph 1:7, 14; 3:11, 16). In the NT the day of the Lord or the day of Christ is correlated with the day Jesus returns, when he delivers those belonging to him and judges those opposed to him (Acts 2:20; 1 Cor 1:8; 5:5; 2 Cor 1:14; 1 Thess 5:2; 2 Thess 2:2; 2 Pet 3:10). Believers should encourage one another, therefore, because the present world will not last, and thus they should urge one another to stay true to Jesus Christ.

---

[513] O'Brien, *Hebrews*, 371.

Bridge

As believers we have rest and peace of heart through Jesus' blood. We know our sins aren't held against us and that we have access to God himself. We rejoice in Jesus our great priest who has offered the final and definitive sacrifice for sins and intercedes for us as the living one. Because we are cleansed from our sins, we can draw near to God with confidence, boldness, and joy. Shame and guilt are no longer ours. We must also hold on to the faith until the end, knowing that God will never abandon us, that he will be faithful to all the promises given to us. Finally, we should consider how to encourage other believers to love and good works and perseverance. Those who abandon the fellowship of the Christian church by failing to attend are in danger of the final judgment. Perseverance is not merely a private matter. It is also reflected in whether believers meet corporately with one another. Refusing and failing to meet regularly with other believers corporately calls into question whether someone truly belongs to God. It is not simply a nice thing for Christians to do. It is necessary preparation for the day of judgment.

Hebrews 10:26–31

Outline

  I. Prologue: Definitive and Final Revelation in the Son (1:1–4)

  II. Don't Abandon the Son Since He Is Greater than Angels (1:5–2:18)

  III. Don't Harden Your Hearts Since You Have a Son and High Priest Greater than Moses and Joshua (3:1–4:13)

  IV. Don't Fall Away from Jesus' Melchizedekian Priesthood Since It Is Greater than the Levitical Priesthood (4:14–10:18)

  V. **Concluding Exhortations and Warnings (10:19–12:29)**

    A. Exhortation to Draw Near, Hold Fast, and Help Others (10:19–25)

    B. **Warning: No Hope of Forgiveness for Those Who Turn from Christ (10:26–31)**

    C. Call to Persevere in Faith (10:32–12:3)

    D. Exhortations to Readers to Endure (12:4–29)

Scripture

²⁶ For if we deliberately sin after receiving the knowledge of the truth, there no longer remains a sacrifice for sins, ²⁷ but a terrifying expectation of judgment and the fury of a fire about to consume the adversaries. ²⁸ If anyone disregards Moses' law, he dies without mercy, based on the testimony of two or three witnesses. ²⁹ How much worse punishment do you think one will deserve who has trampled on the Son of God, regarded as profane the blood of the covenant by which he was sanctified, and insulted the Spirit of grace? ³⁰ For we know the One who has said, Vengeance belongs to Me, I will repay, and again, The Lord will judge His people. ³¹ It is a terrifying thing to fall into the hands of the living God!

Context

The larger context of 10:19–12:29 was sketched under the context section of 10:19–25, and we saw that 10:19–12:29 consists of exhortations to the readers in light of the theology of Jesus' Melchizedekian priesthood (7:1–10:18). The three main admonitions in 10:19–25 were: (1) draw near; (2) hold fast; and (3) help others hold fast. Now the author explains why these admonitions are so important. The "for" (γάρ) in verse 26 indicates that the author provides a reason or ground for the exhortations in verses 19–25. If they intentionally turn away from the gospel, then there will be no forgiveness for them (v. 26). Instead they will face the final judgment of God (v. 27). If those who rejected the law of Moses received an earthly punishment, then those who trample on God's Son, consider the covenant blood unclean, and insult the Holy Spirit will face a more severe judgment (vv. 28–29). As the OT says, they will experience God's vengeance and judgment and fall into the hands of the living God (vv. 30–31; Deut 32:35–36).

Exegesis

10:26

After encouraging the readers to draw near and to hold fast to the gospel, the author now warns the readers about the dangers of falling away (see §5).[514] If they turn away from the gospel after being converted, there will be no forgiveness for them. Sinning "deliberately" ('Εχουσίως) doesn't refer to any and every sin committed. The author has in mind apostasy, the rejection of the Christian faith.[515] Those who repent of their evil demonstrate that they aren't guilty of the apostasy warned against here.[516] The author draws on the OT where defiant sin leads to destruction: "But the person who does anything defiantly, whether he is native or an alien, that one is blaspheming the LORD; and that person shall be cut off from among his people" (Num 15:30 NASB; cf. Deut 1:43; 17:12–13; Ps 19:13). The "knowledge of the truth" refers to conversion, to embracing the Christian faith when one is saved (cf. 1 Tim 2:4; 2 Tim 2:25; 3:7; Titus 1:1). If one defiantly turns away from Christ after salvation, there is no sacrifice for their sins. To say there will be no sacrifice for their sins means there will be no forgiveness for them. Levitical sacrifices will not suffice, for the blood of animals can't take away sins (10:4, 11) or perfect the conscience of worshipers (9:9). They only remind people of their sins repeatedly (10:3). And they can't receive forgiveness from Jesus Christ because they have repudiated him. One can't receive forgiveness through the once-for-all offering of Jesus if one defiantly rejects him. Forgiveness only belongs to those who continue to trust in Jesus for forgiveness.

10:27

Those who sin deliberately, renouncing Christ and the gospel, will not be forgiven of their sins. Instead they await a "terrifying expectation of judgment" and a "fire" that will "consume the adversaries." Clearly this refers to the final judgment, to the day when God's enemies will be completely destroyed. The author reaches back into the OT for the language used here. For instance, Zeph 3:8 says, "For My decision is to gather nations, to assemble kingdoms, in order to pour out My indignation on them, all My burning anger; for the whole earth will be consumed by the fire of My jealousy" (cf. also Zeph 1:18). And Isa 26:11 declares, "The fire for Your adversaries will consume them!" (cf. also Isa 64:2). If the readers revert to the

---

[514] The readers haven't fallen away. They are admonished not to do so (rightly O'Brien, *Hebrews*, 374).

[515] L. Johnson says the author does not refer to "a minor transgression, but apostasy" (*Hebrews*, 262). Cf. Lane, *Hebrews 9–13*, 292; O'Brien, *Hebrews*, 374.

[516] Hughes, *Hebrews*, 420.

Levitical cult and turn away from Jesus, they will identify themselves as enemies of the Lord. They will not enter the heavenly city
but will be destroyed forever, for God's "enemies" (ὑπεναντίους) are
always unbelievers (e.g., Gen 22:17; 24:60; Exod 15:7; 32:25; Lev
26:16; Num 10:9; Deut 32:27; Josh 5:3; 2 Chr 1:11; 20:29; 26:13;
Esth 8:13; Nah 1:2; Isa 1:24; 59:18; 63:18).

10:28

The author is fond of comparing and contrasting the Mosaic law
to the new covenant (2:2–3; 4:2; 12:25; cf. 3:1–6). So too, here, he
contrasts the punishments under the Mosaic law with the judgment
that will be meted out to those who reject the revelation through
Jesus Christ. Those who reject the Mosaic law are condemned to
death on the basis of two or three witnesses. The word "disregards"
(ἀθετήσας) should not be understood merely as a violation of the law
of Moses. The verb is used to describe blatant and outright rebellion
(1 Sam 2:17; 1 Chr 2:7; 5:25), representing Israel's apostasy against
the Lord (Isa 1:2; Jer 3:20; 5:11; 9:1; 12:1; 15:16 LXX; Ezek 22:6;
39:23; Dan 9:27 [Th]).[517] In the same way, the Pharisees rejected
God's purpose in Christ (Luke 7:30), and some reject the words of
Jesus' messengers (Luke 10:16; cf. also John 12:48). Paul warns the
Galatians not to reject God's grace by trusting in the law for salvation (Gal 2:21; cf. also 1 Thess 4:8). Every Israelite transgressed the
law, but the death penalty was assigned to those who egregiously
violated what the law mandated (e.g., Num 35:30; Deut 17:2–7).

10:29

The death penalty was meted out to those who transgressed
certain provisions in the Mosaic law. But the death penalty was an
earthly punishment, and a worse punishment awaits those who reject the revelation of God in Jesus Christ. As we have seen so often
in Hebrews, the earthly punishment forecasts and anticipates a heavenly punishment.[518] Furthermore, there is escalation typologically so
the rejection of a greater revelation leads to a greater punishment.

---

[517] Rightly L. Johnson, *Hebrews*, 263.

[518] Gleason actually reads the warning as if the punishment is physical, just as it
was under the old covenant, maintaining that the readers are warned to flee the literal
destruction of Jerusalem. See Randall C. Gleason, "The Eschatology of the Warning
in Hebrews 10:26–31," *TynB* 53 (2002): 97–120. The language used, however, shows
that a greater punishment than earthly judgment is in view. See O'Brien, *Hebrews*,
380n200; Mackie, *Eschatology and Exhortation in Hebrews*, 129–32.

The "worse punishment" is "deserve[d]" (ἀξιωθήσεται), and therefore, the infliction of wrath on those who turn away from Christ and his sacrifice is just and right.

The author emphasizes the heinousness of apostasy with three phrases. First, if they sin deliberately and shun the gospel, they trample under their feet the "Son of God." "The verb recalls the trampling of the temple by the pagans in Maccabean times."[519] Jesus' sonship points to his divinity and his special relationship with God, and Hebrews often designates Jesus as God's Son (1:2–3, 5, 8; 3:6; 4:14; 5:5, 8; 6:6; 7:3, 28). Clearly those who trample Jesus under their feet reject him fully and scorn him. As L. Johnson says, "The full title [Son of God] emphasizes the shocking character of apostasy: it not only falls from grace, it mocks the giver of grace."[520]

Second, they consider "the blood of the covenant" as "profane" (κοινόν). The word "profane" refers to what is unclean in both Judaism (1 Macc 1:47, 62) and the NT (Mark 7:2, 5; Acts 10:14, 28; 11:8; Rom 14:14; Rev 21:27). The author has argued throughout the letter that Jesus' blood secures "eternal redemption" (9:12), cleanses the conscience (9:14; cf. 12:24), removes sin (9:25–26), gives access to God's presence (10:19), and sanctifies (10:29; 13:12). It is the blood of the covenant (cf. 13:20), in the sense that Jesus' death inaugurates and ratifies the new covenant between God and his people, securing forgiveness of sins (8:13). Those who reject Jesus, however, do not seek purification by his blood. They reject his blood as unclean, tossing it aside as one would throw a menstrual cloth into the garbage.

Third, if they reject Jesus, they insult "the Spirit of grace." The Lord promises to "pour out a spirit of grace" on David's house and Jerusalem in the last days so that they will acknowledge the one they pierced (Zech 12:10). The phrase "Spirit of grace" here probably means the Spirit who grants and gives grace (see §4). Again the language is remarkably strong. Those who reject the blood of Jesus do not merely sin against the Spirit. They insult and despise the Spirit. In a culture where honor and shame were so prominent, the horror of the sin is featured. The sin here is another way of

---

[519] Ellingworth, *Hebrews*, 540. The texts listed include 1 Macc 3:45; 4:60.

[520] L. Johnson, *Hebrews*, 264. But it is too specific to say that the author envisions a rejection of Christ's deity (against Hughes, *Hebrews*, 422).

speaking of blaspheming against the Holy Spirit (Matt 12:31–32; Mark 3:29; Luke 12:10) or is manifested in the resistance to the Spirit in Stephen's hearers (Acts 7:51; cf. also Acts 5:3). The author leaves no doubt that apostasy is egregious since it involves rejecting the Son who is greater than Moses (3:1–6).

We should also note that the author speaks of the blood "by which" the readers were "sanctified" (ἡγιάσθη). Here is powerful evidence that those addressed are truly believers, confirming what was argued in 6:4–5, for Jesus' blood sanctifies and sets them apart (cf. 13:12 and 2:11).[521] Jesus by his once-for-all offering "perfected forever those who are sanctified" (10:14). Sanctification here is definitive and positional rather than progressive. It is awkward and unnatural to see a reference to Jesus in the pronoun instead of believers, for it makes little sense to say Jesus was sanctified by his own blood. Jesus is the one who sanctifies in Hebrews (2:11), not the one who is sanctified. Indeed, in chapters 10 and 13 the author clearly states three times that the death of Jesus sanctifies believers (10:10, 14; 13:12). Nor is it persuasive to say that the sanctification is not saving, comparing it to the sanctification under the old covenant (9:13), which only sanctified externally. The argument fails to persuade, for the point in Hebrews is that Jesus' sacrifice stands in contrast to the sacrifices of the old covenant. His sacrifice is effective and truly brings sanctification. To say that his sacrifice only sanctifies externally, like the sacrifices of the old covenant, misses one of the major themes of the letter. Contrary to OT sacrifices, Jesus' sacrifice truly cleanses the conscience.

10:30

Verse 30 supports ("for," γάρ) the notion that those who sin deliberately (v. 26) will receive worse punishment (v. 29). Two citations from the OT are given (Deut 32:35; 32:36). The first quotation seems to be a translation from the MT, for it is closer to the MT than to the LXX. The second citation matches both the LXX and the MT. Both quotations come from the song of Moses (Deut 32:1–43), which rehearses the Lord's goodness and grace to Israel and Israel's

---

[521] The idea that the sanctification is impersonal and thus nonsaving represents a theological imposition on the text and is not a natural reading (against Guthrie, *Hebrews*, 230, 357; Grudem, "Perseverance of the Saints," 177–78). See here the apposite comments of David Peterson, "The Prophecy of the New Covenant in the Argument of Hebrews," *RTR* 38 (1979): 79.

rebellion against the Lord. Those who trample the Son of God under their feet, treat his blood as unclean, and despise the Spirit of grace will face God's vengeance and justice. They will not be forgiven but will be judged by the Lord.[522] The second citation confirms the same thought. The Lord will judge his people if they depart from him. The words "his people" should not be read to say that God's people will not face final judgment even if they depart from him since they are "his people." Those who depart show that they were only God's people phenomenologically, i.e., in appearance only. Of course, the writer isn't saying that the readers have fallen away. The passage consists of a *warning*. The readers must not fall away as Israel did.

10:31

Our world is used to catastrophes and often shrugs off disasters, but the final judgment is a matter of terror. As L. Johnson says, "The final sentence of the admonition is chilling in its simplicity."[523] The word "terrifying" (φοβερόν) was already used in 10:27 about the future judgment. Here the terrible thing is to fall into the hands of the living God. The expression "fall into the hands of" means to come under the power of another.[524] In some contexts falling into the hands of God refers to his mercy (2 Sam 24:14; 1 Chr 21:13; cf. Sir 2:18), but in this context the final judgment is clearly in view. The idea that the author refers merely to the loss of rewards doesn't fit the severity of the language. God is the "living God" (cf. 3:12; 9:14; 12:22), and departing from him is no idle matter. The threat forecasts 12:29, "For our God is a consuming fire." As L. Johnson says about the readers' inclination toward defection: "It is not a game. It is the most ultimate reality, and therefore, quite properly, 'fearful.'"[525]

---

[522] Attridge argues that in the original context of Deuteronomy 32 both of these citations assure Israel that the Lord will vindicate his people, not that he will judge them. Hence he argues that in Hebrews the meaning of the OT is altered (*Hebrews*, 295–96). O'Brien points out three weaknesses in Attridge's argument: (1) the context of Deuteronomy emphasizes that Israel will be judged if it wanders from God; (2) if God vindicates his people who are faithful, he will of necessity judge them if they are not; (3) God's judgment on his enemies in Hebrews also means that he will vindicate those who are faithful (*Hebrews*, 381–82). Cf. also Allen, *Deuteronomy and Exhortation*, 61–62.

[523] L. Johnson, *Hebrews*, 266.

[524] Ibid., 266.

[525] Ibid., 267.

Bridge

In 10:19–25 believers are encouraged to draw near and to hold fast, but here they are threatened and warned about falling away. Believers need to be warned and comforted so that both the carrot and the stick are used as pastoral tools. One can't renounce Christ and still expect to receive forgiveness of sins. The punishment for those who apostatize will be terrifying. The punishment is great because the sin is heinous since it involves trampling the Son of God, scorning his blood, and despising the Holy Spirit. The things of God can't be belittled without horrific consequences. The author lovingly warns the readers about the judgment to come, urging them to avoid it by staying true to their confession.

Hebrews 10:32–39

Outline

   I. Prologue: Definitive and Final Revelation in the Son (1:1–4)
  II. Don't Abandon the Son Since He Is Greater than Angels (1:5–2:18)
 III. Don't Harden Your Hearts Since You Have a Son and High Priest Greater than Moses and Joshua (3:1–4:13)
 IV. Don't Fall Away from Jesus' Melchizedekian Priesthood Since It Is Greater than the Levitical Priesthood (4:14–10:18)
  V. **Concluding Exhortations and Warnings (10:19–12:29)**
    A. Exhortation to Draw Near, Hold Fast, and Help Others (10:19–25)
    B. Warning: No Hope of Forgiveness for Those Who Turn from Christ (10:26–31)
    C. **Call to Persevere in Faith (10:32–12:3)**
      1. **Don't Abandon Confidence but Endure in Faith (10:32–39)**
      2. Description and Examples of Persevering Faith (11:1–12:3)
    D. Exhortations to Readers to Endure (12:4–29)

Scripture

[32] Remember the earlier days when, after you had been enlightened, you endured a hard struggle with sufferings. [33] Sometimes

you were publicly exposed to taunts and afflictions, and at other times you were companions of those who were treated that way. ³⁴ For you sympathized with the prisoners and accepted with joy the confiscation of your possessions, knowing that you yourselves have a better and enduring possession. ³⁵ So don't throw away your confidence, which has a great reward. ³⁶ For you need endurance, so that after you have done God's will, you may receive what was promised. ³⁷ For yet in a very little while, the Coming One will come and not delay. ³⁸ But My righteous one will live by faith; and if he draws back, I have no pleasure in him. ³⁹ But we are not those who draw back and are destroyed, but those who have faith and obtain life.

Context

The exhortation section, which begins in 10:19, can be summarized in two movements thus far. First, the readers are encouraged to draw near to God and to hold fast their confession (10:19–25). Second, they must not sin defiantly and blatantly, repudiating the good news (10:26–31). Now, third, they should remember their fervor for their faith and willingness to suffer for it in the early days of their Christian life (10:32–34). In 10:35–39 the author draws a conclusion from their willingness to suffer in the past: they must hold on to their confidence and continue trusting God until the end.

In considering 10:32–39 more closely, we see that the author reminds his readers that falling away from the living God doesn't fit with the amazing changes that marked their lives in the past (10:32–34). If the readers recall the first days after their conversion, they endured many sufferings (10:32). They faced reproach themselves and identified with those being mistreated (10:33). They showed compassion to prisoners and even responded in joy to the plunder of their possessions since they were looking to their final reward (10:34). After enduring so much in the past, they must not abandon their boldness now and lose their reward (10:35). For they must endure until the end to receive the promise of the final inheritance (10:36). The readers are assured that the day of promise will arrive, for Jesus will come again (10:37). Those who are righteous will trust in him until the end, but those who turn back will not receive God's favor (10:38). The author ends with a word of assurance (10:39). The readers, he is confident, do not belong to the sort of people who fall away and face destruction, but they will exercise faith and enjoy eschatological preservation.

Exegesis

10:32

The aim of the letter is to provoke the readers to persevere. The readers are encouraged (10:19–25) and warned (10:26–31), and here they are summoned to remember the former days, presumably their early days as believers. They should recall their fervor and passion for the Lord and rekindle their enthusiasm for the things of God. Their current sufferings have given them amnesia about how they responded earlier to the difficulties that beset them. The author reminds them of when they were "enlightened" (φωτισθέντες). The same term was used in 6:4, designating the illumination and understanding that dawned on the readers when they first embraced the gospel. In those days they "endured" (ὑπεμείνατε) while suffering. If they endured then, they can endure now, as long as they reignite their devotion that carried them through the "hard struggle" (ἄθλησιν) of their earlier sufferings. The term is used of athletic events where there were contests.[526] The term could also possibly be translated as "challenge."[527] Fortunately, the meaning of the verse is not greatly affected in either case. The readers are faced with a new struggle and challenge. If they stayed true earlier, they can do so again.

10:33

The nature of the sufferings and struggle experienced by the readers in the earlier days are now rehearsed. They were "publicly exposed" (θεατριζόμενοι) to "taunts and afflictions." They didn't hide their faith in Christ or commitment to the gospel, and consequently they were insulted and mistreated by others. They were the victims of verbal abuse and various sorts of discrimination. They were subject to dishonor, disgrace, and insult because of their allegiance to Christ, and such dishonor was difficult to bear in an honor/shame culture.[528] Perhaps they endured "imprisonment, beatings,

---

[526] L. Johnson, *Hebrews*, 268.

[527] Cf. the two entries in LN 50.3 and 74.13.

[528] See especially David Arthur DeSilva, *Despising the Shame: Honor, Discourse and Community Maintenance in the Epistle to the Hebrews*, SBLDS 152 (Atlanta: Scholars, 1995), 146–64.

and deprivation."[529] Not only did they personally endure vituperation and criticism, but they also shared and identified with fellow believers who were treated in the same way. They didn't shrink back from fellow believers out of fear, in the hopes that they could avoid suffering. They boldly claimed as brothers and sisters those who were afflicted, showing their devotion to Christ. The author recalls them to the courage of earlier days so that they will steel themselves to face the sufferings of the present day.

10:34

The afflictions of the readers after their conversion and their positive response to their situation are elaborated upon further. First, they "sympathized with" or "had compassion on" (ESV, NRSV) those imprisoned. This implies that the readers were not themselves imprisoned but were merciful to those who were suffering in such a way. Such an interpretation would fit with 13:3: "Remember the prisoners, as though you were in prison with them." Alternatively, the readers' participation in the sufferings of those imprisoned may be in view. "You suffered along with those in prison" (NIV; cf. NET, NLT). The term for sympathy may express concern for others when one isn't experiencing the same difficulties (cf. 4 Macc 4:13–14, 18, 20; 15:4, 7, 11), but it may also signify the idea of participation in the same sufferings (Heb 4:15). A decision is difficult to make here, but in both instances the believers' solidarity with those persecuted for their faith stands out. They were willing to be exiles while on earth (see §6).

A fascinating window is opened to the lives of the recipients, one we wish were opened even further. After their conversion they accepted the "confiscation" of their "possessions" "with joy." We don't know what precipitated the seizing of their belongings, but what is remarkable is not that their property was plundered but their response to it. They were filled with joy. Here they fulfilled Jesus' command to rejoice when persecuted (Matt 5:12). Their delight in God and Jesus Christ could hardly be more evident. Still there was a reason for their delight. They knew there was something better than their possessions on earth. They looked to their heavenly inheritance, for they knew the new creation that was coming, the heavenly city (11:10, 13–16; 12:22; 13:14), was a "better" and permanent

---

possession. The word "better" (κρείττονα), which has played such a major role in Hebrews, surfaces again. The heavenly possession is better than the earthly one. The believers rejoiced because they knew a greater joy awaited them. Further, they knew that what awaited them was permanent. It was an "enduring (μένουσαν) possession." The same word is used in 13:14 where the author declares, "For we do not have an enduring city here; instead, we seek the one to come." The author wants the readers to recall their spiritual fervor and joy and to reclaim it for present circumstances. They have forgotten about the city to come. They have put too much hope in the city of man and have forgotten about the city of God.

10:35

The author draws a conclusion ("therefore," οὖν) from the readers' willingness in the past to stand forth for Christ and to identify with other believers (10:32–34). They must not "abandon" (NRSV) their "confidence" (παρρησίαν) or "boldness." The exhortation here fits with the central theme of the letter and thus belongs with the other warning passages in the text. The word "confidence" plays a significant role in the letter. They should hold onto their "confidence" until the end (3:6) and should come to the "throne of grace" boldly (4:16). As L. Johnson remarks, the exhortation demonstrates the readers have not yet committed apostasy but are tempted to do so.[530] It is because of Jesus' blood that they are assured that they have bold access to God (10:19). Their confidence was expressed, according to 10:32–34, in their suffering on behalf of Christ, for such suffering is rooted in a boldness willing to go public. If they retain their boldness or confidence, they will receive a "great reward." The "reward" (μισθαποδοσίαν) here is eschatological, and the context shows (cf. especially 10:39) that the reward is eternal life (see §9). Just as Moses was willing to endure "reproach" "because he was looking ahead to his reward" (11:26 NIV), so too the readers must conclude their lives the way they began them to receive the end-time reward.

10:36

The final reward won't be obtained without endurance. They must persevere to the end to be saved. Endurance manifests itself in faithfully doing the will of God. God's will is something believers are summoned to carry out for the entirety of their lives. It isn't

---

[530] L. Johnson, *Hebrews*, 272.

restricted to spasmodic periods where they are energized for God's sake. If they continue to endure, they will receive the promise. "Promise" (ἐπαγγελίαν) here is eschatological, as is often the case in Hebrews. A number of texts are remarkably similar. The readers must not harden their hearts and miss out on the promised rest (4:1). Those who exercise "faith and patience" will "inherit the promises" (6:12 NRSV). The "promise" for believers was an "eternal inheritance" (9:15). The promises given to the patriarchs are ultimately eschatological as well. They did not receive them during their lifetime (11:9, 13, 17), so it is clear the promise is ultimately the heavenly country and city (11:10, 13–16; 12:22; 13:14).[531] Indeed, none of the OT heroes of faith received the promise (11:39), for they will not obtain it apart from believers in Jesus Christ.

10:37

The promise will be realized soon, and the author quotes Hab 2:3–4 to make his point. The first words cited "for a little while" probably come from Isa 26:20.[532] In Isaiah the Lord promises he will come soon and vindicate his people and judge his enemies. Judah must keep trusting the Lord in the midst of their adversity, knowing that the Lord will intervene on their behalf soon. In the same way the readers should realize that their time of being exiles and sojourners (11:13) is brief compared to the unending reward promised to them.

The allusion to Isaiah 26 fits well with the quotation from Hab 2:3. In its historical context Habakkuk refers to the vision he received from the Lord, which consists of the judgment impending on Judah for its refusal to do the will of God (Hab 1:5–17). In Hebrews, however, the author sees the judgment on Judah as typological of the final judgment. In other words there is an escalation between the historical judgment on Judah and the final judgment to come. What is coming in Hebrews, therefore, is not merely the realization of the vision in Hab 2:3 but Jesus himself. Hebrews turns the participle in Hab 2:3 into a masculine substantival participle to clarify that Jesus himself is coming in the future. The final judgment in history will occur when Jesus returns (9:27–28), rewarding those who have been faithful to him and punishing those have not trusted in or

---

[531] The promise here refers to the fulfillment of the promise (so O'Brien, *Hebrews*, 388).

[532] See here Hughes, *Hebrews*, 434.

obeyed him. We do not have a radical reorientation of Habakkuk, for Habakkuk speaks of the coming of God (Hab 3:3, 8), which for NT believers finds its fulfillment in the future coming of Jesus.[533] Though the time may seem long, Jesus is coming soon, and hence believers must endure until that day arrives.

10:38

Since Jesus is coming soon, the readers are exhorted to continue to trust in God and not to shrink back in unbelief. If they shrink back, God will not be pleased with them, and they will face judgment.

The citation of Habakkuk continues with the citation of Hab 2:4. Hebrews reverses the two clauses so they appear in opposite order found in the LXX. The words "and if he draws back, I have no pleasure in him" are not reflected in the MT but follow the LXX. The words "my righteous one shall live by faith" (NIV) are close to both the MT and the LXX, but one significant difference is related to the pronoun "my." The LXX in the Rahlfs edition should be translated as follows: "The righteous one will live by my faithfulness," while the MT reads, "The righteous one will live by his faith (or faithfulness)." Hebrews clearly deviates from the LXX here, avoiding any notion that the faithfulness in view here is God's. Paul, of course, drops the pronoun altogether, rendering the text, "The righteous shall live by faith" (Rom 1:17 ESV; Gal 3:11).

Jesus is coming soon, but those who belong to God, those who are righteous before him, live by faith. It is clear the author refers to "faith" here and not merely "faithfulness," for verse 38 is part of the introduction to chapter 11, which emphasizes how faith is necessary to receive the final reward. True faith, of course, inevitably leads to faithfulness, and hence the two, though they can be distinguished conceptually, are inseparable in the lives of believers. It is persevering faith that saves, not just a one-time decision, for if one turns back from trusting, then God will not delight in him. Those who turn away from trusting God will not enjoy his pleasure but will experience his anger. They will face judgment rather than salvation.

10:39

Now the author expresses confidence in his readers. They won't shrink back and face God's displeasure. The noun "draw back" (ὑποστολῆς) is picked up from the verb "draws back" (ὑποστείληται)

---

[533] O'Brien, *Hebrews*, 388.

in verse 38. Those shrinking back don't merely lose a reward. They are "destroyed." The word for "destroyed" (ἀπώλειαν) is regularly used for the eschatological destruction awaiting unbelievers (Matt 7:13; John 17:12; Acts 8:20; Rom 9:22; Phil 1:28; 3:19; 2 Thess 2:3; 1 Tim 6:9; 2 Pet 2:1, 3; 3:7, 16; Rev 17:8, 11). The converse of drawing back, as is also the case in verse 38, is faith. The author is confident the readers will continue to believe until the end. And they will "obtain life." More literally, they will "preserve (περιποίησιν) their souls" (ESV). The expression means they will be "saved" (NIV, NRSV),[534] and this is clear since it stands in contrast to the "destruction" (ἀπώλειαν) threatened in the first part of the verse.

Bridge

The author wants his readers to remember the past and to look forward to the future. Apparently they were dispirited and discouraged by their present circumstances. So the author says, remember the past, and your willingness to endure criticism and mistreatment for the sake of the gospel. He reminds them of their solidarity with other Christians who suffered. The readers have not only forgotten the past, but they have ceased to look forward to the future. In the past they rejoiced when their property was stolen because they were looking toward the future, to the heavenly city that was coming. They had lost sight of the city of God because they were becoming ensnared in the trials that beset them in the city of man. The readers can be filled with fresh joy if they recall their past fervor and look forward to their future joy.

The writer doesn't want the readers to give way now. They have shown such devotion to the Lord and his people (10:32–34; cf. 6:9–10). He wants them to keep enduring to receive the final reward of eternal life. They must not draw back and quit believing, for that is the way to destruction and final ruin. Even though the readers are exhorted sharply, the author is convinced they will keep believing and enjoy eternal salvation. He is confident the warnings will be a means God uses to keep them trusting and believing until the end.

---

[534] So Koester, *Hebrews*, 463.

Hebrews 11:1–2

Outline

I. Prologue: Definitive and Final Revelation in the Son (1:1–4)

II. Don't Abandon the Son Since He Is Greater than Angels (1:5–2:18)

III. Don't Harden Your Hearts Since You Have a Son and High Priest Greater than Moses and Joshua (3:1–4:13)

IV. Don't Fall Away from Jesus' Melchizedekian Priesthood Since It Is Greater than the Levitical Priesthood (4:14–10:18)

V. **Concluding Exhortations and Warnings (10:19–12:29)**

  A. Exhortation to Draw Near, Hold Fast, and Help Others (10:19–25)

  B. Warning: No Hope of Forgiveness for Those Who Turn from Christ (10:26–31)

  C. **Call to Persevere in Faith (10:32–12:3)**

    1. Don't Abandon Confidence but Endure in Faith (10:32–39)

    2. **Description and Examples of Persevering Faith (11:1–12:3)**

      a. **Nature of Faith (11:1–2)**

      b. Creation Through Noah (11:3–7)

      c. The Faith of Abraham and His Heirs (11:8–22)

      d. The Faith of Moses and Those Entering the Land (11:23–31)

      e. A Closing Catalog of Faith (11:32–40)

      f. Run the Race Looking to Jesus as Supreme Exemplar of Faith (12:1–3)

  D. Exhortations to Readers to Endure (12:4–29)

Scripture

[1] Now faith is the reality of what is hoped for, the proof of what is not seen. [2] For our ancestors won God's approval by it.

Context

In popular circles Hebrews 11 is often disconnected from the rest of the letter, but it fits with the exhortation section which begins in 10:19. We have seen in 10:19–39 that the author encourages the believers to hold fast and warns them of the danger of falling away. Chapter 10 ends with a call to faith. Those who believe will enjoy eschatological life, but those who shrink back will be destroyed. Chapter 11 is tucked into the exhortation section of the letter by highlighting the nature and character of saving faith. It should be said, however, that chapter 11 itself does not constitute an exhortation but provides examples that serve the exhortation.[535] The writer illustrates the nature of that faith by giving many examples of such faith in the OT.[536] Earlier in the letter the author encourages the readers to imitate those who "inherit the promises through faith and perseverance" (6:12). The examples conclude in chapter 12 with Jesus as the supreme exemplar of faith. The readers must keep believing to be saved on the last day, and they should follow the example of faith set by OT saints and by Jesus to receive final salvation.

L. Johnson captures well the literary impact of the chapter. "Part of the section's dramatic impact comes from the way it begins in such a leisurely fashion, lingering over named figures, with an emphasis on God's promises and rewards, and then builds toward an ever more rapid recitation of hardships suffered by unnamed forebears in the faith."[537]

The author begins by explaining how faith behaves. Faith is confident and sure that what is hoped for will be given; it is assured that what is promised but unseen will come true (v. 1). It is this kind of faith, trusting in what has not yet been seen or given that gave OT ancestors favor before God (v. 2).

Exegesis

11:1

Verse 1 explains the nature of faith, not by completely defining faith but by explaining how faith works. Despite the hesitation of

---

[535] Cf. Cockerill, *Hebrews*, 518. At the end of the day, the difference isn't great, for the examples and exposition are included to motivate the readers to action (Guthrie, *Structure of Hebrews*, 40).

[536] Such example lists were common in both Greco-Roman and Jewish circles. The Jewish background is particularly important (cf. Sirach 44–50; Wisdom 10). Cf. here Cockerill, *Hebrews*, 516. For further discussion of the matter, see Michael R. Cosby, *The Rhetorical Composition and Function of Hebrews 11: In Light of Example Lists in Antiquity* (Macon, GA: Mercer University Press, 1988).

[537] L. Johnson, *Hebrews*, 275. For an excellent study of the literary features and impact of chapter 11, see Cosby, *Rhetorical Composition and Function of Hebrews 11*.

many commentators, a definition of faith, even though partial, is found here.[538] Faith is assured that what is hoped for will become a reality. It is convinced that the unseen promises of God will be fulfilled.

Many scholars dispute this reading of the verse, and they propose an alternate reading. The alternate reading is reflected in the HCSB, "Now faith is the reality of what is hoped for, the proof of what is not seen." The word "reality" (ὑπόστασις) here is translated "confidence" (NIV, NLT) or "assurance" (ESV, NRSV) by other translations.[539] Those who support the translation reflected in the HCSB argue that the word used here (ὑπόστασις) never has the idea of subjective confidence or assurance. For example, BDAG says that confidence "must be eliminated, since examples of it cannot be found."[540] It seems, however, that this judgment is too rash, for the word denotes confidence in Ps 38:8 in the LXX, and the Hebrew word here means "hope" (תּוֹחַלְתִּי) as well.[541] We see the same phenomenon in Ezek 19:5 where the term (ὑπόστασις) renders another Hebrew word for "hope" (תִּקְוָתָהּ). It also seems that the word "confidence" coheres well in 2 Cor 9:4 and 11:7. I argued earlier that such a reading fits with Heb 3:14 also. We have evidence, then, that "confidence" and "assurance" are in the semantic range of the word used here.[542] Most important, "confidence" or "assurance" fit the context of chapter 11. The author concluded chapter 10 by emphasizing the need for persevering faith. The OT ancestors in chapter 11 are saluted because of their trust in God's promises, even when there was no evidence that the promises would come to pass. So the traditional rendering of 11:1 actually accords best with the context of chapter 11.

This should not be interpreted to say that the objective view is entirely without merit, for the subjective and objective meanings are

---

[538] Cf. Koester, *Hebrews*, 479 ("a definition was not expected to be comprehensive but to enhance an argument"); Attridge, *Hebrews*, 307–8.

[539] For a discussion of the various options, see Attridge, *Hebrews*, 308–10. For strong defenses of the objective reading, see Lane, *Hebrews 9–13*, 325–26, 328–29; O'Brien, *Hebrews*, 398–400; Cockerill, *Hebrews*, 520–21.

[540] BDAG. Cf also LN 58.1.

[541] For an excellent discussion of the verse (where it is recognized that the subjective sense could be correct, though it is ultimately rejected), see L. Johnson, *Hebrews*, 277–79.

[542] Cf. especially Richardson, *Pioneer and Perfecter of Faith*, 120–25.

tied together here. Koester rightly captures this in saying: "The subjective side emerges when *hypostasis* is linked with 'faith,' which pertains to the believing person. The objective side emerges when *hypostasis* is connected to 'things hoped for,' since the object of hope lies outside the believer."[543]

A subjective meaning is also suggested in the next line. Even BDAG, which says there is no evidence for the meaning "confidence" or "assurance" in the first line, says the second phrase means "to be sure (ἔλεγχος) about things unseen."[544] A subjective sense for the Greek word here (ἔλεγχος) matches the notion of confidence or assurance in the first line. Faith is convinced that what God promises will most certainly be fulfilled.[545] What is unseen is not completely defined in terms of future promises, for the unseen also describes past realities, such as creation (11:3), or present realities, such as God's existence (11:6, 27), his faithfulness (11:17), and power (11:19).[546]

11:2

Faith and confidence in God's promises are important, for the ancestors recorded in the OT gained approval for their faith, and the writer is about to give us a litany of those ancestors in the forthcoming verses. The word translated "won approval" (ἐμαρτυρήθησαν) often has this meaning (Acts 6:3; 10:22; 16:2; 22:12; 1 Tim 5:10; 2 John 3:12). In the context of Hebrews 11, the author means they won approval before God. Clearly, the author's desire is for the readers to imitate the example of their illustrious ancestors so they will obtain favor before God on the last day.

Bridge

We don't have a dissertation on faith here that is unrelated to the rest of the letter. Faith is introduced because the flip side of apostasy

---

[543] Koester, *Hebrews*, 472.

[544] Other scholars insist that the word means "proof" and that any subjective sense is lacking (Attridge, *Hebrews*, 310; F. Büchsel, "ἔλεγχος," *TDNT* 2:476; Käsemann, *Wandering People*, 41–42; Koester, *Hebrews*, 473), but the meaning of the phrase must be discerned in context.

[545] Richardson rightly argues that the word group has the idea of being convicted and that the notion of being convinced in one's conscience is plausible (*Pioneer and Perfecter of Faith*, 125–28).

[546] Rightly Attridge, *Hebrews*, 311.

is faith. The author doesn't ask the readers to look to themselves and to summon up all their energy to persevere until the end. What it means to endure is to keep trusting God until the end. Endurance comes when we look to God for strength and put our trust in his promises. Faith means we put our trust in what God has promised, even if those promises seem impossible to us. Chapter 11 reminds us that we are not the first to take this journey; many have walked this path ahead of us, and thus we are not alone in our journey of faith.

Hebrews 11:3–7

Outline

I. Prologue: Definitive and Final Revelation in the Son (1:1–4)
II. Don't Abandon the Son Since He Is Greater than Angels (1:5–2:18)
III. Don't Harden Your Hearts Since You Have a Son and High Priest Greater than Moses and Joshua (3:1–4:13)
IV. Don't Fall Away from Jesus' Melchizedekian Priesthood Since It Is Greater than the Levitical Priesthood (4:14–10:18)
V. **Concluding Exhortations and Warnings (10:19–12:29)**
   A. Exhortation to Draw Near, Hold Fast, and Help Others (10:19–25)
   B. Warning: No Hope of Forgiveness for Those Who Turn from Christ (10:26–31)
   C. **Call to Persevere in Faith (10:32–12:3)**
      1. Don't Abandon Confidence but Endure in Faith (10:32–39)
      2. **Description and Examples of Persevering Faith (11:1–12:3)**
         a. Nature of Faith (11:1–2)
         b. **Creation Through Noah (11:3–7)**
         c. The Faith of Abraham and His Heirs (11:8–22)
         d. The Faith of Moses and Those Entering the Land (11:23–31)
         e. A Closing Catalog of Faith (11:32–40)
         f. Run the Race Looking to Jesus as Supreme Exemplar of Faith (12:1–3)
   D. Exhortations to Readers to Endure (12:4–29)

Scripture

³ By faith we understand that the universe was created by God's command, so that what is seen has been made from things that are not visible. ⁴ By faith Abel offered to God a better sacrifice than Cain did. By faith he was approved as a righteous man, because God approved his gifts, and even though he is dead, he still speaks through his faith.

⁵ By faith Enoch was taken away so he did not experience death, and he was not to be found because God took him away. For prior to his removal he was approved, since he had pleased God. ⁶ Now without faith it is impossible to please God, for the one who draws near to Him must believe that He exists and rewards those who seek Him. ⁷ By faith Noah, after he was warned about what was not yet seen and motivated by godly fear, built an ark to deliver his family. By faith he condemned the world and became an heir of the righteousness that comes by faith.

Context

The author writes to encourage his readers to hold on to their faith (10:19–25) so that they don't fall away (10:26–31). They must continue to trust until the end to receive the final reward (10:32–39). In chapter 11 the author provides numerous OT examples of those who trusted in God until the end. Faith holds onto God's promises and believes that what is unseen will be realized. Faith understands that the world was created by the word of God (v. 3). Abel's faith, in contrast to Cain's unbelief, commended him as righteous (v. 4). Enoch was pleasing to God because he trusted in God, and God spared him from death (v. 5). Abel pleased God, even though he died, and Enoch pleased God and didn't die.[547] Both Abel and Enoch anticipate the message of Hebrews 11 as a whole.[548] As Cockerill says, "All, like Abel, will die without the fullness of what God has promised. All, like Enoch, are promised triumph over death,"[549] The author pauses to reflect on the importance of faith (v. 6). One can't please God without it, for to please him one must believe he exists and rewards those who seek him. Noah's faith also stands out (v. 7).

---

[547] Cf. here Lane, *Hebrews 9–13*, 335.

[548] Cf. Cockerill, *Hebrews*, 526.

[549] Ibid., 526.

He believed in what wasn't yet visible when God pronounced judgment on the world. He stood out from the world in preparing an ark for the rescue of his family so that he too was righteous by his faith.

Exegesis

11:3

The author now begins to give examples of faith, beginning with creation (see §7). No one observed the creation, and what happened at the inception of the world can't be verified or reproduced in laboratories. Believers "understand" and comprehend "by faith" that the world was "created" (κατηρτίσθαι) or "formed" (NIV) or "prepared" (NRSV) by the word of God (cf. Pss 73:16; 88:8; Rom 9:22).[550] Here the writer reflects on Genesis 1 where God speaks and his word is effective in that what he speaks becomes a reality so that the things in the world come into existence (Gen 1:3, 6–7, 9, 11, 14, 15, 20–21, 24, 26–27). We find a similar notion in Ps 33:6, "The heavens were made by the word of the LORD" (cf. Ps 148:5).

The result clause could be taken in various ways. The HCSB (cf. also NRSV) rendering indicates that the visible world derives from invisible "things": "so that what is seen has been made from things that are not visible."[551] This could be read to say that visible realities derive from "real things," namely, the word of God.[552] The problem with this reading is that the invisible things are plural (ἐκ φαινομένων) and the word of God is singular.[553] Nor is it likely that the author refers to the earth submerged by the chaos described in Gen 1:2,[554] for the earth though covered was still part of what was visible, and we shouldn't separate the earth and the chaos in the creation narrative (Gen 1:1–2:3).

The NIV and ESV take the negative with the infinitive: "so that what is seen was not made out of what was visible." Grammatically, the ESV and NIV readings are preferable, for it is more likely that the negative modifies the infinitive "made" (γεγονέναι) instead of the prepositional phrase "out of things that are visible" (ἐκ

---

[550] Both psalm texts are from the LXX.

[551] Cf. Attridge, *Hebrews*, 315–16.

[552] So Koester, *Hebrews*, 474; Ellingworth, *Hebrews*, 569; O'Brien, *Hebrews*, 401–2. On this view the negative "not" (μή) modifies the participle "visible" (φαινομένων).

[553] Adams, "Cosmology of Hebrews," 128.

[554] Ibid., 127–28.

φαινομένων).[555] The interpretation favored here fits nicely with what the author is doing in this chapter. The creation of the world is a miracle, and it doesn't derive from preexisting material.[556] Creation out of nothing can't be demonstrated empirically (though neither can the contrary!), and it is embraced by faith (see §1).

11:4

The author moves from creation to Abel and Cain. Abel brought a "better sacrifice" than Cain because of his faith (Gen 4:3–5). What is remarkable is that Genesis says nothing about Abel's faith. It simply records what he did. Perhaps Genesis signals the acceptability of Abel's sacrifice in that he offered "the firstborn of his flock and their fat portions," whereas Cain did not offer what was best from his crops (Gen 4:4).[557] But how does the author of Hebrews see faith when Genesis is silent on the matter? It seems that any act of obedience that pleases God (cf. 11:8 below) flows from faith (cf. the discussion on 3:12–4:11 as well). The wellspring of obedience is always an attitude of trust. It follows, then, that the fundamental sin of Cain was unbelief. His offering was not accepted because he didn't trust in God.

Abel was approved by God as righteous. The author considers here the words of Gen 4:4: "The LORD had regard for Abel and his offering." Such regard shows that Abel was righteous in God's sight, though Hebrews emphasizes that such righteousness stems from his faith. In this regard Hebrews matches Paul's teaching that righteousness is by faith. Abel's gifts were the visible expression of his faith, documenting and ratifying the authenticity of his faith. Abel no longer lives, but his faith lives after him, commending him as an

---

[555] So Lane, *Hebrews 9–13*, 326–27; Hughes, *Hebrews*, 443. For the alternative, see Ellingworth, *Hebrews*, 569.

[556] It is difficult to discern here whether the author argues for creation out of nothing (see Philip E. Hughes, "The Doctrine of Creation in Hebrews 11:3," *BTB* 2 [1972]: 164–77; Lane, *Hebrews 9–13*, 332). It seems to me that this is the best option, but it is difficult to be certain.

[557] Cf. L. Johnson, *Hebrews*, 280; Richardson, *Pioneer and Perfecter of Faith*, 170. Against Walter L. Moberly, who thinks the MT offers no rationale for the preference of Abel's offering ("Exemplars of Faith in Hebrews 11: Abel," in *The Epistle to the Hebrews and Christian Theology*, ed. R. Bauckham, D. R. Driver, T. A. Hart, and N. MacDonald [Grand Rapids, MI: Eerdmans, 2009], 356–58).

example to the present day.[558] The readers of Hebrews should derive inspiration from Abel and follow his example of trusting God.

11:5

Enoch is cited as the next example of faith (Gen 5:21–24). According to Genesis Enoch was 65 years old when his son, Methuselah, was born. Enoch "walked with God" (5:22, 24) for 300 years after Methuselah was born. When Enoch was at the age of 365, God removed him from the earth so that Enoch never died.

Hebrews interprets the story for us. The author concentrates on the fact that Enoch didn't die, mentioning it five different times and in different ways in the verse. The writer did not expect the readers to escape death, and so his point is to see an analogy between the reward given to Enoch and the reward promised to believers. Just as Enoch escaped from death altogether, the readers will finally triumph over death when they are raised from the dead. What was remarkable about Enoch was that he "pleased" (εὐαρεστηκέναι) God. The author draws on the LXX, for the MT speaks of Enoch walking with God. Enoch pleased God, however, by virtue of his faith. His trust in God spurred him to walk with God and to do what was pleasing to him. Clearly the author emphasizes that God rewarded Enoch by sparing him from death,[559] reminding the readers that it is "worth it" to serve the Lord. Perhaps the author also forecasts here the exaltation of Jesus. Just as Enoch was rewarded for his faith, so too Jesus was rewarded by being enthroned by God.[560]

11:6

The indispensability of faith is explained. One cannot please God without faith. Again, the conception seems close to what we find in Pauline theology (cf. Rom 14:23). Human beings are summoned to put their faith in God, entrusting the entirety of their lives to his lordship and love. God is pleased with faith because if he is trusted he is also loved, for trust in God cannot flourish without believing that he is good.

Two comments are made about faith here. First, faith is grounded upon the object of faith. One won't draw near to God unless one believes God exists. Such belief in God is fundamental and basic,

---

[558] Rightly O'Brien, *Hebrews*, 403–4; Richardson, *Pioneer and Perfecter of Faith*, 172.

[559] So L. Johnson, *Hebrews*, 282.

[560] So Richardson, *Pioneer and Perfecter of Faith*, 176–77.

but it is scarcely sufficient. Belief in God is a necessary but not a sufficient condition. One must also believe God "rewards those who seek him." Trust in God will not exist if there isn't any benefit. It believes God "is powerfully active on behalf of the faithful in the present."[561] If the readers truly trust God, they won't depart from Christ and lose the reward of eternal life (10:35). Moses chose to suffer with the people of God because he set his hope on the reward (11:26). The readers are invited to trust in God because ultimately it will bring them the most pleasure. They will "drink from the river of your delights" (Ps 36:8 NRSV).

11:7

Noah functions as the next example in the author's portrait of faith. God instructed Noah about what was not yet seen, informing him that the entire world would be destroyed by a flood (Gen 6:13–18). Noah exercised faith and thus was persuaded that what was not yet seen would become a reality. We have already seen that faith rests in and is convinced by the unseen promises of God (11:1). Faith can't "see" how the world was created but trusts that God made all things. Noah had no conception of the torrent of destruction that would descend on the world, but he believed in what God said even though he had never beheld it. In the same way the readers should look to the unseen and believe that what God promised would be realized.

In "godly fear" (εὐλαβηθείς) Noah believed what God said, and since he was convinced a judgment was coming, he constructed an ark for the deliverance (σωτηρίαν) of his household. The readers should imitate Noah, for deliverance for them is not just physical but relates to whether they will enter the heavenly city. Noah condemned the world by his faith because he showed that he trusted God, had given himself to God, and belonged to God. He didn't give himself over to evil as the culture of his day had. He submitted his will to God. And thus he received a right relationship with God "that comes by faith" (ESV). The world was condemned because it wasn't rightly related to God, and its inhabitants weren't rightly related to God because they didn't trust in him or obey him.[562] On the other

---

[561] Cockerill, *Hebrews*, 531.

[562] Hence, there isn't any notion here of Noah preaching to his contemporaries (O'Brien, *Hebrews*, 408; Cockerill, *Hebrews*, 533).

hand, the inheritance described here may not fit the "Pauline" category sketched in above.[563] Perhaps Noah received the inheritance in part at his death (12:23) and will enjoy its fullness on the final day (10:25). The author would be emphasizing, then, that Noah receives the kingdom promised to believers (12:28). Another possibility is that the author conceives of the postflood world as the inheritance Noah received. It was, so to speak, a new world that was purified and restored. If this last option is preferred, the author of Hebrews would see the inheritance given to Noah as anticipating the future kingdom (12:28) and the heavenly city (11:10–16; 12:22; 13:14).

Bridge

Faith looks to what is unseen, trusting in the promise of God. Faith isn't irrational. It believes in a God who truly created the world, who rescued Enoch from death and Noah from the flood. But faith doesn't see these things from the beginning. It believes God will reward those who seek him. It trusts God, as Abel did, even though death is the immediate consequence. Faith doesn't rely on the contemporary events or perceptions but puts its trust and hope in the word of God and in his promises for his people.

Hebrews 11:8–22

Outline

   I. Prologue: Definitive and Final Revelation in the Son (1:1–4)
  II. Don't Abandon the Son Since He Is Greater than Angels (1:5–2:18)
 III. Don't Harden Your Hearts Since You Have a Son and High Priest Greater than Moses and Joshua (3:1–4:13)
 IV. Don't Fall Away from Jesus' Melchizedekian Priesthood Since It Is Greater than the Levitical Priesthood (4:14–10:18)
  V. **Concluding Exhortations and Warnings (10:19–12:29)**
    A. Exhortation to Draw Near, Hold Fast, and Help Others (10:19–25)

---

[563] For a good discussion of the various options, see Richardson, *Pioneer and Perfecter of Faith*, 179–83.

B. Warning: No Hope of Forgiveness for Those Who Turn
from Christ (10:26–31)

C. **Call to Persevere in Faith (10:32–12:3)**

  1. Don't Abandon Confidence but Endure in Faith
  (10:32–39)

  2. **Description and Examples of Persevering Faith
  (11:1–12:3)**

    a. Nature of Faith (11:1–2)

    b. Creation Through Noah (11:3–7)

    c. **The Faith of Abraham and His
    Heirs (11:8–22)**

    d. The Faith of Moses and Those Entering the Land
    (11:23–31)

    e. A Closing Catalog of Faith (11:32–40)

    f. Run the Race Looking to Jesus as Supreme
    Exemplar of Faith (12:1–3)

D. Exhortations to Readers to Endure (12:4–29)

Scripture

⁸ By faith Abraham, when he was called, obeyed and went out
to a place he was going to receive as an inheritance. He went out,
not knowing where he was going. ⁹ By faith he stayed as a for-
eigner in the land of promise, living in tents with Isaac and Jacob,
co-heirs of the same promise. ¹⁰ For he was looking forward to
the city that has foundations, whose architect and builder is God.
¹¹ By faith even Sarah herself, when she was unable to have children, received power to conceive offspring, even though she was
past the age, since she considered that the One who had promised
was faithful.

¹² Therefore from one man—in fact, from one as good as
dead—came offspring as numerous as the stars of heaven and as
innumerable as the grains of sand by the seashore. ¹³ These all
died in faith without having received the promises, but they saw
them from a distance, greeted them, and confessed that they were
foreigners and temporary residents on the earth. ¹⁴ Now those who
say such things make it clear that they are seeking a homeland.
¹⁵ If they were thinking about where they came from, they would
have had an opportunity to return. ¹⁶ But they now desire a better place—a heavenly one. Therefore God is not ashamed to be

called their God, for He has prepared a city for them. [17] By faith Abraham, when he was tested, offered up Isaac. He received the promises and he was offering his unique son, [18] the one it had been said about, Your seed will be traced through Isaac. [19] He considered God to be able even to raise someone from the dead, and as an illustration, he received him back. [20] By faith Isaac blessed Jacob and Esau concerning things to come. [21] By faith Jacob, when he was dying, blessed each of the sons of Joseph, and he worshiped, leaning on the top of his staff. [22] By faith Joseph, as he was nearing the end of his life, mentioned the exodus of the Israelites and gave instructions concerning his bones.

Context

The exhortation section begins with a summons to keep clinging to Christ and to avoid falling away (10:19–31). The readers must not throw away their boldness but continue to trust in God until they receive the final reward (10:32–39). In chapter 11 the author illustrates the character of the faith that saves. Faith puts its confidence in God's promises that are not yet seen (11:1). By such faith the ancestors of old gained approval (11:2), whether one thinks of Abel (11:3–4), Enoch (11:5–6), or Noah (11:7). All of them pleased God. Verses 8–22 reflect on the faith of Abraham and his heirs. By faith Abraham left his homeland even though he didn't know what land was promised to him (11:8). Abraham, Isaac, and Jacob lived in the land of promise as exiles (11:9). They received strength to live as sojourners because they looked forward to the city of God (11:10). By faith Abraham and Sarah trusted in the promise of offspring, which would be as numerous as the stars of heaven (11:11–12). Still, Abraham, Isaac, and Jacob did not see the promises fulfilled and lived as exiles (11:13). It was clear from this that they were seeking a heavenly homeland (11:14–15). On account of this, God was pleased to be their God and has prepared a city for them (11:16). Abraham offered up Isaac in faith, trusting that God would raise him from the dead if necessary (11:17–19). Isaac, Jacob, and Joseph also exercised faith, for they looked forward to the future and were confident that God would fulfill his promises (11:20–22). Faith, as this section particularly emphasizes, trusts God for the future. It looks to him for a future reward.

Exegesis

11:8

The parade of faith continues, and Abraham naturally follows Noah. The author reflects on Gen 12:1 (NASB), "Now the LORD said to Abram, 'Go forth from your country, and from your relatives and from your father's house, to the land which I will show you.'" And we read in Gen 12:4, "So Abram went." Hebrews summarizes what occurred in the words, "By faith Abraham, when he was called, obeyed." It is obvious that he obeyed, but Hebrews adds that Abraham's obedience flowed from his faith. It is clear from what the writer tells us here that Abraham's first act of faith did not take place in Gen 15:6, even though Gen 15:6 is the first time we are told that Abraham believed. He dared to leave his homeland only because he trusted in God. Such a comment does not contradict Paul's declaration that Abraham was justified by faith in appealing to Gen 15:6 (Rom 4:3; Gal 3:6). In fact, it confirms what Paul teaches, showing that faith is the root and obedience is the fruit.

Abraham was promised a land (Gen 12:1), which would be his inheritance (11:8), but he wasn't told the location of the land when he set out.[564] He trusted that God would reveal the place of his inheritance and that God would give it to him. Faith, the author instructs the readers, does not see the end at the beginning. Faith always trusts in the promises of God, even when it looks as if they won't be fulfilled. The readers should do the same: they must cast themselves entirely on God and believe he will give them the final inheritance.

11:9

When Abraham arrived in the land, he didn't take immediate possession. Indeed, he didn't possess it at all! It seemed as if God's promise wasn't true. He lived in the land as a sojourner and as an exile (cf. Gen 17:8; 20:1; 21:34; 24:37; 1 Chr 16:19). He didn't establish a domicile but lived as a shepherd in tents, constantly on the move. And life was the same for Isaac and Jacob. They didn't possess the land during their lifetimes either. They too lived as sojourners traveling from place to place in the land (Gen 26:3; 37:1; 47:9). Even though the promise was not realized in their lifetime, they clung to the promise.

---

[564] We see here the future orientation of faith. So Attridge, *Hebrews*, 322.

11:10

How could Abraham keep trusting God when the promise of land wasn't being realized? The author argues that he was anticipating something in the future, something greater than the earthly land of Canaan. He was looking forward to the coming of a city, and this city will have "foundations," i.e., it is an unshakable city. The promise of a city hearkens back to OT promises about Jerusalem, which we are told will be secure in the future (Isa 33:20; 54:11–12; cf. Ps 87:1–3). The expectation of a new Jerusalem in the future is also found in Second Temple Judaism (*2 Bar.* 4:1–7; *4 Ezra* 13:36; *T. Dan.* 5:12; *Sib. Or.* 5.420–33), and is present elsewhere in the NT (Gal 4:26; Phil 3:20; Rev 21:1–22:5). Nothing can shatter or displace this city. A similar thing is said about the kingdom in 12:28; it is "a kingdom that cannot be shaken." The city can't be dislodged, for its "architect and builder is God."[565] No human being can overthrow the city of God. The city of man is temporary, but the city of God is eternal. We see again the typology of the writer. The land of Canaan points to something greater, something more profound and lasting than any location on earth. It points to the city of God. Abraham began to realize that there was something greater than Canaan awaiting him, that he would inherit the city of God.

11:11

Most versions understand Sarah to be the subject of the main verb.[566] However, the meaning of the verse is contested.[567] The alternate interpretation is captured by the NRSV, "By faith he [Abraham] received power of procreation, even though he was too old—and Sarah herself was barren—because he considered him faithful who had promised."[568] According to the NRSV and other interpreters,

---

[565] The words "architect" and "builder" are roughly synonymous here (see L. Johnson, *Hebrews*, 290).

[566] For this reading see, p[13vid], ℵ, A, D², M, Augustine. In defense of Sarah as the subject, see L. Johnson, *Hebrews*, 291–92; Hughes, *Hebrews*, 472–75. In defense of the notion that Hebrews is not anti-women, see Carl Mosser, "No Lasting City: Rome, Jerusalem and the Place of Hebrews in the History of Earliest 'Christianity'" (Ph.D. diss., St. Andrews University, 2004), 245–52.

[567] My discussion of the verse is largely dependent upon the work of L. Johnson, *Hebrews*, 291–92.

[568] In this case Sarah herself, being barren, is construed as dative (Bruce, *Hebrews*, 299–302; Attridge, *Hebrews*, 324–26; Ellingworth, *Hebrews*, 586–88). Or the reference to Sarah is parenthetical (Koester, *Hebrews*, 488). Lane sees it as a concessive

Abraham is the subject instead of Sarah. The most important reason for seeing a reference to Abraham is the expression the "power of procreation" (δύναμιν εἰς καταβολὴν σπέρματος), literally "the power for laying down of seed." The activity described here fits with what men do rather than women.[569] On this reading Abraham received the ability to produce sperm that could beget children even when he was an old man. If Abraham is the subject, the phrase about Sarah could be construed as a dative, which could be translated "with Sarah herself who was barren." Or possibly the feminine participle "being" (οὖσα) is implied, so the verse says Abraham received the ability to procreate even though Sarah was barren.[570] Seeing Abraham as the subject is also supported because the words "from one man" in 11:12 are clearly limited to Abraham. It is also noted that Sarah did not have faith in giving Hagar to Abraham in Genesis 16 and laughed in disbelief when the angel of the Lord told her she would have a son (Gen 18:9–12).

Despite the arguments supporting Abraham as the subject, the subject is probably Sarah for the following reasons. First, "Sarah" is clearly nominative in Greek, and there is no textual evidence for the dative. Inserting the implied participle "being" (οὖσα) seems like an unlikely solution, for it isn't evident that the participle is elided in reading the verse, and thus the best solution grammatically is to accept Sarah as the subject. Second, Sarah may have laughed in disbelief when initially hearing the promise, but Abraham probably disbelieved in the case of Hagar and Ishmael as well (Genesis 16) and also laughed when hearing the promise (Gen 17:17). Ultimately they both ended up believing despite initial doubts. Third, the role of the one man in verse 12 doesn't preclude Sarah's participation and faith in having children.[571] Fourth and finally, the most difficult problem is the expression about laying down seed. The phrase could be understood as a purpose clause so that Sarah receives the sperm produced by Abraham and conceives. Alternatively, the language of

---

clause (*Hebrews 9–13*, 344–45). Ellingworth says that Lane's proposal "attains coherence at the cost of almost intolerable strain on the Greek sentence structure" (*Hebrews*, 587).

[569] See Thayer; BDAG.

[570] The participle would be understood as concessive.

[571] Incidentally, in Jewish tradition women also contributed seed necessary for conception (Ellingworth, *Hebrews*, 587; F. Hauck, "καταβολή," *TDNT*, 3.621n3).

laying down seed should not be pressed and is not used technically here. The author speaks generally of the ability to bear children.

In either case the gift of having children is due to faith on the part of both Abraham and Sarah. The God who promised that they would have children (Gen 12:2; 15:1–6; 17:5–6, 15–21; 18:10–14) was considered to be faithful, and the miraculous took place.

11:12

Therefore (διό), because of Abraham's faith in the promise of God, many offspring were born through him. Having so many descendants was a miracle, for Abraham was as good as dead in terms of his ability to produce offspring. God, however, does what is astonishing, and he particularly works when it seems as if his promise will not be realized. Isaiah 51:2 is alluded to here: "Look to Abraham your father, and to Sarah who gave birth to you in pain. When I called him, he was only one; I blessed him and made him many."[572] Hence, Abraham's offspring were as many as the stars in the sky and the sand on the seashore. The wording here is close to Gen 22:17, and the author clearly appeals to this text (cf. also Gen 15:5). The readers should not faint in their faith, for if they read the OT, they are reminded that God fulfills his promises, but he often does so at a time and in a place that one doesn't expect. Abraham thought Ishmael was the fulfillment of the promise (Gen 17:15–21), but God fulfilled his promise by giving Isaac to Abraham and Sarah. The fulfillment came, however, when they least expected it. Still, at the end of the day, they believed God could and would do what he had pledged.

11:13

On the one hand God fulfills his promises. On the other hand the patriarchs died without seeing the promises fulfilled in their fullness. They had children but certainly not as many as the stars of the sky. They were "foreigners and temporary residents on the earth" (cf. Gen 23:4; cf. Ps 39:12; see §6), and yet they didn't lament their social status but "confessed" that they didn't live in the land as citizens but as exiles. The two terms for exiles here shouldn't be distinguished in this context.[573] The patriarchs didn't die with cynicism and disbelief, even though they didn't possess the land of Canaan.

---

[572] So Ellingworth, *Hebrews*, 590.
[573] L. Johnson, *Hebrews*, 292.

Instead, they died in faith, as those who didn't receive the promises. Nevertheless, they "saw" (ἰδόντες) the promises with the eyes of faith.[574] They didn't shut their eyes to reality, for they recognized that the realization of the promises was "far away" (πόρρωθεν). They didn't pretend the promises were fulfilled, and yet they knew God was faithful.[575] They "welcomed" (NIV, ἀσπασάμενοι) the promises, in the sense that they knew they would eventually come to pass. The author wants his readers to see the parallels. They may feel in their current distress that God isn't fulfilling his promises, but a long view reveals that God is always faithful to his word.

11:14

Those who acknowledge that they are sojourners and exiles and strangers on earth make clear that they are seeking a different "homeland" (πατρίδα). If their hope was on earth, they wouldn't long for a domicile that was heavenly. Again this is the word for the readers as well. Their inheritance is heavenly and eschatological. Currently they are resident aliens, and they are awaiting the inheritance to come.

11:15

The patriarchs demonstrated that they didn't long for any earthly land, for when they were exiles and sojourners in Canaan, they could have returned to the land of their origin. Abraham could have gone back to Ur or Haran, and he also stubbornly insisted that his servant never take Isaac back to such a place (Gen 24:6).[576] Jacob could have stayed with Laban instead of returning to Canaan. Their actions indicated their devotion and commitment to the Lord. The readers, on the other hand, are tilting in the other direction. They are tempted to go back to Judaism to enjoy the comfort and security of this world. Judaism was a legal religion in the Roman empire, and they may have been inclined to move in this direction to avoid

---

[574] Bockmuehl rightly observes that faith does not glory in blindness per se. The point is that believers don't see now what God has promised, but they *see* from afar what he has promised by faith. See Markus Bockmuehl, "Abraham's Faith in Hebrews 11," in *The Epistle to the Hebrews and Christian Theology*, ed. R. Bauckham, D. R. Driver, T. A. Hart, and N. MacDonald (Grand Rapids, MI: Eerdmans, 2009), 369–71.

[575] The author says in 6:15 that Abraham received the promise, but he referred there to the promise regarding Isaac, and here in Heb 11:13 the focus is on the promise of the land (Attridge, *Hebrews*, 329).

[576] O'Brien, *Hebrews*, 421.

persecution. Or perhaps they wanted tangible assurance that their sins were forgiven through the concrete and repeated activity of the Levitical cult. They may have justified such a move by saying they were returning to the faith of their fathers. But actually, according to the author, their ancestors didn't look backward but forward. They didn't put their trust in an earthly city but a heavenly one, and the readers should follow the example of Abraham, Isaac, and Jacob.

11:16

The patriarchs were animated by new desires and were fueled with godly longings. They desired a "better" homeland. The word "better" (κρείττονος) plays a major role in Hebrews: Jesus is better than angels (1:4); Melchizedek is better than Abraham (7:7); Jesus brings in a "better hope" (7:19) and a "better covenant" (7:22; 8:6) because he offered "better sacrifices" (9:23); Jesus' blood is "better" than Abel's (12:24). And fitting with this verse in particular, believers anticipate a "better possession" (10:34), and OT saints a "better resurrection" (11:35) and "something better" along with new covenant believers (11:40). The better homeland is the "city" God has prepared for his people. God is the builder of this city (11:10), and it is a heavenly city (12:22). The earthly city of man forecasts a far better heavenly city, the city of God (13:14). In the same way John comforts his readers with the promise of the heavenly city to come (Rev 21:1–22:5).

The promise of a heavenly city is rooted in the OT where there are stunning promises for Jerusalem. We find prayers and promises regarding the future of Jerusalem (Pss 51:18; 122:6; 128:5; 137:5–6; 147:2; Isa 30:19; 33:20; 52:1, 9; Dan 9:25; Joel 3:1, 20; Zeph 3:16–17; Zech 1:14; 2:2, 4, 12; 8:4, 15; 9:9; 12:2–3, 6, 8–10), so that the Lord will "reign as king on Mount Zion in Jerusalem" (Isa 24:23). Jerusalem will be the center of the universe (Isa 2:3; Mic 4:2; cf. Jer 3:17; Zech 8:22; 14:16–17), holy (Isa 4:3–4; Joel 3:17; Zech 8:3), forgiven (Zech 13:10), comforted (Isa 66:13), safe (Jer 33:15; Zech 14:11–12), joyful (Isa 65:18), and blessed marvelously by God (Isa 62:1–12; Zech 1:17). What the OT says about the earthly Jerusalem is fulfilled in the heavenly Jerusalem according to Hebrews. This fits with the earthly-heavenly pattern so often observed in Hebrews. And it also accords with the nature of typology in Hebrews, so that there is escalation from the earthly city to the heavenly city.

Since the ancestors longed for a heavenly homeland and city, and heaven is the residence of God, it is evident they longed for God more than they desired any of the things of this world. Since they longed for God in such a way, he is not ashamed to be called their God. Dwelling in God's presence is their greatest desire, and thus God is not ashamed to be identified as their God. Indeed, he has prepared for them a heavenly city so they may reside with him forever. The author commends the same for his readers. Their desires should not be for earthly comforts but God's heavenly presence, and they should recognize that if they endure in faith and hope until the end that God has prepared a city for them.

11:17

The author turns to one of the most significant events in the OT, Abraham's sacrifice of Isaac (Genesis 22). The author notes that God "tested" Abraham, and the narrative in Gen 22:1 begins with the words, "After these things God tested Abraham." Abraham received promises from God, which pledged to him land, offspring, and blessing (Gen 12:1–3; 13:14–16; 15:4–5, 16; 17:5–6, 15–21; 18:18; 21:10–12; 22:16–18). Central to these promises was the promise of offspring, and the texts cited above make clear that the promise would become a reality through Isaac, not Ishmael. In this sense Isaac was "the unique son" (τὸν μονογενῆ) of Abraham, or as the NIV puts it, his "one and only son." The promises couldn't be fulfilled, however, if Abraham sacrificed Isaac, for the promises couldn't be fulfilled through just any son of Abraham. They were guaranteed to *this son*, to Isaac. Hence, the Lord's command to Abraham didn't make much sense. It contradicted everything God had said. Nevertheless, Abraham trusted God by carrying out his instructions. Abraham had received the promises from God, and thus he did what God commanded, even though it contradicted what God had promised.

11:18

The author confirms that the promises were uniquely and exclusively given to Isaac. He cites Gen 21:12, and the citation matches the LXX exactly. Here we have the story where Sarah wants to evict Ishmael from the house because he was mocking and deriding Isaac (21:9–10). Abraham was grieved and didn't want to carry out his wife's command (Gen 21:11). God, however, confirmed Sarah's word. Abraham must follow her instruction, for the promise will be given through Isaac, not Ishmael. Interestingly, Paul cites the identical account to make the same basic point in both Rom 9:7 and Gal 4:30. In Genesis 17, when the Lord promises Abraham and Sarah a son, Abraham isn't really interested (vv. 15–18). He was satisfied with the promise becoming a reality through Ishmael. But the Lord rejected Abraham's perspective. Though he promised to bless Ishmael, his covenant would be with and through Isaac alone (vv. 19–21). The promises, then, must be secured through Isaac, and yet God demanded that Abraham sacrifice him. If the readers are doubting God, if their circumstances make them wonder if they will receive the final reward, the author reminds them of Abraham's situation. It seemed as if God were contradicting and nullifying his own promise!

11:19

Faced with such a daunting situation, Abraham didn't doubt God's promise. He remained convinced that God would fulfill his promise *through Isaac*. By that point in his life, he had seen God's faithfulness in delivering him repeatedly. For instance God rescued his wife from the clutches of Pharaoh and Abimelech (Gen 12:10–20; 20:1–18). When Abraham trusted God and let Lot choose the "best" land for himself, Abraham actually got the better land, and Lot ended up in Sodom, which was destroyed (Genesis 13). When Abraham attempted to rescue Lot with a paltry number of men (318) against kings who had just won a major victory against many other kings, he succeeded (Gen 14:1–24). And most striking of all, God had given Abraham and Sarah the power to procreate. Isaac was their miracle child born long after the time of childbearing (Gen 17:14–17; 18:9–15; 21:1–7). So Abraham didn't doubt God's pledge that the promises would be fulfilled through Isaac. He was convinced that if he sacrificed Isaac, God would raise him from the dead and fulfill his promises through a miracle. The narrative in Genesis bears out this reading. We read in Gen 22:5, "Then Abraham said to his young men, 'Stay here with the donkey. The boy and I will go over there to worship; then we'll come back to you.'" The words of the narrative here are not incidental or accidental; they are included for a reason. Abraham was convinced that Isaac would return.[577] Somehow and in some way God would fulfill his promise through Isaac.

---

[577] Rightly Hughes, *Hebrews*, 484; O'Brien, *Hebrews*, 424.

Isaac functions, then, as "an illustration" (παραβολῇ) or type or figure of the resurrection of the Son of God, Jesus Christ.[578] Abraham, so to speak, received Isaac back from the dead, but that event anticipated another Son and another Father. In the latter instance the Father actually handed over and sacrificed his Son, and the Son gladly and willingly gave his life for the salvation of his brothers and sisters (2:10–18). Those who obey God are always rewarded, and thus the Father raised his Son from the dead. Isaac's return typologically points to and anticipates that greater resurrection. The readers, like Abraham, are called on to trust God, even when it looks as if everything conspires against the fulfillment of the promise. God's word always comes true, even if it takes a resurrection to bring it to pass. For if God fulfilled his promise to Abraham and was faithful to Jesus, he would be faithful to them as well.

11:20

Faith looks to the future, trusting God that the future will turn out well because God is always faithful to his promises (see §7). The author considers Isaac's blessing of both Jacob (Gen 27:27–29) and Esau (Gen 27:39–40). In both instances Isaac was confident God would fulfill his promises to them in the future. Isaac relied on the same promises as Abraham and was confident God would grant him offspring, land, and universal blessing in accord with the covenant he enacted with Abraham.

11:21

The future-oriented character of faith continues in Jacob's life. Like Isaac, Jacob blessed his sons when he was old. In fact, Jacob was near death. But he didn't view his death as a contradiction or refutation of God's promises, for he prophesied about what God would do in the future in the life of Joseph's sons (Gen 48:1–22). In the MT of Gen 47:31, Jacob gives thanks "at the head of his bed," while in the LXX he worships at the top of his staff. Hebrews clearly follows the LXX here, quoting the exact words found there. It is possible to vocalize the Hebrew so the reference is actually to Jacob's staff. On the other hand, there is evidence that Jacob was in fact in bed (Gen 48:2; 49:33). In either case the main point of the verse is the same: faith looks to the future and trusts in God's promises.

---

[578] Cf. Lane, *Hebrews 9–13*, 363.

11:22

The faith of Joseph is similar to what is said about Isaac and Jacob. When we think about all that could be commented on in the life of Isaac, Jacob, and Joseph, it is remarkable that in every case the author reflects on what they said in their old age or when they were on their deathbed. He doesn't comment on anything these people *did* in their lives that manifested faith. Instead, he zeros in on what they *said*, and how they prophesied about the future when they were about to die. In every case they continued to believe in the promises at their death, even when it became apparent they wouldn't be fulfilled in their lifetimes. Joseph at his death (Gen 50:24–25) reminds his hearers about the promised exodus of Israel. God will deliver Israel from Egypt and bring them to Canaan, and Joseph wants his bones to be brought with them. Joseph is in effect saying that Egypt is not his home. Canaan is his home. The lesson for the Hebrews is clear. Like Joseph they should be looking forward to and trusting in what God will do in the future. He will certainly deliver his people. Furthermore, their home is not on earth. Even though Joseph was a ruler in Egypt, he recognized that he was an exile, that his true home was Canaan. So too, the readers should recognize that their true home is the heavenly city; and like Isaac, Jacob, and Joseph they should trust God's promises even in death.

Bridge

The author highlights here that faith trusts in God for the future. Abraham left Ur even when he didn't know where God was calling him to live. Abraham, Isaac, and Jacob died without seeing the promises realized in their fullness, but they didn't mock the promises of God or dismiss them as fantasies. They trusted that God had a heavenly homeland for them, a heavenly city. So too, when the Lord summoned Abraham to sacrifice Isaac, he didn't shrink back in unbelief. He continued to believe that God would fulfill his promises through Isaac and came to the conviction that God would raise him from the dead if need be. So too, Isaac, Jacob, and Joseph on their deathbeds didn't see God's promises fulfilled; but they spoke about the future in confidence and faith, convinced God would do what he said. Faith trusts God for the future and believes, no matter how improbable it seems, that God will fulfill what he promised.

Hebrews 11:23–31

Outline

I. Prologue: Definitive and Final Revelation in the Son (1:1–4)

II. Don't Abandon the Son Since He Is Greater than Angels (1:5–2:18)

III. Don't Harden Your Hearts Since You Have a Son and High Priest Greater than Moses and Joshua (3:1–4:13)

IV. Don't Fall Away from Jesus' Melchizedekian Priesthood Since It Is Greater than the Levitical Priesthood (4:14–10:18)

V. **Concluding Exhortations and Warnings (10:19–12:29)**

    A. Exhortation to Draw Near, Hold Fast, and Help Others (10:19–25)

    B. Warning: No Hope of Forgiveness for Those Who Turn from Christ (10:26–31)

    C. **Call to Persevere in Faith (10:32–12:3)**

        1. Don't Abandon Confidence but Endure in Faith (10:32–39)

        2. **Description and Examples of Persevering Faith (11:1–12:3)**

            a. Nature of Faith (11:1–2)

            b. Creation Through Noah (11:3–7)

            c. The Faith of Abraham and His Heirs (11:8–22)

            d. **The Faith of Moses and Those Entering the Land (11:23–31)**

            e. A Closing Catalog of Faith (11:32–40)

            f. Run the Race Looking to Jesus as Supreme Exemplar of Faith (12:1–3)

    D. Exhortations to Readers to Endure (12:4–29)

Scripture

²³ By faith, after Moses was born, he was hidden by his parents for three months, because they saw that the child was beautiful, and they didn't fear the king's edict.

²⁴ By faith Moses, when he had grown up, refused to be called the son of Pharaoh's daughter ²⁵ and chose to suffer with the people of God rather than to enjoy the short-lived pleasure of sin. ²⁶ For he considered the reproach because of the Messiah to be

greater wealth than the treasures of Egypt, since his attention was on the reward. [27] By faith he left Egypt behind, not being afraid of the king's anger, for Moses persevered as one who sees Him who is invisible. [28] By faith he instituted the Passover and the sprinkling of the blood, so that the destroyer of the firstborn might not touch the Israelites. [29] By faith they crossed the Red Sea as though they were on dry land. When the Egyptians attempted to do this, they were drowned. [30] By faith the walls of Jericho fell down after being encircled by the Israelites for seven days. [31] By faith Rahab the prostitute received the spies in peace and didn't perish with those who disobeyed.

Context

As noted previously, 10:19 begins a long exhortation section in which the readers are exhorted to keep holding fast, to stay true to Christ, and to persevere in faith until the end so they receive the final reward (10:19–39). Chapter 11 provides illustrations of the faith that receives the final reward. We found in verses 3–7 that faith pleases God, that it sees what is invisible, and that those who exercise faith walk with God and are righteous before him. Verses 8–22 feature the future character of faith, focusing particularly on future promises of blessing that will be given to those who are the Lord's. Verses 23–31, on the other hand, emphasize that faith trusts in God even during suffering. Faith believes it will be rewarded, even if it is currently opposed by the world.

Faith in the midst of suffering is evident in the life of Moses. For example, Moses' parents courageously spared their child's life even when threatened by Pharaoh (v. 23). Moses could have enjoyed the luxury and privilege of being part of Pharaoh's household (v. 24), but he chose to suffer with the people of God instead of enjoying the temporary pleasures of this world (v. 25). He took such a stand because he looked to the future reward that awaited him (v. 26). So too, Moses showed faith in leaving Egypt despite the threats of Pharaoh (v. 27) and expressed his faith by observing the Passover to spare the firstborn in Israel (v. 28). Israel, when confronted by the danger of the Red Sea, crossed it by faith (v. 29), though the Egyptians were destroyed by it. Conquering Jericho was an impossible task, and the walled city was a great danger to Israel, but the walls of the city fell when Israel put their trust in God (v. 30). Finally, Rahab demonstrated that she did not live for the sake of the city of man (Jericho) but for the city of God. She courageously welcomed the Israelite spies and escaped destruction herself (v. 31).

Exegesis

11:23

The author continues to rehearse examples of faith in the history of Israel. We are not surprised to discover that Moses is considered for several verses. The story summarized here follows closely Exod 2:2–3. At the time Moses was born, Pharaoh demanded that Hebrew boys be slain at birth by casting them into the Nile (Exod 1:22). Moses' parents, however, saw the beauty of their child and hid him for three months. What is perhaps most interesting is the author's comment on the story, for he concludes that Moses' parents "didn't fear the king's edict." I noted in the context section above that what links the accounts together in 11:23–31 is how people exercised faith when they were suffering. Presumably the author recounts this story because his readers were fearful of trusting in the Lord and of doing anything that might set them at cross purposes with authorities who could injure them, and thus he sets forth Moses' parents as an example of doing what was right when they would be prone to act in fear.

11:24

In verses 24–29 the faith of Moses himself takes center stage. Verses 24–27 consider Moses' faith that impelled him to align with the people of Israel, while verses 28–29 relate the faith that propelled him to lead Israel out of Egypt. Verse 24 considers the status of Moses. He was the adopted son of Pharaoh's daughter (Exod 2:4–10). Growing up as a son of privilege, he enjoyed all the luxuries of life and the status of belonging to the first family in Egypt. Moses, however, didn't rely on his nobility or his stature. He trusted in God instead and renounced his claim as the son of Pharaoh's daughter.

11:25

Moses' faith was not passive. He sided with Israel, with his people, over against the Egyptians. The author probably refers to Moses' slaying of the Egyptian taskmaster who was beating a Hebrew (Exod 2:11–12). Such an action, even if it was mistaken in some respects, wasn't merely a temporary fit of temper. It signaled where Moses' loyalties were, demonstrating that he associated himself with the people of God rather than with the Egyptians. By siding with the Israelites, Moses renounced the pleasures and joys of Egypt with all its luxuries and comforts. The author acknowledges that sin may bring intense delight and pleasure. Still such pleasures are temporary and evanescent, and Moses recognized that the enjoyment of sin is fleeting.[579]

11:26

Moses' choice should not be considered ultimately as an example of self-denial. He considered the "reproach" (ὀνειδισμόν) he suffered for the sake of the Christ to be "greater wealth than the treasures of Egypt." The "wealth" was the "reward" (μισθαποδοσίαν) he would certainly receive in the future. Moses rejected temporary pleasures and looked to future and eternal riches instead. It is fascinating that the author says Moses suffered the reproach of the Christ since nothing is said about the Messiah in the story. According to NT writers, the promises of redemption and for a king in Israel find their fulfillment in Jesus himself. He is the prophet who is better than Moses (3:1–6; Deut 18:15–22). He is the king promised in the Pentateuch (Gen 17:6, 16; 35:11). The scepter promised to Judah belongs to Jesus (Gen 49:10), and he is the star from Jacob who carries the scepter (Num 24:17) and who will crush the enemies of the Lord (Num 24:17–18). We have already seen as well that the author can take the words of Psalm 102 that refer to the Lord and apply them to Jesus Christ (Heb 1:10–12). It seems that he does something similar here. The reproach Moses suffered for God's sake is attributed to Jesus Christ.

Referring to the reproach of Christ makes the story relevant for the readers as well. The author wants them to suffer for Christ's sake. He also wants them to be like Moses. He can understand and sympathize with their desire for the comforts of the present world. Persecution wasn't a pleasant prospect. The author observes that Moses didn't relish suffering either. The pleasures of sin are real, and following that pathway can bring remarkable delights. But such delights are temporary and fleeting. Far better to join Moses and to

---

[579] L. Johnson argues that the reference is not to the temporary pleasures of sin but the temporary advantages of sin (*Hebrews*, 300). The word can have either meaning, and the overall meaning is not greatly affected in either case.

look to the future reward, a permanent reward that will bring happiness that will never be revoked.

11:27

Moses renounced the joys of Egyptian power and put to death the Egyptian abusing the Hebrew slave (Exod 2:11–12). He became fearful when it was clear that what he did was spreading round the country (Exod 2:14). Pharaoh, upon learning about the slaying, tried to kill Moses, but Moses fled to Midian (Exod 2:15). After reading Exodus, the author's comments on the incident are puzzling, for he says that Moses was not "afraid of the king's anger," when it seems plain from Exodus that he was fearful. One way to solve the conundrum is if the leaving here refers to the later account of the exodus with all of Israel.[580] On that occasion Moses left without fearing Pharaoh. Such a reading is possible, and it would solve our problem.[581] It is possible that the author refers to "a general category (the departure) that contains within it several specific incidents."[582]

It is also possible the author refers to Moses' departure after slaying the Egyptian (Exod 2:15). The chronological order in which the writer recounts the events supports this interpretation.[583] If one adopts this reading, it is difficult to believe the author was unaware of Moses' fear noted in Exod 2:14, for he is well acquainted with the OT and often cites it verbatim. The problem is similar in some ways to his putting the altar of incense inside the most holy place. Indeed, there is some recognition of fear in Hebrews, for otherwise a reason for Moses' departure would be absent. If this interpretation is correct, perhaps the author suggests that Moses' fear was not the ultimate reality in his life. Yes, he feared dying, but at a deeper level he trusted that God would protect him and that his life would be preserved. He persevered through his trial as if he saw the one who can't be seen.[584] The author desired the same for his readers.[585] They

---

[580] Westcott, *Hebrews*, 373.

[581] So O'Brien, *Hebrews*, 434; Cockerill, *Hebrews*, 574–75.

[582] L. Johnson, *Hebrews*, 302 (though Johnson doesn't endorse this view as necessarily correct).

[583] So Bruce, *Hebrews*, 321–22; Hughes, *Hebrews*, 497–500.

[584] In defense of a qualitative reading of the participle "sees" (ὡς ὁρῶν), see O'Brien, *Hebrews*, 434.

[585] Lane suggests that Moses overcame his initial fear and trusted in God's unseen promises (*Hebrews 9–13*, 375).

should see that the unseen one was protecting them, that just as he preserved Moses from danger, so he will preserve them. The author doesn't promise that they will escape death as Moses did. He pledges instead that they will receive the final and better reward even if they surrender their lives.

11:28

The Passover, of course, is one of the signature events in Israelite history (Exodus 12). The Lord put to death all the firstborn in Egypt (Exod 11:5–6; 12:12, 29–30), but he "passed over" and spared those who applied the blood of a lamb to their house (Exod 12:13, 22–23). The Passover celebration commemorates Israel's liberation from Egypt, signifying their day of freedom. Observing the Passover was an act of faith on Moses' part. He trusted God regarding both judgment and redemption. By trusting God and applying the Passover blood, the firstborn in Israel escaped destruction.

11:29

Israel was frightened when, upon fleeing from Egypt, they came face-to-face with the Red Sea (Exod 14:3–13). The Egyptians regretted letting them go and now pursued them with vengeance. The Lord then dried up the sea, and Israel walked through on dry ground (Exod 14:16, 21–22, 29). When the Egyptians followed after them, the waters surged over them, and they perished (Exod 14:23–28). Israel risked its life going into the Rea Sea, but they did so because they believed the Lord would rescue them and he would fight for them against the Egyptians (Exod 14:14). The readers, like the Israelites and like Moses (Exod 14:15), were fearful, and yet if they would trust in the Lord, they would be delivered.

11:30

From Israel's escape and redemption from Egypt, the author moves to the first battle in the conquest: the battle of Jericho (Joshua 6). The battle plan was singularly strange. Israel was to march around the city for six days (Josh 6:3, 6–14). On the seventh day Israel was instructed to march around the city seven times, and while doing so, the priests were to blow on trumpets (Josh 6:4, 15–16). At the end of the march, they were called on to give a loud shout at the "prolonged blast of the horn" (Josh 6:5, 20). The wall collapsed and then Israel took the city. Joshua says nothing about the people's faith in taking the city, but following such an unorthodox battle plan evidenced the faith of Israel, for no one conquers ene-mies with such a "military strategy."

11:31

The destruction of Jericho is intertwined with the story of Rahab's preservation. When the Israelite spies came to Jericho, Rahab hid them from the men of Jericho and informed them how they could escape safely (Joshua 2), and thus Rahab and all who were in her house were spared when the city was destroyed (Josh 6:22–25). It was never forgotten that Rahab was a prostitute, but she was a prostitute who was delivered from her evil, for she trusted in the Lord and gave herself to him. We have a hint here that a sordid past does not preclude one from enjoying forgiveness and a future reward. Her faith manifested itself in believing in the Lord's word (Josh 2:9–11) and in sending away the spies in peace. Rahab is an-other person who trusted in the Lord in a time of danger. How im-probable it seemed that a ragtag army could defeat the walled city of Jericho, and yet Rahab exposed herself to danger in concealing the spies. Mosser may be right in seeing Rahab as the climactic example in chapter 11.[586] She represents someone who was willing to leave her own society and culture and to align herself with the people of God. In other words she functions as a model for the readers since she was willing to go "outside the camp" (13:13) and to suffer the reproach of being identified with the people of God.

Bridge

Whether it was Moses' parents, Moses himself, the battle of Jericho, or Rahab, we see that faith considers God trustworthy in a time of danger. Faith recognizes that God will deliver and rescue his own, just as he rescued Moses from Pharaoh, Israel at the Red Sea, Israel at the battle of Jericho, and Rahab from the leaders in Jericho. Faith takes risks and ventures on God. It doesn't look to society and culture for approval. It trusts in the word of the Lord instead of finding its delight in a life of sin. We again see here the future character of faith. When Moses and Israel and Rahab put their trust in the Lord, they had not yet seen what he would do. Faith came first

---

[586] See Carl Mosser, "Rahab Outside the Camp," in *The Epistle to the Hebrews and Christian Theology*, ed. R. Bauckham, D. R. Driver, T. A. Hart, and N. MacDonald (Grand Rapids, MI: Eerdmans, 2009), 384–404.

and deliverance later. That was the situation of the readers as well. They were not part of the inner circle of society. They were verbally abused and discriminated against. Perhaps worse sufferings would follow. They wanted to enjoy the security and comfort of belonging. The author summons them to trust in God, believing he would deliver them and bring them to the heavenly city.

Hebrews 11:32–40

Outline

I. Prologue: Definitive and Final Revelation in the Son (1:1–4)
II. Don't Abandon the Son Since He Is Greater than Angels (1:5–2:18)
III. Don't Harden Your Hearts Since You Have a Son and High Priest Greater than Moses and Joshua (3:1–4:13)
IV. Don't Fall Away from Jesus' Melchizedekian Priesthood Since It Is Greater than the Levitical Priesthood (4:14–10:18)
V. **Concluding Exhortations and Warnings (10:19–12:29)**
   A. Exhortation to Draw Near, Hold Fast, and Help Others (10:19–25)
   B. Warning: No Hope of Forgiveness for Those Who Turn from Christ (10:26–31)
   C. **Call to Persevere in Faith (10:32–12:3)**
      1. Don't Abandon Confidence but Endure in Faith (10:32–39)
      2. **Description and Examples of Persevering Faith (11:1–12:3)**
         a. Nature of Faith (11:1–2)
         b. Creation Through Noah (11:3–7)
         c. The Faith of Abraham and His Heirs (11:8–22)
         d. The Faith of Moses and Those Entering the Land (11:23–31)
         e. **A Closing Catalog of Faith (11:32–40)**
         f. Run the Race Looking to Jesus as Supreme Exemplar of Faith (12:1–3)
   D. Exhortations to Readers to Endure (12:4–29)

Scripture

³² And what more can I say? Time is too short for me to tell about Gideon, Barak, Samson, Jephthah, David, Samuel, and the prophets, ³³ who by faith conquered kingdoms, administered justice, obtained promises, shut the mouths of lions, ³⁴ quenched the raging of fire, escaped the edge of the sword, gained strength after being weak, became mighty in battle, and put foreign armies to flight. ³⁵ Women received their dead—they were raised to life again. Some men were tortured, not accepting release, so that they might gain a better resurrection, ³⁶ and others experienced mockings and scourgings, as well as bonds and imprisonment.

³⁷ They were stoned, they were sawed in two, they died by the sword, they wandered about in sheepskins, in goatskins, destitute, afflicted, and mistreated. ³⁸ The world was not worthy of them. They wandered in deserts and on mountains, hiding in caves and holes in the ground. ³⁹ All these were approved through their faith, but they did not receive what was promised, ⁴⁰ since God had provided something better for us, so that they would not be made perfect without us.

Context

The great faith chapter appears in the midst of an exhortation section (10:19–12:29) where the author encourages the readers to continue believing until the end and not to fall away (10:19–39). The heroes of faith are introduced so the readers will imitate them and continue believing until the end (11:1–40). Faith is assured that God's promises will be realized even if they are not visible to the human eye (11:1–2). Faith trusts God for the future, and those who believe live in a way that is pleasing to God (11:3–7). Verses 8–22 particularly emphasize that faith looks to God for one's future reward. Abraham, Isaac, and Jacob trusted God's promises even when it seemed humanly impossible for them to be fulfilled. In verses 23–31 the future character of faith continues to be underlined, but here the author emphasizes the centrality of faith when life is difficult.

In the last section of chapter 11, the author realizes the list could keep going on forever, so now he summarizes the rest of the OT and later Jewish tradition (vv. 32–40). In verses 32–35a he focuses on the great exploits of those who exercised faith. The text turns a corner in verses 35b–38, for here the sufferings and afflictions of those who believed are rehearsed. Verses 39–40 consider the whole chapter and the relationship between the ancestors in faith and the readers. There is a framing device in that the author returns to the introduction in 11:2, which affirms that the ancestors were approved because of their faith (11:39). Still they did not receive what was promised. Their faith was forward looking. Believers of the present age, after the cross and resurrection, have "something better," and the ancestors were not perfected apart from NT believers (11:40).

Exegesis

11:32

The words "And what more can I say?" signal that the writer could keep going, but he has abbreviated what he could say. After all, he has stopped with Rahab, and he could have appealed to many more characters in the OT. He recognizes that time and space preclude a detailed exposition. The author lists some of those who could serve as examples of faith, but he doesn't list them in chronological order, for Barak (Judges 4–5) precedes Gideon (Judges 6–8), and Jephthah (Judges 11–12) precedes Samson (Judges 13–16), and Samuel (1 Samuel 1–28) precedes David (1 Samuel 16–2 Samuel 24). Perhaps the writer lists first in every instance the character whom he considered to be more significant. The category "prophets" includes many persons, showing that the discussion could go on for a long time indeed.

One of the striking features of the list is the weakness and sins of those identified as people of faith. Barak wasn't courageous enough to go to battle without Deborah (Judg 4:8). Asking for signs demonstrated Gideon's lack of faith (Judg 6:36–40), and he also made an ephod that catapulted Israel to sin (Judg 8:24–27). Samson's sexual infidelities and impulsive acts are infamous (Judges 13–16). Jephthah foolishly vowed to sacrifice his own daughter (11:30–31, 34–40). It is harder to find blemishes in Samuel, but his sons didn't turn out well, and he appointed them as judges anyway (1 Sam 8:1–3). David committed adultery with Bathsheba and murdered Uriah (2 Samuel 11). Still it is not the sins and faults of these men that are remembered (he doesn't mention the faults of any of them!) but their faith and trust in God, showing that perseverance in faith for the author is not the same thing as perfection. Indeed one may sin dramatically and still persevere in faith. We think of Samson as an example here. The narrator in Judges suggests that the Lord had not abandoned him, despite his dalliance with Delilah, for we are told "his hair began to grow back after it had been shaved" (Judg 16:22). And when Samson put his hands on the pillars, he could do nothing if the Lord were not with him (Judg 16:25–30). The story of Delilah illustrates that when the Lord wasn't with him he was useless. Samson died trusting in the Lord, despite all his foibles.

11:33

Faith trusts in what cannot be seen, but it produces effects in the real world. Faith shows up and manifests itself in concrete ways. Hence faith conquers "kingdoms." He has in mind the victory of Barak over Sisera (Judges 4–5) and Gideon's faith to triumph over Midian when his army was incredibly small and the odds of victory were against him (Judges 6–8). In addition Jephthah triumphed over the Ammonites (Judges 11–12), Samson performed many exploits against the Philistines (Judges 13–16), and Samuel won a significant victory over the Philistines (1 Samuel 7). David, of course, won many battles both as a warrior and as the king of Israel.

Administering "justice" (δικαιοσύνην) was the responsibility of the judges and of kings. The judges weren't kings, but judges like Samuel were responsible to see that what was right and true was practiced in Israel. David, as king, particularly had that responsibility, for one of the main functions of leaders was to see that justice was done in Israel (2 Sam 8:15; 1 Chr 8:14).[587]

The promises given to these men focused especially on victory over their enemies. Barak was promised victory over Sisera's forces (Judg 4:6–7). The angel of the Lord promised Gideon that he would triumph over Midian (Judg 6:12–16). Promises were made that Samson would begin to save Israel from the Philistines (Judg 13:5). David received many promises, including being anointed as king (1 Sam 16:13) and receiving the promise of a dynasty (2 Samuel 7).[588]

Another exploit was shutting "the mouths of lions." Samson tore apart a lion with his bare hands (Judg 14:6–7). David slew lions threatening his flock (1 Sam 17:34–36). Most strikingly lions

---

[587] David may be particularly in view here (Attridge, *Hebrews*, 348).

[588] God's relationship with Israel began with the promises made to Abraham (Gen 12:1–3, etc.).

did not tear Daniel apart when he was cast into the den with them (Daniel 6, see esp. 6:19). Faith trusts in God's promises in risky and dangerous situations.

11:34

Others "quenched" flames of fire. The reference is to Shadrach, Meshach, and Abednego, who defied Nebuchadnezzar and refused to bow down to his statue (Daniel 3). When they were thrown into the fire, the fire did not burn even a hair of their heads, and they were confident that God would deliver them from Nebuchadnezzar (Dan 3:16–18). Escaping the sword, being mighty in war, and putting foreign armies to flight fit many narratives in the OT where Israel or individuals triumphed over their enemies. Threats to the lives of Elijah and Elisha were not realized (1 Kgs 19:2; 2 Kgs 6:31–32; cf. Jer 36:26). Often the point of the accounts is that God's people conquered in spite of their weaknesses. For instance, Gideon triumphed despite his frailty (Judges 6–7). The Lord often put his people in desperate situations so they would trust in him rather than themselves. There are many incidents in the OT where those in Israel became mighty in war and conquered foreign armies, including Joshua, Barak, Gideon, and David. The application for the readers of the letter is clear.

11:35

In two instances women received their sons back from the dead. Elijah raised from the dead the widow of Zarephath's son (1 Kgs 17:17–23), and Elisha raised the Shunammite's son after he died (2 Kgs 4:18–36).

After recounting the great exploits and victories won through faith, the author turns toward those who kept trusting God in the midst of suffering.[589] Some were tortured because of their allegiance to God. They did not, as the NLT puts it, "turn from God in order to be set free" (ἀπολύτρωσιν). The author probably has in mind here the torture of Eleazar that led to his death (2 Macc 6:18–31). Also, seven brothers and a mother were tortured "with whips and thongs" (2 Macc 7:1 NRSV).[590] "The tongue of their spokesman" was "cut out." They "scalp[ed] him and cut off his hands and feet" (2 Macc 7:4). He was then fried in a pan (2 Macc 7:5). They also scalped the

---

[589] For the honor/shame theme, here see deSilva, *Despising Shame*, 195–202.

[590] All references to 2 Maccabees are from the NRSV.

second brother (2 Macc 7:7). And the remaining brothers and mother were tortured and put to death (2 Macc 7:8–42). Torture, however, is not the last word. Those who suffer for God's sake will be raised to life again (7:9, 14, 36). Those who suffer for God's sake receive "a better resurrection" (κρείττονος ἀναστάσεως). The word "better" reveals the author's typological argument. The resurrection is "better" than that received by the sons raised from the dead by Elijah and Elisha. These boys, after all, died again, but their resurrection points to a better and permanent resurrection, a resurrection to a life that never ends.[591] The readers of the letter had not yet experienced death for Christ (12:4), but if they were put to death and tortured for Christ's sake, they too should look to the reward so they would receive "a better resurrection."

11:36

Still others were mocked and scourged. The words of the prophets were mocked and scorned and ignored repeatedly (2 Chr 36:15–16; cf. 2 Chr 30:10). Jeremiah was "beaten" and put in "stocks" (Jer 20:2; cf. 37:15). Still others were imprisoned (cf. Jer 37:14–21). King Asa imprisoned the prophet Hanani when he rebuked him for not trusting in the Lord (2 Chr 16:7–10), and King Ahab imprisoned Micaiah for prophesying his death (1 Kgs 22:26–27). All these suffered in faith, trusting in the Lord's promises despite their afflictions.

11:37

The list of sufferings continues. Some were stoned to death because of their devotion to the Lord. Zechariah was put to death by stoning for rebuking the people (2 Chr 24:20–21; cf. 1 Kgs 21:13; Matt 23:37; Luke 13:34). According to tradition, Jeremiah was stoned to death in Egypt.[592] Others were sawn in two, and according to Jewish tradition this was the fate of Isaiah (*Mart. Ascen. Isa.* 5:11–14). Others were put to death with the sword (cf. 1 Kgs 19:10; Jer 26:23). The clothing of the people of God (cf. 2 Kgs 1:8) signifies their poverty and being forsaken by society. They were poor, "persecuted, tormented" (NRSV; cf. 1 Kgs 18:4, 13; Neh 9:26, 30; Amos 2:12; 7:10–17).

---

[591] So Attridge, *Hebrews*, 350.

[592] For the sources see Attridge, *Hebrews*, 350n74.

11:38

The righteous, the readers are reminded, are often despised by the world, and the world "was not worthy" of such people, showing their unworthiness by their mistreatment and rejection of those who put their trust in the Lord. Some wandered in deserts, such as Elijah and Elisha (1 Kgs 19:4; 2 Kgs 2:8) and those recorded in Maccabees (1 Macc 2:29, 31; 5:24; 9:33, 62; 2 Macc 5:27). The godly sometimes had to flee evil by hiding in caves, just as many prophets were hidden by Obadiah (1 Kgs 18:4, 13), and David hid in a cave from his enemies (1 Sam 22:1; cf. also 2 Macc 6:11; 10:6). Similarly, Israel hid from the Philistines after Saul became king (1 Sam 13:6; cf. 1 Sam 14:11). If the readers expect to be accepted and praised, they need to rethink matters in light of the OT. The people of God have always been a minority people, a pilgrim people, and often despised and forsaken.

11:39

The author returns to the theme of 11:2. God approved the OT saints commended here on account of their faith. Their faith sustained them in good times and bad, in prosperity and suffering. Old Testament saints put their faith in "what was promised" (ἐπαγγελίαν), and yet they did not receive the promise. Remarkably they didn't cease believing, even though the promise was not fulfilled. They experienced the fulfillment of some specific promises (11:11, 33), but they didn't obtain the ultimate fulfillment of the promise.[593] They recognized that they must wait for the fullness of the promise, that the promise would be realized eschatologically. The promise here is another way of speaking of the final inheritance (cf. "inherit the promises" and "heirs of the promise," 6:12, 17), and in 9:15 it is defined as "the eternal inheritance."[594] Similarly the promise is understood as the eschatological rest (4:1), as the realization of final salvation (10:36), and as the coming of the kingdom (12:26, 28).

11:40

God ordained that OT believers would not be perfected apart from NT believers. Despite the remarkable faith of the OT saints, something "better" would only come with the new covenant. The something "better" arrived with Jesus' death and resurrection, with

---

[593] So Peterson, *Hebrews and Perfection*, 156.

[594] Cf. Lane, *Hebrews 9–13*, 392.

the final cleansing of sins through him.[595] Hence, now that Christ has come, those who trust in Jesus have experienced something better even now.[596] This stands in contrast to the notion that the author limits perfection to the final consummation in the heavenly city.[597] Instead the perfection described here shouldn't be equated with the eschatological promise of verse 39. The believer's perfection in the present evil age functions as a guarantee that the promise of the heavenly city will be realized in the future.[598] According to Peterson, perfection refers to the "totality of Christ's work," including both present forgiveness and final salvation.[599] Ribbens may be more precise in saying that perfection refers to access to God.[600] Old covenant saints didn't have full and free access to God apart from the sacrifice of Christ, which has opened the way for new covenant believers who now have a cleansed conscience through Christ's work.

Bridge

Faith trusts God in triumphs and tragedies, in the highs and lows of life. Faith gives itself entirely to God. If he ordains victory through faith, as he did through many of the judges and David, faith rejoices in the goodness God gives. If there is torture, death, and suffering, faith holds on to God, knowing that a "better resurrection" is coming and that the pain and torment of the present world will not last. The readers are called upon to imitate those who have gone before them and to entrust themselves to God. Those who trust God will receive the promise, and the ultimate promise is the resurrection itself.

Hebrews 12:1–3

Outline

   I. Prologue: Definitive and Final Revelation in the Son (1:1–4)
  II. Don't Abandon the Son Since He Is Greater than Angels (1:5–2:18)

---

[595] So Cockerill, *Hebrews*, 598–600.
[596] Peterson, *Hebrews and Perfection*, 156–57.
[597] So Lane, *Hebrews 9–13*, 393.
[598] Rightly Peterson, *Hebrews and Perfection*, 156–57.
[599] Ibid., 158.
[600] Ribbens, "Levitical Sacrifice and Heavenly Cult in Hebrews," 296–97.

III. Don't Harden Your Hearts Since You Have a Son and High
Priest Greater than Moses and Joshua (3:1–4:13)
IV. Don't Fall Away from Jesus' Melchizedekian Priesthood Since
It Is Greater than the Levitical Priesthood (4:14–10:18)
V. **Concluding Exhortations and Warnings (10:19–12:29)**
A. Exhortation to Draw Near, Hold Fast, and Help Others
(10:19–25)
B. Warning: No Hope of Forgiveness for Those Who Turn
from Christ (10:26–31)
C. **Call to Persevere in Faith (10:32–12:3)**
1. Don't Abandon Confidence but Endure in Faith
(10:32–39)
2. **Description and Examples of Persevering Faith
(11:1–12:3)**
a. Nature of Faith (11:1–2)
b. Creation Through Noah (11:3–7)
c. The Faith of Abraham and His Heirs (11:8–22)
d. The Faith of Moses and Those Entering the Land
(11:23–31)
e. A Closing Catalog of Faith (11:32–40)
f. **Run the Race Looking to Jesus as Supreme
Exemplar of Faith (12:1–3)**
D. Exhortations to Readers to Endure (12:4–29)

Scripture

¹ Therefore, since we also have such a large cloud of witnesses
surrounding us, let us lay aside every weight and the sin that so
easily ensnares us. Let us run with endurance the race that lies
before us, ² keeping our eyes on Jesus, the source and perfecter of our faith, who for the joy that lay before Him endured a
cross and despised the shame and has sat down at the right hand
of God's throne. ³ For consider Him who endured such hostility
from sinners against Himself, so that you won't grow weary and
lose heart.

Context

The main point of the entire letter-sermon is this: don't fall
away from Jesus. The readers must hold fast (10:19–25) and must
not let go (10:26–31). They must not abandon their confidence but

continue to believe to receive the final reward (10:32–29). The faith chapter (ch. 11) sketches in what persevering faith looks like. Faith relies on God's promises, believing what he says even if it can't see how they will be fulfilled. Faith looks to the future, banking on the word of God instead of taking its cue from present circumstances. Faith trusts God in danger and distress, knowing he will reward his own. OT ancestors serve as great exemplars of faith, but the supreme example is Jesus himself. As chapter 12 opens, the author applies what he says about OT heroes of faith (see the "therefore," Τοιγαροῦν) to his readers, urging them to run the race with endurance and to lay aside every weight and sin in the race (12:1). The author moves from examples to exhortation.[601] They should keep their eyes on Jesus since he endured the suffering of the cross to obtain the reward of sitting at God's right hand (12:2). By considering the hostility directed against Jesus, they won't grow weary and give up as they run the race (12:3).

Exegesis

12:1

The first word, "therefore" (Τοιγαροῦν), indicates, along with the context, that the author now draws an application from the ancestors of faith in chapter 11. He did not compose the chapter for historical purposes but to motivate the readers of the letter. He encourages the readers to consider the cloud of witness who preceded them and to run the race with endurance until the end, shedding any obstacle and sin that hinders them in the race.

The OT ancestors are described as "a large cloud of witnesses." They are witnesses in the sense that they function as examples for the readers; "the emphasis . . . falls on what Christians see in the host of witnesses, rather than on what they see in Christians."[602] But it is probably also the case that they are conceived of as spectators as well. They witness by their lives, and they "cheer on" those who are in the race.[603] Indeed the word "witnesses" (μαρτύρων) is related

---

[601] Cf. O'Brien, *Hebrews*, 448.

[602] O'Brien, *Hebrews*, 451.

[603] See especially here the evidence presented by N. Clayton Croy, *Endurance in Suffering: Hebrews 12:1–3 in Its Rhetorical, Religious, and Philosophical Context*, SNTSMS 98 (Cambridge: Cambridge University Press, 1998), 58–62. Koester says both notions are present. Those who have gone before are witnesses by their lives,

to the words "gained approval" (from μαρτυρέω), which are used in 11:2, 39 as a framework for the chapter. They witness to the readers by their faith and perseverance, and the readers should follow the train of their example. The author emphasizes the large number of witnesses. Perhaps he does so to impress on the readers that many have run the race before them. They are not alone or the only ones to suffer and endure. The ancestors of faith, as 11:32 demonstrates, were more than could be counted.

The main command, found at the end of the verse, fits with the purpose of the letter as a whole. The readers must "run the race" set before them with perseverance until the end. The ancestors of faith listed in chapter 11 kept running the race when it looked as if they wouldn't triumph and despite suffering and opposition. The middle clause of the verse explains *how* the race is to be run. The readers must "throw off everything that hinders" (NIV) them. Possibly the author refers here to sin that impedes believers as they run the race.[604] Or, alternatively, the author does not refer to sin but to things that may be good in and of themselves, and yet they prevent one from running the race.[605] Probably the author refers generally to anything that can hinder us in a race, whether it is sin or other things in our lives which, though not evil in themselves, can hinder us as we run with perseverance.

Believers should also put off "sin that so easily entangles." The word for "entangles" (εὐπερίστατον) has the idea that sin easily ensnares and trips believers up as they run the race.[606] The author recognizes the power and attractiveness of sin. The Christian life is not easy; it takes strength and discipline, just as ardor and determination are needed to run a race.

---

as those who give approval, and as spectators (*Hebrews*, 522). Cf. also Cockerill, *Hebrews*, 602–3. Lane emphasizes the witness of their lives (*Hebrews 9–13*, 408).

[604] So Attridge, *Hebrews*, 355; Ellingworth, *Hebrews*, 638.

[605] So L. Johnson, *Hebrews*, 316–17.

[606] The variant reading "easily distracting" (εὐπερίσπαστον, 𝔓⁴⁶ and 1739) is clearly secondary (Ellingworth, *Hebrews*, 638–39; but see Lane, *Hebrews 9–13*, 398–99). The word "easily ensnares" (εὐπερίστατον) occurs only here in the NT, but it is surely original. For the meaning supported by the HCSB, see Hughes (*Hebrews*, 520n11) and most commentators.

12:2

The main admonition is found in verse 1. Believers must run the race with endurance, which is just another way of saying they must persevere to the end. The author then tells them *how* to run the race. First, he says in verse 1 that they must lay aside every hindrance to running well, i.e., the sin which can trip believers up in the race. Second, they run with endurance by "keeping [their] eyes on Jesus." Jesus is the supreme exemplar of faith, and believers will be motivated to continue their journey if they look to him.

Jesus is described as "the source and perfecter of our faith" (τὸν τῆς πίστεως ἀρχηγόν καὶ τελειωτήν). The word rendered "source" (ἀρχηγόν) by the HCSB is translated various ways: "founder" (ESV); "pioneer" (NIV, NRSV, NET), and; "champion" (NLT). Jesus is the pathfinder for faith, functioning as an example, which also accords with 2:10. Such an interpretation certainly fits the context here where Jesus is set forth as the supreme exemplar.[607] It seems, however, that the translations of the HCSB and ESV are also fitting.[608] The pairing of the word with "perfecter" suggests that both words should be read together so the verse teaches both that Jesus is the exemplar of faith and that he also initiates and completes the faith of believers.[609] As Lindars says, Jesus perfects their faith "because he enables those who hold fast to the Christian profession to reach the same goal."[610] The author encourages believers, reminding them that the one who was the source and originator of their faith will also complete and perfect it.

Still the main point here is Jesus' example to believers. The believers are to run the race to the end, just as Jesus completed his course.[611] He endured the suffering and shame of the cross. The shame of the cross was proverbial in the ancient world.[612] He was fortified to bear up under the agony of such a death on account of "the joy that lay before him." Hence he could scorn and despise

---

[607] Cf. Lane, *Hebrews 9–13*, 411–12.

[608] See also the commentary on 2:10.

[609] So also Attridge, *Hebrews*, 356–57; Koester, *Hebrews*, 523; Ellingworth, *Hebrews*, 640; Richardson, *Pioneer and Perfecter of Faith*, 96–101.

[610] Lindars, *The Theology of Hebrews*, 45.

[611] For the importance of athletic imagery in chapter 12 and its background in the Greco-Roman world, see Croy, *Endurance in Suffering*, 40–70.

[612] See Martin Hengel, *Crucifixion* (Philadelphia: Fortress, 1977).

the temporary shame, acting bravely since he knew something far better was coming.[613] Jesus' despising the shame means "a rejection of regard for one's reputation, and would include a corresponding negative counter-evaluation of those who would seek to judge one's actions as disgraceful."[614] Jesus was rewarded for his obedience with the reign at God's right hand. The author picks up again one of the central themes of the book. The prophecy of Ps 110:1 is fulfilled in Jesus who is seated at the right hand of God, reigning over all (cf. 1:3, 13; 8:1; 10:12). Just as Moses renounced the temporary pleasures of sin for the sake of the reward that lay before him (11:24–26), so too Jesus endured the cross for the reward.[615] The cross was despised in the ancient world and a shameful way to die. The application to the readers is clear. They too must endure to the end, being willing to endure any suffering since they know they will ultimately enjoy a great reward.

12:3

Jesus' role as an example continues to be expanded upon. The readers must run the race to the end by looking at Jesus who endured the cross. The readers are urged to consider Jesus, and again his endurance is featured, which is just what the readers need as well. Jesus faced remarkable "hostility" (ἀντιλογίαν) of sinners against himself. Probably the author alludes to a similar hostility which the readers experienced, so he calls upon them to consider their brother (2:10–18; 4:14–16) and Lord who was not exempt from the same opposition by sinners. The author is concerned that the readers will "grow weary and lose heart." By considering what Jesus suffered, they will have a fresh resolve in a world that remains unfriendly and opposed. Giving up is another way of describing apostasy. It is the converse to enduring to the end, and Jesus endured by looking to the ultimate reward.

---

[613] For the notion that despising the shame means to be brave or unafraid, see Lane, *Hebrews 9–13*, 414.

[614] deSilva, *Despising Shame*, 172.

[615] For this interpretation see Hughes, *Hebrews*, 523–24n117; Koester, *Hebrews*, 523–24; O'Brien, *Hebrews*, 455–56; deSilva, *Despising Shame*, 173–78; Croy, *Endurance in Suffering*, 177–85. Hence the writer is not saying Jesus endured the cross instead of grasping the joys that life on earth bring (against Lane, *Hebrews 9–13*, 399–400). Even if one adopted Lane's view, the central affirmation of the verse still fits with the message of Hebrews. On this reading believers must not pursue earthly joys now but endure suffering in light of the final reward promised.

Bridge

Believers are in a race, which is hard and difficult and long, and they must run it to the end to receive the prize. They are not alone in the race. Many (see chapter 11) have run it before them. They must throw everything off that hinders them in the race. Jesus is the supreme example for believers, for he endured to the end in his race, suffering agony and the opposition of those who hated him. But he was rewarded for his obedience and endurance, for he now reigns at the right hand of God. So too, the readers must be willing to suffer with Jesus and for him. Jesus is the source of their faith and the one who perfects their faith, but at the same time believers should continue to believe and to keep their eyes on Jesus. The race won't last forever, and knowing there is a great reward ahead should motivate them to keep running.

Hebrews 12:4–13

Outline

I. Prologue: Definitive and Final Revelation in the Son (1:1–4)
II. Don't Abandon the Son Since He Is Greater than Angels (1:5–2:18)
III. Don't Harden Your Hearts Since You Have a Son and High Priest Greater than Moses and Joshua (3:1–4:13)
IV. Don't Fall Away from Jesus' Melchizedekian Priesthood Since It Is Greater than the Levitical Priesthood (4:14–10:18)
V. **Concluding Exhortations and Warnings (10:19–12:29)**
  A. Exhortation to Draw Near, Hold Fast, and Help Others (10:19–25)
  B. Warning: No Hope of Forgiveness for Those Who Turn from Christ (10:26–31)
  C. Call to Persevere in Faith (10:32–12:3)
  D. **Exhortations to Readers to Endure (12:4–29)**
    1. **Endure Discipline for Holiness (12:4–13)**
    2. Pursue Peace and Holiness for the Final Blessing (12:14–17)
    3. You Have Come to Mount Zion Instead of Mount Sinai (12:18–24)
    4. Final Warning: Don't Refuse the One Speaking (12:25–29)

Scripture

[4] In struggling against sin, you have not yet resisted to the point of shedding your blood. [5] And you have forgotten the exhortation that addresses you as sons: My son, do not take the Lord's discipline lightly or faint when you are reproved by Him, [6] for the Lord disciplines the one He loves and punishes every son He receives. [7] Endure suffering as discipline: God is dealing with you as sons. For what son is there that a father does not discipline? [8] But if you are without discipline—which all receive—then you are illegitimate children and not sons. [9] Furthermore, we had natural fathers discipline us, and we respected them. Shouldn't we submit even more to the Father of spirits and live? [10] For they disciplined us for a short time based on what seemed good to them, but He does it for our benefit, so that we can share His holiness. [11] No discipline seems enjoyable at the time, but painful. Later on, however, it yields the fruit of peace and righteousness to those who have been trained by it. [12] Therefore strengthen your tired hands and weakened knees, [13] and make straight paths for your feet, so that what is lame may not be dislocated but healed instead.

Context

Hebrews 12:4–29 concludes the exhortations in the letter though the author adds an epilogue. In 10:19–25 the readers are admonished to hold on to their faith, and 10:26–31 warns them of final judgment if they fall away. In 10:32–39 the readers are exhorted not to throw away their confidence. They must continue to believe until the end to receive final salvation. The heroes of faith in 11:1–40 illustrate persevering faith that leads to final salvation. They trusted in God's promises, believing in the midst of their sufferings that what he promised would come to pass. In 12:1–3 Jesus is presented as the supreme exemplar of faith, and the main point is that the race must be run with endurance until the end.

In the paragraph before us, the readers are encouraged to run the race until the end. They are reminded that they haven't yet suffered as martyrs (12:4). The author applies the athletic games to his readers, for the Greek gymnasium included an emphasis on both physical training and moral education.[616] The difficulties they face

---

[616] So L. Johnson, *Hebrews*, 319.

shouldn't be interpreted as God's punishment but should be understood as his fatherly discipline (12:5).[617] Croy argues that the context indicates that discipline isn't as a result of sin.[618] God isn't punishing believers by disciplining them, but the discipline here is rather general, and so it probably also includes discipline for when believers sin. The adversity faced by the community comes from the outside and includes imprisonment, stealing of their possessions, and slander (10:32–34). Jesus himself endured suffering (12:1–3), but in his case he wasn't being disciplined for his sin. The discipline of believers is rooted in God's love for them (12:6). The main point of the paragraph emerges in verse 7: the readers are to endure discipline as those loved by God. Discipline, in fact, demonstrates that the readers are truly sons (12:8). If the readers respected their earthly fathers who disciplined them, they should gladly submit to God to receive eschatological life (12:9). Parents discipline children in accord with their limited wisdom, but God disciplines so that human beings will be holy (12:10). Discipline isn't pleasant but painful, but ultimately it leads to righteousness (12:11). The readers must not give way to discouragement but strengthen their hands and knees and continue on the right pathway (12:12–13).

Exegesis

12:4

The readers have suffered for the sake of the gospel, but they have not yet spilled their blood. Intriguingly, he describes their life thus far as a struggle against sin.[619] The temptation to fall away, in other words, can also be described as a temptation to yield to sin. The situation facing the readers was not easy, for they were in a battle in which sin threatened to triumph over them; they were tempted to give in to social pressure and thereby avoid persecution. Still he reminds them that they haven't faced the most arduous test. None of them has been called to martyrdom. Here they stand in contrast to Jesus who went to the cross and experienced the ultimate shame (12:2).

---

[617] Cf. Cockerill, *Hebrews*, 617.

[618] Croy, *Endurance in Suffering*, 2–3.

[619] Some think the author refers to boxing here, but Croy argues that the athletic imagery here is rather general (*Endurance in Suffering*, 69–70).

12:5

The readers have forgotten the exhortation given to them in the Scriptures.[620] Clearly the author believes the words recorded in Prov 3:11–12 function as an encouragement for the readers of his day. They are not merely words of antiquity directed to a former generation. What was written long ago is also addressed to contemporary readers. The citation exactly represents the LXX, except for the addition of "my" with "son." Though the MT is close to the LXX, it is clear that the author draws on the LXX here. The author picks up the context of Proverbs, noting that the words instruct them as God's "sons" (υἱοῖς).

The readers should not dismiss the Lord's discipline by taking it lightly. The discipline in view here should not be understood as punitive but as corrective and educative. Still, the discipline here includes both training for godliness in general and discipline for sin. Not all discipline is due to sin, but some discipline is given to wean believers away from sin. It is part of the training God has planned for his children so they grow in righteousness. They should consider its purposes and benefits. Nor should they be discouraged or "grow weary" (ἐκλύου) when they are "reproved" by God. Here the author picks up his admonition from verse 3 where he instructs the readers to consider the opposition Jesus received so they won't "lose heart" (ἐκλυόμενοι). The difficult circumstances in which they find themselves could exhaust and enervate them, but, as the author explains here, they should draw the opposite conclusion. Their sufferings signify that they truly belong to God, that they are his sons, and that they are deeply loved by God.

12:6

The author explains why the readers should not dismiss the Lord's discipline or grow discouraged by it. Discouragement would be the expected reaction if discipline signified the Lord's anger with the readers. But it is precisely the opposite. The Lord is disciplining the readers because he loves them. He "chastises" (ESV; μαστιγοῖ) "every son" he accepts.[621] Their stresses and strains are not unusual

---

[620] Alternatively the verse could be understood as a question (L. Johnson, *Hebrews*, 320).

[621] See Croy, who examines discipline and punishment in the OT and Second Temple Jewish literature. Croy shows various reasons for suffering including punishment, testing, formative discipline, to atone for sin, and to take the punishment

but represent the course of life of everyone who belongs to the family of God. Discipline, in this context, is not a sign of God's anger or punishment but his favor and acceptance.[622]

12:7

The main verb in verse 7, "endure" (ὑπομένετε), could be indicative or imperative. The ESV takes it as an indicative: "It is for discipline that you have to endure" (cf. KJV, NKJV, RSV, NLT).[623] In context it is more likely an imperative: "Endure suffering as discipline" (HCSB; cf. NIV, NET, NRSV).[624] Such a reading fits with the letter as a whole. The writer isn't saying that the readers *are enduring*. Whether they endure is what faces them in their current situation so they are not commended for enduring but are exhorted to endure. The author communicates here the main point of the

---

deserved by others (*Endurance in Suffering*, 83–133). He says the LXX of Prov 3:11–12 has a punitive character (89). Greco-Roman writers, on the other hand, drew a connection less often between suffering and punishment, though the latter idea was certainly not absent (133–58).

[622] See here Koester, *Hebrews*, 538. Fitzgerald sees here a reference to corporal punishment. See John T. Fitzgerald, "Proverbs 3:11–12, Hebrews 12:5–6 and the Tradition of Corporal Punishment," in *Scripture and Traditions: Essays on Early Judaism and Christianity in Honor of Carl R. Holladay*, ed. Patrick Gray and Gail R. O'Day, NovTSup 129 (Leiden: Brill, 2008), 291–317. Croy argues that even though Prov 3:11–12 is punitive in the context of Proverbs, the text as applied in Hebrews is educative and non-punitive, for there is no indication that the readers had misbehaved. Furthermore, the athletic terms used suggest endurance in an athletic contest instead of punishment. Also those commended in chapter 11 were not reproved for sin but set forth as examples of faithful perseverance (Croy, *Endurance in Suffering*, 196–99, 210–14; cf. also Peeler, *You Are My Son*, 151–53). Croy rightly sees in Hebrews that not all discipline is due to sin. Discipline trains the godly to be more godly. Still he goes too far in washing out any reference to discipline for sin in the text. Discipline for sin is not punitive but represents training and correction. Certainly the discipline in Prov. 3:11–12 was corrective, and it is natural to conclude that the same applies in Hebrews. The athletic imagery used doesn't rule out discipline for sin, for the athletic illustrations don't determine the matter clearly one way or the other. Even though discipline for sin is included here, Croy reminds us that discipline has a variety of purposes and hence discipline isn't always because of particular sins in one's life. Often discipline and training are introduced to make the one who is strong even stronger.

[623] For the imperative see Croy, *Endurance in Suffering*, 199–200. In support of the indicative, see L. Johnson, *Hebrews*, 320–21; cf. also Ellingworth, *Hebrews*, 650). Johnson argues that the imperative doesn't make sense because people don't endure in order to be disciplined or educated.

[624] So Lane, *Hebrews 9–13*, 421; O'Brien, *Hebrews*, 464–65.

paragraph, one that fits with the purpose of the letter as a whole. In verses 1–3 they are summoned to run the race, and the thought is similar here. They are commanded to endure to the end, recognizing that endurance is a discipline that entails hardship and suffering.

Such discipline should not surprise them. It is an indication that God is dealing with them as his sons (cf. Prov 13:24; 29:17), so it functions as proof that they are part of the family. What it means to be a son, the author goes on to explain, is to be disciplined and trained by the father. Discipline viewed rightly, then, has an element of encouragement, for it is an indication of God's love.

12:8

The author continues to encourage the readers as they face difficult circumstances. They are to respond by enduring (v. 7), recognizing that "all" who belong to God are disciplined. No true son, no genuine child, is spared by the father. If discipline is withheld, it indicates that one doesn't belong to the family at all, that one is an illegitimate child (νόθοι). Education in the ancient world was limited to legitimate children and wasn't given to children who were illegitimate.[625] Furthermore, illegitimate sons didn't receive any inheritance.[626] Since they are truly God's sons, they experience discipline that comes from the hands of a kind father.

12:9

An analogy is drawn between earthly fathers and the discipline they mete out and God's discipline of his children. Earthly fathers (τοὺς . . . τῆς σαρκὸς ἡμῶν πατέρας) discipline their children, and their children respect and honor them. If that is true of earthly fathers, how much more should this be true of God's fatherly discipline? Often in the letter the earthly is contrasted with the heavenly, and such a disjunction appears again here, and the heavenly is always superior to the earthly. The readers, then, should respect and honor God for the discipline he wisely appoints for them. And it goes even further than this. They should "submit" to such a Father, recognizing that he disciplines them in his wisdom and love. Indeed, he disciplines not to destroy or slay them but so they will "live." Discipline does not jeopardize eschatological life but is the pathway on which life will be realized.

---

[625] L. Johnson, *Hebrews*, 321.
[626] So Koester, *Hebrews*, 528.

The author uses a somewhat strange phrase here: "Father of spirits" (τῷ πατρὶ τῶν πνευμάτων). Usually the word "spirits" alone refers to angels or heavenly beings, but in this context it certainly refers to human beings. It is difficult to know why he uses the word "spirits." Perhaps he does so because he contrasts the earthly and the heavenly. In any case the author emphasizes God's sovereignty and love in the lives of human beings.

12:10

Verse 10 explains further verse 9. Earthly fathers who discipline are respected by their children (v. 9), and yet their discipline is of limited benefit. Parents train their children "based on what seem[s] good to them," and hence it follows that their discipline is imperfect and flawed. Sometimes parents are mistaken in the discipline they apply, even if they have the best intentions in the world. The discipline of parents is limited from another perspective. It is temporary and restricted to the few days in which parents are in charge of their children. God's discipline, on the other hand, does not suffer from a partial vision of the whole. He always knows what his children need, and thus his discipline is always "for our benefit." The benefit is described as participation in God's holiness. God trains believers so they become more righteous. Believers, therefore, should submit to God's discipline (v. 9) and endure since it is for their good.

12:11

The author acknowledges that discipline is distasteful, bringing grief rather than joy. In the long run, though, discipline yields a harvest that makes the painful training worthwhile. The HCSB says discipline produces "the fruit of peace and righteousness" (καρπὸν εἰρηνικόν . . . δικαιοσύνης, cf. also NET, NIV). The phrase may also be rendered "the peaceful fruit of righteousness" (ESV, NRSV; cf. also NLT). The latter seems more likely since there isn't a clear "and" in the Greek text. In other words the "peaceful fruit" *is* righteousness.[627] Righteousness, then, is another way of describing holiness. What is emphasized here is that such righteousness is "peaceful," i.e., it is pleasing and satisfying. The contrast between present pain and future benefits calls to mind what is said about Moses in 11:24–26. He rejected present pleasures and chose to suffer with the people of God to obtain a future reward.

---

[627] So Lane, *Hebrews 9–13*, 425.

12:12

Recognizing and realizing that discipline is for their good should "therefore" (Διό) lead believers to be encouraged despite their present circumstances.[628] They should strengthen hands that are feeble and knees that are weak. The author alludes here to Isa 35:3: "Strengthen the weak hands, steady the shaking knees!" Their weakness corresponds to "their discouragement and dispiritedness."[629] Isaiah's words are in a context which promise the coming kingdom. The desert will blossom, the lame will be healed, streams will flow in the desert, and Israel will return to Zion. The days of exile will be over. "Joy and gladness will overtake them, and sorrow and sighing will flee" (Isa 35:10). The author of Hebrews argues in a similar way, though he maps his words onto his own eschatological framework. The kingdom has come in Jesus Christ, but the final blessings of the kingdom still await the readers. Like Jesus they have joy set before them (12:2), but presently they must strengthen the weak and discouraged with the promise of what is to come. They should strengthen their arms and knees for the race they are running.

12:13

Perhaps the race imagery continues, as the author draws from Isaiah 35 where Israel returned to Zion from exile. But in Hebrews God's people are traveling to a new Zion, the heavenly Jerusalem (11:10, 13–16; 12:22; 13:14). To do so "straight paths" (τροχιὰς ὀρθάς) are needed for their feet. The author also seems to pick up the language of Proverbs here, for the wicked follow "paths" that are "crooked" and "devious" (Prov 2:15). We find the exact phrase used here in Hebrews in Prov 4:15 where the father instructs the son about "straight paths" (cf. also Prov 4:26 LXX).[630] This connection is interesting for another reason since the author has just admonished the readers as sons to pay heed to the discipline of their heavenly father. The straight paths are the paths of righteousness and holiness, and this fits with Isa 35:8. The readers must continue in their moral education.[631] Those who return from exile travel on

---

[628] Attridge rightly argues that 12:12–13 concludes verses 4–11 and belongs with this section (*Hebrews*, 366n6). Against Bruce, who puts verses 12–13 with verses 14–17 (*Hebrews*, 366).

[629] L. Johnson, *Hebrews*, 323.

[630] See Lane, *Hebrews 9–13*, 433.

[631] L. Johnson, *Hebrews*, 323.

"the Holy Way," and "the path" is not for the "unclean." As Koester says, "The emphasis is not so much on making the way smooth for others . . . as on keeping oneself straight."[632]

The language of the lame being "healed" also evokes Isaiah 35, for "the lame will leap like a deer" (Isa 35:6). The readers should make straight paths, i.e., follow righteousness so that the lame should "not be disabled" (NIV) but instead be healed.[633] Hebrews picks up on the figurative meaning of Isaiah. Those who are spiritually lame will find healing if they walk in straight paths, if they continue to follow Jesus. It is also possible that the word translated "disabled" (ἐκτραπῇ, NIV) means "turn aside," for this fits how the verb is typically used (1 Tim 1:6; 5:15; 6:20; 2 Tim 4:4; cf. Amos 5:8).[634] Turning aside, then, would be a way of describing falling away or apostasy. The readers should pursue righteousness so that they do not turn aside from the Lord but instead experience spiritual healing. Alternatively, since the verb is associated in context with healing, it more likely in this context means "disabled" or dislocated.[635] Whatever decision is made here, the referent is the same: the readers should follow the paths of righteousness to avoid apostasy.

Bridge

The readers could overestimate the difficulties they have encountered thus far. They haven't suffered martyrdom. They need a fresh and revised perspective on the difficult circumstances they are encountering. God is disciplining them just as a father disciplines his children. When God disciplines us, we are called upon to endure, to obtain the benefit of the discipline being meted out. Discipline isn't a sign of God's disfavor but his love. It is designed to produce holiness and righteousness in God's children. So even though there is present pain, the readers should look at the long-term gain and embrace the discipline as an indication of God's love. Believers are prone to apostasy if they become unduly discouraged. They must strengthen their hands and feet and continue to run the race.

---

[632] Koester, *Hebrews*, 530; Hughes, *Hebrews*, 535–36 (the concern for others is implicit).

[633] In favor of the word "healed," see Cockerill, *Hebrews*, 630.

[634] So Hughes, *Hebrews*, 535.

[635] Attridge, *Hebrews*, 365; Westcott, *Hebrews*, 405; Bruce, *Hebrews*, 363; O'Brien, *Hebrews*, 471.

Hebrews 12:14–17

Outline

   I. Prologue: Definitive and Final Revelation in the Son (1:1–4)
  II. Don't Abandon the Son Since He Is Greater than Angels
      (1:5–2:18)
 III. Don't Harden Your Hearts Since You Have a Son and High
      Priest Greater than Moses and Joshua (3:1–4:13)
  IV. Don't Fall Away from Jesus' Melchizedekian Priesthood Since
      It Is Greater than the Levitical Priesthood (4:14–10:18)
   V. **Concluding Exhortations and Warnings (10:19–12:29)**
      A. Exhortation to Draw Near, Hold Fast, and Help Others
         (10:19–25)
      B. Warning: No Hope of Forgiveness for Those Who Turn
         from Christ (10:26–31)
      C. Call to Persevere in Faith (10:32–12:3)
      D. **Exhortations to Readers to Endure (12:4–29)**
         1. Endure Discipline for Holiness (12:4–13)
         2. **Pursue Peace and Holiness for the Final Blessing
            (12:14–17)**
         3. You Have Come to Mount Zion Instead of Mount
            Sinai (12:18–24)
         4. Final Warning: Don't Refuse the One Speaking
            (12:25–29)

Scripture

   [14] Pursue peace with everyone, and holiness—without it no one
will see the Lord.

   [15] Make sure that no one falls short of the grace of God and that
no root of bitterness springs up, causing trouble and by it, defiling
many. [16] And make sure that there isn't any immoral or irrever-
ent person like Esau, who sold his birthright in exchange for one
meal. [17] For you know that later, when he wanted to inherit the
blessing, he was rejected because he didn't find any opportunity
for repentance, though he sought it with tears.

Context

The readers are exhorted to hold on to their faith (10:19–25), to resist falling away (10:26–31), and not to abandon their faith (10:32–39). OT saints function as an example of persevering faith, and Jesus is the supreme example (11:1–12:3), and thus they should run the race of faith until the end. In 12:4–13 they are exhorted to endure to the end, recognizing that God is disciplining them as a father disciplines his children, and hence the discipline is for their good. Verses 14–17, then, are a renewed call to run the race to the end (12:1) and to endure (12:7). They should pursue peace and sanctification, for without holiness they will not see the Lord on the final day (12:14). God's grace must abound in the community, and a bitter root must not spring up which leads to apostasy so that many are defiled (12:15). Esau is brought in as an example of one who rejected his birthright, preferring the things of this world to the things of God (12:16). Hence, even though he tearfully longed for the inheritance, he never received it (12:17).

Exegesis

12:14

The next exhortation may seem out of place, for the call to pursue peace with all doesn't seem to follow naturally what preceded.[636] It fits, however, with the notion of seeking righteousness and holiness (12:12–13). In the OT believers are enjoined to "seek peace and pursue it" (Ps 34:14 ESV; cf. also Rom 12:18), and we saw in verse 11 that those who are disciplined yield "the peaceful fruit of righteousness." The author probably alludes to Prov 4:25–27 in the LXX, which emphasizes concentrating on the road ahead of you, making straight paths for one's feet (cf. Heb 12:13), keeping on the right paths, and as a result enjoying peace.[637] Those who seek the Lord are at peace with others, and, as noted earlier, the author probably has fellow believers particularly in mind.[638]

At the same time believers should seek and pursue "holiness" (ἁγιασμόν). Holiness is not optional, for apart from it "no one will see the Lord." Seeking holiness is the opposite of falling away or

---

[636] Lane says that the "all" here are fellow believers (*Hebrews 9–13*, 450).

[637] See here Koester, *Hebrews*, 531.

[638] Attridge, *Hebrews*, 367.

apostasy. Holiness should not be understood in terms of sinlessness but describes those who continue to seek and pursue the Lord. The reward is described here in personal terms. Those who seek holiness will see the Lord, i.e., they will "experience eternal life."[639] Revelation says that saints will see God's face in the new creation (Rev 22:4; cf. 1 John 3:3; 1 Cor 13:12). A similar thought is found in Matt 5:8, "The pure in heart are blessed, for they will see God."

12:15

Continuing on the right pathway and pursuing holiness are not optional. According to the author, life and death are at stake. Hence believers should "watch over" (ἐπισκοποῦντες) one another, exhorting one another not to "[fall] short of the grace of God." Those who fall short commit apostasy since they don't continue in God's grace. The bitterness here could be understood literally, and certainly bitterness defiles and stains when it spreads. But it is more likely that the root of bitterness is metaphorical here, which means that the author has in mind a bitter root that produces terrible consequences. The author draws on Deut 29:18–19,[640]

> Be sure there is no man, woman, clan, or tribe among you today whose heart turns away from the LORD our God to go and worship the gods of those nations. Be sure there is no root among you bearing poisonous and bitter fruit. When someone hears the words of this oath, he may consider himself exempt, thinking, "I will have peace even though I follow my own stubborn heart."

The bitter and poisonous root refers to those who abandon the Lord and worship other gods. They abandon the Lord, and yet think they will be safe and secure from judgment. The author of Hebrews worries that his readers will fall into the same trap. He assures them that they won't be safe from judgment if they abandon the Lord. The word "defiled" (μιανθῶσιν) in the OT refers to those who are unclean (cf. Lev 5:3; 11:24, 43–44; 13:3, 8, 44; 15:31; 18:24–25, 27; 20:3; 21:1; Num 5:3, 14; 6:7; Deut 21:23; Hos 5:3; 9:4; Hag 2:13; Isa 43:28; Jer 2:7; Ezek 4:14; 7:24), and the defilement is sometimes ceremonial and sometimes moral. In Hebrews, however,

---

[639] So O'Brien, *Hebrews*, 473.

[640] For a discussion of the appropriation of the OT text, see Allen, *Deuteronomy and Exhortation in Hebrews*, 83–88; Attridge, *Hebrews*, 368.

the defilement is moral, signifying that those who have given themselves over to apostasy are unclean and outside of the covenant.

12:16

Believers should be on guard so that no one would be sexually immoral or profane like Esau. "He is the foil of the faithful described in 11:1–40."[641] The word "immoral" (πόρνος) always refers
to sexual immorality (Sir 23:17; 1 Cor 5:9–11; 6:9; Eph 5:5; 1 Tim
1:10; Heb 13:4; Rev 21:8; 22:15), and thus it likely has that meaning here as well.[642] But how was Esau sexually immoral? Perhaps
in his decision to marry Hittite women (Gen 26:34).[643] His lack of
concern for holy things is evident in his disdain for his birthright. It
was so trivial to him that he sold it for one meal (Gen 25:29–34),
and hence he "despised his birthright" (Gen 25:34). "God did not
take Esau's blessing from him; Esau traded it away. And God let
him bear the consequences of his action."[644] The author is concerned
that the readers will fall into the same trap as Esau. As Koester says,
"Esau gave up the promise in order to ease his physical discomfort,
listeners might consider giving up the promise in order to ease their
social discomfort."[645] They have been given something precious and
beautiful in the gospel and must not forsake it for the comforts or
joys of the present evil age.

12:17

The consequences of despising the birthright are explained.
Esau longed to inherit the blessing from his father, but Jacob by
deception received it instead (Gen 27:27–30). When Esau discov-
ered the ruse perpetrated by Jacob, he bitterly asked Isaac to bless
him as well (Gen 27:34), but the blessing like the birthright was
irrevocable. Both the blessing and the birthright, which are closely
merged together in the story (Gen 27:36), were given to Jacob, and
hence he would serve as Esau's master (Gen 27:36–40). Hebrews
draws a lesson for the readers: repentance isn't available forever.

---

[641] Cockerill, *Hebrews*, 633.

[642] Some suggest, however, that the term is metaphorical (Lane, *Hebrews 9–13*,
439; Ellingworth, *Hebrews*, 665; O'Brien, *Hebrews*, 475). But against this see
Hughes, *Hebrews*, 540. The term doesn't refer in general to bodily desires (against
Cockerill, *Hebrews*, 639).

[643] Cf. L. Johnson, *Hebrews*, 325.

[644] Koester, *Hebrews*, 542.

[645] Ibid., 542.

Time may run out in receiving the grace of God.[646] Esau's rejection shouldn't be interpreted abstractly, as if he was simply the object of an unfortunate fate, for "there is no indication that Esau recognized his responsibility for what he had done, or the depth of his guilt (Gen. 27:36). His only interest was to reclaim the blessing he had forfeited."[647]

It is unclear what Esau sought. The pronoun "it" (αὐτήν) could refer to either repentance or the blessing since both are feminine nouns. The HCSB could be read as if he sought for repentance since it is the nearest antecedent to the pronoun "it."[648] It is more likely, however, that he sought the blessing.[649] The NIV is probably on target: "Even though he sought the blessing with tears, he could not change what he had done" (cf. also NET, NRSV). "It was his loss, not his profanity, that he mourned."[650] Even if the reference is to repentance rather than to blessing, the meaning doesn't change greatly since repentance was the means to obtain the blessing.[651] Esau wanted the blessing, but the time had passed. The author isn't saying God doesn't allow people to repent even if they wish to. His point is that the time passed when Esau could repent, and he doesn't want the same to happen to the readers. As Koester says,

> This passage is designed to awaken people to danger, not to make them give up hope. Warning is the counterpart to promise; both pertain to the future. Warnings disturb people, while promises encourage them, but together they serve the same end, which is encouraging people to persevere in faith.[652]

Or, as Cockerill says, his "rejection is reflected in a life of callousness that does not desire repentance or seek to turn from its rebellious ways. . . . Thus, any who are truly concerned for their own

---

[646] Lane, *Hebrews 9–13*, 458.

[647] O'Brien, *Hebrews*, 476.

[648] This is the view of many commentators, e.g., Attridge, *Hebrews*, 370.

[649] So Westcott, *Hebrews*, 409; Bruce, *Hebrews*, 368n120; Koester, *Hebrews*, 533; Lane, *Hebrews 9–13*, 440.

[650] Hughes, *Hebrews*, 541.

[651] Cf. Hagner, *Hebrews*, 208; Allen, *Deuteronomy and Exhortation in Hebrews*, 137.

[652] Koester, *Hebrews*, 542.

salvation have not followed the steps of Esau."[653] If they turn away from Christ, they, like Esau, will be filled with bitter regret.

Bridge

The decision facing the readers is momentous. Esau failed to get the blessing because he kicked it away, and when he desired to obtain it, the opportunity to receive it had passed. The readers should not let the comforts of the world beguile them so that they choose them instead of Jesus Christ. They should not turn away from the Lord so that they are defiled and unworthy to enter the heavenly city. They must strengthen themselves to pursue the Lord and holiness so that they will see God and rejoice in him forever.

Hebrews 12:18–24

Outline

   I. Prologue: Definitive and Final Revelation in the Son (1:1–4)
  II. Don't Abandon the Son Since He Is Greater than Angels (1:5–2:18)
 III. Don't Harden Your Hearts Since You Have a Son and High Priest Greater than Moses and Joshua (3:1–4:13)
  IV. Don't Fall Away from Jesus' Melchizedekian Priesthood Since It Is Greater than the Levitical Priesthood (4:14–10:18)
   V. **Concluding Exhortations and Warnings (10:19–12:29)**
    A. Exhortation to Draw Near, Hold Fast, and Help Others (10:19–25)
    B. Warning: No Hope of Forgiveness for Those Who Turn from Christ (10:26–31)
    C. Call to Persevere in Faith (10:32–12:3)
    D. **Exhortations to Readers to Endure (12:4–29)**
        1. Endure Discipline for Holiness (12:4–13)
        2. Pursue Peace and Holiness for the Final Blessing (12:14–17)
        3. **You Have Come to Mount Zion Instead of Mount Sinai (12:18–24)**

---

[653] Cockerill, *Hebrews*, 641.

    4. Final Warning: Don't Refuse the One Speaking
       (12:25–29)
VI. Epilogue: Final Exhortations (13:1–25)

Scripture

¹⁸ For you have not come to what could be touched, to a blazing fire, to darkness, gloom, and storm, ¹⁹ to the blast of a trumpet, and the sound of words. (Those who heard it begged that not another word be spoken to them, ²⁰ for they could not bear what was commanded: And if even an animal touches the mountain, it must be stoned! ²¹ The appearance was so terrifying that Moses said, I am terrified and trembling.) ²² Instead, you have come to Mount Zion, to the city of the living God (the heavenly Jerusalem), to myriads of angels in festive gathering, ²³ to the assembly of the firstborn whose names have been written in heaven, to God who is the Judge of all, to the spirits of righteous people made perfect, ²⁴ to Jesus (mediator of a new covenant), and to the sprinkled blood, which says better things than the blood of Abel.

Context

The paragraph is situated in a context where the readers are exhorted to hold fast and not to fall away (10:19–31). They will hold fast if they believe and run the race to the end as OT saints and Jesus did (11:1–12:3). They are called upon to endure the fatherly discipline they are receiving (12:4–13) and to continue in holiness and godliness so they see God and receive the final reward (12:14–17). Verses 18–24 emphasize why they must continue to persevere in holiness. Hence these verses themselves do not constitute an exhortation. Instead this section "summarizes the main points and themes throughout the theological sections of the epistle," such as, "angels," "heaven," "first-born," "perfection," "Jesus the mediator of the new covenant" and "sprinkled blood."[654] The fundamental reason the believers should endure is that they have not come to Mount Sinai

---

[654] O'Brien, *Hebrews*, 478. The paragraph is not the hermeneutical key to the letter, but it does play a summarizing and climactic role (see Son, *Zion Symbolism in Hebrews*). Son shows how the earlier chapters in Hebrews anticipate and point to the Sinai/Zion themes in 12:18–24, though I don't concur with his view that Melchizedek functioned as a priest in the heavenly Zion.

(12:18–21) but to Mount Zion (12:22–24).[655] Mount Sinai was terrifying because of God's awesome and holy presence, and those who transgressed the boundaries were threatened with God's judgment. In other words, free access to God was denied. Mount Zion, however, is the city of God, the heavenly Jerusalem, where the church of Jesus Christ is already gathered in heaven. The believers must continue until the end because they have come to something better than Mount Sinai; they have come to Jesus who is the mediator of a new and better covenant, to the mountain where they reside in God's presence because their sins are forgiven.

Exegesis

12:18

The readers are urged to stay on the right road, pursue holiness, and live differently from Esau because they have come to a mountain that is far superior to Sinai. So in verses 18–21 the author tells the reader what they have *not* come to. They have not come to Sinai but to Zion. The author never actually mentions "Sinai," but it is clearly in his mind. The word "come to" (προσεληλύθατε) is one of the author's favorites.[656] They should "come to . . . the throne of grace" (4:16). And Jesus will save completely those "coming to" "God through him" (7:25). The sacrifices required in the law can never perfect those coming to God (10:1). Readers are to come to God "with a true heart in full assurance of faith" (10:22). Those who "come to" God must believe he exists and rewards those who pursue him (11:6).

Mount Sinai is an earthly and visible mountain. It can be "touched" and handled, but anyone who touched it when the Lord was present would be slain (Exod 19:12). When the Lord descended to speak with Moses and Israel, it was "blazing with fire" and "darkness, gloom, and storm" (cf. Exod 19:16; 20:21; Deut 4:11; 5:22). The storm and gloom represented the might and power of God, terrifying the people observing it. Smoke billowed up from the mountain, and the mountain was shaking as in an earthquake (Exod 19:18).

---

[655] Cockerill underemphasizes the newness of what is expressed here (*Hebrews*, 643).

[656] The perfect tense is for prominence (see O'Brien, *Hebrews*, 479; cf. Campbell, *Basics of Verbal Aspect*, 111).

12:19

The author continues to convey the terror and dread that cascaded down upon those near Mount Sinai. The sound echoing down the mountain was like a trumpet blasting, and the words were such that the people entreated Moses that they be spared from hearing them (Exod 19:16, 19; 20:18–19; Deut 5:24–27). What they feared was imminent death upon hearing the words of the Lord. Israel was required to cleanse themselves (Exod 19:10), to abstain from sexual relations (Exod 19:15); and they could not touch the mountain (Exod 19:12) or try to break through to see the Lord, or they would face certain death (Exod 19:21, 24).

12:20

The author reminded his readers that under the old covenant the Lord was not accessible (9:8). Only the high priest could enter his presence and only once a year (9:6–7). Those who entered his presence wrongly or without warrant faced the danger of annihilation (cf. Lev 10:1–2). We are not astonished to learn that the Israelites near Sinai begged the Lord to stop speaking, for they couldn't endure the command that even an animal that touched the mountain would be stoned (Exod 19:12–13). Exodus 19:13 actually says that neither human beings nor animals should live if they touched the mountain, that both would be stoned for transgressing the boundaries. The author of Hebrews picks up on the command to execute animals to underscore the strictness of the requirements and the terror the people felt. Even animals, which could not comprehend what was going on, were not spared from punishment if they wandered to the place God prohibited.

12:21

Nor was the terror confined to ordinary Israelites. Even Moses as the leader and deliverer of Israel was filled with dread and fear. The Lord's holiness is so awesome that every person in the world is filled with trembling and fear upon entering his presence.

The terror of gazing at the storm breaking out on the mountain and of hearing the thunder and feeling the mountain shaking was palpable. Moses confessed that he was seized with terror and trembling. The OT actually emphasizes the people shuddering in terror rather than Moses (Exod 19:16; 20:18; Deut 5:5). A reference to Moses' fear is found in the account of the golden calf (Deut 9:19). Perhaps Moses' terror is implied in Exod 19:19 where Moses

397

speaks and God responds with thunder. Such a thunderous reply could doubtless be interpreted to provoke fear in Moses. But it is more likely that the author merges Sinai with the golden calf incident intentionally. Thereby he "evokes Sinai's full implications for Israel."[657] Those who trifle with the Lord and flout his covenant stipulations will be destroyed. As Allen says, "By giving the Sinai narrative its full parameters and recalling the entire old covenant dispensation. . . . Hebrews demonstrates Sinai's inherent inability to deal with sin in the face of divine judgment."[658] The main point is that believers couldn't draw near to God through Sinai, though some did draw near and see God or at least his feet (Exod. 24:9–11).[659] The old dispensation was entirely inadequate.

12:22

The contrast between Mount Sinai and Mount Zion is stunning. Hebrews helps us imagine the difference between the two, for the author paints in striking colors the difference between paralyzing terror and extraordinary joy.

Instead of coming to Mount Sinai, where there is fear and foreboding, the readers have joyfully "come" ($\pi\rho\sigma\epsilon\lambda\eta\lambda\acute{v}\theta\alpha\tau\epsilon$), which is the same term used in 12:18, to Mount Zion. There is an already-but-not-yet dimension to the promise here, for they have come to Zion, and yet the fullness of Zion is not yet theirs.[660] Zion, historically, is part of Jerusalem and was captured by David (2 Sam 5:7; cf. 1 Kgs 8:1), and is henceforth identified with Jerusalem. Zion in the OT is God's "holy mountain" (Pss 2:6; 9:12; 20:2; 74:2; 76:2; 132:13; Mic 4:2; Joel 3:17, 21; Isa 8:18), where he specially dwells. Here in Hebrews Mount Zion is linked with the new Jerusalem, the heavenly city. We are prepared for this in the OT, for Mount Zion is identified as "the city of the great King" (Ps 48:2; cf. Isa 60:14). The promise to rebuild Zion (Ps 102:16) is fulfilled ultimately in the heavenly Zion, for we find in Ps 110:2 (the favorite psalm of the author) that

---

[657] Allen, *Deuteronomy and Exhortation*, 66.

[658] Ibid., 66.

[659] O'Brien, *Hebrews*, 482.

[660] Against Koester, who says that they haven't yet arrived physically in Zion (*Hebrews*, 550; cf. also Harris, "The Eternal Inheritance in Hebrews," 230–32). They haven't arrived physically, but in their conversion they have come to Zion spiritually (see O'Brien, *Hebrews*, 482n200).

the Lord and his Messiah reign from Zion. Zion will not be shaken or destroyed but will endure forever (Ps 125:1; cf. Isa 24:23).

The city of God can't fail, for the living God dwells there, and no one can triumph over him. Psalm 48:8 affirms that "God will establish" the city of God "forever," and it will never end, according to Hebrews, because it is a heavenly city. The city is heavenly, for it is also described as "the heavenly Jerusalem." We see both the vertical and temporal eschatology of the writer. The earthly Jerusalem points upward to the heavenly Jerusalem, and at the same time it points forward in time to the heavenly Jerusalem, to the consummation of God's purposes, for it is described as the city "to come" (Heb 13:14) to which believers are "looking forward" (11:10). In Paul the Jerusalem "above" is the mother of believers (Gal 4:26), and he shares the same vertical imagery, while also reflecting a similar eschatological standpoint. Revelation emphasizes that Jerusalem is the holy city of God that comes from heaven (Rev 3:12; 21:2, 10; cf. *2 Bar.* 4:2). On the one hand the city is something believers anticipate, but at the same time they have already come to that city and are already its citizens.

Believers have also come to "myriads of angels in festive gathering" (μυριάσιν ἀγγέλων, πανηγύρει). "In festive gathering" is appositional to "myriads of angels," just as the heavenly Jerusalem stands in apposition to the city of the living God.[661] The heavenly city is inhabited by countless angels, and the notion that there are thousands with God in the heavenly realms is rooted in the OT (cf. Deut 33:2; Dan 7:10; so also Jude 14; Rev 5:11). The word "festive gathering" (πανηγύρει) is used in the OT for festivals where Israel worshiped the Lord (Hos 2:13; 9:5; Amos 5:21; Ezek 46:11), but we have a picture here of angels enthusiastically gathering to worship (so also ESV, NIV, NRSV). Alternatively, the word "festive gathering" belongs with the next line and describes the church: "to the assembly and congregation of the firstborn" (NET). According to this reading the festive gathering to which believers already belong is the church of Jesus Christ. They are already members of the joyful assembly in heaven. But against this latter interpretation is the structure of the text, for the "and" (καί) is omitted after the reference to the angels, indicating that the "festive gathering" refers to the

---

[661] So Attridge, *Hebrews*, 375; Lane, *Hebrews 9–13*, 467.

gathering of angels. The structure of the text is more difficult to see in the HCSB since it omits the conjunctions ("and" but cf. ESV, NRSV) that separate the items listed.

12:23

The author continues to rejoice in the privileges that belong to believers, emphasizing the joyful confidence that believers have in contrast to old covenant believers. Believers have come to a heavenly assembly, to the place where the names of those who belong to God are inscribed in heaven. Being enrolled in heaven is characteristic of human beings (Luke 10:20; Phil 4:3; Rev 21:27), indicating that human beings rather than angels are described.[662] In the phrase "church of the firstborn" (πρωτοτόκων), the word "firstborn" indicates that believers are beloved of God.[663] Just as Ephraim was God's "firstborn" (Jer 31:9) and Israel was the Lord's "firstborn" (Exod 4:22), so believers are God's children.[664]

Believers haven't just come to the heavenly city, to countless angels, and to the heavenly assembly. They have come to God himself, the one who judges all and determines one's final destiny. Incidentally the references to coming to God and Jesus here constitute important evidence that the perfect tense verb "come" (προσεληλύθατε, v. 22) has an already-but-not-yet dimension. For it would contradict the rest of the letter to say that the readers had not yet come to God and to Jesus Christ. The point of the entire letter is that believers now have access to God through the high priestly atoning work of Jesus Christ.

The word "judge" precedes God, stressing God's awesome holiness. Why does the author refer to God as judge in a paragraph that stresses the joy of coming into God's presence? The hearers are reminded that they will be vindicated on the last day.[665] "This joyful fellowship is not to be taken lightly. God has not relented in his holiness."[666] They come boldly to God's throne where he bestows

---

[662] O'Brien, *Hebrews*, 485.

[663] So L. Johnson, *Hebrews*, 332. The reference is not to the festive gathering of angels here. Against Käsemann, *Wandering People*, 50; Spicq, *L'Épître aux Hébreux*, 2:407.

[664] Hence the writer has all believers throughout history in view here (Hughes, *Hebrews*, 555; O'Brien, *Hebrews*, 485).

[665] Cf. O'Brien, *Hebrews*, 486.

[666] Cockerill, *Hebrews*, 656.

grace because of Jesus (4:16), and they draw near full of assurance (10:22), knowing they will escape judgment because their bodies have been washed and cleansed.

They have also come "to the spirits of righteous people made perfect."[667] The use of the word "spirits" indicates that those described here are no longer in their mortal bodies.[668] On the one hand OT saints are not perfected without NT believers (11:40). On the other hand the author can speak of all believers as already being perfected by virtue of the priestly work of Jesus Christ (10:14). Here he means "they lack nothing in their relationship to God."[669] They "have been cleansed from sin and thus brought into the presence of God through the work of Christ."[670] The writer speaks here of all believers throughout the ages.[671] The perfection described doesn't mean believers already enjoy all God has done for them. It means the perfecting work accomplished for them guarantees their entrance into the heavenly city.[672] The readers are described as God's people, as the gathered assembly whose names are inscribed in heaven. The last phrase relating to spirits is limited to believers who have died but who are perfected because of Jesus' sacrifice on their behalf.

12:24

The author's list climaxes with the reference to Jesus. The joyful access to God described in the previous verses has been opened through the work of Jesus.[673] The readers must not forsake Jesus and his priestly work, for they have come to Mount Zion instead of to Mount Sinai. Mount Sinai was terrifying, but Mount Zion is comforting. Believers are already members of the new Jerusalem, the heavenly city. They have joined the assembly of angels in heaven and the church of Jesus Christ. They have come to God himself and to other righteous believers. Most importantly they have come to Jesus, who is the "mediator of a new covenant." He is not simply

---

[667] The notion that the spirits of the righteous are in God's presence is common in Jewish literature (Attridge, *Hebrews*, 376). He cites a number of texts (376nn82–83).

[668] So L. Johnson, *Hebrews*, 332.

[669] Lane, *Hebrews 9–13*, 471.

[670] Cockerill, *Hebrews*, 657.

[671] So Hughes, *Hebrews*, 550; O'Brien, *Hebrews*, 487; Peterson, *Hebrews and Perfection*, 164.

[672] So Peterson, *Hebrews and Perfection*, 166.

[673] So Cockerill, *Hebrews*, 658.

the mediator of the new covenant (cf. also 9:15). He is also "the mediator of a better covenant" (8:6; cf. 7:22). The old covenant, the old arrangement between God and his people, has been displaced. The readers must not forsake Jesus since they have come to one who has instituted and ratified a new and better covenant, one which guarantees an "eternal inheritance" (9:15), for it secures complete and final forgiveness of sins (10:15–18). Sins are forgiven in the new covenant because of the blood of Jesus, which explains why his blood is better than the blood of Abel. Abel's blood testified to his faith, to his trust in God in offering his sacrifices (Gen 4:4; Heb 11:4). Jesus' blood is superior to Abel's because it sprinkles clean those who trust in him (cf. 10:22).[674] We come again to one of the favorite words of the author: "better" (κρεῖττον). Jesus' blood is better than Abel's because it secures forgiveness, and the heavenly Mount Zion is better than Mount Sinai, for it brings us into God's presence.

Bridge

In this section the author picks up another common theme in the book. Free and confident access to God is granted in the new covenant rather than in the old. Those under the old covenant were afraid to draw near to God on Mount Sinai, and they were terrified as God met them in a thunderstorm and an earthquake, emphasizing his holiness and judgment. Those under the new covenant now come into God's presence boldly. They come to God who is the judge of all with boldness because of Jesus' blood, which cleanses them from all sin. They are already members of the city of God, of the heavenly Jerusalem. They are already participating in heavenly worship with the angels and are members of the heavenly and eschatological assembly of God.

---

[674] Son, *Zion Symbolism in Hebrews*, 101. Or perhaps Jesus' blood is superior because it secures forgiveness, whereas Abel's blood cried out for vengeance (Gen 4:10; so Westcott, *Hebrews*, 417; Spicq, *L'Épître aux Hébreux*, 2:409; Cockerill, *Hebrews*, 658–59). Attridge suggests that Abel's blood may have, like the Maccabean martyrs, had an atoning significance, but Jesus' atonement was far superior (*Hebrews*, 377; cf. also Moberly, "Exemplars of Faith in Hebrews 11," 360). Koester says that the blood speaks to the listeners rather than to God (*Hebrews*, 546). For the inadequacy of this latter interpretation, see O'Brien, *Hebrews*, 489–91.

Hebrews 12:25–29

Outline

I. Prologue: Definitive and Final Revelation in the Son (1:1–4)

II. Don't Abandon the Son Since He Is Greater than Angels (1:5–2:18)

III. Don't Harden Your Hearts Since You Have a Son and High Priest Greater than Moses and Joshua (3:1–4:13)

IV. Don't Fall Away from Jesus' Melchizedekian Priesthood Since It Is Greater than the Levitical Priesthood (4:14–10:18)

V. **Concluding Exhortations and Warnings (10:19–12:29)**

   A. Exhortation to Draw Near, Hold Fast, and Help Others (10:19–25)

   B. Warning: No Hope of Forgiveness for Those Who Turn from Christ (10:26–31)

   C. Call to Persevere in Faith (10:32–12:3)

   D. **Exhortations to Readers to Endure (12:4–29)**

      1. Endure Discipline for Holiness (12:4–13)

      2. Pursue Peace and Holiness for the Final Blessing (12:14–17)

      3. You Have Come to Mount Zion Instead of Mount Sinai (12:18–24)

      4. **Final Warning: Don't Refuse the One Speaking (12:25–29)**

VI. Epilogue: Final Exhortations (13:1–25)

Scripture

[25] Make sure that you do not reject the One who speaks. For if they did not escape when they rejected Him who warned them on earth, even less will we if we turn away from Him who warns us from heaven. [26] His voice shook the earth at that time, but now He has promised, Yet once more I will shake not only the earth but also heaven. [27] This expression, "Yet once more," indicates the removal of what can be shaken—that is, created things—so that what is not shaken might remain. [28] Therefore, since we are receiving a kingdom that cannot be shaken, let us hold on to grace. By it, we may serve God acceptably, with reverence and awe, [29] for our God is a consuming fire.

Context

The exhortation section closes with a final warning before the author concludes with the epilogue of the book (13:1–25). The readers have been exhorted to hold fast to the gospel (10:19–25) and warned about the consequences of falling away (10:26–31). They must not abandon their faith but believe until the end as OT saints and Jesus did (10:32–12:3). So they must run the race to the end (12:1) and endure discipline for their own good (12:4–13). They must pursue holiness so that unlike Esau they will enjoy the final reward (12:14–17). Falling back is really unthinkable, for they have come to Mount Zion instead of to Mount Sinai, to the throne of grace where their sins are cleansed.

The author, then, warns them one last time (12:25–29). They must not refuse the one speaking, for if Israel did not escape when warned on earth, then believers won't escape the one who warns them from heaven (12:25). And no one will escape if they refuse to obey because the one who once shook the earth at Sinai has also promised to shake the heavens (12:26). The shaking means that God will remove the things of this creation (12:27). A new world is coming, a new kingdom is at hand, and therefore believers should give thanks and serve God with awesome fear (12:28), knowing that God is a consuming fire.

Exegesis

12:25

The sermonic character of Hebrews surfaces with the last warning, which begins with the words, "Make sure" (Βλέπετε). The readers should beware that they don't refuse the God speaking to them (see §5). They have the privilege of being addressed with the words of God and must pay heed to them. The author draws the contrast between Israel and the church, between those on earth and those in heaven, just as he has previously (2:1–4; 3:12–4:11).[675] God warned Israel on earth, particularly in the covenant curses that he threatened to impose on those who refused to observe covenant stipulations (Lev 26:14–39; Deut 28:15–68). The curses imposed were earthly curses such as famine, defeat in wars, crops that fail to produce, and

---

[675] But the warning here is stronger than what we find in 2:1–4 (Cockerill, *Hebrews*, 662–63).

disease. Most significantly the culmination of the curses was exile. God's word is an effective word. The curses he promised would
strike Israel indeed came to pass. They did not "escape" (ἐξέφυγον).
The author argues from the lesser to the greater. If those warned on
earth did not escape God's judgment, such is even truer for those
who "turn away" from the one who speaks from heaven. We have
an inclusio here with the first warning in the letter, which also says
there will be no "escape" for those who drift away from the Lord
(2:3). The readers are addressed with a heavenly word because Jesus
"passed through the heavens" into the presence of God (4:14; cf.
7:26; 9:24) and sat down at God's right hand "in the heavens" (8:1).
The "heavenly things" were cleansed with Jesus' sacrifice (9:23),
and so if they refuse what is said, they are rejecting what God has
done through his Son.

12:26

The heaven-earth contrast continues. First, the author thinks
of what happened on Mount Sinai when the old covenant was established (cf. 12:18–21). God shook the earth with his voice, as a
mighty earthquake caused tumult on Mount Sinai (Exod 19:18; Judg
5:5; Pss 68:8; 114:4, 6). The Lord has promised, however, a greater
shaking in the future. The author quotes here Hag 2:6 where the
Lord promises he will shake both the earth and the heavens.

In Haggai 2 Israel is enjoined to work hard at completing the
temple since they have the promise that God is with them and his
Spirit among them (Hag 2:5). This is followed up with the promise
that the Lord will shake both the heavens and the earth (Hag 2:6),
which means he will judge the nations of the world. When he shakes
all nations, the treasures of all nations will fill the temple (Hag
2:7), and there will be greater glory in the new temple than there
was in the old (Hag 2:9). The book concludes with another oracle
where God pledges to shake the heavens and the earth (Hag 2:21).
He promises to dethrone pagan kingdoms and destroy their military
power (Hag 2:22). Then the Lord will rule through his chosen one,
Zerubbabel (Hag 2:23).

The first four words of the citation stem from Hag 2:6, but the
remaining words of the citation are looser, though they still catch
Haggai's meaning. Since Haggai picks up the idea of shaking the
heavens and earth again (Hag 2:21), it seems probable that both texts
are referred to here. The author of Hebrews understands the words

of the prophecy eschatologically, so that it refers ultimately to the coming of the kingdom. In this verse the focus is on the judgment that is impending. The Lord will shake again, but the shaking will be more profound than Sinai and will include all of creation. Hence, Hebrews appropriates these words to refer to the final judgment.[676]

12:27

The temporal character of the prophecy is noted. Hebrews seizes upon the words, "Yet once more" from Hag 2:6. A removal of the present world, the present heavens and earth, is coming. The world will be shaken and changed, and only the unshakeable will remain. This doesn't necessarily mean the present world will be annihilated, though some have interpreted it in such a way.[677] It probably means all that is corruptible and defiling in the present creation will be removed, so the new creation, the new heavens and new earth, will shine with intense beauty (cf. Isa 65:17; 66:22; Rom 8:18–25; 2 Pet 3:10–13; Rev 21:1–22:5). The readers should not sink their hopes into the present world, for the world will not continue as it is. A great disruption is coming before the new world commences.

12:28

What cannot be shaken ultimately is God's kingdom. The coming of the kingdom is another way of speaking of the city to come (13:14; 11:10, 13–16; 12:22) and of the rest God has promised (4:1–11).[678] Nothing can prevent the kingdom of God from triumphing. As Daniel predicted, it is like a great stone that will shatter all other kingdoms and will fill the world (Dan 2:35, 44–45). Or, as we saw in Hag 2:21–23, when God shakes the heavens and earth, he will overturn human kingdoms and rulers and establish his kingdom forever. Since believers have already received that kingdom and are assured of enjoying it in its fullness if they persevere, they should be filled with gratefulness and thankfulness (cf. ESV, NIV, NRSV, NET, NLT). The HCSB translates the phrase, "Let us hold on to grace." The word for "thankful" (χάριν, NRSV) often means grace, but such a meaning is doubtful here. The verb "have" with the noun used here means "give thanks" in other contexts (Luke 17:9; 1 Tim 1:12; 2 Tim 1:3; 2 Macc 3:33; cf. 1 Cor 10:30), and there is no clear

---

[676] Ibid., 666.

[677] So Attridge, *Hebrews*, 381; Moffatt, *Hebrews*, 221; Schenk, *Cosmology and Eschatology in Hebrews*, 125–32.

[678] So also Cockerill, *Hebrews*, 670.

example where the expression refers to God's grace (but cf. 3 Macc 5:20).

Through such gratefulness believers serve God in a way that pleases him. God is honored when those who belong to him give him thanks and praise for his mercy. Such gratefulness is mingled with "reverence and awe." It is a humble gratefulness, a gratefulness mixed with a holy fear, with the realization that the kingdom is an undeserved and precious gift. Hence there is no arrogance or overconfidence in such thankfulness but a joy that is sweetened by a sense of awe.

12:29

The reason gratefulness is mixed with reverence and awe is now explained. "Our God," the God Christians can wonderfully claim as their own God, "is a consuming fire." Here the author picks up on the language of Sinai. Moses explains why he won't be allowed into the promised land and why the people should not fall prey to idolatry (Deut 4:22–23) by informing them that God is "a consuming fire, a jealous God" (Deut 4:24). The covenant with Israel was established in Exodus 24, and the Lord's glory settled on Sinai (Exod 24:16–17), and his glory "was like a consuming fire" (Exod 24:17). The author reminds the readers that God must not be trifled with. Those who heed the heavenly warning will enjoy the kingdom forever, but those who forsake him will face the fire of his anger. Cockerill rightly says these words reinforce "his call for gratitude. Recognition of such potential judgment only heightens the awareness that God is good in providing not only a way of escape, but a way that his own can enjoy eternal fellowship with him."[679] Now the readers, like the Israel of old, are on the cusp of entering the land (the heavenly city), and hence they must remember the awful consequences of failing to believe and obey.[680]

Bridge

We learn from Hebrews that warnings are salutary for the Christian life. The admonitions and warnings have a great urgency, for the warning is not from earth but from heaven, and if those warned on earth didn't escape, then it stands to reason that those

---

[679] Cockerill, *Hebrews*, 673.
[680] Cf. Allen, *Deuteronomy and Exhortation*, 68.

warned from heaven will never escape. A new world is coming. The present world will be shaken so that only the unshakeable world remains. That unshakeable world is nothing less than the kingdom of God, which will certainly come and be consummated. Hence believers should be grateful and full of awe and reverence, realizing that God is a consuming fire, one who destroys all who are opposed to him.

Hebrews 13:1–6

Outline

   I. Prologue: Definitive and Final Revelation in the Son (1:1–4)
  II. Don't Abandon the Son Since He Is Greater than Angels (1:5–2:18)
 III. Don't Harden Your Hearts Since You Have a Son and High Priest Greater than Moses and Joshua (3:1–4:13)
 IV. Don't Fall Away from Jesus' Melchizedekian Priesthood Since It Is Greater than the Levitical Priesthood (4:14–10:18)
  V. Concluding Exhortations and Warnings (10:19–12:29)
 VI. **Epilogue: Final Exhortations (13:1–25)**
    A. **Practical Expressions of Love in the Church (13:1–6)**
    B. Remember Your Leaders and Suffer with Jesus Outside the Camp (13:7–17)
    C. Final Words (13:18–25)

Scripture

¹ Let brotherly love continue. ² Don't neglect to show hospitality, for by doing this some have welcomed angels as guests without knowing it. ³ Remember the prisoners, as though you were in prison with them, and the mistreated, as though you yourselves were suffering bodily. ⁴ Marriage must be respected by all, and the marriage bed kept undefiled, because God will judge immoral people and adulterers. ⁵ Your life should be free from the love of money. Be satisfied with what you have, for He Himself has said, I will never leave you or forsake you. ⁶ Therefore, we may boldly say: The Lord is my helper; I will not be afraid. What can man do to me?

Context

Chapter 13 functions as an epilogue in the letter. A few scholars have questioned whether it belongs with the remainder of the letter, but that is decidedly a minority opinion and rightly so.[681] The content of chapter 13 fits well with the rest of the letter, showing that the chapter belongs with what has preceded. Chapter 13 expands further on what was introduced in chapter 12, i.e., "the vital issue of worship or service that is pleasing to God, and this is explicitly developed in 13:1–21."[682]

The author has argued in the letter that the Son is greater than angels (1:1–2:18), that he is greater than Moses and Joshua (3:1–4:13), and that as Melchizedekian priest he is greater than the Levitical priests (4:14–10:18). The exposition is punctuated by warnings (2:1–4; 3:12–4:13; 5:11–6:8), for the author celebrates Christ's greatness so that the readers will not fall away. We are not surprised, therefore, to discover that the last major section of the letter (10:19–12:29) consists mainly of exhortations.[683]

Chapter 13 is rightly described as an epilogue, for though it is part of the letter, it is not integrated as closely to the remainder of the epistle. At the same time the admonitions fit with the nature of the letter. Indeed the admonitions found here unpack what it means to serve and to please God in 12:28, showing the close connection between 12:28 and what ensues.[684]

The letter concludes with a number of exhortations, beginning in 13:1–6 with practical expressions of love. In one sense the exhortations are rather general, but at the same time the call to love and hospitality and to show solidarity with prisoners fits with the rest of the letter, where the readers are designated as exiles and are suffering (13:1–3). The commands to refrain from sexual sin and greed

---

[681] Rightly Filson, *Yesterday*; Attridge, *Hebrews*, 384–85; Mosser, "No Lasting City," 278–83. Against A. J. M. Wedderburn, "The 'Letter' to the Hebrews and Its Thirteenth Chapter," *NTS* 50 (2004).

[682] O'Brien, *Hebrews*, 503.

[683] The exhortations mark out the church as a distinct social unit, emphasizing their solidarity as believers in a culture in which they were the minority. See Knut Backhaus, "How to Entertain Angels: Ethics in the Epistle to the Hebrews," in *Hebrews: Contemporary Methods—New Insights*, ed. G. Gelardini (Leiden: Brill, 2005), 149–75.

[684] Mosser, "No Lasting City," 329.

are general (13:4–6), though the reference to greed may suggest that the church was experiencing financial pressures (cf. 10:34).

The call to remember their leaders who died (13:7–8) echoes chapter 11 where the readers are encouraged to imitate those who have faith. The reference to leaders opens (13:7) and closes (13:17) this section. In 13:9–16 the readers are called to align themselves with Jesus by worshiping at the new altar rather than the old. They should not try to find grace in the foods and the altar of the old covenant but rely on the grace that is theirs in Jesus Christ. Therefore, they should be willing to suffer reproach outside the community just as Jesus did, realizing that the city to come is their permanent home. What God desires is the sacrifice of praise along with doing good and sharing (13:15–16). In 13:17 the author returns to leaders, but here he refers to leaders who are still alive. The readers should submit to them, for that is the pathway to joy. Such an admonition accords with the rest of the letter, for such obedience is an indication that the readers are following Jesus, that they are not straying onto wrong paths.

The author closes with a number of conventional themes that are often found at the conclusion of letters. He asks the readers to pray for him and for his restoration to them (13:18–19). He prays that the God who raised Jesus from the dead would equip them to do what is pleasing and good before God (13:20–21). Above all, given the rest of the letter, this means they will not commit apostasy. The readers are exhorted to attend to the exhortation in the letter (13:22) and are given news about Timothy (13:23). The letter closes with greetings (13:24) and a grace benediction (13:25).

In this first section we look at 13:1–6 in more detail. The author begins with the admonition to continue in brotherly love (13:1). The rest of the admonitions in these verses unpack the nature of love. Love expresses itself in hospitality, and the author reminds that some have shown hospitality to strangers—unaware that they were actually welcoming angels. Believers are to care for fellow believers in prison as if they were imprisoned themselves and to remember those suffering ill treatment, for they themselves know the trial of bodily pain (13:3).

Marriage and purity in marriage should be honored, knowing that God will judge those who commit adultery (13:4). Believers should be content with what they have, for God promises never to leave or forsake them (13:5), and therefore believers can be confident he will take care of them (13:6).

Exegesis

13:1

The main theme in Hebrews is perseverance, and here the readers are admonished to let "brotherly love continue." The word "continue" (μενέτω) is a synonym for the word "persevere." The readers are not exhorted to practice just any kind of love, for they are admonished to practice "brotherly love" (φιλαδελφία; so also Rom 12:10; 1 Thess 4:9; 1 Pet 1:22; 2 Pet 1:7; cf. also 4 Macc 13:23, 26; 14:1). The emphasis on brotherly love is distinctly Christian, indicating the family relationship that marked out the early Christian movement.[685] The remaining admonitions in 13:1–6 reveal how love expresses itself in various situations.

13:2

Love manifests itself in showing hospitality to others. Hospitality expressed itself in putting up traveling believers and caring for their needs. Leaders in particular traveled and needed to be cared for by those to whom they ministered (cf. 1 *Clem.* 1:2; 10:7; 11:1; 12:1; *Did.* 11:4–6). Those who are brothers and sisters show their concern for one another in meeting practical needs. The importance of hospitality in the early Christian movement is reflected by it being mentioned persistently as a Christian virtue (Rom 12:13; 1 Pet 4:9; cf. Matt 25:35).[686] One can't serve as an overseer if one is not hospitable (1 Tim 3:2; Titus 1:8). Similarly widows shouldn't be supported unless they showed hospitality (1 Tim 5:10). The author reminds the readers of notable examples of hospitality in the OT. Both Abraham and Lot showed hospitality to strangers who ended up being angels (Gen 18:1–8; 19:1–9; cf. Judg 6:11–14; Job 31:32; Isa 58:7). We see from the example of Lot how important hospitality was in the ancient world, for he was willing to sacrifice his daughters for the sake of his guests. His willingness to sacrifice his daughters isn't commendable, but it does indicate how seriously he took his responsibilities as a host.

---

[685] Cf. Attridge, *Hebrews*, 385.

[686] J. Koenig, "Hospitality," *ABD* 3:299–301; G. Stählin, "ξένος," *TDNT* 5:17–25; Wayne Meeks, *The First Urban Christians: The Social World of the Apostle Paul* (New Haven, CT: Yale University Press, 1983), 109–10.

13:3

Brotherly love also means remembering prisoners. The author probably has in mind fellow believers who are imprisoned.[687] It would be tempting to ignore or forget them because of the shame incurred by associating with them.[688] The readers' sympathy and concern for prisoners in the past was noted earlier in the letter (10:34), and such sympathy manifested the vitality of the readers' faith (10:32–33). Presumably those imprisoned were incarcerated for their faith in Jesus Christ, and hence believers showed their solidarity and perseverance in the faith by caring for other believers. Now they are enjoined to care for those imprisoned as if they "were in prison with them." This last expression strengthens the notion that fellow believers were imprisoned, for believers are to join, so to speak, in the suffering of those incarcerated. We saw in 10:32–34 that sympathizing with prisoners was one expression of perseverance, and the same is true here. The readers were tempted to avoid suffering and to fit in with society. The author calls on his readers to identify with fellow believers in prison, showing that their affections are toward the city of God instead of the city of man.

In the same way they are to care actively for those who "are mistreated" (τῶν κακουχουμένων). The parallel in 11:37, which speaks of OT saints who were "mistreated" (κακουχούμενοι), indicates the author refers here to persecution. Once again the readers will demonstrate their allegiance to the gospel if they identify with and care for those suffering for the sake of the gospel. The ethic of the letter is not ethereal but concrete and practical. Believers should empathize and care for those suffering, for they too "are in the body" (ESV). They can imagine the physical hardships of those afflicted and alleviate their pain as opportunity arises.

13:4

Perhaps the reference to the body leads the author to think of marriage and sexual morality. Here we have the kind of general exhortation that characterizes Christian parenesis. At the same time we must note that he speaks to an ordinary and yet vital dimension

---

[687] So O'Brien, *Hebrews*, 508. For the conditions in prisons in the Greco-Roman world, see Koester, *Hebrews*, 564, and especially Brian M. Rapske, *The Book of Acts and Paul in Roman Custody*, vol. 3 in *The Book of Acts in Its First Century Setting*, ed. B. W. Winter (Grand Rapids, MI: Eerdmans, 1994).

[688] L. Johnson, *Hebrews*, 340.

of everyday life. Christians should hold marriage in honor and do all they can to preserve it. The marriage bed must not be defiled by sexual sin and unfaithfulness. The seriousness of the admonition is captured by the last line, for God will judge those who give themselves to sexual immorality[689] and adultery. One way to fall away from the faith is to give oneself over to sexual sin (cf. Gal 5:19, 21; Eph 5:5–6; 1 Cor 6:9; Rev 22:15).

13:5

The practical experiences of life continue to receive the author's attention, and he turns now to financial pressures. Sexual sin and greed were often closely linked in the ancient world (see 1 Cor 5:1–6:20; Eph 5:3–5; Col 3:5; 1 Thess 4:3–7).[690] We have been told earlier that the readers had been robbed of their possessions (10:34), presumably because of their Christian faith. Hence their financial straits may be attributed to their allegiance to Christ. Hence they are admonished here to keep themselves free from the love of money (cf. 1 Tim 6:10). Part of what it means to be devoted to the city of God instead of the city of man is to be content with what God has given, to give him thanks and praise each day for the gifts granted. Nor are the readers at the mercy of other human beings or an impersonal economic structure. They can be content, for God has promised never to fail or forsake them. He will provide what they need every day. He is with them in the most pressing and difficult of times. If they are suffering, they should not interpret it as if God has abandoned them.

The citation is closest to what is found in Deut 31:6 (cf. also Deut 31:8; Josh 1:5), though it doesn't match any OT text precisely.[691] In the context of Deuteronomy, which is actually the same context of Joshua 1, Israel is assured that they need not fear the impending conquest of Canaan, for God will not leave or forsake them.

---

[689] The word "immoral" (πόρνους) refers to sexual sin in general (Ellingworth, *Hebrews*, 698).

[690] L. Johnson, *Hebrews*, 341.

[691] See Attridge, *Hebrews*, 388–89. L. Johnson also sees a possible allusion to Gen 28:15, though he agrees Deut 31:6 and 8 are a "fuller antecedent" (*Hebrews*, 343–44). O'Brien thinks Josh 1:5 is the nearest text (*Hebrews*, 511–12; cf. also Cockerill, *Hebrews*, 686–87). Allen argues that Deut 31:6 is in view (*Deuteronomy and Exhortation*, 68–71), though perhaps Josh 1:5 is also included, so the author appeals to promises given to Israel before entering Canaan. Similarly these promises are addressed to the church, which must persevere to receive the inheritance.

Just as the Lord took care of Israel in the conquest of Canaan, so the author assures his readers he will take care of their everyday needs.

13:6

Since God will never leave or forsake his own, they can confidently say that the Lord is their helper. And if the Lord is their helper, then they need not fear, for human beings can do nothing to believers that has not already passed through God's hands. The comfort provided here fits with the circumstances in which the readers find themselves. They have already been robbed of their possessions because they are believers (10:34) and were tempted to turn away from the gospel in order to gain security and to be spared from difficulties. The last part of the verse is a citation from Ps 118:6. Psalm 118 is a messianic psalm that is often cited or alluded to in the NT (cf. Matt 21:42; Mark 12:10–11; Luke 20:17; Acts 4:11; 1 Pet 2:7), but here it is applied to the lives of the readers. In Psalm 118 the psalmist is surrounded by enemies who threaten to destroy him, but the Lord grants him victory over his foes, and thus he sings praise to God for his goodness. The connection to Hebrews is most interesting, suggesting further that what the author writes about finances is in a context where the readers face enemies. In other words they are probably in financial straits because they are Christians, and thus their contemporaries stand against them. The word from the psalm reminds them, however, that they have no need to fear. Ultimately human beings can do nothing to and against them. The Lord is their helper, and he will strengthen them in the midst of every difficulty.

Bridge

The author gives practical admonitions to a community facing persecution and distress. They should remember that they are a family and show brotherly love to one another. What it means to be a Christian is to show hospitality to brothers and sisters, caring for and supplying the needs of other believers. At the same time there is a solidarity with believers who are imprisoned. They were not to ignore them to avoid getting in trouble themselves. We are to care for those who are being persecuted, knowing the pain of physical suffering. The Christian church should be characterized by sexual purity and faithful marriages, realizing that God will judge those who turn to sexual sin. At the same time there is no need to worry about money and daily provisions. Believers should be content and satisfied, knowing God will never forsake us. No enemy or opponent can finally deprive us of what we need, for the Lord is our helper. We need not fear, for human beings can do nothing apart from God. He is always the Lord in every situation, caring for us and providing every need.

Hebrews 13:7–17

Outline

I. Prologue: Definitive and Final Revelation in the Son (1:1–4)
II. Don't Abandon the Son Since He Is Greater than Angels (1:5–2:18)
III. Don't Harden Your Hearts Since You Have a Son and High Priest Greater than Moses and Joshua (3:1–4:13)
IV. Don't Fall Away from Jesus' Melchizedekian Priesthood Since It Is Greater than the Levitical Priesthood (4:14–10:18)
V. Concluding Exhortations and Warnings (10:19–12:29)
VI. **Epilogue: Final Exhortations (13:1–25)**
    A. Practical Expressions of Love in the Church (13:1–6)
    B. **Remember Your Leaders and Suffer with Jesus Outside the Camp (13:7–17)**
    C. Final Words (13:18–25)

Scripture

[7] Remember your leaders who have spoken God's word to you. As you carefully observe the outcome of their lives, imitate their faith. [8] Jesus Christ is the same yesterday, today, and forever. [9] Don't be led astray by various kinds of strange teachings; for it is good for the heart to be established by grace and not by foods, since those involved in them have not benefited. [10] We have an altar from which those who serve the tabernacle do not have a right to eat. [11] For the bodies of those animals whose blood is brought into the most holy place by the high priest as a sin offering are burned outside the camp. [12] Therefore Jesus also suffered outside the gate, so that He might sanctify the people by His own blood. [13] Let us then go to Him outside the camp, bearing His disgrace. [14] For we do not have an enduring city here; instead, we seek the one to come. [15] Therefore, through Him let us continually offer up to God a sacrifice of praise, that is, the fruit of our lips

that confess His name. ¹⁶ Don't neglect to do what is good and to share, for God is pleased with such sacrifices. ¹⁷ Obey your leaders and submit to them, for they keep watch over your souls as those who will give an account, so that they can do this with joy and not with grief, for that would be unprofitable for you.

Context

The author begins the epilogue with practical instructions about brotherly love (13:1–6). Here he turns aside briefly to remind them of former leaders who have since died. He calls upon them to remember them as those who proclaimed the gospel to them (13:7). The paragraph is framed by the words of exhortation relative to their leaders (13:7 and 13:17).[692] Remembering them doesn't mean just recalling their words, for their instruction was matched by their lives. So they are to "imitate their faith." The affirmation that "Jesus Christ is the same yesterday, today, and forever" (13:8) is linked to the command to remember their leaders. The life and teaching of their leaders "yesterday" is still relevant to the lives of the readers "today," for the Christ whom the leaders served has not changed, for he is always the same.

The transition is rather abrupt in verse 9. Jesus Christ is the same, but the covenants have changed! And the readers should not go backward and live under the old covenant. They should not be carried away by strange teachings but should be strengthened by grace instead of by foods (13:9). Lane presents an interesting chiasm here.[693]

A (13:10) We have an altar from which those who serve the tabernacle do not have the right to eat.	C¹ (13:13) So then (τοίνυν) let us go out to him outside (ἔξω) the camp, bearing the shame he bore.
B (13:11) For (γάρ) . . . their bodies are burned outside (ἔξω) the camp.	B¹ (13:14) for (γάρ) here we do not have a permanent city, but we are expecting intently the city which is to come.
C (13:12) And so (διό) Jesus also suffered death outside (ἔξω) the city gate.	A¹ (13:15–16) Through Jesus, therefore (οὖν), let us continually offer to God a sacrifice consisting in praise.

---

[692] Cockerill, *Hebrews*, 689.
[693] Lane, *Hebrews 9–13*, 503. I am quoting Lane in the table.

The readers should not pay heed to strange teachings or try to be strengthened by the foods of the old covenant, for as Christians we have a better altar than the altar on which animals were sacrificed (13:10). The blood of animals under the old covenant is offered in the holy place, but their bodies were burned outside the camp (13:11). Jesus also suffered outside the city gate (13:12), and thus the readers are to follow Jesus and imitate him, being willing to go outside the camp and to bear his reproach as disciples of Christ (13:13) since they await the city to come (13:14). They are to offer new sacrifices (13:15–16), sacrifices of praise and generosity. Lane again helpfully sees a chiasm in 13:15–16.[694]

A Through him, therefore, let us continually offer a sacrifice of praise to God (15a)	B[1] Do not neglect acts of kindness and generosity (16a)
B this is to say, the fruit of the lips that praise his name (15b)	A[1] for God is pleased because of such sacrifices (16b)

In verse 7 the readers are encouraged to remember former leaders, and the paragraph closes with an exhortation to remember their present leaders. Leaders have a particular responsibility for the lives of those under their authority, and if the readers obey the gospel, the leaders will rejoice instead of groaning. Such obedience doesn't merely redound to the benefit of the leaders. It benefits the readers as well, leading to their final salvation.

Exegesis

13:7

The readers are admonished to remember their leaders. The leaders here are probably to be distinguished from the leaders in 13:17, for they are not called upon to obey them but remember them. It seems probable, then, that the leaders in view here have died. Remembering is not just mental recollection but embraces the whole person. It is a kind of remembering that changes those who do the recollecting. The word for "leaders" (τῶν ἡγουμένων) is also used by the author in 13:17 and 13:24. In the NT the term is used for the Davidic king (Matt 2:6; cf. Gen 49:10), for a leader in general (Luke 22:26), for Joseph as the leader over Egypt (Acts 7:10), and

---

[694] Ibid., 504.

for Judas Barsabbas and Silas as leaders (Acts 15:22). In the OT the term is used for leaders as well (Deut 1:13; 5:23; Josh 13:21; Judg 9:51; 11:6, 11; 1 Sam 15:17; 22:2; 25:30, etc.). The term is a rather general term for leaders, including political leaders as well, but here the reference is clearly to leaders in the church.

Just as the readers must avoid the example of the wilderness generation and Esau (3:7–4:13; 12:16–17) and imitate the saints of the old covenant (11:1–40) and Jesus himself (12:1–3), they should imitate the lives of godly leaders from the past. They should remember their leaders because they "spoke to you the word of God" (ESV). The oral preaching of the leaders is emphasized, and God's word centers on the gospel of Jesus Christ, focusing on his death and resurrection for the forgiveness of sins. Leaders who established the church may be in view here.[695] The readers must not forsake the word proclaimed by their former leaders. They are not only to stay true to the teaching of the leaders but must also "imitate their faith." After examining and remembering "the outcome (ἔκβασιν) of their lives," they should be inspired to live as they did. The word "outcome" could refer to the end of life (Wis 2:17) or more generally the consequence or result of their lives. The term itself doesn't clearly indicate that the leaders have died, but the call to remember and the contrast with 13:17 suggest they are deceased.[696] The transformed life of the leaders is attributed to their faith, to their radical trust in God. Such was the faith of the OT saints in 11:1–40, and it was lack of faith, as the author emphasized earlier, that prevented Israel from entering God's rest (3:12, 19; 4:2–3).

13:8

Verse 8 asserts that Jesus Christ remains the same, picking up the thought from 1:11–12. The author does not suddenly insert here a bit of abstract systematic theology that is unrelated to the context. He exhorts the readers to remember the gospel and the life of leaders who are no longer with them (v. 7). The readers should not fend off these words by thinking that those were different circumstances and a different time so that the life of former leaders is no longer relevant to them. On the contrary the Christ they worshiped is the

---

[695] Cf. Attridge, *Hebrews*, 391; Cockerill, *Hebrews*, 689.
[696] Cf. Attridge, *Hebrews*, 392.

same yesterday and today.[697] Outward circumstances may change, but he doesn't change. Leaders may die, but Jesus remains the same and continues to be faithful.[698] They should look to Jesus who, as 12:1–3 demonstrates, is "the supreme example of faithfulness and constancy."[699] Indeed he remains the same forever. The grace that enabled the leaders to trust in God and to live in a way that pleases God is still available, and it will always be available.

13:9

The readers should stay true to the teaching given by their former leaders (13:7), and "not be carried away" (NIV) by teachings that are alien to the message communicated (cf. ἐβεβαιώθη, confirmed) to them (2:3). The verb "carried away" is used for wind and water that transport things by their force (cf. Eph 4:14–16).[700] The identity of these strange teachings is on first glance uncertain, but as the author unfolds his argument in the subsequent verses, it is clear he refers to teachings derived from the OT law.[701] We have clear evidence, then, that the instructions here accord with the main purpose of the letter in which the author exhorts the readers not to embrace the old covenant and the Levitical cult. The readers must not be swayed by such teachings, for they will not afford them assistance.

The heart (i.e., the whole person) can only be "established" (βεβαιοῦσθαι) and confirmed by grace. It is the grace of God, manifested supremely in the sacrificial death and resurrection of Jesus Christ, that strengthens a person. Foods, on the other hand, do not profit. The foods are most likely the foods of the old covenant. Earlier the author spoke of "physical regulations" and "food and drink" that cannot "perfect the worshiper's conscience" (9:9–10).

---

[697] Lane wrongly says that the statement is not an ontological description of Jesus Christ but refers to the unchanging gospel message (*Hebrews 9–13*, 528). The text actually focuses on Jesus Christ, not the message proclaimed, though in any case we don't want to insert a wedge between the two.

[698] Cf. Attridge, *Hebrews*, 392; Cockerill, *Hebrews*, 691.

[699] Filson, *Yesterday*, 31.

[700] Cf. Attridge, *Hebrews*, 393.

[701] Attridge rightly remarks that "strange" should not be equated with "exotic" (*Hebrews*, 393). The reference is not to pagan meals or to asceticism (Michel, *Der Brief an die Hebräer*, 224), or even a general description of foods. The context of the rest of the letter indicates Jewish practices are in view (Lane, *Hebrews 9–13*, 532).

Such external regulations were not evil.[702] They separated Israel from the nations as the people of God. But neither were they intended to be permanent, and they were certainly not effectual.

13:10

The foods of the old covenant do not profit, for they don't supply grace. They are just external (9:9–10). Believers, on the other hand, have a far better altar. Clearly the author isn't thinking of a literal altar. The altar where sacrifices were offered points to a better altar where Christ was sacrificed to atone for sins.[703] The author doesn't think of a literal altar in heaven, for the imagery shouldn't be pressed to suggest that there is literal altar in the heavenly sanctuary.[704] Hebrews never mentions a heavenly altar.[705] As O'Brien says, "Hebrews nowhere suggests that the heavenly sanctuary contained an altar of sacrifice."[706] Those who attend to the earthly tabernacle have no "right to eat" from the altar of Christ, for they are "behind the times" and are still attending to the old altar.[707] Believers, on the other hand, "eat" from this better altar. He refers to Christ's sacrifice here, the nature of which was explicated previously in the letter.[708] The "eating" again isn't literal. It is a colorful way of describing the grace believers enjoy through the sacrifice of Christ. The author reprises here in a fresh way the Melchizedekian priesthood of Jesus Christ, showing that his "altar" and his "food" are far better than the altar and food of the old covenant (see §2.4).

---

[702] L. Johnson says the author introduces foods as synecdoche for external and material regulations of the old covenant (*Hebrews*, 347–48). See also Ellingworth, *Hebrews*, 708. It is doubtful that we have any reference to the Eucharist here (rightly Hughes, *Hebrews*, 573).

[703] So Hughes, *Hebrews*, 575, 578. There is no basis to see a reference to the Eucharist (rightly Hughes, *Hebrews*, 577).

[704] Rightly Koester, *Hebrews*, 568–69.

[705] "Given only what the eye could see, Christians possessed no altar. But rather than declaring that altars are irrelevant, Hebrews says that Christians have an altar—though one apparent only by faith. . . . In one sense, the altar is the place where Jesus was crucified" (Koester, *Hebrews*, 575).

[706] O'Brien, *Hebrews*, 521.

[707] Those who serve at the altar are Levitical priests, but the author speaks loosely and has in mind all those who attend to the sacrifices of the first covenant (rightly O'Brien, *Hebrews*, 521–22).

[708] Cf. Attridge, *Hebrews*, 396.

13:11

The author in verses 11–12 considers the sacrifice on the two different altars, finding a point of similarity (they were both destroyed outside the camp) and difference (Jesus' sacrifice made them holy). Verse 11 confirms that the author isn't thinking of the altar of incense but the altar where animal sacrifices were offered. The blood of the animals was brought into "the most holy place" (εἰς τὰ ἅγια) by the high priest. The HCSB rightly says that the blood was used for a "sin offering" (περὶ ἁμαρτίας). The author probably has in mind the ritual in Leviticus 16, where the blood of animals was brought into the most holy place to secure forgiveness of sins since he notes that atonement was secured through the high priest (Lev 16:15–16, 27), whereas other priests could offer regular sacrifices (Lev 1:5, 7–8; 3:2, 8). Once again a previous discussion is recalled (Heb 9:7). The practice of burning bulls outside the camp for sin offerings was common (Exod 29:14; Lev 4:12, 21; 9:11). We have seen, however, that other elements in the context suggest a link with Leviticus 16, for the author specifically says the remainder of the bull is to be burned "outside the camp" (Lev 16:27).

13:12

A parallel and a contrast are drawn between Jesus' suffering and the fate of animals. Just as sacrificial animals were burned outside the camp, so Jesus "suffered outside the gate." The gate here refers to the walls of Jerusalem, indicating that Jesus died outside the city limits of Jerusalem (John 19:17–20). The author probably uses the word "suffered" to create a link between the experience of Jesus and the experience of the readers, for even though the readers had not died for their faith (12:3), they were indeed suffering.

The sacrifice of Jesus was also distinct from the sin offerings of the old covenant. For Jesus' blood "sanctified" (ἁγιάσῃ) the people. They were placed into the realm of the holy through his sacrifice. The author echoes here what was taught earlier in the letter, where he affirms, "We have been sanctified through the offering of the body of Jesus Christ once and for all" (10:10), and in 10:29 he affirms that believers are sanctified through Jesus' blood. True cleansing is not secured through animal sacrifices but only through the one to whom the sin offerings pointed. Not the blood of animals but the blood of Jesus cleanses from sin.

13:13

Since Jesus suffered outside the camp, "therefore" (ESV; τοίνυν), believers should join him outside the camp.[709] In the OT being outside the camp meant that one was excluded from the place where God specially dwelt with his people, and hence that which was unclean was not allowed in the camp (Lev 4:12; 10:4–5; 13:46; 14:3; 16:26; Num 5:2–4; 19:7). Jesus' suffering and death show that he was the "unclean" one, despised by human beings. The readers must identify with Jesus. They were tempted to find their identity within the community of Israel, to belong to a group that was welcomed by society.[710] What the author means by these words has been interpreted a number of ways. Some take it generally to say that believers should not be attached to this world. Others have read it specifically. For instance Mosser argues that the author literally exhorts the readers to leave Jerusalem, just as Rahab left Jericho.[711] Such a specific referent is possible but seems less likely. The author calls upon the readers to follow Jesus. They should not find their security and safety in the sacrifices of the old covenant. Such sacrifices should not be the place where they seek forgiveness of their sins. Instead, they should bear the "reproach" (ὀνειδισμόν) of Jesus and stand out as disciples of Jesus. Moses was willing to give up the pleasure of belonging to those who enjoyed nobility and power in Egypt, bearing "the reproach (ὀνειδισμόν) of Christ" (11:26). Similarly the readers endured "reproaches" (ὀνειδισμοῖς) in the past

---

[709] Against Bruce W. Winter ("Suffering with the Saviour: The Reality, the Reasons and the Reward," in *The Perfect Savior: Key Themes in Hebrews*, ed. J. Griffiths [Nottingham: InterVarsity, 2012], 151), I don't take the exile to be literal expulsion from their homeland.

[710] The words here are not a general admonition but exhort believers to leave the comfort and security of Judaism. Against Attridge, *Hebrews*, 399; James W. Thompson, "Outside the Camp: A Study of Heb 13:9–14," *CBQ* 40 (1978): 53–63. Thompson says there is no polemic here against heretical teachings, but see O'Brien, *Hebrews*, 524–25.

[711] Mosser, "No Lasting City," 290–320. Mosser also provides a helpful survey of various interpretations (285–89). Helmut Koester thinks the readers are exhorted to embrace the secular world and to leave the sacred world behind. Christians are called upon to be "worldly" instead of "unworldly" ("'Outside the Camp': Hebrews 13.9–14," *HTR* 55 [1962]: 299–315). Such a reading, however, skews the text with modern notions of sacred and secular.

because of their faith (10:33). They should renew their commitment to Jesus by being willing to suffer for his sake.

13:14

The author explains here why the readers should be willing to bear Christ's reproach and to go outside the camp with him.[712] He doesn't advocate self-denial for its own sake. Moses again serves as an example for the readers. He turned away from the power afforded by his Egyptian upbringing because he no longer put his hope in the comforts of Egypt but looked to the future reward he would receive (11:26). So too, the readers bear Christ's reproach because the city of man, the city of this present world, is not an enduring city. Believers await the eschatological city, the city of God, the heavenly Jerusalem (11:10, 13–16; 12:22; see §9).

13:15

Since believers live for the city to come instead of this present day, they are to offer through Christ "a sacrifice of praise" to God. There is no need to offer sacrifices for atonement (13:9–10), for Christ has atoned for sins and secured final forgiveness with his once-for-all sacrifice (9:25–26; 10:10, 14, 18). Believers give praise to God through Jesus Christ because he has cleansed their consciences so they are free from the guilt of sin. Burnt offerings were to be offered daily to the Lord under the old covenant (Exod 29:38–42), and in the same way praise is to be offered as a sacrifice continually.

The author implicitly contrasts the sacrifices that please God with those that don't please him.[713] The text echoes Psalm 50, which fits with the theology of Hebrews as a whole. The Lord doesn't desire animal sacrifices, for he has need of nothing from human beings (Ps 50:9–13), particularly now that the new covenant has arrived and Christ has given himself as a sacrifice. Twice the psalmist uses the same words found in Heb 13:15. God asks his people to give him a "sacrifice of praise" (θυσίαν αἰνέσεως and θυσία αἰνέσεως in 50:14, 23). Elsewhere a sacrifice of praise is to be rendered to God for

---

[712] Whitlark argues that there is a veiled critique of Roman imperial power here (Jason A. Whitlark, "'Here We Do Not Have a City That Remains': A Figured Critique of Roman Imperial Propaganda in Hebrews 13:14," *JBL* 131 [2012]: 161–79). Whitlark constructs an impressive argument, but I am unconvinced the author employs Greek rhetoric, which undermines Whitlark's thesis.

[713] Mosser, "No Lasting City," 327–28.

his deliverance of his people (Pss 107:22; 116:17), which Hebrews interprets as response to the sacrificial work of Jesus Christ. Such praise is the fruit of lips that confess and acknowledge God's name.[714] Such public acknowledgment takes place among those who recognize that Jesus is the Son of God and the Melchizedekian high priest.

13:16

Sacrifices for atonement are not needed, but God is pleased with those who do good and share with others, and such acts are designated as sacrifices. The word "share" (κοινωνίας) almost certainly refers to giving to meet the material needs of others (cf. Rom 15:26; 2 Cor 8:4; 9:13). In Phil 4:18 the gift the Philippians gave for Paul's ministry is described as "a fragrant offering" and "an acceptable sacrifice." The readers needed to be reminded about the importance of looking outside of themselves and caring for others.

13:17

The charismatic nature of the early church doesn't rule out the need for leadership or submission to authority. The author writes here about current leaders in the church. The readers should obey and submit to them (cf. 1 Cor 16:16; 1 Thess 5:12–13; 1 Pet 5:5). The author assumes in giving this command that the leaders teach and live in accord with the theology articulated in the letter. Hence the call to submit to the leaders is not universal. The readers should not submit if leaders deviate from the gospel. To put it another way, submitting to leaders in Hebrews is an indication that the readers are not repudiating the message preached to them.

The reason for submission is the special responsibility of leaders to "watch over" (ἀγρυπνοῦσιν) the spiritual lives of the readers. This fits with what we find elsewhere in the NT where leaders are identified as "overseers" (ἐπίσκοποι, Acts 20:28; Phil 1:1; 1 Tim 3:2; Titus 1:7), exercising the responsibility of overseeing the flock (1 Pet 5:2; cf. Acts 20:28). Nor do leaders enjoy unbridled power, for they will give account on the final day of their own ministry, and thus their ministry is to be exercised before God (cf. Jas 3:1).

If the readers obey their leaders, then the latter will be full of joy instead of grief and groaning in their ministry. The joy doesn't come from leaders exercising personal and autocratic power because of their selfish will. The leaders are joyful or grieved for God's sake.

---

[714] The name here belongs to Jesus according to Cockerill (*Hebrews*, 706).

If the readers fall away and apostatize, their leaders are grieved, but if the readers stay true to Christ, their leaders will rejoice. The readers' obedience isn't only for the advantage of the leaders. It is the best thing for the recipients of the letter themselves. If the leaders are grieved, then the addressees aren't faithful to the gospel, and if the readers stray from the gospel, then they will face the terrible judgments threatened in the letter, and that would certainly be "unprofitable" to them.[715]

Bridge

The life and teaching of leaders who inspired us should not be forgotten. Their faith continues to be a model and example for us. When we observe their transformation, the truth of the gospel is confirmed to us. We can also take comfort in the truth that Jesus Christ never changes. The grace given to the apostles and other stalwarts throughout church history remains the same, for Jesus has not changed.

In our antiauthoritarian age the call to submit to leaders is often misunderstood. The author isn't supporting the unbridled authority of leaders. If the readers flout the authority of the leaders, they are resisting the gospel itself and are in danger of committing apostasy. Submitting to the leaders, in other words, is one way of submitting to God and to the gospel since the leaders in the churches remain faithful to the gospel. Hence this verse doesn't teach that Christians should obey leaders in every situation. Christians should submit to their leaders as the latter are faithful to the gospel. When believers stay true to the gospel, leaders are full of joy; and if they turn away, then leaders will be grieved.

External matters like foods do not strengthen believers. What they need is the grace of God, and this grace comes from a heavenly altar instead of an earthly altar. God is not pleased with sacrificial animals but with sacrifices that respond to the grace given in Jesus Christ, with such things as praising God and supplying the material needs of others. It is tempting to try to be part of mainstream society, but believers are called upon to identify with Jesus Christ and to bear the same reproach he did. They must be ready to suffer,

---

[715] In support of the notion that the word "unprofitable" refers to the readers' falling away, see Attridge, *Hebrews*, 402.

realizing that their reward isn't found here but will be theirs in the city to come, in the heavenly city.

Hebrews 13:18–25

Outline

I. Prologue: Definitive and Final Revelation in the Son (1:1–4)
II. Don't Abandon the Son Since He Is Greater than Angels (1:5–2:18)
III. Don't Harden Your Hearts Since You Have a Son and High Priest Greater than Moses and Joshua (3:1–4:13)
IV. Don't Fall Away from Jesus' Melchizedekian Priesthood Since It Is Greater than the Levitical Priesthood (4:14–10:18)
V. Concluding Exhortations and Warnings (10:19–12:29)
VI. **Epilogue: Final Exhortations (13:1–25)**
   A. Practical Expressions of Love in the Church (13:1–6)
   B. Remember Your Leaders and Suffer with Jesus Outside the Camp (13:7–17)
   C. **Final Words (13:18–25)**

Scripture

[18] Pray for us; for we are convinced that we have a clear conscience, wanting to conduct ourselves honorably in everything. [19] And I especially urge you to pray that I may be restored to you very soon. [20] Now may the God of peace, who brought up from the dead our Lord Jesus—the great Shepherd of the sheep—with the blood of the everlasting covenant, [21] equip you with all that is good to do His will, working in us what is pleasing in His sight, through Jesus Christ. Glory belongs to Him forever and ever. Amen. [22] Brothers, I urge you to receive this message of exhortation, for I have written to you briefly. [23] Be aware that our brother Timothy has been released. If he comes soon enough, he will be with me when I see you. [24] Greet all your leaders and all the saints. Those who are from Italy greet you. [25] Grace be with all of you.

Context

Thus far the writer gives practical exhortations about life in the community (13:1–6) and warns the readers about finding strength in old covenant practices (13:7–17). They should continue to eat at Jesus' "altar" and suffer reproach with him. They will show that they are willing to suffer such reproach if they obey their leaders (13:17). The letter ends with a call to pray for the author (13:18–19), a prayer wish (13:20–21), one final exhortation (13:22), greetings (13:23–24), and a benediction (13:25). Such matters are often found in the closing of letters. In 13:18–19 the author solicits prayer for himself, for he himself may be in trouble with the authorities. He says he has a clear conscience and expresses his desire to conduct himself in an honorable way. He also asks them to pray that he will be restored to them soon.

As noted above, the final verses of the epilogue have a number of elements that are common in the closings of letters. In 13:20–21 we find a prayer wish, which was typical near the closing of NT letters (Rom 16:25–27; 2 Cor 13:14; Eph 6:23; Phil 4:20; 1 Thess 5:23; 2 Thess 3:16; 1 Pet 5:10). Certainly the prayer wish here is one of the most beautiful and one of the most theologically rich in the NT. The main point of the prayer is that God would equip and strengthen the readers to do his will. In light of the remainder of the letter, he wants the readers to be faithful until the end. The God to whom he prays is the God who acknowledges Jesus Christ as the shepherd of the sheep and who raised him from the dead.

Exegesis

13:18

The author asks the readers to pray for him. The plural "us" here probably refers to the author himself and thus represents a literary plural. The request to pray for the author of a letter is a common feature in NT letters (Rom 15:30–32; Eph 6:19; Col 4:3; 1 Thess 5:25; 2 Thess 3:1). Here the admonition is rather general. Given the other references in the NT, such prayer for the author is probably tied to the spread of the gospel. The comment that the author has "a clear conscience" might suggest that he is under attack from governing authorities, especially when combined with the request to be restored in 13:19. Perhaps he is imprisoned for the sake of the gospel. The righteous life of the author commends the gospel, and hence it is important to him that his conscience is clear and his behavior honorable in all that he does. He doesn't want to bring reproach on the gospel through any sinful behavior.

13:19

Perhaps the author is in prison or is detained from visiting the readers for another reason. In any case he urges them to pray that he should be restored to them soon, so that he can encourage them face-to-face. The language of restoration suggests the author was a member of the church and longed to be with them again.[716]

13:20

The author begins the prayer by designating God as the "God of peace." The phrase is fairly common in Paul (Rom 15:33; 16:20; Phil 4:9; 1 Thess 5:23) and should be interpreted to mean the God who gives peace. The readers, since they were outside the social mainstream, were experiencing significant stress, and hence he reminds them that God grants peace to believers. Furthermore, several exhortations have indicated the importance of peace within the church (12:14; 13:1, 17),[717] and the author reminds the readers that true peace hails from God.

The author also emphasizes the resurrection of Jesus (see §2.6). The resurrection, contrary to the opinion of some scholars, plays a major role in Hebrews. Jesus cried out to God and was saved from death by being raised from the dead (5:7). Jesus enters the heavenly sanctuary as the resurrected and exalted Lord (6:20). He is a Melchizedekian priest who abides as a priest forever by virtue of his resurrection (Ps 110:4; Heb 7:3). What sets apart Jesus as a priest is that "he lives" (7:8), for he has an "indestructible life" (7:16). He isn't like the Levitical priests, who were hindered by death, but he "remains forever" and "always lives" (7:23–25). Jesus is the resurrected Lord, sitting at God's right hand (1:3, 13; 8:1; 10:12; 12:2). The resurrection of Jesus signifies his superiority to all Levitical priests.

Jesus is also "the great Shepherd of the sheep." In the OT God freed Israel from Egypt through Moses as the shepherd of Israel (Isa 63:11 LXX).[718] Jesus' role as shepherd fulfills Ezek 34:23, showing that he is the new and true David, and that as the shepherd he will take care of his flock (cf. also Zech 13:7). Indeed, as "the good shepherd" he gave his life for his sheep (John 10:11 ESV; cf. 10:14;

---

[716] Cf. Attridge, *Hebrews*, 403.

[717] Cf. ibid., 405.

[718] See O'Brien, *Hebrews*, 533–34.

1 Pet 2:25), and such notions are not far from the author's mind since he refers next to the spilling of Jesus' blood. The phrase "with the blood of the eternal covenant" is attached to the phrase "who brought up from the dead our Lord Jesus." The word "with" (ἐν) designates in context the reason Jesus was raised from the dead. His resurrection vindicated his sacrifice, showing that God approved of the yielding of his life for others. We likely have an allusion to Zech 9:11, which says, "Because of the blood of my covenant with you (ἐν αἵματι διαθήκης), I will set your prisoners free from the waterless pit."[719] The shepherd theme also appears in Zech 9:16: "On that day the Lord their God will save them, as the flock his people" (ESV).

The author revisits a major theme in the letter, for the death of Jesus, the blood of Jesus, inaugurates the new covenant and effectively and finally provides forgiveness of sins so that believers enter God's presence boldly (9:12; 10:19). The blood of animals could not cleanse from sins in contrast to the blood of Jesus (9:14). Furthermore, the contrast between the new and old covenant permeates Hebrews. Jesus inaugurated a new and better covenant (8:1–13; 10:15–18). He guarantees a "better covenant" (7:22; cf. 8:6), and it is characterized by full and final forgiveness of sins (10:18). Believers enjoy an "eternal salvation" (5:9), "eternal redemption" (9:12), and an "eternal inheritance" (9:15) secured "through the eternal Spirit" (9:14) because Jesus has instituted through his blood an "eternal covenant" (13:20).

13:21

Since the readers have Jesus as their "great Shepherd" and "Lord," and since by virtue of his sacrificial death they have been forgiven of their sins, and since Jesus now reigns as the risen Lord, they can be confident that the prayer uttered here will be answered. The author prays that his readers will be strengthened to do God's will in every good thing, asking God to work what is pleasing in them through Jesus Christ. Given the rest of the letter, the author is probably thinking particularly of their perseverance, though it is not limited to such. The readers do not have the internal capacity to fulfill what is written here, and thus he prays for God's power to be unleashed in them and at the same time asks that his petition will

---

[719] My thanks to Aubrey Sequeira, who pointed out to me the allusions to Zechariah here.

be fulfilled through Jesus Christ. The God who has done this great work for believers, who has sent the "great Shepherd" to atone for their sins and has instituted a new covenant, deserves all the glory and praise for all time. His magnificent love exhibited to the readers and the wonder of his plan of salvation elevate human hearts so they are drawn to give great praise and glory to God, both now and forevermore. There is some ambiguity as to whether the glory belongs to God or to Jesus Christ here. Still it is most likely that the glory is ascribed to God. In 13:15 praise is given to God through Jesus Christ, and here glory is given to God through Jesus.[720]

13:22

A common verb for exhortation in the NT, "I urge" (Παρακαλῶ), is used here (cf. 13:19; Rom 12:1; 15:30; 16:27; 1 Cor 1:10; 4:16; 16:15; 2 Cor 2:8; 10:1; Eph 4:1; Phil 2:2; 1 Tim 2:1; Phlm 9–10; 1 Pet 2:11; 5:1). The term is well translated here, signifying the importance of carrying out the instructions that follow. The author addresses the readers as "brothers," as fellow members of the people of God. He encourages them to "bear with" (ESV) and "receive" (HCSB) his "message of exhortation" (λόγου παρακλήσεως). The phrase designates a sermon or a homily, and it is used in Acts 13:15 of the synagogue sermon given by Paul in Pisidian Antioch. Hebrews, then, is not a theological treatise or a theological essay but a sermon, an urgent word of warning and admonition given to the readers. "Our author wishes to convey the impression that he is present in the assembly and actually delivering his sermon to them."[721] The main point of the sermon is that they must not fall away from the message they first received, and the author organizes the letter to explain why falling away would be fatal and senseless. Apparently the author thinks he wrote briefly, though that may be a conventional word (cf. 1 Pet 5:12). One can only imagine what the letter would be like if the author wrote everything he desired in its fullness.

13:23

The verb "be aware" (or "know") here is likely an imperative.[722] The author wants the readers to know that Timothy has been freed from prison. The reference to Timothy is fascinating, and it explains

---

[720] Cf. O'Brien, *Hebrews*, 537; Cockerill, *Hebrews*, 718–19.

[721] O'Brien, *Hebrews*, 538.

[722] Cockerill, *Hebrews*, 720.

why some identify Paul as the author, given his close relationship with Timothy. Timothy plays a significant role in the NT, especially in terms of the Pauline mission (Acts 16:1, 3; 17:14–15; 18:5; 19:22; 20:4; Rom 16:21; 1 Cor 4:17; 16:10; 2 Cor 1:1, 19; Phil 1:1; 2:19; Col 1:1; 1 Thess 1:1; 3:2, 6; 2 Thess 1:1; 1 Tim 1:2, 18; 6:20; 2 Tim 1:2; Phlm 1). Apparently Timothy had been imprisoned and was subsequently released.[723] Unfortunately we have no further information about his imprisonment or the reasons for his release. The author hopes that Timothy will join him quickly, and if he does so, they will visit the readers together.

13:24

Final greetings are a staple of early Christian leaders, signifying the love and kinship that characterizes believers in Jesus Christ (Rom 16:3–16, 21–23; 1 Cor 6:19–20; 2 Cor 13:12; Phil 4:21–22; Col 4:10–15; 1 Thess 5:26; 2 Tim 4:19, 21; Tit 3:15; Phlm 23; 1 Pet 5:13–14; 2 John 13; 3 John 15). Interestingly, the "leaders" (τοὺς ἡγουμένους) are singled out for greetings. Indeed, "all" the leaders are to be greeted. The readers should subject themselves to these same "leaders" (13:17) since they teach and live out the message communicated by the author. Greetings are also to be given to "all the saints." The word "saints" (οἱ ἅγιοι) is another common designation for Christians, indicating that they are dedicated to God and set apart from the world (e.g., Acts 9:13, 32, 41; 26:10; Rom 1:7; 12:13; 15:25–26; 1 Cor 1:2; 6:1; 16:1; 2 Cor 1:1; Eph 1:1; 5:3; 1 Thess 3:13; 2 Thess 1:10; Heb 6:10).

The love and affection believers have for one another is evident, for also those who are with the author greet the readers of the letter. The phrase "those who are from Italy" (οἱ ἀπὸ τῆς Ἰταλίας) is ambiguous. It could mean that the author writes from Italy, probably Rome itself, and those who are with him (probably in Rome) greet the readers. In this scenario the readers may be in Palestine, Egypt, or somewhere else. On the other hand the phrase may refer to those who are from Italy (i.e., Rome), and the author and his friends send back their greetings to those at home. The latter seems a bit more likely, for the expression is limited to "those from Italy."[724] He

---

[723] So also Lane, *Hebrews 9–13*, 569.

[724] Attridge slightly prefers the interpretation defended here (*Hebrews*, 409–10). See also Lane, *Hebrews 9–13*, 571; Ellingworth, *Hebrews*, 735–36.

doesn't say, "All those from Italy greet you," or "The churches of Italy greet you." By way of contrast we see expressions like: "The churches of Asia greet you" (1 Cor 16:19). "All the brothers greet you" (1 Cor 16:20). "All the saints greet you" (2 Cor 13:12). "All the saints greet you" (Phil 4:22). "All those who are with me greet you" (Titus 3:15). "The church in Babylon . . . sends you greetings" (1 Pet 5:13). It seems that some from Italy who are currently with the author send greetings to their home.

13:25

A grace benediction at or near the conclusion of letters is common in the NT (Rom 16:20; 1 Cor 16:23; 2 Cor 13:14; Gal 6:18; Eph 6:24; Phil 4:23; Col 4:18; 1 Thess 5:28; 2 Thess 3:18; 1 Tim 6:21; 2 Tim 4:22; Tit 3:15; Phlm 25; cf. also Rev 22:21). Many of Paul's grace benedictions contain references to Jesus Christ or include other statements that make them more complex. The grace benediction in Hebrews is lean and spare. Actually, however, it matches the wording of Titus 3:15 exactly, "Grace be with all of you" (Ἡ χάρις μετὰ πάντων ὑμῶν). Paul is even briefer in 1 Tim 6:21 and 2 Tim 4:22, concluding with the words, "Grace be with you" (ESV). Perhaps he abbreviates the form when writing to friends. The author of Hebrews prays that God's grace will be with all his readers, for the grace of God will keep them from apostasy, and the grace of the new covenant established through the blood of Jesus Christ cleanses them from all sin.

Bridge

The Christian faith expresses itself in mutual care and love for one another. Believers, therefore, turn to God in prayer, asking God to strengthen and help fellow Christians in their journey to the heavenly city. We also recognize that the witness of believers in the world is exemplified in living a godly life so that God is honored by the moral virtue of saints. Finally, the author wants to see the readers so he can minister face-to-face with them, for such ministry is typically the most effective. The church of Jesus Christ is a family. Greetings and news about one another are significant, for every person matters; every person is important. Part of what it means to love one another is to greet one another warmly and in love.

The words in verses 20–21 pick up some of the major themes of the letter. The author reminds his readers that only God gives peace in the midst of the anxieties and worries of everyday life. The believers have a high priest who lives, who has conquered death, and this high priest is also their Shepherd. As their "great Shepherd" he spilled his blood for them so they would enjoy forgiveness of sins and be members of the new covenant. God works what is pleasing to him in his people. He is the one who saves and strengthens them for every good work. Hence all glory and praise and honor belong to God for granting salvation through Jesus. Those who have experienced his great goodness give him great praise.

Hebrews is a sermon. In reading the NT we do not have abstract theology unrelated to life. It was a pastoral issue that precipitated the letter, and we only approach it rightly if we receive it in the same pastoral spirit.

BIBLICAL AND THEOLOGICAL THEMES

When considering some of the themes in Hebrews at the beginning of the commentary, they were investigated in terms of structures of thought in the letter, such as promise and fulfillment, the already-but-not-yet eschatology of the letter, the role of typology, and the role of spatial or vertical thought in the letter. By considering some of the themes in the letter through these lenses, we saw how some major themes fit into the fundamental structures of the book. But it is also important to consider the central theological themes of the letter in their own right, and that task is pursued here.

§1 God in Hebrews

It is easy to overlook God in Hebrews, though he is one of the central characters in the epistle. One reason for this is the centrality of Christ in the letter. We rightly focus on Christ, and fixing our attention on him may lead us to neglect the role of God in the letter.[1] If we attend to the letter closely, God strides throughout the book. Several themes stand out when considering God in Hebrews. The writer often teaches that God is the Creator of the world (1:2; 2:10; 3:4; 4:3–4; 9:26; 11:3).[2] He created the world through the agency of his Son, Jesus Christ (1:2); and as Creator of the world, he is clearly the sovereign ruler over it. God's creative power and sovereignty are

---

[1] See Harold W. Attridge, "God in Hebrews," in *The Epistle to the Hebrews and Christian Theology*, ed. R. Bauckham, D. R. Driver, T. A. Hart, and N. MacDonald (Grand Rapids, MI: Eerdmans, 2009), 95–110.

[2] See especially Adams, who emphasizes that God's creative work is prominent in the letter (Edward Adams, "Cosmology in Hebrews," in *The Epistle to the Hebrews and Christian Theology*, ed. R. Bauckham, D. R. Driver, T. A. Hart, and N. MacDonald [Grand Rapids, MI: Eerdmans, 2009], 124–30).

evident, for all things exist because of him and through him (2:10). God's role as Creator is also featured in chapter 4, for after completing his work of creation, he rested (4:3–4, 10). God's rest doesn't mean he was inactive or inert subsequent to creation. Instead, it signifies that God's initial act of creation was completed. We also see that God is described as the builder of the universe (3:4), which is another way of saying he made all things (cf. Isa 40:28; 43:7; 45:7, 9; Wis 9:2; 11:24; 13:4).

The verse that has provoked the most interest relative to creation is 11:3. The author draws on Genesis in claiming that the world was created by God's word (cf. Gen 1:3, 6, 9, 11, 14, 20, 24, 26). Most of the discussion has centered on whether the verse teaches creation *ex nihilo*. One of the most promising suggestions is that the invisible thing by which the world is created is the word of God.[3] The problem with such a view, however, is that the invisible things (ἐκ φαινομένων) are plural, and hence this doesn't fit well with a reference to the word of God. Alternatively it has been suggested that the invisible things refers to the chaos of Gen 1:2, but chaos isn't invisible, so that doesn't work well either. It is difficult to be certain, but it seems creation out of nothing is the best option for interpreting the verse. In any case Hebrews celebrates God's creation of the world, and as Creator he is the sovereign Ruler and King of the universe.

God's rule over the world is assumed elsewhere in the letter. The angels belong to God; they are his messengers (1:6, 13), and their tasks are appointed by God (1:7). God sovereignly decided that the world would not be subjected to angels but to human beings (2:5, 7, 9). Similarly redemption and forgiveness were not offered to angels but limited to human beings (2:16). God, if he so desired, could have chosen to save angels as well, but he restricted his saving intentions to human beings and did not rescue fallen angels. Even the word "angels" points to their subordinate role, for they carry out the will of God as his envoys and messengers. In the same way, high priests don't serve at their own initiative but are appointed by God (5:1, 4; 8:3; cf. 7:1). God by his own authority and in accord with his own good pleasure instituted the new covenant and declared the old covenant to be obsolete (8:8–13; 10:15–18). The Lord granted signs and wonders and distributions of the Spirit to attest to the

---

[3] See the commentary on 11:3 here.

truthfulness of his revelation in Jesus Christ (2:4), signifying the superiority of the covenant established in Jesus Christ. The sovereignty and rule of God permeate the letter, showing that it is one of the fundamental pillars of the author's thought.

We find eighteen places in the letter that refer to the promises of God (4:1; 6:12–13, 15, 17; 7:6, 28; 8:6; 9:15; 10:23, 36; 11:9, 11, 13, 17, 33, 39; 12:26). Such promises indicate that God has a plan for the world that features the grace of God in Jesus Christ. God planned to bless the world through Abraham, fulfilling that plan through Jesus Christ. The promises reveal God's generosity toward human beings, showing his grace and love and mercy even for those who have rebelled against him. Hence, Jesus by God's grace experienced death for all so that human beings would triumph over death (2:9, 14–15). Human beings are encouraged to seek God in order to receive grace from him (4:16), for God's grace strengthens people to do the will of God (13:9, 25). They should not forsake the grace of God (10:29; 12:15) but hold on to it until the end (12:28).

Another feature of the promise should be noted. God's promise and oath cannot be changed (6:17–18; 7:21), and thus human beings can bank on what God has declared will happen. Similarly, God's promise also points to his character, for by definition what he promises will certainly come to pass. There is no uncertainty about God's promise, for God cannot lie (6:18). Lying is contrary to his character as God, for he is always faithful (11:11).

God's promises and grace point to another truth. God is able to fulfill what he promises. He rules over the world and is able to put into effect what he pledges. The sovereignty and greatness of God form the backdrop for the fulfillment of his gracious promises. God is majestic and great and is worthy of honor and glory because of his majestic greatness (1:3; 8:1). He sits on his throne, ruling over all (4:16; 8:1; 12:2). His sovereignty is evident in the creation of the world, for the Creator is surely also the ruler over all he has made (1:2; 11:3). Since God is the sovereign Ruler, everything in it exists for his glory and his praise (13:15, 21); and nothing can happen, even spiritual growth, apart from his permission (6:3). Indeed, God's name and glory are of fundamental importance, for Jesus came "to proclaim" God's name to all (2:12), and God's name represents his character and being. Similarly believers are called to praise God and to live for the sake of his name (6:10; 13:15). The glory of God, i.e., the praise of his name, is to be the animating principle of all those who live upon the earth.

Nothing can hinder God's promises, for he can strengthen those who are barren or impotent so that they can conceive children (11:11), and he is able to raise the dead if he wishes (11:19). Believers should be full of confidence, for they serve the "living God" (3:12; 9:14; 10:31; 12:22). He is not an inactive God but carries out his promises and his threats. In the new covenant God fulfills his promise by writing the law on the heart of his people (8:8–10; 9:20) so that he equips and strengthens them to do his will (13:21). Similarly the children of God or the brothers and sisters of Jesus are given to Jesus by God (2:13). In other words they become part of Jesus' family by God's grace, by his transforming their hearts. So too, the people of God (2:17; 4:9; 8:10; 11:25), God's household (3:6; 10:21), belong to God. They are his people and he is their God (8:10), which is another way of saying they are his covenant people. Along the same lines peace is not something human beings achieve through hard work but is a gift of God (13:20). God, in fulfillment of his promise to Abraham to bring universal blessing to the world, has prepared a city for his people (11:10, 13–16; 12:22; 13:14).

God's activity in the world is displayed by his voice and his word.[4] He is not absent from the world but vitally involved in it. Hebrews emphasizes repeatedly that God speaks, that he declares his will and purposes in the world. He spoke through the prophets of old and has spoken finally and definitively in his Son (1:1–2). As Griffiths observes, God speaks in his Son in an unexpected way, for he speaks especially through the identity and work of the Son.[5] Hence, as the writer unfolds the Melchizedekian priesthood of Christ and the significance of his atoning work, God is speaking through these words to the readers!

In citing the OT, the author doesn't say the Scriptures "were written" but introduces OT citations by saying that God "speaks" through the Scriptures (1:5–8, 13; 5:5–6; 8:5, 8; 11:18; cf. 4:8).[6] The

---

[4] See especially here Jonathan Griffiths, "The Word of God: Perfectly Spoken in the Son," in *The Perfect Savior: Key Themes in Hebrews*, ed. J. Griffiths (Nottingham: InterVarsity, 2012), 35–48.

[5] Ibid., 36–42.

[6] For an excellent essay on the theology of the Scriptures in Hebrews, see Ken Schenk, "God Has Spoken: Hebrews' Theology of the Scriptures," in *The Epistle to*

emphasis on speaking fits with the sermonic character of Hebrews, communicating the contemporary significance of what God says. God's word is "living and active" so that what is said actually comes to pass (cf. also 6:5). For instance, his voice will shake both the earth and heavens (12:26), and hence human beings should pay heed to his voice (3:7, 15; 4:7). God's word comes to the readers through the letter, through the sermon or "message of exhortation" (13:22) read to the recipients.[7] The writer hopes the word he delivers to them will be the means God uses to keep them from apostasy. God speaks to them through his warnings (12:25) and as he exposits the high priestly work of Jesus Christ. Interestingly, God's word is also delivered through leaders who proclaim his will and ways to the readers (13:7, 17).[8]

God is not impersonal or distant, but human beings are summoned to enjoy a relationship with him: to know him (8:11). The goal of life is seeing him (12:14), which means nothing is more delightful than enjoying him. Human beings should make it their aim to please God (11:5–6; 13:16), to gain his approval (11:2, 4–5, 39), to do his will (10:7, 9, 36; 12:9; 13:21; cf. 10:6, 8), and to have a good conscience before him (13:18) since he is the Lord. Believers are to draw near to God (7:19; 10:22) and come to him, for they will find help at the "throne of grace" (4:16). He forgives those who rely on Jesus as their great high priest (8:12; 10:22). God helps human beings and will never leave or forsake those who depend on him (13:5–6). Human beings direct their prayers to God, which shows that he cares about them and that he has the power to answer their petitions (5:7; 13:18–19). Blessing comes from God (6:7, 14; 12:14), and hence human beings must believe he exists and that it is worthwhile to seek him (11:6), for God calls on us to trust in him, to put our faith in him (3:12, 19; 4:1; 6:1; 10:39; 11:1–40). Those who believe in Jesus and trust in God are his children or sons (2:10, 13–14; 12:5, 7–8). God is their Father (2:11), showing his love for them by disciplining them so they are holy (12:4–11).

No one can deceive or manipulate God, for nothing is hidden from him (4:13). He knows everything that is done on earth. God is

---

the Hebrews and Christian Theology, ed. R. Bauckham, D. R. Driver, T. A. Hart, and N. MacDonald (Grand Rapids, MI: Eerdmans, 2009), 321–36.

[7] See here Griffiths, "The Word of God," 40–46.

[8] Ibid., 46–48.

invisible and can't be manipulated by human beings (11:27). God is just and doesn't tolerate sin (6:10). He is not impassive toward evil but is provoked and angry at those who sin (3:1, 10, 17; 4:3). His anger leads to action with the result that he punishes those who practice evil. Everyone is accountable to God, and so leaders must give an account to God for their ministry (13:17). Those who give themselves over to sexual sin and adultery will be judged by God (13:4). God is "the Judge of all" (12:23). Those who turn away from the salvation in Jesus will not escape his just punishment (2:3; 12:25). They will face his judgment, fury, and vengeance (10:29–30). It is indeed "terrifying . . . to fall into the hands of living God" (10:31) since God "is a consuming fire" (12:29). Thus human beings must worship him "with reverence and awe" (12:28).

The author doesn't unpack the significance of the relationship of God to Jesus as his Son in any detail, but he often refers to Jesus as the Son (1:8, 13; 3:6; 4:14; 6:6; 7:3; 10:29), suggesting the Father's ultimate authority and love for Jesus, for Jesus is designated as the Son and God is his Father (1:5; 2:11; 5:5). As the Son, Jesus obeyed the Father during his ministry (5:8) and was perfected by God through his sufferings (2:10). God appointed the Son as his heir (1:2; cf. 3:2) and high priest (5:6, 10, 7:17, 28), anointing him as the Son who rules the world (1:9). The Son radiates the glory of God, representing his nature to the world (1:3). Because of his obedience, the Son was raised from the dead by the Father (13:20).

Peeler nicely summarizes what Hebrews teaches about God as Father:

> In Hebrews, God is the Father of Jesus and in this relationship utilizes suffering to perfect and exaltation to honor. In precisely the same ways, God is the Father of the members of the congregation themselves, disciplining them so that they might be perfect as he leads them to share his glorious presence. God's status as Jesus' Father reveals the very character of God. He is powerful, intimately involved with his children, and generous. He is one who calls, one who listens, one who rewards, and one who disciplines. He allows suffering and labors for salvation. His abode is one of joy. He is capable of pain, anger, and compassion.

God's standing as Jesus' Father makes his status as Father of humanity a reality.[9]

§2 Jesus Christ

Jesus Christ plays a central role in Hebrews, for the fundamental issue is whether the readers will remain faithful to Jesus Christ and his sacrifice or will turn to OT sacrifices to secure atonement for their sins. The author makes an elegant and passionate case for staying true to Jesus Christ. His argument has many facets, but here and in the next section the identity of the Christ is sketched in. There is no claim here that divinity and humanity represent all the author teaches about Jesus, for Jesus is described as the Messiah, the high priest, the Son of God, and the Lord. On the other hand the divinity and humanity of Jesus are clearly central and major themes for the writer. Along with the discussions on Jesus' priestly work and sacrifice, they help us chart out what the author communicates about Jesus Christ in the letter.

It is also helpful to consider another perspective in considering the author's perspective on Jesus Christ. Small has studied how Jesus is characterized in the letter if one uses rhetorical *topoi* of Greco-Roman literature.[10] Small argues that by using narrative

---

[9]   Amy L. B. Peeler, "The Ethos of God in Hebrews," *PRSt* 37 (2010): 50. Peeler also says: "By analyzing the Father's relationship with the Son, several things about the character of God emerge. First, it is clear that he is a powerful Father. He is the God to whom the priests direct their service, the Creator and controller of all things, who will remain to see the end of all things being subjected to his Son. Second, he has chosen to be in relationship with another, a relationship of intimacy, naming Jesus as his Son. Third, in this relationship he has chosen to involve his Son in his reign and to share his glory. Fourth, he appoints the Son to his vocation as heir and high priest. In so doing, God is portrayed as a Father who listens to His children. Yet God's attendance to their prayers does not mean that he delivers them. Instead, God allows his children to suffer so that they might be perfected and be able to fulfill his plan for them. God's fatherly *ethos* with his firstborn Son is powerful, relational, generous, appointing, attentive, and perfecting. In many ways, this fatherly relationship will be similar with humanity; for, although, he is the firstborn, Christ, too is a Son" (45). For further elaboration of Peeler's understanding of familial teaching in Hebrews, see Amy Peeler, *You Are My Son: The Family of God in the Epistle to the Hebrews*, LNTS 486 (New York: Bloomsbury T&T Clark, 2014).

[10]   Brian C. Small, "The Use of Rhetorical *Topoi* in the Characterization of Jesus in the Book of Hebrews," *PRSt* 37 (2010): 53–69. I have tried to represent Small

criticism the excellency of Jesus is presented. Readers are invited to consider Jesus (3:1; 12:2) and to look to him (12:2). Small says they are to consider Jesus so they would have assurance (3:14; 6:11; 10:22; 11:1), so they would endure and hold on till the end (3:6; 4:16; 10:19, 32, 35–36; 12:1–3) and not fall away (2:1–4; 6:1–8; 10:26, 31; 12:15–17). The various *topoi* presented by Small are drawn from Cicero and Theon. I present briefly here his findings before considering in the sections below the divinity and humanity of Jesus.[11] First, we consider Jesus' origin or race.

Origin/Race	Texts
God's Son	1:2, 5, 8; 3:6; 5:5, 8; 7:28
Son of God	4:14; 6:6; 7:3; 10:29
Begotten	1:5; 5:5
Firstborn	1:6

Small appeals to 7:3 and what is said about Melchizedek ("without father, mother, or genealogy, having neither beginning of days nor end of life"), though I question whether the author intends to depict the deity of Jesus here.[12] Jesus is also depicted as a human being, as one who came from the tribe of Judah (7:14).

Second, the nature of Jesus is set forth. Small takes the word ἀπαύγασμα to say that Jesus is the reflection of God's glory (1:3),[13] though I think it more likely refers to his radiance. At the same time Jesus represents exactly God's character (1:3). He is designated as God (1:8–12) and as eternal (1:11–12; 7:8, 16, 24–25) but is also set forth as human (2:9, 14). Third, Small considers Jesus' training. He was perfected through his suffering (cf. 2:10, 18; 5:8–9; 7:28) and hence can now perfect others (10:14; 12:2).

---

accurately in summarizing his work. Anyone who looks at his article will see that I have drawn upon him closely here, often using the exact words in the charts since the terms regularly come from Hebrews.

[11] The texts cited and the wording here are drawn extensively from Small.

[12] Small, "Rhetorical *Topoi*," 60–61. But see the vigorous and fascinating defense of this notion by Jerome H. Neyrey, "'Without Beginning of Days or End of Life' (Hebrews 7:3): Topos for a True Deity," *CBQ* 53 (1991): 439–55. For my understanding of 7:3, see the commentary on that verse.

[13] Small, "Rhetorical *Topoi*," 61.

Fourth, various names, titles, and roles are given to Jesus.

Names/Titles	Texts
Jesus	2:9; 3:1; 4:14; 6:20; 7:22; 10:19; 12:2, 24; 13:12, 20
Christ	2:9; 3:1; 4:14; 6:20; 7:22; 10:19; 12:2, 24; 13:12, 20
Jesus Christ	10:10; 13:8, 21
Lord	7:14; 13:20; cf. 1:10–12
High priest	2:17; 3:1; 4:14–15; 5:5, 10; 6:20; 7:26; 8:1; 9:11
Priest	5:6; 7:17, 21; 10:21
King	1:3; 8:1; 10:12; 12:2; cf. Ps 110:1; see also 1:5, 8–9
Heir of all things	1:2
Greater than angels	1:4
Pioneer of salvation and faith	2:10; 12:2
Apostle	3:1
Forerunner	6:20
Mediator of new covenant	8:6; 9:15; 12:24
Guarantor of a better covenant	7:22
Minister of sanctuary	8:2
Great Shepherd of the sheep	13:20

Small points out that the author uses the various titles to comprehend various aspects of Jesus' life and destiny. For instance, the word "blood" is used both of Jesus (10:19; 12:24; 13:12, 20) and of Christ (9:14). The term high priest is used both of Jesus (3:1; 4:14; 6:20) and of Christ (5:5; 9:11). Jesus has entered heaven (4:14; 6:20), but the same is said of Christ (9:11, 24). To qualify as a priest, Jesus had to: be human (2:14, 27), be tempted (2:18; 4:15), be without sin (4:15; 7:26–27), suffer (2:10, 18; 5:8), die (9:12; 10:12), and enter into heaven (6:20; 9:11). Jesus is also described in Hebrews as a King who sits at God's right hand (1:3, 13; 8:1; 10:12; 12:2).

Fifth, Small rehearses the actions and events ascribed to Jesus. I describe these matters elsewhere, but it also helpful to list these in short compass so the extent of what Jesus did is seen at a glance.

Action/Events	Texts
Creation	1:2
Entered the world	1:6; 10:5
Proclaimed and praised God's name	2:12
Trusted God	2:13
Did God's will	10:7, 9
Tempted without sin	2:18; 4:15
Prayed to God	5:7
Suffered to learn obedience and to be perfected	2:10; 5:8
Died	2:9, 14; 9:15, 26; 12:2
Offered himself in his death as a sacrifice by shedding his blood	7:27; 9:12, 14, 25–26, 28; 10:10, 12; 13:12
Saved others by his death	5:9; 7:25
Death as redemption	9:12, 15
Bore sins of others	9:28
Cleansed sins	1:3; 9:14
Atoned for sins	2:17
Triumphed over devil so humans don't fear death	2:14–15
Leads humans to glory	2:10
Perfects humans	10:14
Sanctifies humans	2:11; 10:10; 13:12
Raised from dead	13:20
Entered heaven	4:14; 6:19–20; 9:11–12, 24
Crowned with glory and honor	2:9

Action/Events	Texts
Sits at God's right hand	1:3, 13; 8:1; 10:12; 12:2
Appointed high priest	5:10; 6:20; 9:11
Mediator of new covenant	8:6; 9:15; 12:24
Helps human beings	2:16, 18; 4:15; 7:25
Minister of saints and heavenly things	8:5–6
Will come in the future	9:28

Sixth, Small considers the speech of Jesus. Jesus speaks the words of Ps 22:22 to his brothers (2:12), proclaiming and praising God's name. In 2:13 the words of Isa 8:17–18 are attributed to him. Perhaps most remarkably in 10:5–7 the words of Ps 40:7–8 are put on his lips. Jesus also speaks in prayer in 5:7.

Finally, different dimensions of Jesus' death are highlighted.

Action/Events	Texts
His death as an offering	7:27; 9:14, 25, 28; 10:10
A voluntary offering	10:7, 9
His death for the sake of all people	2:9
To break the devil's power	2:14
To release humans from slavery and fear	2:15
To remove sin	7:27; 9:26, 28
To sanctify	13:12
Once for all	9:26, 28; 10:10, 12, 14

§2.1 Divine Son

When we think of authorial strategy, it is evident that the author wanted to highlight Jesus' divinity from the outset of the book, for his divinity is emphasized in chapter 1 more than any other chapter. Any question about whether the author refers to Jesus' deity is removed in chapter 1, for God "made the universe through Him" (1:2).

Some scholars, however, question such a reading, for they postulate wisdom as the framework and background for the author's comment. In the OT the Lord created the world through wisdom (Ps 104:24; Prov 3:19; 8:22–31). It is difficult to see, though, how the deity and preexistence of Christ can be denied here, for even though wisdom in the OT is personified, Jesus Christ is clearly a person.[14] He is not merely an ideal person but a real person. The Son's role as an agent of creation indicates his deity, for creation is a work of God, and in the OT God's creation of the world sets him apart from idols as the one true God (Gen 1:1–2:3; Isa 45:7, 8, 12, 18).[15] God is also said to

---

[14] Against James D. G. Dunn, *Christology in the Making: A New Testament Enquiry into the Origins of the Doctrine of the Incarnation,* 2nd ed. (Grand Rapids, MI: Eerdmans, 1996), 206–9. Kenneth Schenk says ("Keeping His Appointment: Creation and Enthronement in Hebrews," *JSNT* 66 [1997]: 104–15) that the Son preexisted in a sense but suggests that he did not personally preexist since the preexistence language draws on wisdom and logos themes prominent in Judaism. Schenk goes on to say that a number of texts attribute creation to God (e.g., 2:10; 3:4; 11:3), and Christ is viewed as the agent of creation. It seems to me, however, that Schenk blunts the texts that emphasize Christ's eternal preexistence. For instance, in 1:10–12 creation is clearly predicated of the Son, and, against Schenk, the text can't be reduced to the fact that he is eternal. Similarly identifying the Son as God (1:8) clearly indicates his preexistence as an eternal person. Hence what the author says about Jesus, though drawing on wisdom and logos themes, indicates that Jesus transcends wisdom and word in the OT. Rightly John P. Meier, "Symmetry and Theology in the Old Testament Citations of Heb 1,5–14," *Bib* 66 (1985), 531–33. Lindars says the Son of God preexisted but Jesus did not (Barnabas Lindars, *The Theology of the Letter to the Hebrews*, New Testament Theology (Cambridge: Cambridge University Press, 1991), 34). Lindars is correct in stating it so precisely, for the Son of God only assumed humanity at the incarnation.

[15] Against those who claim that chapter 1 is only about Christ's humanity and not his divinity. For such a perspective, see G. B. Caird, "Son by Appointment," in *The New Testament Age: Essays in Honor of Bo Reicke*, ed. W. Weinrich, 2 vols. (Macon, GA: Mercer University Press, 1984), 73–81; Lincoln D. Hurst, "The Christology of Hebrews 1 and 2," in *The Glory of Christ in the New Testament: Studies in Christology*, ed. L. D. Hurst and N. T. Wright (Oxford: Clarendon, 1987), 151–64. For a convincing critique of this view, see John Webster, "One Who Is Son: Theological Reflections on the Exordium to the Epistle to the Hebrews," in *The Epistle to the Hebrews and Christian Theology*, ed. R. Bauckham, D. R. Driver, T. A. Hart, and N. MacDonald (Grand Rapids, MI: Eerdmans, 2009), 69–94; cf. also Jody A. Barnard, *The Mysticism of Hebrews: Exploring the Role of Jewish Apocalyptic Mysticism in the Epistle to the Hebrews*, WUNT 2/331 (Tübingen: Mohr Siebeck, 2012), 264–66; Peeler, *You Are My Son*, 26–28.

work what is pleasing in believers "through Jesus Christ" (13:21), and Jesus' mediatorial role suggests his equality with God.

Jesus' role in creation is reiterated in 1:10–12 where the author cites Ps 102:25–27, identifying Jesus as Lord here. Again the author picks up language that reminds us of wisdom's role in creation (Prov 8:29). The Son laid the earth's foundations at the beginning of time (1:10). There is no question, though, of this work simply being "ideal" instead of "real," for the author cites an OT psalm that attributes creation to Yahweh, and Yahweh's work of creation isn't merely ideal. It is harder to discern *why* the author attributed the work of creation in this psalm to Jesus. There is no doubt *that* the Son is the Creator here. Perhaps via wisdom traditions any text that speaks of creation can also be attributed to the Son. The language is reminiscent of Gen 1:1 where we have a merism, for God is the Creator of "the heavens and the earth" "in the beginning" (ἐν ἀρχῇ). The same comprehensiveness is evident here. The Son "in the beginning" (κατ᾽ ἀρχάς) laid the earth's foundations and created the heavens. The allusion to Gen 1:1 demonstrates that Jesus shares the same stature and identity as God.

The created world will not persist forever, but the Son will "remain" (1:11). The Son is divine because he is eternal; his "years will never end," and he is always "the same" (1:12). We should recall again that this psalm was originally written about Yahweh, so there is no doubt that the eternality and unchangeableness of the Son are qualities of deity (cf. Mal 3:6; Jas 1:17). The same notion is communicated in the unforgettable words of Heb 13:8, "Jesus Christ is the same yesterday, today, and forever." The unchangeableness of Jesus points to his divinity, for creatures inevitably change over time. But Jesus Christ has never changed, whether one thinks of the past (yesterday), the present (today), or the future (forever). Jesus Christ's divinity, his role as Creator, his eternality and unchangeableness are not simply shared with the readers so they have such facts in their head. The author teaches that abandoning the Son of God would be fatal. They are not merely abandoning a religion if they fall away. They are turning their backs on the Creator of the world, the one who never changes, the one whose saving work was effective yesterday, still saves today, and will save for all time.

Jesus did not only create the world but upholds it: "He sustains all things by His powerful word" (1:3). Paul says something similar about Christ: "by him all things hold together" (Col 1:17). No human being or angel is ever said to sustain and preserve the created world, and hence the conservation of the universe demonstrates the Son's divinity.

The deity of the Son is confirmed and strengthened in 1:3. The Son "is the radiance of God's glory." The word "radiance" (ἀπαύγασμα) could mean that Jesus "reflects" God's glory (NRSV), or that God's glory shines forth or radiates from the Son (HCSB, NIV, NET, ESV, NLT). The same term is used of wisdom in Wis 7:26, and there also we have the question whether the word means "reflection" or "radiance." In either case, the deity of Christ is affirmed, for whether he reflects God's glory or radiates it, he shares the glory of God. If the idea is one of reflection, Jesus reflects the glory of God perfectly, and that is only true of one who is fully divine. If the meaning is radiance, which I slightly prefer, Jesus radiates the very glory of God because he fully possesses God's glory.

The next line confirms a reference to Jesus' deity. He is the "exact expression of His nature" (1:3). Even though NT scholars tend to be wary of ontological statements, it is hard to deny that we have such here. The word "nature" (ὑποστάσεως) certainly has an ontological character, and the text says that Jesus exactly represents (χαρακτήρ) or reproduces the nature of God. Since Jesus shares God's nature, he is truly and fully God. He shares the same identity as God, and yet the Father and the Son are also distinct. The author doesn't work out the doctrine of the Trinity, but we have some of the raw materials for that doctrine here.

The divinity of the Son is also taught in 1:6 where the writer cites Deut 32:43, which summons the angels to worship the Son. The use of the OT and other features of the verse are discussed in the commentary. What should be attended to here is the angelic worship of the Son. Such an action by the angels demonstrates that the Son shares the same identity as God, and hence the readers must not turn back to a revelation mediated by the angels instead of relying on the revelation given by the Son. In Jewish thought worship belongs only to God, and thus John is corrected and rebuked by an angel for worshiping him, for the angel insists that only God should be worshiped (Rev 19:10; 22:8–9). This accords with the OT which teaches that there is only one God and that he alone should be worshiped (Exod 20:3, 5; Deut 5:7; 6:13; 7:16; 8:19; 10:12; 11:13; Josh 24:14–16,

20–21; 2 Kings 17:35; Isa 43:10; 45:21, 22; 46:9). In the Jewish and biblical framework in which Hebrews is written, it is clear that the writer identifies the Son as divine.

The deity of the Son is specifically taught in 1:8, for Jesus as the Messiah and the King is identified in the words of Ps 45:6 as "God." In the original context of Psalm 45 the Davidic king is called "God." The words should not be read literally in their historical context, for the psalm also teaches that the king will be succeeded by his sons (Ps 45:16).[16] In Exod 7:1 Moses is "like God to Pharaoh," and it is obvious that the title isn't literal. Similarly, judges in Israel are called "gods" (Ps 82:6) by virtue of their judicial responsibility. The title is obviously metaphorical in Psalm 82, for the judges are reminded in the next verse of their impending death (Ps 82:7). Despite all this, it is obvious in the context of Hebrews 1 that the author literally describes the Son as God and is not using the term metaphorically or poetically. In chapter 1, as has been noted, the Son is identified as the Creator of the universe, as one who shares God's nature, and is to be worshiped as God. Apparently the author reads Psalm 45 typologically. What is true of Davidic kings at one level is true at a deeper and more profound level of David's greater Son. We have an example here of typological escalation. There is some preparation for this in the OT itself. The favorite psalm of the author, Psalm 110, asserts in the first verse that one of David's heirs will be his Lord. Similarly, Isa 9:6 says the son born in David's line will be the "Mighty God." Hebrews 11:26 supports this judgment, for Moses suffered reproach for Christ's sake. Such a statement implies an identity between Christ and God since Christ isn't explicitly named in the Pentateuchal narrative, and the verse also implies that the Christ preexisted so that Moses could suffer for his sake. The author of Hebrews ascribes divinity to Jesus and identifies him as God. The readers, therefore, should not repudiate the message of one who is so exalted.

Hebrews often identifies Jesus as the Son or the Son of God. Does the title Son point to Jesus' deity? If we consider the OT, Israel is God's son and his firstborn (Exod 4:22; Jer 31:9; Hos 11:1), and there is no suggestion here of deity. Similarly, the Davidic king is also said to be God's son and firstborn (2 Sam 7:14; Pss 2:7; 89:27;

---

[16] See further discussion in the commentary on 1:8.

1 Chr 22:10), but once again there is no suggestion that sonship indicates deity. On the other hand we have already seen the typological and eschatological character of biblical revelation. Typology is marked by escalation, and thus titles which are restricted to human beings in the OT may have a greater significance in the NT.[17]

I would suggest that the title Son is not one dimensional in Hebrews, and hence it refers to both Jesus' deity and his humanity. This is a way of saying that Chalcedonian Christology does not impose its theology on the NT but accords with it. More will be said to Jesus' humanity below, but that his deity and humanity are in view is supported by the first mention of the Son in the book, for the Son is both the "heir of all things" (humanity) and the Creator of the universe (deity, 1:2). God's speaking by his Son (1:2), then, is not merely a human word but is also a divine word. Just as God made the universe through the agency of his Son, so he speaks to human beings via his Son.

I am not claiming that every usage of the word "Son" emphasizes deity, only that in some instances the notion of deity is certainly present and that in the last analysis a sharp division between humanity and deity introduces a dichotomy not intended by the writer. The close relationship between sonship and deity is evident in 1:8: "But about the Son: Your throne, God, is forever and ever." It is possible, of course, that the author sharply distinguishes sonship from deity here, but it seems more natural that sonship includes the notion of deity since the Son is identified as God. If this reading is correct, then Jesus' superiority over Moses as the Son includes the idea that he is better because he is divine and Moses was merely human. Such an interpretation is supported by 3:6, for Christ is not merely part of God's household but rules over the household.

Jesus' priesthood should be interpreted along the same lines. As "the Son of God" he "passed through the heavens" and entered God's presence (4:14). Certainly Jesus was a human priest, for he was from the tribe of Judah (7:13–14), but the author's argument is more profound than simply saying Jesus was the ideal and best representation of human priesthood. As priest he is both divine and

---

[17] Though Schenk would not endorse all my conclusions, I agree with him when he says that in terms of identity Jesus was always God's Son, but he is only enthroned as Son at his resurrection/ascension ("Creation and Enthronement in Hebrews," 92–100).

human. The humanity of Jesus will be considered more in the next section, but it is appropriate here to consider 7:3. The writer remarks that Melchizedek was "without father, mother, or genealogy, having neither beginning of days nor end of life, but resembling the Son of God." As I argued in the commentary, the author is not thinking literally here, for he believed Melchizedek had a father and a mother. He exploits the silence of the text to make a point. At the same time the silences in the text point to someone who is greater than Melchizedek. As a human being, Jesus had a mother and beginning of days. But as the Son of God he is eternal (cf. 1:10–12!). He is both a divine and a human priest. Athanasius rightly expressed the message of Hebrews in his essay *On the Incarnation* (even though his essay was on the entire Bible), for Jesus saves from sin both because he is truly human and because he is fully divine. He is the human and divine high priest, and hence trampling under one's feet God's Son is no light matter (10:29). It is an egregious and heinous sin that warrants eschatological punishment.

Does the Son's sitting at God's right hand signal deity? The author of Hebrews in one of the main emphases of the book affirms that Jesus has sat down at God's right hand since his atoning work is finished as the exalted Son of God (1:3, 13; 8:1; 10:12; 12:2). In the remainder of the NT, in dependence upon Ps 110:1, Jesus' sitting at God's right hand is assigned great significance (Matt 22:44; 26:64; Mark 12:36; 14:62; Luke 20:42; 22:69; Acts 2:33–34; 5:31; 7:55–56;[18] Rom 8:34; Eph 1:20; Col 3:1; 1 Pet 3:22).[19] The angels stand at God's right and left hand as he consults them (1 Kgs 22:19; 2 Chr 18:18). Bathsheba sits at Solomon's right hand (1 Kgs 2:19), which seems to signal that she shares at that moment Solomon's rule. It seems in the NT that sitting at God's right hand is a claim to deity as well. The charge of blasphemy follows Jesus' claim that he will come in power seated at God's right hand (Matt 26:64–65; Mark 14:62–64; Luke 22:69–71).[20] Indeed, as the one seated at

---

[18] In Acts 7:55–56 Jesus stands by God's right hand, but space is lacking to pursue that theme here.

[19] Some of these texts do not specifically say that Jesus is seated (cf. Acts 2:33; Rom 8:34; 1 Pet 3:22).

[20] See Darrell Bock, *Blasphemy and Exaltation in Judaism and the Final Examination of Jesus: A Philological-Historical Study of the Key Jewish Themes Impacting Mark 14:61–64* (Grand Rapids, MI: Baker, 2000).

God's right hand, he grants forgiveness and repentance, which are divine prerogatives (Acts 5:31). Similarly his intercession for believers appears to be a divine activity (Heb 7:25; cf. Rom 8:34), and divine stature is indicated by angelic powers being subjected to him (Heb 1:4–14; 2:5, 16; cf. 1 Pet 3:22).

None of the texts about Jesus' sitting at God's right hand in Hebrews necessarily point to his deity, for they also certainly relate to his exaltation as a human being and as the Davidic king. At the same time the language of sitting at God's right probably designates divinity as well for three reasons. First, the divinity of Jesus, as we have seen, is emphasized elsewhere in Hebrews, and thus it is likely present here as well. Second, elsewhere in the NT Jesus' sitting at the right hand communicates his deity, and so it is probable that the phrase functions in the same way in Hebrews. Third, the meaning of Ps 110:1 implies divinity, for the One spoken of there is not merely the son of David but also his lord.

§2.2 The Humanity of the Son

Certainly there is the danger of abstraction in distinguishing Jesus' humanity from his divinity for the sake of analysis. The whole Christ belongs to the readers, not a parceled out Christ. On the other hand it can be helpful to separate out strands of the author's teaching so we can see different aspects of it more clearly. The emphasis on the humanity of the Son in Hebrews is striking. At some points in discussing Jesus' humanity, I will note his high priestly ministry, but most of what could be said about his priesthood will be reserved for the next section.

The section that is the most important for understanding Jesus' humanity in Hebrews is 2:5–18. Here the author distinguishes between God's plan for angels and human beings. It was never God's intention that angels rule the world for him (2:5). By way of contrast, he called Adam and Eve at the beginning to be his vice-regents so they would rule the world under divine authority (1:26–27; 2:15). Hebrews quotes Psalm 8 in 2:6–8 to elaborate on God's plan for the world. Psalm 8 is a creation psalm that considers the role of human beings in creation, echoing what is taught in Genesis 1–2. Human beings feel insignificant when they consider the marvels of creation and the majesty of God, and yet they were made to be the rulers of the world. The author of Hebrews reads Psalm 8, however, in light of the entire biblical story, recognizing that the world is not currently subjected to human beings (2:8). Something is radically wrong with the world, and as we continue to read, we see that death (2:14–15) and sin (2:17) have frustrated human potential. The divine plan for the world has not been realized.

The role intended for human beings in the garden has been fulfilled by Jesus Christ. He succeeded as a human being where everyone else has failed. Because of his suffering and death, he was "crowned with glory and honor" (2:9). The role intended for Adam, rule over the world, was obtained by Jesus through his suffering on the cross. Jesus, as 2:10 says, was perfected through his sufferings. Clearly such sufferings indicate that Jesus was composed of "flesh and blood" (2:14). Jesus is the elder brother of all believers (2:11–12), and he is "like His brothers in every way" (2:17). He can help those facing temptation since he himself as a human being experienced suffering and temptation. Jesus as a human being sympathizes with the human condition, for he shared the weakness and frailty of human life (4:15) and was tempted just as other human beings are. On earth he endured "loud cries and tears" (5:7). As a human being he had to learn obedience and thus obtained perfection through his obedience (5:8–9).

Jesus' humanity is evident because of his death (12:2). Hebrews emphasizes in particular that Jesus gave his life as a sacrifice (cf. 9:11–10:18). God is immortal, and thus Jesus' death confirms his true humanity and is the clearest expression of his suffering (2:9, 14; 5:7; 6:6; 13:20).

Jesus lived a truly human life, knowing human suffering and temptation. He didn't live a privileged existence separated from the travails of ordinary human beings. He knew the anguish of temptation and the sorrows that blight human existence. He learned obedience in the midst of his sufferings and temptations. Jesus' humanity is confirmed by his family background, for he is from the tribe of Judah (7:13–14). The humanity of Jesus and the reality of his temptations do not mean he sinned. Quite the contrary. Hebrews emphasizes that he was without sin (4:15; 7:26). The portrait of Jesus' humanity shows that sin is not intrinsic to human nature. Jesus was fully human and yet he never sinned, demonstrating that it is not human to sin. Sin is characteristic of fallen human beings but is not native to human nature per se.

I argued above that we should resist a simple either-or in our categories relating to Jesus' deity and humanity. Even though the author doesn't work matters out theologically or philosophically, it is clear that Jesus is fully human and fully divine. We saw evidence in the above section that Jesus as the high priest is divine, but it is also the case that he is a human high priest. The author emphasizes that the high priest is a human being in 5:1–4 and goes on to show Jesus' humanity as high priest (5:7–9).

The humanity of Jesus is also evident in that he is the Messiah, the son of David—one from the tribe of Judah (7:13–14). The Messiah may be more than a human being, but he is certainly not less than a human being. The OT clearly teaches that the Messiah will come from David's line (2 Samuel 7; Hos 3:5; Mic 5:2–4; Isa 9:1–7; 11:1–10; 55:3; Jer 23:5–6; 30:9; 33:15–17; Ezek 34:23–24; 37:24–25; Zech 9:9). The title "Christ" shows that Jesus was the son of David and a human being (3:6, 14; 5:5; 6:1; 9:11, 14, 24, 28; 10:10; 11:26; 13:8, 21). Jesus fulfills the promise made to David and ultimately to Abraham in that he is the "heir of all things" (1:2). God's promises for the renewal and salvation of the world will be realized in Jesus, as the son of David. As the Christ, Jesus is the King, the Ruler of the world, fulfilling the promises in the OT that the Messiah would inherit "the ends of the earth" (Ps 2:8; cf. 16:6). As a human being Jesus became greater than the angels when he was exalted to God's right hand (1:4, 9, 13). He was rewarded as the faithful Son (3:2, 6).

The language of sonship, then, doesn't merely designate divinity but also includes the notion of Jesus' humanity. The term, as it is used in Hebrews, is complex and defies simple analysis. This is not a case of imposing upon the text results from systematic theology. Rather, the divinity and humanity relative to Jesus as the Son of God are both emphasized and impressed upon the reader with the result that both themes should be included when referring to Jesus as God's Son and as high priest.

§2.3 The Priesthood of Jesus[21]

One of the central themes of Hebrews is that Jesus is the great high priest, and hence believers should not attach or entrust themselves to any other high priest. As Lindars says about Hebrews, "Two ideas are unique in the New Testament. The priesthood of Jesus after the order of Melchizedek is entirely new. . . . Similarly his use of the ceremonial Day of Atonement to expound upon the sacrificial death of Jesus goes beyond any previous expositions of the faith that 'Christ died for our sins' (1 Cor. 15.3)."[22] The importance of the high priestly theme is evident from Heb 8:1, "Now the main point of what is being said is this: We have this kind of high priest, who sat down at the right hand of the throne of the Majesty in the heavens." What is striking here is that the author says the main point in his discourse is that Jesus is a high priest who has sat down at God's right hand. In other words, Jesus is a different kind of high priest from Levitical high priests, for his work as high priest is completed and finished, and hence he has sat down at God's right hand.[23] The Levitical high priests, on the other hand, continually stand (10:11), for their work as priests is never completed, which demonstrates the inadequacy and ineffectiveness of their priesthood.

---

[21] Scholars have often discussed when Jesus' high priesthood began, and this issue, though it is touched on here and in the commentary, is not examined in detail here. The letter itself is vague enough to lead scholars to various conclusions. Vos argues that Hebrews emphasizes Jesus' priesthood upon his exaltation, though he functioned as a priest at his death as well. But, says Vos, the author doesn't focus on Jesus priesthood before his death, and hence there is not a notion that Jesus served as a priest during his entire ministry (Geerhardus Vos, "The Priesthood of Christ in Hebrews," in *Redemptive History and Biblical Interpretation: The Shorter Writings of Geerhardus Vos*, ed. R. B. Gaffin Jr. [Phillipsburg, NJ: Presbyterian & Reformed, 1980], 154–59). See also Richard B. Gaffin Jr. "The Priesthood of Christ: A Servant in the Sanctuary," in *The Perfect Savior: Key Themes in Hebrews*, ed. J. Griffiths (Nottingham: InterVarsity, 2012), 49–68.

[22] Lindars, *The Theology of Hebrews*, 1.

[23] Scholer rightly says that Jesus' heavenly priesthood depends on and is founded on his earthly ministry as a priest (John M. Scholer, *Proleptic Priests: Priesthood in the Epistle to the Hebrews*, JSNTSup 49 [Sheffield: Sheffield Academic, 1991], 88). We can reject the notion, therefore, that Jesus only became a priest when he was exalted, but this doesn't resolve the question of whether Jesus was a priest throughout his entire earthly ministry or only during his suffering on the cross.

The Levitical priesthood, then, is "a copy and shadow" of a better priesthood (8:5), a heavenly priesthood (8:4), which introduces a "better covenant" (8:6). The Levitical priesthood was not evil or contrary to the will of God. The Lord designed it to function for a certain period of salvation history, but it was never intended to be permanent. Jesus is a better priest, for he enters as priest into God's presence and secures "eternal redemption" (9:11–12), whereas the high priest from Aaron has limited access to God, entering his presence in the most holy place only once a year (9:7, 25).

The author encourages the readers to draw near to God since they have such a great high priest (10:21–22). Jesus has "passed through the heavens" and entered the presence of God (4:14). The exhortation to draw near makes sense in light of what has been taught about the high priest in the entire letter. The readers should be full of confidence in God's presence since Jesus as high priest has secured permanent access to God for them. We can understand why the author says elsewhere that Jesus should be considered as the "high priest of our confession" (3:1).

Jesus' high priesthood is closely tied to his sacrifice, a theme we will consider in the next section. Jesus' priesthood is effective because he made satisfaction for the sins of the people (2:17). The various themes in Hebrews interlock together, and Jesus' priesthood is tied to his humanity. He could only be a "merciful and faithful high priest" if he was "like His brothers in every way" (2:17). High priests must be human (5:1), and Jesus is merciful and sympathetic because he has been tempted like all human beings (4:15). He is not an exalted high priest untouched by the sufferings of the human condition. As high priest he knew the anguish of temptation and the suffering of the cross.

Jesus was not an ordinary priest but a priest after the order of Melchizedek. He did not exalt himself and choose the vocation of high priesthood. Rather, God appointed him to the priesthood (5:5), so it was an honor bestowed by God. The words of appointment relative to Jesus hail from Ps 110:4, demonstrating that Jesus is a priest like Melchizedek (5:6, 10; 6:20). Jesus' priesthood is explained in terms of his election and appointment by God and cannot be attributed to his selfish will or to his desire for a vocation.

Melchizedek in the OT is a mysterious figure, appearing only in Genesis 14 and Ps 110:4. The writer of Hebrews is not the only author who shows interest in Melchizedek, for he also appears in the Qumran writings. In 11QMelch Melchizedek plays a major role at the final judgment, proclaiming liberty to Israel at Jubilee and announcing the forgiveness of their sins. Indeed he is even called "God," which fits with his role at the final judgment. It is doubtful that the divine role of Melchizedek was taken literally, as if he were literally God, even at Qumran. There is no evidence of rival "gods" at Qumran or elsewhere in Judaism.[24] What we do see, though, is that Melchizedek played an important eschatological role in some Jewish circles. It is evident from Qumran that the author of Hebrews was not alone in spying out significance in the person of Melchizedek.[25]

In the OT Melchizedek surfaces after Abraham rescued Lot from those who captured him (Gen 14:16). In celebration Melchizedek brings out "bread and wine" and is identified as "a priest to God Most High" (14:18). He proceeds to bless Abraham, and Abraham gave him a tenth of his plunder (14:19–20). We don't hear of Melchizedek again in the OT until Ps 110:4 where he appears as unexpectedly in the psalm as he does in the narrative in Genesis 14. The author has already told us of one who will be David's lord (Ps 110:1), showing that he is a kingly figure. Suddenly he declares with an oath that this one will also be a priest like Melchizedek (Ps 110:4). The historical character of the revelation is important here, for the promise from the psalmist comes after the appearance of Melchizedek in Genesis, demonstrating that another Melchizedekian priest is coming.

Hebrews identifies the priest of Ps 110:4 as the Son of God, Jesus Christ (5:6, 10; 7:17, 21). Peeler rightly says that Jesus' sonship

---

[24] For a fuller investigation into this question, which considers the matter in Judaism in general, see Larry Hurtado, *One God, One Lord: Early Christian Devotion and Ancient Jewish Monotheism* (Philadelphia: Fortress, 1988); idem, *Lord Jesus Christ: Devotion to Jesus in Earliest Christianity* (Grand Rapids, MI: Eerdmans, 2003).

[25] For a wider discussion on Melchizedek, including his role in other sources beyond Qumran, see M. Delcor, "Melchizedek from Genesis to the Qumran Texts and the Epistle to the Hebrews," *JSJ* 2 (1971); Eric F. Mason, *"You Are a Priest Forever": Second Temple Jewish Messianism and the Priestly Christology of the Epistle to the Hebrews*, STDJ 74 (Leiden: Brill, 2008); and especially Fred L. Horton Jr., *The Melchizedek Tradition: A Critical Examination of the Sources to the Fifth Century A.D. and in the Epistle to the Hebrews*, SNTSMS 30 (Cambridge: Cambridge University Press, 1976).

and priesthood don't clash but are "reciprocal identities both located within and existing because of the paternal actions of God."[26] Jesus' role as Son qualifies him to be a priest, and hence his filial status has priority over the priestly.[27] Some throughout the history of the church have said that Melchizedek was the preincarnate Christ. The evidence for this reading is impressive. Melchizedek suddenly appears on earth, as if out of nowhere, celebrating Abraham's victory with bread and wine. Furthermore, Heb 7:3 seems to identify him as an eternal person, one who didn't have a mother or father, neither the beginning of life nor the end of days. Despite the impressive evidence supporting such a reading, it is more persuasive to identify Melchizedek as a human being. When we read Genesis 14 carefully, it is evident that Melchizedek isn't a divine figure. He is "the king of Salem" (14:18), and therefore he reigned as king at a particular place and at a specific time in history. Nor does the wording in 7:3 lend itself to the idea that Melchizedek was the preincarnate Christ. The text doesn't say that Melchizedek "was" the Son of God but that he was made like the Son of God (7:3). He isn't identified as the Son of God but compared to him. It is probable from the wording used here that Melchizedek was a type anticipating the coming of the Christ. The author exploits the silence of the text to draw a correspondence between Jesus Christ and Melchizedek. Unlike Levitical priests, no genealogy is presented for Melchizedek, showing that he is a priest of a different type.

The material on Melchizedek might seem arcane or even strange to us, but the writer wants to show that he is a different kind of priest and a better priest than the Levitical priests. Melchizedek was greater than Abraham, for Abraham gave a tenth of his plunder to Melchizedek and was blessed by him (7:4–8). Indeed, Levi, in a sense, gave a tenth to Melchizedek since he descended from Abraham (7:9–10). So Melchizedek is better than Levi as well. The reason all of this is important is that Jesus is a Melchizedekian priest, and hence Jesus is superior to Levitical priests. The readers, then, should not put their faith in the Levitical priesthood to obtain forgiveness of sins, for in doing so they are relying on an inferior priesthood.

---

[26] Peeler, *You Are My Son*, 108.

[27] Ibid., 124, 137.

The author piles up arguments supporting the superiority of Christ's priesthood. First, if perfection were truly granted through the Levitical priesthood, then the Lord would not predict and institute another priesthood, a Melchizedekian one, later (7:11–12). The Lord would not inaugurate a new priesthood if the Levitical priesthood were truly effective. Second, neither should one make the argument that the priesthood had not changed, for Jesus was obviously not a Levitical priest (7:13–14). Jesus descended from the tribe of Judah, and hence he was not qualified to be a Levitical priest. He was clearly a priest of a different order.

Third, the author reverts to the prophecy of the Melchizedekian priesthood (7:15–17). Such a prophecy demonstrates that the Levitical priesthood was temporary in nature. There wouldn't be a prophecy about a new priesthood if the old priesthood was effective and sufficient. The Melchizedekian priesthood is inherently superior, for it is "based on the power of an indestructible life" (7:16) since Jesus conquered death. Fourth, the Levitical priesthood is defective because of its weakness (7:18). By way of contrast, Jesus' priesthood is qualitatively different, for believers are brought into fellowship with God (7:19). Fifth, the superiority of the Melchizedekian priesthood is not just a retrospective matter (7:20–22). God swore on an oath that the Melchizedekian priesthood would be perpetual. On the other hand, no oath accompanied the Levitical priesthood, and there was no promise that it would persist.

Sixth, the inadequacy of the Levitical priesthood is evident when one considers the nature of the priesthood. The office of priest constantly changes, for the priests keep dying (7:23). Jesus' priesthood, conversely, never ends, for he has conquered death (7:24). And since Jesus has triumphed over death, his saving power, as the ever-living and interceding one, never ends (7:25). Seventh, the Melchizedekian priesthood of Jesus is better because Jesus is a sinless priest, whereas Levitical priests were weak and sinful (7:26–28).

The author gives a battery of arguments supporting the superiority of Jesus' priesthood, but he does so for pastoral reasons. The readers must not forsake Jesus as their high priest. Jesus is their Melchizedekian priest-king who has sat down at God's right hand because his work is finished, and the readers should rest entirely in what Jesus has done for them.

§2.4 Jesus' Better Sacrifice and Human Anthropology

The sacrifice of Jesus is closely tied to his priesthood, for his sacrifice is effective because of the nature of his priesthood. The author emphasizes that Jesus' sacrifice is better than the sacrifices offered under the old covenant (9:23). The tabernacle and its furniture on earth are a copy of what is in heaven, and "the heavenly things" are cleansed with a better sacrifice. Jesus offers a better sacrifice because he gave of himself on a better "altar" (13:10). His "sprinkled blood" is "better" than Abel's (12:24), for in contrast to Abel his blood actually cleanses from sin.

Before saying more about Jesus' sacrifice, a word should be said about the author's anthropology. It should be noted at the outset that the author doesn't explicitly set forth an anthropological vision of human beings. His anthropology must be derived from the letter as a whole. Still we can't understand Jesus' priesthood if we don't grasp Hebrews's conception of human beings. It is evident from Heb 2:5–8, where the author cites Psalm 8, that human beings are considered to be magnificent. God made them to be his vice-regents, and hence they are called upon to rule the world for him. But even in this context, it is evident that something tragic and terrible has happened to prevent human beings from realizing their calling.

Whitlark nicely summarizes the anthropological pessimism found in Hebrews.[28] The writer believes human beings are defiled by sin. Our conscience needs to be cleansed since we are stained by sin (9:14; 10:2), and forgiveness for transgressions can only be granted if blood is shed (9:22). The sacrifice of Jesus provides such forgiveness (10:17–18), indicating that human beings have failed to do what God requires and need absolution for the evil done, for what the author calls "dead works" (6:1; 9:14). Dead works signifies

---

[28] Jason A. Whitlark, *Enabling Fidelity to God: Perserverance in Hebrews in Light of Reciprocity Systems in the Ancient Mediterranean World* (Milton Keynes, UK: Paternoster, 2008), 163–66. At the same time Whitlark shows that deSilva's view of reciprocity in Hebrews is flawed for several reasons (138–46). First, the reciprocity theme is not prominent in Hebrews. Second, the fundamental motivation for believers is faith in God's future promises instead of gratitude for his past benefits. Third, the readers are warned about lack of faith, and the focus is not on lack of gratitude. Fourth, deSilva assumes an optimistic anthropology in his conception of reciprocity, and hence the focus on the need for God's grace and the human need for divine empowering is lacking.

works that lead to death, and because of such works human beings need atonement for the evil they have perpetrated. Human beings are also unholy and hence need to be sanctified and inducted into the realm of the holy (2:11; 10:10, 14, 29; 13:12). Sanctification becomes a reality through the work of Jesus Christ, but what we should observe is that apart from Christ human beings are outside the realm of the holy and are corrupted by sin.

The plight of human beings is also signaled by the rule of death over their lives (2:14–15). Indeed the author says they are under Satan's power and will face final judgment (9:27). Clearly human beings need to be freed from the power of Satan, from death, and from judgment. In the same way the warnings in the letter (e.g., 2:1–4; 3:7–4:13; 6:4–8; 10:26–31; 12:25–29) indicate the severity of judgment warranted for those who give themselves to sin, who fail to trust in Jesus. The corruption and evil of human beings are such that they will face death and final judgment unless their sins are atoned for.

When the author reflects on Jesus' sacrifice, he thinks covenantally. The author explains that the old covenant was inaugurated with blood sacrifices (9:15–22). In Exod 24:5–8 the covenant was inaugurated with Israel. During the ceremony the blood of bulls was sprinkled on both the altar and the people. The author, apparently, doesn't limit himself to this event, for he includes the blood of goats and the role of "water, scarlet wool, and hyssop" (9:19) along with the blood being sprinkled on "the scroll." Perhaps these other features are included from tradition. We find such practices reflected in the ritual of the heifer which purified Israelites (Num 19:1–22), for sprinkling, water, blood, hyssop, and scarlet yarn all play a role in purification (19:4, 6, 12–13, 17–21; cf. also Lev 14:4, 49). Hyssop and blood are also used in the Passover sacrifice (Exod 12:22). In any case the author of Hebrews emphasizes that almost everything in the old covenant was cleansed with blood and that forgiveness is not possible without "the shedding of blood" (9:22).

The old covenant typologically anticipated the new (9:23–24), demonstrating that purification and forgiveness could only come through blood, i.e., through a sacrificial death. Old Testament sacrifices were ordained by God and are not rejected as evil. They point to the final and ultimate sacrifice. Here we can agree with Ribbens that OT sacrifices are christological and sacramental types of the

461

sacrifice of Christ.[29] They forgave sins under the old covenant because they pointed forward to the final and effective sacrifice of Jesus Christ. The violence and blood of sacrifices send a message about the evil of humanity, showing that sin is a great offense against God that can only be satisfied by the death of another, by a substitute that takes the penalty deserved by human beings. The "sins of the people" had to be "propitiated" and "expiated" (ἱλάσκεσθαι, 2:17). There had to be appeasement for the sins committed, and sins needed to be erased and blotted out for forgiveness to be granted.

Jesus' sacrifice is superior to the sacrifices of the old covenant for many reasons. The law and its sacrifices are "a shadow of the good things to come" (10:1), showing that God intended animal sacrifices to function as a type and anticipation of a future sacrifice which would bring permanent cleansing from sins. Sacrifices are perpetually offered under the old covenant, but they are not efficacious. The author argues that the repetition of sacrifices reveals their inadequacy (10:2). If they truly worked, if they truly cleansed from sin, there wouldn't be any need to continue offering them. The repeated offering of such sacrifices has the opposite effect; it reminds worshipers that their sins have not been truly removed (10:3). And indeed their sins haven't been cleansed entirely, for animal sacrifices can't "take away sins" (10:4). What the author says here resonates with us, for it makes sense that the sacrifice of unwilling animals can't atone for human sin. Animals can't comprehend why they are being slain, and as brute victims lacking in consciousness of what is happening to them, they can't cleanse human beings of their sin before God.

The sacrifice of Jesus is dramatically different from animal sacrifices, and in contrast to them his sacrifice truly and finally cleanses from sin. Upon coming into the world, Jesus recognized his vocation in the words of Ps 40:6–8. God did not ultimately find delight in burnt offerings and sin offerings (10:5–6, 8), for such offerings could not finally remove sin. What God wanted from Jesus, his will for Jesus, was that Jesus would give of himself (10:5, 7, 9). Jesus was called to do the will of God, and this meant he would offer himself

---

[29] Ribbens makes this case in his dissertation (Benjamin J. Ribbens, "Levitical Sacrifice and Heavenly Cult in Hebrews" [Ph.D. diss., Wheaton College, 2013]). I am not endorsing every aspect of his dissertation, but the fundamental argument about the role of OT sacrifices is correct.

as a sacrifice for sins (10:10). We see clearly here why Jesus' sacrifice was better. Instead of the sacrifice of unwilling animals, he willingly and gladly gave himself to God and surrendered his life for human beings.[30] The significance of Jesus' sacrifice could hardly be greater. Here we have the sacrifice of one who is fully divine and fully human, and hence his one sacrifice atones for sins forever.

Jesus' sacrifice is better, then, because of who he is. And who he is can't be separated from what he accomplished. Indeed, it is the foundation for what he accomplished. His one sacrifice was definitive and complete, and hence there is no further need for other sacrifices to atone for sins. Since final cleansing of sins has been accomplished, Jesus "sat down at the right hand of the Majesty on high" (1:3). Jesus sat down because his work as priest is finished (1:13; 8:1; 10:12; 12:2). His sacrifice doesn't save halfway but is completely effective in delivering those who belong to God (7:25).

The connection between ontology (who Jesus is) and function (what he accomplished) is communicated in 7:26–28. Jesus' freedom from all defilement and uncleanness and sin is featured here. Unlike the high priests he isn't stained by sin. Instead he is a priest who has been "perfected" (7:28). So he has no need to offer sacrifices for his own sins. On the contrary, as the sinless Son of God and as the Melchizedekian priest, he atoned for sins through the one offering of himself. According to the law, the high priests entered the most holy place yearly to procure atonement with the blood of animals (9:25). But Jesus' way was completely different. One sacrifice removed sin for all time, and thus he doesn't need to suffer over and over (9:26, 28). His once-for-all sacrifice suffices to cleanse from sin forever.

The author pounds home this truth in 10:11–14. Priests stand "day after day," offering over and over the same sacrifices, but they don't remove sins. The repetition conveys the futility of the entire enterprise. But Jesus "after offering one sacrifice for sins forever, sat down" at God's right hand (10:12). His work is finished, since "by one offering He has perfected forever those who are sanctified" (10:14). The completeness and efficacy of what Christ has done is

---

[30] Cf. John Dunnill, *Covenant and Sacrifice in the Letter to the Hebrews*, SNTSMS 75 (Cambridge: Cambridge University Press, 1992), 231.

communicated by the truth that there is no need for further sacrifices. The work is finished with the one sacrifice.

Jesus' one sacrifice opened up access to God, for as God's Son and high priest he "passed through the heavens" (4:14), which means he entered the presence of God. Jesus entered the true "inner sanctuary behind the curtain" (6:19), signifying again the presence of God. He entered God's presence as the "forerunner" (πρόδρομος), and he is the forerunner by virtue of his sacrifice. Because of Jesus' sacrifice, believers are enabled to "draw near to God" (7:19). The ritual on the Day of Atonement reveals that the way into God's presence wasn't secured through the old covenant (9:7–8). Jesus won "eternal redemption" with his own blood and thereby entered into the "perfect tabernacle" (9:11–12). This tabernacle isn't part of created reality, signifying that it represents God's presence. The author isn't suggesting that there is a real tabernacle in heaven. The language related to the tabernacle is analogical and not literal. The earthly points to the heavenly, but the heavenly stands for the presence of God, so it is not as if there is a literal tabernacle in heaven with distinct compartments.

The significance of Jesus' blood and the shedding of blood in sacrifices have often been discussed.[31] Jesus' shed blood doesn't include the notion of the release of his life, as if his life is mystically found in his blood. Instead his blood signifies life that has been given up in death. The spilling of Jesus' blood indicates that he has given up his life, that he has died. We should not separate in Jesus' case the shedding of the blood from the application of the blood in the sanctuary. The blood shed by Jesus has been applied to the heavenly sanctuary, just as the blood of animals was applied in the tabernacle/temple. The author is not suggesting that Jesus' blood was literally brought into a literal heavenly sanctuary. He appropriates the language of the cult to denote what Jesus has accomplished, and thus we have analogical rather than literal or univocal language here. The author uses the symbolism of what took place in the earthly

---

[31] See most recently Hermann V. A. Kuma, *The Centrality of Αἷμα (Blood) in the Theology of the Epistle to the Hebrews: An Exegetical and Philological Study* (Lewiston, NY: Edwin Mellen, 2012), though my own reading is closer to Morris than to Kuma. See Leon Morris, *The Apostolic Preaching of the Cross,* 3rd ed. (London: Tyndale, 1965), 112–29.

tabernacle to convey the truth that Jesus' death brings believers into God's presence.

The blood of Jesus in Hebrews is sacrificial, denoting that his blood makes access to God possible. Believers, by virtue of Jesus' sacrificial blood, have the same "boldness" to enter God's presence (the most holy place, 10:19) as Jesus did. The curtain is not open only once a year as it was under the old covenant (9:6–7), but it has been torn open for every believer through the flesh of Jesus (10:20). We might say that access to God is more important than the sacrifice since it is the goal of the sacrifice, but such a judgment could also be misleading. Those who have access to God's presence will never forget how or why they have such access.

Access to God means the sins of human beings are forgiven. Human beings suffered under God's wrath (2:17) and experienced death (2:9, 14–15) because of sin. Now sins are expiated and propitiated because of Jesus' death (2:17). God is not angry with human beings who are the brothers of Jesus but counts them as his children (2:12–14, 16). Their sins have been forgotten and forgiven because of Jesus' sacrificial work on the cross (8:13). God's forgetting of sins, in accord with the new covenant (Jer 31:34), means there is full and final forgiveness, and hence there isn't a need for further sacrificial offerings (10:17–18).

Forgiveness means freedom and complete cleansing from sin. The author seems particularly concerned to emphasize that believers need not fear the defilement and shame that sin engenders. Animal sacrifices provide only an external purification (9:13). The sacrificial nature of 9:14 is evident, for the author refers to Jesus' blood, and blood was a central element in the offering of sacrifices under the old covenant.[32] Furthermore, Jesus "offered himself unblemished." The language of "offering" (προσήνεγκεν) hails from OT

---

[32] See Jay Sklar, "Sin and Impurity: Atoned or Purified? Yes!," in *Perspective on Purity and Purification in the Bible*, ed. Baruch J. Schwartz, David P. Wright, Jeffrey Stackert, and Naphtali S. Meshel, LHBOTS 474 (New York: T&T Clark, 2002), 18–31. Sklar argues that sin defiles and hence purification is needed, and sin also places one's life is in danger, and hence ransom is required. See idem, *Sin, Impurity, Sacrifice, Atonement: The Priestly Conceptions*, HBM 2 (Sheffield: Sheffield Phoenix, 2005). For a thorough discussion of the role of sacrifices and the cult, see Roy E. Gane, *Cult Character: Purification Offerings, Day of Atonement, and Theodicy* (Winona Lake, IN: Eisenbrauns, 2005).

sacrifices (cf. Gen 4:7; Exod 32:6; Lev 1:2–3; 3:6; 4:23; 16:9, etc.; see also Heb 5:1, 3; 8:3–4; 9:7, 9, 25; 10:1–2, 8, 11; 11:4, 17) as does the word "unblemished" (ἄμωμον; cf. Exod 29:1, 38; Lev 1:3, 10; 3:1; 4:14, etc.). Jesus "offered" himself "once" to take away sins (9:28; cf. 10:12). His sacrificial blood is effective, for he "cleanse[s] our consciences" so that believers are freed from the shame that disables us (9:14). As a result we are liberated "to serve the living God" (9:14). One can't serve God joyfully if one feels defiled, unclean, and shameful before God. Believers may now gladly "draw near [to God] with a true heart in full assurance of faith" (10:22). We have such assurance because through Christ's blood our "evil conscience" has been cleansed. The warnings in the letter have more weight because of what the readers would be leaving behind if they abandoned Christ. As the author says, they would repudiate the only "sacrifice for sins" available if they renounced Christ (10:26). Assurance, boldness to enter God's presence, and future hope would all be lost if they turned away from the one who gave his blood as a once-for-all sacrifice to atone for sins forever.

§2.5 Perfection and Assurance[33]

In considering perfection in Hebrews, we shall explore two dimensions: the perfection of Jesus and the perfection of human beings. It is remarkable that the author speaks of the perfection of Jesus since he emphasizes that Jesus is without sin (4:15; 7:26). In giving himself to God as an offering, he was "without blemish" (9:14). Such claims about Jesus help us see at the outset that being perfected doesn't mean he was previously stained by sin.

In 2:10 Jesus is said to be perfected through his sufferings. He wasn't purified of existing sin in his sufferings since he was already without sin, but he was qualified to serve as high priest by his sufferings. Merely being without sin did not qualify Jesus to serve as high priest. He needed to experience life, to be tested, and to suffer

---

[33] See David G. Peterson's excellent dissertation, *Hebrews and Perfection: An Examination of the Concept of Perfection in the "Epistle to the Hebrews,"* SNTSMS 47 (Cambridge: Cambridge University Press, 1982). See also his more popular and accessible essay, David G. Peterson, "Perfection: Achieved and Experienced," in *The Perfect Savior: Key Themes in Hebrews*, ed. J. Griffiths (Nottingham: InterVarsity, 2012), 125–45.

(2:18). The fullness of human experience was his (2:17), for he knows what it is like to be tempted (4:15) and to feel the anguish of human life. His sinlessness is all the more remarkable, for it was worked out in the anvil of human experience. He "learned obedience" in his sufferings (5:8), and in that sense was perfected (5:9; cf. 7:28). Irenaeus's recapitulation theory regarding Christ's person reflects Hebrews to some extent. For Jesus could not atone for sin as a child or even as a teenager. He needed to experience what it was like to obey God as he grew older so that his life of obedience had a depth and profundity that was lacking earlier. Jesus' perfection, then, had an experiential quality to it, and he demonstrated that he was wholly God's in the midst of tears and anguish (5:7).

Jesus' perfection included his suffering on the cross, for the sufferings culminated in his death on the cross by which he stripped the devil of his power and freed human beings from being enslaved to death (2:10, 14–15). The perfecting of Jesus, then, includes the expiatory and propitiatory work on the cross. He was qualified to serve as a high priest because of his obedience in his sufferings and the atonement accomplished on the cross. Jesus' high priestly work stands in contrast to the Levitical priesthood in that he truly brought perfection (7:11, 19; 10:1), which means that through him believers enjoy bold access to God.[34] Furthermore, Jesus' perfection also included his exaltation, for as a result of his sufferings and exaltation (5:7–10), he became "the source of eternal salvation" (5:9). Hence his sufferings, death, and exaltation qualified him to serve as high priest. As Peterson says, "Perfecting involved a whole sequence of events: his proving in suffering, his redemptive death to fulfill the divine requirements for the perfect expiation of sins and his exaltation to glory and honour."[35] Therefore, we should reject the idea that Jesus' perfection is exclusively eschatological, so that he was only perfected as the reigning priest-king.[36] Peterson sums up perfection

---

[34] Ribbens argues that perfection in Hebrews always has the idea of access to God ("Levitical Sacrifice and Heavenly Cult in Hebrews," 227–39, 328–36). Certainly this notion is present, but in some texts it seems that the idea of qualification fits better (see 2:9; 5:9).

[35] Peterson, *Hebrews and Perfection*, 73.

[36] Against Scholer, *Proleptic Priests*, 84.

in this way: "His proving in temptation, his death as a sacrifice for sins and his heavenly exaltation."[37]

Hebrews is also interested in the perfection or maturity of human beings. The letter investigates what qualifies human beings to stand before God. It is imperative that the readers progress on to "maturity" (τελειότητα, 6:1), for if they are not "mature" (τελείων), they will not receive the eschatological reward. In other words, those who are mature cling to Christ in faith until the end. They do not fall away from the faith.

Hebrews insists that perfection can't be obtained through the OT priesthood and law. "Perfection" (τελείωσις) can't be achieved through Levitical priesthood (7:11) since the law "perfected" (ἐτελείωσεν) nothing (7:19). What the author means is that human beings couldn't have fellowship in God's presence through the law. The law, instead of granting access to God, reveals that human beings are too unclean and defiled to enter God's presence. The Levitical priesthood, therefore, couldn't really cleanse the conscience and bring forgiveness of sins: it "cannot perfect (τελειῶσαι) the worshiper's conscience" (9:9). On the contrary, it reminded people of their sins (10:3), for the same sacrifices offered repeatedly "can never perfect (τελειῶσαι) the worshipers" (10:1). On the other hand Jesus "by one offering . . . has perfected (τετελείωκεν) forever those who are sanctified" (10:14). The word "perfected" in Hebrews has affinities with how Paul uses the word justification, for believers aren't made morally perfect by virtue of Jesus' sacrifice. In other words they aren't transformed so that they are without sin and perfectly holy in their everyday lives. But they are perfect before God by virtue of Christ's sacrifice, i.e., their sins are forgiven, and their consciences are cleansed so that they may boldly enter God's presence.

We have seen perfection means the conscience is cleansed so believers are qualified to enter God's presence, and it also means believers have access to God's power and grace on a daily basis.[38] The perfecting of the conscience isn't limited to the past. It frees and strengthens believers so they are empowered by the grace of God, so they boldly draw on God's mercy and grace in their present trials. In

---

[37] Peterson, *Hebrews and Perfection*, 118. These words are italicized in Peterson.

[38] See Whitlark, *Enabling Fidelity to God*, 156–57.

other words perfection is closely related to assurance. As Whitlark says, "Christ's cleansing of the conscience does not only stand at the beginning of the Christian's pilgrimage but is the basis of the empowering that the pilgrim experiences to approach God throughout the pilgrimage to the heavenly Jerusalem."[39]

In a few texts the word "sanctify" (ἁγιάζω) seems to be remarkably close in meaning to "perfection" in Hebrews. Believers are now "sanctified" through the once-for-all offering of Jesus Christ (10:10). In 10:14, cited in the previous paragraph, we find both the word "perfected" and the word "sanctified," and both are accomplished through the one sacrifice of Christ. On two other occasions as well in Hebrews, sanctification is attributed to Christ's blood (10:29; 13:14), to his atoning death. The term "sanctify" signifies Christ's work by which he consecrates and sets apart those who belong to him. Their holiness hails not from themselves but from the once-for-all sacrifice of Jesus. Believers are assured they are holy before God; they stand without blemish before him.

Final perfection is an eschatological reality, for OT saints will not be perfected without NT believers (11:40). New Testament believers, insofar as they are perfected now, enjoy an eschatological preview of what will be theirs in a fuller sense on the last day. In one sense believers are perfected now by virtue of Christ's definitive and final sacrifice; they are positionally holy. At the same time a day is coming when every remnant of sin will be fully removed from those who are Christ's. The author's comment in 12:23 suggests that this is true of believers who are with the Lord now before the day of the resurrection. Their spirits are perfected, though they wait for the day of final resurrection.

Perfection in Hebrews is closely associated with the new covenant and the assurance of salvation.[40] Believers can be assured of final salvation since Jesus "by one offering . . . has perfected forever those who are sanctified" (Heb 10:14). The conscience of believers has been perfected and cleansed forever through the sacrifice

---

[39] Ibid., 157.

[40] For an excellent summary of Hebrews' soteriology, see I. Howard Marshall, "Soteriology in Hebrews," in *The Epistle to the Hebrews and Christian Theology*, ed. R. Bauckham, D. R. Driver, T. A. Hart, and N. MacDonald (Grand Rapids, MI: Eerdmans, 2009), 253–77; Brenda B. Colijn, "'Let us Approach': Soteriology in the Epistle to the Hebrews," *JETS* 39 (1996): 571–86.

of Jesus Christ (9:9; 10:1). Forgiveness of sins is an accomplished reality, and what has been secured will not be undone. What characterizes the new covenant (8:8–12; 10:15–18) is full forgiveness of sins and the writing of the law upon the heart. Since God is the one who imprints the law upon the heart, what he has inscribed upon the heart cannot and will not be erased.

Believers are empowered and strengthened to persevere to the end because the God who raised Jesus from the dead is the one who equips believers to do his will (13:20–21).[41] The writer implies that they have resurrection power, the power that defeated death, to enable them to do what is pleasing in God's sight. Believers are assured not only of forgiveness of sins but of God's presence and power in their daily lives.

Confidence of perseverance comes from the work of God. In the OT we read regularly that God is the one who sanctifies and sets apart Israel as his own (cf. Lev 20:8; 21:8, 15, 23; 22:9, 16, 32). The author of Hebrews says Jesus is the one who sanctifies his people (2:11). Whitlark observes that God's sanctifying his people is closely associated with his electing and redeeming work in Lev 22:31–33.[42] God's election of his people is also communicated in 2:13 where the words of Isaiah are placed on the lips of Jesus: "Here I am with the children God gave Me." Jesus' brothers and sisters have been given to him by God himself, demonstrating that their belonging to God is the work of God, the product of his electing grace. Along the same lines the reference to the names of the first-born "written in heaven" (12:23) may point to election. The perfect passive tense suggests they are enrolled "by God's initiative."[43]

Identifying his hearers as "Abraham's offspring" (2:16) also resonates with the OT and the grace of God in choosing his people. The author draws on Isa 41:8–10 where Abraham is identified as God's "chosen" (ἐξελεξάμην, 41:8–9) and God's "beloved" (ἠγάπησα, 41:8). The word "beloved" is often associated with election (e.g., Rom 9:13). By alluding to Isa 41:8–10 and by describing the hearers as the offspring of Abraham, the author calls attention

---

[41] For a helpful study of the texts examined here, which influenced my own comments, see Whitlark, *Enabling Fidelity to God*, 146–63.

[42] Ibid., 148.

[43] Ibid., 150.

to God's election. Just as Israel was chosen by the Lord, so now believers in Christ are his chosen ones.

The author says in Heb 9:15 that the hearers "are called" to receive an "eternal inheritance." Calling signifies God's effective work by which he summons people to put their faith in him. It should not be confused with an invitation but connotes instead God's supernatural work that creates faith in God. Interestingly we see another allusion to Isa 41:9 where God's calling is closely connected to his electing grace.[44] God's electing grace assures believers that he has granted them and will grant them the grace to endure until the final day. On the one hand believers are called upon to persevere, but election reminds the hearers of the letter that their endurance is ultimately ascribed to God. Indeed it suggests that God will see to it that they do not forsake him, that he will give them the resources to bear whatever comes their way. Those whom God has perfected and sanctified and chosen will, by his grace, persevere in faith until the end, for those who are sanctified and perfected by the atoning death of Jesus have been perfected forever.

§2.6 Jesus' Resurrection and Exaltation

Sometimes it is said that Hebrews considers the resurrection of Jesus to be a minor theme; but when we examine the letter closely, it is evident that the resurrection and exaltation of Jesus play a major role in the letter.[45] The texts that affirm that Jesus reigns or that he entered God's presence with his blood also affirm, at least implicitly, the resurrection. Hence, the resurrection of Jesus, his entrance into the heavenly tabernacle, and his exaltation are closely intertwined in Hebrews.

The author doesn't often directly refer to the resurrection, but it is clearly vital to the message of the letter as a whole. The clearest reference to the resurrection is in Heb 13:20, where we are told that

---

[44] See Ibid., 151.

[45] See especially here, David M. Moffitt, *Atonement and the Logic of the Resurrection in the Epistle to the Hebrews*, SuppNovT 141 (Leiden: Brill, 2011), 145–214. I don't agree with all of Moffitt's arguments, but I think he rightly demonstrates the centrality of Jesus' physical resurrection. For the importance of the resurrection, see also Gareth L. Cockerill, "The Better Resurrection (Heb. 11:35): A Key to the Structure and Rhetorical Purpose of Hebrews 11," *TynB* 51 (2000): 215–34.

God raised Jesus from the dead as "the great Shepherd of the sheep" (13:20). The sheep trust in and obey a living Shepherd, one who can strengthen them during this life and guarantee that in the future they too will not be defeated by death.

Jesus prayed with anguish to be saved from death, and his prayer was answered (5:7). The author certainly doesn't mean Jesus was spared from dying, for nothing is clearer in the letter than Jesus' sacrificial death. Therefore, his prayer for deliverance from death was answered at the resurrection. In addition, Jesus by his death destroyed the one who exercised the power of death, i.e., the devil (2:14). The devil's power was stripped not only by Jesus' death but also by his resurrection, and hence believers are now freed from the fear of death since they can be confident of the future resurrection. Isaac's rescue from death at the last moment is a parable of the resurrection (11:19), presumably of the resurrection of the Christ and all those who belong to him.

The author takes pains to demonstrate that Jesus' Melchizedekian priesthood is superior to the Levitical priesthood (7:1–28). Jesus' claim to the priesthood does not rest on his genealogy and the legal requirements of the law (7:16). He was qualified to serve as priest because of his "indestructible life" (7:16). In other words the resurrection of Jesus demonstrated conclusively that his priesthood was qualitatively better than the Levitical priesthood. Indeed the author finds a prophecy of Christ's resurrection in Ps 110:4, for the Melchizedekian priest serves as priest "forever" (7:17). A perpetual priesthood is only possible if one conquers death, and hence there is a reference here to Christ's resurrection. One of the fundamental reasons for Jesus' better priesthood is that Levitical priests die and so cannot continue their priestly ministry (7:23). Jesus, however, has triumphed over death and so "He remains forever" (7:24). As the resurrected Lord his priesthood doesn't have a termination point. Hence his saving power is not limited, for, as noted in 2:14–15, he saves from death those who are terrified of dying. As the one who has been raised from the dead, he saves from death those who rely on him for victory (7:25). Indeed, as the ever-living one, he "intercedes" for believers (7:25), asking God to give them whatever they need for final salvation.

Jesus' resurrection is implied in texts that speak of his exaltation. For example, in 1:2 Jesus is said to be the "heir of all things."

But he can only receive this inheritance as the living one. Indeed, his inheritance is closely tied to his sitting down at God's right hand, which is, in dependence on Ps 110:1, a recurrent theme in the letter (1:3, 13; 8:1; 10:12; 12:2). Jesus' resurrection doesn't merely indicate that he is still alive. It is tied to his rule at God's right hand, in fulfillment of God's purpose when he created human beings. He is "exalted above the heavens" (7:26). The rule of Jesus signifies that everything is right (or will be right) in the universe.

By virtue of Jesus' resurrection, God's intention for the world will be realized. Jesus at his exaltation assumes a "higher . . . rank" than angels (1:4), for it was never God's purpose that angels would rule over human beings (2:5). Jesus as the resurrected Lord is "crowned with glory and honor" (2:9). He is the "Son over His household" (3:6). He has been exalted over his companions because of his obedience (1:9). His exaltation took place at his resurrection in accord with Ps 2:7. In the historical context of Psalm 2, the "begetting" of the son took place at the king's coronation, when he was appointed by God as the ruler. The author of Hebrews, as is the case with other writers in the NT (cf. Acts 13:33; Matt 3:17 par.), reads the psalm typologically and prophetically. Ultimately what is said here is true of a greater king than David, for it was prophesied that David's dynasty would endure (2 Samuel 7), that a new David was coming (Hos 3:5; Mic 5:2–4; Isa 9:1–7; 11:1–10; 55:3; Jer 23:5–6; 30:9; 33:15–17; Ezek 34:23–24; 37:24–25; Zech 9:9), and that the future heir of David would be greater than he was (Ps 110:1). Jesus' begetting, then, does not refer in 1:5 and 5:5 to his eternal generation as the Son of the Father or to his conception in the virgin Mary's womb. The reference in Hebrews is to Jesus' resurrection and exaltation, to his being installed as the messianic king at God's right hand. This is not to say that Jesus was not the Messiah or God's Son before his exaltation. The point is that he was not the reigning and ruling Messiah and Son of God until he was exalted by God.

Jesus' resurrection and exaltation mean that he has access to God. He has "passed through the heavens" (4:14) and entered into the presence of God. He has pierced through the curtain by virtue of his death so that he is now the "forerunner" of believers (6:19–20). Jesus' access to God isn't a matter of historical interest. It is meant to provide "strong encouragement" to believers so they would be full of hope, for since Jesus entered God's presence as a forerunner, entrance into God's presence is what believers enjoy as well. As 9:24 says, the Christ entered God's true sanctuary, into "heaven itself" to "appear in the presence of God for us." Here the words "for us" should be noted. Christ's access to God means access for believers. Hence believers "have boldness to enter the sanctuary through the blood of Jesus" (10:19). The resurrection and exaltation of Jesus are central, for they mean that sins are truly forgiven, death has been defeated, and human beings who trust in Christ will enjoy God's presence forever.

§3 The New Covenant[46]

Jesus is better than Levitical priests because he inaugurates a better covenant, a new covenant, for his sacrifice is "better" than old covenant sacrifices (9:23). By virtue of his priestly work, there is a "better hope" (7:19), and believers have a "better possession" (10:34; cf. 11:16). Jesus is also the "guarantee" and "mediator" of a "better covenant" (7:22; 8:6), which has "better promises" (8:6). The author refers to the "new" covenant (8:8, 13; 12:24), to the

---

[46] See Susanne Lehne, *The New Covenant in Hebrews*, JSNTSup 44 (Sheffield: Sheffield Academic, 1990); Peter Gräbe, "The New Covenant and Christian Identity in Hebrews," in *Cloud of Witnesses: The Theology of Hebrews in Its Ancient Contexts*, ed. R. Bauckham, D. Driver, T. Hart, and N. MacDonald, LNTS 387 (London: T&T Clark, 2008), 119–27; David Peterson, "The Prophecy of the New Covenant in the Argument of Hebrews," *RTR* 38 (1979): 74–81; Peter O'Brien, "The New Covenant and Its Perfect Mediator," in *The Perfect Savior: Key Themes in Hebrews*, ed. J. Griffiths (Nottingham: InterVarsity, 2012), 13–33. Hays underestimates the newness of the new covenant in saying that only the cultic law is abolished and in suggesting that the author may have believed that Jews who did not trust in Jesus as Messiah may be saved. On the other hand he rightly points to the many areas in which there is no critique of Judaism in the letter. Skarsaune rightly calls into question Hays's suggestion that the author of Hebrews may have believed Jews could be saved without belief in Jesus the Messiah. See Richard B. Hays, "'Here We Have No Lasting City': New Covenantalism in Hebrews," in *The Epistle to the Hebrews and Christian Theology*, ed. R. Bauckham, D. R. Driver, T. A. Hart, and N. MacDonald (Grand Rapids, MI: Eerdmans, 2009), 151–73; Oskar Skarsaune, "Does the Letter to the Hebrews Articulate a Supersessionist Theology? A Response to Richard Hays," in *The Epistle to the Hebrews and Christian Theology*, ed. R. Bauckham, D. R. Driver, T. A. Hart, and N. MacDonald (Grand Rapids, MI: Eerdmans, 2009), 174–82. For a helpful study of the new covenant that embraces the whole Bible, see David G. Peterson, *Transformed by God: New Covenant Life and Ministry* (Downers Grove, IL: InterVarsity, 2012).

"second" one (8:7), or to the "everlasting covenant" (13:20). The new covenant stands in contrast to the "old" covenant (8:13) or to the "first" covenant (8:7; 9:1, 18). The Sinai covenant is identified as the first covenant and the old covenant. Now what is first and old can be better than what comes later and is new. But that is certainly not the case in this instance. The Sinai covenant is not only first and old, but it is also obsolete and inferior. The author specifically argues that a second covenant was needed because the first was flawed (8:7). The new covenant or the second covenant is a "better" covenant and "everlasting." The author clearly teaches that the old covenant, the covenant made with Moses (9:15–22), is no longer in force. The old covenant was intended to rule over the people of God for a certain period in salvation history. But that day has ended. Now a better and superior administration has arrived. Hence believers are not bound to the stipulations and regulations of the old covenant. They are certainly not required to offer animal sacrifices as the old covenant requires, for those sacrifices have passed away now that Christ has come (10:1–18). They were not effective in any case, and they point forward to the better sacrifice of Jesus Christ (9:1–28).

What makes the new covenant better? The author says the promises of the new covenant are better, and the nature of those better promises is explained in the citation of Jer 31:31–34 in 8:8–12. Certainly there was grace in the old covenant, for the Lord delivered Israel from Egypt because of his mercy. The covenant wasn't defective because of some imperfection in God or his plan. Some say that the new covenant in Hebrews is a superior covenant because it is unconditional in contrast to the Sinai covenant. Such an interpretation is attractive but doesn't get it quite right.[47] The warning passages in Hebrews make clear that there are conditions in the covenant.[48]

The difference between the two covenants doesn't lie in whether there are conditions. Instead, Israel didn't keep the covenant stipulations (8:9) under the Sinai covenant. They experienced the

---

[47] Wellum and Gentry rightly argue that the fundamental difference between the covenants isn't based on whether they are conditional or unconditional. See Peter W. Gentry and Stephen J. Wellum, *Kingdom Through Covenant: A Biblical-Theological Understanding of the Covenants* (Wheaton, IL: Crossway, 2012), 608–11.

[48] Rightly Allen, *Deuteronomy and Exhortation in Hebrews*, 116–19; Dunnill, *Covenant and Sacrifice in Hebrews*, 133; Lehne, *The New Covenant in Hebrews*, 104–8.

cursings of the covenant, particularly exile, because they didn't obey commands of their covenant king (Lev 26:14–39; Deut 28:15–68; 2 Kings 17 and 25). The first covenant, then, was flawed by virtue of human nature. Israel knew what they were enjoined to do, and yet they failed to keep what was prescribed, and hence the promises of rule and victory did not come to pass in Israel.

The new covenant is better, for it represents an even greater outpouring of the grace of God. The Lord inscribes the law on the heart of his people (8:10; 10:16), and thus believers have an internal desire to do what he commands.[49] The law is no longer an external standard that does not conform to the desire of the heart. God's requirements are now within his people so believers find their greatest delight in obeying the Lord. Such a promise accords with Ezek 36:26–27, where the Lord gives his people the Holy Spirit and takes away their stony hearts, granting them a heart of flesh. As a result they are empowered to do what God prescribes. It doesn't follow that believers are sinless, for the new covenant is inaugurated but not consummated, and thus believers continue to struggle with sin, even though the law is implanted in their hearts.

The covenant formula is realized in the new covenant: God is their God, and they are his people (8:10; cf., Gen 17:7–8; Exod 29:45; Lev 26:45; Jer 24:7; 32:38; Ezek 11:20; 14:11; 37:23, 27; Zech 8:12; 10:6). God will be their God because every covenant member knows the Lord (8:11). In the old covenant one was a covenant member from birth, and the covenant was theocratic in nature. Israel was both a national and political entity (a distinct nation) and a religious entity (formed to worship the Lord). Membership in the old covenant didn't mean that one truly knew God. Inclusion in the national entity of Israel did not mean one was genuinely and truly a believer. The new covenant, however, is different in nature. Every member of the new covenant knows the Lord. The author particularly emphasizes this point: "They will *all* know Me, from *the least* to *the greatest* of them" (8:11). That all new covenant members know the Lord isn't surprising since God writes the law on the heart. Therefore, new covenant members don't have to say, as they did under the old covenant, to other covenant members: know the Lord. Such an exhortation was fitting under the old covenant where many

---

[49] See here Peterson, "The Prophecy of the New Covenant," 78–79.

covenant members weren't regenerate, but the distinctiveness of the new covenant is that every covenant member is regenerate.

The new covenant is effective in another way. Covenant members are truly forgiven of their sins.[50] God doesn't remember their sins since they have been completely wiped away (8:13; 10:17). Because their sins are forgiven, there is no longer a need for old covenant offerings and sacrifices (10:18). Such sacrifices were not of long-term help anyway, for they didn't take away sins (10:1–4). The new covenant, then, is an "everlasting covenant" (13:21) since it is linked to the sacrifice of Christ who offered himself through the "eternal Spirit" (9:14).

The permanence and efficacy of the new covenant can be traced to Christ as "the mediator of a new covenant" so that an "eternal inheritance" is obtained through his sacrificial death (9:15). Even under the old covenant death was necessary to receive redemption from sins that were committed (9:15). Apparently sacrifices had to be offered for Israel to be cleansed of their sins. Such is always the case when it comes to covenants (9:15–22). They are only valid where blood has been spilt to establish the covenant, and hence the Sinai covenant was "inaugurated with blood" (9:18; Exod 24:3–8). The blood purified the tabernacle, its articles, and the people (9:19–22). The people needed to be purified because of their sin, as 9:22 makes clear. Without blood there would be no forgiveness. So too, in the new covenant the blood of Jesus had to be shed for the covenant to be effective (9:23–26). The people of God could only have access to him if they were forgiven of their sins. Jesus' blood cleanses from sin (12:24) and inducts believers into the realm of the holy (10:29; 13:20). The new covenant is better than the old because through the blood of Jesus sins are truly forgiven, and thus human beings have access to God.

§4 The Spirit in Hebrews[51]

The Holy Spirit is only mentioned seven times in Hebrews, and thus he doesn't play a major role. On the other hand the references to

---

[50] O'Brien rightly points out that we have a new covenant, not just a renewed covenant, since in the new covenant there is perfection (7:11, 19), the final cleansing of sin, and an unbreakable covenant ("The New Covenant," 21).

[51] See Martin Emmrich, *Pneumatological Concepts in the Epistle to the Hebrews: Amtscharisma, Prophet, and Guide of the Eschatological Exodus* (Lanham, MD:

the Spirit are interesting, showing a vibrant, although limited, view of the Spirit's presence. Of course, we need to remind ourselves that what we find in an occasional letter like Hebrews doesn't represent the entirety of the author's theology. So what is said about the Spirit is likely the tip of the iceberg in the author's theology.

First, the Spirit is the gift of the new age that is fulfilled in Jesus Christ. The references to the Spirit fit with the author's eschatology. The "end of the ages" has dawned in Jesus Christ and his sacrificial death (9:26). The author can't countenance turning back to the law, for then the readers would step backward in salvation history. Neglecting their great salvation would be outrageous, for God attested to its truthfulness by granting "signs, wonders," and "miracles" (2:3–4). He also verified such a salvation through the gifts given by the Holy Spirit (2:4). The gifts of the Spirit are the gifts of the new age, testifying that God has spoken the definitive and final word in Jesus Christ (1:2).

Along the same lines believers are said to be those who "have shared in the Holy Spirit" (6:4 ESV). One of the fundamental eschatological promises in the OT was the granting of the Holy Spirit (Isa 32:15; 44:3; Ezek 36:26–27; 37:14; 39:29; Joel 2:28; Zech 12:10). When the Spirit was given, Israel would return from exile, the wilderness would bloom, they would keep the Lord's commands, repent of their sin, speak forth God's word, and God's great promises to Israel would come to pass. Now we are told in 6:4 that the readers were sharers in or partakers of the Holy Spirit. Clearly the end of history had arrived, for believers in Jesus Christ had received the Holy Spirit (cf. Gal 3:2, 5; Acts 15:7–11). Nevertheless the readers were on the verge of marching backward in salvation history, as if the new era of the Spirit had not yet come. Such a prospect, according to the writer, is unthinkable.

The Spirit also plays a role in the great redemptive events that have been fulfilled in Jesus Christ. For instance, when Christ gave himself as a sacrificial offering to God, an offering without blemish (9:14), he did so "through the eternal Spirit." A few commentators

University Press of America, 2003); Steve Motyer, "The Spirit in Hebrews: No Longer Forgotten?," in *The Spirit and Christ in the New Testament and Christian Theology: Essays Presented in Honor of Max Turner*, ed. I. H. Marshall, V. Rabens, and C. Bennema (Grand Rapids, MI: Eerdmans, 2012), 213–27, though he over reads the prophetic role of the Spirit (222–26).

have seen a reference to Christ's human spirit, but most agree that the Holy Spirit is intended here. For the Spirit in Hebrews, except for one instance, is always the Holy Spirit (4:12); and it doesn't make much sense to say that Jesus' human spirit was eternal. Furthermore, if the author wanted to designate Jesus' human spirit, he could have added the pronoun "his" to make this clear. But what does the author mean in saying Christ offered himself through the eternal Spirit? It is difficult to be sure. At least we can say that the Holy Spirit played a central role in Christ's self-giving. Perhaps the author here draws on what we see in the Gospel of Luke where Jesus is empowered by the Holy Spirit in his ministry (Luke 3:21–22; 4:1, 14, 18). Jesus was the Spirit-anointed Messiah, and the Spirit of the Lord rested on him (Isa 11:2; 61:1). We have a trinitarian reference here, for Jesus gave himself to God as an offering through the work of the Holy Spirit. The atonement, which secured "redemption" and the "eternal inheritance" (9:15), was the work of the Father, the Son, and the Spirit.

Rather similar to this is the reference to "the Spirit of grace" (10:29). The expression almost certainly means the Spirit who gives or grants grace. But in context the grace of the Spirit is tied to "the blood of the covenant," which sanctifies believers (10:29). The Spirit grants grace, then, through the sacrificial blood of Jesus Christ. The grace isn't a diffuse grace granted in a general way. The grace given by the Spirit is dispensed through Jesus Christ and his atoning work. The readers should not despise this grace, for that would be apostasy.

When considering what Hebrews teaches about God, we saw that he is a God who speaks. The author makes the same point relative to the Holy Spirit.[52] The words of Ps 95:7–11 are the words of the Holy Spirit (3:7).[53] As Schenk says, "The author thinks of God and the Holy Spirit as the same speaker. . . . The Holy Spirit speaking is God speaking."[54] The Spirit addresses the church of the author's day through the Scriptures. The Scriptures aren't a dead letter but contain the living voice of the Spirit of God. Similarly,

---

[52] Hence, Lindars wrongly rejects the idea of the Spirit's personality in Hebrews (*The Theology of Hebrews*, 57).

[53] But Emmrich goes too far in saying we have a "*new*" oracle" in 3:7–11 by virtue of the Spirit (*Pneumatological Concepts in Hebrews*, 29, cf. also p. 32, italics his).

[54] Schenk, "God Has Spoken," 334–35.

the Spirit also bears witness and testifies to the readers in the words of Jer 31:33–34 (10:15–17). We might expect that the writer would attribute these words to God, but he refers to the Holy Spirit. It seems clear that the author puts the Holy Spirit on par with God. He doesn't formally explicate or work out a doctrine of the Trinity, but we are on the way to such a doctrine with statements like these. Lastly the writer sees the Holy Spirit speaking through OT events. The high priest enters the most holy place only once a year on the Day of Atonement (9:7; cf. Lev 16:1–34). The author concludes that the Spirit was speaking (for those who have ears to hear) through such a practice (9:8). It was clear that access to God wasn't available under the old covenant. The Spirit was revealing that a new way and a new day were coming, a day in which there would be regular access to God through the atoning sacrifice of Jesus Christ.

§5 Warnings and Exhortations[55]

The warning passages in Hebrews have been debated in both popular and scholarly circles for centuries.[56] It is actually difficult to determine where the warnings begin and end. For our purposes a resolution of this issue isn't crucial, for where one delimits the passages doesn't make much difference in terms of how one understands the warnings. For the purposes of the study here, the warnings will be restricted to 2:1–4; 3:12–4:13; 6:4–8; 10:26–31; 12:25–29.

Scholars propose a number of different views of the warnings, but here I will restrict myself to four interpretations.[57]

---

[55] See also Thomas R. Schreiner, "Warning and Assurance: Run the Race to the End," in *The Perfect Savior: Key Themes in Hebrews*, ed. J. Griffiths (Nottingham: InterVarsity, 2012), 89–106.

[56] For a useful survey, see B. J. Oropeza, "The Warning Passages in Hebrews: Revised Theologies and New Methods of Interpretation," *CBR* 10 (2011): 81–101. See also H. W. Bateman IV, ed., *Four Views on the Warning Passages in Hebrews* (Grand Rapids, MI: Kregel, 2007).

[57] Another view can be labeled as the Federal Vision view. According to this reading, the warnings are addressed to Christians who are members of the covenant, and believers can lose their covenant status by committing apostasy. There are two fundamental problems with this view. First, it doesn't adequately interpret the new covenant. The old covenant was broken because of the unfaithfulness and apostasy of Israel; but the new covenant, by way of contrast, will not and cannot be broken since God writes the law on the heart of his people. The new covenant is a better

View	To Whom Are the Warnings Addressed?	What Is the Sin Warned Against?	What Are the Consequences of the Sin Warned Against?
Arminian	Christians	Apostasy	Loss of salvation
Free Grace	Christians	Lack of fruitfulness	Loss of rewards
Tests of Genuineness	Almost Christians/ mixed audience	Apostasy	Never were saved
Means of Salvation	Christians	Apostasy	Loss of salvation

The Arminian view is the most common one among commentators today and has the virtue of being a straightforward reading. The author warns the readers who are believers that they will be damned if they fall away. It seems beside the point to give a warning if believers can't fall away, and hence it follows, according to the Arminian reading, that true believers may renounce and abandon the salvation they once had. The warnings are given to encourage the readers not to do so. The Free Grace view agrees that the warnings are addressed to Christians but argues from other texts that loss of salvation is impossible. When the warnings are examined carefully, according to this reading, they are not about salvation at all. The issue is actually about fruitfulness in one's everyday life. The sin warned against is compared to the sin of Israel in the wilderness (cf.

---

covenant with better promises because it ensures the obedience of those who are covenant members. Second, the Federal Vision view segregates election from covenant inclusion. In other words not all of those who are in the covenant are elected by God to final salvation. Such matters take us into theological reflection that goes beyond the boundaries of Hebrews. Suffice it to say that the gift of the new covenant is the Holy Spirit, and there is no warrant in the NT to say that some who receive the regenerating Spirit are nonelect. The Spirit is the guarantee of the end-time inheritance (Eph 1:13–14), and thus all who are members of the covenant are also elect. For a brief discussion of these matters, see Thomas R. Schreiner, *Run to Win the Prize: Perseverance in the New Testament* (Wheaton, IL: Crossway, 2010), 90–94. For a response to the interpretations of covenant theologians who believe the warnings of Hebrews imply that there are non-elect members of the new covenant who will commit apostasy, see Christopher W. Cowan, "The Warning Passages of Hebrews and the Nature of the New Covenant," in *Progressive Covenantalism*, ed. S. Wellum and B. Parker (Nashville: B&H Academic, forthcoming).

2:2–3; 3:12–4:13; 10:28–29; 12:25–27). Israel's sin was not rejection of salvation itself. Instead, they received earthly punishment for their transgressions, and the same kind of earthly punishments are now described relative to the church.

The third view argues that those receiving the warnings are a mixed audience, composed of both Christians and non-Christians.[58] Those who fail to heed the warning were never Christians at all. Often the warnings are explained as a test of genuineness, i.e., the warnings are intended to provoke the readers to self-examination to see if they are truly believers. True believers, it is argued, can't lose their salvation, and so the warnings function as a test to determine whether one is truly saved. On the other hand those who fall away were never believers in the first place. Those described in 6:4–6 are, according to this interpretation, almost Christians. The writer doesn't describe his readers as those who are actually saved. They are close to salvation but are not actually part of the people of God. It is important to understand that in the mixed audience view those described in 6:4–6 are not a mixed audience: they are non-Christians.

The view that will be defended here is that the warnings are addressed to Christians.[59] They aren't merely about rewards, but eschatological salvation is at stake. In other words those who fall away will experience the judgment destined for the wicked. In all these respects my view is similar to the Arminian view. I will also argue, in contrast to the Arminian view, that the warnings are always effective in the lives of the elect, and thus the warnings are the means by which believers are preserved in their faith.

In examining the text, four questions will be answered: (1) To whom are the warnings addressed? (2) What is the issue at stake in the warnings? (3) What are the consequences of falling away? (4) How should the warnings be assessed as a whole?

We begin by asking who is addressed in the warnings. It should be noted that of the four views sketched above all agree Christians

---

[58] For a good presentation of this view, along with a fine historical survey and critique of the various views, see C. Adrian Thomas, *A Case for Mixed-Audience with Reference to the Warning Passages in the Book of Hebrews* (New York: Peter Lang, 2008).

[59] For a concise but helpful pastoral application of the text, see Donald A. Hagner, *Hebrews* (New York: Harper & Row, 1983), 73.

are warned except for the tests of genuineness view, which maintains that a mixed audience is in view and that those who are described in 6:4–6 are not Christians.

It is clear that the warnings are addressed to believers. The readers are identified as "brothers," which means they are fellow Christians (3:12). Often the second person plural is used in the warnings, which is most naturally understood as being directed to the readers (3:12–13, 15; 4:1, 7; 5:11–12; 10:30; 12:25). The author naturally addresses the audience as "you" and as "Christians," but such identifications don't necessarily mean every reader was a believer. The author could be generalizing, and hence the second-person plural doesn't prove believers are necessarily addressed. On the other hand the pronouns indicate that Christians are certainly included in the warnings, for second-person pronouns aren't designed to address non-Christians.

Perhaps even more striking is the use of the first-person plurals in the warnings. The author includes himself among those who need the warning, using "we" and "us" (2:1, 3; 3:14; 4:1–3, 11; 10:26; 12:25, 28; cf. 3:6; 6:1). Again this doesn't preclude the mixed audience reading, for including Christians in the warning doesn't necessarily exclude unbelievers. But once again we naturally conclude that Christians are described in the first-person pronouns.

The decisive issue is the identity of those described in 6:4–6, and the commentary on those verses should be consulted for further discussion. I would argue that those described in those verses are most naturally identified as Christians. The notion that they are "almost Christians" can't be sustained. When the author says they were "once enlightened" (ἅπαξ φωτισθέντας, 6:4), this most naturally refers to their conversion, as the use of the same term in 10:32 attests. What is most decisive is the statement that the readers have "shared in the Holy Spirit" (6:4 ESV). The word "shared" (μετόχους) and its cognates don't point to a "false" sharing. Jesus truly "shared" in flesh and blood (2:14). Believers "share" a heavenly calling (3:1) and are "partakers" or "sharers" in Christ (3:14). The author refers to "partaking" of milk (5:13), and there is no sense that one only "sips" at the milk. All children "share" in discipline (12:8).

It is clear the author doesn't refer to "almost Christians," for *the mark* that one is a Christian is reception of the Holy Spirit. Paul appeals to the fact that the Galatians have received the Spirit to show they don't need to be circumcised to be saved (Gal 3:2, 5). Peter makes the same argument at the Apostolic Council in Acts 15, declaring that circumcision must not be necessary for salvation since God gave the Spirit apart from circumcision (15:7–11). What it means to be a Christian, according to Rom 8:9, is to be a person of the Spirit, for those who don't have the Spirit aren't believers.

It is irrelevant, then, to argue that the readers aren't Christians since Hebrews doesn't say in 6:4–6 that they are forgiven of their sin or that they are sanctified or justified.[60] We can't impose criteria upon the author that are foreign to his purpose, and he actually uses the clearest evidence possible to demonstrate that the readers are Christians: they share in the Holy Spirit. As we have seen, the word "sharing" here doesn't suggest a partial or insubstantial sharing.

The author also says the readers have tasted three things: "the heavenly gift" (6:4), which is probably salvation; "God's good word," which is the gospel (6:5); and, "the powers of the coming age" (6:5). Nothing here suggests deficiency. These are all normal and standard ways of describing what it means to be a Christian. Indeed, "the powers of the coming age" signify that the OT promises have become reality in Jesus Christ.

Some object to what I am arguing here by saying the word "taste" means the experiences depicted here are partial and inadequate. But there is no evidence in Hebrews that the word "taste" should be understood this way. After all, the author uses the same verb to say Jesus "tasted" death (2:8), and this certainly doesn't mean Jesus just sipped death. He experienced death in all its fullness.

All this is to say the warnings are most naturally interpreted to be directed to Christians. The author is not intending in 6:4–6 to speak to those who are almost Christians, nor does he suggest that he addresses a mixed audience. He *describes those addressed as Christians*. He is not asking readers to be introspective and to consider whether they have been truly saved, as the test of genuineness view teaches. Such a perspective on Hebrews 6 makes this text different from all the other warning passages, which is unlikely. Scot McKnight has rightly argued that the warning passages should

---

[60] Against Wayne Grudem, "Perseverance of the Saints: A Case Study from the Warning Passages in Hebrews," in *Still Sovereign*, ed. T. R. Schreiner and B. A. Ware (Grand Rapids, MI: Baker, 2000), 133–82.

be read synoptically.[61] In other words they mutually interpret one another. Hebrews is a sermon (13:22) with one main point: don't fall away from Jesus. It is unlikely that chapter 6 has a different function from all the other warning passages in this sermon. Hence the author doesn't write to provoke the readers to question whether they are truly believers. He writes to encourage them to keep following Jesus.

The participles strung together (6:4–6) do not, in light of the rest of the letter, indicate that some have already fallen away. Nor is the author writing about other Christians who are unrelated to the readers. When the author speaks of falling away, he warns the readers, just as he did in the other warning passages. The immediately following verses indicate that the author isn't saying the readers *have fallen away*. He is admonishing them not to fall away, and we see from 6:9–12 that he is confident they won't fall away. The author apparently believes the warnings will be effective, that they will succeed in preserving the readers in the faith.

One more word should be said about the test of genuineness view. I am not denying that there was probably a mixed audience in the church. It is unlikely that every single person addressed was genuinely a Christian! And thus we must be precise and careful here. The question that must be asked centers on the descriptions found in 6:4–6: How are the readers described? I have argued in the commentary that the author specifically targets Christians and describes Christians in these verses. He doesn't direct his warnings against almost Christians. Now this is not to deny that some who appeared to be believers probably fell away from the faith in the churches or church addressed. That was a common experience in the early church (cf. 1 John 2:19; 1 Cor 11:19). The point I am making here is that the warnings are actually addressed to believers, not to those who aren't quite believers. We must attend to the literary function of the warnings, and they are specifically addressed to believers. And, as I will argue later, the warnings were intended to be a means to preserve the believers from apostasy. I conclude, then, that the almost Christian view or the mixed-audience view should be rejected

---

[61] See Scot McKnight, "The Warning Passages of Hebrews: A Formal Analysis and Theological Conclusions," *TrinJ* 13 (1992): 21–59.

since it doesn't satisfactorily interpret the descriptions of the readers in 6:4–6.

That brings us to the second issue: What is at stake in the warnings? Perhaps it should be noted again that the warnings are just that. They are admonitions and warnings. They are not declarations about what has happened. They warn the readers about the consequences if they fall away. I would argue with most interpreters that what is at stake in the warnings is apostasy: renunciation of salvation. In 2:1 the readers are warned about drifting away (2:1) and neglecting *salvation* (2:3).

It is even clearer in 3:12–4:11 that the issue is apostasy. The readers are admonished not to "fall away (ἀποστῆναι) from the living God" (ESV). They should beware of hardness of heart (3:13, 15; 4:7), of rebellion (3:15–16), of disobedience (3:18; 4:6, 11), of unbelief (3:12, 19; 4:2–3), and of falling short (4:1). In 6:6 the sin is described as falling away (παραπεσόντας).[62] Falling away constitutes a recrucifixion of Jesus and treats him with contempt (6:6). Crucifying Jesus again describes those who have totally repudiated him and doesn't refer to those who are merely losing out on their rewards. Putting Jesus to death again is the action of his enemies, not his friends.

It is imperative to recall that the warnings should be read synoptically, and thus the author uses a variety of terms to describe the same reality. Thus the notion that apostasy is in view in all the texts is strengthened by the descriptions of the sin in 10:26–31. First, the sin is deliberate (Ἐκουσίως . . . ἁμαρτανόντων, 10:26). In other words, it is akin to defiant sin in the OT (Num 15:30; Deut 17:2), sin for which there was no forgiveness. It is difficult to believe the writer just has unfruitfulness in view, for the sins are described as trampling Jesus as God's Son under one's feet, considering the covenant blood of Jesus to be as unclean as a menstrual cloth, and insulting the Holy Spirit (10:29). The severity of the descriptions makes it impossible to think that the sin here is anything other than apostasy. The author rounds out his warnings in 12:25 by exhorting the readers not to reject the one who has warned them from heaven.

What are the consequences of the falling away or apostasy? I will argue that the consequences are final judgment, exclusion from

---

[62] In support of a reference to apostasy here, see the commentary on 6:6.

his gracious presence. In 2:1 and 12:25 the author warns them that they will not escape if they turn away from the one who admonishes them. The word "escape" functions as a framework or envelope for the warning passages since it occurs in the first and last warning. The word "escape" is rather general, and one can see why some might think the text refers only to losing one's reward. Still there are two decisive points against such a reading. First, the consequences described in the warning passages should be read synoptically, and the other texts make clear that something more than losing rewards is intended. Second, the Free Grace view actually turns upside down what the author is doing. In both 2:2–3 and 12:25–26, the author draws a parallel between judgments that occurred in Israel with the judgment that will be meted out to those who turn against the Son. The Free Grace interpretation, noting the parallel, argues that the threatened judgment is earthly, just as it was under the old covenant. But such an interpretation actually misses what the author does, for he argues typologically and escalates the argument. He doesn't merely draw a parallel between Israel and the church of Jesus Christ. He contends that believers will face a greater judgment for neglecting a greater salvation. In other words the judgment isn't just earthly but also heavenly (12:25). We see another example here of the escalation that is a common feature of NT typology.[63]

It is also clear in 3:12–4:11 that the consequences of apostasy are not merely loss of rewards but final judgment. The author again argues from the earthly to the heavenly. Israel failed to enter earthly rest in Canaan because of its disobedience and hardness of heart.[64] But the rest envisioned for the readers is not merely an earthly rest but a heavenly one. It is God's Sabbath rest (4:9), the rest intended for human beings since the creation of the world. The point of the text is that the rest under Joshua was not ultimate but provisional,

---

[63] In support of what is said here, see the commentary for the interpretation of the passages under consideration.

[64] On the theme of rest in Hebrews, see Jon Laansma, *"I Will Give You Rest": The Rest Motif in the New Testament with Special Reference to Mt 11 and Heb 3–4*, WUNT 2/98 (Tübingen: Mohr Siebeck, 1997); Judith Hoch Wray, *Rest as a Theological Metaphor in the Epistle to the Hebrews and the Gospel of Truth: Early Christian Homiletics of Rest*, SBLDS 166 (Atlanta: Scholars,1988). Laansma's work is insightful and theologically rich. Wray fails to see how the rest theme integrates with the remainder of Hebrews.

so that it pointed to and anticipated a greater rest to come. The Free Grace view, then, fails to understand the typology and theology of Hebrews. The earthly rest points to the heavenly rest, indeed to the heavenly city promised for believers (11:10, 13–16; 12:22; 13:14). If they fail to enter God's rest, they will not be in his presence but will experience torment instead.

The consequences of falling away in 6:4–8 come to the forefront in the illustration of land that receives rain but fails to bear fruit. Ultimately such land is "worthless," will be "burned," and is "about to be cursed" (6:8). Free Grace advocates think the text supports their reading, for they claim that those who don't produce fruit but rather "thorns and thistles" (6:8) are not damned. The penalty, according to the Free Grace reading, is that they won't enjoy a life that is fruitful on earth. I would suggest, however, that the Free Grace interpretation fails, for they fail to see the point of the illustration. In the illustration the "land" ($\gamma\tilde{\eta}$, ESV) stands for the person. It should be observed that verse 8 doesn't say crops are destroyed and burned. Instead, if the land is unfruitful, then the *land* will "be burned," is near a curse and is worthless. The judgment is inflicted on the land (i.e., the person), not on the fruit (the person's works). Indeed, the word "worthless" is regularly used in the NT to designate those who are unqualified at the final judgment, for those who are unbelievers (Rom 1:28; 1 Cor 9:27; 2 Cor 13:5–7; 2 Tim 3:8; Titus 1:16). To say they are "near a curse" doesn't mean they will escape the curse. The nearness is temporal, not spatial.

The judgments described in 10:26–31 also demonstrate that the readers would not merely lose rewards if they apostatized. If they turned away from Christ, there would be no sacrifice for their sins (10:26); and if there is no sacrifice, then there is no atonement and forgiveness, and the only prospect is final judgment. The ensuing verses confirm this reading. Those who turn against Christ are his enemies and will face a "terrifying expectation of judgment and the fury of a fire" (10:27). The argument again compares the punishments to those given under Moses, but he argues that the punishment meted out to those who reject Christ is a "worse punishment" (10:29). Those who violated the Mosaic covenant received judgment on earth, but those who refuse Christ will be banned from fellowship with God forever. They won't have any access to God's presence. They will face God's vengeance and final judgment (10:30) and will realize how "terrifying" it is "to fall into the hands of the living God" (10:31). I conclude, then, that the Free Grace view isn't persuasive; for when we examine the warning texts together, the sin warned against is apostasy, and the judgment threatened is final damnation.

Perhaps it would seem from the above that the view defended here is the same as the loss of salvation of view. I argue, however, that the warnings are always effective in the lives of those elected and chosen by God. The admonitions and warnings are prospective, not retrospective. The author doesn't declare that the readers *have* fallen away. He warns them not to fall away. I argue that for all those who have been enlightened and who have received the Holy Spirit (6:4–6), i.e., all believers, the warnings are one of the means by which believers are kept until the end. All those who are indwelt by the Holy Spirit heed the warnings and thus obtain final salvation. To say that believers are saved by heeding the warnings is not works-righteousness, for those who heed the warnings keep *trusting* God (11:1–40). Those who respond rightly to the author's admonitions continue to believe in God instead of turning away from him.[65]

Such a view of the warnings will not be persuasive to those convinced that believers can lose or forsake their salvation. This is not the place to defend the notion that those who have received the Holy Spirit and are saved will never apostatize. There is abundant evidence to support such a conclusion in the NT (e.g., John 6:37–44; 10:28–29; Rom 8:28–39; 1 Cor 1:8–9; Eph 1:13–14; Phil 1:6; 1 Thess 5:23–24; 1 Pet 1:5; Jude 24–25).

A common objection is that warnings are superfluous and beside the point if believers can't apostatize. Such an objection, though it initially sounds plausible, reads the biblical text as an abstraction and does not take into account that God is a God of both means and ends. Nor is it correct, biblically speaking, to say that the means are pointless if the end will be secured. For instance God has elected who will be saved before the foundation of the world, from all eternity (e.g., Rom 9:11–13; 1 Cor 1:26–28; Eph 1:4; 2 Thess 2:13–14; 1 Pet 1:1–2). Such a truth does not rule out the use of means, for those who are elected must still repent and believe in order to be saved (Acts 2:38; 16:31), for those who don't repent and believe will

---

[65] I will expand on this matter in the section below on "Faith, Obedience, and the Situation of the Readers."

face the last judgment. Furthermore, the gospel must be proclaimed so people can put their faith in Christ (Rom 10:14–17). The fact that the end (election) will certainly be obtained doesn't preclude the use of means (preaching the gospel and believing). Indeed the means must be present for the end to be obtained.

The same pattern of means and end applies to perseverance. God promises that all those who are justified and chosen by him will never be forsaken, that they will never totally and finally fall away from God. Such a promise doesn't preclude the use of means, and it is argued here that the warnings are one of the primary means God uses to preserve his own from falling away. The end is not cast in doubt by the means that should be employed but is actually supported and undergirded by the means.

There are many examples in Scripture where means are used when the end is certain. For instance, Daniel prays fervently that God would fulfill the promise from Jeremiah (Jer 25:11–12; 29:10) that Israel would return from Babylon after 70 years (Dan 9:1–23). The Lord promised Israel would return from exile, and hence one might think Daniel's prayer was superfluous, but Daniel believed his prayer was one of the means by which the promise would be secured. Similarly in Acts 27, during the midst of a raging storm at sea, Paul received the promise that every single person on the ship, all 276 of them, would live (27:21–26). Shortly thereafter, however, he warned the centurion and soldiers that they would not survive if they allowed the sailors to escape on the smaller boat (27:30–31). What was the purpose of the warning since God had already promised that the lives of all on the ship would be saved? Clearly Paul believed the warning was one of the means by which the promise would come to pass. Finally, Jesus teaches that it is impossible for the elect to believe in false messiahs and false prophets (Mark 13:20, 22). God will protect them from such deception. And yet he warns his disciples in the same text in the strongest terms possible to be on guard and constantly alert (Mark 13:21, 23, 33, 35, 37). Why should believers stay alert if they can't be deceived? The warning is one of the means by which the promises of God are secured.

Another objection should be answered briefly. Is the view proposed here saying that no one falls away from the faith, that every person addressed in Hebrews was truly a believer, and hence that no one addressed falls away? Such a scenario is implausible, for we know it was common for people to fall away from the faith (cf. 2 Pet 2:1–22; 1 John 2:19). I am not denying there was a mixed audience in Hebrews, nor am I suggesting that every single person persevered to the end and was saved. Such a state of affairs is highly doubtful. The point being made is more specific. It is evident from 6:4–6 that the writer addresses Christians, that he warns believers about what will happen if they fall away. His purpose in the warning isn't to pause and to say, "Some of those I am addressing are not truly believers." Believers are addressed in the admonitions. I am asking, therefore, how the warnings functioned in the lives of those specifically addressed by the author (Christians), and I am contending that the warnings were a means used to preserve them in the faith until the end. Another way to put it is this: the author doesn't attend to a question that often holds our attention. He doesn't consider whether some of those addressed aren't truly believers, for to do so would be to distract him from his main purpose and would blunt the force of the warning.

§6 Sojourners and Exiles

The warnings given to the readers fit with their status as sojourners and exiles.[66] In that sense the readers are like the Israelites who were in the wilderness before finding rest in the land of Canaan (3:12–4:13). The readers are on a journey to enter their heavenly rest, but they face perils on the way, just as Israel did on the way to the land of promise. The readers are warned not to harden their hearts and rebel against God. Israel gave way to unbelief and disobedience, and the readers must not follow their example. Unbelief and disobedience threaten because the wilderness period is exasperating,

---

[66] This theme was especially emphasized by Ernst Käsemann, *The Wandering People of God: An Investigation of the Letter to the Hebrews*, trans. R. A. Harrisville and I. L. Sundberg (Minneapolis, MN: Augsburg, 1984), though he wedded it to a Gnostic framework for the letter, which is now dismissed by nearly everyone. Still, the notion that the readers are exiles and wanderers is prominent in the letter. See David M. Allen, *Deuteronomy and Exhortation in Hebrews: A Study in Narrative Representation*, WUNT 2/238 (Tübingen: Mohr Siebeck, 2008), 191–98; Benjamin Dunning, "The Intersection of Alien Status and Cultic Discourse in the Epistle to the Hebrews," in *Hebrews: Contemporary Methods—New Insights*, ed. G. Gelardini (Leiden: Brill, 2005), 179–98; M. Thiessen, "Hebrews 12.5–13, the Wilderness Period, and Israel's Discipline," *NTS* 55 (2009): 366–79.

exhausting, and trying. Believers long to be in the heavenly city and to enjoy their heavenly rest, but instead they encounter the pressures and opposition of life in the world.

Their experience as "foreigners and temporary residents" (11:13) is also comparable to the patriarchs: Abraham, Isaac, and Jacob. These men also received promises that were not realized during their lifetimes, but they persevered knowing that a homeland, a city awaited them (11:10, 13–16; 12:22; 13:14). But life in the wilderness, life as exiles, is frustrating and can be dispiriting. Chapter 11 was written so the readers would keep trusting in God and would put their hope in him until the promises were realized. The readers should understand that life as exiles is not unique to them. The saints who preceded them also lived without seeing the final fulfillment of the promise. As exiles they must put their trust in God's promises for a happy future, believing that he will bring to pass what he has pledged.

A specific window into life in the wilderness is provided in 10:32–34. The readers experienced all kinds of sufferings: verbal abuse and discrimination, the plundering of their possessions and economic deprivation. Perhaps they wanted to come under the umbrella of Judaism since it was a legal religion in the Roman Empire. Then they would be free from the constant attacks that plagued them. The author encourages them to endure in faith. Life as exiles, life in the wilderness, is like growing up as children in a family (12:4–13). God is using their time in the wilderness to educate and train them.

The author uses here metaphors from education and physical training. They are in God's school and are being trained like athletes. God's purpose and design are for their holiness so they will be mature Christians. As parents discipline their children, so they will live productive and fruitful lives, so God is using the time in exile to form the character of his children.

God knows they are in the wilderness, and Jesus himself has experienced the sorrow and anguish of human life (2:17–18; 4:14–16; 5:7–8). The warnings and encouragements in the letter are intended to bring them to their heavenly rest, to the city to come. The days of exile and wandering will soon be over, and thus the readers must follow the example of Jesus and the saints who preceded them, trusting and obeying God until the end. Furthermore, they have access to God's presence through the atoning work of Jesus. They can enter

God's presence with confidence and joy, knowing that he will grant strength and grace for every trial (4:14–16). They shouldn't shrink back from God in fear but come with boldness since Jesus is their great high priest who has cleansed all their sins (10:19–22).

§7 Faith, Obedience, and the Situation of the Readers

A word about the situation of the readers might be helpful before considering the role faith and obedience play in the letter.[67] The readers after their conversion displayed love to fellow Christians in remarkable ways by serving others (6:10). They experienced considerable difficulty and opposition and ridicule (10:32–33). Even when their possessions were stolen, they responded with joy since they looked forward to "a better and enduring possession" (10:32–34).

Apparently, however, they had grown weary and sluggish (5:11; 6:12). The opposition against them was wearing on them. They were tired of facing opposition and wanted some relief (12:4–11). Perhaps they wanted to integrate with Judaism since it was a legal religion in the empire. The writer reminds them that Jesus shed his own blood (12:3–4) and was rejected by the social elites of his day (13:12). The suffering and discrimination they were experiencing were actually part of the Lord's discipline (12:4–11), and they should recognize that God was using these pressures for their holiness and righteousness. Hence they are encouraged to be like Abraham, Isaac, and Jacob and live out of step with their culture (11:8–16). They should, like Moses, choose the reproach of Christ instead of the comfort of Roman approval (11:23–26). They should follow Jesus and suffer outside the gate (13:12–13).

The warnings in Hebrews are severe and bracing, and thus interpreters may actually misunderstand what the author is calling for. The author doesn't summon the readers to heroism or to autonomous works. They are being called upon to trust in God and to rest in him instead of turning elsewhere to get a cleansed conscience. They are called on to believe in God and to look to him for their final reward, which is entrance into the heavenly city.

---

[67] For a helpful study on spirituality in Hebrews, see Kevin B. McCruden, *A Body You Have Prepared for Me: The Spirituality of the Letter to the Hebrews* (Collegeville, MN: Liturigical, 2013).

What it means to commit apostasy is to harden one's heart against God (3:8, 15; 4:7). The wilderness generation went "astray in their hearts" (3:10) and could not enter God's rest because of "unbelief" (3:19). The readers are admonished against letting their hearts grow hard and allowing an "evil, unbelieving heart" to take root in them (3:12). Only those who believe until the end will enter God's eschatological rest (4:2–3; 6:12). The author presents them with a clear choice in 10:38–39. Either the readers continue to believe or they commit apostasy, for faith is necessary to "obtain life" (10:39).

The function of the great faith chapter (chapter 11), then, is to explain the nature of the faith that obtains a final reward. Faith trusts in the promises and work of God instead of looking at what is visible. For instance, it can't be proven that the universe was created by God, but faith believes that the created world derives from the word of God (11:3). The readers saw that those who sided with Rome were rewarded, but the author encourages them to remember God's promises, which in the nature of the case are future and not visible now. Faith is convinced that what is not seen now will become a reality (11:1). Faith is certain that there will be a reward in the future for those who trust God (11:6).

The future character of faith is evident in Noah's case. He believed that he would be rewarded for constructing an ark, even when there was no evidence that a flood would strike the land (11:7). Similarly, Abraham left his homeland, trusting God's promise that he would give him the land. Isaac and Jacob followed the same pattern, and they all believed God would give them a homeland in the future, even though they never possessed the land of Canaan during their lives on earth (11:8–16).

God's promises would be fulfilled in the future, even if the fulfillment seemed to be impossible. Hence, Abraham believed God would raise Isaac from the dead if necessary (11:17–19). God, after all, promised that Isaac would be Abraham's offspring; and thus even if Abraham sacrificed Isaac on the altar, the Lord would fulfill his promise regarding Isaac, which meant that he would raise him from the dead. The author wants the readers to see that God always keeps his promises so they will keep trusting him despite the fact that his promises seem to be "unbelievable."

The author specifically remarks on the words of Isaac, Jacob, and Joseph as they were dying (11:20–22). Each one of them looked forward in the future and foresaw days of blessing for Israel. They didn't die in despair or in hopelessness but were convinced God would keep the promises he made to his people. Along the same lines Moses repudiated the pleasures of Egypt and chose to suffer with Israel because he knew God would reward him in the future (11:24–26). Others faced torture, but even in their agony they put their hope in the promise of the resurrection (11:35). The author underscores the truth that their OT ancestors continued to trust God, even though they didn't receive what was promised (11:39–40), encouraging, thereby, the readers to do the same. The supreme example, of course, is Jesus. He suffered the pain of the cross "for the joy that lay before Him" (12:2). Jesus trusted God as he was crucified because he believed God would reward him with a joy that would never end by raising him from the dead and seating him at God's right hand.

Another dimension of faith, which has already been touched on, emerges in Hebrews. Faith is willing to suffer, to take risks, because it contemplates the reward. That is, faith does not immediately access the promise. Faith meant Abraham, Isaac, and Jacob weren't at home in the world (11:9, 13). Faith expressed itself in Abraham's being willing to sacrifice his only son if God demanded it (11:17). Faith revealed itself when Moses chose to suffer with Israel instead of reveling in Egyptian luxury (11:25–26). Faith meant some were tortured, mocked, imprisoned, slain, and cast outside of society (11:35–38). Jesus demonstrated his faith in going to the cross (12:2–3).

What is implicit in the above paragraph needs to be made explicit. A faith that suffers is a faith that obeys. We noticed earlier that the wilderness generation failed to enter the promised rest because of unbelief, but the author emphasizes with equal force that they did not enter because of disobedience (3:18; 4:6, 11) because of sin (3:17). The old covenant was defective because Israel didn't keep covenant stipulations (8:9). Jesus is the "source of eternal salvation" to those who obey him (5:9). The warnings that punctuate the letter (2:1–4; 3:12–4:13; 5:11–6:8; 10:26–31; 12:25–29) demonstrate that obedience is necessary to obtain an eternal reward. We also see the importance of obedience in the exhortations that conclude the letter in chapter 13. Believers should love, practice hospitality, care for prisoners and the mistreated, be sexually pure, avoid love for money, obey their leaders, refuse defective teaching, suffer with Jesus, praise God, do good, and pray (13:1–18).

What is the relationship between faith and obedience in Hebrews? It is captured best by 11:8, "By faith Abraham . . . obeyed." Faith inevitably expresses and manifests itself as obedience. Abraham would not have truly believed in God's promise if he refused to go to the land God promised. If Moses didn't suffer with God's people but threw his lot in with the Egyptians, he would demonstrate that he didn't actually believe there was greater pleasure for those who trusted in the Lord. Faith is inseparable from obedience. "By faith Abel offered" his sacrifice (11:4). "By faith Noah . . . built an ark" (11:7). "By faith Abraham . . . offered up Isaac" (11:17). "By faith [Moses] left Egypt" (11:27). "By faith they crossed the Red Sea" (11:29). "By faith Rahab the prostitute received the spies" (11:31). The heroes of old "by faith conquered kingdoms, administered justice, obtained promises, shut the mouths of lions, quenched the raging of fire, escaped the edge of the sword, gained strength after being weak, became mighty in battle, and put foreign armies to flight" (11:33–34). If obedience is lacking, then faith is a charade. To say that faith is inseparable from obedience is not to say that faith and obedience are the same thing. Faith and obedience are distinguishable but inseparable. Faith is the root and obedience is the fruit. True faith always reveals itself in works, as James also teaches.

§8 Assurance

Hebrews is characterized by admonitions and warnings, but the theme of assurance is present too.[68] The author doesn't exclusively warn readers about the dangers of falling away, but he also emphasizes the assurance they have as followers of Jesus Christ. One of the fundamental themes of the letter is that the sins of the readers are truly forgiven. Jesus expiated and propitiated for their sins at the

---

[68] See especially Christopher W. Cowan, "'Confident of Better Things': Assurance of Salvation in the Letter to the Hebrews" (Ph.D. diss., The Southern Baptist Theological Seminary, 2012).

cross (2:17). They are freed from the fear of death because they are now brothers and sisters with Jesus (2:14–15). Their sins have been cleansed forever, and the evidence that their sins are forgiven is that Jesus, in fulfillment of Ps 110:1, has sat down at God's right hand (1:3; cf. 1:13; 8:1; 10:12; 12:2). The readers were tempted to rely on the Levitical priesthood for the cleansing of their conscience and the forgiveness of sins, but the priesthood of Jesus offers "a better hope" because believers actually "draw near to God" through Jesus (7:19). Jesus entered the most holy place with his own blood and cleanses the conscience of its evil (9:11–12, 14, 24). As a result believers can approach God's throne boldly through Christ as the high priest (4:14–16). They can be full of confidence, and even boldness, so that they enter into the presence of God by virtue of Christ's blood (10:19) and hence "draw near" to God with "full assurance of faith" (10:22). They know that since Jesus' priesthood never ceases he will save them completely (7:25). His "one offering . . . has perfected forever those who are sanctified" (10:14).

From one angle Hebrews can be read as a call to assurance. The warnings and admonitions are also given so the readers will be convinced they are on the right path, that they are truly clean before God by virtue of what Christ has done. The warnings aren't meant to cast doubt about the readers' assurance but to strengthen and confirm it. The author doesn't want them to doubt whether they are Christians but to be encouraged to keep living as Christians.

The author seems to be convinced that the warnings will have a salutary effect. He is persuaded that the urgent warnings will provoke the readers to "better things" (6:9), to final salvation. The readers, after all, are recipients of God's promises. God promises to bless them as he did Abraham (6:13–20). The promise is not uncertain, for God swore to bless Abraham (6:13–14). There was no question, then, whether Abraham would receive the blessing. God took an oath to underscore "His unchangeable purpose," which he guarantees to those who belong to him (6:17). The promise is given as an encouragement so believers would "seize the hope set before us" (6:18). Hope functions as an "anchor" for their lives, which can't be dislodged, for Jesus has entered through the curtain into the presence of God (6:19). Lindars says about hope: "It is like a place of refuge for those in need. It is like an anchor in rough seas. It is like admission beyond the veil of the sanctuary, which is the place of the presence of God himself."[69]

The new covenant promise also provides assurance (8:6–12; 10:15–17), for the new covenant is God's work by which he inscribes his law on the hearts of his people. The new covenant is like the oath God gives to his people. It is unilateral and flows from God's mercy alone. The new covenant, unlike the old covenant, can't be revoked, nor will it be cancelled by human disobedience, for God promises that his people will obey his commands. The promise of obedience sets the new covenant apart from the old. It follows, then, that the new covenant grants assurance; for the law is written indelibly by God in their hearts, and believers enjoy forgiveness of sins through Christ's sacrifice. God will certainly complete what he has started in them, for that is the promise of the new covenant. They will not fall away as Israel did.

§9 The Future Reward

A discussion of the future reward in Hebrews is closely related to the promise of assurance, for we have just seen that assurance means one has confidence that one will receive the final reward. Here I want to examine a bit more closely the final reward in Hebrews, and that reward is described in a variety of ways.

I begin with the notion of salvation. Salvation in Hebrews is an eschatological notion, for salvation ultimately means rescue from the end-time wrath of God. In Hebrews, however, there is an already-but-not-yet dimension to salvation. "Eternal salvation" now belongs to those who have given themselves to Jesus (5:9). Even now believers enjoy salvation through their brother Jesus (2:3, 10). He saves now and for all time those who belong to God through him (7:25). Believers are saved, and yet salvation is fundamentally future. They will ultimately "inherit salvation" on the last day (1:14) and will be saved if they heed the warnings given (6:9). Jesus will bring salvation to his own when he comes again (9:28), which clearly demonstrates that salvation is ultimately a future gift.

It is also interesting to notice the convergence between the terms *promise* and *inheritance*, which point to the eschaton. Believers don't just inherit salvation, but they also inherit the promises (6:12) and the

---

[69] Lindars, *The Theology of Hebrews*, 71.

blessing (12:17).[70] It is plain that in 6:13–20 the promise is not yet fully realized, for believers are "heirs of the promise" (6:17) given to Abraham. This promise is their hope (6:18–19), a hope that will finally be realized on the day of resurrection (6:11). Because of Christ's redemptive work, believers enjoy the "promise of the eternal inheritance" (9:15); and if they persevere, they will receive what God has promised (10:35). The reception of the promise is correlated with the final "reward" (10:35; cf. 11:26). Another way of describing the final reward is the promise of the resurrection (11:35; cf. 6:2).

Often the future reward is described as "rest" (3:11, 18; 4:1, 3, 5, 8–11). I argued earlier that there was an already-but-not-yet dimension to the rest, but the rest is mainly eschatological, denoting the final blessing that will belong to the believers when Jesus returns (9:28) or when they die. Believers will cease from laborious activity when their earthly sojourn has ended (4:10). A Sabbath rest is appointed for the people of God (4:9), where believers will rest from the labors of this life, just as God rested because he was finished with the work of creation.

The future reward is also referred to in terms of a city. Believers anticipate the city, which will be perfect since God is its builder (11:10). It is not corrupt and defiled by sin like the city of man. Believers are exiles on earth and look forward eagerly to the heavenly city God has prepared for them (11:16). The city of man doesn't endure, but the city of God will most certainly come (13:14), and it is the hope of every believer. There is a sense in which believers have already arrived at "the heavenly Jerusalem" (12:22), but the full revelation of the city belongs to a future day (Rev 21:1–22:5).

The heavenly city represents the entire universe under God's lordship. His kingdom (12:28) will arrive in its fullness, and God will rule over all things and all people. The promise of victory over the serpent (Gen 3:15) and defeat of the devil and death (2:14–15) will be fully realized. Believers will enjoy God's presence without interruption and without the blight of sin. The days of wilderness will be over, and the days of rest will have begun, and they will never, ever end.

---

[70] For an excellent study on the inheritance in Hebrews, see Dana M. Harris, "The Eternal Inheritance in Hebrews: The Appropriation of the Old Testament Inheritance Motif by the Author of Hebrews" (Ph.D. diss., Trinity Evangelical Divinity School, 2009).

Bibliography

Adams, Edward. "The Cosmology of Hebrews." Pages 122–39 in *The Epistle to the Hebrews and Christian Theology*. Edited by R. Bauckham, D. R. Driver, T. A. Hart, and N. MacDonald. Grand Rapids, MI: Eerdmans, 2009.

Allen, David L. *Hebrews*. NAC 35. Nashville, TN: B&H, 2010.

———. *Lukan Authorship of Hebrews*. Nashville, TN: B&H, 2010.

Allen, David M. *Deuteronomy and Exhortation in Hebrews: A Study in Narrative Re-presentation*. WUNT 2/238. Tübingen: Mohr Siebeck, 2008.

Anderson, Charles P. "Who Are the Heirs of the New Age in the Epistle to the Hebrews?" Pages 255–77 in *Apocalyptic and the New Testament: Essays in Honor of J. Louis Martyn*. Edited by J. Marcus and M. L. Soards. JSNTSup 24. Sheffield: Sheffield Academic, 1989.

Attridge, Harold W. "God in Hebrews." Pages 95–110 in *The Epistle to the Hebrews and Christian Theology*. Edited by R. Bauckham, D. R. Driver, T. A. Hart, and N. MacDonald. Grand Rapids, MI: Eerdmans, 2009.

———. *The Epistle to the Hebrews*. Hermeneia. Philadelphia: Fortress, 1989.

———. "The Uses of Antithesis in Hebrews 8–10." *HTR* 79 (1986): 1–9.

Backhaus, Knut. "How to Entertain Angels: Ethics in the Epistle to the Hebrews," Pages 149–75 in *Hebrews: Contemporary Methods—New Insights*. Edited by G. Gelardini. Leiden: Brill, 2005.

Barnard, Jody A. *The Mysticism of Hebrews: Exploring the Role of Jewish Apocalyptic Mysticism in the Epistle to the Hebrews*. WUNT 2/331. Tübingen: Mohr Siebeck, 2012.

Barrett, C. K. "The Eschatology of the Epistle to the Hebrews." Pages 363–93 in *The Background of the New Testament and Its Eschatology*. Edited by W. D. Davies and D. Daube. Cambridge: Cambridge University Press, 1956.

Bateman, Herbert W., IV. *Early Jewish Hermeneutics and Hebrews 1:5–13: The Impact of Early Jewish Exegesis on the Interpretation of a Significant New Testament Passage.* New York: Peter Lang, 1997.

Bauckham, Richard. "The Divinity of Jesus Christ in the Epistle to the Hebrews." Pages 15–36 in *The Epistle to the Hebrews and Christian Theology.* Edited by R. Bauckham, D. R. Driver, T. A. Hart, and N. MacDonald. Grand Rapids, MI: Eerdmans, 2009.

Bauer, Walter. *A Greek-English Lexicon of the New Testament and Other Early Christian Literature.* 3rd edition. Revised and edited by Frederick William Danker, William F. Arndt, and F. Wilbur Gingrich. Chicago: University of Chicago Press, 2000.

Behm, J. "αἷμα." *TDNT* 1:172–77.

Berger, K. "χαρακτήρ." *EDNT* 3:456.

Black, David Alan. *The Authorship of Hebrews: The Case for Paul.* Gonzalez, FL: Energion, 2013.

———. "The Problem of the Literary Structure of Hebrews: An Evaluation and Proposal." *GTJ* 7 (1986): 163–77.

———. "Who Wrote Hebrews? The Internal and External Evidence Re-examined." *Faith and Mission* 18 (2001): 3–26.

Blomberg, Craig L. "'But We See Jesus': The Relationship Between the Son of Man in Hebrews 2.6 and 2.9 and the Implications for English Translations." Pages 88–99 in *A Cloud of Witnesses: The Theology of Hebrews in Its Ancient Contexts.* Edited by R. Bauckham, D. Driver, T. Hart, and N. MacDonald. LNTS 387. London: T&T Clark, 2008.

Bock, Darrell. *Blasphemy and Exaltation in Judaism and the Final Examination of Jesus: A Philological-Historical Study of the Key Jewish Themes Impacting Mark 14:61–64.* Grand Rapids, MI: Baker, 2000.

Bockmuehl, Markus. "Abraham's Faith in Hebrews 11." Pages 364–73 in *The Epistle to the Hebrews and Christian Theology.* Edited by R. Bauckham, D. R. Driver, T. A. Hart, and N. MacDonald. Grand Rapids, MI: Eerdmans, 2009.

Brooks, Walter Edward. "The Perpetuity of Christ's Sacrifice in the Epistle to the Hebrews." *JBL* 89 (1970): 205–14.

Bruce, F. F. *The Epistle to the Hebrews.* Rev. ed. NICNT. Grand Rapids: Eerdmans, 1990.

———. "'To the Hebrews' or 'To the Essenes'?" *NTS* 9 (1962–63): 217–32.

Büchsel, F. "ἔλεγχος." *TDNT* 2:476.

Caird, G. B. "Son by Appointment." Pages 73–81 in vol. 1 of *The New Testament Age: Essays in Honor of Bo Reicke.* Edited by W. C. Weinrich. Macon, GA: Mercer University Press, 1984.

———. "The Exegetical Method of the Epistle to the Hebrews." *Canadian Journal of Theology* 5 (1959): 44–51.

Caneday, Ardel B. "The Eschatological World Already Subjected to the Son: The Οἰκουμένη of Hebrews 1:6 and the Son's Enthronement." Pages 28–39 in *A Cloud of Witnesses: The Theology of Hebrews in Its Ancient Contexts*. Edited by R. Bauckham, D. Driver, T. Hart, and N. MacDonald. LNTS 387. London: T&T Clark, 2008.

Chester, A. N. "Hebrews: The Final Sacrifice." Pages 57–72 in *Sacrifice and Redemption: Durham Essays in Theology*. Edited by S. W. Sykes. Cambridge: Cambridge University Press, 1991.

Cockerill, Gareth L. "Structure and Interpretation in Hebrews 8:1–10:18: A Symphony in Three Movements." *BBR* 11 (2001): 179–201.

———. "The Better Resurrection (Heb. 11:35): A Key to the Structure and Rhetorical Purpose of Hebrews 11." *TynB* 51 (2000): 215–34.

———. *The Epistle to the Hebrews*. NICNT. Grand Rapids, MI: Eerdmans, 2012.

———. "The Melchizedek Christology in Hebrews 7:1–28." Ph.D. diss., Union Theological Seminary, 1976.

Cody, Aelred. *Heavenly Sanctuary and Liturgy in the Epistle to the Hebrews: The Achievement of Salvation in the Epistle's Perspectives*. St. Meinrad, IN: Grail, 1960.

Colijn, Brenda B. "'Let Us Approach': Soteriology in the Epistle to the Hebrews." *JETS* 39 (1996): 571–86.

Compton, Jared. "The Origin of σῶμα in Heb 10:5: Another Look at a Recent Proposal." *TrinJ* 32 (2011): 19–29.

Cosby, Michael R. *The Rhetorical Composition and Function of Hebrews 11: In Light of Example Lists in Antiquity*. Macon, GA: Mercer University Press, 1988.

Cowan, Christopher W. "'Confident of Better Things': Assurance of Salvation in the Letter to the Hebrews." Ph.D. diss., The Southern Baptist Theological Seminary, 2012.

———. "The Warning Passages of Hebrews and the Nature of the New Covenant." In *Progressive Covenantalism*. Edited by S. Wellum and B. Parker. Nashville: B&H Academic (forthcoming).

Croy, N. Clayton. *Endurance in Suffering: Hebrews 12:1–3 in Its Rhetorical, Religious, and Philosophical Context*. SNTSMS 98. Cambridge: Cambridge University, 1998.

Cullmann, Oscar. *Christ and Time: The Primitive Christian Conception of Time and History*. Translated by F. V. Filson. Philadelphia: Westminster, 1950.

Davidson, Richard M. "Christ's Entry 'Within the Veil' in Hebrews 6:19–20: The Old Testament Background." *AUSS* 39 (2001): 175–90.

Decker, Rodney J. "The Intentional Structure of Hebrews." *The Journal of Ministry & Theology* 4 (2000): 80–105.

―――. "The Warning of Hebrews 6." *The Journal of Ministry & Theology* 5 (2001): 26–48.

Deenick, Karl. "Priest and King or Priest-King in 1 Samuel 2:35." *WTJ* 73 (2011): 325–39.

DeSilva, David A. *Despising Shame: Honor Discourse and Community Maintenance in the Epistle to the Hebrews.* SBLDS 152. Atlanta: Scholars, 1995.

―――. *Perseverance in Gratitude: A Socio-Rhetorical Commentary on the Epistle to the Hebrews.* Grand Rapids, MI: Eerdmans, 2000.

Dunnill, John. *Covenant and Sacrifice in the Letter to the Hebrews.* SNTSMS 75. Cambridge: Cambridge University Press, 1992.

Dunning, Benjamin. "The Intersection of Alien Status and Cultic Discourse in the Epistle to the Hebrews." Pages 179–98 in *Hebrews: Contemporary Methods—New Insights.* Edited by G. Gelardini. Leiden: Brill, 2005.

Eberhart, Christian A. "Characteristics of Sacrificial Metaphors." Pages 37–64 in *Hebrews: Contemporary Methods—New Insights.* Edited by G. Gelardini. Leiden: Brill, 2005.

Eisenbaum, Pamela M. "Locating Hebrews within the Literary Landscape of Christian Origins." Pages 213–37 in *Hebrews: Contemporary Methods—New Insights.* Edited by G. Gelardini. Leiden: Brill, 2005.

Ellingworth, Paul. "Jesus and the Universe in Hebrews." *EvQ* 58 (1986): 337–50.

―――. *The Epistle to the Hebrews: A Commentary on the Greek Text.* NIGTC. Grand Rapids: Eerdmans, 1993.

Elliott, J. K. "Is Post-Baptismal Sin Forgivable?" *Bible Translator* 28 (1977): 330–32.

Emmrich, Martin. "Hebrews 6:4–6—Again! (A Pneumatological Inquiry)." *WTJ* 65 (2003): 83–95.

―――. *Pneumatological Concepts in the Epistle to the Hebrews: Amtscharisma, Prophet, and Guide of the Eschatological Exodus.* Lanham, NY: University Press of America, 2003.

Fanning, Buist M. "A Classical Reformed View." Pages 172–219 in *Four Views on the Warning Passages in Hebrews.* Edited by Herbert W. Bateman IV. Grand Rapids, MI: Kregel, 2007.

Filson, Floyd V. *"Yesterday": A Study of Hebrews in the Light of Chapter 13.* SBT 2/4. Naperville, IL: Allenson, 1967.

Fitzgerald, John T. "Proverbs 3:11–12, Hebrews 12:5–6 and the Tradition of Corporal Punishment." Pages 291–317 in *Scripture and Traditions: Essays on Early Judaism and Christianity in Honor of Carl R.*

Holladay. Edited by Patrick Gray and Gail R. O'Day. NovTSup 129. Leiden: Brill, 2008.

France, R. T. "The Son of Man in Hebrews 2:6: A Dilemma for Bible Translators." Pages 81–96 in *New Testament Theology in Light of the Church's Mission: Essays in Honor of I. Howard Marshall*. Edited by Jon C. Laansma, Grant R. Osborne, and Ray Van Neste. Eugene, OR: Cascade, 2011.

———. "The Writer of Hebrews as a Biblical Expositor." *TynB* 47 (1996): 245–76.

Gaffin, Richard B., Jr. "A Sabbath Rest Still Awaits the People of God." Pages 33–51 in *Pressing Toward the Mark: Essays Commemorating Fifty Years of the Orthodox Presbyterian Church*. Edited by C. G. Dennison and R. C. Gamble. Philadelphia: The Committee for the Historian of the Orthodox Presbyterian Church, 1986.

———. "The Priesthood of Christ: A Servant in the Sanctuary." Pages 49–68 in *The Perfect Saviour: Key Themes in Hebrews*. Edited by J. Griffiths. Nottingham: InterVarsity, 2012.

Gane, Roy E. *Cult Character: Purification Offerings, Day of Atonement, and Theodicy*. Winona Lake, IN: Eisenbrauns, 2005.

Gentry, Peter J., and Stephen J. Wellum, *Kingdom Through Covenant: A Biblical-Theological Understanding of the Covenants*. Wheaton, IL: Crossway, 2012.

Gleason, Randall C. "A Moderate Reformed View." Pages 336–77 in *Four Views on the Warning Passages in Hebrews*. Edited by Herbert W. Bateman IV. Grand Rapids, MI: Kregel, 2007.

———. "The Eschatology of the Warning in Hebrews 10:26–31." *TynB* 53 (2002): 97–120.

Gräbe, Peter. "The New Covenant and Christian Identity in Hebrews." Pages 119–27 in *A Cloud of Witnesses: The Theology of Hebrews in Its Ancient Contexts*. Edited by R. Bauckham, D. Driver, T. Hart, and N. MacDonald. LNTS 387. London: T&T Clark, 2008.

Gray, Patrick. "The Early Reception of Hebrews 6:4–6." Pages 321–39 in *Scripture and Traditions: Essays on Early Judaism and Christianity in Honor of Carl R. Holladay*. Edited by Patrick Gray and Gail R. O'Day. NovTSup 129. Leiden: Brill, 2008.

Griffiths, Jonathan. "The Word of God: Perfectly Spoken in the Son." Pages 35–48 in *The Perfect Saviour: Key Themes in Hebrews*. Edited by J. Griffiths. Nottingham: InterVarsity, 2012.

Grudem, Wayne. "Perseverance of the Saints: A Case Study from the Warning Passages in Hebrews." Pages 133–82 in *Still Sovereign*. Edited by T. R. Schreiner and B. A. Ware. Grand Rapids, MI: Baker, 2000.

Guthrie, George H. *Hebrews*. NIVAC. Grand Rapids: Zondervan, 1998.

———. "Hebrews." Pages 919–95 in *Commentary on the New Testament Use of the Old Testament*. Edited by G. K. Beale and D. A. Carson. Grand Rapids, MI: Baker, 2007.

———. "Hebrews' Use of the Old Testament: Recent Trends in Research." *CBR* 1 (2003): 271–94.

———. "The Case for Apollos as the Author of Hebrews." *Faith and Mission* 18 (2001): 41–56.

———. *The Structure of Hebrews: A Text-Linguistic Analysis*. NovTSup 73. Leiden: Brill, 1994.

Guthrie, George H., and Russell D. Quinn. "A Discourse Analysis of the Use of Psalm 8:4–6 in Hebrews 2:5–9." *JETS* 49 (2006): 235–46.

Haber, Susan. "From Priestly Torah to Christ Cultus: The Re-vision of Covenant and Cult in Hebrews." *JSNT* 28 (2005): 105–24.

Hagner, Donald A. *Hebrews*. New York: Harper & Row, 1983.

———. *The New Testament: A Historical and Theological Introduction*. Grand Rapids, MI: Baker, 2012.

Hahn, Scott W. "Covenant, Cult, and the Curse-of-Death: Διαθήκη in Hebrews 9:15–22." Pages 65–88 in *Hebrews: Contemporary Methods—New Insights*. Edited by G. Gelardini. Leiden: Brill, 2005.

———. "A Broken Covenant and the Curse of Death: A Study of Hebrews 9:15–22." *CBQ* 66 (2004): 416–36.

Hamilton, James M., Jr. *God's Indwelling Presence: The Holy Spirit in the Old and New Testaments*. NACSBT. Nashville: B&H, 2006.

Harris, Dana M. "The Eternal Inheritance in Hebrews: The Appropriation of the Old Testament Inheritance Motif by the Author of Hebrews." Ph.D. diss., Trinity Evangelical Divinity School, 2009.

Hauck, F. "καταβολή." *TDNT* 3.620–21.

Hay, David M. *Glory at the Right Hand: Psalm 110 in Early Christianity*. SBLMS 18. Nashville: Abingdon, 1973.

Hays, Richard B. "'Here We Have No Lasting City': New Covenantalism in Hebrews." Pages 151–73 in *The Epistle to the Hebrews and Christian Theology*. Edited by R. Bauckham, D. R. Driver, T. A. Hart, and N. MacDonald. Grand Rapids, MI: Eerdmans, 2009.

Heen, E. M., and P. W. D. Krey, eds. *Hebrews*. Ancient Christian Commentary on Scripture. Downers Grove, IL: InterVarsity, 2005.

Heil, John Paul. *Worship in the Letter to the Hebrews*. Eugene, OR: Wipf and Stock, 2011.

Hengel, Martin. *Studies in Early Christology*. Edinburgh: T&T Clark, 1995.

Hewitt, Thomas. *The Epistle to the Hebrews*. TNTC. Grand Rapids: Eerdmans, 1960.

Hofius, O. "ἀπαύγασμα." *EDNT* 1:117–18.

————. *Der Vorhang vor dem Thron Gottes: Eine exegetisch-religionsges-chichtliche Untersuchung zu Hebräer 6,19f. und 10,19f.* WUNT 14. Tübingen: Mohr Siebeck, 1972.

————. *Katapausis: Die Vorstellung vom endzeitlichen Ruheort im Hebräerbrief.* WUNT 11. Tübingen: Mohr Siebeck, 1970.

Hooker, Morna. "Christ, the 'End' of the Cult." Pages 189–212 in *The Epistle to the Hebrews and Christian Theology.* Edited by R. Bauckham, D. R. Driver, T. A. Hart, and N. MacDonald. Grand Rapids, MI: Eerdmans, 2009.

Horbury, W. "The Aaronic Priesthood in the Epistle to the Hebrews." *JSNT* 19 (1983): 52–59.

Horton, Fred L., Jr. *The Melchizedek Tradition: A Critical Examination of the Sources to the Fifth Century A.D. and in the Epistle to the Hebrews.* SNTSMS 30. Cambridge: Cambridge University Press, 1976.

Hughes, Graham. *Hebrews and Hermeneutics: The Epistle to the Hebrews as a New Testament Example of Biblical Interpretation.* SNTSMS 36. Cambridge: Cambridge University Press, 1979.

Hughes, J. J. "Hebrews IX 15ff. and Galatians III 15ff.: A Study in Covenant Practice and Procedure." *NovT* 21 (1979): 27–96.

Hughes, Philip Edgcumbe. *A Commentary on the Epistle to the Hebrews.* Grand Rapids, MI: Eerdmans, 1977.

————. "Doctrine of Creation in Hebrews 11:3." *BTB* 2 (1972): 164–77.

Hurst, L. D. "The Christology of Hebrews 1 and 2." Pages 151–64 in *The Glory of Christ in the New Testament: Studies in Christology in Memory of George Bradford Caird.* Edited by L. D. Hurst and N. T. Wright. Oxford: Clarendon, 1987.

————. *The Epistle to the Hebrews: Its Background of Thought.* SNTSMS 65. Cambridge: Cambridge University Press, 1990.

Hurtado, Larry. *Lord Jesus Christ: Devotion to Jesus in Earliest Christianity.* Grand Rapids, MI: Eerdmans, 2003.

————. *One God, One Lord: Early Christian Devotion and Ancient Jewish Monotheism.* Philadelphia: Fortress, 1988.

Isaacs, Marie E. "Hebrews 13.9–16 Revisited." *NTS* 43 (1997): 268–84.

————. *Sacred Space: An Approach to the Theology of the Epistle to the Hebrews.* JSNTSup 73. Sheffield: Sheffield Academic, 1992.

Jennings, Mark A. "The Veil and the High Priestly Robes of the Incarnation: Understanding the Context of Heb 10:20." *PRSt* 37 (2010): 85–97.

Jewett, Robert. *Letter to Pilgrims: A Commentary on the Epistle to the Hebrews.* New York: Pilgrim, 1981.

Jipp, Joshua W. "The Son's Entrance into the Heavenly World: The Soteriological Necessity of the Scriptural Catena in Hebrews 1:5–14." *NTS* 56 (2010): 557–75.

Jobes, Karen H. "Rhetorical Achievement in the 'Misquote' of Psalm 40." *Bib* 72 (1991): 387–96.

———. "The Function of Paronomasia in Hebrews 10:5–7." *TrinJ* 13 (1992): 181–91.

Johnson, Luke Timothy. *Hebrews: A Commentary*. NTL. Louisville, KY: Westminster/John Knox, 2006.

Johnson, Richard W. *Going Outside the Camp: The Sociological Function of the Levitical Critique in the Epistle to the Hebrews*. JSNTSup 209. London: Sheffield Academic, 2001.

Johnston, George. "Christ as Archegos." *NTS* 27 (1981): 381–85.

Joslin, Barry C. "Can Hebrews Be Structured? An Assessment of Eight Approaches." *CBR* 6 (2007): 99–129.

———. "Christ Bore the Sins of Many: Substitution and Atonement in Hebrews." *SBJT* 11 (2007): 74–103.

———. "Hebrews 7–10 and the Transformation of the Law." Pages 100–17 in *A Cloud of Witnesses: The Theology of Hebrews in Its Ancient Contexts*. Edited by R. Bauckham, D. Driver, T. Hart, and N. MacDonald. LNTS 387. London: T&T Clark, 2008.

———. *Hebrews, Christ, and the Law: The Theology of the Mosaic Law in Hebrews 7:1–10:18*. Paternoster Biblical Monograph. Carlisle, England: Paternoster, 2008.

———. "'Son of Man' or 'Human Beings'? Hebrews 2:5–9 and a Response to Craig Blomberg." *JBMW* 14 (2009): 41–50.

———. "Whose Name? A Comparison of Hebrews 1 and Philippians 2 and Christ's Inheritance of the Name." Unpublished paper.

Kaiser, Walter C., Jr. "The Abolition of the Old Order and Establishment of the New: Psalm 40:6–8 and Hebrews 10:5–10." Pages 19–37 in *Tradition and Testament: Essays in Honor of Charles Lee Feinberg*. Edited by J. S. Feinberg and P. D. Feinberg. Chicago: Moody, 1981.

Kang, Dae-I. "The Royal Components of Melchizedek in Hebrews 7." *Perichoresis* 10 (2012): 95–124.

Käsemann, Ernst. *The Wandering People of God: An Investigation of the Letter to the Hebrews*. Translated by R. A. Harrisville and I. L. Sundberg. Minneapolis: Augsburg, 1984.

Kelber, G. "χαρακτήρ." *TDNT* 9:418–23.

Kibbe, Michael. "Is It Finished? When Did It Start? Hebrews, Priesthood, and Atonement in Biblical, Systematic, and Historical Perspective." *JTS* 65 (2014): 25–61.

Kistemaker, Simon J. "Atonement in Hebrews." Pages 163–75 in *The Glory of the Atonement: Biblical, Theological, and Practical Perspectives. Essays in Honor of Roger Nicole*. Edited by C. E. Hill and F. A. James III. Downers Grove, IL: InterVarsity, 2004.

Kittel G. "ἀπαύγασμα." *TDNT* 1:508.

Koenig, J. "Hospitality." *ABD* 3:299–301.

Koester, Craig R. *Hebrews: A New Translation with Introduction and Commentary*. AB 36. New Haven, CT: Yale University Press, 2001.

———. *The Dwelling of God: The Tabernacle in the Old Testament, Intertestamental Jewish Literature, and the New Testament*. CBQMS 22. Washington, DC: Catholic Biblical Association of America, 1989.

Koester, H. "ὑπόστασις." *TDNT* 8:572–89.

———. "'Outside the Camp': Hebrews 13.9–14." *HTR* 55 (1962): 299–315.

Köstenberger, Andreas J. "Jesus, the Mediator of a 'Better Covenant': Comparatives in the Book of Hebrews." *Faith and Mission* 21 (2004): 30–49.

Kuma, Hermann V. A. *The Centrality of Αἷμα (Blood) in the Theology of the Epistle to the Hebrews: An Exegetical and Philological Study*. Lewiston, NY: Edwin Mellen, 2012.

Laansma, Jon C. "Hebrews and the Mission of the Earliest Church." Pages 327–46 in *New Testament Theology in Light of the Church's Mission: Essays in Honor of I. Howard Marshall*. Edited by Jon C. Laansma, Grant R. Osborne, and Ray Van Neste. Eugene, OR: Cascade, 2011.

———. "Hidden Stories in Hebrews: Cosmology and Theology." Pages 9–18 in *A Cloud of Witnesses: The Theology of Hebrews in Its Ancient Contexts*. Edited by R. Bauckham, D. Driver, T. Hart, and N. MacDonald. LNTS 387. London: T&T Clark, 2008.

———. *"I Will Give You Rest": The Rest Motif in the New Testament with Special Reference to Mt 11 and Heb 3–4*. WUNT 2/98. Tübingen: Mohr Siebeck, 1997.

———. "The Cosmology of Hebrews." Pages 125–43 in *Cosmology and New Testament Theology*. Edited by Jonathan T. Pennington and Sean M. McDunough. LNTS 355. London: T&T Clark, 2008.

Laansma, Jon C., and Daniel J. Trier, eds. *Christology and Hermeneutics of Hebrews: Profiles from the History of Interpretation*. LNTS 423. London: T&T Clark, 2012.

Lane, William L. *Hebrews 1–8*. WBC. Dallas: Word, 1991.

———. *Hebrews 9–13*. WBC. Dallas: Word, 1991.

Lehne, Susanne. *The New Covenant in Hebrews*. JSNTSup 44. Sheffield: Sheffield Academic, 1990.

Leithart, Peter J. "Womb of the World: Baptism and the Priesthood of the New Covenant in Hebrews 10.19–22." *JSNT* 78 (2000): 49–65.

Leschert, Dale F. *Hermeneutical Foundations of Hebrews: A Study in the Validity of the Epistle's Interpretation of Some Core Citations from the Psalms*. NABPRDS 10. Lewiston, NY: Edwin Mellen, 1994.

Lewis, C. S. *Mere Christianity*. Revised ed. San Francisco: HarperCollins, 2001.

Lincoln, A. T. "Sabbath, Rest, and Eschatology in the New Testament." Pages 197–220 in *From Sabbath to Lord's Day: A Biblical, Historical, and Theological Investigation*. Edited by D. A. Carson. Grand Rapids, MI: Zondervan, 1982.

Lindars, Barnabas. "The Rhetorical Structure of Hebrews." *NTS* 35 (1989): 382–406.

———. *The Theology of the Letter to the Hebrews*. New Testament Theology. Cambridge: Cambridge University Press, 1991.

Loader, W. R. G. "Christ at the Right Hand—Ps. cx.l in the New Testament." *NTS* 24 (1977–78): 199–217.

Louw, Johannes P., and Eugene A. Nida, eds. *Greek-English Lexicon of the New Testament Based on Semantic Domains*. 2 vols. New York: United Bible Societies, 1988.

Mackie, Scott D. "Ancient Jewish Mystical Motifs in Hebrews' Theology of Access and Entry Exhortations." *NTS* 58 (2011): 88–104.

———. "Early Christian Eschatological Experience in the Warnings and Exhortations of the Epistle to the Hebrews." *TynB* 63 (2012): 93–114.

———. *Eschatology and Exhortation in the Epistle to the Hebrews*. WUNT 2/223. Tübingen: Mohr Siebeck, 2007.

———. "Heavenly Sanctuary Mysticism in the Epistle to the Hebrews." *JTS* 62 (2011): 77–117.

MacLeod, David J. "The Cleansing of the True Tabernacle." *BSac* 152 (1995): 60–71.

———. "The Literary Structure of the Book of Hebrews," *BSac* 146 (1989): 185–97.

MacRae, George W. "Heavenly Temple and Eschatology in the Letter to the Hebrews." *Semeia* 12 (1978): 179–99.

Manson, Thomas W. "The Problem of the Epistle to the Hebrews." *BJRL* 32 (1949): 1–17.

Marshall, I. Howard. "Soteriology in Hebrews." Pages 253–77 in *The Epistle to the Hebrews and Christian Theology*. Edited by R. Bauckham, D. R. Driver, T. A. Hart, and N. MacDonald. Grand Rapids, MI: Eerdmans, 2009.

Martin, Michael W., and Jason A. Whitlark. "Choosing What Is Advantageous: The Relationship Between Epideictic and Deliberative Syncrisis in Hebrews." *NTS* 58 (2012): 379–400.

———. "The Encomiastic Topics of Syncrisis as the Key to the Structure and Argument of Hebrews." *NTS* 57 (2011): 415–39.

Martin, Oren R. *"Bound for the Promised Land*. NSBT. Downers Grove: InterVarsity, 2015.

Mason, Eric F. "Hebrews and the Dead Sea Scrolls: Some Points of Comparison." *PRSt* 37 (2010): 457–79.

———. "The Epistle (Not Necessarily) to the 'Hebrews': A Call to Renunciation of Judaism or Encouragement to Christian Commitment?" *PRSt* 37 (2010): 7–20.

———. *'You Are a Priest Forever': Second Temple Jewish Messianism and the Priestly Christology of the Epistle to the Hebrews.* STDJ 74. Leiden: Brill, 2008.

Matheson, Dave. "Reading Heb 6:4–6 in Light of the Old Testament." *WTJ* 61 (1999): 209–25.

McCruden, Kevin B. *A Body You Have Prepared for Me: The Spirituality of the Letter to the Hebrews.* Collegeville, MN: Liturgical, 2013.

———. *Solidarity Perfected: Beneficent Christology in the Epistle to the Hebrews.* BZNW 159. Berlin: Walter de Gruyter, 2008.

McKelvey, R. J. *Pioneer and Priest: Jesus Christ in the Epistle to the Hebrews.* Eugene, OR: Pickwick, 2013.

McKnight, Scot. "The Warning Passages of Hebrews: A Formal Analysis and Theological Conclusions." *TrinJ* 13 (1992): 21–59.

Meeks, Wayne. *The First Urban Christians: The Social World of the Apostle Paul.* New Haven, CT: Yale University Press, 1983.

Meier, John P. "Structure and Theology in Heb 1:1–4." *Bib* 66 (1985): 168–89.

———. "Symmetry and Theology in the Old Testament Citations of Heb. 1:5–14." *Bib* 66 (1985): 504–33.

Michaelis, W. "σκηνή." *TDNT* 7:368–94.

Michel, Otto. *Der Brief an die Hebräer*, 13th ed. KEK. Göttingen: Vandenhoeck & Ruprecht, 1975.

Mitchell, Alan C. *Hebrews.* SP. Collegeville, MN: Michael Glazier, 2007.

Moberly, Walter L. "Exemplars of Faith in Hebrews 11: Abel." Pages 353–63 in *The Epistle to the Hebrews and Christian Theology.* Edited by R. Bauckham, D. R. Driver, T. A. Hart, and N. MacDonald. Grand Rapids, MI: Eerdmans, 2009.

Moffat, James A. *A Critical and Exegetical Commentary on the Epistle to the Hebrews.* ICC. New York: Scribner's, 1924.

Moffitt, David M. *Atonement and the Logic of the Resurrection in the Epistle to the Hebrews.* NovTSup 141. Leiden: Brill, 2011.

———. "'If Another Priest Arises': Jesus' Resurrection and the High Priestly Christology of Hebrews." Pages 68–79 in *A Cloud of Witnesses: The Theology of Hebrews in Its Ancient Contexts.* Edited by R. Bauckham, D. Driver, T. Hart, and N. McDonald. London: T&T Clark, 2008.

———. "Unveiling Jesus' Flesh: A Fresh Assessment of the Relationship Between the Veil and Jesus' Flesh in Hebrews 10:20." *PRSt* 37 (2010): 71–84.

Moo, Douglas J. "Nature in the New Creation: New Testament Eschatology and the Environment," *JETS* 49 (2006): 459–69.

Moore, Nicholas J. "Jesus as 'the One Who Entered His Rest': The Christological Reading of Hebrews 4.10." *JSNT* 36 (2014): 1–18.

Morris, Leon. *The Apostolic Preaching of the Cross.* 3rd ed. London: Tyndale, 1965.

Morrison, Michael D. *Who Needs a New Covenant? Rhetorical Function of the Covenant Motif in the Argument of Hebrews.* Eugene, OR: Pickwick, 2008.

Mosser, Carl. "No Lasting City: Rome, Jerusalem and the Place of Hebrews in the History of Earliest 'Christianity.'" Ph.D. diss., St. Andrews University, 2004.

———. "Rahab Outside the Camp." Pages 384–404 in *The Epistle to the Hebrews and Christian Theology.* Edited by R. Bauckham, D. R. Driver, T. A. Hart, and N. MacDonald. Grand Rapids: Eerdmans, 2009.

Motyer, Steve. "The Spirit in Hebrews: No Longer Forgotten?" Pages 214–27 in *The Spirit and Christ in the New Testament and Christian Theology: Essays Presented in Honor of Max Turner.* Edited by I. Howard Marshall, Volker Rabens, and Cornelius Bennema. Grand Rapids, MI: Eerdmans, 2012.

Nash, Ronald H. "The Notion of Mediator in Alexandrian Judaism and the Epistle to the Hebrews." *WTJ* 40 (1977): 89–115.

Nauck, Wolfgang. "Zum Aufbau des Hebräerbriefes." Pages 199–206 in *Judentum-Urchristentum-Kirche: Festschrift für Joachim Jeremias.* Edited by W. Eltester. Berlin: Alfred Töpelmann, 1960.

Neeley, Linda Lloyd. "A Discourse Analysis of Hebrews." *OPTAT* 3–4 (1987): 1–146.

Neyrey, Jerome H. "'Without Beginning of Days or End of Life' (Hebrews 7:3): Topos for a True Deity." *CBQ* 53 (1991): 439–55.

Nicole, Emile. "Atonement in the Pentateuch: 'It Is the Blood That Makes Atonement for One's Life.'" Pages 35–50 in *The Glory of the Atonement.* Edited by Charles E. Hill and Frank A. James III. Downers Grove, IL: InterVarsity, 2004.

O'Brien, Peter T. *The Letter to the Hebrews.* PNTC. Grand Rapids, MI: Eerdmans, 2010.

———. "The New Covenant and Its Perfect Mediator." Pages 13–33 in *The Perfect Saviour: Key Themes in Hebrews.* Edited by J. Griffiths. Nottingham: InterVarsity, 2012.

Olbricht, T. H. "Hebrews as Amplification." Pages 375–87 in *Rhetoric and the New Testament: Essays from the 1992 Heidelberg Conference.* Edited by S. E. Porter and T. H. Olbricht. JSNTSup 90. Sheffield: Sheffield Academic, 1993.

Oropeza, B. J. "The Warning Passages in Hebrews: Revised Theologies and New Methods of Interpretation." *CBR* 10 (2011): 81–100.

Ounsworth, Richard. *Joshua Typology in the New Testament.* WUNT 2/328. Tübingen: Mohr Siebeck, 2012.

Owen, John. *Hebrews.* Crossway Classic Commentaries. Wheaton, IL: Crossway, 1998.

Peeler, Amy L. B. "The Ethos of God in Hebrews." *PRSt* 37 (2010): 37–51.

_____. *You Are My Son: The Family of God in the Epistle to the Hebrews.* LNTS 486. New York: Bloomsbury T&T Clark, 2014.

Peterson, David G. *Hebrews and Perfection: An Examination of the Concept of Perfection in the 'Epistle to the Hebrews.'* SNTSMS 47. Cambridge: Cambridge University Press, 1982.

———. "Perfection: Achieved and Experienced." Pages 125–45 in *The Perfect Saviour: Key Themes in Hebrews.* Edited by J. Griffiths. Nottingham: InterVarsity, 2012.

———. "The Prophecy of the New Covenant in the Argument of Hebrews." *RTR* 38 (1979): 74–81.

———. *Transformed by God: New Covenant Life and Ministry.* Downers Grove, IL: InterVarsity, 2012.

Pitts, Andrew W., and Joshua F. Walker. "The Authorship of Hebrews: A Further Development in the Luke-Paul Relationship." Pages 143–84 in *Paul and His Social Relations.* Edited by Stanley E. Porter and Christopher D. Land. Leiden: Brill, 2012.

Rapske, Brian M. *The Book of Acts and Paul in Roman Custody.* Vol. 3 of *The Book of Acts in Its First Century Setting.* Edited by B. W. Winter. Grand Rapids, MI: Eerdmans, 1994.

Rhee, Victor. "The Role of Chiasm for Understanding Christology in Hebrews 1:1–14." *JBL* 131 (2012): 341–62.

Ribbens, Benjamin J. "A Typology of Types: Typology in Dialogue." *Journal of Theological Interpretation* 5 (2011): 81–96.

———. "Levitical Sacrifice and Heavenly Cult in Hebrews." Ph.D. diss., Wheaton College, 2013.

Richardson, Christopher A. *Pioneer and Perfecter of Faith: Jesus' Faith as the Climax of Israel's History in the Epistle to the Hebrews.* WUNT 2/338. Tübingen: Mohr Siebeck, 2012.

Robertson, A. T. *A Grammar of the Greek New Testament in the Light of Historical Research.* 2nd ed. Nashville: Broadman, 1934.

Rooke, Deborah W. "Jesus as Royal Priest: Reflections on the Interpretation of the Melchizedek Tradition in Heb 7." *Bib* 81 (2000): 81–94.

Schenk, Kenneth L. "A Celebration of the Enthroned Son: The Catena of Hebrews 1." *JBL* 120 (2001): 469–86.

———. *Cosmology and Eschatology in Hebrews: The Settings of the Sacrifice*. SNTSMS 143. Cambridge: Cambridge University Press, 2007.

———. "God Has Spoken: Hebrews' Theology of the Scriptures." Pages 321–36 in *The Epistle to the Hebrews and Christian Theology*. Edited by R. Bauckham, D. R. Driver, T. A. Hart, and N. MacDonald. Grand Rapids: Eerdmans, 2009.

———. "Keeping His Appointment: Creation and Enthronement in Hebrews." *JSNT* 66 (1997): 91–117.

———. "Philo and the Epistles to the Hebrews: Ronald Williamson's Study after Thirty Years." *SPhilo* 14 (2002): 112–35.

———. *Understanding the Book of Hebrews: The Story Behind the Sermon*. Louisville, KY: Westminster/John Knox, 2003.

Scholer, John M. *Proleptic Priests: Priesthood in the Epistle to the Hebrews*. JSNTSup 49. Sheffield: Sheffield Academic, 1991.

Schreiner, Thomas R. "Goodbye and Hello: The Sabbath Command for New Covenant Believers," in *Progressive Covenantalism*. Edited by S. Wellum and B. Parker. Nashville: B&H Academic (forthcoming).

———. *Run to Win the Prize: Perseverance in the New Testament*. Wheaton, IL: Crossway, 2010.

———. "Warning and Assurance: Run the Race to the End." Pages 89–106 in *The Perfect Saviour: Key Themes in Hebrews*. Edited by J. Griffiths. Nottingham: InterVarsity, 2012.

Seid, Timothy W. "Synkrisis in Hebrews 7: The Rhetorical Structure and Strategy." Pages 322–47 in *The Rhetorical Interpretation of Scripture: Essays from the 1996 Malibu Conference*. Edited by S. E. Porter and D. L. Stamps. JSNTSup 180. Sheffield: Sheffield Academic, 1999.

Selby, Gary S. "The Meaning and Function of συνείδησις in Hebrews 9 and 10." *ResQ* 28 (1985–86): 145–54.

Silva, Moises. "Perfection and Eschatology in Hebrews." *WTJ* 39 (1976): 60–71.

Skarsaune, Oskar. "Does the Letter to the Hebrews Articulate a Supersessionist Theology? A Response to Richard Hays." Pages 174–82 in *The Epistle to the Hebrews and Christian Theology*. Edited by R. Bauckham, D. R. Driver, T. A. Hart, and N. MacDonald. Grand Rapids, MI: Eerdmans, 2009.

Skehan, Patrick W. "A Fragment of the 'Song of Moses' (Deut. 32) from Qumran." *BASOR* 136 (1954): 12–15.

Sklar, Jay. "Sin and Impurity: Atoned or Purified? Yes!" Pages 18–31 in *Perspective on Purity and Purification in the Bible*. Edited by Baruch J. Schwartz, David P. Wright, Jeffrey Stackert, and Naphtali S. Meshel. LHBOTS 474. New York: T&T Clark, 2002.

———. *Sin, Impurity, Sacrifice, Atonement: The Priestly Conceptions*. Hebrew Bible Monographs 2. Sheffield: Sheffield Phoenix, 2005.

Small, Brian C. "The Use of Rhetorical *Topoi* in the Characterization of Jesus in the Book of Hebrews." *PRSt* 37 (2010): 53–69.

Son, Kiwoong. *Zion Symbolism in Hebrews: Hebrews 12:18–24 as a Hermeneutical Key to the Epistle*. Paternoster Biblical Monographs. Waynesboro, GA: Paternoster, 2005.

Spicq, Ceslas. *L'Épître aux Hébreux*. 2nd ed. 2 vols. EB. Paris: Gabalda, 1953.

Stählin, G. "ξένος." *TDNT* 5:17–25.

Stanley, Steve. "Hebrews 9:6–10: The 'Parable' of the Tabernacle." *NovT* 37 (1995): 385–99.

———. "The Structure of Hebrews from Three Perspectives." *TynB* 45 (1994): 245–71.

Stegemann, Ekkehard W., and Stegemann, Wolfgang. "Does the Cultic Language in Hebrews Represent Sacrificial Metaphors? Reflections on Some Basic Problems." Pages 13–24 in *Hebrews: Contemporary Methods—New Insights*. Edited by G. Gelardini. Leiden: Brill, 2005.

Steyn, Gert J. "The Eschatology of Hebrews: As Understood Within a Cultic Setting." Pages 429–50 in *Eschatology of the New Testament and Some Related Documents*. Edited by J. G. van der Watt. WUNT 2/315. Tübingen: Mohr Siebeck, 2012.

Still, Todd D. "*Christos as Pistos:* The Faith(fullness) of Jesus in the Epistle to the Hebrews." Pages 40–50 in *A Cloud of Witnesses: The Theology of Hebrews in Its Ancient Contexts*. Edited by R. Bauckham, D. Driver, T. Hart, and N. MacDonald. LNTS 387. London: T&T Clark, 2008.

Stokl, Daniel. *The Impact of Yom Kippur on Early Christianity*. WUNT 163. Tübingen: Mohr Siebeck, 2003.

Stott, W. "Conception of 'Offering' in the Epistle to the Hebrews." *NTS* 9 (1962–3): 62–67.

Svendsen, Stefan Nordgaard. *Allegory Transformed: The Appropriation of Philonic Hermeneutics in the Letter to the Hebrews*. WUNT 2/269. Tübingen: Mohr Siebeck, 2009.

Swetnam, James. "A Suggested Interpretation of Hebrews 9,15–18." *CBQ* 27 (1965): 373–90.

————. "Christology and the Eucharist in the Epistle to the Hebrews." *Bib* 70 (1989): 74–95.

————. "Greater and More Perfect Tent: A Contribution to the Discussion of Hebrews 9:11." *Bib* 47 (1966): 91–106.

————. *Jesus and Isaac: A Study of the Epistle to the Hebrews in the Light of the Aqedah*. AnBib 94. Rome: Pontifical Biblical Institute, 1981.

————. "Jesus as λόγος in Hebrews 4,12–13." *Bib* 62 (1981): 214–24.

————. "The Crux at Hebrews 5,7–8." *Bib* 81 (2000): 347–61.

Swinson, L. Timothy. "'Wind' and 'Fire' in Hebrews 1:7: A Reflection upon the Use of Psalm 104 (103)." *TrinJ* 28 (2007): 215–28.

Thiessen, M. "Hebrews 12.5–13, the Wilderness Period, and Israel's Discipline." *NTS* 55 (2009): 366–79.

Thomas, C. Adrian. *A Case for Mixed-Audience with Reference to the Warning Passages in the Book of Hebrews*. New York: Peter Lang, 2008.

Thompson, James W. "Outside the Camp: A Study of Heb 13:9–14." *CBQ* 40 (1978): 53–63.

————. *The Beginnings of Christian Philosophy*. CBQMS 13. Washington, DC: The Catholic Biblical Association of America, 1982.

————. "The New Is Better: A Neglected Aspect of the Hermeneutics of Hebrews." *CBQ* 73 (2011): 547–61.

Thornton, T. C. G. "The Meaning of αἱματεκχυσίας in Heb. ix.22." *ExpT* (1964): 63–65.

Vanhoye, Albert. *La Structure littéraire de l'épître aux Hébreux*. StudNeot 1. 2nd. ed. Paris: Desclée de Brouwer, 1976.

————. *Structure and Message of the Epistle to the Hebrews*. SubBi 12. Rome: Pontifical Biblical Institute, 1989.

Verbrugge, Verlyn D. "Towards a New Interpretation of Hebrews 6:4–6." *CTJ* 15 (1980): 61–73.

von Harnack, Adolf. "Probabilia über die Addresse und den Verfasser des Hebräerbriefes." *ZNW* 1 (1900): 16–41.

Vos, Geerhardus. "The Priesthood of Christ in Hebrews." Pages 126–60 in *Redemptive History and Biblical Interpretation: The Shorter Writings of Geerhardus Vos*. Edited by R. B. Gaffin Jr. Phillipsburg, NJ: Presbyterian & Reformed, 1980.

Wallace, Daniel B. *Greek Grammar Beyond the Basics: An Exegetical Syntax of the New Testament*. Grand Rapids, MI: Zondervan, 1996.

Walser, Georg Q. *Old Testament Quotations in Hebrews*. WUNT 2/356. Tubingen: Mohr Siebeck, 2013.

Watson, Duane F. "Rhetorical Criticism of Hebrews and the Catholic Epistles since 1978." *CurBS* 5 (1997): 175–207.

Webster, John. "One Who Is Son: Theological Reflections on the Exordium to the Epistle to the Hebrews." Pages 69–94 in *The Epistle to the Hebrews and Christian Theology*. Edited by R. Bauckham, D. R. Driver, T. A. Hart, and N. MacDonald. Grand Rapids, MI: Eerdmans, 2009.

Wedderburn, A. J. M. "The 'Letter' to the Hebrews and Its Thirteenth Chapter." *NTS* 50 (2004): 390–405.

Weiss, Harold. "*Sabbatismos* in the Epistle to the Hebrews." *CBQ* 58 (1996): 674–89.

Westcott, B. F. *The Epistle to the Hebrews: The Greek Text with Notes and Essays*. Reprint. Grand Rapids, MI: Eerdmans, 1977.

Westfall, Cynthia Long. *A Discourse Analysis of the Letter to the Hebrews: The Relationship Between Form and Meaning*. LNTS 297. London: T&T Clark, 2005.

Whitfield, Bryan J. *Joshua Traditions and the Argument of Hebrews 3 and 4*. BZNW 194. Berlin: Walter de Gruyter, 2013.

Whitlark, Jason A. *Enabling Fidelity to God: Perseverance in Hebrews in Light of Reciprocity Systems in the Ancient Mediterranean World*. Paternoster Biblical Monographs. Milton Keynes, UK: Paternoster, 2008.

———. "'Here We Do Not Have a City That Remains': A Figured Critique of Roman Imperial Propaganda in Hebrews 13:14." *JBL* 131 (2012): 161–79.

Williamson, Ronald. "Eucharist and the Epistle to the Hebrews." *NTS* 21 (1975): 300–12.

———. "Hebrews 4:15 and the Sinlessness of Jesus." *ExpT* 86 (1974): 4–8.

———. *Philo and the Epistle to Hebrews*. ALGHJ. Leiden: Brill, 1970.

———. "The Incarnation of the Logos in Hebrews." *ExpT* 95 (1983): 4–8.

Winter, Bruce W. "Suffering with the Saviour: The Reality, the Reasons and the Reward." Pages 147–67 in *The Perfect Saviour: Key Themes in Hebrews*. Edited by J. Griffiths. Nottingham: InterVarsity, 2012.

Wray, Judith Hoch. *Rest as a Theological Metaphor in the Epistle to the Hebrews and the Gospel of Truth: Early Christian Homiletics of Rest*. SBLDS 166. Atlanta: Scholars, 1988.

Young, Norman H. "'Tout Estin Sarkos Autou' (Heb. X.20): Apposition, Dependent, or Explicative?" *NTS* 20 (1973): 100–104.

———. "The Day of Dedication or the Day of Atonement? The Old Testament Background to Hebrews 6:19–20 Revisited." *AUSS* 40 (2002): 61–68.

———. "The Gospel According to Hebrews 9." *NTS* 27 (1981): 198–210.

NAME INDEX

Adams, Edward *45–49, 343, 435, 501*
Allen, David L. *2, 4, 8, 45, 66, 80, 182,*
 187, 189–90, 328, 391, 393, 398,
 407, 413, 475, 491, 501
Allen, David M. *2, 4, 8, 45, 66, 80,*
 182, 187, 189–90, 328, 391, 393,
 398, 407, 413, 475, 491, 501
Anderson, Charles P. *106, 217, 501*
Attridge, Harold W. *3, 6, 8, 11, 15, 53,*
 56, 60, 63, 71, 73, 75, 79–80, 94, 96,
 99, 102, 107–9, 114, 116, 118, 122,
 129, 134–36, 146–47, 152, 157–58,
 163–66, 169–70, 180–81, 183–84,
 188–89, 191, 195, 201–2, 220–21,
 226, 233, 237–38, 241–44, 246,
 249–51, 254, 257, 260, 262, 266–68,
 270, 276–77, 279, 283, 285, 290,
 295–96, 304, 310, 315, 317–18, 328,
 339–40, 343, 350–51, 354, 370, 372,
 377–78, 387–88, 390–91, 393, 399,
 401–2, 406, 409, 411, 413, 418–20,
 422, 425, 428, 431, 435

Backhaus, Knut *409, 501*
Barnard, Jody A. *16, 48, 57, 60, 73,*
 243, 319, 446, 501
Barrett, C. K. *16, 136, 501*
Bateman, Herbert W. *65–66, 68, 73,*
 480, 502
Bauckham, Richard *58–60, 65, 210,*
 502
Bauer, Walter *502*
Behm, J. *270, 502*
Berger, K. *57, 502*
Black, David Alan *2, 4, 12, 502*
Blomberg, Craig L. *87, 502*
Bock, Darrell *451, 502*
Bockmuehl, Markus *354, 502*

Brooks, Walter Edward *271, 502*
Bruce, F. F. *16, 59, 73, 90, 98, 122,*
 162, 242, 262, 276, 283, 351, 364,
 387–88, 393, 502
Büchsel, F. *340, 502*

Caird, G. B. *15, 56, 446, 502*
Calvin, John *3, 4*
Campbell, Constantine R. *305–6, 396*
Caneday, Ardel B. *68–69, 503*
Carson, D. A. *vii*
Chester, A. N. *503*
Childs, Brevard *vii*
Cockerill, Gareth L. *4, 10, 40, 55, 57,*
 60, 70, 73, 81, 87–88, 90, 96, 99,
 101, 107, 109, 114, 119, 126–27,
 129, 131, 136, 151–52, 158–60, 163,
 165, 168, 171–72, 175, 180, 183–84,
 188, 190, 195, 204, 210, 212, 216,
 220, 223, 231, 233–34, 237–39, 242,
 255, 260, 264, 267–69, 272, 276,
 283, 285, 291, 298, 301, 304, 306,
 310–11, 313, 315, 338–39, 342, 346,
 364, 374, 377, 382, 388, 392–94,
 396, 400–401, 404, 406–7, 413, 416,
 418–19, 424, 430, 471, 503
Cody, Aelred *283, 503*
Colijn, Brenda B. *469, 503*
Compton, Jared *297, 503*
Cosby, Michael R. *338, 503*
Cowan, Christopher W. *481, 496, 503*
Croy, N. Clayton *376, 378–79,*
 382–84, 503
Cullmann, Oscar *304, 503*

Davidson, Richard M. *203, 503*
Davids, Peter H. *vii*
Decker, Rodney J *12, 187, 504*

519

Deenick, Karl   *115, 504*
Delcor, M.   *207, 457*
deSilva, David A.   *7, 11, 331, 371, 379, 460, 504*
Dunnill, John   *319, 463, 475, 504*
Dunning, Benjamin   *491, 504*
Dunn, James D. G.   *446*

Eberhart, Christian A.   *269, 504*
Eisenbaum, Pamela M.   *5, 504*
Ellingworth, Paul   *6, 9, 46, 57, 74, 77, 79, 82, 88, 90, 95, 97, 107, 109, 113, 119, 122, 126, 129, 136, 143, 146, 151, 162–63, 169, 171–72, 175, 184, 187, 189, 201, 203, 216–17, 226, 230, 233, 238, 242–43, 257, 259–60, 262–64, 267, 269–71, 274–79, 283, 304, 306, 315, 318, 326, 343–44, 351–53, 377–78, 384, 392, 413, 420, 431, 504*
Elliott, J. K.   *189, 504*
Emmrich, Martin   *180, 183–84, 186, 271, 319, 477, 504*

Fanning, Buist M.   *119, 128, 504*
Filson, Floyd V.   *10, 409, 419, 504*
Fitzgerald, John T.   *384, 504*
France, R. T.   *11, 505*

Gabler, J. P.   *viii*
Gaffin, Richard B., Jr.   *136, 210, 455, 505*
Gane, Roy E.   *465, 505*
Gentry, Peter J.   *475, 505*
Gleason, Randall C.   *190, 325, 505*
Gräbe, Peter   *474, 505*
Gray, Patrick   *181, 505*
Griffiths, J.   *200, 202, 438–39, 505*
Grudem, Wayne   *182, 193–94, 327, 484, 505*
Guthrie, George H.   *3, 7, 11–13, 61, 65, 87–88, 116, 182, 190, 249, 268, 313, 327, 338, 506*

Haber, Susan   *6, 506*
Hagner, Donald A.   *5, 7, 60, 175, 204, 260, 270, 283, 393, 482, 506*
Hahn, Scott W.   *276, 506*
Hamilton, James M., Jr.   *184, 506*
von Harnack, Adolf   *4, 516*
Harris, Dana M.   *275, 398, 499, 506*
Harris, Murray J.   *71–72*

Hauck, F.   *352, 506*
Hay, David M.   *58, 506*
Hays, Richard B.   *474, 506*
Heen, E. M.   *1, 90, 506*
Heil, John Paul   *506*
Hengel, Martin   *58, 234, 304, 378, 506*
Hewitt, Thomas   *4, 506*
Hofius, O.   *15, 56, 129, 134–36, 267, 506–7*
Hooker, Morna   *14, 507*
Horton, Fred L., Jr.   *207, 209, 457, 507*
Hughes, Graham   *16, 279, 507*
Hughes, J. J.   *276*
Hughes, Philip E.   *3, 65, 73, 77, 80, 88, 90, 95, 98, 104, 107, 110, 114–15, 126, 129, 136, 138, 147, 153, 162, 164, 170–71, 176–77, 180–81, 184, 188, 193, 207, 210, 212, 220, 234, 237–38, 243, 249, 254, 259–60, 262, 269–71, 276–77, 279, 283, 285, 292, 300, 324, 326, 334, 344, 351, 357, 364, 377, 379, 388, 392–93, 400–401, 420, 507*
Hurst, L. D.   *15–16, 56, 446, 507*
Hurtado, Larry   *457, 507*

Isaacs, Marie E.   *16, 507*

Jennings, Mark A.   *317, 507*
Jewett, Robert   *4, 60, 507*
Jipp, Joshua W.   *64, 507*
Jobes, Karen H.   *297, 508*
Johnson, Luke Timothy   *6, 10–11, 16, 54, 56–57, 60, 66, 68, 75, 85, 95–96, 98, 105, 107, 114, 116, 131, 144, 146, 154, 161, 169–70, 181, 187–88, 193, 204, 215, 220, 222, 226, 242, 254, 260, 262–63, 270, 290, 317, 320, 324–26, 328, 331, 333, 338–39, 344–45, 351, 353, 363–64, 377, 381, 383–85, 387, 392, 400–401, 412–13, 420, 508*
Johnston, George   *96, 508*
Joslin, Barry C.   *12–13, 60, 87, 217, 251–52, 271, 287, 291, 508*

Kaiser, Walter C., Jr.   *296, 508*
Kang, Dae-I.   *208–9, 508*
Käsemann, Ernst   *15, 183, 300, 340, 400, 491, 508*
Kelber, G.   *57, 508*
Kibbe, Michael   *160, 285, 508*

Kistemaker, Simon J. *109, 508*
Kittel, G. *56, 509*
Koenig, J. *411, 509*
Koester, Craig R. *7, 11, 65, 68, 79–80,
84, 96–98, 107, 109, 122, 136, 148,
161, 164, 176–77, 180–81, 188, 193,
210, 216–17, 223, 230, 234, 237,
242–44, 249, 252, 254, 267, 269–70,
275, 279, 298, 317–18, 336, 339–40,
343, 351, 376, 378–79, 384–85,
388, 390, 392–93, 398, 402, 412,
420, 509*
Koester, H. *57, 129, 422, 509*
Krey, P. W. D. *1, 90, 506*
Kuma, Hermann V. A. *464, 509*
Laansma, Jon C. *1, 15, 46, 130, 134,
136, 143, 487, 509*
Lane, William L. *6, 9–11, 13–14,
48, 63, 65–66, 68, 79, 83, 86, 88,
90, 95–96, 98, 102, 104–5, 107–8,
114–15, 123, 129, 135–36, 138, 143,
146–47, 153, 157, 163–65, 169, 176,
181, 188–89, 195, 200, 215–17,
222–23, 226, 234, 240, 243, 246,
249, 263, 267, 269–70, 276–77, 283,
308, 315, 317–18, 324, 339, 342,
344, 351–52, 358, 364, 373–74,
377–79, 384, 386–87, 390, 392–93,
399, 401, 416–17, 419, 431, 509*
Lehne, Susanne *474–75, 509*
Leithart, Peter J. *318, 509*
Leschert, Dale F. *40, 71, 87, 134, 509*
Lewis, C. S. *111, 510*
Lincoln, A. T. *136, 510*
Lindars, Barnabas *6, 11, 15, 80, 92,
259, 378, 446, 455, 479, 497–98,
510*
Loader, W. R. G. *58, 510*
Long, D. Stephen *65*
Louw, Johannes P. *510*

Mackie, Scott D. *7, 16–17, 33, 147,
154, 238, 283, 325, 510*
MacLeod, David J. *12, 282, 510*
MacRae, George W. *283, 510*
Manson, Thomas W. *60, 510*
Marshall, I. Howard *469, 510*
Martin, Michael W. *11, 510*
Martin, Ralph P. *vii*
Mason, Eric F. *7–8, 207, 457, 511*
Matheson, Dave *180, 183–84, 186,
190, 511*

McCruden, Kevin B. *89, 97, 493, 511*
McKelvey, R. J. *96, 283, 511*
McKnight, Scot *485, 511*
Meeks, Wayne *411, 511*
Meier, John P. *56, 60, 63, 68, 73, 446,
511*
Michaelis, M. *267, 511*
Michel, Otto *237, 243, 419, 511*
Mitchell, Alan C. *90, 511*
Moberly, Walter L. *344, 402, 511*
Moffat, James A. *7, 511*
Moffitt, David M. *64, 68–69, 73, 86,
88, 96, 98, 222, 238, 244, 267–68,
271, 285, 300–301, 471, 511*
Moo, Douglas J. *76, 512*
Moore, Nicholas J. *16, 145, 512*
Morris, Leon *269–70, 279, 464, 512*
Morrison, Michael D. *512*
Mosser, Carl *9, 10, 366, 409, 422–23,
512*
Motyer, Steve *83, 185, 478, 512*

Nash, Ronald H. *17, 60, 512*
Nauck, Wolfgang *12, 150, 512*
Neeley, Linda Lloyd *12, 512*
Neyrey, Jerome H. *442, 512*
Nicole, Emile *109, 512*

O'Brien, Peter T. *6–7, 9, 11–13, 55,
57–58, 67, 72–73, 77, 79, 81, 85, 88,
91, 95–96, 101, 105, 108–9, 112,
114, 119, 128–29, 143, 145, 147,
153, 159, 162, 165, 170–72, 183,
186, 188, 190, 195, 203–4, 210, 216,
219, 227, 231, 238, 257, 260, 262,
267, 270, 275–77, 283, 285, 300,
304, 306, 310, 315–16, 319–21, 324,
325, 332, 334–35, 339, 343, 345–46,
354, 357, 364, 376, 379, 384, 388,
391–93, 395–96, 398, 400–402, 409,
412, 420, 422, 428, 430, 474, 512*
Olbricht, T. H. *11, 513*
Oropeza, B. J. *480, 513*
Ounsworth, Richard *37, 123, 134, 136,
143–44, 513*
Owen, John *105, 513*

Peeler, Amy L. B. *55, 58, 68, 384,
440–41, 446, 457–58, 513*
Peterson, David G. *96–98, 153, 161,
163, 171, 216, 223, 237, 243, 257,*

266, 300–301, 304–6, 327, 373–74,
  401, 466–68, 474, 476, 513
Pitts, Andrew W.   513

Quinn, Russell D.   87–88, 506

Rapske, Brian M.   412, 513
Rhee, Victor   63, 513
Ribbens, Benjamin J.   37, 109, 267,
  279, 306, 374, 462, 513
Richardson, Christopher A.   98, 101,
  103, 114, 244, 298, 339, 344–45,
  347, 378, 513
Robertson, A. T.   126, 513
Rooke, Deborah W.   208, 514

Schaffer, Francis   92
Schenk, Kenneth L.   14, 16, 33, 55, 60,
  87, 136, 245, 262, 267, 276, 406,
  438, 446, 479, 514
Scholer, John M.   319, 455, 467, 514
Schreiner, Thomas R.   144, 480–81,
  514
Seid, Timothy W.   11, 514
Selby, Gary S.   6–7, 514
Sequeira, Aubrey   xi, 429
Silva, Moisés   96, 514
Skarsaune, Oskar   474, 514
Skehan, Patrick W.   66, 515
Sklar, Jay   465, 515
Small, Brian C.   441–42, 515
Son, Kiwoong   210, 395, 402, 515
Spicq, Ceslas   3, 8, 16, 68, 117, 183,
  400, 402, 515
Stählin, G.   411, 515
Stanley, Steve   10, 12, 263, 515
Stegemann, Ekkehard W.   269, 515
Stegemann, Wolfgang   269, 515
Steyn, Gert J.   45–46, 515

Still, Todd D.   101, 515
Stott, W.   285, 515
Svendsen, Stefan Nordgaard   36, 515
Swetnam, James   98, 146, 163, 266,
  515–16
Swinson, L. Timothy   70, 516

Thiessen, M.   491, 516
Thomas, C. Adrian   182, 482, 516
Thompson, James W.   16, 142, 422,
  516
Thornton, T. C. G.   279, 516
Trier, Daniel J.   1, 509

Vanhoye, Albert   12, 266, 516
Verbrugge, Verlyn D.   181, 516
Vos, Geerhardus   111, 455, 516

Wallace, Daniel B.   126, 128, 516
Walser, Georg Q.   65, 516
Watson, Duane F.   11, 516
Webster, John   446, 517
Wedderburn, A. J. M.   10, 409, 517
Weiss, Harold   143, 517
Wellum, Stephen J.   144, 475, 505, 514
Westcott, B. F.   68, 90, 135–36, 171,
  262, 270, 364, 388, 393, 402, 517
Westfall, Cynthia Long   12, 313, 517
Whitfield, Bryan J.   142, 517
Whitlark, Jason A.   11, 423, 460,
  468–70, 510, 517
Williamson, Ronald   16, 146, 153,
  245, 517
Winter, Bruce W.   9–10, 412, 422, 517
Wray, Judith Hoch   487, 517

Young, Norman H.   203, 262, 285,
  317, 517

Subject Index

A

Abel 21, 344–45, 402
Abraham 21, 197–98, 200–201, 207–8, 350–53
Adam 20, 89
already-not-yet eschatology 27, 29, 33–36, 91, 134, 136–37, 186, 253–54, 304, 399–400, 498
angels 59–78, 80–81, 106, 399–400, 448
apostasy 79–80, 84, 126–27, 132, 171, 181, 187–91, 253–54, 321, 324–27, 335, 486–89
approach, draw near 154, 227, 233–34, 317, 466
assurance of salvation 193, 469–70, 496–97
atonement 42, 91, 99, 110, 159, 202, 254, 317, 400
    Christus Victor 105, 472
    limited atonement 110
    penal substitution 105, 110, 287, 298
    ransom theory 105

B

background
    apocalyptic 16, 134, 267
    Gnosticism 15
    Plato, Philo 5, 16–17, 46–48, 134, 170, 245, 268, 290
    Qumran 8, 16, 207, 457
baptism 318–19
better, superior 59, 78, 130, 148, 151, 227, 230, 242, 245, 248, 300, 355, 372, 459–60, 462, 474–75

blood
    blood of animals 268–69, 292, 421
    blood of Christ 43, 204, 268–69, 293, 318, 326, 402, 421, 429, 464–65
    for purification 278–80, 477

C

Christ
    as Creator 57–58, 73–74, 116, 447–48
    death of 91, 164
    deity of 58, 223, 304
    divinity of 31, 53, 56–57, 70–71, 445–51
    humanity of 31, 73, 89–90, 92, 103, 105, 110, 153, 162, 452–54, 467
    incarnation of 67, 89–90, 285–86, 295, 299
    sinlessness of 154, 237, 467
church 144
    assembly, gathering 127, 321
    covenant community 252–53, 476
cleansing, purification 42, 58, 264, 269, 271–72, 282–83, 292, 318–19, 465–66
confidence 129, 204, 315, 317–18, 333, 466
conscience 263, 269, 271–72, 292, 318, 468
cosmology. *See* heaven and earth, spatial orientation
covenant
    covenant ratification 276, 477
    covenant satisfaction 42

Davidic Covenant   *24, 30, 32, 116, 299*
New covenant   *26, 32, 66, 245–46, 248–55, 274, 301, 309–10, 401–2, 474–81, 498*
Old Covenant, Sinai Covenant   *22, 66, 250–51, 254–55, 263, 274–75, 277–78, 299–300, 475*
creation   *343, 436*

D

Davidic kingship, Davidic king   *24–26, 32, 38–39, 54–55, 64–65, 71, 77, 102, 116, 161, 209, 219, 297, 299, 449, 454, 473*
Day of Atonement   *158–60, 204, 238, 243, 261–62, 279, 292*
Day of the Lord   *25, 321*
death   *286*
    fear of death   *94, 106*
    power of death   *104, 461, 472*
    rescue from death   *102, 104–6, 472*
devil, Satan   *104, 472*
discipline   *383–88*
disobedience, unbelief   *122, 126, 131, 166, 249*

E

encouragement, exhortation   *127, 320, 383, 387*
Esau   *392–94*
eschatology   *43*
exaltation   *237*
exile   *24, 81, 250, 475*
exodus, from Egypt   *21–22, 95, 365*

F

faith   *35, 135, 335, 337–74, 494–97*
    future orientation   *494*
    relationship to obedience   *131, 141, 166, 335, 350, 495–96*
faithfulness, obedience   *131*
    of Christ   *73, 97, 109, 164, 239, 298, 378–79*
fall of man   *20, 89, 92–93, 104*
final judgment   *191*
firstborn   *67, 69, 400*

G

grace   *154, 391, 406, 419, 432, 471*

H

heaven and earth, spatial orientation   *45–49, 74–75, 152, 243, 266–67, 283–85, 399, 404–5, 487*
heavenly calling   *113*
heavenly city, city of God   *49, 87, 113, 134, 332–33, 351, 355–56, 398, 423, 499*
Hebrews
    addresses, recipients   *6–8*
    authorship   *2–5*
    authorship, Luke   *4*
    authorship, Pauline   *82*
    date   *5–6*
    destination   *8–10*
    genre   *10–11, 51*
    history of interpretation   *1*
Luke   *4*
Pauline   *4*
    oral character   *10–11*
    outline   *17–20*
    purpose   *13–15*
    religious historical background   *15–17*
    rhetorical features   *11*
    situation of recipients   *9–10, 493–94*
    structure   *11–13*
    title   *7*
holy of holies, most holy place   *203, 258–62, 283–85, 421*
Holy Spirit   *25, 27, 35, 42, 84, 121, 146, 174, 177, 180, 185, 253, 262–63, 270–71, 275, 309, 326, 405, 477–79, 483*
hospitality   *411–12*
house, household of God   *115*
human beings, rule of   *20, 85–86, 88, 92–93, 100, 103, 452*

I

inheritance, inherit, heir   *55, 60, 146, 274–75, 473, 498*
intercession   *234–37*
Isaac   *356–58*
Israel, Israelites   *22, 144, 249–50, 475*

J

Johannine theology   *113*
Joshua   *22, 96, 135, 142*

judgment, retribution   *81, 324–25, 327–28, 407*

K

kingdom of God   *25, 49, 65, 77, 91–92, 104, 137, 187, 208, 351, 404, 406, 499*

L

leaders   *417–18, 424–25*
Levi, Levites   *206, 211–12*

M

mediator   *202, 230, 245, 274–75, 401–2, 477*
Melchizedek   *40–41, 206–13, 456–58*
mercy, merciful   *109, 151, 154, 456*
Mosaic law   *80, 84, 216–17, 226–27, 290–92, 325*
Moses   *38, 95–96, 112, 114–20, 362–65, 397–98, 407*
Mount Sinai   *22, 48, 396–97, 407*
Mount Zion, heavenly Jerusalem   *48, 87, 398*

N

new creation   *26, 49, 144, 406*
new exodus   *95*
Noah   *21, 346–47*

O

oath   *131, 198–202, 229, 239–40*
offspring   *20–21, 40, 64, 94, 106–7, 199, 353, 470*
Old Testament story line   *20–25, 27, 71, 144*

P

Parousia, Second Coming   *67, 287–88, 304, 334–35*
patriarchs   *33, 334, 353–59, 354–55, 492*
Pauline theology   *107, 145, 350*
perfection   *34–35, 97, 165–66, 215, 225–26, 236, 239, 263–64, 291, 305–6, 373, 401–2, 466–71*
persecute, persecution   *6, 9, 14, 105, 163, 180, 195, 321, 331–32, 355, 382, 412, 414*

perseverance, persevere   *14, 84, 95, 118–19, 128, 149, 319–20, 333–36, 376–77, 384, 430, 468, 490*
prayer, prayers, pray   *163, 427–28*
priesthood
    Aaronic priesthood, Levitical priesthood   *41, 157, 160, 210–11, 215–17, 221–23, 227, 229–42, 303–4, 456*
    Christ's priesthood   *152–53, 161–62, 211, 219–23, 229–43, 304, 317, 450–51, 455–60*
    Melchizedekian priesthood, Melchizedekian priest   *31, 40–41, 76, 108, 160–61, 166, 210, 215–17, 221–23, 229–42*
promised land, Canaan, homeland   *21, 33, 45, 87, 134, 350–51, 354–56*
promise-fulfillment   *30–33, 100, 107, 252, 354, 373, 437–38*
propitiation, expiation   *109*

R

Rahab   *366*
redemption   *269, 275–76*
repentance   *175, 181, 392–93*
rest, Sabbath rest   *23, 33, 36, 44–45, 120–48, 151, 166, 201, 487, 491, 499–500*
resurrection   *26, 43, 162, 164, 177, 211, 220, 222–23, 233, 316, 357, 371–72, 428, 471–73, 499*
retribution   *196*
return from exile   *26, 387*
revelation
    God speaking   *52–53, 138, 438, 479*
    in OT Scriptures   *88*
    in Son   *54, 82, 84, 450*
reward   *146, 333, 363, 379, 423, 495, 498–99*

S

sacrifice
    Christ's sacrifice   *28, 58, 235, 238, 254, 269–70, 287, 297–98, 300–301, 304–5, 317, 420, 462–64*
    Old Testament sacrifices   *29, 32, 42, 254, 261–62, 287, 297–98, 303–4, 421–62*
    sacrifice of praise   *423–24*

salvation   *34, 166–67, 233–34, 287, 498*

sanctification, holiness   *34, 97–98, 301, 306, 327, 390–91, 421, 469*

Servant of the Lord   *209*

signs and wonders   *22, 83, 102, 478*

sojourners and exiles   *33, 36, 45, 49, 75, 334, 349–50, 353–54, 491–92*

solidarity   *99, 101, 103, 108, 110, 151, 153, 158, 162, 166, 412, 422*

Son of God   *26, 39, 64, 152, 206, 326, 449*

Son of Man   *26, 88, 92*

sonship
    in OT   *38, 54*
    of believers   *94, 383–86*
    of Christ   *52, 54, 59–61, 64–67, 164, 440, 457*

suffering   *95, 163–64, 331–32, 363–64, 371–32, 379, 384, 422, 466–67*

T

tent, tabernacle, sanctuary
    earthly   *47, 244, 257, 263, 266, 284*
    heavenly   *46, 48, 204, 243–44, 266–67, 284–85, 315*

tithes, tithing   *206, 211–13*

Trinity   *74, 448*
    eternal generation   *65, 473*

typology   *28, 36–45, 118, 143–44, 210, 269, 282, 284, 290–91, 293, 297, 334, 351, 358, 449–50, 461, 473, 487*

U

use of OT in Hebrews   *67, 69–71, 73–74, 87, 89, 99–104, 121, 296–98, 334–35, 363–64, 405–6*

V

veil   *203, 227, 258, 316–17*

W

warnings, warning passages   *13–14, 35, 79–84*
    addressees   *134, 181–86, 193, 327, 482–85*
    Arminian view   *481*
    escalation   *78, 81–82, 325–26, 404–5, 487–88*
    Federal Vision view   *480*
    loss of rewards view   *187, 191*
    means of salvation   *84, 192–93, 482, 489*
    synoptical reading   *14, 484–85*
    tests of genuineness   *480–81*
    warning passages   *323–24*

wilderness generation   *22, 28, 44, 122–24, 166*

will, testament   *276*

wisdom, wisdom Christology   *55, 446*

word of exhortation   *10, 430*

Word of God   *146–47*

world, coming world, heavenly world   *69, 86–87*

worship   *257, 407*

Z

Zerubbabel   *115*

Scripture Index

Genesis
1   343
1:1   45, 74, 447
1:1–2:3   343, 447
1:1–31   146
1–2   452
1:2   343, 436
1:3   343, 436
1:6   343
1:6–7   343
1:9   343
1–11   21
1:11   343
1:14   343
1:15   343
1:20   343
1:20–21   343
1:24   343
1:26   343
1:26–27   20, 39, 343
1:28   89
2:1   45
2:2   133, 138
2–3   104
2:3   44
2:15   39
2:17   109
3   20
3:3   109
3:15   20, 22–23, 30, 67, 199, 499
3:24   261
4:3–5   344
4:4   344, 402
4:7   466
4:10   402

4:25   21
5:21–24   345
6:2   64, 66
6:4   64
6–9   21
6:13–18   346
8:1   310
9:15   310
9:15–16   310
9:29   310
11:1–9   21
12:1   350
12:1–3   21, 30, 33, 198, 200, 356, 370
12:2   60, 353
12:3   64, 100
12:4   350
12:10–20   357
13   357
13:14–16   356
13:14–17   33
14   209–10, 457–58
14:1–24   357
14:16   457
14:17   207
14:17–18   208
14:18   207–8
14:18–20   161
14:19   207, 212
14:20   207
15:1–6   353
15:4–5   356
15:5   353
15:6   350
15:16   356
15:18–21   33
16   352

17   253, 357
17:5–6   353, 356
17:6   363
17:7   476
17:8   252, 350
17:14–17   357
17:15–21   353, 356
17:16   363
17:17   352
18:1–8   411
18:1–15   210
18:9–12   352
18:9–15   357
18:10–14   353
18:17–18   198
18:18   356
18:18–19   39
19   23
19:1–9   411
20:1   350
20:1–18   357
21:10–12   356
21:11   356
21:12   356
21:34   350
22   200, 356
22:1   356
22:4   43
22:5   357
22:16–18   356
22:17   199, 325, 353
22:17–18   198–99
22:18   64
23:4   353
24:6   354
24:37   350

24:60 *325*
25:29–34 *392*
25:34 *392*
26:3 *33, 350*
26:4 *100*
26:5 *39*
26:34 *392*
27:27–29 *358*
27:27–30 *392*
27:34 *392*
27:36 *392*
27:36–40 *392*
27:39–40 *358*
28:4 *33*
28:13–15 *33*
28:14 *100*
28:15 *413*
30:22 *310*
35:11 *363*
35:12 *33*
37:1 *350*
45:5 *178*
45:7–8 *178*
47:9 *350*
47:31 *358*
48:1–22 *358*
48:2 *358*
48:14 *176*
49:1 *54*
49:10 *23, 363, 417*
49:33 *358*
50:20 *178*
50:24–25 *359*

Exodus
1–18 *22*
1:22 *362*
2:2–3 *362*
2:4–10 *362*
2:11–12 *362, 364*
2:14 *364*
2:15 *364*
2:24 *310*
3:8 *67*
3:10 *114*
3:13–15 *61*
4:22 *22, 38, 54, 67, 400, 449*
4:22–23 *59*
6:5 *310*
6:7 *252*
6:8 *67*

7:1 *39, 71, 207, 449*
7:3 *83*
11:5–6 *365*
12 *365*
12:12 *365*
12:13 *365*
12–14 *269*
12:22 *461*
12:22–23 *365*
12:29–30 *365*
13:21 *183*
14:3–13 *365*
14:14 *365*
14:15 *365*
14:16 *365*
14:21–22 *365*
14:23–28 *365*
14:29 *365*
15:6 *58*
15:7 *325*
15:12 *58*
16:23 *143*
16:30 *143*
16:31–35 *259*
16:34 *259*
19:4 *250*
19:5–6 *22*
19:10 *397*
19:12 *396–97*
19:12–13 *397*
19:13 *397*
19:15 *397*
19:16 *396–97*
19:18 *397, 405*
19:19 *397–98*
19:21 *397*
19–24 *22*
19:24 *397*
20:1 *250*
20:3 *448*
20:5 *448*
20:11 *143*
20:18 *397*
20:18–19 *397*
20:21 *396*
21:1–22:20 *81*
23:12 *143*
24 *271, 274, 278, 407*
24:3 *277*
24:3–8 *477*

24:4 *278*
24:5–8 *461*
24:6 *278*
24:7 *277*
24:8 *274, 278, 318*
24:16–17 *407*
24:17 *407*
25:9 *42*
25:10–16 *259*
25:16 *258*
25:18–20 *261*
25:22 *261*
25:23–29 *258*
25:30 *258, 261*
25–31 *244, 258*
25:31–39 *258*
25–40 *22*
25:40 *42, 47, 242, 244–45*
26:14 *310*
26:30 *42*
26:33 *258–59, 316*
26:35 *258*
26:45 *310*
27:8 *42*
27:20 *261*
28:1 *160, 219*
28:3–4 *219*
28–29 *158, 239*
28:41 *72, 219*
29:1 *270, 466*
29:4 *264, 318*
29:7 *72*
29:9 *219*
29:10 *177, 268*
29:14 *421*
29:15 *176*
29:19 *176*
29:21 *278*
29:22 *96*
29:26 *96*
29:30 *219*
29:36 *58*
29:36–37 *272*
29:38 *303, 466*
29:38–42 *238, 261, 423*
29:40–42 *298*
29:44 *219*
29:45 *476*
30:1–5 *259*
30:6 *260, 316*

30:7   *260*
30:7–9   *259*
30:8   *261*
30:10   *58, 259,*
    261–62, 272
30:19–21   *264*
30:30   *72, 219*
31:10   *219*
31:18   *258*
32:6   *270, 466*
32:13   *310*
32:25   *325*
34:28   *258*
35:12   *316*
35–40   *244, 258*
37:1–5   *259*
37:7–9   *261*
37:10–16   *258*
37:17–24   *258*
37:25–28   *259*
40:3   *259, 316*
40:5   *260*
40:12   *264, 318*
40:13–15   *219*
40:21   *258–59, 316*
40:21–22   *316*
40:22–24   *258*
40:26   *316*

Leviticus

1:1–17   *158, 298*
1:2   *270, 466*
1:3   *270, 466*
1:4   *158, 238, 303*
1:5   *268, 270, 421*
1–7   *22, 159, 263,*
    275, 279
1:7   *421*
1:7–8   *421*
1:10   *270, 466*
1:13   *270*
1:13–15   *270*
2:1–16   *158, 279*
3:1   *270, 466*
3:1–17   *158*
3:2   *421*
3:6   *270, 466*
3:8   *421*
3:12   *268*
4:1–35   *158, 298*
4:2   *158*
4:3   *159, 268, 270*

4:6   *278*
4:7   *259*
4:12   *421–22*
4:13   *158*
4:14   *159, 466*
4:15   *177*
4:17   *278*
4:21   *421*
4:23   *268, 270, 466*
4:28   *159, 270*
4:32   *270*
4:35   *159*
5:1–19   *158*
5:3   *391*
5:6–9   *159*
5:11   *159*
5:15   *270*
5:18   *158*
7:12   *158*
7:13   *158*
7:15   *158*
7:37   *96*
8:2   *268*
8:6   *318*
8:14   *177*
8:15   *272*
8:18   *177*
8:19   *278*
8:22   *96, 177*
8:24   *278*
8:30   *278*
9:2   *270*
9:7   *159, 238*
9:11   *421*
9:12   *278*
10   *22*
10:1–2   *109, 397*
10:4   *422*
10:4–5   *422*
11:1–44   *264*
11:24   *391*
11:25   *264*
11:40   *318*
11:43–44   *391*
12:7–8   *272*
13:3   *391*
13:6   *264*
13:6–7   *272*
13:8   *391*
13:13   *272*
13:17   *272*
13:44   *391*

13:46   *422*
14:1–9   *278*
14:2   *272*
14:3   *422*
14:4   *272, 461*
14:8–9   *264, 318*
14:10   *270*
14:32   *58*
14:49   *461*
15:5   *318*
15:5–6   *318*
15:5–8   *264*
15:13   *272*
15:28   *272*
15:31   *391*
16   *42, 159, 203,*
    243, 262, 271,
    275, 279, 292, 421
16:1–34   *158, 317,*
    480
16:2   *203, 261, 316*
16:3   *262, 268, 285,*
    298
16:4   *318*
16:5   *262, 298*
16:5–11   *285*
16:6   *159, 238, 262*
16:8–19   *260*
16:9   *262, 298, 466*
16:11   *262, 298*
16:12   *316*
16:14   *262*
16:14–15   *278*
16:14–20   *285*
16:15   *238, 262,*
    298, 316, 421
16:15–16   *421*
16:18   *262, 272*
16:19   *262*
16:21   *177*
16:21–22   *262*
16:24   *285, 318*
16:24–25   *285*
16:25   *298*
16:26   *264, 318,*
    422
16:27   *262, 298,*
    421
16:30   *272*
16:34   *261*
17:11   *279–80*
17:15   *318*

17:16 *264*
18:24–25 *391*
18:27 *391*
19:18 *310*
20:3 *391*
20:8 *98, 470*
20:10 *43*
20:13 *43*
21:1 *391*
21:8 *98, 470*
21:15 *98, 470*
21:23 *98, 470*
22:6 *318*
22:9 *98, 470*
22:16 *98, 470*
22:19 *270*
22:31–33 *470*
22:32 *98, 470*
23:27 *261*
24:2 *261*
24:3 *316*
24:4 *261*
24:5–7 *261*
24:8 *261*
24:14 *177*
25:29 *269*
26 *22, 81, 250*
26:1 *284*
26:14–39 *404, 476*
26:16 *325*
26:30 *284*
26:45 *476*
29:48 *269*

Numbers
3:5–9 *212*
3:10 *316*
5:2 *422*
5:3 *391, 422*
5:3–4 *422*
5:14 *391*
5:22–29 *158*
6:3 *264*
6:7 *391*
6:9–21 *27*
6:14 *270*
8:2–3 *261*
8:10 *177*
8:12 *177*
10:9 *325*
10:33 *259*
11:16–30 *184*

11:25 *309*
11:25–26 *309*
11:29 *309*
12 *117*
12:1–2 *38*
12:3 *38*
12:7 *38, 117*
12:8 *38, 117*
13:2–3 *96*
13–14 *122*
14 *123, 126, 130*
14:1–38 *130*
14:4 *96*
14:9 *126*
14:11 *126*
14:22 *123*
14:23 *123*
14:29 *130*
14:30 *123*
14:32 *130*
14:39–45 *147*
14:44 *259*
14:49 *461*
15:30 *262, 324,
486*
15:30–31 *159*
17:1–13 *259*
18:1–32 *212*
18:21 *211*
18:26 *211*
19 *269, 271*
19:1–22 *461*
19:2 *270*
19:4 *278, 461*
19:6 *278, 461*
19:7 *318, 422*
19:7–8 *264, 318*
19:9 *269*
19:12 *269*
19:13 *461*
19:17 *269*
19:17–21 *461*
19:18 *278*
23:19 *202*
24:2 *309*
24:14 *54*
24:17 *219–20, 363*
24:17–18 *363*
24:17–19 *23*
27:23 *177*
28:3 *270, 303*
28:3–8 *261*

28:9 *270*
28:11 *270*
28:19 *270*
28:27 *270*
28–29 *238*
28:31 *270*
29:7 *261*
35:30 *325*

Deuteronomy
1:13 *418*
1:43 *262, 324*
3:20 *142*
4:11 *396*
4:13 *258*
4:22–23 *407*
4:24 *407*
4:30 *67*
4:38 *55*
5:5 *397*
5:7 *448*
5:22 *258, 396*
5:23 *418*
5:24–27 *397*
6:4–5 *310*
6:10 *67*
6:13 *448*
6:22 *83*
7:16 *448*
8:3 *259*
8:6 *123*
8:16 *259*
8:19 *448*
9:19 *397*
9:27 *310*
10:4 *258*
10:5 *258*
10:8 *259, 303*
10:12 *123, 448*
11:1 *190*
11:13 *448*
12:9 *55*
12:9–12 *144*
12:10 *142, 144*
12:12 *144*
14:3–21 *264*
17:2 *486*
17:2–7 *325*
17:12 *262, 324*
17:12–13 *159, 324*
17:13 *262*
18:7 *303*

18:15 *118*
18:15–22 *363*
18:18–19 *118*
21:23 *391*
23:11 *264*
23:12 *318*
25:19 *142*
26:8 *83*
26–28 *250*
27–28 *81*
28:15–68 *404, 476*
29:3 *83*
30:6 *251*
31:6 *413*
31:8 *413*
31:9 *259*
32 *328*
32:1–43 *327*
32:8 *86*
32:27 *325*
32:35 *327*
32:35–36 *323*
32:36 *327*
32:43 *66–67, 448*
33:2 *80, 399*
34:9 *177*
34:11 *83*

Joshua
1 *413*
1:5 *413*
1:13 *142*
1:15 *142*
2 *366*
2:9–11 *366*
3:3 *259*
3:6 *259*
3:8 *259*
3:10 *127*
3:11 *259*
4:7 *259*
4:9 *259*
5:2–9 *147*
5:3 *325*
5:13–15 *210*
6 *365*
6:3 *365*
6:4 *365*
6:5 *365*
6:6–14 *365*
6:15–16 *365*
6:20 *365*

6:22–25 *366*
8:33 *259*
11:23 *55, 142*
13:21 *418*
14:15 *142*
21:4 *23*
21:43 *186*
21:44 *143*
21:44–45 *44*
22:4 *23, 44, 143*
22:24 *163*
23:1 *23, 44, 143*
23:15 *186*
24:14–16 *448*
24:20–21 *449*

Judges
4–5 *369–70*
4:6–7 *370*
4:8 *369*
5:5 *405*
6–7 *371*
6–8 *369–70*
6:11–14 *411*
6:12–16 *370*
6:36–40 *369*
8:24–27 *369*
9:51 *418*
11:6 *418*
11:11 *418*
11–12 *369–70*
13:5 *370*
13–16 *369–70*
14:6–7 *370*
14:9 *172*
16:22 *370*
16:25–30 *370*
20 *23*
20:27 *259*

1 Samuel
2:17 *325*
4:4 *259*
4:5 *259*
7 *370*
8:1–3 *369*
10:10 *309*
13:6 *373*
14:11 *373*
15:1 *72*
15:17 *418*
16:3 *72*

16:12 *72*
16:13 *370*
17:6 *23*
17:16 *23*
17:34–36 *370*
19:20 *309*
19:23 *309*
22:1 *373*
22:2 *418*
23:2 *309*
25:30 *418*
35:11 *23*

2 Samuel
5:7 *398*
6:2 *261*
7 *24, 30, 61, 297, 370, 454, 473*
7:9 *60–61*
7:13 *61, 66*
7:14 *32, 54, 65, 299, 449*
7:21 *61*
7:23 *61*
7:26 *61*
8:15 *370*
11 *24, 369*
15:24 *259*
22:3 *101*
24:14 *328*

1 Kings
2:3 *123*
2:19 *451*
3:15 *259*
6:20 *260*
6:22 *260*
6:23–28 *261*
8:1 *259, 398*
8:9 *258*
17:17–23 *371*
18:4 *372–73*
18:13 *372–73*
18:28 *279*
19:2 *371*
19:4 *373*
19:10 *372*
19:16 *72*
21:13 *372*
22:19 *451*
22:26–27 *372*

2 Kings

1:8 *372*
2:8 *373*
4:18–36 *371*
6:31–32 *371*
17 *476*
17:35 *449*
19:4 *127*
19:16 *127*
25 *476*

1 Chronicles

2:7 *325*
5:25 *325*
8:14 *370*
9:32 *261*
12:18 *309*
16:19 *350*
17 *297*
17:11–12 *116*
17:14 *115*
21:13 *328*
22:10 *450*
23:13 *160*
23:28 *58*

2 Chronicles

3:10–13 *261*
4:19 *261*
5:10 *258*
13:11 *261*
15:1 *309*
16:7–10 *372*
18:18 *451*
20:14 *309*
24:20 *309*
24:20–21 *372*
26:19 *259*
29:31 *158*
30:10 *372*
31:4–5 *211*
36:15–16 *372*

Ezra

8:52 *136*
13:36 *351*

Nehemiah

5:19 *310*
7:64 *41*
7:64–65 *209*

9:12 *183*
9:13 *186*
9:26 *372*
9:30 *372*
10:37–38 *211*
10:37–39 *212*
13:14 *310*

Esther

6:10 *187*
8:13 *325*

Job

1:6 *64, 66*
2:1 *64, 66*
26:6 *148*
28:24 *148*
31:32 *411*
38:7 *64, 66*

Psalms

2 *65, 473*
2:6 *398*
2:7 *32, 54, 64, 157,*
 160–62, 450, 473
2:7–12 *59*
2:8 *32, 55, 454*
2:8–9 *64*
5:5–6 *31*
8 *39, 49, 85–92,*
 103–5, 108,
 452–53, 460
8:4–6 *49, 87, 506*
8:5 *87–88*
16:6 *454*
16:8 *58*
19:12 *264*
19:13 *262, 324*
20:6 *58*
22 *99–101*
22:7 *100*
22:15 *100*
22:18 *100*
22:22 *94, 99, 445*
22:26 *100*
22:27 *100*
22:28 *100–101*
22:29 *100*
25:4 *123*
25:7 *310*
25:10 *123*

29:1 *67*
33:6 *146, 343*
33:13 *148*
34:14 *390*
36:8 *346*
38:8 *339*
39:7 *129*
39:12 *353*
40 *295–99, 301,*
 508
40:6 *297*
40:6–8 *296, 462,*
 508
40:7–8 *445*
40:12 *299*
42:2 *127*
45 *39, 71–72, 74,*
 449
45:4–5 *74*
45:6 *39, 71, 74,*
 449
45:6–7 *71*
45:7 *71*
45:16 *71*
45:16 *449*
48:2 *398*
48:8 *399*
50 *423*
50:9–13 *423*
50:14 *158*
51:18 *355*
68:8 *405*
72:1–20 *59*
72:7 *208*
72:8 *100*
72:17 *64*
73:16 *343*
73:23 *58*
74:2 *310*
78:24 *259*
79:8 *310*
82 *449*
82:1 *71*
82:6 *71, 449*
82:7 *449*
84:2 *127*
87:1–3 *351*
89 *69, 161, 297*
89:6 *67*
89:27 *38, 69*
89:30–32 *299*

95   *44–45, 121,*
   124–25, 130, 133,
   135, 141–42, 148,
   309
95:7   *121, 127, 142*
95:7–8   *129*
95:7–11   *121, 142,*
   479
95:8   *127, 130*
95:10   *130*
95:11   *44, 131, 133,*
   139
97:7   *66–67*
102   *73–74, 363*
102:12   *74*
102:15   *74*
102:16   *398*
102:25–27   *48, 73,*
   447
103:7   *123*
103:20–21   *70*
104   *70, 516*
104:4   *69–70*
104:24   *55, 446*
105:26   *160*
105:39   *183*
107:20   *147*
107:22   *424*
110   *30–31, 40–41,*
   58, 76–77, 161,
   223, 229, 239,
   449, 506
110:1   *31, 33, 40,*
   58, 76, 91, 161,
   223, 237, 241–42,
   270, 304, 317,
   379, 443, 451–52,
   457, 473, 497
110:2   *161, 398*
110:4   *31, 40–41,*
   76, 161–62, 168,
   207, 211, 215,
   221, 223–25, 229,
   236, 239, 242,
   316, 428, 456–57,
   472
110:5–7   *161*
111:9   *269*
118   *414*
118:6   *414*
125:1   *399*
135:9   *83*

138:1   *67*
145:8   *109*
148:5   *343*

Proverbs
2:1–5   *172*
2:9   *172*
2:10   *172*
2:15   *387*
3:11–12   *383–84,*
   504
3:19   *55, 446*
4:15   *387*
4:25–27   *390*
4:26   *387*
8:22–31   *55, 74,*
   446
8:29   *447*
13:24   *385*
17:18   *230*
22:26   *230*
28:14   *163*
29:17   *385*

Isaiah
1:2   *325*
1:10–15   *292*
2:3   *355*
4:3–4   *355*
8:17–18   *445*
8:18   *398*
9:1–7   *25, 32, 454,*
   473
9:6   *209, 449*
10:11   *284*
11:1   *220*
11:1–10   *25, 32,*
   102, 454, 473
11:2   *479*
13:6–13   *321*
16:2   *284*
19:1   *284*
21:9   *284*
24:23   *355, 399*
26:19   *26*
26:20   *334*
30:19   *355*
31:7   *284*
32:1   *209*
32:15   *25, 35, 478*
32:17   *209*
33:20   *351, 355*

34:8   *321*
35   *387–88*
35:3   *387*
35:6   *388*
35:8   *387*
35:10   *387*
40:28   *436*
41:8–9   *470*
41:8–10   *470*
41:9   *471*
43:7   *436*
43:10   *449*
43:25   *310*
43:28   *391*
44:3   *25, 35, 478*
45:7   *447*
45:8   *446*
45:12   *446*
45:18   *446*
45:21   *449*
45:22   *449*
46:6   *284*
46:9   *449*
51:2   *353*
52:1   *355*
52:9   *355*
53   *26*
53:5   *209, 298*
53:10   *298*
53:11–12   *298*
53:12   *287, 300*
54:11–12   *351*
55:3   *25, 32, 454,*
   473
58:7   *411*
60:14   *398*
61:1   *309, 479*
62:1–12   *355*
63:11   *428*
63:18   *325*
64:2   *324*
64:9   *310*
65:17   *406*
65:18   *355*
66:3   *292*
66:13   *355*
66:22   *406*

Jeremiah
2:7   *391*
3:16   *259–60*
3:17   *355*

3:20 *325*
4:4 *251*
5:11 *325*
7:21–23 *292*
8:8–12 *32*
9:1 *325*
9:25–26 *251*
10:10 *127*
10:11 *45*
10:12 *55*
10:15–18 *32*
12:1 *325*
14:21 *310*
15:15 *310*
15:16 *325*
20:2 *372*
23:5 *220*
23:5–6 *25, 32, 454, 473*
23:20 *54*
24:7 *476*
25:11–12 *490*
25:19 *54*
26:23 *372*
29:10 *490*
30:9 *25, 32, 454, 473*
30:22 *252*
30–33 *249*
31 *35, 309*
31:9 *38, 400, 449*
31:31 *309*
31:31–34 *25, 32, 35, 248–49, 309, 475*
31:32 *108*
31:33 *309*
31:33–34 *308–11, 480*
31:34 *26, 465*
32:20 *83*
32:21 *83*
32:38 *476*
33:8 *272*
33:15 *220, 355*
33:15–17 *25, 32, 454, 473*
36:26 *371*
37:14–21 *372*
37:15 *372*
38:32 *108*

Lamentations
5:1 *310*

Ezekiel
4:14 *391*
7:24 *391*
8:11 *259*
11:5 *309*
11:20 *252, 476*
13:5 *321*
14:11 *476*
14:13 *187*
15:8 *187*
16:60 *310*
18:22 *310*
18:24 *187*
19:5 *129, 339*
20:27 *187*
22:4 *187*
22:6 *325*
30:2–3 *321*
34:23 *428*
34:23–24 *25, 32, 454, 473*
36:25 *264*
36:25–26 *319*
36:26–27 *25, 35, 250, 253, 476, 478*
36:28 *252*
36:33 *264*
37 *26*
37:14 *35, 478*
37:23 *252, 264, 476*
37:24–25 *25, 32, 454*
37:27 *252, 476*
39:23 *325*
39:29 *35, 478*
43:22 *270*
43:23 *270*
43:25 *270*
45:19 *278*
46:11 *399*

Daniel
1:15 *172*
2:35 *406*
2:44–45 *406*
3 *371*

3:16–18 *371*
5 *136*
5:4 *284*
5:23 *284*
6 *371*
6:8 *284*
7 *92*
7:9–14 *26*
7:10 *399*
7:13 *88*
9:1–23 *490*
9:25 *355*
9:27 *325*
10:13 *86*
10:14 *54*
10:20 *86*
12:2 *26*

Hosea
2:13 *399*
3:5 *25, 32, 54, 454, 473*
5:3 *391*
6:6 *292*
7:2 *310*
8:13 *310*
9:4 *391*
9:5 *399*
9:9 *310*
11:1 *449*

Joel
1:15 *321*
2:1–2 *321*
2:11 *321*
2:28 *25, 35, 309, 478*
3:1 *355*
3:17 *355, 398*
3:20 *355*
3:21 *398*

Amos
2:12 *373*
5:8 *388*
5:18 *321*
5:20 *321*
5:21 *399*
5:22 *292*
7:10–17 *372*

Obadiah
15 *321*

Micah
2:7 *309*
3:8 *309*
4:1 *54*
4:2 *355, 398*
5:2–4 *25, 32, 454, 473*
6:6–8 *292*

Nahum
1:2 *325*

Habakkuk
1:5–17 *334*
2:3 *334*
2:3–4 *334*
2:4 *335*
3:3 *335*
3:8 *335*

Zephaniah
1:7 *321*
1:14 *321*
1:18 *324*
3:8 *324*
3:16 *321*
3:16–17 *355*

Haggai
2 *405*
2:5 *405*
2:6 *405–6*
2:7 *405*
2:9 *405*
2:13 *391*
2:20–23 *115*
2:21 *405*
2:21–23 *406*
2:22 *405*
2:23 *405*

Zechariah
1:14 *355*
1:17 *355*
2:2 *355*
2:4 *355*
2:12 *355*
3 *142*

3:8 *220*
4:10 *116*
4:13 *116*
6:12 *220*
6:13 *116*
7:12 *309*
8:3 *355*
8:4 *355*
8:12 *476*
8:15 *355*
8:22 *355*
9:9 *25, 32, 355, 454, 473*
9:11 *429*
9:16 *429*
10:6 *476*
12:2 *355*
12:2–3 *355*
12:6 *355*
12:8 *355*
12:8–10 *355*
12:10 *326, 478*
13:1 *264*
13:7 *428*
13:10 *355*
14:11–12 *355*
14:16–17 *355*

Malachi
3:6 *75, 447*
4:1–2 *220*

Matthew
1:21 *26*
1:23 *26*
2:6 *417*
3:11–12 *25*
3:16–17 *65, 72*
3:17 *473*
5:8 *391*
5:12 *332*
7:13 *336*
10:40 *114*
12:29 *105*
12:31–32 *327*
12:32 *187*
13:39–40 *187*
13:49 *187*
15:24 *114*
16:28 *90, 184*
19:13 *177*
19:15 *177*

20:28 *26*
21:42 *414*
22:5 *82*
22:34–40 *320*
22:41–46 *76*
22:44 *304, 451*
23:37 *372*
24 *6*
24:3 *187*
25:35 *411*
26:26–29 *26*
26:28 *246, 250*
26:36–45 *162*
26:64 *451*
26:64–65 *452*
27:34 *184*
27:43 *100*
27:46 *99*
28:20 *187*

Mark
1:14–15 *176*
3:29 *327*
5:23 *177*
6:5 *177*
7:2 *326*
7:4 *176*
7:5 *326*
8:23 *177*
8:25 *177*
8:31 *163*
9:31 *163*
9:37 *114*
10:16 *177*
10:30 *187*
10:32–34 *163*
10:45 *26, 91*
12:10–11 *414*
12:36 *451*
13:20 *490*
13:21 *490*
13:22 *490*
13:23 *490*
13:33 *490*
13:35 *490*
13:37 *490*
14:24 *91, 246, 250*
14:61–64 *451, 502*
14:62 *451*
14:62–64 *452*
15:24 *100*
15:29 *100*

15:34 *99*

Luke

1:5–23 *260*
1:35 *271*
3:21–22 *479*
3:22 *271*
4:1 *271, 479*
4:14 *271, 479*
4:18 *114, 271, 479*
4:40 *177*
4:43 *114*
7:30 *325*
9:48 *114*
10:16 *114, 325*
10:20 *400*
10:21 *271*
12:10 *327*
13:11 *233*
13:13 *177*
13:34 *372*
14:24 *90, 184*
17:9 *406*
18:30 *187*
20:17 *414*
20:35 *187*
20:42 *451*
21:36 *82*
22:19–20 *26*
22:20 *91, 246, 250*
22:26 *417*
22:69 *451*
22:69–71 *452*
23:34 *100*
23:41 *153*

John

1:1 *57, 72*
1:1–18 *26*
1:3 *55, 57, 74*
1:14 *103, 286*
1:18 *57*
1:29 *26*
3:25 *176*
3:34 *113*
4:10 *184*
4:34 *113*
5:23 *26, 113*
5:24 *113*
5:30 *113*
5:36 *113*
5:37 *113*

5:38 *113*
5:44 *160*
6:29 *113*
6:37–44 *489*
6:38 *113*
6:39 *113*
6:44 *113*
6:50–58 *317*
6:51 *26, 91*
7:18 *113, 153*
7:28 *113*
7:29 *113*
7:33 *113*
7:42 *65*
8:16 *113*
8:18 *113*
8:26 *113*
8:29 *113*
8:42 *113*
8:44 *104*
8:46 *153*
8:52 *90, 184*
8:58 *26*
10:11 *429*
10:14 *428*
10:28–29 *489*
11:49–52 *26*
12:31 *104*
12:48 *325*
13 *431*
13:34–35 *320*
14:9 *57*
14–16 *26*
14:30 *104, 153*
15 *431*
17:12 *336*
19:17–20 *421*
19:23–24 *100*
19:28 *100*
19:30 *1*
20:28 *72*

Acts

2 *27*
2:20 *321*
2:23 *178*
2:33 *451*
2:34 *76, 451*
2:38 *27, 29, 176, 184, 490*
2:43 *83*
3:1–10 *27*

3:19 *176*
3:26 *114*
4:2 *177*
4:11 *414*
4:12 *27, 29*
4:27–28 *178*
4:30 *83*
4:36 *3*
5:3 *327*
5:12 *83*
5:31 *76, 176, 451–52*
6:3 *340*
6:6 *177*
7:10 *418*
7:48 *284*
7:51 *327*
7:53 *60, 80*
7:55 *451*
7:55–56 *451*
7:56 *451*
8:9–24 *185*
8:12 *176*
8:17 *177*
8:19 *177*
8:20 *336*
9:12 *177*
9:13 *431*
9:17 *177*
9:32 *431*
9:41 *431*
10:1–11:18 *27*
10:14 *326*
10:22 *340*
10:28 *326*
10:43 *176*
11:8 *326*
11:18 *176*
11:21 *176*
13:3 *177*
13:15 *10, 430*
13:33 *65, 473*
13:39 *176*
14:3 *83*
14:15 *127*
15 *185, 484*
15:1–21 *27*
15:7 *176*
15:7–11 *84, 185, 478*
15:8 *185*
15:12 *83*

15:22   *418*
15:39   *320*
16:1   *431*
16:2   *340*
16:3   *431*
16:31   *27, 176, 489*
17:14   *431*
17:14–15   *431*
17:15   *431*
17:18   *177*
17:24   *284*
17:30   *176*
17:31   *27*
18:2   *8*
18:5   *431*
18:18   *27*
18:24   *3*
19:4   *176*
19:6   *177*
19:22   *431*
20:4   *431*
20:11   *184*
20:21   *176*
20:28   *424*
21:23–26   *27*
22:12   *340*
23:6   *177*
23:14   *184*
24:22   *177*
24:25   *177*
26:10   *431*
26:20   *176*
27   *490*
28:8   *177*

Romans

1:7   *431*
1:28   *488*
3:28   *176*
4:3   *350*
4:24   *176*
5:6–10   *91*
8:9   *484*
8:18–25   *406*
8:23   *288*
8:25   *288*
8:28–39   *489*
8:30   *275, 305*
8:34   *451–52*
9:7   *275, 357*
9:11–13   *489*
9:12   *275*

9:13   *470*
9:22   *343*
9:24–26   *275*
9:33   *176*
10:9   *176*
10:14–17   *490*
12:1   *430*
12:10   *411*
12:13   *411, 431*
12:18   *390*
14:11   *74*
14:23   *345*
15:25   *431*
15:25–26   *431*
15:26   *424*
15:30   *430*
15:30–32   *427*
15:33   *428*
16:3–16   *431*
16:20   *428, 432*
16:21   *431*
16:21–23   *431*
16:25–27   *427*
16:27   *430*

1 Corinthians

1:2   *431*
1:7   *288*
1:8   *321*
1:8–9   *489*
1:9   *275*
1:10   *430*
1:20   *187*
1:26–28   *489*
1:31   *74*
2:6   *187*
2:16   *74*
3:18   *187*
4:16   *430*
4:17   *431*
5:1–6:20   *413*
5:5   *321*
5:9   *392*
5:9–11   *392*
6:1   *431*
6:3   *86*
6:9   *392, 413*
6:14   *177*
6:19   *431*
6:19–20   *431*
7:31   *187*
8:6   *55*

9:27   *488*
10:11   *54, 286*
10:22   *74*
10:26   *74*
10:30   *406*
11:19   *485*
11:25   *250*
12:1–31   *84*
13:1–13   *320*
13:12   *391*
14:1–40   *84*
15:2   *176*
15:12–19   *177*
15:25   *77, 304*
16:1   *431*
16:10   *431*
16:15   *430*
16:16   *424*
16:19   *432*
16:20   *432*
16:23   *432*

2 Corinthians

1:1   *431*
1:14   *321*
1:19   *431*
2:8   *430*
3:6   *250*
4:4   *104, 187*
4:4–6   *183*
4:14   *177*
5:21   *153*
8:4   *424*
9:4   *129, 339*
9:13   *424*
10:1   *430*
10:17   *74*
11:7   *339*
11:17   *129*
12:12   *83*
13:5   *488*
13:5–7   *190*
13:7   *488*
13:12   *431–32*
13:14   *427, 432*

Galatians

1:4   *187*
1:6   *275*
1:11–17   *83*
1:15   *275*
2:16   *176*

2:21 *325*
3:1–5 *84, 185*
3:2 *478, 484*
3:5 *478, 484*
3:6 *350*
3:6–9 *107*
3:11 *335*
3:19 *80*
4 *170*
4:4 *114*
4:9 *170*
4:26 *351, 399*
4:30 *357*
5:5 *288*
5:19 *413*
5:21 *413*
6:18 *432*

Ephesians
1:1 *431*
1:4 *489*
1:13–14 *481, 489*
1:20 *77, 451*
1:21 *59, 187*
2:2 *104*
2:11 *284*
4:1 *275, 430*
4:11–16 *84*
4:14–16 *419*
5:3 *431*
5:3–5 *413*
5:5 *392*
5:5–6 *413*
6:19 *427*
6:23 *427*
6:24 *432*

Philippians
1:1 *424, 431*
1:6 *489*
1:28 *336*
2 *60, 508*
2:2 *430*
2:9–11 *59*
2:10–11 *74*
2:19 *431*
3:9 *176*
3:11 *177*
3:19 *336*
3:20 *288, 351*
4:3 *400*

4:9 *428*
4:18 *424*
4:20 *427*
4:21–22 *431*
4:22 *432*
4:23 *432*

Colossians
1:1 *431*
1:15 *57, 291*
1:15–18 *59*
1:16 *74*
2:17 *290*
2:21 *184*
3:1 *77, 451*
3:5 *413*
3:15 *320*
4:3 *427*
4:10–15 *431*
4:18 *432*

1 Thessalonians
1:1 *431*
1:10 *176*
3:2 *431*
3:13 *431*
4:3–7 *413*
4:6 *74*
4:8 *325*
4:9 *411*
5:2 *321*
5:3 *82*
5:12–13 *424*
5:23 *427–28*
5:23–24 *489*
5:24 *275*
5:25 *427*
5:26 *431*
5:28 *432*

2 Thessalonians
1:1 *431*
1:7–8 *74*
1:10 *431*
2:2 *321*
2:3 *336*
2:13–14 *489*
2:14 *275*
3:1 *427*
3:16 *427*
3:18 *432*

1 Timothy
1:2 *431*
1:6 *388*
1:10 *392*
1:12 *406*
1:18 *431*
2:1 *430*
2:4 *324*
2:5 *246*
2:7 *55*
3:2 *411, 424*
4:14 *177*
5:10 *340, 411*
5:15 *388*
5:22 *177*
6:9 *336*
6:10 *413*
6:17 *187*
6:20 *388, 431*
6:21 *432*

2 Timothy
1:2 *431*
1:3 *406*
1:6 *177*
1:9 *275*
1:11 *55*
2:19 *74*
2:25 *176, 324*
3:7 *324*
3:8 *190, 488*
4:4 *388*
4:10 *187*
4:19 *431*
4:21 *431*
4:22 *432*

Titus
1:1 *324*
1:7 *424*
1:8 *411*
1:16 *190, 488*
2:13 *72*
3:15 *432*

Philemon
1 *431*
9 *430*
9–10 *430*
23 *431*
25 *432*

Hebrews

1:1–4   *51–62*
1:5–14   *62–78*
2:1–4   *78–84*
2:5–9   *84–93*
2:10–18   *93–111*
3:1–6   *111–20*
3:7–11   *120–24*
3:12–19   *124–32*
4:1–5   *132–39*
4:6–13   *139–48*
4:14–16   *149–56*
5:1–10   *155–66*
5:11–14   *167–72*
6:1–3   *173–78*
6:4–8   *178–91*
6:9–12   *192–97*
6:13–20   *196–204*
7:1–10   *205–14*
7:11–12   *214–17*
7:13–14   *218–21*
7:15–17   *220–24*
7:18–19   *224–27*
7:20–22   *228–31*
7:23–25   *231–35*
7:26–28   *235–40*
8:1–6   *240–46*
8:7–13   *247–55*
9:1–10   *255–64*
9:11–14   *265–72*
9:15–22   *272–80*
9:23–28   *280–88*
10:1–4   *288–93*
10:5–10   *293–302*
10:11–14   *302–7*
10:15–18   *307–11*
10:19–25   *311–21*
10:26–31   *322–29*
10:32–39   *329–37*
11:1–2   *337–41*
11:3–7   *341–48*
11:8–22   *347–59*
11:23–31   *360–67*
11:32–40   *367–75*
12:1–3   *374–80*
12:4–13   *380–88*

12:14–17   *389–94*
12:18–24   *394–402*
12:25–29   *403–8*
13:1–6   *408–15*
13:7–17   *415–26*
13:18–25   *426–33*

James

1:17   *75, 447*
1:21   *377*
2:14–26   *496*
3:1   *424*

1 Peter

1:1–2   *489*
1:5   *489*
1:19   *153, 270*
1:20   *286*
1:22   *411*
2:1   *377*
2:7   *414*
2:8   *55*
2:9   *319*
2:11   *430*
2:22   *153*
2:25   *429*
3:18   *153*
3:22   *59, 77, 451–52*
4:9   *411*
4:10–11   *84*
4:17   *177*
5:1   *430*
5:2   *424*
5:5   *424*
5:10   *427*
5:12   *430*
5:13   *431–32*
5:13–14   *431*

2 Peter

1:1   *72*
1:5–11   *195*
1:7   *411*
1:21   *309*
2:1   *336*
2:1–22   *491*

2:3   *177, 336*
3:7   *336*
3:10   *75, 170, 321*
3:10–13   *406*
3:12   *75, 170*
3:13   *75*
3:16   *336*

1 John

2:2   *91*
2:19   *253, 485, 491*
3:3   *391*
3:5   *153*
4:9   *113*
4:9   *113*
4:10   *91, 113*
4:14   *113*
5:19   *104*

2 John

3:12   *340*
13   *431*

3 John

15   *431*

Jude

4   *177*
14   *399*
24–25   *489*

Revelation

3:12   *399*
5:11   *399*
6:14   *75*
17:11   *336*
21:1–22:5   *406, 499*
21:2   *399*
21:8   *392*
21:10   *399*
21:27   *400*
22:4   *391*
22:15   *392, 413*
22:21   *432*